# Survival Communications
# in New Hampshire

# John E. Parnell, KK4HWK

ISBN 978-1-62512-051-9

Cover design by:
Lynda Colón
FREELANCE GRAPHIC DESIGN &
MARKETING COMMUNICATIONS
www.hirelynda.webs.com

**Titles available in this series:**

Survival Communications in Alabama
Survival Communications in Alaska
Survival Communications in Arizona
Survival Communications in Arkansas
Survival Communications in California
Survival Communications in Colorado
Survival Communications in Connecticut
Survival Communications in Delaware
Survival Communications in Florida
Survival Communications in Georgia
Survival Communications in Hawaii
Survival Communications in Idaho
Survival Communications in Illinois
Survival Communications in Indiana
Survival Communications in Iowa
Survival Communications in Kansas
Survival Communications in Kentucky
Survival Communications in Louisiana
Survival Communications in Maine
Survival Communications in Maryland
Survival Communications in Massachusetts
Survival Communications in Michigan
Survival Communications in Minnesota
Survival Communications in Mississippi
Survival Communications in Missouri

Survival Communications in Montana
Survival Communications in Nebraska
Survival Communications in Nevada
Survival Communications in New Hampshire
Survival Communications in New Jersey
Survival Communications in New Mexico
Survival Communications in New York
Survival Communications in North Carolina
Survival Communications in North Dakota
Survival Communications in Ohio
Survival Communications in Oklahoma
Survival Communications in Oregon
Survival Communications in Pennsylvania
Survival Communications in Rhode Island
Survival Communications in South Carolina
Survival Communications in South Dakota
Survival Communications in Tennessee
Survival Communications in Texas
Survival Communications in Utah
Survival Communications in Vermont
Survival Communications in Virginia
Survival Communications in Washington
Survival Communications in West Virginia
Survival Communications in Wisconsin
Survival Communications in Wyoming

The above titles are available from your favorite online or brick-and-mortar bookstore or directly from the publisher at Tutor Turtle Press LLC, 1027 S. Pendleton St. – Suite B-10, Easley, SC 29642.

# TABLE OF CONTENTS

## Appendix A – New Hampshire Ham Radio Clubs

### ARRL Affiliated Amateur and Ham Radio Clubs – By City

## Appendix B – New Hampshire Ham Licensees by City

# Survival Communications in New Hampshire

Perhaps you have prepared for WTSHTF or TEOTWAWKI with respect to food, water, self-defense and shelter. But what about communication?

Whenever there is a disaster (hurricane, earthquake, economic collapse, nuclear war, EMF, solar eruption, etc.), the normal means of communication that we're all reliant upon (cell phone, land line phone, the Internet, etc.) will probably be, at best, sporadic and at worst, non-existent.

As this author sees it, short of smoke signals and mirrors, there are three options for communication in "trying times": (1) GMRS or FRS radios; (2) CB radios; and (3) ham or amateur radio. Let's consider each of these options to come up with the most acceptable one.

## GMRS (General Mobile Radio Service) / FRS (Family Radio Service)

GMRS (General Mobile Radio Service) / FRS (Family Radio Service) radios work optimally over short distances where there is minimal interference. Originally designed to be used as pagers, particularly inside a building or other such confined area, these radios are low-cost and convenient to carry. Unfortunately their small size and light weight comes with a trade-off – short range and short battery life. These radios are supposed to be able to communicate for up to 25-30 miles. Right. That's on level terrain, without buildings or trees getting in the way. While battery life technology is constantly improving, you will need spare batteries to keep communicating or someway of recharging the ones in the radio. In this author's opinion, GMRS/FRS radios are not first choice when concerned with medium or long range communication.

## CB (Citizens Band)

CB (Citizens Band) radios operate in a frequency range originally reserved for ham or amateur radio operation. Because of the overwhelming number of people wishing quick, low-cost, regulation-free communication, the FCC (Federal Communication Commission) split off a portion of the frequency spectrum and allowed anyone to purchase a CB radio and start communicating. No test. No license. Just personal/business communication. Today, CB radios are readily available in such outlets as eBay and Craigslist. This author has seen them at yard/garage/tag sales and at flea markets.

CB radios come in a variety of "flavors." Fixed units, sometimes referred to as base units are intended for home use. For the most part, they derive their power from the utility company. In the event of loss of electricity, most base units can also be connected to a 12-volt battery, like that in your car/truck. If you choose to obtain a fixed unit, make sure you know how to connect the unit to the battery – ahead of time. Trying to figure this out when you're under extra stress is not a good situation.

A second type of CB radio is designed to be mobile, that is, installed in your car/truck. It gets its power from the vehicle's battery. You can either attach an antenna permanently to the vehicle or have a removable, magnetic type antenna.

The third type of CB radio is designed for handheld use. They are small and light. Most weigh less than a pound and operate on batteries. Yes, using batteries in a CB poses the same limitations as those by the GMRS/FRS radios, but have the added advantage that most handheld units come with a cigarette lighter adapter. Comes in handy when you are on the move and wish to be able to communicate both from a vehicle and also when you have to abandon it.

While they have a greater range than GMRS/FRS radios, CB radios are, legally, limited to operate on 40 channels, with a power rating of four (4) watts or less. Yes, it is possible to alter CB radios to get around these limitations, but not legally,

## Ham/Amateur Radio

Ham/Amateur radio is very appealing. With a ham radio, you are not limited to less than 50 miles, but can communicate with anyone in the world (who also has access to a ham radio, of course).

## Standardized Amateur Radio Prepper Communications Plan

In the event of a nationwide catastrophic disaster, the nationwide network of Amateur Radio licensed preppers will need a set of standardized meeting frequencies to share information and coordinate activities between various prepper groups. This Standardized Amateur Radio Communications Plan establishes a set of frequencies on the 80 meter, 40 meter, 20 meter, and 2 meter Amateur Radio bands for use during these types of catastrophic disasters.

Routine nets will not be held on all of these frequencies, but preppers are encouraged to use them when coordinating with other preppers on a routine basis. Routine nets may be conducted by The American Preparedness Radio Net (TAPRN) on these or other frequencies as they see fit. However, TAPRN will promote the use of these standardized frequencies by all Amateur Radio licensed preppers during times of catastrophic disaster. The promotion of this Standardized Amateur Radio Communications Plan is encouraged by all means within the prepper community, including via Amateur Radio, Twitter, Facebook, and various blogs.

---

### Standardized Frequencies and Modes

80 Meters – 3.818 MHz LSB (TAPRN Net: Sundays at 9 PM ET)
40 Meters – 7.242 MHz LSB
40 Meters Morse Code / Digital – 7.073 MHz USB (TAPRN: Sundays at 7:30 PM ET on
    CONTESTIA 4/250)
20 Meters – 14.242 MHz USB
2 Meters – 146.420 MHz FM

---

**Nets and Network Etiquette**

In times of nationwide catastrophic disaster, the ability of any one prepper to initiate and sustain themselves as a net control may be limited by the availability of power and other resource shortages. However, all licensed preppers are encouraged to maintain a listening watch on these frequencies as often as possible during a catastrophic disaster. Preppers may routinely announce themselves in the following manner:

• This is [Your Callsign Phonetically] in [Your State], maintaining a listening watch on [Standard Frequency] for any preppers on frequency seeking information or looking to provide information. Please call [Your Callsign Phonetically]. Preppers exchanging information that may require follow up should agree upon a designated time to return to the frequency and provide further information. If other stations are utilizing the frequency at the designated time you return, maintain watch and proceed with your communications when those stations are finished. If your communications are urgent and the stations on frequency are not passing information of a critical nature, interrupt with the word "Break" and request use of the frequency.

For More Information

Catastrophe Network: http://www.catastrophenetwork.org or @CatastropheNet on Twitter The American Preparedness Radio Network: http://www.taprn.com or @TAPRN on Twitter

© 2011 Catastrophe Network, Please Distribute Freely

In order to use a ham radio, legally, one must be licensed to do so by the FCC (other countries have analogous governmental bodies to regulate ham radio). To obtain a license is quite easy – take a test and pay your license fee. There are currently three classes of license – Technician, General, and Amateur Extra. With each of these licenses come specific abilities.

Technician class is the beginning level. The exam consists of 35 multiple choice questions randomly drawn from a pool of 395 questions. The question pool is readily available online for free downloading (http://www.ncvec.org/downloads/Revised%20Element%202.Pdf) or in such publications at *Ham Radio License Manual Revised 2nd Edition* (ISBN 978-0-87259-097-7). The current Technician pool of questions is to be used from July 1, 2010 to June 30, 2014. Be sure the question pool you are studying from is current. You will need to score at least 26 correct to pass. (Do not worry, Morse Code is no longer on the test, although many ham operators use it anyway.) You do not need to take a formal class in order to qualify to take the exam. You can learn the material on your own. Most people spend 10-15 hours studying and then successfully take the exam. The cost of taking the exam is under $20. The exam is given in MANY locations throughout the US. Usually the exam is given by area ham clubs. You do not have to belong to the club to take the exam. Check Appendix A for a listing of clubs in New Hampshire.

**Topics for the Technician License in Amateur Radio**

The Technician license exam covers such topics as basic regulations, operating practices, and electronic theory, with a focus on VHF and UHF applications. Below is the syllabus for the Technician Class.

---

**Subelement T1 – FCC Rules, descriptions and definitions for the amateur radio service, operator and station license responsibilities**

*[6 Exam Questions – 6 Groups]*

T1A – Amateur Radio services; purpose of the amateur service, amateur-satellite service, operator/primary station license grant, where FCC rules are codified, basis and purpose of FCC rules, meanings of basic terms used in FCC rules

T1B – Authorized frequencies; frequency allocations, ITU regions, emission type, restricted sub-bands, spectrum sharing, transmissions near band edges

T1C – Operator classes and station call signs; operator classes, sequential, special event, and vanity call sign systems, international communications, reciprocal operation, station license licensee, places where the amateur service is regulated by the FCC, name and address on ULS, license term, renewal, grace period

T1D – Authorized and prohibited transmissions

T1E – Control operator and control types; control operator required, eligibility, designation of control operator, privileges and duties, control point, local, automatic and remote control, location of control operator

T1F – Station identification and operation standards; special operations for repeaters and auxiliary stations, third party communications, club stations, station security, FCC inspection

---

**Subelement T2 – Operating Procedures**

*[3 Exam Questions – 3 Groups]*

T2A – Station operation; choosing an operating frequency, calling another station, test transmissions, use of minimum power, frequency use, band plans

T2B – VHF/UHF operating practices; SSB phone, FM repeater, simplex, frequency offsets, splits and shifts, CTCSS, DTMF, tone squelch, carrier squelch, phonetics

T2C – Public service; emergency and non-emergency operations, message traffic handling

---

**Subelement T3 – Radio wave characteristics, radio and electromagnetic properties, propagation modes**

*[3 Exam Questions – 3 Groups]*

T3A – Radio wave characteristics; how a radio signal travels; distinctions of HF, VHF and UHF; fading, multipath; wavelength vs. penetration; antenna orientation

T3B – Radio and electromagnetic wave properties; the electromagnetic spectrum, wavelength vs. frequency, velocity of electromagnetic waves

T3C – Propagation modes; line of sight, sporadic E, meteor, aurora scatter, tropospheric ducting, F layer skip, radio horizon

## Subelement T4 - Amateur radio practices and station setup

*[2 Exam Questions – 2 Groups]*

T4A – Station setup; microphone, speaker, headphones, filters, power source, connecting a computer, RF grounding

T4B – Operating controls; tuning, use of filters, squelch, AGC, repeater offset, memory channels

## Subelement T5 – Electrical principles, math for electronics, electronic principles, Ohm's Law

*[4 Exam Questions – 4 Groups]*

T5A – Electrical principles; current and voltage, conductors and insulators, alternating and direct current

T5B – Math for electronics; decibels, electronic units and the metric system

T5C – Electronic principles; capacitance, inductance, current flow in circuits, alternating current, definition of RF, power calculations

T5D – Ohm's Law

## Subelement T6 – Electrical components, semiconductors, circuit diagrams, component functions

*[4 Exam Groups – 4 Questions]*

T6A – Electrical components; fixed and variable resistors, capacitors, and inductors; fuses, switches, batteries

T6B – Semiconductors; basic principles of diodes and transistors

T6C – Circuit diagrams; schematic symbols

T6D – Component functions

## Subelement T7 – Station equipment, common transmitter and receiver problems, antenna measurements and troubleshooting, basic repair and testing

*[4 Exam Questions – 4 Groups]*

T7A – Station radios; receivers, transmitters, transceivers

T7B – Common transmitter and receiver problems; symptoms of overload and overdrive, distortion, interference, over and under modulation, RF feedback, off frequency signals; fading and noise; problems with digital communications interfaces

T7C – Antenna measurements and troubleshooting; measuring SWR, dummy loads, feedline failure modes

T7D – Basic repair and testing; soldering, use of a voltmeter, ammeter, and ohmmeter

## Subelement T8 – Modulation modes, amateur satellite operation, operating activities, non-voice communications

*[4 Exam Questions – 4 Groups]*

T8A – Modulation modes; bandwidth of various signals

T8B – Amateur satellite operation; Doppler shift, basic orbits, operating protocols

T8C – Operating activities; radio direction finding, radio control, contests, special event stations, basic linking over Internet

T8D – Non-voice communications; image data, digital modes, CW, packet, PSK31

## Subelement T9 – Antennas, feedlines

*[2 Exam Groups – 2 Questions]*

T9A – Antennas; vertical and horizontal, concept of gain, common portable and mobile antennas, relationships between antenna length and frequency

T9B – Feedlines; types, losses vs. frequency, SWR concepts, matching, weather protection, connectors

## Subelement T0 – AC power circuits, antenna installation, RF hazards

*[3 Exam Questions – 3 Groups]*

T0A – AC power circuits; hazardous voltages, fuses and circuit breakers, grounding, lightning protection, battery safety, electrical code compliance

T0B – Antenna installation; tower safety, overhead power lines

T0C – RF hazards; radiation exposure, proximity to antennas, recognized safe power levels, exposure to others

Once your name and call sign are available in the FCC database, you have the privilege of operating on all VHF (2 m) and UHF (70 cm) frequencies above 30 megahertz (MHz) and HF frequencies 80, 40, and 15 meter, and on the 10 meter band using Morse code (CW), voice, and digital mode. For a Technician license in New Hampshire, your call sign will consist of a two-letter prefix beginning with K or W, the number one (1), and a three-letter suffix. The single digit number in the call sign is determined according to which area of the US you obtain your first license. Even though you may move to another state, you keep this number in your call sign. This is also true should you upgrade to a higher license and get a new call sign. The numeral portion of your call sign stays the same.

**Call Sign Numbers**

Below is a chart showing the various numbers and the state(s) in which you would obtain the number.

| Call Sign Number | State(s) |
|---|---|
| 0 | CO, IA, KS, MN, MO, NE, ND, SD |
| 1 | CT, ME, MA, NH, RI, VT |
| 2 | NJ, NY |
| 3 | DE, DC, MD, PA |
| 4 | AL, FL, GA, KY, NC, SC, TN, VA |
| 5 | AR, LA, MS, NM, OK, TX |
| 6 | CA |
| 7 | AZ, ID, MT, NV, OR, WA, UT, WY |
| 8 | MI, OH, WV |
| 9 | IL, IN, WI |

Residents of Alaska may have any of the following call sign prefixes assigned to them: AL0-7, KL0-7, NL0-7, or WL0-7. Likewise, residents of Hawaii may have the prefix AH6-7, KH6-7, NH6-7, or WH6-7 assigned.

Once you obtain your Technician license, do not stop there. Go and get your General license.

General is the second of three ham license classes. Like the Technician license, to get a General license, you merely have to take a 35-question multiple choice exam and pay your license fee. Passing is still at least 26 correct answers and the fee is the same (less than $20). Again the question pool is available for free online (http://www.ncvec.org/page.php?id=358). It is also available in such print publications as *The ARRL General Class License Manual 7th Edition* (ISBN 978-0-87259-811-9). The current General pool of questions is to be used from July 1, 2011 to June 30, 2015. Be sure the question pool you are using is current. Being a bit more comprehensive than the Technician license, the General license usually requires 15-20 hours of study to learn the material. Check Appendix A for a listing of clubs in New Hampshire where you might take your exam. Once your name and NEW call sign is listed in the FCC database, you're good to go. For a General license in New Hampshire, your call sign will consist of a one-letter prefix beginning with K, N or W, the number one (1), and a three-letter suffix.

**Topics for the General License in Amateur Radio**

The General license exam covers regulations, operating practices and electronic theory. Below is the syllabus for the General Class.

---

**Subelement G1 – Commission's Rules**

*(5 Exam Questions – 5 Groups)*
G1A – General Class control operator frequency privileges; primary and secondary allocations
G1B – Antenna structure limitations; good engineering and good amateur practice, beacon operation; restricted operation; retransmitting radio signals
G1C – Transmitter power regulations; data emission standards
G1D – Volunteer Examiners and Volunteer Examiner Coordinators; temporary identification
G1E – Control categories; repeater regulations; harmful interference; third party rules; ITU regions

---

**Subelement G2 – Operating procedures**

*(5 Exam Questions – 5 Groups)*
G2A – Phone operating procedures; USB/LSB utilization conventions; procedural signals; breaking into a OSO in progress; VOX operation
G2B – Operating courtesy; band plans, emergencies, including drills and emergency communications

G2C – CW operating procedures and procedural signals; Q signals and common abbreviations; full break in

G2D – Amateur Auxiliary; minimizing interference; HF operations

G2E – Digital operating; procedures, procedural signals and common abbreviations

## Subelement G3 – Radio wave propagation

*(3 Exam Questions – 3 Groups)*

G3A – Sunspots and solar radiation; ionospheric disturbances; propagation forecasting and indices

G3B – Maximum Usable Frequency; Lowest Usable Frequency; propagation

G3C – Ionospheric layers; critical angle and frequency; HF scatter; Near Vertical Incidence Sky waves

## Subelement G4 – Amateur radio practices

*(5 Exam Questions – 5 Groups)*

G4A – Station Operation and setup

G4B – Test and monitoring equipment; two-tone test

G4C – Interference with consumer electronics; grounding; DSP

G4D – Speech processors; S meters; sideband operation near band edges

G4E – HF mobile radio installations; emergency and battery powered operation

## Subelement G5 – Electrical principles

*(3 Exam Questions – 3 Groups)*

G5A – Reactance; inductance; capacitance; impedance; impedance matching

G5B – The Decibel; current and voltage dividers; electrical power calculations; sine wave root-mean-square (RMS) values; PEP calculations

G5C – Resistors; capacitors and inductors in series and parallel; transformers

## Subelement G6 – Circuit components

*(3 Exam Questions – 3 Groups)*

G6A – Resistors; capacitors; inductors

G6B – Rectifiers; solid state diodes and transistors; vacuum tubes; batteries

G6C – Analog and digital integrated circuits (ICs); microprocessors; memory; I/O devices; microwave ICs (MMICs); display devices

## Subelement G7 – Practical circuits

*(3 Exam Questions – 3 Groups)*

G7A – Power supplies; schematic symbols

G7B – Digital circuits; amplifiers and oscillators

G7C – Receivers and transmitters; filters, oscillators

## Subelement G8 – Signals and emissions

*(2 Exam Questions – 2 Groups)*

G8A – Carriers and modulation; AM; FM; single and double sideband; modulation envelope; overmodulation

G8B – Frequency mixing; multiplication; HF data communications; bandwidths of various modes; deviation

## Subelement G9 – Antennas and feed lines

*(4 Exam Questions – 4 Groups)*

G9A – Antenna feed lines; characteristic impedance and attenuation; SWR calculation, measurement and effects; matching networks

G9B – Basic antennas

G9C – Directional antennas

G9D – Specialized antennas

## Subelement G0 – Electrical and RF safety

*(2 Exam Questions – 2 Groups)*

G0A – RF safety principles, rules and guidelines; routine station elevation

G0B – Safety in the ham shack; electrical shock and treatment, safety grounding, fusing, interlocks, wiring, antenna and tower safety

With a General license, you can use all VHF and UHF frequencies and most of the HF frequencies. You would have access to the 160, 30, 17, 12, and 10 meter bands and access to major parts of the 80, 40, 20, and 15 meter bands. Of course, this is in addition to all bands available to Technician license holders.

Amateur Extra is the third of three ham license classes. Like the Technician and General classes, you merely have to pass a test and pay your fee to get your Amateur Extra license. This class of license is more comprehensive than the lower license classes. The exam is longer – 50 questions – and the minimum passing score is higher – 37. However, once you get your Amateur Extra license, all ham frequencies, VHF, UHF and HF are available for your enjoyment. The Extra exam covers regulations, specialized operating practices, advanced electronics theory, and radio equipment design.

Like for the other license classes, the question pool for the Amateur Extra license is available online for downloading (http://www.ncvec.org/downloads/REVISED%202012-2016%20Extra%20Class%20Pool.doc). It is also available in print form in such publications as *The ARRL Extra Class License Manual Revised 9th Edition* (ISBN 978-0-87259-887-4).

**Topics for the Extra License in Amateur Radio**

Below is the syllabus for the Amateur Extra Class for July 1, 2012 to June 30, 2016.

## Subelement E1 – Commission's Rules

[6 Exam Questions – 6 Groups]

E1A – Operating Standards: frequency privileges; emission standards; automatic message forwarding; frequency sharing; stations aboard ships or aircraft

E1B – Station restrictions and special operations: restrictions on station location; general operating restrictions, spurious emissions, control operator reimbursement; antenna structure restrictions; RACES operations

E1C – Station control: definitions and restrictions pertaining to local, automatic and re-mote control operation; control operator responsibilities for remote and automatically controlled stations

E1D – Amateur Satellite service: definitions and purpose; license requirements for space stations; available frequencies and bands; telecommand and telemetry operations; re-strictions, and special provisions; notification requirements

E1E – Volunteer examiner program: definitions, qualifications, preparation and admin-istration of exams; accreditation; question pools; documentation requirements

E1F – Miscellaneous rules: external RF power amplifiers; national quiet zone; business communications; compensated communications; spread spectrum; auxiliary stations; reciprocal operating privileges; IARP and CEPT licenses; third party communications with foreign countries; special temporary authority

## Subelement E2 – Operating procedures

[5 Exam Questions – 5 Groups]

E2A – Amateur radio in space: amateur satellites; orbital mechanics; frequencies and modes; satellite hardware; satellite operations

E2B – Television practices: fast scan television standards and techniques; slow scan tele-vision standards and techniques

E2C – Operating methods: contest and DX operating; spread-spectrum transmissions; selecting an operating frequency

E2D – Operating methods: VHF and UHF digital modes; APRS

E2E – Operating methods: operating HF digital modes; error correction

## Subelement E3 – Radio wave propagation

[3 Exam Questions – 3 Groups]

E3A – Propagation and technique, Earth-Moon-Earth communications; meteor scatter

E3B – Propagation and technique, trans-equatorial; long path; gray-line; multi-path prop-agation

E3C – Propagation and technique, Aurora propagation; selective fading; radio-path hori-zon; take-off angle over flat or sloping terrain; effects of ground on propagation; less common propagation modes

## Subelement E4 – Amateur practices

[5 Exam Questions – 5 Groups]

E4A – Test equipment: analog and digital instruments; spectrum and network analyzers, antenna analyzers; oscilloscopes; testing transistors; RF measurements

E4B – Measurement technique and limitations: instrument accuracy and performance limitations; probes; techniques to minimize errors; measurement of "Q"; instrument calibration

E4C – Receiver performance characteristics, phase noise, capture effect, noise floor, image rejection, MDS, signal-to-noise-ratio; selectivity

E4D – Receiver performance characteristics, blocking dynamic range, intermodulation and cross-modulation interference; 3rd order intercept; desensitization; preselection

E4E – Noise suppression: system noise; electrical appliance noise; line noise; locating noise sources; DSP noise reduction; noise blankers

## Subelement E5 – Electrical principles

*[4 Exam Questions – 4 Groups]*

E5A – Resonance and Q: characteristics of resonant circuits: series and parallel resonance; Q; half-power bandwidth; phase relationships in reactive circuits

E5B – Time constants and phase relationships: RLC time constants: definition; time constants in RL and RC circuits; phase angle between voltage and current; phase angles of series and parallel circuits

E5C – Impedance plots and coordinate systems: plotting impedances in polar coordinates; rectangular coordinates

E5D – AC and RF energy in real circuits: skin effect; electrostatic and electromagnetic fields; reactive power; power factor; coordinate systems

## Subelement E6 – Circuit components

*[6 Exam Questions – 6 Groups]*

E6A – Semiconductor materials and devices: semiconductor materials germanium, silicon, P-type, N-type; transistor types: NPN, PNP, junction, field-effect transistors: enhancement mode; depletion mode; MOS; CMOS; N-channel; P-channel

E6B – Semiconductor diodes

E6C – Integrated circuits: TTL digital integrated circuits; CMOS digital integrated circuits; gates

E6D – Optical devices and toroids: cathode-ray tube devices; charge-coupled devices (CCDs); liquid crystal displays (LCDs); toroids: permeability, core material, selecting, winding

E6E – Piezoelectric crystals and MMICs: quartz crystals; crystal oscillators and filters; monolithic amplifiers

E6F – Optical components and power systems: photoconductive principles and effects, photovoltaic systems, optical couplers, optical sensors, and optoisolators

## Subelement E7 – Practical circuits

*[8 Exam Questions – 8 Groups]*

E7A – Digital circuits: digital circuit principles and logic circuits: classes of logic elements; positive and negative logic; frequency dividers; truth tables

E7B – Amplifiers: Class of operation; vacuum tube and solid-state circuits; distortion and intermodulation; spurious and parasitic suppression; microwave amplifiers

E7C – Filters and matching networks: filters and impedance matching networks: types of networks; types of filters; filter applications; filter characteristics; impedance matching; DSP filtering

E7D – Power supplies and voltage regulators

E7E – Modulation and demodulation: reactance, phase and balanced modulators; detectors; mixer stages; DSP modulation and demodulation; software defined radio systems

E7F – Frequency markers and counters: frequency divider circuits; frequency marker generators; frequency counters

E7G – Active filters and op-amps: active audio filters; characteristics; basic circuit design; operational amplifiers

E7H – Oscillators and signal sources: types of oscillators; synthesizers and phase-locked loops; direct digital synthesizers

## Subelement E8 – Signals and emissions

*[4 Exam Questions – 4 Groups]*

E8A – AC waveforms: sine, square, sawtooth and irregular waveforms; AC measurements; average and PEP of RF signals; pulse and digital signal waveforms

E8B – Modulation and demodulation: modulation methods; modulation index and deviation ratio; pulse modulation; frequency and time division multiplexing

E8C – Digital signals: digital communications modes; CW; information rate vs. bandwidth; spread-spectrum communications; modulation methods

E8D – Waves, measurements, and RF grounding: peak-to-peak values, polarization; RF grounding

## Subelement E9 – Antennas and transmission lines

*[8 Exam Questions – 8 Groups]*

E9A – Isotropic and gain antennas: definition; used as a standard for comparison; radiation pattern; basic antenna parameters: radiation resistance and reactance, gain, beamwidth, efficiency

E9B – Antenna patterns: E and H plane patterns; gain as a function of pattern; antenna design; Yagi antennas

E9C – Wire and phased vertical antennas: beverage antennas; terminated and resonant rhombic antennas; elevation above real ground; ground effects as related to polarization; take-off angles

E9D – Directional antennas: gain; satellite antennas; antenna beamwidth; losses; SWR bandwidth; antenna efficiency; shortened and mobile antennas; grounding

E9E – Matching: matching antennas to feed lines; power dividers

E9F – Transmission lines: characteristics of open and shorted feed lines: 1/8 wavelength; 1/4 wavelength; 1/2 wavelength; feed lines: coax versus open-wire; velocity factor; electrical length; transformation characteristics of line terminated in impedance not equal to characteristic impedance

E9G – The Smith chart

E9H – Effective radiated power; system gains and losses; radio direction finding antennas

Once your new call sign is listed in the FCC database, you are good to go. For an Amateur Extra license in New Hampshire, your call sign will consist of a prefix of K, N or W, the number one (1), and a two-letter suffix, or a two-letter prefix beginning with A, N, K or W, the number one (1), and a one-letter suffix, or a two-letter prefix beginning with A, the number one (1), and a two-letter suffix.

Ham radio equipment can be expensive or you can do it "on the cheap." The cost will run from a couple hundred dollars to well in the thousands, depending on what you have available. eBay, and Craigslist are good places to start looking. Most ham clubs do some sort of hamfest annually wherein club members or others are willing to part with older equipment. See Appendix A for a list of clubs in New Hampshire.

Another excellent source of equipment, as well as advice on setting the equipment up and how to use it properly, is current ham operators. In Appendix B, the author has listed all the FCC licensed ham operators in New Hampshire, listed by city, and then sorted by street and house number on the street. Who knows, maybe someone who lives close to you is a ham operator. Be a good neighbor, stop by and have a chat with him/her.

Like CB radios, ham radios come in three formats – base, mobile, and handheld. They can use the electric company for power, or operate off a car battery. In the opinion of this author, in spite of the slightly higher cost of the equipment and having to take a test to legally use the equipment, ham radio is the way to go when concerned about communication during times of crisis.

**Canadian Call Sign Prefixes**

Because of our proximity to Canada, many times ham contact is made with our northern neighbors. Below is a chart showing the origin of Canadian call sign prefixes.

| Call Sign Prefix | Provence or Territory |
|---|---|
| CY0 | Sable Island |
| CY9 | St. Paul Island |
| VA1, VE1 | New Brunswick, Nova Scotia |
| VA2, VE2 | Quebec |
| VA3, VE3 | Ontario |
| VA4, VE4 | Manitoba |
| VA5, VE5 | Saskatchewan |
| VA6, VE6 | Alberta |
| VA7, VE7 | British Columbia |
| VE8 | North West Territories |
| VE9 | New Brunswick |
| VO1 | Newfoundland |

| | |
|---|---|
| VO2 | Labrador |
| VY0 | Nunavut |
| VY1 | Yukon |
| VY2 | Prince Edward Island |

## Common Radio Bands in the United States

Certain radio bands are more popular with ham radio enthusiasts than others. Below is a chart showing these bands and when they are most popular.

| | Band (meter) | Frequency (MHz) | Use |
|---|---|---|---|
| **HF** | 160 | 1.8 – 2.0 | Night |
| | 80 | 3.5 – 4.0 | Night and Local Day |
| | 40 | 7.0 – 7.3 | Night and Local Day |
| | 30 | 10.1 – 10.15 | CW and Digital |
| | 20 | 14.0 – 14.350 | World Wide Day and Night |
| | 17 | 18.068 – 18.168 | World Wide Day and Night |
| | 15 | 21.0 – 21.450 | Primarily Daytime |
| | 12 | 24.890 – 24.990 | Primarily Daytime |
| | 10 | 28.0 – 29.70 | Daytime during Sunspot highs |
| **VHF** | 6 | 50 – 54 | Local to World Wide |
| | 2 | 144 – 148 | Local to Medium Distance |
| **UHF** | 70 cm | 430 – 440 | Local |

## Common Amateur Radio Bands in Canada

### 160 Meter Band - Maximum bandwidth 6 kHz
1.800 - 1.820 MHz - CW
1.820 - 1.830 MHz - Digital Modes
1 830 - 1.840 MHz - DX Window
1.840 - 2.000 MHz - SSB and other wide band modes

### 80 Meter Band - Maximum bandwidth 6 kHz
3.500 - 3.580 MHz - CW
3.580 - 3.620 MHz - Digital Modes
3.620 - 3.635 MHz - Packet/Digital Secondary
3.635 - 3.725 MHz - CW
3.725 - 3.790 MHz - SSB and other side band modes*
3.790 - 3.800 MHz - SSB DX Window
3.800 - 4.000 MHz - SSB and other wide band modes

### 40 Meter Band - Maximum bandwidth 6 kHz
7.000 - 7.035 MHz - CW
7.035 - 7.050 MHz - Digital Modes
7.040 - 7.050 MHz - International packet

7.050 - 7.100 MHz - SSB
7.100 - 7.120 MHz - Packet within Region 2
7.120 - 7.150 MHz - CW
7.150 - 7.300 MHz - SSB and other wide band modes

## 30 Meter Band - Maximum bandwidth 1 kHz

10.100 - 10.130 MHz - CW only
10.130 - 10.140 MHz - Digital Modes
10.140 - 10.150 MHz - Packet

## 20 Meter Band - Maximum bandwidth 6 kHz

14.000 - 14.070 MHz - CW only
14.070 - 14.095 MHz - Digital Mode
14.095 - 14.099 MHz - Packet
14.100 MHz - Beacons
14.101 - 14.112 MHz - CW, SSB, packet shared
14.112 - 14.350 MHz - SSB
14.225 - 14.235 MHz - SSTV

## 17 Meter Band - Maximum bandwidth 6 kHz

18.068 - 18.100 MHz - CW
18.100 - 18.105 MHz - Digital Modes
18.105 - 18.110 MHz - Packet
18.110 - 18.168 MHz - SSB and other wide band modes

## 15 Meter Band - maximum bandwidth 6 kHz

21.000 - 21.070 MHz - CW
21.070 - 21.090 MHz - Digital Modes
21.090 - 21.125 MHz - Packet
21.100 - 21.150 MHz - CW and SSB
21.150 - 21.335 MHz - SSB and other wide band modes
21.335 - 21.345 MHz - SSTV
21.345 - 21.450 MHz - SSB and other wide band modes

## 12 Meter Band - Maximum bandwidth 6 kHz

24.890 - 24.930 MHz - CW
24.920 - 24.925 MHz - Digital Modes
24.925 - 24.930 MHz - Packet
24.930 - 24.990 MHz - SSB and other wide band modes

## 10 Meter Band - Maximum band width 20 kHz

28.000 - 28.200 MHz - CW
28.070 - 28.120 MHz - Digital Modes
28.120 - 28.190 MHz - Packet

28.190 - 28.200 MHz - Beacons
28.200 - 29.300 MHz - SSB and other wide band modes
29.300 - 29.510 MHz - Satellite
29.510 - 29.700 MHz - SSB, FM and repeaters

## 160 Meters (1.8-2.0 MHz)

1.800 - 2.000 CW
1.800 - 1.810 Digital Modes
1.810 CW QRP
1.843-2.000 SSB, SSTV and other wideband modes
1.910 SSB QRP
1.995 - 2.000 Experimental
1.999 - 2.000 Beacons

## 80 Meters (3.5-4.0 MHz)

3.590 RTTY/Data DX
3.570-3.600 RTTY/Data
3.790-3.800 DX window
3.845 SSTV
3.885 AM calling frequency

## 40 Meters (7.0-7.3 MHz)

7.040 RTTY/Data DX
7.080-7.125 RTTY/Data
7.171 SSTV
7.290 AM calling frequency

## 30 Meters (10.1-10.15 MHz)

10.130-10.140 RTTY
10.140-10.150 Packet

## 20 Meters (14.0-14.35 MHz)

14.070-14.095 RTTY
14.095-14.0995 Packet
14.100 NCDXF Beacons
14.1005-14.112 Packet
14.230 SSTV
14.286 AM calling frequency

## 17 Meters (18.068-18.168 MHz)

18.100-18.105 RTTY
18.105-18.110 Packet

## 15 Meters (21.0-21.45 MHz)

21.070-21.110 RTTY/Data

21.340 SSTV

## 12 Meters (24.89-24.99 MHz)

24.920-24.925 RTTY
24.925-24.930 Packet

## 10 Meters (28-29.7 MHz)

28.000-28.070 CW
28.070-28.150 RTTY
28.150-28.190 CW
28.200-28.300 Beacons
28.300-29.300 Phone
28.680 SSTV
29.000-29.200 AM
29.300-29.510 Satellite Downlinks
29.520-29.590 Repeater Inputs
29.600 FM Simplex
29.610-29.700 Repeater Outputs

## 6 Meters (50-54 MHz)

50.0-50.1 CW, beacons
50.060-50.080 beacon subband
50.1-50.3 SSB, CW
50.10-50.125 DX window
50.125 SSB calling
50.3-50.6 All modes
50.6-50.8 Nonvoice communications
50.62 Digital (packet) calling
50.8-51.0 Radio remote control (20-kHz channels)
51.0-51.1 Pacific DX window
51.12-51.48 Repeater inputs (19 channels)
51.12-51.18 Digital repeater inputs
51.5-51.6 Simplex (six channels)
51.62-51.98 Repeater outputs (19 channels)
51.62-51.68 Digital repeater outputs
52.0-52.48 Repeater inputs (except as noted; 23 channels)
52.02, 52.04 FM simplex
52.2 TEST PAIR (input)
52.5-52.98 Repeater output (except as noted; 23 channels)
52.525 Primary FM simplex
52.54 Secondary FM simplex
52.7 TEST PAIR (output)
53.0-53.48 Repeater inputs (except as noted; 19 channels)
53.0 Remote base FM simplex
53.02 Simplex
53.1, 53.2, 53.3, 53.4 Radio remote control

53.5-53.98 Repeater outputs (except as noted; 19 channels)
53.5, 53.6, 53.7, 53.8 Radio remote control
53.52, 53.9 Simplex

## 2 Meters (144-148 MHz)

144.00-144.05 EME (CW)
144.05-144.10 General CW and weak signals
144.10-144.20 EME and weak-signal SSB
144.200 National calling frequency
144.200-144.275 General SSB operation
144.275-144.300 Propagation beacons
144.30-144.50 New OSCAR subband
144.50-144.60 Linear translator inputs
144.60-144.90 FM repeater inputs
144.90-145.10 Weak signal and FM simplex (145.01,03,05,07,09 are widely used for
    packet)
145.10-145.20 Linear translator outputs
145.20-145.50 FM repeater outputs
145.50-145.80 Miscellaneous and experimental modes
145.80-146.00 OSCAR subband
146.01-146.37 Repeater inputs
146.40-146.58 Simplex
146.52 National Simplex Calling Frequency
146.61-146.97 Repeater outputs
147.00-147.39 Repeater outputs
147.42-147.57 Simplex
147.60-147.99 Repeater inputs

## 1.25 Meters (222-225 MHz)

222.0-222.150 Weak-signal modes
222.0-222.025 EME
222.05-222.06 Propagation beacons
222.1 SSB & CW calling frequency
222.10-222.15 Weak-signal CW & SSB
222.15-222.25 Local coordinator's option; weak signal, ACSB, repeater inputs, control
222.25-223.38 FM repeater inputs only
223.40-223.52 FM simplex
223.52-223.64 Digital, packet
223.64-223.70 Links, control
223.71-223.85 Local coordinator's option; FM simplex, packet, repeater outputs
223.85-224.98 Repeater outputs only

## 70 Centimeters (420-450 MHz)

420.00-426.00 ATV repeater or simplex with 421.25 MHz video carrier control links and
    experimental
426.00-432.00 ATV simplex with 427.250-MHz video carrier frequency

432.00-432.07 EME (Earth-Moon-Earth)
432.07-432.10 Weak-signal CW
432.10 70-cm calling frequency
432.10-432.30 Mixed-mode and weak-signal work
432.30-432.40 Propagation beacons
432.40-433.00 Mixed-mode and weak-signal work
433.00-435.00 Auxiliary/repeater links
435.00-438.00 Satellite only (internationally)
438.00-444.00 ATV repeater input with 439.250-MHz video carrier frequency and re-
    peater links
442.00-445.00 Repeater inputs and outputs (local option)
445.00-447.00 Shared by auxiliary and control links, repeaters and simplex (local option)
446.00 National simplex frequency
447.00-450.00 Repeater inputs and outputs (local option)

## 33 Centimeters (902-928 MHz)

902.0-903.0 Narrow-bandwidth, weak-signal communications
902.0-902.8 SSTV, FAX, ACSSB, experimental
902.1 Weak-signal calling frequency
902.8-903.0 Reserved for EME, CW expansion
903.1 Alternate calling frequency
903.0-906.0 Digital communications
906-909 FM repeater inputs
909-915 ATV
915-918 Digital communications
918-921 FM repeater outputs
921-927 ATV
927-928 FM simplex and links

## 23 Centimeters (1240-1300 MHz)

1240-1246 ATV #1
1246-1248 Narrow-bandwidth FM point-to-point links and digital, duplex with 1258-
    1260.
1248-1258 Digital Communications
1252-1258 ATV #2
1258-1260 Narrow-bandwidth FM point-to-point links digital, duplexed with 1246-1252
1260-1270 Satellite uplinks, reference WARC '79
1260-1270 Wide-bandwidth experimental, simplex ATV
1270-1276 Repeater inputs, FM and linear, paired with 1282-1288, 239 pairs every 25
    kHz, e.g. 1270.025, .050, etc.
1271-1283 Non-coordinated test pair
1276-1282 ATV #3
1282-1288 Repeater outputs, paired with 1270-1276
1288-1294 Wide-bandwidth experimental, simplex ATV
1294-1295 Narrow-bandwidth FM simplex services, 25-kHz channels
1294.5 National FM simplex calling frequency

1295-1297 Narrow bandwidth weak-signal communications (no FM)
1295.0-1295.8 SSTV, FAX, ACSSB, experimental
1295.8-1296.0 Reserved for EME, CW expansion
1296.00-1296.05 EME-exclusive
1296.07-1296.08 CW beacons
1296.1 CW, SSB calling frequency
1296.4-1296.6 Crossband linear translator input
1296.6-1296.8 Crossband linear translator output
1296.8-1297.0 Experimental beacons (exclusive)
1297-1300 Digital Communications

## 2300-2310 and 2390-2450 MHz

2300.0-2303.0 High-rate data
2303.0-2303.5 Packet
2303.5-2303.8 TTY packet
2303.9-2303.9 Packet, TTY, CW, EME
2303.9-2304.1 CW, EME
2304.1 Calling frequency
2304.1-2304.2 CW, EME, SSB
2304.2-2304.3 SSB, SSTV, FAX, Packet AM, Amtor
2304.30-2304.32 Propagation beacon network
2304.32-2304.40 General propagation beacons
2304.4-2304.5 SSB, SSTV, ACSSB, FAX, Packet AM, Amtor experimental
2304.5-2304.7 Crossband linear translator input
2304.7-2304.9 Crossband linear translator output
2304.9-2305.0 Experimental beacons
2305.0-2305.2 FM simplex (25 kHz spacing)
2305.20 FM simplex calling frequency
2305.2-2306.0 FM simplex (25 kHz spacing)
2306.0-2309.0 FM Repeaters (25 kHz) input
2309.0-2310.0 Control and auxiliary links
2390.0-2396.0 Fast-scan TV
2396.0-2399.0 High-rate data
2399.0-2399.5 Packet
2399.5-2400.0 Control and auxiliary links
2400.0-2403.0 Satellite
2403.0-2408.0 Satellite high-rate data
2408.0-2410.0 Satellite
2410.0-2413.0 FM repeaters (25 kHz) output
2413.0-2418.0 High-rate data
2418.0-2430.0 Fast-scan TV
2430.0-2433.0 Satellite
2433.0-2438.0 Satellite high-rate data
2438.0-2450.0 WB FM, FSTV, FMTV, SS experimental

## 3300-3500 MHz

| 3456.3-3456.4 Propagation beacons |
| --- |

| **5650-5925 MHz** |
| --- |
| 5760.3-5760.4 Propagation beacons |

| **10.00-10.50 GHz** |
| --- |
| 10.368 Narrow band calling frequency 10.3683-10.3684 Propagation beacons<br>10.3640 Calling frequency |

Now that you have your license (you do, don't you?), and your equipment, you are ready to go live. Below is a suggested start.

1) Assuming you have the HT set up to the appropriate frequency, and offset, press the mic button on the HT and say, "KK4HWX listening." Replace the KK4HWX with your own call sign, the one assigned to you by the FCC (it's the law). If no one responds to your call, you may wish to try again. Hopefully someone will respond to your call.

2) Once you get a response, it will be in the form of something like, "KK4HWX this is ??1??? in Eastport returning. My name is Florence. Back to you. ??1???" then a tone. Let us examine the response more closely. She first acknowledged your call sign (KK4HWX), then identified hers (??1???). From the 1 in her call sign, you know that she first got her license in Region 1, meaning she got it while a resident of CT, ME, MA, NH, RI, or VT. She then told you where she's transmitting from (Eastport). The term "returning" means that she is returning your call. Her name is Florence. The phrase, "Back to you" indicates that she is turning over the conversation to you. She then repeats her call sign. The tone indicates to you that it is okay to proceed with your response. BTW if she had used the term "Over" instead of "Back to you," it would mean the same thing, just fewer words.

3) At this point, press the mic button and continue with the conversation. You should restate your call sign often during the conversation (perhaps every 10 minutes or less and whenever you begin transmitting). Don't forget to say, "Over" or "Back to you" whenever you are giving Florence control of the conversation again.

4) When you are ready to stop the conversation, you should say goodbye or use the phrase "73", meaning "best wishes." Your conversation would end something like, "??1??? 73, this is KK4HWX clear and monitoring." The "clear and monitoring" indicates that you are going to continue to monitor the frequency. If you are not going to continue monitoring, you may wish to end the conversation with Florence with, "clear and QRT" instead. The QRT means that you are stopping transmissions.

**Call Sign Phonics**

Because of different accents of various people, sometimes it is difficult to understand call sign letters when spoken. For this reason, most ham operators verbalize their call sign using phonics. Below is a table listing the accepted phonics for letters and numbers.

| | |
|---|---|
| A = ALFA | S = SIERRA |
| B = BRAVO | T = TANGO |
| C = CHARLIE | U = UNIFORM |
| D = DELTA | V = VICTOR |
| E = ECHO | W = WHISKEY |
| F = FOXTROT | X = X-RAY |
| G = GOLF | Y = YANKEE |
| H = HOTEL | Z = ZULU (ZED) |
| I = INDIA | 1 = ONE |
| J = JULIETT | 2 = TWO |
| K = KILO | 3 = THREE (TREE) |
| L = LIMA | 4 = FOUR |
| M = MIKE | 5 = FIVE (FIFE) |
| N = NOVEMBER | 6 = SIX |
| O = OSCAR | 7 = SEVEN |
| P = PAPA (PA-PA') | 8 = EIGHT |
| Q = QUEBEC (KAY-BEK') | 9 = NINE (NINER) |
| R = ROMEO | 0 = ZERO |

The words in parentheses are the pronunciation or the alternate pronunciations for the words or numbers, but you will hear both used. With the letter Z, (ZED) is by far the most commonly used. With the number 9, NINER is the most common and easiest to understand ON THE AIR.

If you wish to use Morse code (CW) instead of voice communication, the "conversation" would follow the same steps, with a few modifications. To type out each word would require a lot of typing and translating. If you are like this author, more means more, i.e., more typing means more typos are likely. To help with this situation, CW enthusiasts have developed a language all their own – they use abbreviations for common phrases. Below is a chart showing some of these abbreviations.

| Abbreviation | Use |
|---|---|
| AR | Over |
| de | From or "this is" |
| ES | And |
| GM | Good Morning |
| K | Go |
| KN | Go only |
| NM | Name |
| QTH | Location |
| RPT | Report |
| R | Roger |
| SK | Clear |

| tnx | Thanks |
|---|---|
| UR | Your, you are |
| 73 | Best Wishes |

## Morse Code and Amateur Radio

If you wish to use CW, but are concerned about accuracy, you might consider purchasing a Morse code translator. This is an electronic device that you place in front of your speakers. It takes the CW sounds and translates them into English and displays the transmission on an LCD display. For the reverse, you can pick up a CW keyboard. With the keyboard, you type in your message and it converts the text to Morse code. The translator does not need to be attached to your ham equipment, whereas the keyboard would.

For your convenience, below is a table showing the Morse code signals and their meaning.

| Character | Code |
|---|---|
| A | · — |
| B | — · · · |
| C | — · — · |
| D | — · · |
| E | · |
| F | · · — · |
| G | — — · |
| H | · · · · |
| I | · · |
| J | · — — — |
| K | — · — |
| L | · — · · |
| M | — — |
| N | — · |
| O | — — — |
| P | · — — · |
| Q | — — · — |
| R | · — · |
| S | · · · |
| T | — |
| U | · · — |
| V | · · · — |
| W | · — — |
| X | — · · — |
| Y | — · — — |
| Z | — — · · |
| 0 | — — — — — |
| 1 | · — — — — |

| | |
|---|---|
| 2 | · · — — — |
| 3 | · · · — — |
| 4 | · · · · — |
| 5 | · · · · · |
| 6 | — · · · · |
| 7 | — — · · · |
| 8 | — — — · · |
| 9 | — — — — · |
| Ampersand [&], Wait | · — · · · |
| Apostrophe ['] | · — — — — · |
| At sign [@] | · — — · — · |
| Colon [:] | — — — · · · |
| Comma [,] | — — · · — — |
| Dollar sign [$] | · · · — · · — |
| Double dash [=] | — · · · — |
| Exclamation mark [!] | — · — · — — |
| Hyphen, Minus [-] | — · · · · — |
| Parenthesis closed [)] | — · — — · — |
| Parenthesis open [(] | — · — — · |
| Period [.] | · — · — · — |
| Plus [+] | · — · — · |
| Question mark [?] | · · — — · · |
| Quotation mark ["] | · — · · — · |
| Semicolon [;] | — · — · — · |
| Slash [/], Fraction bar | — · · — · |
| Underscore [_] | · · — — · — |

An advantage of using Morse Code is that when broadcasting CW, you are using reduced power, thereby saving your battery. Your battery is used only while actually transmitting or receiving.

**International Call Sign Prefixes**

As was stated earlier, all ham radio call signs begin with letters (or numbers) taken from blocks assigned to each country of the world by the *ITU - International Telecommunications Union,* a body controlled by the United Nations. The following chart indicates which call sign series are allocated to which countries.

| Call Sign Series | Allocated to |
|---|---|
| **AAA-ALZ** | **United States of America** |
| AMA-AOZ | Spain |
| APA-ASZ | Pakistan (Islamic Republic of) |
| ATA-AWZ | India (Republic of) |
| AXA-AXZ | Australia |
| AYA-AZZ | Argentine Republic |

| | |
|---|---|
| A2A-A2Z | Botswana (Republic of) |
| A3A-A3Z | Tonga (Kingdom of) |
| A4A-A4Z | Oman (Sultanate of) |
| A5A-A5Z | Bhutan (Kingdom of) |
| A6A-A6Z | United Arab Emirates |
| A7A-A7Z | Qatar (State of) |
| A8A-A8Z | Liberia (Republic of) |
| A9A-A9Z | Bahrain (State of) |
| BAA-BZZ | China (People's Republic of) |
| CAA-CEZ | Chile |
| CFA-CKZ | Canada |
| CLA-CMZ | Cuba |
| CNA-CNZ | Morocco (Kingdom of) |
| COA-COZ | Cuba |
| CPA-CPZ | Bolivia (Republic of) |
| CQA-CUZ | Portugal |
| CVA-CXZ | Uruguay (Eastern Republic of) |
| CYA-CZZ | Canada |
| C2A-C2Z | Nauru (Republic of) |
| C3A-C3Z | Andorra (Principality of) |
| C4A-C4Z | Cyprus (Republic of) |
| C5A-C5Z | Gambia (Republic of the) |
| C6A-C6Z | Bahamas (Commonwealth of the) |
| C7A-C7Z | World Meteorological Organization |
| C8A-C9Z | Mozambique (Republic of) |
| DAA-DRZ | Germany (Federal Republic of) |
| DSA-DTZ | Korea (Republic of) |
| DUA-DZZ | Philippines (Republic of the) |
| D2A-D3Z | Angola (Republic of) |
| D4A-D4Z | Cape Verde (Republic of) |
| D5A-D5Z | Liberia (Republic of) |
| D6A-D6Z | Comoros (Islamic Federal Republic of the) |
| D7A-D9Z | Korea (Republic of) |
| EAA-EHZ | Spain |
| EIA-EJZ | Ireland |
| EKA-EKZ | Armenia (Republic of) |
| ELA-ELZ | Liberia (Republic of) |
| EMA-EOZ | Ukraine |
| EPA-EQZ | Iran (Islamic Republic of) |
| ERA-ERZ | Moldova (Republic of) |
| ESA-ESZ | Estonia (Republic of) |
| ETA-ETZ | Ethiopia (Federal Democratic Republic of) |
| EUA-EWZ | Belarus (Republic of) |
| EXA-EXZ | Kyrgyz Republic |
| EYA-EYZ | Tajikistan (Republic of) |

| | |
|---|---|
| EZA-EZZ | Turkmenistan |
| E2A-E2Z | Thailand |
| E3A-E3Z | Eritrea |
| E4A-E4Z | Palestinian Authority |
| E5A-E5Z | New Zealand - Cook Islands (WRC-07) |
| E7A-E7Z | Bosnia and Herzegovina (Republic of) (WRC-07) |
| FAA-FZZ | France |
| GAA-GZZ | United Kingdom of Great Britain and Northern Ireland |
| HAA-HAZ | Hungary (Republic of) |
| HBA-HBZ | Switzerland (Confederation of) |
| HCA-HDZ | Ecuador |
| HEA-HEZ | Switzerland (Confederation of) |
| HFA-HFZ | Poland (Republic of) |
| HGA-HGZ | Hungary (Republic of) |
| HHA-HHZ | Haiti (Republic of) |
| HIA-HIZ | Dominican Republic |
| HJA-HKZ | Colombia (Republic of) |
| HLA-HLZ | Korea (Republic of) |
| HMA-HMZ | Democratic People's Republic of Korea |
| HNA-HNZ | Iraq (Republic of) |
| HOA-HPZ | Panama (Republic of) |
| HQA-HRZ | Honduras (Republic of) |
| HSA-HSZ | Thailand |
| HTA-HTZ | Nicaragua |
| HUA-HUZ | El Salvador (Republic of) |
| HVA-HVZ | Vatican City State |
| HWA-HYZ | France |
| HZA-HZZ | Saudi Arabia (Kingdom of) |
| H2A-H2Z | Cyprus (Republic of) |
| H3A-H3Z | Panama (Republic of) |
| H4A-H4Z | Solomon Islands |
| H6A-H7Z | Nicaragua |
| H8A-H9Z | Panama (Republic of) |
| IAA-IZZ | Italy |
| JAA-JSZ | Japan |
| JTA-JVZ | Mongolia |
| JWA-JXZ | Norway |
| JYA-JYZ | Jordan (Hashemite Kingdom of) |
| JZA-JZZ | Indonesia (Republic of) |
| J2A-J2Z | Djibouti (Republic of) |
| J3A-J3Z | Grenada |
| J4A-J4Z | Greece |
| J5A-J5Z | Guinea-Bissau (Republic of) |
| J6A-J6Z | Saint Lucia |
| J7A-J7Z | Dominica (Commonwealth of) |

| | |
|---|---|
| J8A-J8Z | Saint Vincent and the Grenadines |
| **KAA-KZZ** | **United States of America** |
| LAA-LNZ | Norway |
| LOA-LWZ | Argentine Republic |
| LXA-LXZ | Luxembourg |
| LYA-LYZ | Lithuania (Republic of) |
| LZA-LZZ | Bulgaria (Republic of) |
| L2A-L9Z | Argentine Republic |
| MAA-MZZ | United Kingdom of Great Britain and Northern Ireland |
| **NAA-NZZ** | **United States of America** |
| OAA-OCZ | Peru |
| ODA-ODZ | Lebanon |
| OEA-OEZ | Austria |
| OFA-OJZ | Finland |
| OKA-OLZ | Czech Republic |
| OMA-OMZ | Slovak Republic |
| ONA-OTZ | Belgium |
| OUA-OZZ | Denmark |
| PAA-PIZ | Netherlands (Kingdom of the) |
| PJA-PJZ | Netherlands (Kingdom of the) - Netherlands Antilles |
| PKA-POZ | Indonesia (Republic of) |
| PPA-PYZ | Brazil (Federative Republic of) |
| PZA-PZZ | Suriname (Republic of) |
| P2A-P2Z | Papua New Guinea |
| P3A-P3Z | Cyprus (Republic of) |
| P4A-P4Z | Netherlands (Kingdom of the) - Aruba |
| P5A-P9Z | Democratic People's Republic of Korea |
| RAA-RZZ | Russian Federation |
| SAA-SMZ | Sweden |
| SNA-SRZ | Poland (Republic of) |
| SSA-SSM | Egypt (Arab Republic of) |
| SSN-STZ | Sudan (Republic of the) |
| SUA-SUZ | Egypt (Arab Republic of) |
| SVA-SZZ | Greece |
| S2A-S3Z | Bangladesh (People's Republic of) |
| S5A-S5Z | Slovenia (Republic of) |
| S6A-S6Z | Singapore (Republic of) |
| S7A-S7Z | Seychelles (Republic of) |
| S8A-S8Z | South Africa (Republic of) |
| S9A-S9Z | Sao Tome and Principe (Democratic Republic of) |
| TAA-TCZ | Turkey |
| TDA-TDZ | Guatemala (Republic of) |
| TEA-TEZ | Costa Rica |
| TFA-TFZ | Iceland |
| TGA-TGZ | Guatemala (Republic of) |

| | |
|---|---|
| THA-THZ | France |
| TIA-TIZ | Costa Rica |
| TJA-TJZ | Cameroon (Republic of) |
| TKA-TKZ | France |
| TLA-TLZ | Central African Republic |
| TMA-TMZ | France |
| TNA-TNZ | Congo (Republic of the) |
| TOA-TQZ | France |
| TRA-TRZ | Gabonese Republic |
| TSA-TSZ | Tunisia |
| TTA-TTZ | Chad (Republic of) |
| TUA-TUZ | Côte d'Ivoire (Republic of) |
| TVA-TXZ | France |
| TYA-TYZ | Benin (Republic of) |
| TZA-TZZ | Mali (Republic of) |
| T2A-T2Z | Tuvalu |
| T3A-T3Z | Kiribati (Republic of) |
| T4A-T4Z | Cuba |
| T5A-T5Z | Somali Democratic Republic |
| T6A-T6Z | Afghanistan (Islamic State of) |
| T7A-T7Z | San Marino (Republic of) |
| T8A-T8Z | Palau (Republic of) |
| UAA-UIZ | Russian Federation |
| UJA-UMZ | Uzbekistan (Republic of) |
| UNA-UQZ | Kazakhstan (Republic of) |
| URA-UZZ | Ukraine |
| VAA-VGZ | Canada |
| VHA-VNZ | Australia |
| VOA-VOZ | Canada |
| VPA-VQZ | United Kingdom of Great Britain and Northern Ireland |
| VRA-VRZ | China (People's Republic of) - Hong Kong |
| VSA-VSZ | United Kingdom of Great Britain and Northern Ireland |
| VTA-VWZ | India (Republic of) |
| VXA-VYZ | Canada |
| VZA-VZZ | Australia |
| V2A-V2Z | Antigua and Barbuda |
| V3A-V3Z | Belize |
| V4A-V4Z | Saint Kitts and Nevis |
| V5A-V5Z | Namibia (Republic of) |
| V6A-V6Z | Micronesia (Federated States of) |
| V7A-V7Z | Marshall Islands (Republic of the) |
| V8A-V8Z | Brunei Darussalam |
| **WAA-WZZ** | **United States of America** |
| XAA-XIZ | Mexico |
| XJA-XOZ | Canada |

| | |
|---|---|
| XPA-XPZ | Denmark |
| XQA-XRZ | Chile |
| XSA-XSZ | China (People's Republic of) |
| XTA-XTZ | Burkina Faso |
| XUA-XUZ | Cambodia (Kingdom of) |
| XVA-XVZ | Viet Nam (Socialist Republic of) |
| XWA-XWZ | Lao People's Democratic Republic |
| XXA-XXZ | China (People's Republic of) - Macao (WRC-07) |
| XYA-XZZ | Myanmar (Union of) |
| YAA-YAZ | Afghanistan (Islamic State of) |
| YBA-YHZ | Indonesia (Republic of) |
| YIA-YIZ | Iraq (Republic of) |
| YJA-YJZ | Vanuatu (Republic of) |
| YKA-YKZ | Syrian Arab Republic |
| YLA-YLZ | Latvia (Republic of) |
| YMA-YMZ | Turkey |
| YNA-YNZ | Nicaragua |
| YOA-YRZ | Romania |
| YSA-YSZ | El Salvador (Republic of) |
| YTA-YUZ | Serbia (Republic of) (WRC-07) |
| YVA-YYZ | Venezuela (Republic of) |
| Y2A-Y9Z | Germany (Federal Republic of) |
| ZAA-ZAZ | Albania (Republic of) |
| ZBA-ZJZ | United Kingdom of Great Britain and Northern Ireland |
| ZKA-ZMZ | New Zealand |
| ZNA-ZOZ | United Kingdom of Great Britain and Northern Ireland |
| ZPA-ZPZ | Paraguay (Republic of) |
| ZQA-ZQZ | United Kingdom of Great Britain and Northern Ireland |
| ZRA-ZUZ | South Africa (Republic of) |
| ZVA-ZZZ | Brazil (Federative Republic of) |
| Z2A-Z2Z | Zimbabwe (Republic of) |
| Z3A-Z3Z | The Former Yugoslav Republic of Macedonia |
| 2AA-2ZZ | United Kingdom of Great Britain and Northern Ireland |
| 3AA-3AZ | Monaco (Principality of) |
| 3BA-3BZ | Mauritius (Republic of) |
| 3CA-3CZ | Equatorial Guinea (Republic of) |
| 3DA-3DM | Swaziland (Kingdom of) |
| 3DN-3DZ | Fiji (Republic of) |
| 3EA-3FZ | Panama (Republic of) |
| 3GA-3GZ | Chile |
| 3HA-3UZ | China (People's Republic of) |
| 3VA-3VZ | Tunisia |
| 3WA-3WZ | Viet Nam (Socialist Republic of) |
| 3XA-3XZ | Guinea (Republic of) |
| 3YA-3YZ | Norway |

| | |
|---|---|
| 3ZA-3ZZ | Poland (Republic of) |
| 4AA-4CZ | Mexico |
| 4DA-4IZ | Philippines (Republic of the) |
| 4JA-4KZ | Azerbaijani Republic |
| 4LA-4LZ | Georgia (Republic of) |
| 4MA-4MZ | Venezuela (Republic of) |
| 4OA-4OZ | Montenegro (Republic of) (WRC-07) |
| 4PA-4SZ | Sri Lanka (Democratic Socialist Republic of) |
| 4TA-4TZ | Peru |
| 4UA-4UZ | United Nations |
| 4VA-4VZ | Haiti (Republic of) |
| 4WA-4WZ | Democratic Republic of Timor-Leste (WRC-03) |
| 4XA-4XZ | Israel (State of) |
| 4YA-4YZ | International Civil Aviation Organization |
| 4ZA-4ZZ | Israel (State of) |
| 5AA-5AZ | Libya (Socialist People's Libyan Arab Jamahiriya) |
| 5BA-5BZ | Cyprus (Republic of) |
| 5CA-5GZ | Morocco (Kingdom of) |
| 5HA-5IZ | Tanzania (United Republic of) |
| 5JA-5KZ | Colombia (Republic of) |
| 5LA-5MZ | Liberia (Republic of) |
| 5NA-5OZ | Nigeria (Federal Republic of) |
| 5PA-5QZ | Denmark |
| 5RA-5SZ | Madagascar (Republic of) |
| 5TA-5TZ | Mauritania (Islamic Republic of) |
| 5UA-5UZ | Niger (Republic of the) |
| 5VA-5VZ | Togolese Republic |
| 5WA-5WZ | Samoa (Independent State of) |
| 5XA-5XZ | Uganda (Republic of) |
| 5YA-5ZZ | Kenya (Republic of) |
| 6AA-6BZ | Egypt (Arab Republic of) |
| 6CA-6CZ | Syrian Arab Republic |
| 6DA-6JZ | Mexico |
| 6KA-6NZ | Korea (Republic of) |
| 6OA-6OZ | Somali Democratic Republic |
| 6PA-6SZ | Pakistan (Islamic Republic of) |
| 6TA-6UZ | Sudan (Republic of the) |
| 6VA-6WZ | Senegal (Republic of) |
| 6XA-6XZ | Madagascar (Republic of) |
| 6YA-6YZ | Jamaica |
| 6ZA-6ZZ | Liberia (Republic of) |
| 7AA-7IZ | Indonesia (Republic of) |
| 7JA-7NZ | Japan |
| 7OA-7OZ | Yemen (Republic of) |
| 7PA-7PZ | Lesotho (Kingdom of) |

| | |
|---|---|
| 7QA-7QZ | Malawi |
| 7RA-7RZ | Algeria (People's Democratic Republic of) |
| 7SA-7SZ | Sweden |
| 7TA-7YZ | Algeria (People's Democratic Republic of) |
| 7ZA-7ZZ | Saudi Arabia (Kingdom of) |
| 8AA-8IZ | Indonesia (Republic of) |
| 8JA-8NZ | Japan |
| 8OA-8OZ | Botswana (Republic of) |
| 8PA-8PZ | Barbados |
| 8QA-8QZ | Maldives (Republic of) |
| 8RA-8RZ | Guyana |
| 8SA-8SZ | Sweden |
| 8TA-8YZ | India (Republic of) |
| 8ZA-8ZZ | Saudi Arabia (Kingdom of) |
| 9AA-9AZ | Croatia (Republic of) |
| 9BA-9DZ | Iran (Islamic Republic of) |
| 9EA-9FZ | Ethiopia (Federal Democratic Republic of) |
| 9GA-9GZ | Ghana |
| 9HA-9HZ | Malta |
| 9IA-9JZ | Zambia (Republic of) |
| 9KA-9KZ | Kuwait (State of) |
| 9LA-9LZ | Sierra Leone |
| 9MA-9MZ | Malaysia |
| 9NA-9NZ | Nepal |
| 9OA-9TZ | Democratic Republic of the Congo |
| 9UA-9UZ | Burundi (Republic of) |
| 9VA-9VZ | Singapore (Republic of) |
| 9WA-9WZ | Malaysia |
| 9XA-9XZ | Rwandese Republic |
| 9YA-9ZZ | Trinidad and Tobago |

**Third-Party Communications and Amateur Radio**

If all of this information about ham radios is somewhat intimidating, do not despair. "You" can still use ham radios for communications without being a licensed operator. Yes, you do have to have a ham license in order to legally transmit by ham equipment (or be under the direct supervision of someone else who is licensed), but there is an alternative – third-party communication.

Third-party communications occur when a licensed operator sends either written or verbal messages on behalf of unlicensed persons or organizations. There are two "controls" on third-party communication.

First, the communication must be noncommercial and of a personal nature. Asking a ham operator to contact another ham operator located in an area just hit by tornados and, be-

31

cause of being without power, phones do not work in Grandma Sally's city so you can check up on her, is okay. Asking a ham to send a message out that you have an old Chevy for sale would not be okay.

Second, the message must be going to a permitted area. Transmitting from a US location to another US location is okay, but transmitting from the US to another country may not. Because third-party communications bypass a country's normal telephone and postal systems, many foreign governments forbid such communications. In order to transmit from one country to another, the other country must have signed a third-party agreement with the US. What follows is a list of those countries that do have third-party a communications agreement with the US.

| V2 | Antigua / Barbuda |
|---|---|
| LU | Argentina |
| VK | Australia |
| V3 | Belize |
| CP | Bolivia |
| T9 | Bosnia-Herzegovina |
| PY | Brazil |
| VE | Canada |
| CE | Chile |
| HK | Colombia |
| D6 | Comoros (Federal Islamic Republic of) |
| TI | Costa Rica |
| CO | Cuba |
| HI | Dominican Republic |
| J7 | Dominica |
| HC | Ecuador |
| YS | El Salvador |
| C5 | Gambia, The |
| 9G | Ghana |
| J3 | Grenada |
| TG | Guatemala |
| 8R | Guyana |
| HH | Haiti |
| HR | Honduras |
| 4X | Israel |
| 6Y | Jamaica |
| JY | Jordan |
| EL | Liberia |
| V7 | Marshall Islands |
| XE | Mexico |
| V6 | Micronesia, Federated States of |
| YN | Nicaragua |
| HP | Panama |

| | |
|---|---|
| ZP | Paraguay |
| OA | Peru |
| DU | Philippines |
| VR6 | Pitcairn Island |
| V4 | St. Christopher / Nevis |
| J6 | St. Lucia |
| J8 | St. Vincent and the Grenadines |
| 9L | Sierra Leone |
| ZS | South Africa |
| 3DA | Swaziland |
| 9Y | Trinidad / Tobago |
| TA | Turkey |
| GB | United Kingdom |
| CX | Uruguay |
| YV | Venezuela |
| 4U1ITUITU | Geneva |
| 4U1VICVIC | Vienna |

Remember, before TSHTF, keep your pantry well stocked, your powder dry, and your batteries fully charged. 73

# APPENDIX A

## American Radio Relay League

## Affiliated Amateur Radio Clubs in

## New Hampshire

| | |
|---|---|
| ARRL Affiliated Club: | **White Mountain Amateur Radio Club** |
| City: | Conway, NH |
| Call Sign: | W1MWV |
| Section: | NH |
| Links: | www.w1mwv.com / www.w1mwv.org, http://www.w1mwv.com or http://www.w1mwv.org |

| | |
|---|---|
| ARRL Affiliated Club: | **Interstate Repeater Society, Inc.** |
| City: | Derry, NH |
| Call Sign: | K1CA |
| Section: | NH |
| Links: | http://www.irs.nhradio.org |

| | |
|---|---|
| ARRL Affiliated Club: | **Great Bay Radio Association** |
| City: | Dover, NH |
| Call Sign: | W1FZ |
| Section: | NH |
| Links: | www.w1fz.org |

| | |
|---|---|
| ARRL Affiliated Club: | **NHradio Inc.** |
| City: | Goffstown, NH |
| Call Sign: | K1AKS |
| Section: | NH |
| Links: | www.nhradio.org |

| | |
|---|---|
| ARRL Affiliated Club: | **Port City Amateur Radio Club** |
| City: | Greenland, NH |
| Call Sign: | W1WQM |
| Section: | NH |
| Links: | www.w1wqm.org |

| | |
|---|---|
| ARRL Affiliated Club: | **Twin State Radio Club, Inc.** |
| City: | Hanover, NH |
| Call Sign: | W1FN |
| Section: | NH |
| Links: | http://www.w1fn.org |

| | |
|---|---|
| ARRL Affiliated Club: | **Contoocook Valley Radio Club** |
| City: | Henniker, NH |
| Call Sign: | K1BKE |
| Section: | NH |
| Links: | http://www.qsl.net/k1bke |

| | |
|---|---|
| ARRL Affiliated Club: | **Cheshire County DX ARC** |
| City: | Keene, NH |
| Call Sign: | AD1T |
| Section: | NH |
| Links: | http://www.ccdx.org/ |

| | |
|---|---|
| ARRL Affiliated Club: | **68 Boyscout Amateur Radio Club** |
| City: | Laconia, NH |
| Call Sign: | KB1RSP |
| Section: | NH |
| Links: | nhtroop68.org |

| | |
|---|---|
| ARRL Affiliated Club: | **Central New Hampshire Amateur Radio Club** |
| City: | Laconia, NH |
| Call Sign: | W1JY |
| Section: | NH |
| Links: | www.cnharc.org |

| | |
|---|---|
| ARRL Affiliated Club: | **New Hampshire Scouting Service Club** |
| City: | Manchester, NH |
| Call Sign: | WB1BSA |
| Section: | NH |

| | |
|---|---|
| ARRL Special Service Club: | **Granite State Amateur Radio Association** |
| City: | Manchester, NH |
| Call Sign: | N1QC |
| Section: | NH |
| Links: | www.gsara.org |

| | |
|---|---|
| ARRL Affiliated Club: | **Nashua Area Radio Club** |
| City: | Nashua, NH |
| Call Sign: | N1FD |
| Section: | NH |
| Links: | http://www.n1fd.org |

| | |
|---|---|
| ARRL Affiliated Club: | **New Hampshire Interconnect Team** |
| City: | North Hampton, NH |
| Call Sign: | N1HIT |
| Section: | NH |
| Links: | http://www.n1hit.org |

| | |
|---|---|
| ARRL Affiliated Club: | **Saddleback Repeater Associates Inc.** |
| City: | Rochester, NH |
| Call Sign: | W1SRA |
| Section: | NH |
| Links: | http://www.sra.nhradio.org |

# APPENDIX B

## Amateur Radio License Holders

## in

## New Hampshire
## (by City)

## FCC Amateur Radio Licenses in Acworth

Call Sign: N1UUO
Bruce H Adams
Acworth NH 03601

Call Sign: KB1TVV
Deanne R Sanville
Acworth NH 03601

Call Sign: KB1TVW
Daniel R Sanville
Acworth NH 03601

Call Sign: KB1TYU
Shirley B Sanville
Acworth NH 03601

Call Sign: KB1TYY
Stephen Olson
Acworth NH 03601

## FCC Amateur Radio Licenses in Alexandria

Call Sign: KB1UGU
Richard Gonzalez
144 Walker Rd
Alexandria NH 03222

Call Sign: N1NYY
Richard Gonzalez
144 Walker Rd
Alexandria NH 03222

## FCC Amateur Radio Licenses in Allenstown

Call Sign: KC1JO
Abraham J Blow
14 Albin Ave
Allenstown NH 03275

Call Sign: KD1TT
William R Kirby Jr
389 Deerfield Rd
Allenstown NH 03275

Call Sign: K1RBE
William R Kirby Jr
389 Deerfield Rd
Allenstown NH 03275

Call Sign: N1RKR
Eric J Tingley
414 Deerfield Rd
Allenstown NH 03275

Call Sign: KB1GWE
Michael P Viar
41 Dowst Rd
Allenstown NH 03275

Call Sign: N1OVL
Michael G Valley
24 Emile Dr.
Allenstown NH 03275

Call Sign: KB1EUC
Thomas J Matthew
7 Fullam Cir
Allenstown NH 03275

Call Sign: W1MCE
David J Shrader
13 Lubern Ave
Allenstown NH 03275

Call Sign: N1QXK
Richard C Brown
4 Meadow Ln
Allenstown NH 03275

Call Sign: KB1MEQ
Maria E Brown
4 Meadow Ln
Allenstown NH 03275

Call Sign: KB1QVK
Jeffrey M Radzik
5 Monroe Ave
Allenstown NH 03275

Call Sign: K1RVP
Edward P Juranty
5 Pine Acres Rd
Allenstown NH 03275

Call Sign: N1TOB
James F Powers
73 River Rd
Allenstown NH 03275

Call Sign: KB1HOF
Matthew G Bouley
63 School St
Allenstown NH 03275

Call Sign: KA1MTE
Brian R Ernst
Swiftwater Dr
Allenstown NH 03275

Call Sign: N1MWX
Debra J Caswell
16 Town House Rd
Allenstown NH 03275

Call Sign: KB1OSY
James A Bernier
27 Webster St
Allenstown NH 03275

Call Sign: KA1YRV
Eric J Woodman
22 Woodridge Dr
Allenstown NH 03275

## FCC Amateur Radio Licenses in Alstead

Call Sign: KB1EGZ

Randall M Bois
Box 136a
Alstead NH 03602

Call Sign: N1KCA
Laura P Bascom
Box 138
Alstead NH 03602

Call Sign: N1TTE
Debra A Hunter
Box 144
Alstead NH 03602

Call Sign: N1IRK
Earl W Kathan Jr
Box 152a
Alstead NH 03602

Call Sign: KC7GTT
Harry E Chesley
Cobb Hill
Alstead NH 03602

Call Sign: KA1ZZB
Richard A Sonosky
1209 Forest Rd
Alstead NH 03602

Call Sign: KB1LDH
Hans J Waldmann
105 Homestead Rd
Alstead NH 03602

Call Sign: KE1HU
Robert L Bromley
142 Homestead Rd
Alstead NH 03602

Call Sign: N1HZM
Cary J Stratford
198 Murphy Hill Rd
Alstead NH 03602

Call Sign: KB1OWG

George J Moore
430 Old Settlers Rd
Alstead NH 03602

Call Sign: KA1TKU
Benjamin D Howard
Alstead NH 03602

Call Sign: KE1CM
Robert L Anderson
Alstead NH 036020232

Call Sign: N1PBY
Michael A Di Chiara
Alstead NH 03602

## FCC Amateur Radio Licenses in Alton

Call Sign: N1GZI
Edward J Lyons
Abednego Rd
Alton NH 03809

Call Sign: K1HPD
Allan W Young
72 Bowman Rd
Alton NH 03102

Call Sign: N1LRG
Gerald E Verrette
Box 197l Hamwoods Rd
Alton NH 03809

Call Sign: KB4DPJ
Jean B Whitehouse
Box 236a2
Alton NH 03809

Call Sign: N4DAM
Francis E Whitehouse
Box 236a2
Alton NH 03809

Call Sign: N1AYT

William M Chatman
321 Dudley Rd
Alton NH 03809

Call Sign: W1GWU
Robert V Tiffany
102 Lockes Corner Rd
Alton NH 03809

Call Sign: N1SDW
John T Conboy
Main St
Alton NH 03809

Call Sign: N1DBW
Warren C Buchanan
8 Mitchell Ave
Alton NH 03809

Call Sign: N1XBF
Conal B Dochartaigh
P.O. 972
Alton NH 03809

Call Sign: KB1OVB
Lawrence A Poliquin
314 Powder Mill Rd
Alton NH 03809

Call Sign: W1PAL
Lawrence A Poliquin
314 Powder Mill Rd
Alton NH 03809

Call Sign: N1VAR
Donald E Smith
155 Roberts Cove Rd
Alton NH 03809

Call Sign: N4NJB
Kathryn M Hedspeth
62 Stockbridge Corner Rd
Alton NH 03809

Call Sign: AC1Z

Robert W Daniels
208 Stockbridge Corner Rd
Alton NH 03809

Call Sign: KB1ELJ
Jamie S Tuttle
86 Stonewall Rd.
Alton NH 03809

Call Sign: KB1BFZ
Donald O Best
29 Suncook Valley Rd
Alton NH 03809

Call Sign: KB1RQN
Janet M Stumpf
55 Valley Rd
Alton NH 03809

Call Sign: KB1RQO
David G Tuttle
55 Valley Rd
Alton NH 03809

Call Sign: KJ1CBF
Janet M Stumpf
55 Valley Rd
Alton NH 03809

Call Sign: KD1CBF
David G Tuttle
55 Valley Rd
Alton NH 03809

Call Sign: KB1Z
Henry B Stevens
Alton NH 03809

Call Sign: N1NLP
Jeffrey B Kantar
Alton NH 03809

Call Sign: N6PMM
John J Lauer
Alton NH 03809

### FCC Amateur Radio Licenses in Alton Bay

Call Sign: N1CMF
Robert A Peck
Box 449
Alton Bay NH 03810

Call Sign: KA3KTS
Stuart A Siegler
45 County Rd
Alton Bay NH 03810

Call Sign: KB1IK
Timothy J Goodwin
Gedney Court
Alton Bay NH 03810

Call Sign: KB1FAE
William D Shurbert
9 Happy Hollow Dr
Alton Bay NH 03810

Call Sign: K1MPK
William D Shurbert
9 Happy Hollow Dr
Alton Bay NH 03810

Call Sign: KA1QIP
Marty J Tippett
Hc West Box 449
Alton Bay NH 03810

Call Sign: WA1HXH
Peter J George
6 Legal Lane
Alton Bay NH 03810

Call Sign: NF1V
Arthur E Richardson
16 Mill Cove Rd
Alton Bay NH 038104076

Call Sign: KA1MF

Donald R Hughes Jr
92 Minge Cove Rd
Alton Bay NH 038104063

Call Sign: N1ROH
Levon Maserian
2 Mt Pleasant Ave
Alton Bay NH 03810

Call Sign: K1DYY
Thomas B Newman Jr
15 Olive St
Alton Bay NH 03810

Call Sign: K1DZU
Thomas Toleos
Rand Hill Rd
Alton Bay NH 03810

Call Sign: WA1QBZ
Gay L Lamoureux
201 Route 11-D
Alton Bay NH 03810

Call Sign: WA1RVF
Kenneth T Leach
Trask Rd
Alton Bay NH 03810

Call Sign: N1VZV
John T Cheshire Jr
Alton Bay NH 03810

Call Sign: N1ZEZ
Clarisse Kersch
Alton Bay NH 03810

Call Sign: KB1EQY
Walter E Gibbs Jr
Alton Bay NH 03810

### FCC Amateur Radio Licenses in Amherst

Call Sign: K1ZDI

Henry J Perras
2 Aglipay Dr
Amherst NH 03031

Call Sign: W1QNH
Robert C Treadwell Jr
133 Amherst St
Amherst NH 030310327

Call Sign: K4NEH
Vernon L Townsend Sr
7 Austin Rd
Amherst NH 030312519

Call Sign: KA1JDL
Nancy E Townsend
7 Austin Rd
Amherst NH 03031

Call Sign: KA1UEQ
Nathan E Townsend
7 Austin Rd
Amherst NH 03031

Call Sign: KB1ODK
Dean P Marirea
17 B Deerwood Dr
Amherst NH 030312002

Call Sign: W2TUJ
Morris M Weisberg
128 Baboosic Lake Rd
Amherst NH 030311920

Call Sign: KY1N
New Hampshire Council Of
Ves
6 Birch Dr
Amherst NH 030311807

Call Sign: W1DES
Dead Ender Society
6 Birch Dr
Amherst NH 030311807

Call Sign: WA1UXA
Balinski Amateur Radio
Fellowship
6 Birch Dr
Amherst NH 030311807

Call Sign: WW1Y
James M Heedles
6 Birch Dr
Amherst NH 030311807

Call Sign: WD2DW
David P Worrall
11 Briarwood Ln
Amherst NH 03031

Call Sign: KA1PDW
Kevin N Corriveau
24 Broadway St
Amherst NH 03031

Call Sign: N1JLE
Jeremy L Prine
20 Brook Rd
Amherst NH 03031

Call Sign: KY1D
Cynthia Hensley
29 Brook Rd
Amherst NH 030312409

Call Sign: N1WDY
Richard D Lefebvre
31 Buckridge Dr
Amherst NH 03031

Call Sign: AA1EI
Edward A Urbanik
9 Candlewood Dr
Amherst NH 03031

Call Sign: W1PSU
Edward A Urbanik
9 Candlewood Dr
Amherst NH 03031

Call Sign: KD6PPC
Jerry J Redington
2 Chatham Court
Amherst NH 03031

Call Sign: KD6TAM
Martha S Redington
2 Chatham Court
Amherst NH 03031

Call Sign: W5SWE
Denny R Townson
58 Chestnut Hill Rd
Amherst NH 03031

Call Sign: K1WFE
Jo An M Tyrrell
96 Chestnut Hill Rd
Amherst NH 03031

Call Sign: K1JMT
Jo An M Tyrrell
96 Chestnut Hill Rd
Amherst NH 03031

Call Sign: KA1JMS
Choral E Maxwell
104 Chestnut Hill Rd
Amherst NH 03031

Call Sign: KA1LUC
Darren A Jones
Chestnut Hill Rd
Amherst NH 03031

Call Sign: KA1LRG
Phillip A Jones
Chestnut Hill Rd
Amherst NH 03031

Call Sign: N1LPQ
Calvin E Stow
52 Christian Hill Rd
Amherst NH 03031

Call Sign: N1IBF
Carol L Lewis
29 Colonel Wilkins Rd
Amherst NH 03031

Call Sign: KA1YGC
Sheila G Tymowicz
6 Douglas Dr
Amherst NH 03031

Call Sign: N1VEF
Theodore G Carr
6 Greenbriar Ln
Amherst NH 03031

Call Sign: WB2WZL
Thomas J Lewis
29 Colonel Wilkins Rd
Amherst NH 03031

Call Sign: WA1PGE
Richard J Nixon
9 Douglas Dr
Amherst NH 03031

Call Sign: KB1NRO
Micheal F Glisson
8 Hemlock Hill
Amherst NH 03031

Call Sign: N1ZUF
Timothy Parker
11 Courthouse Rd
Amherst NH 03031

Call Sign: N4FPU
Gary J Strauch
16 Dream Lake Dr
Amherst NH 03031

Call Sign: KB1MAX
Matthew W Kincaid
17 Hickory Dr
Amherst NH 03031

Call Sign: N1PHO
Brian P Quick
27 Cricket Corner Rd
Amherst NH 03031

Call Sign: KR1TD
Kevin M Fiebke
15 Edgewood Run
Amherst NH 03031

Call Sign: KB1FBI
Gary E Kaufman
12 Highland Dr
Amherst NH 03031

Call Sign: WA1ALL
Michael J Morelli
6 Cricket Hill Dr
Amherst NH 03031

Call Sign: W1GHE
Thomas P Kustes
10 Fairway Dr
Amherst NH 030312715

Call Sign: N1THP
Albert E Denis
167 Hollis Rd
Amherst NH 03031

Call Sign: N3CZO
Paul R Bendeck
29 Cross Rd
Amherst NH 030312124

Call Sign: KB3RKQ
Hammad Iqbal
4 Farmington Rd
Amherst NH 03031

Call Sign: W1JR
Joseph H Reisert Jr
3 Hubbard Rd
Amherst NH 03031

Call Sign: KB1LMN
Gregory G Smith
6 Deer Hollow Dr
Amherst NH 03031

Call Sign: KB3TFK
Uzma Iqbal
4 Farmington Rd
Amherst NH 03031

Call Sign: N2RJG
Douglas J Kaputa Mr
1 Jennifer Lane
Amherst NH 030312721

Call Sign: WA4LDL
Stephen J Uurtamo
13 Deer Hollow Dr
Amherst NH 030311808

Call Sign: NO1I
Victor L Bennison
2 Georgetown Dr
Amherst NH 03031

Call Sign: KF6NFI
Diane Loux
29 Josiah Bartlett Rd
Amherst NH 03031

Call Sign: KA1YGB
Martin F Tymowicz
6 Douglas Dr
Amherst NH 03031

Call Sign: KB1JPF
Timothy J Rogers
5 Greenbriar Ln
Amherst NH 03031

Call Sign: N1QXP
George L Riel
37 Josiah Bartlett Rd.
Amherst NH 03031

Call Sign: WB7TXK
Roger V Wegehoft
2 Juniper Dr
Amherst NH 03031

Call Sign: W1UN
Edward W Hanna
13 Nathanial Dr
Amherst NH 03031

Call Sign: W1CAT
Michael J Badzinski
29 Pond Parish Rd
Amherst NH 03031

Call Sign: WB7UBO
Deborah D Wegehoft
2 Juniper Dr
Amherst NH 03031

Call Sign: KB1TLA
Madison E Colby
12 Nicholas Rd
Amherst NH 03031

Call Sign: W1OL
Michael J Badzinski
29 Pond Parish Rd
Amherst NH 03031

Call Sign: KB1HIC
Bradford H Maxwell
15 Juniper Dr
Amherst NH 03031

Call Sign: KB1TJZ
Walter D Colby
12 Nichols Rd
Amherst NH 03031

Call Sign: W1ZQ
Michael J Badzinski
29 Pond Parish Rd
Amherst NH 03031

Call Sign: N1IZL
Fred Iannelli Ii
6 Lakeview St
Amherst NH 03031

Call Sign: K1EYE
Arthur L Hebert
50 Old Manchester Rd
Amherst NH 03031

Call Sign: W1CYB
William E Rose Jr
8 Ponemah Hill Rd
Amherst NH 030312808

Call Sign: KB1TFM
Donald B Holden
23 Manchester Rd
Amherst NH 03031

Call Sign: K1HS
Phillip S Rutledge
54 Old Manchester Rd
Amherst NH 03031

Call Sign: W1DAB
Roberta F Rose
8 Ponemah Hill Rd
Amherst NH 03031

Call Sign: W1DJH
Frank M Weinstein
3 Martingale Rd Box 116
Amherst NH 030310116

Call Sign: W1RX
Steven J Grossman
14 Old Mt Vernon Rd
Amherst NH 03031

Call Sign: WW1Z
John T Rose
8 Ponemah Hill Rd
Amherst NH 03031

Call Sign: KB1RUD
John G Bachman
100 Merrimack Rd
Amherst NH 03031

Call Sign: K1ACC
C Thomas Carson
5 Pinewood Dr
Amherst NH 03031

Call Sign: KA1SNW
Frederick R Geis
1 Ponemah Rd
Amherst NH 030313003

Call Sign: W1JGB
John G Bachman
100 Merrimack Rd
Amherst NH 03031

Call Sign: AA1CO
Raymond C Hall
27 Pinewood Dr
Amherst NH 03031

Call Sign: KA1TLO
Anne Y Bellefontaine
1 Ponemah Rd
Amherst NH 03031

Call Sign: WA4RLG
Jeffrey R Harrow
2 Nathan Lord Rd
Amherst NH 03031

Call Sign: NG7A
George Cooley
Po Box 112
Amherst NH 03031

Call Sign: WB1DZT
Thomas A Geis
1 Ponemah Rd
Amherst NH 03031

Call Sign: WB1FRE
Georgeann M Geis
1 Ponemah Rd
Amherst NH 030313003

Call Sign: KB1GKL
Gregory M Geis
1 Ponemah Rd
Amherst NH 030313003

Call Sign: K1ZQ
Thomas A Geis
1 Ponemah Rd
Amherst NH 030313003

Call Sign: KA1SSS
John A Sotiriou
13 River Rd
Amherst NH 03031

Call Sign: KB1CMO
Richard G Mc Kenzie
31 Schoolhouse Rd
Amherst NH 03031

Call Sign: KA1SRC
Brent C Talbot
9 Shadow Ln
Amherst NH 03031

Call Sign: WB3LRK
David S Beach
25 Simeon Wilson Rd
Amherst NH 030312142

Call Sign: W1ETC
John K Webb
Southfield Rd
Amherst NH 030310747

Call Sign: KB1RWI
John M Wight
98 Spring Rd
Amherst NH 03031

Call Sign: N1DGA
B Richard Fow
100 State Route 101a
Amherst NH 03031

Call Sign: N1JDY
Kevin C Zalondek
53 The Flume
Amherst NH 03031

Call Sign: KB1HFR
Cynthia A Schmidt
53 The Flume
Amherst NH 03031

Call Sign: N1SXJ
Richard P Perry
40 Thorntons Ferry Rd 1
Amherst NH 03031

Call Sign: KB1PWV
Kenneth J Breeman Iii
4 Tranquility Lane
Amherst NH 03031

Call Sign: KB1EFK
Joshua D Robinson
14 Veterans Rd 22
Amherst NH 03031

Call Sign: K0BQF
Raymond D Townson
11 Veterans Rd.   Apt #214
Amherst NH 03031

Call Sign: N1FLP
Robert C Schaumann
14 Village Woods Dr
Amherst NH 03031

Call Sign: W1FKW
Caldwell P Smith
4 Washington Dr
Amherst NH 03031

Call Sign: N1JDP
Rodney D Bowes
7 Wilkins Rd
Amherst NH 03031

Call Sign: KB1LSR
Henry J Wisneski
11 Windsor Dr
Amherst NH 030312105

Call Sign: N1WWU
David R Mc Kenna
30 Windsor Dr
Amherst NH 03031

Call Sign: KB1IC
Peter J Kajenski
33 Windsor Dr
Amherst NH 03031

Call Sign: N1QGG
Carleton L Kingsford
4 Winterberry Dr
Amherst NH 03031

Call Sign: KD6BU
Jared Kondratuk
5 Woodbine Ln
Amherst NH 03031

Call Sign: K1PH
Pauer Family Radio Club
Amherst NH 03031

Call Sign: KA1JMB
Benjamin Brewster
Amherst NH 03031

Call Sign: KB1DJA
Stephen S Corbin
Amherst NH 030310938

Call Sign: KB1T
John G David

Amherst NH 03031

Call Sign: KM3T
David H Pascoe
Amherst NH 03031

Call Sign: N5VUP
Brett A Pauer
Amherst NH 03031

Call Sign: W1DAY
David E Day
Amherst NH 030311212

Call Sign: W6PH
Kurt B Pauer
Amherst NH 03031

Call Sign: WW1D
Augustus H Rice Jr
Amherst NH 03031

Call Sign: KB1FLS
Paul Macphee
Amherst NH 03031

Call Sign: AB1CD
Stephen S Corbin
Amherst NH 030310938

Call Sign: NE1V
Stephen S Corbin
Amherst NH 030310938

Call Sign: W1PH
Pauer Family Radio Club
Amherst NH 03031

Call Sign: KB1QOD
Eugene A Heighton
Amherst NH 030310836

Call Sign: KF7HPX
Olenka N Cooley
Amherst NH 03031

**FCC Amateur Radio
Licenses in Andover**

Call Sign: KB1UJD
Heather H Makechnie
158 Boston Hill Rd
Andover NH 03216

Call Sign: N1DMF
Robert D Bussey
207 Cilleyville Rd
Andover NH 03216

Call Sign: N1DIY
Robert D Bussey
207 Cilleyville Rd
Andover NH 03216

Call Sign: KC7ZFA
Jeffrey B Woodward
456 Franklin Hwy
Andover NH 03216

Call Sign: KB4QC
Joel E Provost
11 Kearsarge Mountain Rd
Andover NH 03216

Call Sign: KB1KSP
Ronald Vasquez
66 Sam Hill Rd
Andover NH 03216

Call Sign: K1TMD
Peter C Aube
84 W Shore Dr
Andover NH 03216

Call Sign: N1XHV
Barbara J Aube
84 West Shore Dr
Andover NH 03216

Call Sign: N1XGK

Henry J Aube
84 West Shore Dr
Andover NH 03216

Call Sign: KB1ICM
Michael J Wiley
Andover NH 03216

**FCC Amateur Radio
Licenses in Antrim**

Call Sign: K1JNJ
Harry B Smith Iii
Box 411
Antrim NH 034409207

Call Sign: N1NQY
Chad S Moody
Box 53a
Antrim NH 03440

Call Sign: WA1LHE
William A Mc Kinnon
37 Bridle Rd
Antrim NH 03440

Call Sign: KB1VME
Vincent S Lyon
26 Buttercup Ln
Antrim NH 03440

Call Sign: K2SYA
A. Fred Anderson
5 Forest St
Antrim NH 034403603

Call Sign: WB8GLQ
Michael J Nugent Jr
17 Grove St
Antrim NH 03440

Call Sign: WB1AAZ
Michael C Morton
23 High St
Antrim NH 03440

Call Sign: KB1JYM
Ralph L Morton
23 High St
Antrim NH 03440

Call Sign: WB1AKF
David A Dubois
45 Miltimore Rd
Antrim NH 03440

Call Sign: KA1JRS
Richard B Hodges Iii
52 Old N Branch Rd
Antrim NH 03440

Call Sign: N1WWM
Glenn E Beebe
52 Old N Branch Rd
Antrim NH 03440

Call Sign: N1WWN
Travis S Beebe
52 Old N Branch Rd
Antrim NH 03440

Call Sign: N1DZZ
Ralmond H Burgess
103 Old Pound Rd
Antrim NH 03440

Call Sign: W1IPS
Ralmond H Burgess
103 Old Pound Rd
Antrim NH 03440

Call Sign: N1MDH
Souly A Loizos
349 Pleasant Ave
Antrim NH 03440

Call Sign: KA7TRA
Bruce E Berwick
72 Reed Carr Rd
Antrim NH 034403203

Call Sign: N1CXF
Barbara I Berwick
72 Reed Carr Rd
Antrim NH 034403203

Call Sign: AA1DF
Souly Loizos
Antrim NH 03440

Call Sign: WB2HDQ
Sandy A Larson
Antrim NH 03440

Call Sign: K1SAL
Sandy A Larson
Antrim NH 03440

## FCC Amateur Radio Licenses in Ashland

Call Sign: KB1EOE
Patrick J Abear
62 Hicks Hill Rd
Ashland NH 03217

Call Sign: KB1SKM
Susannah L Voniderstine
111 North Ashland Rd
Ashland NH 03217

Call Sign: KB1QGT
Gordon F Mccormack Sr
101 Riverside Dr
Ashland NH 03217

Call Sign: KB1PKU
Gordon F Mccormack Jr
101 Riverside Dr
Ashland NH 03217

Call Sign: NV1G
Gordon F Mccormack Sr
101 Riverside Dr
Ashland NH 03217

Call Sign: W1YWC
Daniel J Rafferty Jr
West Shore Rd Lake
Winona
Ashland NH 032170622

Call Sign: KB1FCY
Jennifer M Head
Ashland NH 03217

Call Sign: KB1VVU
Thomas E Mcnamara Jr
Ashland NH 03217

## FCC Amateur Radio Licenses in Ashuelot

Call Sign: W2HTA
Eugene W Clark
23 Broad Brook Rd
Ashuelot NH 03441

Call Sign: W9KDY
Lawrence B Smith Sr
161 Main St Apt 1
Ashuelot NH 03441

Call Sign: WA4MST
Maryan G Morrell
Ashuelot NH 03441

Call Sign: KB1NQM
Christopher J Platz
Ashuelot NH 03441

## FCC Amateur Radio Licenses in Atkinson

Call Sign: N1HFF
Lloyd G Swanburg
13 Amberwood Dr
Atkinson NH 03811

Call Sign: KA1GR

Loren O Albright
18 Bittersweet Lane
Atkinson NH 03811

Call Sign: WA1AUM
Robert H Dahlquist
8 Brookside Ter
Atkinson NH 03811

Call Sign: AH2V
Desmond D Kinnersley
18 Brookside Terrace
Atkinson NH 03811

Call Sign: K1MDX
Dorothy G Conley
14 Conley Rd
Atkinson NH 03811

Call Sign: WA2KOL
Warner A Reed
7 Cottontail Ln
Atkinson NH 03811

Call Sign: KB1DFG
Jeanne V Schipelliti
7 Dearborn Ridge Rd
Atkinson NH 038112229

Call Sign: WB1GEX
Peter Schipelliti
7 Dearborn Ridge Rd
Atkinson NH 038112229

Call Sign: N1VDR
Theodore J Sattley
94 East Rd
Atkinson NH 038112224

Call Sign: N2RP
Robert D Peck
16 Emery Dr
Atkinson NH 03811

Call Sign: KB1FBJ

Donald L Doughty
4 Forest Rd
Atkinson NH 03811

Call Sign: WB2ELF
Marc E Goldfarb
5 Green Hill Dr
Atkinson NH 038112506

Call Sign: N1EBB
Stephen E Toohey
24 Heald Bailey Rd.
Atkinson NH 03811

Call Sign: K1SET
Stephen E Toohey
24 Heald Bailey Rd.
Atkinson NH 03811

Call Sign: WB1EAL
Walter P Stiebitz
16 Ironwood Ln
Atkinson NH 03811

Call Sign: W1OUV
Vernon C Mac Neill Jr
35 Island Pond Rd
Atkinson NH 03811

Call Sign: KB1WLE
Paul A Gilberti Jr
42 Island Pond Rd
Atkinson NH 03811

Call Sign: N1FDH
Claire T Lussier
Main St
Atkinson NH 038110968

Call Sign: N1APV
Thomas W Christenson
3 Meeting Rock Dr
Atkinson NH 03811

Call Sign: KB1LT

Donald P Jackman
6 Oak Hill Cir
Atkinson NH 03811

Call Sign: N1DHF
Harriet C Jackman
6 Oak Hill Cir
Atkinson NH 03811

Call Sign: W1ILC
Douglas E Wilson
34 Overlook Dr
Atkinson NH 03811

Call Sign: K1KEO
John H Bradshaw
14 Pine Knoll Dr
Atkinson NH 03811

Call Sign: KA1MLC
Charles J Mc Carthy
51 Providence Hill Rd
Atkinson NH 03811

Call Sign: N1HSM
Stanley J Graziano
1 Rockingchair Lane
Atkinson NH 03811

Call Sign: N1ITI
Nancy B Graziano
1 Rockingchair Lane
Atkinson NH 03811

Call Sign: KB1ELF
Christopher R Page
18 Sawyer Ave
Atkinson NH 03811

Call Sign: N1TZW
Terence E Banville
30 Sleepy Hollow Rd
Atkinson NH 03811

Call Sign: W1OTR

Jean C Sanders
1 Stonewall Ter
Atkinson NH 03811

Call Sign: K1WS
William J Sanders
1 Stonewall Terr
Atkinson NH 03811

Call Sign: KB1MKV
Robert S Kugler
36 Summit Dr
Atkinson NH 03811

Call Sign: W1CCD
Herbert G Witherell
17 Sunset Dr
Atkinson NH 03811

Call Sign: N1QLY
James K Ligouri
7 Sycamore Ct
Atkinson NH 03811

Call Sign: KB1WOA
Michael W Cronin
9 Upland Rd
Atkinson NH 03811

Call Sign: KB1WYL
Paul R Cronin
9 Upland Rd
Atkinson NH 03811

Call Sign: WA1HSD
Dean B Killam
West Side Dr
Atkinson NH 03811

Call Sign: KB1PBC
Matthew S Jasiak
22 Wood Dr
Atkinson NH 03811

Call Sign: WA1UJN

Louise L Waters
6 Woodlawn Ave
Atkinson NH 03811

Call Sign: W1GPV
Frederick J Waters Sr
Woodlawn Ave
Atkinson NH 03811

Call Sign: K1RJW
Howard Potter
Atkinson NH 03811

Call Sign: N1FLZ
Bertha M Potter
Atkinson NH 03811

Call Sign: N1HM
Harold P Mierop
Atkinson NH 038110753

Call Sign: N1KUP
Patricia I Mierop
Atkinson NH 03811

Call Sign: N1TAE
Michael A Costanzo
Atkinson NH 03811

Call Sign: W1UV
Loren O Albright
Atkinson NH 03811

Call Sign: KB1UYO
Peter E Torosian
Atkinson NH 03811

Call Sign: W1CBY
Peter E Torosian
Atkinson NH 03811

**FCC Amateur Radio
Licenses in Auburn**

Call Sign: N1CPZ

Ronald A Langley
273 Bunker Hill Rd
Auburn NH 03032

Call Sign: KB1HYO
Michael A Dignard
627 Bunker Hill Rd
Auburn NH 03032

Call Sign: W1YVM
Michael A Dignard
627 Bunker Hill Rd
Auburn NH 03032

Call Sign: N1WDT
Thomas J Lorden
11 Button Dr
Auburn NH 03032

Call Sign: N1UJE
John J Riik
170 Chester Rd
Auburn NH 03032

Call Sign: N1IOF
Shepard L Siegel
287 Chester Rd
Auburn NH 030323503

Call Sign: N1HHI
David Blumberg Jr
514 Chester Rd
Auburn NH 03032

Call Sign: KA1KI
Richard C Guerin
631 Chester Rd.
Auburn NH 03032

Call Sign: N1KOY
Louis W Rouleau
28 Dearborn Rd
Auburn NH 03032

Call Sign: N1OOW

Christopher S Taylor
26 Deerneck Lane
Auburn NH 03032

Call Sign: N5AGS
Almond J Cote
191 Eaton Hill Rd
Auburn NH 03032

Call Sign: KB1WQN
Robert C Glosner
111 Grapevine Dr
Auburn NH 03032

Call Sign: N1JUT
Georges J B Saucier
72 Hooksett Rd
Auburn NH 03032

Call Sign: N1SBV
Joseph J Allwood
229 Hooksett Rd
Auburn NH 03032

Call Sign: W1EIE
Donald K Mac Corkle
783 Hooksett Rd.
Auburn NH 03032

Call Sign: W1VAX
David E Baxter
368 Manchester Rd
Auburn NH 03032

Call Sign: N1WDZ
Miriam A Overman
21 Olde Towne Rd.
Auburn NH 03032

Call Sign: KA1LYE
William C Hallstrom I
115 Pingree Hill Rd
Auburn NH 030321810

Call Sign: W1YVM

Robert G Norris Sr
20 Raymond Rd
Auburn NH 03032

Call Sign: N1IXV
Richard J Miville
132 Rockingham Rd
Auburn NH 03032

Call Sign: KB1IEB
Zachary P Driscoll
38 Sagharbor Dr
Auburn NH 03032

Call Sign: W1LIM
Hubert J Topliff
34 Squirrel Dr Rfd 2
Auburn NH 030323954

Call Sign: WA2ROY
Lawrence S Gould
21 Steam Mill Rd
Auburn NH 030323815

Call Sign: KB1WDU
Kevin R Wood
32 Westford Dr
Auburn NH 03032

Call Sign: N1FBS
James R Tillery
17 Wood Hill Dr
Auburn NH 03032

Call Sign: N1XES
Michael G Barber
Auburn NH 03032

Call Sign: KB1MOT
Elizabeth A O'donnell
Auburn NH 03032

**FCC Amateur Radio
Licenses in Barlett**

Call Sign: KA1WSB
David B Pomfret
394 Rolling Ridge
Barlett NH 03812

**FCC Amateur Radio
Licenses in Barnstead**

Call Sign: N1TLS
Alberton A Berry
Evans Mt Rd
Barnstead NH 03218

Call Sign: KB1HOI
Richard G Simomeau
15 Garland Rd
Barnstead NH 03218

Call Sign: N1DOU
David A Weiss
224 Gray Rd
Barnstead NH 03218

Call Sign: N1CKM
Wayne W Santos
163 Hartshorn Rd
Barnstead NH 03218

Call Sign: KL1WD
Elizabeth G Santos
163 Hartshorn Rd
Barnstead NH 03218

Call Sign: KB1LRY
J Richard Jaques Sr
78 John Tasker Rd
Barnstead NH 03218

Call Sign: KD1CT
Robert L Emory
206 John Tasker Rd
Barnstead NH 03218

Call Sign: KB1JCX
George R Richards

4 Newport Dr
Barnstead NH 03225

Call Sign: N1QBO
Paul A King
55 Parade Hill Rd
Barnstead NH 03218

Call Sign: KB1MAW
Ronald A Panneton
387 Parade Rd
Barnstead NH 03218

Call Sign: KC1FP
John D Perkins
886 Province Rd
Barnstead NH 032180266

Call Sign: KB1MIX
Robin I Panneton
Barnstead NH 03218

## FCC Amateur Radio Licenses in Barrington

Call Sign: N1XCL
Pamela J Sprowl
5 Amys Ln
Barrington NH 03825

Call Sign: N1ZAK
Thomas J Morris
67 Atwood Dr
Barrington NH 03825

Call Sign: N1YOG
Barbara W Morris
67 Atwood Rd
Barrington NH 03825

Call Sign: KB1MCR
David C Perron
Barrington Rd
Barrington NH 03825

Call Sign: K1ZJY
Richard S Brooks
192 Beauty Hill  Box 165
Barrington NH 038250165

Call Sign: WW1G
Donald W Kielbasa
91 Beauty Hill Rd
Barrington NH 03025

Call Sign: KB1SXC
Richard R Merrill Iii
249 Beauty Hill Rd
Barrington NH 03825

Call Sign: NW1R
Richard R Merrill Iii
249 Beauty Hill Rd
Barrington NH 03825

Call Sign: KB1QPL
Judith E Roun
7 Bellamy Rd
Barrington NH 03825

Call Sign: N1SDT
Ronald F Dondero
13 Bellamy Rd.
Barrington NH 03825

Call Sign: KA1CQZ
Leonard P Greaney Jr
8 Calef Island Rd
Barrington NH 03825

Call Sign: N1SDV
Michael J Mawson
110 Canaan Back Rd
Barrington NH 03825

Call Sign: KB1RVF
Gregory L Wieder
5 Century Pines
Barrington NH 03825

Call Sign: KA1TSF
Charles G Skoolicas
1 Century Pines Dr
Barrington NH 03825

Call Sign: WA1UNU
Adam M Perkins
11 Century Pines Dr
Barrington NH 03825

Call Sign: KB1IOB
Michael J Roscoe
13 Chesley Dr
Barrington NH 03825

Call Sign: KB1JCC
Ted M Bergeron
6 Cross Lane
Barrington NH 03825

Call Sign: KB1JCD
Trevor J Bergeron
6 Cross Lane
Barrington NH 03825

Call Sign: KB1CUZ
Frederick H Dodge
33 Emerald Acres
Barrington NH 03825

Call Sign: K1VQS
Thomas E Voss
1402 Franklin Pierce
Highway
Barrington NH 03825

Call Sign: KB1TUT
John H Ramsdell
40 Goldfinch Rd
Barrington NH 03825

Call Sign: N1HLX
James E Lewis
12 Hall Rd
Barrington NH 03825

Call Sign: KA1FYQ
John P Wormell
20 Ham Rd
Barrington NH 03825

Call Sign: AA1TF
Scott J Mayo
93 Ham Rd
Barrington NH 03825

Call Sign: W1XER
Scott J Mayo
145 Ham Rd
Barrington NH 03825

Call Sign: KB1EMM
Joseph N Kazura Iii
10 Highland Ridge Rd
Barrington NH 038253004

Call Sign: N0JNK
Joseph N Kazura Iii
10 Highland Ridge Rd
Barrington NH 038253004

Call Sign: N1VRB
Bruce R Stocker
12 Highland Ridge Rd
Barrington NH 038253004

Call Sign: K1BRS
Bruce R Stocker
37 Highland Ridge Rd
Barrington NH 038253004

Call Sign: N1TLY
Jonathan E Cardin
5 Maple Wood Dr
Barrington NH 03825

Call Sign: K1BQT
Frederick H Littlefield
Mc Daniel Shore Dr
Barrington NH 03825

Call Sign: WR1CK
Frederick H Littlefield
Mc Daniel Shore Dr
Barrington NH 03825

Call Sign: KA1STC
Terry L Northup
Mc Daniel Shore Dr
Barrington NH 03825

Call Sign: K1BQT
Frederick H Littlefield
528 Mcdaniel Shore Dr
Barrington NH 03825

Call Sign: N1LVA
Celeste A Hall
7 Melodie Ln
Barrington NH 03825

Call Sign: KE1FC
Dan C Cui
17 Mica Point Rd
Barrington NH 03825

Call Sign: KB1SXD
Christopher B Peabody
158 Michael Dr
Barrington NH 03825

Call Sign: WA5RVU
Howard E Mixon
82 Oak Hill Rd
Barrington NH 038253820

Call Sign: WB1FGW
Frank C Spiers
181 Pond Hill Rd
Barrington NH 03825

Call Sign: N1LBH
Kristann L Moody
77 Priest Rd
Barrington NH 03825

Call Sign: N1XEP
Kristopher D Cui
701 Route 202
Barrington NH 03825

Call Sign: N1XEQ
Debra M Cui
701 Route 202
Barrington NH 03825

Call Sign: KB1FRU
Michaela A Cui
701 Route 202
Barrington NH 03825

Call Sign: N1ZTC
Sean R Ramsey
326 Route 4
Barrington NH 03825

Call Sign: N1KGK
Donald J Norris
630 Scruton Pond Rd
Barrington NH 03820

Call Sign: KA1ODJ
Dennis R Dutra Jr
9 Sherborne Rd
Barrington NH 03825

Call Sign: KA1RAA
Tracy N Hallock
Star Route
Barrington NH 03825

Call Sign: K1ZAC
Robert E Potter
65 Tolend Rd
Barrington NH 038250333

Call Sign: N1NXS
Mark C Porter
165 Tolend Rd
Barrington NH 03825

Call Sign: KA1VDO
Launcelot C Nash
Valentine Dr
Barrington NH 03825

Call Sign: KC2MHU
Robert J Hall
752 Washington St
Barrington NH 03825

Call Sign: K1CUI
Dan C Cui
761 Washington St
Barrington NH 03825

Call Sign: K3CUI
Debra M Cui
761 Washington St
Barrington NH 03825

Call Sign: KA1PJS
Omer A Hebert
Barrington NH 03825

Call Sign: KA1RLE
John R Mc Kinney
Barrington NH 03825

Call Sign: KA1TFV
Pamela J Jessurun
Barrington NH 03825

Call Sign: N1VZX
David D Robinson
Barrington NH 03825

Call Sign: KB1OGA
Normand H Boucher
Barrington NH 03825

Call Sign: KB1QOW
Jason P Jasper
Barrington NH 03825

Call Sign: K1FDP
Jason P Jasper
Barrington NH 038250086

## FCC Amateur Radio Licenses in Bath

Call Sign: N1TXX
David A Wheeler
55 Goose Ln
Bath NH 03740

Call Sign: KD1VL
Timothy B Parker
84 Monroe Rd
Bath NH 03740

Call Sign: AB1LQ
Timothy B Parker
84 Monroe Rd
Bath NH 03740

Call Sign: N1KZ
Roger E Fournier Sr
90 Monroe Rd
Bath NH 03740

Call Sign: N1QNZ
Roger E Fournier Jr
90 Monroe Rd
Bath NH 03740

Call Sign: KB1JIE
Everett L Rust
102 Pettyboro Rd
Bath NH 03740

Call Sign: WB2LDG
Francis B Murray
Rr 1
Bath NH 03740

Call Sign: KB1PQH
Robert L Harris
Bath NH 03740

Call Sign: K9UDX
Robert L Harris
Bath NH 03740

## FCC Amateur Radio Licenses in Bedford

Call Sign: KA1HFE
Willard J Foss Jr
35 Appledor Rd
Bedford NH 03110

Call Sign: N1TRI
Michelle S Collier
7 Appleleaf Dr
Bedford NH 031100665

Call Sign: N1TRR
Michael A Collier
7 Appleleaf Dr
Bedford NH 03110

Call Sign: N1HWP
Richard J Garabedian
6 Arbor Lane
Bedford NH 03110

Call Sign: N1VPX
William D Granfield
248 Back River Rd
Bedford NH 03110

Call Sign: KB1ANS
Gerard J Gagne
279 Back River Rd
Bedford NH 03110

Call Sign: N1AED
Richard M Roux
288 Back River Rd
Bedford NH 03110

Call Sign: N1DQY
Andrea J Roux

288 Back River Rd
Bedford NH 03110

Call Sign: K1MR
David A Rosenzweig
10 Balsam Ct
Bedford NH 03110

Call Sign: K1ESM
Tate J Keegan
61 Barr Farm Rd
Bedford NH 03110

Call Sign: KB1OP
Robert Di Meo
14 Bayberry Ct
Bedford NH 03110

Call Sign: KB1LCY
Roland Garbe
94 Beals Rd
Bedford NH 03110

Call Sign: AB1DZ
Roland Garbe
94 Beals Rd
Bedford NH 03110

Call Sign: KB1UWK
Kevin B Hale
212 Beals Rd
Bedford NH 03110

Call Sign: W1UAD
John A Jackman
8 Beaudoin St
Bedford NH 031106700

Call Sign: NE1J
John Ton
50 Bedford Center Rd
Bedford NH 03110

Call Sign: KD6LFW
Bob D Peret

34 Birchwood Circle
Bedford NH 03110

Call Sign: WA1WFI
Tina E Packhem
86 Blanford Pl
Bedford NH 03110

Call Sign: KB1MXG
Tom R Grimmett
120 Blanford Place
Bedford NH 03110

Call Sign: KB1HII
Randy L Schneiderheinze
424 Boynton St
Bedford NH 031105144

Call Sign: N1VLA
Leo M Capillo
35 Briar Rd
Bedford NH 03110

Call Sign: W1LMC
Leo M Capillo
35 Briar Rd
Bedford NH 03110

Call Sign: WA1YDI
Robert Richards
30 Brick Mill Rd
Bedford NH 03102

Call Sign: NA1RR
Robert Richards
30 Brick Mill Rd
Bedford NH 03110

Call Sign: W2FZ
Daniel M Monfried
20 Burgundy Terrace
Bedford NH 03110

Call Sign: KA1BN
Carl J Bernier

12 Butterfield Ln
Bedford NH 03110

Call Sign: KB1SRC
Frederick C Aumann Iii
8 Cabot Lane
Bedford NH 03110

Call Sign: KB1RLZ
Martin J Lavin
61 Camelot Dr
Bedford NH 03110

Call Sign: N1THL
Stanley J Popielarz
70 Camelot Dr
Bedford NH 03110

Call Sign: KB1MFB
Christopher M Woodsum
70 Campbell Rd
Bedford NH 03110

Call Sign: KB1POZ
Paul M Goldberg
17 Chipping Horton Ln
Bedford NH 031106066

Call Sign: KB1PPA
Mary B Cotter-Goldberg
17 Chipping Norton Ln
Bedford NH 031106066

Call Sign: N1YOV
Mark G V Williams
9 Churchill Ct
Bedford NH 03110

Call Sign: N1JDK
Stephen W Maloney
16 Clifton Rd
Bedford NH 03102

Call Sign: KB1LKG
Derek D Hodgkins

7 Colby Ct Pmb 292
Bedford NH 03110

Call Sign: KB1LLJ
Kelly J Hodgkins
7 Colby Ct Pmb 292
Bedford NH 03110

Call Sign: W6KBJ
Richard G Harris
54 Colonel Daniels Dr
Bedford NH 03110

Call Sign: KC1LX
Robert H Hughes
23 Cricket Hill Rd
Bedford NH 03110

Call Sign: WD8KXN
Raymond W Ninness
8 Davies St
Bedford NH 03110

Call Sign: K1KXN
Raymond W Ninness
8 Davies St
Bedford NH 03110

Call Sign: N1UUH
Normand P Binette
33 Dery St
Bedford NH 03110

Call Sign: KA1QKZ
Henry Douville
384 Donald St
Bedford NH 03110

Call Sign: KB1HOH
Constance M Gagnon
2 Dunnington Wey
Bedford NH 03110

Call Sign: N1YBS
Joe V Lupo Jr

76 Eagle Dr
Bedford NH 03110

Call Sign: K1YLA
Elton B Conley Jr
Elk Dr
Bedford NH 03102

Call Sign: KA1YZL
Brendon S Browne
3 Essex Rd
Bedford NH 03102

Call Sign: N1LTC
John F Browne
3 Essex Rd
Bedford NH 03110

Call Sign: WB1HCG
Sandra P Mackey
11 Federation Rd
Bedford NH 03110

Call Sign: W1SPM
Sandra P Mackey
11 Federation Rd
Bedford NH 03110

Call Sign: K1KA
David L Mackey
11 Federation Rd
Bedford NH 03110

Call Sign: KA1UIX
Jennifer L Jolicoeur
8 Flintlock Rd
Bedford NH 03102

Call Sign: KC1EP
Paul R Hitchcock
46 Forest Dr
Bedford NH 03110

Call Sign: KA1SIN
Jay M Niederman

11 French Dr
Bedford NH 03102

Call Sign: KA1RQD
Alfred R Boisvert
29 Garrison Dr
Bedford NH 03102

Call Sign: KB1HGG
Laura M Hines
50 Golden Dr
Bedford NH 03110

Call Sign: KB1MTK
Thomas P Hines
50 Golden Dr
Bedford NH 03110

Call Sign: KB1MEO
Lynne T Bishop
22 Grafton Dr
Bedford NH 03110

Call Sign: KB1MEP
Seth A Bishop
22 Grafton Dr
Bedford NH 03110

Call Sign: WA1ELS
Joseph Silvia
74 Grafton Dr
Bedford NH 03110

Call Sign: W0RRI
Robert H Burton
3 Grey Rock Rd
Bedford NH 03110

Call Sign: W1RRI
Robert H Burton
3 Grey Rock Rd
Bedford NH 03110

Call Sign: KB1OOQ
Scott R Traurig

50 Hardy Rd
Bedford NH 03110

Call Sign: WU2O
Scott R Traurig
50 Hardy Rd
Bedford NH 03110

Call Sign: KB1GZC
Kalila Touba
15 Harrod Ln
Bedford NH 03110

Call Sign: KB1GZD
Zachary J Touba
15 Harrod Ln
Bedford NH 03110

Call Sign: N1XYI
Ryan M Sutton
38 Hawthorne Dr
Bedford NH 03110

Call Sign: KA1HRH
David B Gaudes Sr
65 Hawthorne Dr
Bedford NH 03110

Call Sign: W1YQL
Agnes M Warrington
70 Hawthorne Dr South Rm
103
Bedford NH 03110

Call Sign: W1HZH
John D Adamson Sr
28 Hickory Ln
Bedford NH 03102

Call Sign: KB1FIS
Norma J Adamson
28 Hickory Ln
Bedford NH 03110

Call Sign: KB1WIM

R Christopher Richards
25 Highland Farms Dr
Bedford NH 03110

Call Sign: W1PRH
Paul R Hitchcock
127 Hitching Post Lane
Bedford NH 03110

Call Sign: WB1EDF
Marc D Hebert
155 Hitching Post Ln
Bedford NH 03110

Call Sign: K1LHT
James B Waterman Iii
1 Horizon Dr
Bedford NH 03110

Call Sign: N1ODL
Aron A Brown
40 Horizon Dr
Bedford NH 03110

Call Sign: NN1F
Aron A Brown
40 Horizon Dr
Bedford NH 03110

Call Sign: KB1PSN
Nathan C Palmer
3 Hunters Rd
Bedford NH 03110

Call Sign: KB1KCH
William H Devane Jr
15 Iron Horse Dr Bldg G
Apt 303
Bedford NH 03110

Call Sign: KB1HBQ
Craig W Child
15 Iron Horse Dr Unit C-
208
Bedford NH 03110

Call Sign: NO1E
Frank M Milos
40 John Goffe Dr
Bedford NH 03110

Call Sign: KB1MPT
Benjamin C Shaffer
49 John Goffe Dr
Bedford NH 03110

Call Sign: KA1JHQ
Ward F Gravel
56 John Goffe Dr
Bedford NH 03102

Call Sign: KB1PSO
Steven R Palmer
107 Joppa Hill Rd
Bedford NH 03110

Call Sign: WB2TKP
Robert A Bersak
10 Lancaster Lane
Bedford NH 031104518

Call Sign: WA6HZX
James L Dillard
21 Lancaster Lane
Bedford NH 031104518

Call Sign: KA1ZUF
Daniel R Bersak
10 Lancaster Ln
Bedford NH 03110

Call Sign: KB1MES
Keenan P Dillard
21 Lancaster Ln
Bedford NH 03110

Call Sign: KB1HHI
Stephen J Kalil
15 Laurel Dr
Bedford NH 03110

Call Sign: N1AXQ
William A Beers
174 Liberty Hill Rd
Bedford NH 03110

Call Sign: N1LVB
Robert W Cushman
242 Liberty Hill Rd
Bedford NH 03110

Call Sign: AB1PJ
Sujit Basu
300 Liberty Hill Rd
Bedford NH 03110

Call Sign: N1NYG
James J Denhup
3 Mc Afee Farm Rd
Bedford NH 03110

Call Sign: KB1UMY
Donald L Demark
186 Mcallister Rd
Bedford NH 03110

Call Sign: AB1NF
Donald L Demark
186 Mcallister Rd
Bedford NH 03110

Call Sign: WR7M
Donald L Demark
186 Mcallister Rd
Bedford NH 03110

Call Sign: WA6DVA
Matt S Magoun
35 Mcquade Brook Rd
Bedford NH 031105018

Call Sign: K1EL
Steven T Elliott
43 Meadowcrest Dr
Bedford NH 03110

Call Sign: KB1PSR
Peter M Labombarde
66 Meadowcrest Dr
Bedford NH 03110

Call Sign: KB1RFZ
Evan P Labombarde
66 Meadowcrest Dr
Bedford NH 03110

Call Sign: W1OMZ
Evan P Labombarde
66 Meadowcrest Dr
Bedford NH 03110

Call Sign: WA1CEZ
Robert A Rasanen
39 Ministerial Branch
Bedford NH 03102

Call Sign: KA1HYR
Linda J Gaudes
63 Ministerial Branch
Bedford NH 03102

Call Sign: N1ULK
Ellen N Poole
9 Muirfield
Bedford NH 03110

Call Sign: W1TWP
Thomas W Poole
9 Muirfield Rd
Bedford NH 03110

Call Sign: KA1SWF
Chris J Seichter
318 N Amherst Rd
Bedford NH 03110

Call Sign: WA1YSU
Churchill S Miller
38 Nathan Cutler Dr
Bedford NH 03110

Call Sign: KA1ZAG
Amanda L Fiedler
46 Nathan Cutler Dr
Bedford NH 03102

Call Sign: KB1MSY
John A Hallett
72 New Boston Rd
Bedford NH 03110

Call Sign: KB1MSZ
Christine A Hallett
72 New Boston Rd
Bedford NH 03110

Call Sign: KB1TUQ
Brian Cohen
104 New Boston Rd
Bedford NH 03110

Call Sign: N1JUS
Earl J Sandford
597 New Boston Rd
Bedford NH 031024111

Call Sign: N1MPN
Bruce W Breining
49 New Merrimac Rd
Bedford NH 03110

Call Sign: WB1DOF
Brian J Krol
40 New Merrimack Rd
Bedford NH 03110

Call Sign: N1IMW
Dennis M Markell
47 Old Farm Rd
Bedford NH 03110

Call Sign: N1WKC
Christopher D Kaprielian
68 Old Farm Rd
Bedford NH 03110

Call Sign: AA1G
R Gregg Keary
3 Old Stone Way
Bedford NH 031104641

Call Sign: N1QXM
Millard A Dill
32 Old Stone Way
Bedford NH 03110

Call Sign: KA1UDG
Daniel F Gruhl
16 Olde English Rd
Bedford NH 03102

Call Sign: K1API
Wilfrid J Ott
6 Olde Lantern Rd
Bedford NH 031104814

Call Sign: N5SEV
Charles W Woolford
30 Olde Lantern Rd
Bedford NH 03110

Call Sign: N1TMP
Troy N Tauro
57 Olde Lantern Rd
Bedford NH 03110

Call Sign: K1RD
M Ralph Dieter
78 Olde Lantern Rd
Bedford NH 031104814

Call Sign: KB1UXR
John W Grubmuller
14 Orchard Hill Cir
Bedford NH 03110

Call Sign: K1XF
John W Grubmuller
14 Orchard Hill Cir
Bedford NH 03110

Call Sign: KD1LZ
Denis R A Gagnon
P.O. Box 10664
Bedford NH 031100664

Call Sign: KA1VMW
Mark J Zimarowski
43 Palomino Ln
Bedford NH 03102

Call Sign: K1EHZ
Jay L Taft
5 Parker Lane
Bedford NH 03110

Call Sign: N1BTT
William F Stone
1 Pebble Beach Dr
Bedford NH 03110

Call Sign: KA1SBC
Gary W Wenzel
43 Pheasant Run Rd
Bedford NH 03110

Call Sign: KB1WIN
Robert E Schneider Iii
35 Pimlico Ct
Bedford NH 03110

Call Sign: N1DRW
Christopher G Carter
7 Pinewood Ter
Bedford NH 031105537

Call Sign: W1YHI
Albert F Haworth
20 Plummer Rd
Bedford NH 031106409

Call Sign: WA1QBY
Richard F Barr
9 Polly Peabody Rd
Bedford NH 03110

Call Sign: KD1TH
Paul T Leonard
5 Presidential Rd
Bedford NH 03110

Call Sign: W1IJB
Richard J Bellerose
16 Privet Hedge Lane
Bedford NH 03110

Call Sign: AC1J
Thomas O Perkins Iii
194 Pulpit Rd
Bedford NH 03110

Call Sign: N1QC
Granite State Amateur
Radio Association
194 Pulpit Rd
Bedford NH 03110

Call Sign: KB1PSQ
Donald G Anderson
194 Pulpit Rd
Bedford NH 03110

Call Sign: N1LPC
William J Delaney
41 Quincy Dr
Bedford NH 03110

Call Sign: N1CNY
Ronald J Natale
40 Random Rd
Bedford NH 031105605

Call Sign: KB1WQL
David R Dewyngaert
12 Roblin Rd
Bedford NH 03110

Call Sign: KA1JHO
W Ray Walker
11 Roosevelt Dr

Bedford NH 03102

Call Sign: AA5QL
David H Penrose
52 Rosewell Rd
Bedford NH 03110

Call Sign: K1DHP
David H Penrose
52 Rosewell Rd
Bedford NH 03110

Call Sign: KB1MTD
Donald R Byrne
84 Rosewell Rd
Bedford NH 03110

Call Sign: KB1GOE
Scott G Fraser
243 Route 101
Bedford NH 031105103

Call Sign: KA1JGZ
Joseph A Komisarek
424 Rt 101
Bedford NH 031105029

Call Sign: W1ETJ
Richard N Sansoucie
38 S Hill Dr
Bedford NH 03102

Call Sign: AA1RG
Jonathan D Eastment
49 Sandstone Dr
Bedford NH 031105825

Call Sign: N1DNU
Barry Onigman
49 Sandstone Dr
Bedford NH 031105825

Call Sign: N1USK
Isaac J Onigman
49 Sandstone Dr

Bedford NH 03110

Call Sign: K1HHM
George B Cleaver
17 Sebbins Pond Dr
Bedford NH 03102

Call Sign: W1FGM
Guglielmo Marconi
Foundation Usa Inc
45 Shaw Dr
Bedford NH 031106050

Call Sign: N1LJL
Wilfred L Masse
14 Silver Spring Dr
Bedford NH 031026612

Call Sign: KB1MTA
Frederick D Goode
12 Smithfield Ln
Bedford NH 03110

Call Sign: KC5GJI
Bruce T Hellen
19 Sonoma Dr
Bedford NH 03110

Call Sign: KC5GWW
Frances H Hellen
19 Sonoma Dr
Bedford NH 03110

Call Sign: K9DM
Donald C Mills
22 Spartan Dr.
Bedford NH 03110

Call Sign: K1JXK
James D Jenkins
31 Spring Hill Rd
Bedford NH 03110

Call Sign: NG1J
James D Jenkins

31 Spring Hill Rd
Bedford NH 03110

Call Sign: AA1J
James D Jenkins
31 Spring Hill Rd
Bedford NH 03110

Call Sign: KF4EKF
Richard J Millard
21 Stowell Rd
Bedford NH 031104714

Call Sign: K1UIL
Richard J Millard
21 Stowell Rd
Bedford NH 031104714

Call Sign: WB4ZUS
Robert A Neidorff
39 Stowell Rd
Bedford NH 03110

Call Sign: AB1FR
Robert A Neidorff
39 Stowell Rd
Bedford NH 03110

Call Sign: AB1AP
Thomas M Taylor
73 Stowell Rd
Bedford NH 03110

Call Sign: K1RHM
Ronald H Michaud
21 Tirrell Rd
Bedford NH 03110

Call Sign: KB1SXE
Stephen M Pereira
72 Tirrell Rd
Bedford NH 03110

Call Sign: KB1RIL
Dorothy E Cazamichaud

21 Tirrell Rd.
Bedford NH 03110

Call Sign: K1CAZ
Dorothy E Cazamichaud
21 Tirrell Rd.
Bedford NH 03110

Call Sign: AB1FD
George B Melnikov
24 Veronica Dr
Bedford NH 03110

Call Sign: KB1MMV
Russian Speaking
Americans Arc
24 Veronica Dr
Bedford NH 03110

Call Sign: NU3C
George B Melnikov
24 Veronica Dr
Bedford NH 03110

Call Sign: WU3A
Russian Speaking
Americans Arc
24 Veronica Dr
Bedford NH 03110

Call Sign: KJ5CM
Alexej Jalyschko
24 Veronica Dr.
Bedford NH 03110

Call Sign: W3UA
Gene Shablygin
24 Veronica Dr.
Bedford NH 031106304

Call Sign: KB1TDF
Martin W Koechel
30 Wellesley Dr
Bedford NH 03110

Call Sign: K9AMG
Martin W Koechel
30 Wellesley Dr
Bedford NH 03110

Call Sign: KB1ULI
Tara L Koechel
30 Wellesley Dr
Bedford NH 03110

Call Sign: KB1UVM
Kevin M Koechel
30 Wellesley Dr
Bedford NH 03110

Call Sign: W1WSQ
Robert E Westcott
52 Wentworth Dr
Bedford NH 03110

Call Sign: W1ZYS
George B Lucas Jr
7 West Dr
Bedford NH 031104937

Call Sign: KB1EOL
Gerald K Johnson
14 Weymouth Dr
Bedford NH 031105026

Call Sign: NL7OI
Peter G Allen
9 Whitney Ct
Bedford NH 03110

Call Sign: KA1HFF
Kathleen M Thies
28 Windsong Cir
Bedford NH 03110

Call Sign: N1BON
Robert W Thies
28 Windsong Cir
Bedford NH 03110

Call Sign: W2SBC
Robert W Thies
28 Windsong Cir
Bedford NH 03110

Call Sign: N1IQS
Thomas L Carder
87 Worthley Rd
Bedford NH 03110

Call Sign: N1QBY
Scott K Therrien
3 York Rd
Bedford NH 03110

Call Sign: W1SWP
John J O Reilly Jr
Bedford NH 03110

Call Sign: KB1UCP
Roy A Duddy
231 North Amherst Rd
Beford NH 03110

---

**FCC Amateur Radio
Licenses in Belmont**

Call Sign: KA1HFQ
Eugene F Mazzei
117 Bean Hill Rd
Belmont NH 03220

Call Sign: N1THM
Christopher M Mazzei
117 Bean Hill Rd
Belmont NH 03220

Call Sign: KA1DPZ
Curtis A Appleyard
193 Bean Hill Rd
Belmont NH 03220

Call Sign: N1YXG
Thomas E Garfield
307 Bean Hill Rd

Belmont NH 03220

Call Sign: KB1CUW
Charles H Hampe
49 C Shaker Rd
Belmont NH 03220

Call Sign: KB1QLY
David H Champagne
20 Cherry St
Belmont NH 03220

Call Sign: KB1RJZ
Bonnie L Champagne
20 Cherry St
Belmont NH 03220

Call Sign: KB1RKV
Tyler S Foley
50 Cherry St
Belmont NH 03220

Call Sign: KB1RKW
Adam B Foley
50 Cherry St
Belmont NH 03220

Call Sign: N1RKW
Adam B Foley
50 Cherry St
Belmont NH 03220

Call Sign: KA1INY
Jared A Willson
26 Countryside Cir
Belmont NH 03220

Call Sign: KB1LEI
John K Feeley
21 Cycle Ln
Belmont NH 03220

Call Sign: KB1RKL
Bruce W Simpson
351 Depot St

Belmont NH 03220

Call Sign: KB1FBN
James D Woodbury Sr
77 Durrell Mountain Rd
Belmont NH 03220

Call Sign: KB1GQO
Jack S Lahue
44 Highcrest Dr
Belmont NH 03220

Call Sign: N1PKF
Robert C Fitzbag
36 Hoadley Rd
Belmont NH 03220

Call Sign: WB1DMV
Thomas J Bon Enfant Sr
356 Laconia Rd  Apt 1
Belmont NH 03220

Call Sign: K1VP
Edward E Lawson Jr
231 Leavitt Rd
Belmont NH 032203219

Call Sign: KB1UXW
Francis J Martin Jr
25 Magnolia Ln
Belmont NH 03220

Call Sign: KB1DXT
Marjorie E Ashton
72 Main St
Belmont NH 032200253

Call Sign: N1WXQ
Dana P Ashton Sr
72 Main St
Belmont NH 032200253

Call Sign: KB1ESJ
Gary R Johnson
153 Milehill Rd

Belmont NH 03220

Call Sign: K1ESJ
Gary R Johnson
153 Milehill Rd
Belmont NH 03220

Call Sign: N1KWH
Robert P Murphy
Morgan Rd
Belmont NH 03220

Call Sign: W3CWO
Raymond T Peterson
29 Rogers Rd
Belmont NH 03220

Call Sign: K1ZMA
Frederic N Porfert
230 South Rd
Belmont NH 03220

Call Sign: N1JHF
Peter D Chase
30 St Josephs Dr
Belmont NH 03220

Call Sign: KB1PIF
Armol F Walrath Jr
24 Sturtevant Dr
Belmont NH 03220

Call Sign: KB1VVQ
Lisa J Vermacy
278 Union Rd
Belmont NH 03220

Call Sign: KB1VVR
Sheila M Vermacy
278 Union Rd
Belmont NH 03220

Call Sign: K1VPO
John A Morrison Jr
340 Union Rd

Belmont NH 032203458

Call Sign: KE1KG
Roland H Bjelf
605 Union Rd
Belmont NH 03220

Call Sign: N1MVD
Robert E Brobst
11 Wildlife Blvd
Belmont NH 03220

Call Sign: KB1UJB
Alan L Macrae
128 Wildlife Blvd
Belmont NH 03220

Call Sign: W1ALM
Alan L Macrae
128 Wildlife Blvd
Belmont NH 03220

Call Sign: N1SFS
Richard H Brown
Belmont NH 03220

Call Sign: KB1FBQ
James C Brown
Belmont NH 03220

Call Sign: KB1JWD
Catherine A Brown
Belmont NH 03220

Call Sign: KB1LEJ
William H Hamel
Belmont NH 03220

## FCC Amateur Radio Licenses in Bennington

Call Sign: KB1TOW
James E Bronson
76 N Bennington Rd
Bennington NH 03442

Call Sign: KB1TOX
Elizabeth H Bronson
76 N Bennington Rd
Bennington NH 03442

Call Sign: N1XDV
Nathan W Schroeder
329 N Bennington Rd
Bennington NH 03442

Call Sign: N1XJO
Daniel S Schroeder
329 N Bennington Rd
Bennington NH 03442

Call Sign: N1SWT
Linda M Magoon
81 Old Greenfield Rd
Bennington NH 03442

## FCC Amateur Radio Licenses in Benton

Call Sign: KB1OYB
John Viscomi
509 Bradley Hill Rd
Benton NH 03785

Call Sign: KB1QMT
Patricia H Viscomi
509 Bradley Hill Rd
Benton NH 03785

Call Sign: N1YBX
Francesco M Pesce Jr
527 Coventry Rd
Benton NH 03785

Call Sign: WB1ACM
Wayne R Klingler
277 Tunnel Stream Rd
Benton NH 03785

## FCC Amateur Radio Licenses in Berlin

Call Sign: N1WTL
Laurent G Riendeau
32 7th St
Berlin NH 03570

Call Sign: KB1DZP
Anita Berry
15 Bret St
Berlin NH 035703801

Call Sign: N1XEB
John M Berry
15 Bret St
Berlin NH 03570

Call Sign: N1TAD
David E Derosier
610 Burgess St
Berlin NH 03570

Call Sign: WB1GGQ
Ronald M Ramsey
205 Cates Hill Rd
Berlin NH 03570

Call Sign: KR1Z
Alexander A Radsky
384 First Ave
Berlin NH 03570

Call Sign: N1SHS
Carl B Leveille
399 First Ave
Berlin NH 03570

Call Sign: KA1MAX
Elsa B S De Bartolomao
55 High St
Berlin NH 03670

Call Sign: KB1CRP
Pauline C Couture

740 Hillside Ave
Berlin NH 03570

Call Sign: N1XEA
Darryl A Couture
740 Hillside Ave
Berlin NH 03570

Call Sign: K1KTY
Pauline C Couture
740 Hillside Ave
Berlin NH 03570

Call Sign: KA1PCK
Lawrence W La Fontaine
812 Kent St
Berlin NH 035703600

Call Sign: N1JNH
Paul J Herman
625 Lincoln Ave
Berlin NH 03570

Call Sign: N1SLX
Steve M Couture
227 Madison Ave
Berlin NH 03570

Call Sign: N1XEF
Robert J Barbieri
464 Norway St
Berlin NH 03570

Call Sign: N1XEG
Barbara J Barbieri
464 Norway St
Berlin NH 03570

Call Sign: N1QGL
Jon J Frenett
123 Park St
Berlin NH 03570

Call Sign: N1QOA
Melissa M Frenette

123 Park St
Berlin NH 03570

Call Sign: N1SHM
Larry L Laflamme
474 Second Ave
Berlin NH 03570

Call Sign: W1JIY
Nicholas C Darchik
126 Shepard St
Berlin NH 03570

Call Sign: N1OUA
George K Grande
168 Washington St
Berlin NH 03570

Call Sign: KA1JPJ
George E Fennessey
21 Winter St
Berlin NH 03570

## FCC Amateur Radio Licenses in Berwick

Call Sign: KB1MIQ
Thomas Akin Iii
28 Bell St
Berwick NH 03901

## FCC Amateur Radio Licenses in Bethlehem

Call Sign: N1MTM
Jason A Beard
144 James St
Bethlehem NH 03574

Call Sign: N1PP
George E Foss Iii
187 Lehan Rd
Bethlehem NH 03574

Call Sign: KO1J

Robert F Kimmerle Sr
1574 Main St
Bethlehem NH 03574

Call Sign: N1DFI
Richard I Inghram
Maple St
Bethlehem NH 03574

Call Sign: W8FNE
James I Ash
206 Otter Pond Rd
Bethlehem NH 035744336

Call Sign: KC1FX
Gary W Miller
100 Parker Rd
Bethlehem NH 03574

Call Sign: WD9HMY
Michael G Kindred
40 Peppersass Rd
Bethlehem NH 03574

Call Sign: KB1QKB
Julian Czarny
845 Swazey Lane
Bethlehem NH 03574

Call Sign: KB1UMR
Nancy B Czarny
845 Swazey Lane
Bethlehem NH 03574

Call Sign: KB1MDZ
Jodi A Olsen
504 Westside Rd
Bethlehem NH 03574

Call Sign: KB1MEA
Alden J Bolduc
504 Westside Rd
Bethlehem NH 03574

Call Sign: KB1OKX

Eric E Lougee
40 Whitcomb Hill Rd
Bethlehem NH 03574

Call Sign: KD1VO
John L Kimball
Bethlehem NH 03574

Call Sign: KB1OON
Lisa W Lougee
Bethlehem NH 03574

## FCC Amateur Radio Licenses in Boscawen

Call Sign: KB1HHV
Richard A Boucher
42 Bailey Dr
Boscawen NH 03303

Call Sign: W1SGP
George R Burton
44 Chandler St
Boscawen NH 033031202

Call Sign: KB1DXV
Albert R Higgins
325 Daniel Webster
Highway
Boscawen NH 03303

Call Sign: KB1VOD
Jean M Doherty
51 Daniel Webster Hway
Boscawen NH 03303

Call Sign: K1EFQ
Edward A Maloof
55 Daniel Webster Hwy
Boscawen NH 033032406

Call Sign: KB1MM
Timothy P Vendt
216 Daniel Webster Hwy
Boscawen NH 03303

Call Sign: N1MRL
Jeremy E Littlefield
56 Forest Ln
Boscawen NH 03303

Call Sign: KB1JHD
Joseph A Mann
14 Keneval Ave
Boscawen NH 03303

Call Sign: AB1HA
Kerry W Wentworth
85 N Main St
Boscawen NH 03303

Call Sign: KA1VAV
Steven M Harris
35 N Water St
Boscawen NH 03303

Call Sign: K3RZG
Mark W Barker
10 Prospect St
Boscawen NH 033031216

Call Sign: N1JIN
Scott C Mc Grath
4 Robin St
Boscawen NH 03303

Call Sign: KB1QGG
Carl S Glover Jr
4 Valley Of Industry
Boscawen NH 03303

Call Sign: K1SPG
Carl S Glover Jr
4 Valley Of Industry
Boscawen NH 03303

## FCC Amateur Radio Licenses in Bow

Call Sign: N1URJ

Juliette G Eaton
2 Allen Rd
Bow NH 03304

Call Sign: N1URK
Donald W Eaton
2 Allen Rd
Bow NH 03304

Call Sign: N2FVM
Robert M Lux
7 Allen Rd
Bow NH 03304

Call Sign: N1SSD
Jennifer A Kezer
70 Allen Rd
Bow NH 03304

Call Sign: KB0OJC
Robin L Narkis
8 Asa Dr
Bow NH 03304

Call Sign: N0VLO
Michael R Narkis
8 Asa Dr
Bow NH 03304

Call Sign: KB1EDR
Claire G Metzger
5 Belaview Dr
Bow NH 03304

Call Sign: KA1WYF
Stephen E Holdsworth
3 Bettys Ln
Bow NH 03304

Call Sign: N1EYF
Allen J Bardwell
14 Bow Bog Rd
Bow NH 03304

Call Sign: KG4SRB

Joseph M Myers Ii
48 Bow Bog Rd
Bow NH 03304

Call Sign: KB1JWE
Joseph M Myers Ii
48 Bow Bog Rd
Bow NH 03304

Call Sign: KB1IIT
Philip J Sletten
163 Bow Bog Rd
Bow NH 033044001

Call Sign: KB1QV
Robert J Sletten
163 Bow Bog Rd.
Bow NH 033044001

Call Sign: KA1JOG
Frederick Weddleton
6 Bow Center Rd
Bow NH 03304

Call Sign: N1JUN
Eric B Fiske
36 Bow Center Rd
Bow NH 03304

Call Sign: KB1KPS
Michael S Fiske
36 Bow Center Rd
Bow NH 03304

Call Sign: N1IIC
Jason D Greene
63 Bow Center Rd
Bow NH 03304

Call Sign: KB1OLO
No Replacement For
Displacement Rc
63 Bow Center Rd
Bow NH 03304

Call Sign: WA2SLO
No Replacement For
Displacement Rc
63 Bow Center Rd
Bow NH 03304

Call Sign: KB1EFJ
HELEN M Greene
63 Bow Center Rd
Bow NH 03304

Call Sign: KB1MK
Sarah E Burton-Knight
10 Branch Londonderry
Tpke
Bow NH 03304

Call Sign: K1AFH
Harold P Eaton Jr
40 Brown Hill Rd
Bow NH 03301

Call Sign: KA1SU
James E Fowler
2 Chelsea Dr
Bow NH 03304

Call Sign: N1GHE
Beth L Fowler
2 Chelsea Dr
Bow NH 03304

Call Sign: N1TAB
Curtis G Johnson
8 Chelsea Dr
Bow NH 03304

Call Sign: KA1IGW
Elaine E Giguere
23 Clearview Dr
Bow NH 03304

Call Sign: KA1IHX
Dennis D Giguere
23 Clearview Dr

Bow NH 03304

Call Sign: KB1DBC
Abigail L Gagnon
9 Dean Ave
Bow NH 03304

Call Sign: KW1I
Dale E Gagnon
9 Dean Ave
Bow NH 033043906

Call Sign: N1HHG
Philip H Gagnon
9 Dean Ave
Bow NH 03304

Call Sign: KB1EDL
Greg C Mc Kinnon
22 Dean Ave
Bow NH 03304

Call Sign: KB1TQI
Thomas R Chagnon
7 Erin Dr
Bow NH 03304

Call Sign: W1QLB
Thomas R Chagnon
7 Erin Dr
Bow NH 033043908

Call Sign: KB1BDL
Judith A Chalk
3 Everett Ave
Bow NH 03304

Call Sign: N1QYS
H Mead Herrick
7 Evergreen Dr
Bow NH 03304

Call Sign: K1MXJ
Arthur J Lagios
9 Evergreen Dr

Bow NH 03304

Bow NH 03304

Bow NH 03304

Call Sign: N2FVL
Mary E Lux
Fauen Rd
Bow NH 03304

Call Sign: KB1TKX
Jennifer M Ordway
19 Hooksett Turnpike
Bow NH 03304

Call Sign: KB1VUM
Jordan K Engel
19 N Bow Dunbarton Rd
Bow NH 03304

Call Sign: KB1LCX
Stephen A Piroso
7 Heather Ln
Bow NH 03304

Call Sign: NI1F
Mike J Conroy
19 Hooksett Turnpike
Bow NH 03304

Call Sign: NS1O
Allen J Bardwell
6 Page Rd
Bow NH 03304

Call Sign: KC1WX
Gary J Light
10 Heidi Ln
Bow NH 03304

Call Sign: K1BWB
Leslie P Le Blanc Sr
37 Johnson Rd
Bow NH 03301

Call Sign: KB1VOK
Andrea L Jordan
132 Page Rd
Bow NH 03304

Call Sign: N1RAN
Vincent J Salerno Jr
584 Highway 3a
Bow NH 03304

Call Sign: KB1EFH
Spafford W Hutchinson
14 Jonathan Ln
Bow NH 033043713

Call Sign: W1RMY
Normand A Saucier
137 Page Rd
Bow NH 03304

Call Sign: N1IDJ
John C Baier Jr
10 Hollow Rd
Bow NH 03304

Call Sign: KB1OTH
Dale P Moore
42 Knox Rd
Bow NH 03304

Call Sign: W1ENM
Harold C Moffett
150 Page Rd
Bow NH 033044710

Call Sign: KB1OSZ
Mark K Hendryx
157 Hooksch Turnpike
Bow NH 03304

Call Sign: WA1CBP
Halstead N Colby Jr
12 Logging Hill Rd
Bow NH 03301

Call Sign: W1XV
Ben B Hutton
3 Pepin Dr
Bow NH 03304

Call Sign: N1LYC
David C Parente
8 Hooksett Tpke
Bow NH 03304

Call Sign: KB1EDO
Ingar F Andersen
16 Logging Hill Rd
Bow NH 03304

Call Sign: KB1OOR
Craig R Beaulac
5 Rand Rd
Bow NH 03304

Call Sign: KB1WBN
Donald M Bennert
5 Hooksett Tpke Rd
Bow NH 03304

Call Sign: KB1CSI
John H Moore
31 Logging Hill Rd
Bow NH 03304

Call Sign: KB1OTD
Ronald R Beaulac
5 Rand Rd
Bow NH 03304

Call Sign: KB1SXM
Mike J Conroy
19 Hooksett Turnpike

Call Sign: KB1WYF
Deborah E Moore
31 Logging Hill Rd

Call Sign: W1BFT
Carl B Evans
River Rd

Bow NH 03304

Call Sign: WB3ECL
John J Hoglund
20 Rosewood Dr.
Bow NH 03304

Call Sign: KA1TOZ
Stephen D Corliss Sr
24 S Bow Rd
Bow NH 03301

Call Sign: N1PXG
William Cheney
60 S Bow Rd
Bow NH 03304

Call Sign: KB1JYN
Travis J Mitchell
51 South Bow Rd
Bow NH 03304

Call Sign: KB1KJI
William A Mitchell
51 South Bow Rd
Bow NH 03304

---

**FCC Amateur Radio
Licenses in Bradford**

---

Call Sign: KB2UZG
Steven R Endres
81 A Fairgrounds Rd
Bradford NH 03221

Call Sign: KB1IQD
Nicole L Leister
Box 332
Bradford NH 03221

Call Sign: KA1HJF
Lois M Donnelly
Box 84
Bradford NH 03221

Call Sign: KB1IDQ
Dennis R Howland
203 Davis Rd
Bradford NH 03221

Call Sign: KB1EMC
Christopher C Leister
93 Johnson Hill Rd
Bradford NH 03221

Call Sign: KB1TJ
Beatrice P Howe
140 Marshall Hill Rd
Bradford NH 032213310

Call Sign: KY1M
Dexter S Howe
140 Marshall Hill Rd
Bradford NH 032213310

Call Sign: N1CCL
Christopher C Leister
Po Box 332
Bradford NH 03221

Call Sign: AB1CG
Kristi S Upton
188 Route 114
Bradford NH 03221

Call Sign: KB1CKT
Shawn D Upton
188 Rt 114
Bradford NH 03221

Call Sign: KB1SFQ
Andrew G Rushia
351 West Rd
Bradford NH 03221

---

**FCC Amateur Radio
Licenses in Brentwood**

---

Call Sign: N1OYN
Richard P Zacher Jr

72 Dudley Rd
Brentwood NH 03833

Call Sign: N1LUE
Aaron M La Branche
57 North Rd
Brentwood NH 03833

Call Sign: KB1PQP
Johnathan J Richard
57 North Rd
Brentwood NH 03833

Call Sign: KB1PQR
Monica M Labranche
57 North Rd
Brentwood NH 03833

Call Sign: KA1OPS
Hermon L Winch Jr
206 Pickpocket Rd
Brentwood NH 038336419

Call Sign: WB1GJF
Stephen J Kolacz Jr
144 Scrabble Rd
Brentwood NH 03833

Call Sign: N1TXS
Russell W Kenney
145 Scrabble Rd
Brentwood NH 03833

Call Sign: KB1DOR
Scott M Standen
24 Skim Milk Ln
Brentwood NH 03833

---

**FCC Amateur Radio
Licenses in Bridgewater**

---

Call Sign: WA1PBJ
John J Donovan Iii
2834 Dick Brown Rd
Bridgewater NH 03264

Call Sign: KE6SRR
Frank W Denson
94 Foxtail Lane
Bridgewater NH 03222

Call Sign: KB1OYF
Kay T Denson
94 Foxtail Lane
Bridgewater NH 03222

Call Sign: W1EQS
Paul T Hart
44 Mohawk Trail
Bridgewater NH 03222

Call Sign: KB1EMO
Stephen J Emanouil
311 Whittemore Point Rd
Bridgewater NH 03222

## FCC Amateur Radio Licenses in Bristol

Call Sign: N1QFI
John F Feist
Box 500
Bristol NH 03222

Call Sign: W1JY
Olof W H Johnson
Box 63
Bristol NH 03222

Call Sign: K1HPJ
Lawrence A Mc Kinley Jr
1 Chandler
Bristol NH 03222

Call Sign: WA1ZOQ
Forrest R Webber
1336 Dick Brown Rd
Bristol NH 03222

Call Sign: WA1ZLG

Robert W Gillespie
858 Hall Rd
Bristol NH 03222

Call Sign: KB1DXY
Ronald C Surels
31 Hemp Hill Rd.
Bristol NH 03222

Call Sign: KA1IGV
Kathleen M Blish
586 Hundred Acre Wood
Rd
Bristol NH 03222

Call Sign: NU1S
Bernard A Doehner
21 Redbone Dr
Bristol NH 032220330

Call Sign: W5JT
James L Thayer Sr.
22 Remick Rd
Bristol NH 032223473

Call Sign: W1NKA
William R Beharrell
1635 Summer St
Bristol NH 03222

Call Sign: KB1FEY
Walter White Jr
44 Sunset Dr
Bristol NH 032223671

Call Sign: KB2CYK
Kevin J Farrell
Bristol NH 03222

Call Sign: N1ZAJ
Darlene L Mac Pherson
Bristol NH 03222

Call Sign: NX1N
John F Mc Grath

Bristol NH 03222

Call Sign: WB1AOB
Helen R Johnson
Bristol NH 03222

Call Sign: WX1B
Maxwell W Mac Pherson Jr
Bristol NH 03222

Call Sign: KB1RKF
Karen A Nunes
Bristol NH 03222

## FCC Amateur Radio Licenses in Brookfield

Call Sign: WA8TMA
William D Fredericks
7 Garney Rd
Brookfield NH 03872

Call Sign: KD1WM
Carol A Tully
320 Governors Rd
Brookfield NH 03872

Call Sign: KB1RKZ
Janet S Williamson
2 Lyford Rd
Brookfield NH 03872

Call Sign: KB1RLA
Bradford N Williamson
2 Lyford Rd
Brookfield NH 03872

Call Sign: KB1DNR
Janet S Williamson
2 Lyford Rd
Brookfield NH 03872

Call Sign: KA1PTW
William G Nelson Sr
98 Lyford Rd

Brookfield NH 03872

Call Sign: K1NXR
Robert G Byrne Jr
300 Stoneham Rd
Brookfield NH 038727404

Call Sign: KB0UQP
John A Nelson
67 Tucker Rd
Brookfield NH 038720561

## FCC Amateur Radio Licenses in Brookline

Call Sign: KC0YYC
Derek J Fry
6 Ames Rd.
Brookline NH 03033

Call Sign: KB1UFN
Vivian Claramitaro
5 Averill Rd
Brookline NH 03033

Call Sign: N2LAW
Adam L Jacobs
5 Averill Rd
Brookline NH 03033

Call Sign: N1RUY
Mark T Bisbee
51 Averill Rd
Brookline NH 03033

Call Sign: K1BIZ
Mark T Bisbee
51 Averill Rd
Brookline NH 03033

Call Sign: N1FDG
Priscilla M Mc Gan
11 Bohannon Bridge Rd
Brookline NH 03033

Call Sign: N1SLR
Rebeccah T Sherman
11 Bond St
Brookline NH 03033

Call Sign: N2OYK
Dejan Radosavljevic
27 Captain Seaver Rd
Brookline NH 030332481

Call Sign: KB1RTW
Jon R Maurer
21 Dupaw Gould Rd
Brookline NH 03033

Call Sign: W1JFK
Barry P Green
34 Dupaw Gould Rd
Brookline NH 03033

Call Sign: N1OJI
Jennifer S Metcalf
7 Flint Meadow Dr
Brookline NH 03033

Call Sign: W8JAC
John A Cockerham
9 Flint Meadow Dr
Brookline NH 03033

Call Sign: KB1FNS
Boy Scout
122 Greenville Nh
Brookline NH 03033

Call Sign: K3EVB
James C Dempsey
3 Hillside Dr
Brookline NH 03033

Call Sign: KB1LSP
Robert L Berube Jr
24 Hillside Dr
Brookline NH 03033

Call Sign: AB1EO
Robert L Berube Jr
24 Hillside Dr
Brookline NH 03033

Call Sign: WB2SKC
Paul R Nocella
25 Hillside Dr
Brookline NH 03033

Call Sign: W1CVV
Christopher Van Veen
38 Laurel Crest Dr
Brookline NH 030332138

Call Sign: KB1UIE
Christopher Van Veen
38 Laurel Crest Dr
Brookline NH 03033

Call Sign: W1CVV
Christopher Van Veen
38 Laurel Crest Dr
Brookline NH 03033

Call Sign: KB1SEF
Jonathan D Fickett
49 Mason Rd
Brookline NH 03033

Call Sign: KB1RTU
George W Foley Iii
4 Maxwell Dr
Brookline NH 03033

Call Sign: NV1A
Robert L Metcalf
8 Mcdaniels Dr
Brookline NH 03033

Call Sign: KB1BND
Mark A Levesque
2 Millbrook Rd.
Brookline NH 03033

Call Sign: K8LT
Gary L Grebus
16 N Mason Rd
Brookline NH 030332452

Call Sign: N1IMH
Colleen M Grebus
16 N Mason Rd
Brookline NH 03033

Call Sign: KB1OBT
Marie G Anne
109 N Mason Rd
Brookline NH 03033

Call Sign: KB1OBU
Eric H Nickerson
109 N Mason Rd
Brookline NH 03033

Call Sign: KB1DFE
Marc A Slater
11 Nightingale Rd
Brookline NH 03033

Call Sign: K1ARA
Robert A Riedel
18 Oak Hill Rd
Brookline NH 03033

Call Sign: KB1EFG
Richard L Gribble
23 Oak Hill Rd
Brookline NH 030332020

Call Sign: KB1EMN
Christopher A Gribble
23 Oak Hill Rd
Brookline NH 030332020

Call Sign: N1BIG
Shane A Mc Laughlin
89 Oak Hill Rd.
Brookline NH 03033

Call Sign: N1EYS
Calvin K Sandford
83 Old Milford Rd
Brookline NH 03033

Call Sign: K2DWR
Gary M Smetana
132 Old Milford Rd
Brookline NH 03033

Call Sign: W1EBM
Gary M Smetana
132 Old Milford Rd
Brookline NH 03033

Call Sign: WA1SLO
Timothy H Sagear
Old Milford Rd
Brookline NH 03033

Call Sign: K1KEC
Stephen J Murray
84 Pepperell Rd
Brookline NH 03033

Call Sign: KA1QEK
Peter W Bretschneider
5 Pope Rd
Brookline NH 03033

Call Sign: KB1RTY
Ronald F Olsen
5 Potanipo Hill Rd
Brookline NH 03033

Call Sign: KB1PYA
Lorna J Spargo
6 Regina Rd
Brookline NH 03033

Call Sign: K1MFQ
Ture A Heline Jr
12 Rocky Pond Rd
Brookline NH 03033

Call Sign: N1ZSC
Richard J Zore
265 Route 13
Brookline NH 03033

Call Sign: KB1WDF
Lawrence Thibeault
7 Smith Rd
Brookline NH 03033

Call Sign: K1LGQ
Dennis Marandos
11 South Main St
Brookline NH 03033

Call Sign: N1JSJ
Doug F Barnett
28 South Main St
Brookline NH 03033

Call Sign: N1GCW
David C Arigoni
8 Taylor Dr
Brookline NH 03033

Call Sign: KB1JNN
Richard P Abato
16 Taylor Dr
Brookline NH 03033

Call Sign: K4JTA
Robert W Johnson
39 W Hill Rd
Brookline NH 03033

Call Sign: KB1VEO
Wendell B Fisher Jr
8 Wallace Brook Rd
Brookline NH 03033

Call Sign: W2BFJ
Wendell B Fisher Jr
8 Wallace Brook Rd
Brookline NH 03033

Call Sign: N1DND
Eric K Pauer
12 Westview Dr
Brookline NH 03033

Call Sign: N1ZLR
Dawn S Catalanotti
19 Westview Rd
Brookline NH 03033

Call Sign: KB1WWT
David J Coffey
41 Westview Rd
Brookline NH 03033

Call Sign: N7VEU
Christopher R Winters
6 Woodland Dr
Brookline NH 03033

Call Sign: KA1WLI
William M Snyder
Brookline NH 03033

Call Sign: N1RYR
Joseph Plodzik
Brookline NH 03033

Call Sign: KB1ETC
Susan J Wagoner
Brookline NH 03033

Call Sign: KB1GTN
Matthew D Wagoner
Brookline NH 03033

## FCC Amateur Radio Licenses in Campton

Call Sign: KA1JNK
David L La Brie
61 Ames Rd.
Campton NH 03223

Call Sign: NN3RC

Robert A Clewell Jr
560 Bog Rd
Campton NH 03223

Call Sign: K1PQV
Sidney L Cheney
Box1377
Campton NH 03223

Call Sign: N1ZPQ
Shawn S Turmelle
12 Carla Court
Campton NH 03223

Call Sign: K0DNV
M Eugene Mockabee
23 Cider Mill Dr
Campton NH 03223

Call Sign: KE1KP
John F Petrycki
Campton NH 03223

Call Sign: W1NXM
William F Byers
Campton NH 032230366

Call Sign: AA1VR
John F Petrycki
Campton NH 03223

Call Sign: AB1B
John F Petrycki
Campton NH 03223

Call Sign: KC8RZG
Alex J Dria
Campton NH 03223

Call Sign: KC2TDB
Jamie L Tuttle
Campton NH 03223

Call Sign: KB1VVS
Paul D Steele Jr

Campton NH 03223

## FCC Amateur Radio Licenses in Canaan

Call Sign: KA1VDW
Randall J Labbie
Box 21a
Canaan NH 03741

Call Sign: KA1RPU
James W Crowell
Box 88
Canaan NH 03741

Call Sign: KB1DLD
Gail M Schmitt
Chiefs Dr
Canaan NH 03741

Call Sign: N1YMQ
Alan M Bradford
Eringlen Way
Canaan NH 03741

Call Sign: NO1P
Alan M Bradford
Eringlen Way
Canaan NH 03741

Call Sign: AE1H
Alan M Bradford
Eringlen Way
Canaan NH 03741

Call Sign: KB1HZP
Matt R Bradford
281 Fernwood Farms Rd
Canaan NH 03741

Call Sign: W1SKE
Matt R Bradford
281 Fernwood Farms Rd
Canaan NH 03741

Call Sign: KB1UYZ
Jody L Bradford
281 Fernwood Farms Rd
Canaan NH 03741

Call Sign: W1NNE
Jody L Bradford
281 Fernwood Farms Rd
Canaan NH 03741

Call Sign: N1VLK
Mark J Farrell
158 Gristmill Hill Rd.
Canaan NH 03741

Call Sign: N1HAC
David G Mc Gaw
185 Roberts Rd
Canaan NH 03741

Call Sign: K1GE
Glenn C Edson
19 Shelly Ln
Canaan NH 03741

Call Sign: N1HMK
Benjamin R Geoghegan
South Rd
Canaan NH 03741

Call Sign: KA1WCF
James C Geoghegan
South Rd Box 224
Canaan NH 03741

Call Sign: N1VJU
Peter K Arnold
74 Split Rock Rd
Canaan NH 03741

Call Sign: AA1DI
William D Simpson
66 Strawbrook Lane
Canaan NH 03741

Call Sign: KB1VOI
Bethany Hill
Canaan NH 03741

Call Sign: KB1VOJ
Wilbert J Hill
Canaan NH 03741

## FCC Amateur Radio Licenses in Candia

Call Sign: N1ZFZ
Derek P Bond
422 Baker Rd
Candia NH 030340165

Call Sign: N1LTL
Richard A Cox Jr
452 Brown Rd
Candia NH 03034

Call Sign: KB1WJM
Brodie J Kio
292 Chester Rd
Candia NH 03034

Call Sign: K1HJC
Myrle H Morgan Jr
572 Chester Tpke
Candia NH 03034

Call Sign: KB1UBH
Nicole D French
512 Chester Turnpike
Candia NH 03034

Call Sign: N1KVY
Robert L Walker
47 Diamond Hill Rd
Candia NH 03034

Call Sign: K1NTP
Richard E Clark
158 Healey Rd
Candia NH 03034

Call Sign: K1ZEP
Delmont E Weeks
643 High St
Candia NH 03034

Call Sign: W1FBH
Noel B Desilets
669 High St
Candia NH 030342005

Call Sign: KA1UXN
Michael D Kief
37 Hook Rd
Candia NH 03034

Call Sign: N1XRP
Jason M Runcie
11 Island Rd
Candia NH 03034

Call Sign: AA1YH
Steven V Hovater
46 Jane Dr
Candia NH 03034

Call Sign: K1DFM
Francis R Cartier Jr
159 Merrill Rd
Candia NH 03034

Call Sign: N1FDQ
William A Jarres
188 Merrill Rd
Candia NH 03034

Call Sign: W1IOJ
John J Rollston
31 Murray Hill Rd
Candia NH 03034

Call Sign: N1JHE
Sandra J Rollston
31 Murray Hill Rd
Candia NH 03034

Call Sign: N1QGJ
Paul A Hunter
606 N Rd
Candia NH 03034

Call Sign: W1ASS
Paul A Hunter
606 N Rd
Candia NH 03034

Call Sign: KB1OZ
Ronald M Sinclair
706 North Rd
Candia NH 03034

Call Sign: N1LKV
Robin S Brooks
230 Patten Hill Rd
Candia NH 03034

Call Sign: N1GOU
Bruce R Larson
2 Patten Hill Rd Box 181
Candia NH 03034

Call Sign: KB1EOF
William E Beebe
162 Raymond Rd
Candia NH 03034

Call Sign: KB1IZW
Edward C Harvey
313 South Rd
Candia NH 03034

Call Sign: KB1CMY
Bryce B Watts
133 Tower Hill Rd
Candia NH 03034

Call Sign: WA1KKH
Edward H Cunningham
230 Tower Hill Rd
Candia NH 03034

Call Sign: WA1SEC
Mary E Cunningham
230 Tower Hill Rd
Candia NH 03034

Call Sign: W1EBC
Edward H Cunningham
230 Tower Hill Rd
Candia NH 03034

Call Sign: W1CGS
Courtland G Sandberg
Candia NH 03034

**FCC Amateur Radio
Licenses in Canterbury**

Call Sign: K1PDY
Ronald T Herman
74 Baptist Hill Rd
Canterbury NH 03224

Call Sign: N1MGK
Laura A Herman
74 Baptist Hill Rd
Canterbury NH 03224

Call Sign: KB1MSX
Frederick G Norton
165 Baptist Rd
Canterbury NH 03224

Call Sign: N1FSL
Allen F Crabtree Iii
310 Baptist Rd
Canterbury NH 03224

Call Sign: KA1MCN
Carol L Prospere
119 Clough Pond Rd
Canterbury NH 03224

Call Sign: KB1NM
Richard E Prospere

119 Clough Pond Rd
Canterbury NH 03224

Call Sign: WA1CQN
Harold L Dakin Jr
6 Foster Rd
Canterbury NH 03224

Call Sign: KB1PL
Lee R Savary
136 Foster Rd
Canterbury NH 03224

Call Sign: KA1GEQ
Steven M Lundahl
33 Layton Dr
Canterbury NH 032242017

Call Sign: KB1IFM
Sumner A Dole Iii
192 Old Tilton Rd
Canterbury NH 032240161

Call Sign: KB1LBT
Peter C Keeler
12 Pickard Rd
Canterbury NH 03224

Call Sign: W1YXA
Vernon P Girard
35 Pickard Rd
Canterbury NH 03224

Call Sign: KB1RKA
David R Leclair
637 Shaker Rd
Canterbury NH 03224

Call Sign: N1HAN
David R Leclair
637 Shaker Rd
Canterbury NH 03224

Call Sign: KC1YM
David A Bailey

Wilson Rd
Canterbury NH 03224

## FCC Amateur Radio Licenses in Carroll

Call Sign: N1OUB
Stephen M Vendt
573 Route 115
Carroll NH 03598

Call Sign: KB1GYB
David P Vendt
260 Rt 115
Carroll NH 03598

## FCC Amateur Radio Licenses in Center Barnstead

Call Sign: KA1UHB
Donna L Martin
282 Narrows Rd
Center Barnstead NH 03225

Call Sign: N1HVP
Earl P Martin
282 Narrows Rd
Center Barnstead NH 03225

Call Sign: WA1FHJ
Mark A Fritz
272 Narrows Rd
Center Barnstead NH 03225

Call Sign: N1ELB
Robert P Tousignant
83 North Shore Dr.
Center Barnstead NH 03225

Call Sign: K1RDX
Robert P Tousignant
83 North Shore Dr.
Center Barnstead NH 03225

Call Sign: N1IHF
Brian M Lamarsh
61 S Barnstead Rd Apt C
Center Barnstead NH
032253629

Call Sign: KA1LPE
Robert G Goode Sr
39 Spruce Ct
Center Barnstead NH
032253453

Call Sign: N1VMA
Frank E Kirkland
Upper Suncook Ln
Center Barnstead NH 03225

## FCC Amateur Radio Licenses in Center Conway

Call Sign: KB1TUP
Richard G Sieberg
1095 Brownfield  Rd
Center Conway NH 03813

Call Sign: KB1RJH
Joann Lafontaine
17 Church St
Center Conway NH 03813

Call Sign: KA1PWO
Kathryn A Knowles
62 Davis Hill Rd
Center Conway NH 03813

Call Sign: W1KJ
James A Knowles
62 Davis Hill Rd
Center Conway NH 03813

Call Sign: N1CCB
David B Hobbs
10 Hiram Philbrook Rd

Center Conway NH
038130247

Call Sign: KB1QAY
Richard J Sears
117 Mill St
Center Conway NH 03813

Call Sign: KF6NVR
Shane A Conder
1316 Stark Rd
Center Conway NH 03813

Call Sign: W1UJJ
Arthur A Theophelakes
Center Conway NH
038130565

Call Sign: KB1KBZ
Brandon P Records
Center Conway NH 03813

Call Sign: KB1QAZ
Rebecca A Chase
Center Conway NH 03813

Call Sign: KB1RJI
Christine Sears
Center Conway NH 03813

## FCC Amateur Radio Licenses in Center Harbor

Call Sign: K1DUC
Patrick J Mohan
Bean Rd
Center Harbor NH 03226

Call Sign: KB1CST
Victor L Hamke
Box 112
Center Harbor NH
032267702

Call Sign: N1CHB

Carlton R Bennett
Box 240a
Center Harbor NH 03226

Call Sign: KB1LGL
Renee M Paine
Box 489d
Center Harbor NH 03226

Call Sign: KB1LGM
Scott M Paine
Box 489d
Center Harbor NH 03226

Call Sign: N1QVZ
Patrick E O Neil
Box 503m
Center Harbor NH 03226

Call Sign: KC1E
Harold J Tate
15 Eagle Ridge Rd Unit 4
Center Harbor NH 03226

Call Sign: N1EO
Edward L O Hearn Jr
132 Follett Rd
Center Harbor NH 03226

Call Sign: KB1KHL
Amy P O Hearn
132 Follett Rd
Center Harbor NH 03226

Call Sign: W1LEW
Lewis E Woodaman
14 Lakeshore Dr
Center Harbor NH 03226

Call Sign: WB1EZM
Charles L Fritz
Po Box 606
Center Harbor NH 03226

Call Sign: N1WMI

Arthur F Abbott
Rfd Box 225
Center Harbor NH 03226

Call Sign: KA1UVL
Robert J Probst
Center Harbor NH
032260381

Call Sign: KA1WLW
George R Mottram
Center Harbor NH 03226

Call Sign: KA1ZR
Donald S Banks
Center Harbor NH 03226

Call Sign: N1KPM
Darlene M Fritz
Center Harbor NH
032260606

Call Sign: N1RJN
Richard Mc Cahan
Center Harbor NH 03226

Call Sign: N1WDD
Richard F Kennedy
Center Harbor NH 03226

Call Sign: N1ZWB
Christopher E Morrill
Center Harbor NH 03226

Call Sign: N1ZYI
Kathleen Morrill
Center Harbor NH 03226

Call Sign: N3NBS
Peter L Wright
Center Harbor NH
032260220

Call Sign: W1RRN
Joseph L Fermano

Center Harbor NH
032261233

Call Sign: W7VGW
Carl E Ellingson
Center Harbor NH 03226

Call Sign: WA1GQL
James G Ingham
Center Harbor NH 03226

Call Sign: WA1NSD
Bernard I Kimmel
Center Harbor NH 03226

Call Sign: WB1GEO
John R Elmore Sr
Center Harbor NH 03226

Call Sign: KB1IFN
Greg F Janaitis
Center Harbor NH 03226

Call Sign: KB1KHK
Howard T Trevor
Center Harbor NH 03226

Call Sign: K1HZR
Frank J Raffaele Jr
7 Piper Hill Rd
Center Harbour NH 03226

**FCC Amateur Radio
Licenses in Center Ossipee**

Call Sign: W1QVK
George M Dewey Jr
23 Bay Rd
Center Ossipee NH
038140653

Call Sign: KA1AHE
James F Mc Kinnon Jr
52 Chickville Rd

Center Ossipee NH
038140815

Call Sign: AB1GP
James F Mc Kinnon Jr
52 Chickville Rd
Center Ossipee NH
038140815

Call Sign: N1BO
James F Mc Kinnon Jr
52 Chickville Rd
Center Ossipee NH
038140815

Call Sign: KB1RIZ
William F O'brien
25 Deer Cove Rd
Center Ossipee NH 03814

Call Sign: N1TPL
Carol M Mc Conkey
Joshua Rd
Center Ossipee NH 03814

Call Sign: KB1DUE
Matthew A Meserve
64 Joshua Rd
Ctr Ossipee NH 03814

Call Sign: KB1NMW
James P Hazard
40 Knox Mtn Rd
Center Ossipee NH 03814

Call Sign: N1HAZ
James P Hazard
40 Knox Mtn Rd
Center Ossipee NH 03814

Call Sign: W1LKM
Anthony P Fiore Sr
30 Leisure Dr
Center Ossipee NH 03814

Call Sign: K1HTN
Bruce C Beaman
22 Lovell River Rd.
Center Ossipee NH
038146111

Call Sign: WA1PWZ
Thomas L Galante I
Nichols Rd
Center Ossipee NH 03814

Call Sign: N1TTK
Mark E Mc Conkey
Skandia Estates
Center Ossipee NH 03814

Call Sign: KA1STT
David A Nicholson Sr
625 Townhouse Raod
Center Ossipee NH
038149507

Call Sign: W1YBR
David A Nicholson Sr
625 Townhouse Rd
Center Ossipee NH
038149507

Call Sign: W1UDZ
Carleton D Wilson
Center Ossipee NH 03814

**FCC Amateur Radio
Licenses in Center
Sandwich**

Call Sign: W1BJD
John N Dyer
Box 266
Center Sandwich NH 03227

Call Sign: N1NI
Charles H Gray
451 Mt Israel Rd
Center Sandwich NH 03227

Call Sign: W1KWE
William J Goodwin
46 Palmer Hill Rd
Center Sandwich NH 03227

Call Sign: WB1BUT
Dale H Mac Kay
92 Smithville Rd
Center Sandwich NH 03227

Call Sign: W1DHM
Dale H Mac Kay
92 Smithville Rd
Center Sandwich NH 03227

Call Sign: WA1PAX
Denny C Kalette
Center Sandwich NH 03227

**FCC Amateur Radio
Licenses in Center
Strafford**

Call Sign: KB1HPN
Brian A Sargent
Box 115
Center Strafford NH 03815

Call Sign: N1DHA
Richard O Skidgel
28 Sloper Rd
Center Strafford NH 03815

**FCC Amateur Radio
Licenses in Center
Tuftonboro**

Call Sign: KB1MGN
Joseph L Kowalski
7 Birch Ln
Ctr Tuftonboro NH 03816

Call Sign: N1FTI
Kristine F Kenison

21 Butternut Ln
Center Tuftonboro NH
03816

Call Sign: K1IEB
Timothy J Reardon
25 Fir Tree Dr
Center Tuftonboro NH
03816

Call Sign: KB1KXO
Donald E Ditullio
164 Ledge Hill Rd
Center Tuftonboro NH
03816

Call Sign: KJ1D
Donald E Ditullio
164 Ledge Hill Rd
Center Tuftonboro NH
03816

Call Sign: WA1FVM
Wolfgang W Kaiser
92 Hidden Valley Dr
Center. Tuftonboro NH
038165922

## FCC Amateur Radio Licenses in Charleston

Call Sign: K1SR
Robert J Ravlin Jr
1466 Acworth Rd
Charlestown NH 03603

Call Sign: N1YNX
Justin M Poirier
1 Blueberry Hill
Charlestown NH 03603

Call Sign: KB1DSL
Joseph H Desharnais
Box 127a
Charlestown NH 03603

Call Sign: KA1WGG
Walter E Walmsley
Box 204
Charlestown NH 03603

Call Sign: N1TYW
Kurth Bemis
1942 Claremont Rd
Charlestown NH 03603

Call Sign: N1PEV
Robert J Young
David Ave
Charlestown NH 03603

Call Sign: KN1H
John T Collins
19 Fairbrother Ave.
Charlestown NH 03603

Call Sign: N1UUK
Jane E Collins
19 Fairbrother Ave
Charlestown NH 03603

Call Sign: N1JEC
Jane E Collins
19 Fairbrother Ave
Charlestown NH 03603

Call Sign: KB1VHY
Clarence J Smith Jr
532 Hackett Swamp Rd
Charlestown NH 03603

Call Sign: WI1V
Brian S Rivette
169 Hillview Circle
Charlestown NH 03603

Call Sign: N1YSX
Thomas C Platt
61 Morways Pk
Charlestown NH 03603

Call Sign: KB1RZB
Allan F Exley
450 Morse Hill Rd
Charlestown NH 03603

Call Sign: N1MSB
Charles E Baraly
10 N Taylor Hill
Charlestown NH 03603

Call Sign: WA1ZPU
Elwin L Balla
Old Claremont Rd Box 659
Charlestown NH 03603

Call Sign: KB1MBK
Eugene J Augustinowicz
59 Old Ferry Rd
Charlestown NH 03603

Call Sign: AB1FN
Eugene J Augustinowicz
59 Old Ferry Rd
Charlestown NH 03603

Call Sign: KB1ROX
Eric J Augustinowicz
59 Old Ferry Rd
Charlestown NH 03603

Call Sign: KD1NZ
David N Grey
77 Perry Ave
Charlestown NH 03603

Call Sign: KB1RZI
Harry E Chesley
358 S Hemlock Rd
Charlestown NH 03603

Call Sign: K1SZR
Robert L Lamountain
45 Snumshire Lane
Charlestown NH 03603

Call Sign: W1UJP
Ernest S Lanphear
10 Summer St Box 261
Charlestown NH 03603

Call Sign: N1PBW
Judith A Baraly
10 Taylor Hill Rd - P O Box
169
Charlestown NH 03603

Call Sign: N1TZA
Lois M Corcoran
76 Weeks Rd
Charlestown NH 03603

Call Sign: KB1BLC
Stephen J Bailey
67 West St
Charlestown NH 03603

Call Sign: N1ZCM
William C Van De Water
55 Windy Acres
Charlestown NH 03603

Call Sign: N1TYX
Michael C Weaver
Charlestown NH 03603

Call Sign: N1UUN
George T Platt
Charlestown NH 036030543

Call Sign: KB1JHG
Vincent F Augustinowicz
Charlestown NH 03603

Call Sign: W1SUL
Sullivan Nhares Club
Charlestown NH 03603

Call Sign: NX1DX
Vincent F Augustinowicz

Charlestown NH 03603

Call Sign: W1KAD
Kenneth A Domey
Charlestown NH 03603

Call Sign: KB1CPU
Shaun J Smith
Charlestown
NH 3603 0

Call Sign: N1IOK
Scott Mickelbank
Charlestown
NH 36030305 0

**FCC Amateur Radio
Licenses in Chatham**

Call Sign: WA1JUF
D Kenyon King
184 Butter Hill Rd
Chatham NH 03813

**FCC Amateur Radio
Licenses in Chester**

Call Sign: WA1GCJ
George J Lyons
Box 12
Chester NH 03036

Call Sign: N1HUU
Robert H Brackett
449 Derry Rd
Chester NH 03036

Call Sign: KB1JSZ
Arvin B Congleton
37 Fremont Rd
Chester NH 030364107

Call Sign: K1ORG
A Louise Holmes
12 Great Oak Dr

Chester NH 03036

Call Sign: W6OX
Robert D Smith
186 Halls Village Rd
Chester NH 03036

Call Sign: N1OYW
James R Dore
304 Halls Village Rd
Chester NH 03036

Call Sign: N1PMP
Diane M Dore
304 Halls Village Rd
Chester NH 03036

Call Sign: N1PJZ
Scott C Rice
16 Haverhill Rd
Chester NH 03036

Call Sign: W1FCK
Gary J Welch
17 Haverhill Rd
Chester NH 03036

Call Sign: KA1WUT
Marilyn C Harding
49 Haverhill Rd
Chester NH 03036

Call Sign: KA1WUU
Gary R Harding
49 Haverhill Rd
Chester NH 03036

Call Sign: W1GJS
Carl E Wonser
424 Haverhill Rd
Chester NH 03036

Call Sign: N1YES
Barbara A Albright
656 Haverhill Rd

Chester NH 03036

Call Sign: K1OX
Theodore R Gamlin
669 Haverhill Rd
Chester NH 03036

Call Sign: N1NVZ
William P Berkeley
31 Isinalass Lane
Chester NH 03036

Call Sign: N1UBE
Dennis P Glynn Ii
96 Lane Rd
Chester NH 03036

Call Sign: N1LTK
Douglas V Thompson
234 Old Chester Tpke
Chester NH 03036

Call Sign: N1MWZ
Nora J Thompson
234 Old Chester Tpke
Chester NH 03036

Call Sign: KB1PAR
Lisa J Dimambro
182 Old Chester Turnpike
Chester NH 03036

Call Sign: KB1PAS
Christopher R Dimambro
182 Old Chester Turnpike
Chester NH 03036

Call Sign: KB1PAU
Frank P Dimambro
182 Old Chester Turnpike
Chester NH 03036

Call Sign: K1TVR
Lisa J Dimambro
182 Old Chester Turnpike

Chester NH 03036

Call Sign: KB1END
David D Smith
126 Old Sandown Rd
Chester NH 030364122

Call Sign: KB1DYL
Margaret A Voss
189 Old Sandown Rd
Chester NH 03036

Call Sign: KC1CR
Richard B Voss
189 Old Sandown Rd
Chester NH 030364124

Call Sign: K1WX
Richard B Voss
189 Old Sandown Rd
Chester NH 030364124

Call Sign: K1DYL
Margaret A Voss
189 Old Sandown Rd
Chester NH 03036

Call Sign: KA1QNS
David G Gagne
75 Parker Rd
Chester NH 03036

Call Sign: KB1KQV
Michael R Noyes
491 Raymond Rd
Chester NH 03036

Call Sign: KB1KOV
Jeffrey A Venner
86 Rod Gun Club Rd
Chester NH 03036

Call Sign: N1VRR
Ellen M Boda
81 Shepard Home Rd

Chester NH 03036

Call Sign: KB1AK
Joseph A Lombardo
21 Stonebridge Dr
Chester NH 03036

Call Sign: KB1RMA
Christopher A Snyder
160 Town Farm Rd
Chester NH 03036

Call Sign: WA2WSX
Edward Swiderski Jr
63 Trillium Lane
Chester NH 03036

Call Sign: K1RXX
Daniel R Leite
Chester NH 03036

Call Sign: KB1TKY
John M Cavaretta
Chester NH 03036

**FCC Amateur Radio
Licenses in Chesterfield**

Call Sign: KB1VJR
Matthew W Kowalski
109 Crowningshield Rd
Chesterfield NH 03443

Call Sign: K1YXP
Matthew W Kowalski
109 Crowningshield Rd
Chesterfield NH 03443

Call Sign: N1HZT
Winfield R Brown
Old Chesterfield Rd
Chesterfield NH 03443

Call Sign: N1NNT
Peter Petschik

Old Chesterfield Rd Box 67
Chesterfield NH 03443

Call Sign: N1YHM
Kevin A Bruce
908 Rte 9
Chesterfield NH 034430144

Call Sign: N1YHN
Irvin A Bruce
Chesterfield NH 03443

Call Sign: KB1HPO
Keith Bruce
Chesterfield NH 03443

Call Sign: KB1MJB
Nancy A Bruce
Chesterfield NH 03443

Call Sign: KB1MJC
Kenneth I Bruce
Chesterfield NH 03443

Call Sign: KB1MJD
Katherine G Bruce
Chesterfield NH 034430144

**FCC Amateur Radio
Licenses in Chichester**

Call Sign: N1VZZ
Steven J Tumasz
266 Bear Hill Rd
Chichester NH 03258

Call Sign: KB1LVM
Merideth J Tumasz
266 Bear Hill Rd
Chichester NH 03258

Call Sign: N1LZO
James L Batchelder
Bear Hill Rd
Chichester NH 03263

Call Sign: KB1QBF
John D Prickett
33 Bear Rd
Chichester NH 03258

Call Sign: WA1OWC
Ray W Munsey
108 Canterbury Rd
Chichester NH 03234

Call Sign: N1THZ
Richard L Moore
21 Fred Wood Dr
Chichester NH 03258

Call Sign: WA1WGR
Richard C Sanborn
Granny Howe Rd
Chichester NH 03263

Call Sign: KA1NDU
Linda M Booth
45 Hilliard Rd
Chichester NH 03263

Call Sign: KB1VEN
Dennis L Lavertu
71 Hilliard Rd
Chichester NH 03258

Call Sign: WB1ALX
Paul E Spaulding
29 Horse Corner Rd
Chichester NH 032586012

Call Sign: KB1GYS
Donald R Beland
30 Horse Corner Rd
Chichester NH 03258

Call Sign: KB1OYH
Gary L Kerr
224 Horse Corner Rd
Chichester NH 03258

Call Sign: KB1JSS
Fred A Ruoff
12 Hutchinson Rd
Chichester NH 03258

Call Sign: N1DRN
James E Palmquist
Kaime Rd Box 3645
Chichester NH 03263

Call Sign: N1QXJ
Richard F Bean
10 Kara Dr
Chichester NH 032586546

Call Sign: W1HUR
Richard F Bean
10 Kara Dr
Chichester NH 032586546

Call Sign: KA1SGP
Henriette M Schwab
200 Main St
Chichester NH 03234

Call Sign: KA1SGQ
Dennis R Schwab
200 Main St
Chichester NH 03234

Call Sign: K1NA
James E Power Jr
52 Pleasant St
Chichester NH 03258

**FCC Amateur Radio
Licenses in Chocorua**

Call Sign: KB1TX
Arthur L Smith
42 Beaver Lane
Chocorua NH 03817

Call Sign: N1DUZ

Marilyn F Smith
42 Beaver Lane
Chocorua NH 03817

Call Sign: KB1VIF
Ruth F Halpin
611 Page Hill Rd
Chocorua NH 038170231

Call Sign: K1ERP
Ruth F Halpin
611 Page Hill Rd
Chocorua NH 038170231

Call Sign: K1ERO
Joseph D Halpin
611 Page Hill Rd
Chocorua NH 03817

**FCC Amateur Radio
Licenses in Claremont**

Call Sign: KB1UUR
Kenneth A Domey
465 2nd Nh Turnpike
Claremont NH 03743

Call Sign: KA1QCG
Joseph R Tardiff
25 Beechmont St
Claremont NH 03743

Call Sign: K1LBY
Colby C Martin
25 Beechmont St.
Claremont NH 03743

Call Sign: N2MJO
William Schimek
144 Bible Hill Rd
Claremont NH 03743

Call Sign: KB1KCJ
Frank W Eastman
2 Bond St

Claremont NH 03743

Call Sign: KA1TZU
Keith A Rivette
Bonmark Dr
Claremont NH 03743

Call Sign: KA1MCO
Daniel D Haynes
Box 111a
Claremont NH 03743

Call Sign: WA1DYP
Lloyd G Page
Box 299
Claremont NH 037439308

Call Sign: KB1AVC
Randy S Coupal
Box 307
Claremont NH 03743

Call Sign: KA1SOE
Mark C Waldmann
Box 401
Claremont NH 03743

Call Sign: W1AXL
John H Stoughton
Box 440
Claremont NH 03743

Call Sign: AL7DJ
David W Walton
Box 487
Claremont NH 03743

Call Sign: N1NTL
Paul L Rollins
Box 601
Claremont NH 03743

Call Sign: KA7OES
Lyman W Fitzgearld
20 Briggs St

Claremont NH 03743

Call Sign: N0NNI
Robert N Harrington Jr
243 Broad St Apt 114
Claremont NH 03743

Call Sign: KA1INN
Douglas A Benoit
19 Butler Terrace
Claremont NH 03743

Call Sign: KA1UAG
Dave J Decelles Jr
3 Cedar St
Claremont NH 03743

Call Sign: WA1SKY
Kevin A Halevan
30 Chase St
Claremont NH 037433202

Call Sign: KB1THP
Alfred D Ensley
89 Chestnut St
Claremont NH 03743

Call Sign: KA1POX
Henry E Gogan
Clay Hill Rd
Claremont NH 03743

Call Sign: KA1QCH
Eunice S Damren
4 Clifton Ave
Claremont NH 03743

Call Sign: WB1EAE
Leigh A Damren
4 Clifton Ave
Claremont NH 03743

Call Sign: WB1FIC
Clifford T Blair Jr
16 Collin Place

Claremont NH 03743

Call Sign: KA3SYI
John F Rushmore
71 Durham Ave
Claremont NH 03743

Call Sign: N1PHU
James R Gosselin
79 Durham Ave
Claremont NH 03743

Call Sign: N1XIB
Nathan F Gosselin
79 Durham Ave
Claremont NH 03743

Call Sign: KU1R
David W Walton
598 Elm St
Claremont NH 03743

Call Sign: KA1MXA
Richard B Doody Jr
10 Fenway Lane
Claremont NH 03743

Call Sign: KB1GOM
Steven Prepost
8 Fitch Manor
Claremont NH 03743

Call Sign: WA1UJA
David C Belisle
9 Foisy Hill Rd
Claremont NH 03743

Call Sign: KB1AIJ
Allen R Damren
40 Grove St
Claremont NH 03743

Call Sign: KB1UTZ
Colby C Martin
91 Hanover St Apt 1

Claremont NH 03743

Call Sign: WA1ZFY
Steven R Eisenberg
91 Hanover St Apt. 3
Claremont NH 03743

Call Sign: N1PHS
Robert I Batchelder
Heritage Dr
Claremont NH 03743

Call Sign: KA1OPA
Charles B Mc Dermott
39 Ledgewood Dr
Claremont NH 03743

Call Sign: KB1JIO
Green Mountain Amateur
Radio Society
27 Maple Ave
Claremont NH 03743

Call Sign: K1VNA
Hamilton H Webb
73 Maple Ave
Claremont NH 03743

Call Sign: KA1PNE
Daniel C Lawry
163 Maple Ave
Claremont NH 03743

Call Sign: KA1IHH
Theresa H Marvin
67 Maple Ave Apt 212
Claremont NH 03743

Call Sign: N1FSR
Joseph J Grey
13 Mckenzie Dr
Claremont NH 03743

Call Sign: N1PHQ
Richard A Benoit Jr

6 Meadow St
Claremont NH 03743

Call Sign: KA1ZHN
Kimbal L Bergstrom
Mica Mine Rd Rr1
Claremont NH 03743

Call Sign: KA1BGT
Jeanne A Wood
185 Mulberry St
Claremont NH 03743

Call Sign: KA1GOG
Philip W Wood
185 Mulberry St
Claremont NH 03743

Call Sign: N1PWT
Jeffrey E Semprebon
72 Myrtle St
Claremont NH 03743

Call Sign: N1MS
Michael C Schmitt
8 Nelmar Hts
Claremont NH 03743

Call Sign: AB1BF
Gail M Schmitt
8 Nelmar Hts
Claremont NH 03743

Call Sign: N1WOO
Charles K Barnes
10 Oak St #3
Claremont NH 03743

Call Sign: N1TIA
Kenneth E Mastro
63 Park Ave
Claremont NH 03743

Call Sign: WA1VFV
Leon C Osborne

48 Pearl St
Claremont NH 03743

Call Sign: N1GKZ
Richard H Lowe
237 Pleasant St
Claremont NH 037433156

Call Sign: NL7SH
Dave J Numme
94 Roberts Hill Rd
Claremont NH 03743

Call Sign: KB1JHF
John M Carton
64 South St
Claremont NH 03743

Call Sign: N1VFU
Gary L Herbert
16 Spring Farm Rd
Claremont NH 03743

Call Sign: N1SSF
Barbara E Kramer
353 Stage Rd
Claremont NH 037430369

Call Sign: N1PEX
William H Cummings Jr
32 W Pleasant St
Claremont NH 037433055

Call Sign: KB1OGK
Charles V Chandler
425 Washington St -110
Claremont NH 03743

Call Sign: KB1DOF
Robert E Vogel
11 Wildwood Ave
Claremont NH 03743

Call Sign: N1SCK
John D Howald

2 Winter St
Claremont NH 03743

Call Sign: KA1DUN
Cecil C Adams Jr
Winter St Ext
Claremont NH 03743

Call Sign: AA1IR
Robert J Noll
Claremont NH 03743

Call Sign: AA1TT
Billy R Michaud
Claremont NH 037431616

Call Sign: KA1AKC
Henry L Courtemanche
Claremont NH 03743

Call Sign: KA1MYT
Robert W Michaud
Claremont NH 037431616

Call Sign: KB1CCA
Goshen Lempster
Educational Amateur Radio
Soc
Claremont NH 037431076

Call Sign: KC2EEA
Viola Marie Lozito
Claremont NH 037431466

Call Sign: KC2EEB
Patrick A Lozito
Claremont NH 037431466

Call Sign: N1CQX
Wayland W Bailey
Claremont NH 03743

Call Sign: N1MEV
Timothy M Donovan
Claremont NH 03743

Call Sign: N1PKP
Gary A De Poyster
Claremont NH 03743

Call Sign: N1PPO
Barry M Brunelle
Claremont NH 03743

Call Sign: N1WWO
Evan H De Poyster
Claremont NH 03743

Call Sign: N1WZQ
Barbara L De Poyster
Claremont NH 03743

Call Sign: N1WZR
Ethan J De Poyster
Claremont NH 03743

Call Sign: W1EEK
Colin H Skelding
Claremont NH 03743

Call Sign: KB1JCM
Eric D Zeiner
Claremont NH 03743

Call Sign: WX1NH
Green Mountain Amateur
Radio Society
Claremont NH 03743

Call Sign: KB1LBY
Eric D Zeiner
Claremont NH 03743

Call Sign: KB1WLP
James R Morse
Claremont NH 03743

**FCC Amateur Radio
Licenses in Clarksville**

Call Sign: N1WEH
Robert J Purcell
443 Clarksville Pond Rd
Clarksville NH 03592

Call Sign: KB1LDI
Joanna L Vaughan
443 Clarksville Pond Rd
Clarksville NH 03592

Call Sign: K1GZL
Charles L Morgan
388 Nh Route 145
Clarksville NH 03592

Call Sign: W1COS
Coos Nhares Club
14 Tower Rd
Clarksville NH 03592

Call Sign: K1AVR
Androscoggin Valley
Amateur Radio Club
14 Tower Rd
Clarksville NH 03592

Call Sign: KB1IZU
Robert R Martin
14 Tower Rd.
Clarksville NH 03592

**FCC Amateur Radio
Licenses in Colebrook**

Call Sign: KB1UVS
Pierre Forest
3 Angels Rd
Colebrook NH 03576

Call Sign: KA1FSD
Gordon A Bishop
Box 361
Colebrook NH 03576

Call Sign: K1NCR

North Country Amateur
Radio Club
Box 409
Colebrook NH 03576

Call Sign: KB1OKI
Edwin C Calhoun
10 Cedar St
Colebrook NH 03576

Call Sign: WM1R
Peter Rauert
34 Colby St
Colebrook NH 03576

Call Sign: KA1UN
Thomas R Bearor Mr.
65 Johnson Lane
Colebrook NH 03576

Call Sign: WA1JVV
Thomas R Mangels
7 Mangels' Dr
Colebrook NH 03576

Call Sign: K1RIX
Gerard C Laperle
12 Parsons St
Colebrook NH 035761306

Call Sign: K1BHD
Kenneth C Douglas
14 Pleasant St
Colebrook NH 03576

Call Sign: N1ADS
Peter C Lear
Reed Rd
Colebrook NH 03576

Call Sign: KB1RXG
Bruce D Latham
26 Russell Rd
Colebrook NH 03576

Call Sign: K1ATC
John H Taylor
Colebrook NH 03576

Call Sign: K1JO
John G Hipp
Colebrook NH 03576

Call Sign: KA1BRF
Marie H Stewartson
Colebrook NH 03576

Call Sign: KA1BRG
Arthur L Stewartson
Colebrook NH 035760086

Call Sign: N1XEC
Barbara A Schnetz
Colebrook NH 03576

Call Sign: N3ICM
Mark S Santangelo
Colebrook NH 035760402

Call Sign: W1HJF
Laurence M Rappaport
Colebrook NH 035760158

Call Sign: W1WMO
Charles P Corbett
Colebrook NH 035760325

**FCC Amateur Radio
Licenses in Concord**

Call Sign: KB1BTW
New Hampshire Wing Civil
Air Patrol Ama Rad Grp
51 Airport Rd
Concord NH 03301

Call Sign: N1YXH
Justin P Garfield
317 Alton Woods Dr
Concord NH 03301

Call Sign: K1EEB
Joseph S Malinowski Jr
916 Alton Woods Dr
Concord NH 03301

Call Sign: W1QXP
Richard L Dunnell
1006 Altonwoods Dr
Concord NH 03301

Call Sign: N1JH
John W H Hopkins
17 Americana Dr
Concord NH 03301

Call Sign: W1JJD
James P Moran
66 Auburn
Concord NH 03301

Call Sign: K9OWM
John B Welch
48 Auburn St
Concord NH 03301

Call Sign: K1NQR
Harold J Denoncour Jr
16 Boanza Dr
Concord NH 03303

Call Sign: N1PGG
Peter Venne
29 Bog Rd 24
Concord NH 033032018

Call Sign: W1VEN
Peter Venne
29 Bog Rd 56
Concord NH 033032018

Call Sign: KA1YIV
David J Fournier Jr
Box 285a
Concord NH 03303

Call Sign: N1RSU
Thomas A Hettinger
58 Branch Tpk #83
Concord NH 03301

Call Sign: N1VTV
Dan T Hebert
12 Branch Tpke
Concord NH 03301

Call Sign: WA6SIE
Robert A Engh
84 Branch Turnpike 145
Concord NH 033015725

Call Sign: N1XEZ
Alfred Flint
84 Branch Turnpike 93
Concord NH 03301

Call Sign: KD1WY
Eugene A Morrill Jr
84 Branch Turnpike Rd 58
Concord NH 03301

Call Sign: N1PHY
Andre H Martel
1 Broad Ave
Concord NH 03301

Call Sign: KB1UMX
Elizabeth A Thorpe
160 Broadway
Concord NH 03301

Call Sign: N1JI
Jock B Irvine
5 Celtic St
Concord NH 03301

Call Sign: KC1CL
Roscoe E Sanborn
33 Christian Ave
Concord NH 03301

Call Sign: WB2IIU
Paul M Oves
17 Clinton St
Concord NH 03301

Call Sign: WB1DVL
Michael J Robbins
99 Clinton St #418
Concord NH 03244

Call Sign: W1YUU
Harold R Moffett
99 Clinton St Unit 301
Concord NH 033012251

Call Sign: KB1AIM
Sungki Lee
99 Clinton St Unit E6
Concord NH 03301

Call Sign: KB1MQO
Yeong Hwan Son
99 Clinton St Unit E6
Concord NH 03301

Call Sign: N1CPI
Richard C Gifford
26 Commercial St Apt 202b
Concord NH 03301

Call Sign: KB1WTI
Jeffrey L Shaw
Concord Gardens
Concord NH 03301

Call Sign: KB1QXG
Robert J Lucier
21 Concord Gardens -1
Concord NH 03301

Call Sign: KB1OEG
Jennifer M Eastman
16 Concord Gardens Apt 12
Concord NH 03301

Call Sign: K1JNE
Jennifer M Eastman
16 Concord Gardens Apt 12
Concord NH 03301

Call Sign: KB0TXW
Barnett Hughes
10 Court St
Concord NH 033014306

Call Sign: K1MA
George R Rickley
82 Currier Rd
Concord NH 03301

Call Sign: KA1IGF
Kenneth C Jameson
10 Daphne Ct
Concord NH 03301

Call Sign: KA1IAR
Richard J Harrison
17 Dartmouth St
Concord NH 03301

Call Sign: NI1B
John M Harrison
17 Dartmouth St
Concord NH 03301

Call Sign: N1ZIG
Jonathan W Balinski
53 Downing St
Concord NH 03301

Call Sign: WD8QLZ
Darin L Ninness
3 Dudley Dr
Concord NH 03301

Call Sign: N1IQG
Bruce L Gowan
Dunklee Rd P.O. Box 317
Concord NH 03302

Call Sign: KB1LVJ
Ronald A Wilbur
21 Dwinell Dr
Concord NH 03301

Call Sign: K1JQE
Ronald A Wilbur
21 Dwinell Dr
Concord NH 03301

Call Sign: WA1UFW
Alfred M Russ
149 E Side Dr
Concord NH 03301

Call Sign: W1OGZ
George N Davis
202 E Side Dr
Concord NH 033015469

Call Sign: K1RDW
John T Bartlett
208 E Side Dr
Concord NH 033015469

Call Sign: WA1SRU
Norman A Collishaw
22 East Side Dr
Concord NH 03301

Call Sign: N1CUD
John E Enos
149 East Side Dr 304-43a
Concord NH 033015410

Call Sign: N1PHW
David S Chase
38 Eastman St
Concord NH 03301

Call Sign: KB1OTZ
Nicholas J Horangic
20 Emerson Rd
Concord NH 03301

Call Sign: KB1PPG
Nicole Varasteh
20 Emerson Rd
Concord NH 03301

Call Sign: KB1EJY
James C Van Dongen
10 Farmwood Rd
Concord NH 033016926

Call Sign: KB1VBA
Alexander W Seiger
12 Farmwood Rd
Concord NH 03301

Call Sign: WA1VVX
Richard O Blanchard Ii
6 Fisher St
Concord NH 03301

Call Sign: KB1NKC
Shaun E Schafer
20 Forest St
Concord NH 03301

Call Sign: KB1WIJ
PATRICK Mcguinness
5 FRANKLIN ST
Concord NH 03301

Call Sign: KA1TCX
Richard E Clymer
19 Freedom Acres Dr
Concord NH 03301

Call Sign: KA1TCY
Wendy S Clymer
19 Freedom Acres Dr
Concord NH 03301

Call Sign: KB1VQI
Karl F Blake
4 Garvins Falls Rd Apt 28
Concord NH 03301

Call Sign: KA1UUM
Mark R Johnson
19 Gilmore St
Concord NH 03301

Call Sign: ND1Q
Peter J Stohrer
9 Gladstone St.
Concord NH 03301

Call Sign: K1PJS
Peter J Stohrer
9 Gladstone St.
Concord NH 03301

Call Sign: N1SLT
Gary M Janinda
9 Granite Ave
Concord NH 03301

Call Sign: KB1JCV
Oliver R Northcott
35 Grappone Dr.
Concord NH 03301

Call Sign: N1SZW
Lawrence E Taylor
24 Greenwich St
Concord NH 03301

Call Sign: WC1WAC
William A Champney
22 Harvard St
Concord NH 033012318

Call Sign: KB1CFL
New Hampshire Ofc Of
Emerg Mngmnt Amt Rad
Clb
Hazen Dr
Concord NH 03305

Call Sign: KA4TMD
Robert V Byron Sr

37 Highridge Trail
Concord NH 03301

Call Sign: KG6TCF
Margaret F Sells
12 Hoit Rd
Concord NH 03301

Call Sign: KA1XT
Thomas P Hopper
210 Hoit Rd
Concord NH 03301

Call Sign: N1HCI
Thomas L Taylor
167 Hopkinton Rd
Concord NH 03301

Call Sign: N1XKR
Karl D Deans
170 Hopkinton Rd
Concord NH 03301

Call Sign: W1WQL
Richard L Deans
170 Hopkinton Rd
Concord NH 03301

Call Sign: N1UIZ
Steven R Arndt
173 Hopkinton Rd
Concord NH 03301

Call Sign: KB1QKS
Sky Is No Limit Amateur
Radio Club
2 Institute Dr
Concord NH 03301

Call Sign: KA1SKY
Sky Is No Limit Amateur
Radio Club
2 Institute Dr
Concord NH 03301

Call Sign: K1TEC
New Hampshire Technical
Institute Amt Rad Clb
11 Institute Dr Paramedic
Dept
Concord NH 033017412

Call Sign: N1ZIF
Seth W Angeloro
8 Jefferson St
Concord NH 03301

Call Sign: KB1QGB
Matthew D Eastman
42 Jennings Dr
Concord NH 03301

Call Sign: N1VPG
Jeffrey A Guimond
53 Joffre St
Concord NH 03301

Call Sign: KB1QGA
Robert F Spencer
3 Kent St
Concord NH 03301

Call Sign: KB1QGD
Emily P Spencer
3 Kent St
Concord NH 03301

Call Sign: KA1KJR
Mary J Ham
40 Lake St
Concord NH 033013214

Call Sign: W1ICU
Norman E Brown
18 Little Pond Rd
Concord NH 03301

Call Sign: KB1KCP
Tristan P Donovan
42 Long Pond Rd

Concord NH 03301

Call Sign: KB1KCQ
Philip J Donovan Jr
42 Long Pond Rd
Concord NH 03301

Call Sign: N1UNH
Philip J Donovan Jr
42 Long Pond Rd
Concord NH 03301

Call Sign: K1UNH
Tristan P Donovan
42 Long Pond Rd
Concord NH 03301

Call Sign: KC1YY
Paul R Leclerc
203 Loudon Rd #417
Concord NH 03301

Call Sign: KB1TZA
Jennifer C Jones
203 Loudon Rd #706
Concord NH 03301

Call Sign: KA1PQL
Horace L Johnson
185 Loudon Rd Apt 21
Concord NH 03301

Call Sign: KC0YHP
Alex Samuel
203 Loudon Rd Unit 119
Concord NH 03301

Call Sign: K6MNT
Richard A Magoon
203 Loudon Rd Unit 216
Concord NH 03301

Call Sign: K1YWT
Arnold H Taylor
20 Lyndon St

Concord NH 033014418

Call Sign: KB1FDX
American Redcross
Concord Nh Chapter
2 Maitland St
Concord NH 03301

Call Sign: N1PZP
James R Geschwindner Jr
192 Manchester St #8
Concord NH 03301

Call Sign: KB1WTJ
Keith G Bean
190 Manchester St Lot 10
Concord NH 03301

Call Sign: KB1VUO
Robert E Upson
192 Manchester St Lot 10
Concord NH 03301

Call Sign: N1SJP
Steven J Patrick
62 Manor Rd
Concord NH 03303

Call Sign: AB1DK
John C Huntley
99 Manor Rd
Concord NH 033031928

Call Sign: KE6WWS
Alicia A Huntley
99 Manor Rd
Concord NH 033031928

Call Sign: K1OGW
Otis G Gamsby
3 Maple Lane
Concord NH 03301

Call Sign: W1ATU
Robert S Mc Carthy

25 Meadow
Concord NH 033012242

Call Sign: N1KNC
Mark S Kritlow
16 Merrimack
Concord NH 03301

Call Sign: KC1IU
Neil J Jorgensen
37 Misty Oak Dr
Concord NH 03301

Call Sign: KA1DQB
Linda C Montgomery
20 Monroe St
Concord NH 03301

Call Sign: KB1HZ
Stuart Montgomery
20 Monroe St
Concord NH 03301

Call Sign: KB1OBX
Phill C Davies
21 Monroe St 2
Concord NH 03301

Call Sign: WB2IXH
Daniel Bucciano Sr
34 Monroe St.
Concord NH 03301

Call Sign: K1FLI
Frank L Irvine Jr
39 Mountain Rd
Concord NH 03301

Call Sign: W1FTZ
Winston L Blake
560 Mountain Rd  Rfd 11
Concord NH 033011814

Call Sign: KB1AUD
Forrest A Downing

456 Mt Rd
Concord NH 03301

Call Sign: N1IIL
Walter A Smith
121 N State
Concord NH 03301

Call Sign: KB1GSB
Christine H Metcalf
232 N State St
Concord NH 03301

Call Sign: N1ZIH
Donald A Curtis
353 N State St Apt 1
Concord NH 03301

Call Sign: KB1JCW
Charles M Virgin
353 N State St Apt 2
Concord NH 03301

Call Sign: N1AWR
Matthew F Caldwell
556 No State St
Concord NH 03301

Call Sign: KA1OSD
Eric P Duclos
38 Oak Hill Rd
Concord NH 03301

Call Sign: KB1OTC
James H Miller
60 Oak Hill Rd
Concord NH 03301

Call Sign: K1JHM
James H Miller
60 Oak Hill Rd
Concord NH 03301

Call Sign: KD1CQ
Raymond A Fournier

184 Oak Hill Rd
Concord NH 03301

Call Sign: KA1UHI
J T Sargent
80 Old Loudon Rd
Concord NH 03301

Call Sign: N1HCU
Thomas R Sargent
80 Old Loudon Rd
Concord NH 03301

Call Sign: WA1UFY
Edward Ferman
12 Orion St
Concord NH 03301

Call Sign: KB1PSU
Stephen T Black
45 Pekoe Dr
Concord NH 03301

Call Sign: WB0VJA
Keith D Mc Clune
52 Pembroke Rd
Concord NH 03301

Call Sign: N1PGF
Edward P Young Iii
68 Penacook St
Concord NH 033013149

Call Sign: KO1P
Arnold O Goodman
97 Pillsbury St
Concord NH 03301

Call Sign: KB1GSA
Daniel N Daly
17 Pine Acres Rd
Concord NH 03301

Call Sign: W1TTU
Edgar H Preston

12 Pine Acres Rd Suite
1207
Concord NH 033016077

Call Sign: K1RTM
Margaret V Pelich
42 Pinewood Trail
Concord NH 03301

Call Sign: K1TVZ
George Pelich
42 Pinewood Trail
Concord NH 03301

Call Sign: NN1N
Allison L Lloyd
15 Pitman St Apt 303
Concord NH 03301

Call Sign: W1QL
Harold E Kimball Sr
227 Pleasant St
Concord NH 03301

Call Sign: N1CPX
Kenneth L Mac Laughlin
239 Pleasant St
Concord NH 033017504

Call Sign: KB1NUC
St Pauls School Amateur
Radio Station
325 Pleasant St
Concord NH 03301

Call Sign: KB1NVF
St Pauls School Amateur
Earth Station
325 Pleasant St
Concord NH 03301

Call Sign: W1SPS
St Pauls School Amateur
Radio Station
325 Pleasant St

Concord NH 03301

Call Sign: K1SPS
St Pauls School Amateur
Earth Station
325 Pleasant St
Concord NH 03301

Call Sign: N1WWS
Michael N Martin
61 Pleasant St Apt 1
Concord NH 03301

Call Sign: W1MIP
Theodore E Noyes
5 Portsmouth St
Concord NH 03301

Call Sign: K1NUQ
George S Crane
24 Portsmouth St
Concord NH 03301

Call Sign: KB1DXU
Curtis J Boyden
124 Portsmouth St
Concord NH 03301

Call Sign: N1OCR
Donald E Williams
169 Portsmouth St   Apt
#137
Concord NH 03301

Call Sign: N1VQO
Theron S Longley Jr
169 Portsmouth St 68
Concord NH 03301

Call Sign: K1BZZ
Daniel E Salo
169 Portsmouth St Unit 167
Concord NH 03301

Call Sign: W1KBX

Daniel E Salo
169 Portsmouth St Unit 167
Concord NH 03301

Call Sign: N1VUT
Jeffrey L Lahey
5 Putney Ave
Concord NH 03301

Call Sign: N1YRP
Robert J Bouchard
17 Quail Ridge Rd
Concord NH 03301

Call Sign: WA1UEF
Winston J Bridge
18 Quail Ridge Rd
Concord NH 03301

Call Sign: N1HCH
Stephen J Naylor
14 Redwing Rd
Concord NH 03301

Call Sign: N1JDO
Michael J Frappier
9 Robin Rd
Concord NH 03301

Call Sign: N1QJN
Barbara J Freeman
135 Rumford St
Concord NH 03301

Call Sign: KB1QFX
David B Mcdonald
26 S Main St 103
Concord NH 03301

Call Sign: W2LPI
Charles L Nenninger Jr
103 School St
Concord NH 03301

Call Sign: N2DEY

Leo L Marin Jr
54 Shawmut St
Concord NH 03301

Call Sign: KA1DGQ
Leroy R Quimby
264 Sheep Davis Rd
Concord NH 03301

Call Sign: KB1JPE
Aaron J Fracht-Monroe
9 Short St
Concord NH 03301

Call Sign: KA2QFX
Mark W Sedutto
204 Silk Farm Rd
Concord NH 03301

Call Sign: K1DND
Daniel N Daly
53 South Main St Apt 2a
Concord NH 03301

Call Sign: KB1LDP
Mark D Handley
26 South Main St Pmb 212
Concord NH 03301

Call Sign: KB1LDQ
Judith M Handley
26 South Main St Pmb 212
Concord NH 03301

Call Sign: KB1IBG
Walter A Kahn
53 South Spring St
Concord NH 03301

Call Sign: KA1FMQ
Ida M Valla
91 South St
Concord NH 03301

Call Sign: W1CUE

Stephen J Valla
91 South St
Concord NH 03301

Call Sign: N1JDL
Warren N Runde
168 South St
Concord NH 03301

Call Sign: W8NCL
Warren N Runde
168 South St
Concord NH 03301

Call Sign: KA1ZSK
Daniel S Mabry
321 South St
Concord NH 03301

Call Sign: KB1GQE
Gordon C Thompson
58 South St A-3
Concord NH 03301

Call Sign: KB1TYX
Christy L Roberts
39 Stone St
Concord NH 03301

Call Sign: NH6IK
Patrick F Cassell Jr
4 Sulloway St
Concord NH 03301

Call Sign: KB1IQO
Alan W Magnuson
9 Sylvester St
Concord NH 03303

Call Sign: WB9WWE
Vernon A Miller
1 Tow Path Ln
Concord NH 033016913

Call Sign: KA1QBE

Deborah L Fortuna
55 Tremont St
Concord NH 03301

Call Sign: KB1ECK
Richard G Morin
12 Union St
Concord NH 033014250

Call Sign: K1CF
Wayne F Dailey Jr
18 Union St
Concord NH 03301

Call Sign: WA1MXN
David W Burnham
16 Valley St
Concord NH 03301

Call Sign: K1BBQ
Gerald S Blanchard Sr
8 Venne Cir
Concord NH 033012705

Call Sign: N1JV
Patrick J Poirier Sr
167 W Parish Rd
Concord NH 03303

Call Sign: W1KA
Patrick J Poirier Sr
167 W Parish Rd
Concord NH 03303

Call Sign: KB1TNB
Kelly M Clancy
97 Warren St
Concord NH 03301

Call Sign: N1KBZ
Robert E Phipps
72 Washington St Apt 1
Concord NH 03301

Call Sign: KA1WFV

Robert E Brodeur
6 Wilson Ave
Concord NH 03301

Call Sign: N1QXO
Harold L Rice
23 Wilson Ave
Concord NH 03301

Call Sign: K1UK
David L Breck
6 Windham Dr
Concord NH 03301

Call Sign: K1OJA
Ira R Evans
Concord NH 03302

Call Sign: KA1LMR
Christopher M Merchant
Concord NH 03302

Call Sign: N1JHJ
Steven M Jones
Concord NH 03301

Call Sign: N2LUG
Paul A Halvorsen
Concord NH 03302

Call Sign: N2LZZ
Penny Y Halvorsen
Concord NH 03302

Call Sign: W1OC
Concord Brasspounders
Concord NH 03302

Call Sign: KB1IWP
Heidi C Scott
Concord NH 03302

Call Sign: KB1KFT
Gregory J Van Ermen
Concord NH 03302

Call Sign: AJ1Q
Ian M Hoffman
Concord NH 03302

Call Sign: KB1OYE
Austin C Wiggin
Concord NH 033021125

Call Sign: W1ACW
Austin C Wiggin
Concord NH 033021125

Call Sign: AB1KX
Ian M Hoffman
Concord NH 03302

Call Sign: KB1UCQ
Mark T Hillson
Concord NH 03302

Call Sign: W1MR
Christopher M Merchant
Concord NH 03302

## FCC Amateur Radio Licenses in Condonderry

Call Sign: N1FIE
Frank A Marconi
42 Trolleycar Lane
Condonderry NH
030532931

## FCC Amateur Radio Licenses in Contoocook

Call Sign: N1JHO
Henry R Simonds Iii
210 Amesbury Rd
Contoocook NH 03229

Call Sign: N1ZGO
Robert S Clay
1677 Bound Tree Rd

Contoocook NH 03229

Call Sign: KA1ONM
Karlis D Serzans
Box 27
Contoocook NH 03229

Call Sign: KA1WFB
John K Grant
Box 481
Contoocook NH 03229

Call Sign: N1IVG
George B Foote
Box 495
Contoocook NH 03229

Call Sign: KA1RJD
Anne M Black-Thoits
67 Burnham Intervale Rd
Contoocook NH 03229

Call Sign: K1MID
Kenneth B Wilkens
146 Carriage Ln
Contoocook NH 03229

Call Sign: KB1IVT
Stephen M Power
151 Carriage Ln
Contoocook NH 032293302

Call Sign: N1FOJ
John C Moore
320 Dustin Rd
Contoocook NH 03229

Call Sign: KA1SYS
Thomas R Hencke
436 Gould Hill Rd
Contoocook NH 03229

Call Sign: N1KJW
Robert W Donnelly Sr
1855 Hopkinton Rd

Contoocook NH 03229

Call Sign: KG4RGF
Mark P Faulkner
49 Kearsarge Ave
Contoocook NH 03229

Call Sign: K1DKA
David A Forest
28 Knollwood Cir
Contoocook NH 03229

Call Sign: N1NSI
Keith D Wallace
157 Little Tooky Rd.
Contoocook NH 03229

Call Sign: KA1DOK
Bruce A Metzger
614 Main St
Contoocook NH 03229

Call Sign: W1CWP
Earl S Woods
631 Main St
Contoocook NH 032293007

Call Sign: K1OPQ
David B Perrin Sr
1161 Penacook Rd
Contoocook NH 03229

Call Sign: N1GPD
Susan S Perrin
1161 Penacook Rd
Contoocook NH 032293032

Call Sign: N1NPN
Casey-Lyn P Knight
1161 Penacook Rd
Contoocook NH 03229

Call Sign: N1BHE
Ronald E Romer
831 Pine St

Contoocook NH 03229

Call Sign: W1EAW
Richard W Cressy Jr
916 Pine St
Contoocook NH 032293131

Call Sign: W1IN
Robert E Hall
50 Sunset Dr
Contoocook NH 03229

Call Sign: KB1LPE
Keith M Harrison
53 Woodland Dr
Contoocook NH 032292533

Call Sign: W1DAE
Peter Clarner
168 Woodland Dr
Contoocook NH 03229

Call Sign: N1SSE
Cynthia J Stopa
178 Woodland Dr
Contoocook NH 03229

Call Sign: K1DBL
George A Langwasser
Contoocook NH 03229

Call Sign: N1HXO
Stephen R Ingham
Contoocook NH 03229

Call Sign: KB1EVJ
Veronica M Meisser
Contoocook NH 03229

Call Sign: N1KYJ
Mark P Faulkner
Contoocook NH 03229

**FCC Amateur Radio
Licenses in Conway**

Call Sign: N1KAM
Brian L King
Box 907
Conway NH 03818

Call Sign: WA1UFO
Hans K Hildebrand
99 E Main St
Conway NH 03818

Call Sign: WA1FUH
Armand H Query Jr
70 Grandview Rd
Conway NH 03818

Call Sign: KA1IIQ
Stanley A Cressey
33 Lamplighters Dr
Conway NH 03818

Call Sign: AA1WV
Richard A Ferraro
34 Main St. #22
Conway NH 03818

Call Sign: KB1PTI
Edward F Duffy
224 Poliquin Dr
Conway NH 03818

Call Sign: KB0VCC
Dale S Anderson
27 River St
Conway NH 038186192

Call Sign: AB1S
Charles A Harrow
Tasker Hill Rd
Conway NH 03818

Call Sign: WA3RTJ
Charles L Harrow
Conway NH 03818

Call Sign: K1JCU
Peter H Gibson
Conway NH 038180356

Call Sign: K1QNZ
Richard F Norris
Conway NH 03818

Call Sign: N1XER
Michael W Clark
Conway NH 03818

Call Sign: W1MWV
White Mountain Amateur
Radio Club
Conway NH 03818

Call Sign: KB1GZQ
David C Andrzejewski
Conway NH 03818

Call Sign: KB1OOM
Richard C Amaral Jr
Conway NH 03818

**FCC Amateur Radio
Licenses in Cornish**

Call Sign: KA1RBU
Anne C Bauerdorf
Box 138
Cornish NH 03745

Call Sign: AA1TQ
Stephen J Hopkins
670 Center Rd
Cornish NH 03745

Call Sign: N1UUM
Bernard W Stone
1124 Nh Rt 120
Cornish NH 037454823

Call Sign: KB1NNV
James R Liggett

973 Nh Rt 12a
Cornish NH 03745

Call Sign: K1JRL
James R Liggett
973 Nh Rt 12a
Cornish NH 03745

Call Sign: KE1IW
David B Haseman
300 Paget Rd
Cornish NH 03745

Call Sign: N2FRA
Raymond P Kendall
107 Sunset Strip Rd
Cornish NH 03745

Call Sign: WB2NWR
Howard J Katchen
192 Tandy Brook Rd
Cornish NH 03745

Call Sign: KB1JSO
Lynn S Kneedler
52 Tifft Rd
Cornish NH 03745

Call Sign: K1DAN
Daniel G Martin
13 Town Line Dr.
Cornish NH 03745

Call Sign: KB1JSR
Jonathan T Nichols
Cornish Flat NH 03746

Call Sign: KA1FKV
Richard P Cota
Cornish Flat NH 03746

FCC Amateur Radio
Licenses in Croydon

Call Sign: KB1ICV

Patrick P Hayward
249 Reeds Mill Rd
Croydon NH 03277

FCC Amateur Radio
Licenses in Dalton

Call Sign: KB1ACX
Marilyn M Komisarek
21 Achorn Hill Rd
Dalton NH 03598

Call Sign: N1EII
Edward J Tomashek
558 Dalton Rd
Dalton NH 035985727

Call Sign: KA2EBX
Thomas J Livingston
814 Dalton Rd
Dalton NH 03598

Call Sign: WA1HRH
Thomas F Barker
329 Faraway Rd
Dalton NH 03598

Call Sign: KB1FFX
Scott J Ramsdell
46 Meadowmist Dr
Dalton NH 03598

FCC Amateur Radio
Licenses in Danbury

Call Sign: KB1CSV
Jon A Johnson
505 Nh Rt 104
Danbury NH 03230

Call Sign: KB1VVO
Richard A Swift
420 North Rd
Danbury NH 03230

Call Sign: N1NKC
Glen P Harding
116 Restful Rd
Danbury NH 03230

Call Sign: N1SMD
COLLEEN E Harding
116 Restful Rd
Danbury NH 03230

Call Sign: W1FNJ
Glen P Harding
116 Restful Rd
Danbury NH 03230

Call Sign: KB1IFH
Janette K Hillsgrove
203 Waukeena Lake Rd
Danbury NH 03230

Call Sign: KB1GNI
Lee R Hillsgrove Sr
203 Waukeena Lake Rd
Danbury NH 03230

Call Sign: N2LGX
Frederick J Maddage
Danbury NH 03230

FCC Amateur Radio
Licenses in Danville

Call Sign: N1KOX
Bruce P Skaff
37 Beechwood Dr
Danville NH 03819

Call Sign: K1NQ
David F Jordan
26 Crestwood Dr
Danville NH 03819

Call Sign: KB1IJA
John S Castle
73 Johnson Rd

Danville NH 03819

Call Sign: N1ORT
David T Cianfrini
229 Kingston Rd
Danville NH 03819

Call Sign: WA1FCV
Paul D Canfield
58 Long Pond Rd
Danville NH 03819

Call Sign: KB1DYI
Robin W Lewis
232 Long Pond Rd
Danville NH 03819

Call Sign: W1AUA
John S Howland
207 Main St
Danville NH 03819

Call Sign: KB1IHQ
Matthew J Goss
23 Moose Hollow Rd
Danville NH 03879

Call Sign: N1HEX
George P Sullivan
217 Sandown Rd
Danville NH 03819

Call Sign: W1EHF
Francis R Vernon
Danville NH 03819

Call Sign: W1IOO
Wallace H Cooledge Jr
Danville NH 03819

Call Sign: KB1MGD
K Ross Chapman Jr
Danville NH 03819

Call Sign: KB1PMJ

Eileen B O'gorman
Danville NH 03819

## FCC Amateur Radio Licenses in Dartmouth College

Call Sign: KC0GKJ
Seth Y Maxson
Hinman Box 3167
Dartmouth College NH
03755

## FCC Amateur Radio Licenses in Deerfield

Call Sign: KB1AAX
Jacob A Pena
14 Birch Rd
Deerfield NH 03037

Call Sign: N1GT
G Donald Tomilson
30 Birch Rd
Deerfield NH 03037

Call Sign: KB1DYC
Walter C Turgeon Jr
44 Church St
Deerfield NH 030370382

Call Sign: KB1FXY
Scott A Sybert
93 Coffeetown Rd
Deerfield NH 03037

Call Sign: W1TLX
Scott A Sybert
93 Coffeetown Rd
Deerfield NH 03037

Call Sign: KT1C
Timothy D Rogers
39 Middle Rd
Deerfield NH 03037

Call Sign: KB1LTH
Christopher E Valade
122 Middle Rd
Deerfield NH 03037

Call Sign: N1TC
Anthony P Capelle
233 Middle Rd
Deerfield NH 03037

Call Sign: KB1ESO
Stephen A Hills
265 Middle Rd
Deerfield NH 03037

Call Sign: KB1ESP
PHILIP J Hills
265 Middle Rd
Deerfield NH 03037

Call Sign: KB1GYV
Bethany L Hills
265 Middle Rd
Deerfield NH 03037

Call Sign: KB1GYW
Brenda A Hills
265 Middle Rd
Deerfield NH 03037

Call Sign: KB1GYX
Brian P Hills
265 Middle Rd
Deerfield NH 03037

Call Sign: KB1WSU
Jonathan D Lacy
71 Mount De Light Rd
Deerfield NH 03037

Call Sign: KE1KX
David W Lacy
71 Mount Delight Rd
Deerfield NH 03037

Call Sign: W1TDR
David G Holloway
137 Mount Delight Rd
Deerfield NH 03037

Call Sign: WK1Y
Joseph R Boyle
181 Mt. Delight Rd.
Deerfield NH 03037

Call Sign: KB1PPB
Jennifer R Hutchins
135 Nottingham Rd
Deerfield NH 03037

Call Sign: N1HVU
Caroline A Boyle
181 Mount Delight Rd
Deerfield NH 03037

Call Sign: KB1NLV
David W Smith
139 North Rd
Deerfield NH 03037

Call Sign: N1JDR
Kenneth W Watts
Old Centre Rd
Deerfield NH 03037

Call Sign: KB1QGC
Malcolm E Cameron Jr
91 Mountain View Rd
Deerfield NH 03037

Call Sign: WB1ESP
William V Carozza
294 North Rd
Deerfield NH 03037

Call Sign: N1NSF
Barbara S Watts
52 Old Centre Rd N
Deerfield NH 03037

Call Sign: KB1LOX
David E Guild
113 Mountain View Rd
Deerfield NH 03037

Call Sign: N1DCG
Wayne R Murray Jr
352 North Rd
Deerfield NH 03037

Call Sign: KB1OBH
John P Dubiansky
5 Parade Rd
Deerfield NH 03037

Call Sign: KB1LEK
Jacqueline E Lacy
71 Mt Delight Rd
Deerfield NH 03037

Call Sign: N1UDB
Dorothy S Anderson
47 Nottingham Rd
Deerfield NH 03037

Call Sign: KB1VLE
Thomas G Dionne
47 Pleasant Hill Rd
Deerfield NH 03037

Call Sign: N1VBM
Paula J Dunigan
169 Mt Delight Rd
Deerfield NH 03037

Call Sign: KB1FIH
William A Cartier
106 Nottingham Rd
Deerfield NH 03037

Call Sign: N1AKD
Sigrid Marble
61 Pleasant Hill Rd
Deerfield NH 03037

Call Sign: N1VBL
Thomas F Dunigan
169 Mt Delight Rd
Deerfield NH 03037

Call Sign: K1BNH
William A Cartier
106 Nottingham Rd
Deerfield NH 03037

Call Sign: N1AKE
Bradford G Marble
61 Pleasant Hill Rd
Deerfield NH 03037

Call Sign: N1VBL
Thomas F Dunigan
169 Mt. Delight Rd
Deerfield NH 03037

Call Sign: KA1FJC
Lynn B Garland
135 Nottingham Rd
Deerfield NH 03037

Call Sign: KA1ZCQ
Aaron W Major
49 Pleasent Lake
Deerfield NH 03037

Call Sign: KB1IMI
Thomas F Dunigan
169 Mt. Delight Rd
Deerfield NH 03037

Call Sign: KA1JM
Charles A Garland
135 Nottingham Rd
Deerfield NH 03037

Call Sign: KB1LEL
Robert E Kilham Jr
1 Ridge Rd
Deerfield NH 03037

Call Sign: K1VC
Victor L Carozza
31 Ridge Rd
Deerfield NH 03037

Call Sign: N3ULG
Brenda J Carr
76 Ridge Rd
Deerfield NH 03037

Call Sign: WB3CXC
Jeffrey S Carr
76 Ridge Rd
Deerfield NH 03037

Call Sign: KB1BBR
Sarah N Muller
92 Ridge Rd
Deerfield NH 03037

Call Sign: KA1QWT
Cory Cummings Snow
Ridge Rd
Deerfield NH 03037

Call Sign: N1OWS
Cynthia M B Maimone
3 Swamp Rd
Deerfield NH 03037

Call Sign: KB1RDA
Otis R Bruce
Deerfield NH 03037

Call Sign: KB1UXL
Burton R Bush
Deerfield NH 03037

Call Sign: N1ZOI
Eric R Kangas
2063 2nd Nh Tpke

Deering NH 03244

Call Sign: WB2IHH
Louann Caron
62 Blueberry Hill Rd
Deering NH 03244

Call Sign: WB2IJC
Bruce A Caron
62 Blueberry Hill Rd.
Deering NH 03244

Call Sign: KB1HVN
Erik L Parker
55 Farrell Hill Rd
Deering NH 03244

Call Sign: K1HNK
Henry H Drake
40 Manselville Rd
Deering NH 03244

Call Sign: K1TKY
Patricia L Drake
40 Manselville Rd
Deering NH 03244

Call Sign: N1LM
Linda S Morehouse
405 Tubbs Hill Rd
Deering NH 032446538

Call Sign: N7NH
George D Morehouse
405 Tubbs Hill Rd
Deering NH 032446538

Call Sign: N1LQL
Kirt E Tonken
104 Union St
Deering NH 03244

Call Sign: KB1DHY
Timothy R Giglio
17 Wyman Rd.

Deering NH 03244

Call Sign: KB1MAT
Dennis E Jacobs
16 Abbott St
Derry NH 03038

Call Sign: KM4NZ
Charles L Wyrick
62 Adams Pond Rd
Derry NH 03038

Call Sign: KB1MIU
Michael D Kline
6 Al St
Derry NH 03038

Call Sign: N1GUB
Joseph A Zimmer
3 Aladdin Cr Apt 2
Derry NH 03038

Call Sign: KB1AZI
David W Mc Grath
4 Aladdin Village Apt 28
Derry NH 03038

Call Sign: N1GYH
Stephen J Parrott
19 Alyssa Dr
Derry NH 03038

Call Sign: N1RKD
Dennis H Dean
51 Amherst Dr
Derry NH 03038

Call Sign: N1ROK
Nathan J Dean
51 Amherst Dr
Derry NH 03038

Call Sign: KA1VMS
Brian A George
20 B Conifer Place
Derry NH 03038

Call Sign: KA1TPU
Richard H Ruh Iii
65 Bedard Ave
Derry NH 03038

Call Sign: KA1NAU
James A Hannah
3 Belle Brook Ln
Derry NH 03038

Call Sign: W1OOQ
Woodrow J Madison
17 Berry Rd
Derry NH 03038

Call Sign: N1EVK
Robert J Beaulieu
29 Berry Rd
Derry NH 03038

Call Sign: KA1UEL
Andrew J Ralph
3 Birch St
Derry NH 03038

Call Sign: KA1ULL
Kelley A Ralph
3 Birch St
Derry NH 03038

Call Sign: W1HCP
Joseph W Smith Jr
51 Birch St
Derry NH 03038

Call Sign: WA1DMV
William S Polewarczyk Jr
59 Birch St
Derry NH 03038

Call Sign: WA1RPQ
Joseph L Wall
1 Bisbee Cir
Derry NH 03038

Call Sign: W8AOT
Merle A Centner
2 Bisbee Cir
Derry NH 03038

Call Sign: KC1ZF
Bo H Strandnes
Box 3
Derry NH 03038

Call Sign: KB1TMW
Gail A Dunn
12 Bradford St
Derry NH 03038

Call Sign: KA1SNJ
Jack W Mann
8 Brady Ave
Derry NH 03038

Call Sign: N1KTL
Jay W Stone
44 Brady Ave
Derry NH 03038

Call Sign: KB1FOW
Timothy J Stone
44 Brady Ave
Derry NH 03038

Call Sign: N1OBA
Frederick H Gould Jr
14 Brandywyne Common
Derry NH 03038

Call Sign: KB1DYE
Dale T Stancik
14 Briarwood St
Derry NH 03038

Call Sign: K6OOZ
George E Hause
10 Brier Ln
Derry NH 030384844

Call Sign: N1PZM
Donald L Bodwell Sr
22 Brook St
Derry NH 03038

Call Sign: N1KTN
Gerald S Lavery
13 Brookview Dr
Derry NH 03038

Call Sign: N1ZCL
James F Shanley
7 Buttonwood Dr
Derry NH 03038

Call Sign: KP4ARS
Arthur S Glawson
C/O C Saunders
Derry NH 03038

Call Sign: KD9BI
Cynthia K Adams
4 Cedar St
Derry NH 030382206

Call Sign: KB1HMZ
Stephen L Witley
413 Chases Grove
Derry NH 03038

Call Sign: N1RKU
Brian K Wiggin
Chases Grove Ln 2
Derry NH 03038

Call Sign: N1RKE
Scott T Fuller
48 Chester Rd
Derry NH 03038

Call Sign: N1SRD
Kathleen M Fuller
48 Chester Rd
Derry NH 03038

Call Sign: KF4NHV
Jami M Carroll
6 Cilley Rd
Derry NH 03038

Call Sign: KB1UXO
Michael R Deveau
1 Claire Ave
Derry NH 03038

Call Sign: KE1JS
Salvatore Gioe
89 Conleys Grove Rd
Derry NH 030389507

Call Sign: WA2CYS
Leonard A Epstein
8 Corwin Dr
Derry NH 03038

Call Sign: KA1FDF
Harold G Hurd
3 Cote Ln
Derry NH 03038

Call Sign: KA1DGD
Robert P Hamm
27 Cove Dr
Derry NH 03038

Call Sign: KA1VWC
Richard N Marshall
5 Crescent St
Derry NH 03038

Call Sign: N1OMF
Alexandra G Blais
4 Crystal Ave Apt 2
Derry NH 03038

Call Sign: KB1WXR
Wayne F Pearson Jr
5 Damren Rd
Derry NH 03038

Call Sign: KA1VMT
Michael S Trachtman
Derryfield Rd
Derry NH 03038

Call Sign: KA1TUK
Lawrence C Costa
Derryfield Rd
Derry NH 03038

Call Sign: KB1PMK
John C Green
6 Derryway Apt 12
Derry NH 03038

Call Sign: KG1OWL
John C Green
6 Derryway Apt 12
Derry NH 03038

Call Sign: N1WMY
Gary A Raphanella
Dexter St
Derry NH 03038

Call Sign: KB1PEY
Christopher A Bourque
2 Donmac Dr
Derry NH 03038

Call Sign: N1RUZ
Joyce T Bourque
2 Donmac Dr
Derry NH 030383716

Call Sign: W1AJI
Merrimack Valley Contest
Club
2 Donmac Dr
Derry NH 030383716

Call Sign: WB1FLD
David W Bourque
2 Donmac Dr
Derry NH 030383716

Call Sign: N3GQW
William F Gardei
1 Drake Ln
Derry NH 03038

Call Sign: N3TJL
Kenneth W Gardei
1 Drake Ln
Derry NH 03038

Call Sign: N3TJM
Douglas W Gardei
1 Drake Ln
Derry NH 030384131

Call Sign: N3VQZ
Donna M Gardei
1 Drake Ln
Derry NH 03038

Call Sign: KB1UMK
George R Feole
5 Drake Ln
Derry NH 03038

Call Sign: N1YXE
Bryan L Scanlon
61 Drew Rd
Derry NH 03038

Call Sign: W1LSO
Laurier A St Onge
11 Drew Woods Dr
Derry NH 03038

Call Sign: N1YEN
Geoffrey A Lundy
46 Drew Woods Dr
Derry NH 03038

Call Sign: KB1FQC
Christopher D Case
80 E Broadway Apt C
Derry NH 03038

Call Sign: KB1HN
Frederick U Meier
116 East Broadway Apt 2
Derry NH 030381800

Call Sign: N1GD
Gianni M Dintino
10 Eastgate Rd
Derry NH 03038

Call Sign: KA1SVI
Warren E Towne Jr
7 Emerald Dr
Derry NH 03038

Call Sign: N8CMS
Donald J Cook
77 English Range Rd
Derry NH 03038

Call Sign: KA1DCA
Robert M Berry
2 Erin Ln
Derry NH 03038

Call Sign: KA1BX
John J Mc Cormack Sr
18 Everett St
Derry NH 030382237

Call Sign: NQ1O
Michael T Mc Cormack
18 Everett St
Derry NH 030382237

Call Sign: N1TRH
Roger M Swanson
1 Fairway Apt 311
Derry NH 03038

Call Sign: KB1HMX
Jeremy P Lakin
15 Fairway Dr 21
Derry NH 03038

Call Sign: N1ZWU
Matthew S Dydo
11 Fairway Dr Apt #20
Derry NH 03038

Call Sign: N1QCQ
Susan M Bilodeau
8 Fairway Dr Apt 258
Derry NH 03038

Call Sign: KB1FFZ
George A Moranian
11 Fairway Dr. Apt. 33
Derry NH 03038

Call Sign: N1TRN
Joshua J Hodson
13 Floyd Rd
Derry NH 03038

Call Sign: KA1TOP
Charles F Pacheco
63 Franklin St
Derry NH 03038

Call Sign: KB1EDQ
Tracy J Horacek
19 Franklin St 1
Derry NH 03038

Call Sign: N1MWK
Bion R Estabrook
22 Frost Rd
Derry NH 03038

Call Sign: WB1FXS
Mark J Donovan
63 Frost Rd
Derry NH 03038

Call Sign: KB1WQM
Leszek Rompa
64 Frost Rd
Derry NH 03038

Call Sign: K1YRM
Clyde G Hayward
Frost Rd
Derry NH 03038

Call Sign: N1SJF
James L Puffer
4 Gaita Dr
Derry NH 03038

Call Sign: KC1Q
David F Jordan
32 Gulf Rd
Derry NH 03038

Call Sign: N1LTD
Robert W Donnell Jr
77 Gulf Rd
Derry NH 03038

Call Sign: WB4HTD
John T Orr
24 Hampshire Dr
Derry NH 03038

Call Sign: KA1UVH
Michael P Pelletier
138 Hampstead Rd
Derry NH 03038

Call Sign: K1WRK
West Rockingham Nhares
Club
138 Hampstead Rd
Derry NH 03038

Call Sign: KD1UC
Michael E Dawson
264 Hampstead Rd

Derry NH 03038

Call Sign: N1UWB
James C Overman
1 Hanover Lane
Derry NH 030381200

Call Sign: N1WIX
William M O Connor
3 Heather Ln
Derry NH 03038

Call Sign: N1XEI
Michael J Therrien
Hemlock Springs Rd
Derry NH 03038

Call Sign: N1PJT
David A Rousseau
3 Hemlock Springs Rd.
Derry NH 03038

Call Sign: N1KAN
Jon A Cabbe
28 High St
Derry NH 03038

Call Sign: KB1WSM
Linda A Lyons
34 High St 2nd Flr
Derry NH 03038

Call Sign: K0KVR
Ray L Thompson
5 Highland Ave
Derry NH 03038

Call Sign: KA1KUL
Robert M Ahern
103 Hillside Ave
Derry NH 030532605

Call Sign: WB1FET
Leslie S F Brown
6 Hood Rd

Derry NH 03038

Call Sign: K1STH
Frederick R Tupper
15 Hoodkroft Dr
Derry NH 03038

Call Sign: KB5LHG
Shannon M Delgado
6 Hunter Dr
Derry NH 03038

Call Sign: KD5GZR
Carlos S Delgado
6 Hunter Dr
Derry NH 03038

Call Sign: N1EPB
Charles E Naylor
1 Island Pond Rd
Derry NH 03038

Call Sign: W1GHB
Chester A Ellison
48 Island Pond Rd
Derry NH 03038

Call Sign: KB1UXZ
Carol B Spoerl
242 Island Pond Rd
Derry NH 03038

Call Sign: KB1CBS
Carol B Spoerl
242 Island Pond Rd
Derry NH 03038

Call Sign: KA1YAW
Jamie Rios
Island Pond Rd
Derry NH 03038

Call Sign: KA1SOA
Michele L Cabana
3 James St

Derry NH 03038

Call Sign: W1FI
Glenn E Cabana
3 James St
Derry NH 03038

Call Sign: KB1PUZ
Darrell W Park
6 Joan St
Derry NH 03038

Call Sign: WA2HZV
Myron C Hollingsworth
Juniper Rd
Derry NH 03038

Call Sign: KA1ZFQ
Andrew J Cote
30 Kendall Pd Rd
Derry NH 03038

Call Sign: KA1UKL
Paula A Natola
72 Kendall Pond Rd
Derry NH 03038

Call Sign: KB1EUM
Thomas D Wagner
66 Kilrea Rd
Derry NH 03038

Call Sign: N1CSA
Thomas D Wagner
66 Kilrea Rd
Derry NH 03038

Call Sign: WB1GPC
Kenneth A Hepworth
32 Kingsbury St
Derry NH 03038

Call Sign: N7YNJ
Bonnie M Drake
6 Larauq Ct 213

Derry NH 03038

Call Sign: K1YHE
Theodore A Poreda
8 Laraway Ct Apt 1d
Derry NH 03038

Call Sign: KB1PAV
Christopher M Marsh
44 Lawrence Rd
Derry NH 03038

Call Sign: N1TEC
Steven D Hutzley
8 Liberty Circle
Derry NH 03038

Call Sign: W1IPI
Carroll W Saunders
1 Linda Rd
Derry NH 03038

Call Sign: KA1KUE
John F Flynn
17 Linlew Dr A22
Derry NH 03038

Call Sign: KB1QMI
Jason A Dubrow
7 Linlew Dr Apt 12
Derry NH 03038

Call Sign: KA1SHL
Jeffrey P Petrin
28 Linlew Dr Apt 8
Derry NH 03038

Call Sign: KB1NJQ
William R Fournier Jr
9 Linlew Dr. Apt. 3
Derry NH 03038

Call Sign: KA1LEV
John E O Neill
2 London Rd

Derry NH 03038

Call Sign: W1DDY
Wilber W Bridge
Mallard Ct
Derry NH 03038

Call Sign: N1OEZ
Nancy J Webb
25 Maxwell Dr
Derry NH 03038

Call Sign: KA1UVI
Joseph F Stowers
5 Mecca Ln
Derry NH 03038

Call Sign: KB1IDG
John E D Errico
Mill Rd
Derry NH 03038

Call Sign: N1ERF
John E D'errico
Mill Rd
Derry NH 03038

Call Sign: KA1RCA
Anne M Mac Cord
3 Miltimore Rd
Derry NH 03038

Call Sign: KB1XI
Donald A Mac Cord
3 Miltimore Rd
Derry NH 03038

Call Sign: AC1U
Donald A Mac Cord
3 Miltimore Rd
Derry NH 03038

Call Sign: WA1EFX
William F Gruning
23 Miltimore Rd

Derry NH 030384442

Call Sign: KA1JZT
Jeffrey R Angle
5 Montgomery Farm Rd
Derry NH 03038

Call Sign: KB1EWO
Heather N Cooney
11 Morningside Dr
Derry NH 03038

Call Sign: WA1RRW
Earle E Kelley
41 N Main St
Derry NH 030381208

Call Sign: N1NYZ
Gardner O Dauphinais
12 Nesmith St
Derry NH 03038

Call Sign: WA1EZE
Mario R Natola
4 Newell Rd
Derry NH 03038

Call Sign: WB9TSS
Michael W Faber
100 Old Auburn Rd
Derry NH 03038

Call Sign: WB2TFZ
Pamela J Otis
65 Old Chester Rd
Derry NH 03038

Call Sign: KB1DQB
Mary S Desautel
20 Olesen Rd
Derry NH 03038

Call Sign: N1OIJ
Colleen R Desautel
20 Olesen Rd.

Derry NH 03038

Call Sign: W1IA
Brent R Desautel
20 Olesen Rd.
Derry NH 03038

Call Sign: W1ELA
Colleen R Desautel
20 Olesen Rd.
Derry NH 03038

Call Sign: KB1KKI
Andrea R Desautel
20 Oleson Rd
Derry NH 03038

Call Sign: N1INI
Lawrence H Boise
20 Overledge Dr
Derry NH 03038

Call Sign: KB1FFB
Alexander C Hoch
22 Overledge Dr
Derry NH 03038

Call Sign: N1RLC
Gregory S Hamilton
17 Oxbow Lane
Derry NH 03038

Call Sign: NW1Y
Paul E Heintel
24 Partridge Ln
Derry NH 03038

Call Sign: KA1QWH
Dana R Richardson
23 Paul Ave
Derry NH 030383810

Call Sign: K1RWT
Lois E Sieg
2 Pembroke Dr 4

Derry NH 03038

Call Sign: WF1K
John C Sieg
2 Pembroke Dr 4
Derry NH 03038

Call Sign: N1PFB
Paul F Beasley
4 Pembroke Dr Unit 11
Derry NH 03038

Call Sign: KB1UFM
Kathleen A Peterson
4 Pembroke Dr Unit 11
Derry NH 03038

Call Sign: KB1TQK
Paul F Beasley
4 Pembroke Dr Unit 111
Derry NH 03038

Call Sign: KB1WKM
Southern New Hampshire
Dstar Group
4 Penbroke Dr - #11
Derry NH 03038

Call Sign: K1QVC
Southern New Hampshire
Dstar Group
4 Penbroke Dr - #11
Derry NH 03038

Call Sign: KA1YSP
Joan F Durling
4 Pierce Ave
Derry NH 03038

Call Sign: N1GXB
Robert J Landers
20 Pinehurst Ave
Derry NH 03038

Call Sign: KA1TDU

Norman L Cousins Jr
18 Pinkerton St
Derry NH 03038

Call Sign: KB1POY
Morgan S Gaythorpe
5 R Morningside Dr
Derry NH 03038

Call Sign: KB1PZ
Michael W Bernock
22 Redfield Cir
Derry NH 030384839

Call Sign: N1IW
Michael W Bernock
22 Redfield Cir
Derry NH 030384839

Call Sign: NM1D
Richard J Bono
7 Redfield Circle
Derry NH 03038

Call Sign: N1PML
Leonard J Ouellette
21 Rita Ave
Derry NH 03038

Call Sign: KB1JYF
Patricia A Baum
21 Rita Ave
Derry NH 03038

Call Sign: N1VBN
James H Shanks
192 Rt 28
Derry NH 03038

Call Sign: N1SJI
Richard F Gillaspie
116 Scobie Pond Rd
Derry NH 03038

Call Sign: N1SUB

Allison M Gillaspie
116 Scobie Pond Rd
Derry NH 03038

Call Sign: N1YYZ
Keith D Flanagan
3 Silvestri Circle Unit 3
Derry NH 03038

Call Sign: WB1EUB
Robert J Letourneau
30 South Ave
Derry NH 03038

Call Sign: N1NHT
Ronald C Chase
22 Spinnaker Dr N
Derry NH 03038

Call Sign: KB1SZG
Phil J Whittemore
87 Stonegate Lane
Derry NH 03038

Call Sign: K1HON
Phil J Whittemore
87 Stonegate Lane
Derry NH 03038

Call Sign: KB1QXI
Stephen P Morton
14 Stonegate Lane
Derry NH 03038

Call Sign: N1KCB
Mary E Barrett
75 Stonegate Ln
Derry NH 03038

Call Sign: K1GEX
Anthony J Syvinski
Summer Hill Condos 8d
Sundown Dr
Derry NH 03038

Call Sign: K1RIZ
Richard N Hayes
1 Summit Ave
Derry NH 03038

Call Sign: N1TJY
Nancy M Hayes
1 Summit Ave
Derry NH 03038

Call Sign: KB1CSE
William H Durocher
Sundown Dr
Derry NH 03038

Call Sign: N1IIG
Roy S Dumas
15 Sundown Dr Unit D
Derry NH 03038

Call Sign: N1GBC
Roy S Dumas
15 Sundown Dr Unit D
Derry NH 03038

Call Sign: KB1RYP
Gary M Simard
Sunnyside Lane
Derry NH 03038

Call Sign: W1DGE
John T Holgate
6 Sunset Ave
Derry NH 030384243

Call Sign: K1VUB
Robert E Cole
14 Sunset Ave
Derry NH 030384244

Call Sign: KA1YIJ
H Trevor Williams
1 Taryn Rd
Derry NH 03038

Call Sign: AJ1V
John A Ingerowski
2 Thames Rd
Derry NH 03038

Call Sign: N1DDQ
Judith M Ingerowski
2 Thames Rd
Derry NH 03038

Call Sign: N1YIH
Darrell R Beers
3 True Ave
Derry NH 03038

Call Sign: K1BF
John B Foster Jr
1 Tsienneto 20
Derry NH 03038

Call Sign: N2STJ
Lawrence A Deck
5 Tsienneto Rd Unit 119
Derry NH 03038

Call Sign: N1YEO
Ann L Hodson
4 Twin Brook Dr
Derry NH 03038

Call Sign: N1TRM
Randall M Hodson
4 Twinbrook Dr
Derry NH 03038

Call Sign: N1WEL
Randall M Hodson Ii
4 Twinbrook Dr
Derry NH 03038

Call Sign: N1OUE
Joseph R Holt
14 Village Brook Ln
Derry NH 03038

Call Sign: K1FIP
Paula Walach
95 Walnut Hill Rd
Derry NH 03038

Call Sign: K1CA
Laurent J Blouin
52 Warner Hill Rd
Derry NH 03038

Call Sign: WA1MEK
Joan A Blouin
52 Warner Hill Rd
Derry NH 03038

Call Sign: KA1FEM
Arthur J Harvey
17 Wentworth Ln
Derry NH 03038

Call Sign: N1YET
J Scott Harvey
17 Wentworth Ln
Derry NH 03038

Call Sign: N1RST
Richard Leto
22 Wentworth Ln
Derry NH 03038

Call Sign: WD8KEL
Rickey L Hampton
4 Westerly Dr
Derry NH 030384124

Call Sign: KG4GMJ
Elizabeth A Hampton
4 Westerly Dr
Derry NH 030384124

Call Sign: KG4QKX
Matthew T Hampton
4 Westerly Dr
Derry NH 030384124

Call Sign: N1QGM
Marc P Fraser
4 Willow St
Derry NH 03038

Call Sign: K1MLH
Glen D Belinsky
18 Windham Depot Rd
Derry NH 03038

Call Sign: KB1QVM
Christopher J Martin
19 Windham Rd
Derry NH 03038

Call Sign: KA1HLC
Marie E Lamontagne
Derry NH 03038

Call Sign: KA1SSO
Eric R Hamm
Derry NH 03038

Call Sign: KA1VMV
Timothy N Swan
Derry NH 03038

Call Sign: N1BIP
Gary A Delong
Derry NH 03038

Call Sign: N1BIU
Robert J Bohn
Derry NH 03038

Call Sign: N1GLT
Walter J O'donnell
Derry NH 03038

Call Sign: N1HKO
William A Fleming
Derry NH 030381116

Call Sign: N1ING
Joseph C Sheehan

Derry NH 03038

Call Sign: N1WJB
Robert G Dinoto Sr
Derry NH 03038

Call Sign: N1XRI
April M Bonderud
Derry NH 03038

Call Sign: WA1UBC
Derry Amateur Radio Club
Derry NH 03038

Call Sign: WA1WGN
John W Morris
Derry NH 03038

Call Sign: WT1M
Kokopelli ARC
Derry NH 030381116

Call Sign: KB1IDP
Donald L Burtoft
Derry NH 03038

Call Sign: KB1OED
Niel R Raiche
Derry NH 03038

Call Sign: KB1OWJ
Robert B Tarquinio
Derry NH 03030

Call Sign: N1AMF
Robert J Bohn
Derry NH 03038

Call Sign: KB1QCI
Ryan M Pratt
Derry NH 030386535

Call Sign: KB1QFY
Bretton O Raiche
Derry NH 03038

Call Sign: KB1QOA
Interstate Repeater Society
Derry NH 03038

Call Sign: K1IRS
Interstate Repeater Society
Derry NH 03038

Call Sign: WF1R
Elizabeth A O'donnell
Derry NH 03038

Call Sign: AB1MM
Ryan M Pratt
Derry NH 030386535

Call Sign: NB1G
Ryan M Pratt
Derry NH 030386535

---

**FCC Amateur Radio
Licenses in Dover**

---

Call Sign: N3VMT
William D Harding
79 Adelle Dr
Dover NH 03820

Call Sign: W1SMK
Stephen M Ketel
4 Allan St
Dover NH 03820

Call Sign: AA1FF
Richard L Jacques
2 Amy Ln
Dover NH 03820

Call Sign: N1XHY
Leonard H Daum
30 Back River Rd
Dover NH 03820

Call Sign: NW1L

Carlos Z Cate
35 Belknap St
Dover NH 03820

Call Sign: KB1MBD
Steven C Diamond
14 Bird Dr
Dover NH 03820

Call Sign: K1ZDS
Barry R Sansoucie
Box 756
Dover NH 03820

Call Sign: KB1TCU
Christopher N Janvrin
38 Bridle Path
Dover NH 03820

Call Sign: N1JMV
James L Miller Sr
10 Brookmoor Rd
Dover NH 03820

Call Sign: KL7IHC
Richard H Pomeroy
14 Cedarbrook Dr
Dover NH 03820

Call Sign: N1UXC
Peter H Menounos Jr
720 Central Ave
Dover NH 03820

Call Sign: N1RVG
Frederick G Slama
240 Central Ave Apt A
Dover NH 03820

Call Sign: N1WFJ
Dana M Virgin
3 Cherokee St
Dover NH 03820

Call Sign: WA2FLF

David J Rivoire
11 Cielo Dr
Dover NH 03820

Call Sign: KB1ASZ
Parks L Christenbury Iii
98 Cocheco St
Dover NH 03820

Call Sign: KJ1J
John G Maglio
38 Constitution Way
Dover NH 03820

Call Sign: W1CTB
James E Welch Sr
40 Constitution Way
Dover NH 03820

Call Sign: N1EAD
Scott C Goodreau
11 Country Club Estates
Dover NH 03820

Call Sign: NX1H
Scott C Goodreau
11 Country Club Estates
Dover NH 03820

Call Sign: KA1TGP
Diane M Myles
186 County Farm Rd
Dover NH 03820

Call Sign: KC8RAC
Paul S Walker
23 Court St
Dover NH 03820

Call Sign: N1EOT
Ernest S Dunham
Dover Neck Rd
Dover NH 03820

Call Sign: N1OXF

Jonathan G Newcomb
22 Dover St
Dover NH 03820

Call Sign: NE4G
Furman C Wilson Jr
Edgar Bois Ter
Dover NH 03820

Call Sign: W1VST
Ernest B Shackford Sr
5 Fairview Ave
Dover NH 03820

Call Sign: KB1ELI
Adam G Pennington
13 Fairway Dr
Dover NH 038205103

Call Sign: N1OM
Richard R Pelletier
25 Fairway Dr
Dover NH 038205103

Call Sign: W1ATM
Richard H Craig
47 Fieldstone Dr
Dover NH 038205205

Call Sign: N1WYS
Douglas B Scadding
48 Fieldstone Dr
Dover NH 03820

Call Sign: KA1WFH
James B Austin
40 Fisher St
Dover NH 03820

Call Sign: N1WEC
Samuel T Lingeman
52 Forest St
Dover NH 03820

Call Sign: W1BOF

George R Whitehead
85 Fourth St
Dover NH 03820

Call Sign: N1LUN
Michael P Quinlan
54 French Cross Rd
Dover NH 03820

Call Sign: KC1XG
John H Lovering
24 Gladiola Way
Dover NH 03820

Call Sign: N1JLO
Melanie V Lovering
24 Gladiola Way
Dover NH 03820

Call Sign: K1SIE
Michael R Latour
36 Gladiola Way
Dover NH 03820

Call Sign: N1HPI
Arthur B Corte
81 Glenhill Rd
Dover NH 03820

Call Sign: KA1SSU
Raymond M De Roy
48 Glenwood Ave
Dover NH 03820

Call Sign: KC1KA
Richard M Ellis Sr
48 Glenwood Ave
Dover NH 038202416

Call Sign: W1ZUD
Raymond M De Roy
48 Glenwood Ave
Dover NH 03820

Call Sign: N1ELP

Seth F Hunt
55 Glenwood Ave
Dover NH 03820

Call Sign: KA1SZW
William M Foley
Greenfield Dr
Dover NH 03820

Call Sign: KB1TFI
Chapman B Baetzel
Grove St
Dover NH 03827

Call Sign: KB1FUB
Wayne H Stickney
23 Ham St Apt B
Dover NH 038203152

Call Sign: N1LCJ
Michael W Snader
98 Henery Low Ave Apt 27
Dover NH 03820

Call Sign: KB1CAD
Ethan A Burns
19 High Ridge Dr
Dover NH 03820

Call Sign: N1EX
Richard D Sedgewick
100 Horne St
Dover NH 03820

Call Sign: KB1QBX
Michael A Thomas Jr
9 Ironwood Dr
Dover NH 03820

Call Sign: W1GEK
Michael A Thomas Jr
9 Ironwood Dr
Dover NH 03820

Call Sign: KB1RWF

Christy L Thomas
9 Ironwood Dr
Dover NH 03820

Call Sign: W1UBG
Robert P King
6 Kelley Dr
Dover NH 03820

Call Sign: KB1FAM
Michael L King
6 Kelley Dr
Dover NH 03820

Call Sign: KB1DIG
Steven W Merrill
9 Kelley Dr
Dover NH 03820

Call Sign: KB1GTR
Kimberly L Merrill
9 Kelley Dr
Dover NH 03820

Call Sign: KB1RVD
James F Ormond
18 Lisa Beth Circle
Dover NH 03820

Call Sign: AB7OY
Wilhelm Schommer
78 Littleworth Rd
Dover NH 038204331

Call Sign: K1BD
William A Dodge
78 Littleworth Rd
Dover NH 03820

Call Sign: N1TOI
Egbert Hertsen
78 Littleworth Rd
Dover NH 03820

Call Sign: W1FZ

Great Bay Radio Assn
78 Littleworth Rd
Dover NH 038204331

Call Sign: WB1ALO
Shirley K Dodge
78 Littleworth Rd
Dover NH 03820

Call Sign: W1ALO
Shirley K Dodge
78 Littleworth Rd
Dover NH 038204331

Call Sign: KB1VSA
John W Laakso
74 Long Hill Rd
Dover NH 03820

Call Sign: N1VLF
Timothy A Sprowl
46 Maple St
Dover NH 03820

Call Sign: AA1SX
Nicole E Glines
816 Marthas Way
Dover NH 03820

Call Sign: WA1MNG
Robert E Ferri
11 Mc Kenna St
Dover NH 03820

Call Sign: W1JYJ
Henry J Ellis Sr
449 Middle Rd
Dover NH 03820

Call Sign: KB1KBB
Jonathan A Beckwith
9 Milk St Apt 3
Dover NH 03820

Call Sign: KB1RDB

Jared Simms
32 Mill St
Dover NH 03820

Call Sign: KB1LHS
Frederick J Schonberger
1 Mill St 114
Dover NH 03820

Call Sign: N1JKS
Joseph A Consiglio
1 Mill St Mail Box 31
Dover NH 03820

Call Sign: W1LSR
Larry Ricard
1 Mill St Unit 105
Dover NH 03820

Call Sign: KB1DAB
Shawn M Kimball
18 Monroe
Dover NH 038204011

Call Sign: KB1FXM
James R Overbey
175 Mt Vernon St
Dover NH 03820

Call Sign: N1CUZ
Robert P Walker
53 New Rochester Rd 14
Dover NH 038202159

Call Sign: KB1AQB
James M Stein
53 New Rochester Rd Apt
18
Dover NH 03820

Call Sign: KB1UWV
Alan A Stone
3 Oak Hill Dr
Dover NH 03820

Call Sign: N1UFZ
Burchell K Emerson Jr
44 Old Rocherster Rd
Dover NH 038202020

Call Sign: N1PXJ
Benjamin A Laquerre
8 Old Rochester Rd
Dover NH 03820

Call Sign: K1GOE
Joseph J Pazyra
40 Old Rochester Rd
Dover NH 03820

Call Sign: KB1RVB
Judith L Caron
7 Phillip St
Dover NH 03820

Call Sign: KB1RVC
Daryl J Caron
7 Phillip St
Dover NH 03820

Call Sign: WA1SHR
Richard H Craig
48 Piscataqua Rd
Dover NH 038205205

Call Sign: N1VXC
Edmund C Chevalier
61 Polly Ann Pk
Dover NH 03820

Call Sign: KD5MTO
Robert C Parish
4 Portland Ave 4
Dover NH 03820

Call Sign: N1XUR
Armand P Jacques
61 Prospect St
Dover NH 03820

Call Sign: KG6GBV
Patrick R Mcelhiney
12 Renaud Ave
Dover NH 03820

Call Sign: KB1QPE
David A Keeler
8 Reyners Brook Dr
Dover NH 03820

Call Sign: K1AAT
John D Davis
3 Rivers Farm Rd 92
Dover NH 03820

Call Sign: KB1WHT
Francisco Santiago
Gonzalez
18 Rutland St
Dover NH 03820

Call Sign: KA1MLL
Charles A Clement
39 Rutland St
Dover NH 03820

Call Sign: KB2EWN
Lloyd W Rosevear
39 Rutland St
Dover NH 03820

Call Sign: N1KAI
Virgil Mehalek
5 Samuel Hanson Ave
Dover NH 03820

Call Sign: K1TOE
Lawrence T Hamilton
17 Sandpiper Dr
Dover NH 03820

Call Sign: KB1WTZ
Brendan R Powers
25 School St Apt 1
Dover NH 03820

Call Sign: KB1NQA
James W Hyland
11 Seaborne Dr
Dover NH 03820

Call Sign: K1GP
George E Perrine
107 Silver St
Dover NH 03820

Call Sign: N1PXI
Catherine A Cheney
9 Snows Ct
Dover NH 03820

Call Sign: N1VBQ
Linda L H Ross
1 South Pine St
Dover NH 03820

Call Sign: N1GIP
Brian F Flynn
2 Spruce Ln
Dover NH 038204410

Call Sign: KA1IHW
Robert E Blair
50 Spur Rd
Dover NH 03820

Call Sign: WB3AXE
James C Gardner
3 Steppingstone Rd Lee
Dover NH 03820

Call Sign: WA1NYP
Brian F Flynn
5 Sullivan Dr.
Dover NH 03820

Call Sign: KD6ZVZ
James F Goodrich Jr
31 Surrey Run
Dover NH 093824442

Call Sign: K1WNZ
David G Stuart
29 Surrey Run The Paddock
Dover NH 03820

Call Sign: KB1PZZ
Thomas E Hurton Iii
Sylvan Dr
Dover NH 03820

Call Sign: W3TEH
Thomas E Hurton Iii
Sylvan Dr
Dover NH 03820

Call Sign: N1UXG
Sylvia M Crosman
3 Tennyson Ave
Dover NH 03820

Call Sign: K1DWE
David W Economos
22 Union Ct
Dover NH 03820

Call Sign: N1QJL
Robert E Anderson
3 Varney Rd Ext
Dover NH 038206102

Call Sign: N1HNQ
Lawrence E Lehman
22 W Concord St
Dover NH 03820

Call Sign: N1VWV
Chet Farwell
247 Washington St
Dover NH 03820

Call Sign: W1RKO
Chet Farwell
247 Washington St
Dover NH 03820

Call Sign: WN1I
Edward V Hammond
347 Washington St
Dover NH 03820

Call Sign: KB1UGT
Thomas J Doster
381 Washington St
Dover NH 03820

Call Sign: N1VDS
George R Tibbetts
Washington St
Dover NH 03820

Call Sign: KA1MTN
Daniel C Peduzzi
9 West Knox Marsh Rd
Dover NH 038204346

Call Sign: K1SHR
Kenneth J Cayer
3 Willard Rd
Dover NH 03820

Call Sign: K1FZB
Arnold M Ashley
Dover NH 038200246

Call Sign: KA1HVM
Karen L Whitcomb
Dover NH 03821

Call Sign: KA1SHA
Gail M Conway
Dover NH 03820

Call Sign: KB2AVX
Anna E Porter
Dover NH 03821

Call Sign: W1FSK
Stephen E Marshall
Dover NH 03820

Call Sign: KB1NSL
Neil Holtzhausen
Dover NH 03821

Call Sign: K1HLM
Milton H Todd
49 New Rochester Rd.
Apt#5
Dover, NH 03820

## FCC Amateur Radio Licenses in Drewsville

Call Sign: KB1SMO
Downey J Page
Drewsville NH 03604

## FCC Amateur Radio Licenses in Dublin

Call Sign: KB1AEC
Blake C Anderson
Box 445
Dublin NH 03444

Call Sign: KB1AED
Timothy H B Stoneman
Box 445
Dublin NH 03444

Call Sign: KB1RNH
Stephen J Bordner
27 Camp Rockne Lane
Dublin NH 03444

Call Sign: KB1LDS
Mark S Donovan
1266 Main St 142
Dublin NH 034440142

Call Sign: KB1UIC
Debora L Lauzon
571 Main St 3
Dublin NH 03444

Call Sign: WB6ERG
Michael N Clifford
1541 Main St.
Dublin NH 03444

Call Sign: KA1QLV
Kendra M Sandford
42 Marstaller Dr
Dublin NH 034448314

Call Sign: N1DJC
Neil R Sandford
42 Marstaller Dr
Dublin NH 034448314

Call Sign: N1EUE
Elaine H Sandford
42 Marstaller Dr
Dublin NH 034448314

Call Sign: N1KDC
Craig K Sandford
42 Marstaller Dr
Dublin NH 034448314

Call Sign: KB1GTF
Clyde W Sandford
42 Marstaller Dr
Dublin NH 034448314

Call Sign: KB1MGO
Kayla R Sandford
42 Marstaller Dr
Dublin NH 034448314

Call Sign: KB1AVV
Brian E Rohde
26 Spring Rd
Dublin NH 0344

Call Sign: KB1VOM
Brett A Koskela
290 Valley Rd
Dublin NH 03444

Call Sign: KA1TQ
John S Albano
Dublin NH 03444

Call Sign: KB1EEB
Clyde W Sandford
Dublin NH 034440445

Call Sign: N1MXJ
Michael J Paulin
Dublin NH 03444

Call Sign: N1QBX
Daniel E Stockwell Jr
Dublin NH 03444

Call Sign: W1QYY
Thomas B Greenhalgh
Dublin NH 03444

## FCC Amateur Radio Licenses in Drummer

Call Sign: N1WAZ
Roger O Meserve
151 Blake Rd
Dummer NH 03588

## FCC Amateur Radio Licenses in Dunbarton

Call Sign: KB1VSC
Marc P Lambert
40 A Long Pond Rd
Dunbarton NH 03046

Call Sign: K1BVU
Louis P Faustini
1112 Black Brook Rd
Dunbarton NH 03045

Call Sign: N1KMY
Donald J Rollins
179 Concord Stage Rd

Dunbarton NH 03045

Call Sign: N1XWH
Alfred F Lively
1215 Gorham Pond Rd
Dunbarton NH 03045

Call Sign: N1ONM
John Van Loendersloot
3 Jewett Rd
Dunbarton NH 03046

Call Sign: N1WTF
Jason A Dubrow
155 Kimball Pond Rd
Dunbarton NH 03046

Call Sign: N1LFS
Joseph F Spadaro
10 Little Ln
Dunbarton NH 03045

Call Sign: WA7QEX
Paul A Cuda
21 Long Pond Rd
Dunbarton NH 030454430

Call Sign: W7QEX
Paul A Cuda
21 Long Pond Rd
Dunbarton NH 030464430

Call Sign: KB1DXE
William R Gardner Iii
54 Long Pond Rd
Dunbarton NH 03046

Call Sign: K7ETI
William J Crilly Jr
87 Mansion Rd
Dunbarton NH 03046

Call Sign: N1PKH
Arthur E Wilson Jr
210 Mansion Rd

Dunbarton NH 03045

Call Sign: N1PKI
Andrea R Wilson
210 Mansion Rd
Dunbarton NH 03045

Call Sign: AA1QR
David V Kane
30 Millie's Way
Dunbarton NH 03046

Call Sign: K1YEU
Peter A Magoun
40 North Woods Rd
Dunbarton NH 03046

Call Sign: WB1GWH
Wayne A Bracy
19 Olde Mill Brook Rd
Dunbarton NH 03045

Call Sign: N1NEW
Alain B Biron
39 Olde Mill Brook Rd
Dunbarton NH 030464405

Call Sign: KB1GNE
L Mark Kibler
8 Ray Rd
Dunbarton NH 03046

Call Sign: KB1POR
Geoffrey Johnson
222 Stark Highway North
Dunbarton NH 03046

Call Sign: N1KPZ
Dennis W Little
161 Stark Highway South
Dunbarton NH 03046

Call Sign: WP4LYV
John N Van Loendersloot
Stark Highway South

Dunbarton NH 03046

Call Sign: NK1R
Roger E Gray
49 Stinson Dr
Dunbarton NH 03046

Call Sign: N1LJM
Richard Averill
160 Twist Hill Rd
Dunbarton NH 03046

Call Sign: N1QGU
Gloria L Averill
160 Twist Hill Rd
Dunbarton NH 03046

## FCC Amateur Radio Licenses in Durham

Call Sign: N1SJQ
Gerald J Needell
36 Bagdad Rd
Durham NH 03824

Call Sign: KB1VMF
Allen D Drake
55 Bagdad Rd
Durham NH 03824

Call Sign: AA1AH
Karen M Garrison
Box 605
Durham NH 03824

Call Sign: W1WUO
Thomas B Merrick
7 Canney Rd
Durham NH 03824

Call Sign: WB1DKB
Chris T Ogden
35 Canney Rd
Durham NH 03824

Call Sign: K1FEZ
Matthew E Last
Cedar Point Rd
Durham NH 03824

Call Sign: WB1GGB
Charles A Benning
Colony Cove Rd
Durham NH 03824

Call Sign: W1AM
Arthur S Westneat Jr
15 Davis Ave
Durham NH 03824

Call Sign: N1WUX
Scott A Thrasher
8 Denbow Rd
Durham NH 03824

Call Sign: WB1EKD
Raymond J Halloran
12 Denbow Rd
Durham NH 038243105

Call Sign: WB1EKE
Peter R Halloran
12 Denbow Rd
Durham NH 03824

Call Sign: WA1NNT
Charles H Lilly
42 Dover Rd
Durham NH 03824

Call Sign: W2OMN
Frederic G Greenberg
59 Durham Point Rd
Durham NH 03824

Call Sign: KB1VRZ
Emily K Slama
367 Durham Pt Rd
Durham NH 03824

Call Sign: KB1VUF
Benjamin F Slama
367 Durham Pt Rd
Durham NH 03824

Call Sign: KB1URQ
Frederick G Slama
367 Durham Pt Rd
Durham NH 03824

Call Sign: N1FGS
Frederick G Slama
367 Durham Pt Rd
Durham NH 03824

Call Sign: W1UNH
Adam M Perkins
25 Garden Lane
Durham NH 03824

Call Sign: N1CLM
Robert A Messier
28 James Farm Rfd 1
Durham NH 03824

Call Sign: N1GCA
Craig Lund
3 Langley Rd
Durham NH 038243424

Call Sign: KA1SQY
Elizabeth A Lund
16 Langley Rd
Durham NH 03824

Call Sign: KA1WZU
Thomas F Richardson
11 Littlehale Rd
Durham NH 038242106

Call Sign: AB1CL
Thomas F Richardson
11 Littlehale Rd
Durham NH 038242106

Call Sign: W1CVG
Kenneth S Poole
38 Madbury Rd
Durham NH 038242039

Call Sign: W1YZB
Richard A Bernard
127 Madbury Rd
Durham NH 03824

Call Sign: N1IKA
Merrill R Clark
4 Mathes Cove Rd
Durham NH 03824

Call Sign: W1PP
Edward J Durnall
26 Mathes Cove Rd Tides
Reach
Durham NH 03824

Call Sign: W4CLG
Robert J Levins
63 Newmarket Rd
Durham NH 03824

Call Sign: K1MLC
Richard L Kaufmann
19 Oyster River Rd
Durham NH 03824

Call Sign: K1HKY
David N Williams
144 Packers Falls Rd
Durham NH 03824

Call Sign: KC1KZ
Joan G Carreiro
118 Piscataqua
Durham NH 03824

Call Sign: KD1BT
Carol R Miller
118 Piscataqua
Durham NH 03824

Call Sign: WM1H
Mary E Miller
118 Piscataqua
Durham NH 03824

Call Sign: KC1KS
Pamela Ranheim
118 Piscataqua Rd
Durham NH 03824

Call Sign: NU1L
Shelbourne Miller
118 Piscataqua Rd
Durham NH 03824

Call Sign: KA1MGV
Eugene J Mc Manus
54 Ross Rd
Durham NH 03824

Call Sign: KB1MVU
Gifford A Hammar
29 Sandy Brook Dr
Durham NH 03824

Call Sign: WB1DMI
John S Gianforte
57 Sandybrook Dr
Durham NH 03824

Call Sign: N1FIM
Philip M Zarrow
12 Sunnyside Dr
Durham NH 03824

Call Sign: K1ORS
Philip M Zarrow
12 Sunnyside Dr
Durham NH 03824

Call Sign: KR1G
Theodore J Demopoulos
20 Tall Pines Rd
Durham NH 03824

Call Sign: K8CN
Michael J Carter
4 Willey Rd
Durham NH 038243118

Call Sign: N1CJP
Michael E Singer
46 Woodridge Rd
Durham NH 03824

Call Sign: N1NSK
Timothy S Talbot
Durham NH 03824

## FCC Amateur Radio Licenses in East Alstead

Call Sign: KA1BLF
Dwight M Swisher
Box 196
East Alstead NH 03602

## FCC Amateur Radio Licenses in East Andover

Call Sign: KA1QFT
Susan L Aste
Chase Hill Rd
East Andover NH 03231

Call Sign: WA1VTS
Francis P Aste
Chase Hill Rd
East Andover NH 03231

Call Sign: KB1CIM
Reid L Mullett
East Andover NH 03231

## FCC Amateur Radio Licenses in East Derry

Call Sign: WA1JIJ
Richard P Apgar

7 Old Chester Rd
East Derry NH 030410014

Call Sign: KC2LT
David F Unkles
East Derry NH 03041

Call Sign: N0CUL
Sue Ann Mc Donald
East Derry NH 03041

## FCC Amateur Radio Licenses in East Hampstead

Call Sign: KB1AMJ
James L Gariepy
22 Atwood Dr
East Hampstead NH 03826

Call Sign: KB1AMK
Diane M Gariepy
22 Atwood Dr
East Hampstead NH 03826

Call Sign: KD4YIA
Kevin Hodge
13 Catherine Ave
East Hampstead NH
038265400

Call Sign: KC1NP
Richard L Bloomfield
48 Checkerberry Rd
East Hampstead NH 03826

Call Sign: N1GHF
Laurie T Bloomfield
48 Checkerberry Rd
East Hampstead NH 03826

Call Sign: KB1DTO
Donald L Kirkpatrick
9 Lewis Ln. #16
East Hampstead NH 03826

Call Sign: KB1LRM
Carlene M Kirkpatrick
9 Lewis Ln. #16
East Hampstead NH 03826

Call Sign: N1GWB
George W Bryant Sr
12 Odd Fellows Rd.
East Hampstead NH
038265404

Call Sign: KA1WLD
Annmarie Georgopolis
44 Pitman Rd
East Hampstead NH 03826

Call Sign: WF1D
Gerald J Georgopolis
44 Pitman Rd
East Hampstead NH 03826

Call Sign: WA1HZK
Keith S Clark
Rt 121a
East Hampstead NH 03826

Call Sign: KB1IZX
James W Gilbert
2 Sean Dr
East Hampstead NH 03826

Call Sign: N1OKD
Donald F Bartlett
35 Webber Rd
East Hampstead NH 03826

Call Sign: KB1DTH
Robert C Beals
East Hampstead NH 03826

Call Sign: W1BAH
Fred F Drag
East Hampstead NH 03826

Call Sign: WA1VKO
Michael W Murphy
East Hampstead NH
038261024

Call Sign: WB1EAK
Nicholas F Maselli
East Hampstead NH 03826

Call Sign: KB1JNK
Curtis H Moller
East Hampstead NH 03826

Call Sign: W1RLT
Robert C Beals
East Hampstead NH 03826

## FCC Amateur Radio Licenses in East Kingston

Call Sign: N1BWP
William A Anderson Jr
74 Depot Rd Box 61
East Kingston NH 03827

Call Sign: WB1DSW
Herbert H Salls
122 Giles Rd
East Kingston NH 03827

Call Sign: K1KZX
Michael P Polletta
61 Main St
East Kingston NH
038272014

Call Sign: KA1ICG
Carl F Johnnen
6 Maplevale Rd
East Kingston NH
038272070

Call Sign: KB1MSW
Michael R Prescott
13 Pheasant Run

East Kingston NH 03827

Call Sign: W1RFW
Michael R Prescott
13 Pheasant Run
East Kingston NH 03827

Call Sign: N1FCC
David L Taylor
30 Pheasant Run
East Kingston NH 03827

Call Sign: KB1TIX
Seacoast Digital Association
30 Pheasant Run
East Kingston NH 03827

Call Sign: KB1UVD
Seacoast Digital Association
30 Pheasant Run
East Kingston NH 03827

Call Sign: KB1UVE
Seacoast Digital Association
30 Pheasant Run
East Kingston NH 03827

Call Sign: KB1VTL
Seacoast Digital
30 Pheasant Run
East Kingston NH 03827

Call Sign: K1TCI
Arthur E Haley Jr
13 Rowell Rd
East Kingston NH 03827

Call Sign: WN1KXB
John R Poulin
Rowell Rd
East Kingston NH 03827

Call Sign: KB1OCL
David A Hobson
3 Woldridge Ln

East Kingston NH 03827

Call Sign: KB1KEW
Linda M Andrzejewski
East Kingston NH
038270148

## FCC Amateur Radio Licenses in East Lempster

Call Sign: KB1BYQ
Emily K Roberts
Box 62
East Lempster NH 03605

Call Sign: KA1YEQ
Nick G Wirkkala
E Lempster 1
East Lempster NH 03605

Call Sign: K1NOR
John E Hussey
134 South Rd Box 149
East Lempster NH
036050149

Call Sign: KA1WFW
Amy S Jacobsen
5 Woodland Manor
East Lempster NH 03605

Call Sign: KA1VGK
Jeffrey B Skrocki
East Lempster NH 03605

Call Sign: KA1YES
Tyler B House
East Lempster NH 03605

Call Sign: N1APM
Daniel H Cooley
East Lempster NH 03605

Call Sign: N1YLZ
James P Lupold

East Lempster NH 03605

Call Sign: KB1ASX
Wayne F Mc Carthy
30 Cocheco Ave
East Rochester NH 03868

Call Sign: NY1O
Donald R Chick Sr
30 Main St
East Rochester NH 03868

Call Sign: K1YRE
Walter A Aukstikalnis
47 Spring St
East Rochester NH 03868

Call Sign: N1ZTE
Victor J Schultz
East Rochester NH 03868

**FCC Amateur Radio Licenses in East Sullivan**

Call Sign: AL7AV
Vladimir W Luban
Box 380
East Sullivan NH
034459703

**FCC Amateur Radio Licenses in East Swanzey**

Call Sign: N1KWE
Dale W Freihofer Jr
429 Massey Hill Rd
East Swanzey NH 03446

Call Sign: N1NGD
Cynda G Freihofer
431 Massey Hill Rd
East Swanzey NH 03446

Call Sign: W1KVW
Ellison B Brooks
796 Old Homestead Hwy
East Swanzey NH 03446

Call Sign: N1JLF
Neal L Starr Sr
935 Old Homestead Hwy
East Swanzey NH 03446

Call Sign: W1UGT
Benjamin A Nelson
East Swanzey NH 03446

Call Sign: N1PPN
Dale W Freihofer Sr
440 Massey Hill Rd
East Swnzey NH 03446

**FCC Amateur Radio Licenses in East Wakefield**

Call Sign: W1DBG
James E Kunkle
745 Acton Ridge Rd
East Wakefield NH 03830

Call Sign: N1JMW
James L Miller Jr
76 Blaney Rd
East Wakefield NH 03830

Call Sign: KB1WAW
Robert D Turner
30 North Desmond Dr
East Wakefield NH 03830

Call Sign: W1LEH
Robert E Bass
3669 Province Lake Rd
East Wakefield NH 03830

Call Sign: KA1ZIR
Phillip C Blay

Rt 153
East Wakefield NH 03830

Call Sign: K1WLP
William L Perreault
East Wakefield NH 03830

**FCC Amateur Radio Licenses in Eaton Center**

Call Sign: W1BPI
Alexander A Mc Kenzie
5 Ridge Rd
Eaton Center NH 03832

Call Sign: KB1DQA
Richard W Shaw
Eaton Center NH 03832

Call Sign: NM1H
John M Hartman
Eaton Center NH 03832

Call Sign: W2APF
Thaire B Bryant
Eaton Center NH 03832

Call Sign: KB1VMO
Jeanne M Basile
Eaton Center NH 03832

**FCC Amateur Radio Licenses in Effingham**

Call Sign: KF3AS
Jeffery O Best
65 Green Mountain Rd
Effingham NH 03882

Call Sign: KB1SAY
Benjamin A Nicholson
737 Green Mt Rd
Effingham NH 03882

Call Sign: KB1MNX

Donna L Nicholson
625 Townhouse Rd
Effingham NH 03882

Call Sign: KA1TAW
Donna L Nicholson
625 Townhouse Rd
Effingham NH 03882

## FCC Amateur Radio Licenses in Elkins

Call Sign: KB1QXJ
William T Hopwood
706 Bunker Rd
Elkins NH 03233

Call Sign: W1KYC
Bruce B Bottomley
617 Sugarhouse Rd
Elkins NH 032330066

Call Sign: KF4QJJ
Victoria B Gulker
Elkins NH 03233

Call Sign: NS1O
Roger E Prior
Elkins NH 03233

Call Sign: W2STU
Stuart P Gulker
Elkins NH 03233

Call Sign: KB1RKJ
Mary F Miller
Elkins NH 03233

Call Sign: K1RRX
Mary F Miller
Elkins NH 03233

## FCC Amateur Radio Licenses in Ellsworth

Call Sign: N1WQL
Paul D Jeffrey
Ellsworth NH 03223

Call Sign: WA1KUN
Paul D Jeffrey
Ellsworth NH 03223

## FCC Amateur Radio Licenses in Enfield

Call Sign: KA1VZP
Donald G Hammond Jr
151 Choate Rd
Enfield NH 037483402

Call Sign: KA1VZR
Susan M Hammond
151 Choate Rd
Enfield NH 03748

Call Sign: K1MAT
Charles F Mason
45 Cogswell Way
Enfield NH 03748

Call Sign: N1USU
John R Largent Iii
Jones Hill Rd
Enfield NH 03748

Call Sign: KB1KID
Philip A Macvicar
552 Lockehaven Rd
Enfield NH 03748

Call Sign: KE8VA
Anne G Esler
22 Main St
Enfield NH 03748

Call Sign: KB1CXC
John R Bannister
680 Methodist Hill Rd
Enfield NH 03748

Call Sign: N1FGE
Thomas G Brodeur
590 Nh Rt 4a
Enfield NH 03748

Call Sign: KA1TYP
Richard R Adams
94 Palmer Rd
Enfield NH 03748

Call Sign: KA1UNC
Yvonne A Adams
94 Palmer Rd
Enfield NH 03748

Call Sign: KB1QAK
Richard I Pruitt
1531 Rte 4a
Enfield NH 03748

Call Sign: KA1YVL
James B Harlow Jr
Enfield NH 03745

Call Sign: N1JAD
Steven E Goldsmith
Enfield NH 03748

Call Sign: N1TFD
Ian P Messier
Enfield NH 03748

## FCC Amateur Radio Licenses in Enfield Center

Call Sign: KB1GPA
Martel D Wilson Jr
Enfield Center NH 03749

Call Sign: KB1PNZ
Scott A Thompson
Enfield Center NH 03749

Call Sign: N1LZU
Harold G Robertson
30 Blake Rd
Epping NH 03042

Call Sign: KB1WYJ
Christopher H Bigelow
15 Bridle Ln
Epping NH 03042

Call Sign: W1LXZ
Robert H Saunders
290 Calef Hwy C 19
Epping NH 03042

Call Sign: N1UVO
Robert C Fauci
20 Cote Dr
Epping NH 03042

Call Sign: N1VNW
Nancy A Fauci
20 Cote Dr
Epping NH 03042

Call Sign: N1TCI
James Russo Jr
33 Depot Rd
Epping NH 03842

Call Sign: N1YEQ
Douglas E Fairbanks
47 Elm St
Epping NH 03042

Call Sign: N1LAM
Jonathan P Morang
19 Fox Ridge Rd
Epping NH 03042

Call Sign: N1ICK
Stewart G Kenly

8 Gatchell Way
Epping NH 03042

Call Sign: WS3F
Brian L Matheny
37 Gatchell Way
Epping NH 03042

Call Sign: KA1RVR
Jay D Carter
20 Harvey Ln
Epping NH 030421704

Call Sign: N2TQS
Richard D Scalzo
238 Hedding Rd
Epping NH 030421522

Call Sign: N1RDS
Richard D Scalzo
238 Hedding Rd
Epping NH 03042

Call Sign: N1CTP
Raymond E Lake
41 High St
Epping NH 03042

Call Sign: KA1BYD
Vincent E Burridge Jr
39 High St Rfd 2
Epping NH 03042

Call Sign: KB1ELN
Steven M Illsley
14 Holt Rd
Epping NH 03042

Call Sign: N1WQO
David T Mylott
37 Jenness Rd
Epping NH 03042

Call Sign: WB1ESO
Kenneth W Morrison

8 Ladds Ln Rt 3
Epping NH 03042

Call Sign: KA1JWP
Marilyn L Mims Dow
30 Long Meadow Farm Dr
Epping NH 03042

Call Sign: N1VOX
Donald S Shappell
88 Main St
Epping NH 030420115

Call Sign: KB1UCT
Robert G Thibedore
193 Main St
Epping NH 03042

Call Sign: KB1UCY
Joanne I Hanna
193 Main St
Epping NH 03042

Call Sign: N1WQN
James M Lawrence Jr
10 Mallileau Ave
Epping NH 03042

Call Sign: KB1TOP
Chris F Leone
16 Mast Rd
Epping NH 03042

Call Sign: N1ZBE
Sharon L Kenney
7 Mill Pond Rd Apt 4
Epping NH 03042

Call Sign: N2JZZ
Roy T Everett
25 Mill St
Epping NH 03042

Call Sign: K1JLP
Glenn D Johnson

153 Old Hedding Rd 5
Epping NH 03042

Call Sign: W1TTM
Edgar E Graham
85 Old Hedding Rd Lot 4
Epping NH 03042

Call Sign: KB1MZC
Lee J Wurzel
153 Old Heddingrd 3
Epping NH 030420549

Call Sign: KA1SVB
Edward R Mann
229 Old Nottingham Rd
Epping NH 03042

Call Sign: W1HJM
Wilbur G Remick
Pine & Pond Pk Box 541
Epping NH 03042

Call Sign: KB1UYA
Kevin R Zukas
28 Pleasant St
Epping NH 03042

Call Sign: N1JCG
Craig L Johnson
14 School St
Epping NH 03042

Call Sign: KB1GTS
Gregory E Johnson
14 School St
Epping NH 03042

Call Sign: K1GTS
Gregory E Johnson
14 School St
Epping NH 03042

Call Sign: N1KTV
Jeffrey S Falkingham

27 Winslow Way
Epping NH 03042

Call Sign: KC4WWF
Thomas J Schmidt
3 Witchole Rd
Epping NH 03042

Call Sign: KE4CMO
Thomas H Schmidt
Epping NH 03042

Call Sign: W1LJW
Lee J Wurzel Sr.
Epping NH 03042

## FCC Amateur Radio Licenses in Epsom

Call Sign: W1VJM
Victor J Mailloux Iii
4 Bishop Lane
Epsom NH 03234

Call Sign: W1PZI
Carleton T Rand
85 Black Hall Rd
Epsom NH 03234

Call Sign: KB1RKD
Shawn W Lawrence
152 Black Hall Rd
Epsom NH 03234

Call Sign: N1ATL
William D Coburn
Box 59
Epsom NH 03234

Call Sign: WA1MGC
Dorothy M Sanborn
Bx 367a Rte 28s Webster
Pk Ln
Epsom NH 03234

Call Sign: KB1QGU
William C Meagher Iii
32 Colby Rd
Epsom NH 03055

Call Sign: N1GHS
Westley J Bailey Jr
33 Colonial Dr
Epsom NH 032344405

Call Sign: KB1URP
Aaron Vrooman
93 Copperline Rd
Epsom NH 03234

Call Sign: NT1W
Aaron Vrooman
93 Copperline Rd
Epsom NH 03234

Call Sign: N1LIB
Robert L Smith
4 Elm St
Epsom NH 032344261

Call Sign: KB1GKQ
Paul W Erickson
27 Elm St
Epsom NH 03234

Call Sign: KB1IVQ
Jeff A Fowler
5 Lincoln St
Epsom NH 03234

Call Sign: KB1SKV
Michael A Officer
274 Mountdelight Rd
Epsom NH 03234

Call Sign: KB1RSZ
Richard L Harkness Jr
92 Munroe Rd
Epsom NH 03234

Call Sign: N1VQU
Derek O Connell
55 N Pembroke Rd
Epsom NH 03234

Call Sign: KA1JZH
Clinton J Ellsworth
Windymere Dr
Epsom NH 03234

Call Sign: KB1VT
Donald E White Jr
Epsom NH 032340402

Call Sign: N1KR
Kenneth P Rollock
Epsom NH 03234

Call Sign: WA1NBI
Dale A Sanborn
Epsom NH 032340458

FCC Amateur Radio<br>Licenses in Errol

Call Sign: W1YZN
Vernon J Le Duc Sr
Rt 26w
Errol NH 03579

Call Sign: KA1AUK
Neal A Wells Jr
Errol NH 03579

Call Sign: N1VZY
Leo P Cellupica
Errol NH 03579

Call Sign: KB1MEG
John D Mcewan
Errol NH 03579

Call Sign: KB1NJN
Gladys I Mcewan
Errol NH 03579

FCC Amateur Radio<br>Licenses in Etna

Call Sign: N1LCA
Young C Shin
Box 211
Etna NH 03750

Call Sign: AA1KL
Rex G Carr
341 Dogford Rd
Etna NH 03750

Call Sign: KB1MIS
Southern Grafton Amateur
Radio Emergency Service
341 Dogford Rd
Etna NH 03750

Call Sign: AB1OB
Donato C Ian
288 Hanover Center Rd
Etna NH 03750

Call Sign: W1ECT
Michael H Mcamis
433 Hanover Center Rd
Etna NH 03750

Call Sign: KB1HSR
Upper Valley Dx
Association
433 Hanover Center Rd
Etna NH 03750

Call Sign: W1DXA
Upper Valley Dx
Association
433 Hanover Center Rd
Etna NH 03750

Call Sign: AA1OE
Robert Morris
9 King Rd

Etna NH 03750

Call Sign: AC4E
Yorke J Brown
96 King Rd
Etna NH 03750

Call Sign: N1JRC
Charles B Burke
Etna NH 03750

FCC Amateur Radio<br>Licenses in Exeter

Call Sign: K1RSD
Alfred P Markey
10 Ash St
Exeter NH 03833

Call Sign: N1ZLP
Paul J Markey
10 Ash St
Exeter NH 03833

Call Sign: WA1PHV
Richard R Hyman
21 Ash St
Exeter NH 03833

Call Sign: KB1RYM
Carribean Dx Contest Club
89 Beech Hill Rd
Exeter NH 03833

Call Sign: KB1JMU
Benjamin C Pepper
5 Bell Ave
Exeter NH 038333001

Call Sign: KB1PCC
Gregory S Pratt
9 Carriage Dr
Exeter NH 03833

Call Sign: K1VMR

Arthur R Lewis
22 Cass St
Exeter NH 03833

Call Sign: N1GBG
David W Chase
11 Chestnut St
Exeter NH 03858

Call Sign: KA9KXD
Keith W Clanton
10 Chestnut St 2106
Exeter NH 03833

Call Sign: N1KPP
William W Burke White
10 Chestnut St Apt 2302
Exeter NH 03833

Call Sign: N1RUX
Jessica M Boyd
12 Columbus Ave
Exeter NH 03833

Call Sign: W1LSN
Gerald B Le Roy
137 Court St
Exeter NH 03833

Call Sign: W1HKR
Benjamin E Madison
4 Cragmere Heights
Exeter NH 03833

Call Sign: W1NB
Scott A Madison
4 Cragmere Heights
Exeter NH 03833

Call Sign: KA1VJS
Edmund J Comeau
12 Cross Rd
Exeter NH 03833

Call Sign: KB1KGT

Nathan R Scolamiero
59 Deep Meadows
Exeter NH 03833

Call Sign: KB1MHS
Cynthia J Scolamiero
59 Deep Meadows
Exeter NH 038334102

Call Sign: K1KYW
Richard H Streeter
Drinkwater
Exeter NH 03833

Call Sign: KB1NZF
Jonathan K Freshour
1 Eno Dr
Exeter NH 03833

Call Sign: KB1OOP
Kent A Freshour
1 Eno Dr
Exeter NH 03833

Call Sign: K1HRT
Scott A Marquis
39 Ernest Ave Unit 104
Exeter NH 03833

Call Sign: K1LLR
Paul D Kenyon Mr
97 Exeter  River Landing
Exeter NH 03833

Call Sign: KB1HFH
Eugene L Lambert
2 Exeter Farms Rd
Exeter NH 03833

Call Sign: AB1CK
Eugene L Lambert
2 Exeter Farms Rd
Exeter NH 03833

Call Sign: N1JT

John G Tefft
16 Folsom St
Exeter NH 03833

Call Sign: N1QDN
Susan J Tefft
16 Folsom St
Exeter NH 03833

Call Sign: N1REY
Jonathan R Tefft
16 Folsom St
Exeter NH 03833

Call Sign: N1TPF
Rebecca J Tefft
16 Folsom St
Exeter NH 03833

Call Sign: K1KR
Kenneth P Roberts
18 Folsom St
Exeter NH 038332924

Call Sign: KB1MWA
Paul D Kenyon
1 Franklin St
Exeter NH 03833

Call Sign: N1RMX
Marshall E Quandt
45 Franklin St
Exeter NH 03833

Call Sign: KB1BCX
James S Black
150 Front St 29
Exeter NH 03833

Call Sign: N1TXU
Ronald L Pulliam Jr
10 Green Hill Rd
Exeter NH 03833

Call Sign: N1UE

James D Rives Iii
18 Grove St
Exeter NH 03833

Call Sign: KB1OMP
Christopher P Dixson
22 Hampton Falls Rd
Exeter NH 03833

Call Sign: K1PRD
Christopher P Dixson
22 Hampton Falls Rd
Exeter NH 03833

Call Sign: W1SX
Richard M Purinton
17 Hampton Rd Apt 125
Exeter NH 03833

Call Sign: K1EKI
Ethel B Reed
22 Haven Ln
Exeter NH 03833

Call Sign: WA1RMS
John R Donnell
25 High St
Exeter NH 03833

Call Sign: K1KKE
Roland J Roberge
56 High St
Exeter NH 03833

Call Sign: W1ZQR
Joseph L Kenick Jr
10 Hobart St
Exeter NH 038332005

Call Sign: AA1SB
Neil J Collesidis
121 Kingston Rd
Exeter NH 038334356

Call Sign: KB1HML

James D Rives Iii
88 Linden St
Exeter NH 03833

Call Sign: KC2VUU
Christopher Barsi
8 Lindenshire Ave
Exeter NH 03833

Call Sign: AB1QN
Christopher Barsi
8 Lindenshire Ave
Exeter NH 03833

Call Sign: KB1KKX
Bryce E Lambert
18 Locust Ave
Exeter NH 03833

Call Sign: KA1WTK
Mark F Allen
1 Meadow Ln
Exeter NH 03833

Call Sign: KB1DTR
Louis H Comeau
15 Minuteman Ln
Exeter NH 03833

Call Sign: N1QGR
Anthony M Callendrello
28 Park St
Exeter NH 03833

Call Sign: KB1WYM
John W Dudley
237 Pickpocket Rd
Exeter NH 03833

Call Sign: KA1QT
Mark F Sinclair
18 Pleasant View Dr
Exeter NH 03833

Call Sign: W1AZE

Renald J Sirois
1 Pleasantview Dr
Exeter NH 03833

Call Sign: K1VUF
Josephine K Parker
19 Prospect St
Exeter NH 03833

Call Sign: KA1MDD
Richard A Zecchini
8 Sumac St
Exeter NH 03833

Call Sign: K1ED
Edmund L Burke
13 Tamarind Ln
Exeter NH 03833

Call Sign: KB1WFK
Michael G Griffin
9 Vine St
Exeter NH 03833

Call Sign: N1PLQ
Wilbert W Brown
32 Watson Rd
Exeter NH 03833

Call Sign: N1MLH
Matthew A Therrien
48 Watson Rd
Exeter NH 03833

Call Sign: K1KN
Philip R Lyster
Watson Rd
Exeter NH 03833

Call Sign: N1QYO
Michael L Daigle
2 Wayside Dr
Exeter NH 03833

Call Sign: KA7LRK

Jay H Martin
1 Wyndbrook Circle
Exeter NH 03833

Call Sign: KB1KHT
Thomas W Beaudet
Exeter NH 03833

## FCC Amateur Radio Licenses in Farmington

Call Sign: N1YAV
Mark W Brown
433 A Chestnut Hill Rd
Farmington NH 03835

Call Sign: KA1HNX
Ernest M Jones
14 Blaine St
Farmington NH 03835

Call Sign: N1SDY
Cyle J Dore
Box 227
Farmington NH 03835

Call Sign: N1QER
Joseph L Hale
Box 298
Farmington NH 03835

Call Sign: KA1LBH
Louis W Mattia
232 Camelot Shore Dr
Farmington NH 03835

Call Sign: K1DPE
Louis W Mattia
232 Camelot Shore Dr
Farmington NH 03835

Call Sign: N1WQQ
Alvin R Glover
134 Central St
Farmington NH 03835

Call Sign: KB1LFV
Ronald E Muise
370 Chestnut Hill Rd
Farmington NH 03835

Call Sign: N1ABB
Ronald E Muise
370 Chestnut Hill Rd
Farmington NH 03835

Call Sign: N1XIG
Gregory T Kuder
560 Chestnut Hill Rd
Farmington NH 03835

Call Sign: N1LCP
George M Berry
52 Civic St
Farmington NH 03835

Call Sign: KA1RNA
Rudolph W Blanchard
19 Elm St
Farmington NH 03835

Call Sign: KB1AEZ
Patrick C Smart
30 Elm St
Farmington NH 03835

Call Sign: KB1KSA
Charles M Woodworth
227 Elm St
Farmington NH 03835

Call Sign: KB1TBW
Douglas M Houston
21 Glen St
Farmington NH 03835

Call Sign: W1DMH
Douglas M Houston
21 Glen St
Farmington NH 03835

Call Sign: KB1QGV
John A Baker Iii
209 Governors Rd
Farmington NH 03835

Call Sign: KA1ZVT
Peter W Russell
17 Hancock St
Farmington NH 03835

Call Sign: WZ1F
Lee R Russell
17 Hancock St
Farmington NH 03835

Call Sign: KB1DHZ
Richard A Catruch
290 Main St.
Farmington NH 03835

Call Sign: KA1WCG
Philip E Jolles
Marstons Ct
Farmington NH 03835

Call Sign: KB1VAW
Robert C Nienhouse
394 Meaderboro Rd
Farmington NH 03835

Call Sign: N1ODK
Gail E Merrill
N Main St
Farmington NH 03835

Call Sign: N1MMK
Clyde R Glidden
167 Nh Rt 11
Farmington NH 03835

Call Sign: W1FZ
James E Thayer
65 North Main St
Farmington NH 03835

Call Sign: W1TZ
Roger E Graves Jr
30 Pleasant St
Farmington NH 03835

Call Sign: KA1YMK
Robert W Gibbons
Rfd 59a
Farmington NH 03835

Call Sign: KB1JQR
Jack L Weber
14 School St
Farmington NH 03835

Call Sign: KB1LVK
Patricia M Weber
20 School St
Farmington NH 03835

Call Sign: N1MMH
Richard A Bailey Jr
573 South Main St
Farmington NH 03835

Call Sign: KB1AQA
Matthew A Desroches
891 Ten Rod Rd
Farmington NH 03835

Call Sign: KB1DIA
Robert G Boucher
1166 Ten Rod Rd.
Farmington NH 03835

Call Sign: KA1TAW
Donna L Nicholson
Thurston Rd
Farmington NH 03835

Call Sign: KB1UTX
Nelson R Morton
167 Waldron Rd
Farmington NH 03835

Call Sign: KB1AQC
Kimberly A Blackden
Farmington NH 03835

Call Sign: KB1AQD
Brian K Blackden
Farmington NH 03835

Call Sign: KB1DOK
Charles K Williams
Farmington NH 03835

Call Sign: N1HVJ
Neil D Smart
Farmington NH 03835

Call Sign: N1HVV
Warren E Merrill
Farmington NH 038350201

Call Sign: KB1VTA
David J Montenegro
Farmington NH 03835

Call Sign: W1TAO
David J Montenegro
Farmington NH 03835

### FCC Amateur Radio Licenses in Fitzwilliam

Call Sign: KA8WAQ
Dorothy M Gustin
Box 237d Hwy 119
Fitzwilliam NH 03447

Call Sign: KB1DVT
Barry P Hilton
19 Crane Rd
Fitzwilliam NH 03447

Call Sign: KB1ECE
Barry P Hilton Jr
19 Crane Rd

Fitzwilliam NH 03447

Call Sign: N1PH
Potters Place Ham Club
661 Fullam Hill Rd
Fitzwilliam NH 03447

Call Sign: N1SP
Scott W Porter
661 Fullam Hill Rd
Fitzwilliam NH 03447

Call Sign: W1GAN
John J Bilodeau
733 Fullam Hill Rd
Fitzwilliam NH 03447

Call Sign: N1NNJ
Eric O Prigge
Lower Troy Rd
Fitzwilliam NH 03447

Call Sign: K1KAF
Richard H Carter
519 Nh Rt 119e
Fitzwilliam NH 034473161

Call Sign: N3YJA
Robert N Wolfe
73 Old Troy Rd
Fitzwilliam NH 03447

Call Sign: N1BTN
Ronnie A Nickerson
86 Old Troy Rd
Fitzwilliam NH 03447

Call Sign: KB1KCT
Christopher K Ramsey Sr
478 Royalston Rd
Fitzwilliam NH 03447

Call Sign: KA1VYE
Jeremy A Goddard
Royalston Rd Box 282a

Fitzwilliam NH 03447

Call Sign: K3KMO
Fitzwilliam Amateur Radio
Telegraphy Society
258 Upper Troy Rd
Fitzwilliam NH 03447

Call Sign: W1AB
Albert M Brogdon
258 Upper Troy Rd
Fitzwilliam NH 03447

Call Sign: N1PDH
Lawrence A Croteau
W Lake Rd
Fitzwilliam NH 03447

Call Sign: KB1LKF
Gene W Hytonen
12 Westminster Dr
Fitzwilliam NH 034473542

Call Sign: N1PPR
Matthew W Prigge
Fitzwilliam NH 03447

Call Sign: N1YVM
Paul R Fortin
Fitzwilliam NH 03447

## FCC Amateur Radio Licenses in Francestown

Call Sign: KB1HAL
Michael S Greenberg
282 Bible Hill Rd
Francestown NH 03043

Call Sign: KB1WTH
Richard L Welch
1097 Bible Hill Rd
Francestown NH 03043

Call Sign: KB1LCW

Raymond N Capes
24 Champagne Rd
Francestown NH 03043

Call Sign: K1JKN
Raymond N Capes
24 Champagne Rd
Francestown NH 03043

Call Sign: KB1FT
John G Quin
83 Dennison Pond Rd
Francestown NH 03043

Call Sign: KB1VLL
Daniel T Russell
475 Dennison Pond Rd
Francestown NH 03043

Call Sign: W1NLB
Thorvald H Tenney Jr
685 Dodge Hill Rd
Francestown NH 03043

Call Sign: WA1HGE
Louis Wiederhold
219 Main St
Francestown NH
030430300

Call Sign: N1ZPP
Christopher S Bradford
28 Mountainside Lane #2
Francestown NH 03043

Call Sign: N1THQ
William W Bennert
28 Mountainside Ln Unit 2
Francestown NH 03043

Call Sign: WA3NIJ
Randolph P Walker
229 Oak Hill Rd
Francestown NH 03043

Call Sign: AA1PW
Robert T Schwinger
80 Scoby Rd
Francestown NH 03043

Call Sign: KB1OTF
Christopher O Smith
228 Wilson Hill Rd
Francestown NH 03043

Call Sign: N1BHG
Steven H Lape
361 Wilson Hill Rd
Francestown NH 03043

Call Sign: KB1LPR
Matthew H Lape
361 Wilson Hill Rd
Francestown NH 03043

Call Sign: AB1EG
Matthew H Lape
361 Wilson Hill Rd
Francestown NH 03043

Call Sign: N1UD
Steven H Lape
361 Wilson Hill Rd
Francestown NH 03043

Call Sign: N1XB
Matthew H Lape
361 Wilson Hill Rd
Francestown NH 03043

Call Sign: KA1JDQ
Carole L Lape
361 Wilson Hill Rd
Francestown NH 03043

Call Sign: N1XBB
Mark D Limbert
15 Dennison Pond Rd
Francetown NH 03043

Call Sign: W1HAM
Donald Eastman
31 Dow Ave
Franconia NH 03580

Call Sign: N1WBC
Robert W Sherburn Jr
2059 Easton Rd
Franconia NH 03580

Call Sign: N1YZG
Richard G Robinson
139 Gibson Rd
Franconia NH 03580

Call Sign: AA1UX
Richard G Robinson
139 Gibson Rd
Franconia NH 03580

Call Sign: AA1OF
Jerome Terres
27 Indian Pipe Rd
Franconia NH 03580

Call Sign: W1YJE
Michael P Morley
404 Lafayette Rd
Franconia NH 03580

Call Sign: N1MAV
Jane A Giroux
Magowan Hill Rd
Franconia NH 03580

Call Sign: N1FBH
Darrel R Dietlein
308 Park View Dr
Franconia NH 03580

Call Sign: N1YNH
Darrel R Dietlein
308 Park View Dr
Franconia NH 03580

Call Sign: KB1AGY
Charles T Bonnett
Franconia NH 03580

Call Sign: N1IMF
Patrick C Mitchell
Franconia NH 03580

Call Sign: N1LPK
Nelson B Howe
Franconia NH 03580

Call Sign: N1WOH
Barry E Bernstein
Franconia NH 035800546

Call Sign: N1YBQ
Julia B Howe
Franconia NH 03580

Call Sign: KB1NRS
Edmund H Sears
Franconia NH 035800431

Call Sign: KB1PPF
Ronald J Taksar
Franconia NH 03580

Call Sign: KB1RXM
Mary A Nehring
Franconia NH 03580

Call Sign: WB1RJT
Ronald J Taksar
Franconia NH 03580

Call Sign: AB1NN
Ronald J Taksar
Franconia NH 03580

Call Sign: N1HD
Christopher M Read
29 Dearborn St
Franklin NH 03235

Call Sign: KA1ZBF
Tim N Hopkins
35 Easy St
Franklin NH 03235

Call Sign: N1CHY
Armand J Le Page Jr
60 Evergreen Ave
Franklin NH 03235

Call Sign: KB1RKK
James L Richardson
8 Fairway Dr
Franklin NH 03235

Call Sign: KA1BUC
Richard H Hansen
32 Liberty Ave
Franklin NH 032351232

Call Sign: KA1BUD
Marcia A Hansen
32 Liberty Ave
Franklin NH 032351232

Call Sign: KB1DXW
Andrew J Hurd
4 Madeline St
Franklin NH 03235

Call Sign: KB1RZS
Jonathan A Glines
46 Mark Rd
Franklin NH 03235

Call Sign: KB1CIL
Michael M Nawoj
24 N Shore Lane
Franklin NH 03235

Call Sign: N1KEW
June B Robinson
Oak Hill Rd
Franklin NH 03235

Call Sign: N1SRS
Warren R Cline
42 Pearl St
Franklin NH 03235

Call Sign: KD1IC
Gilbert A Lambert
328 Prospect St
Franklin NH 03235

Call Sign: KB1IFJ
William S Stacey
94 Range Rd
Franklin NH 03235

Call Sign: KB1JVX
Stephen K Foster
123 S Main St
Franklin NH 03235

Call Sign: KB1HTD
Robert A Lucas
170 Sterling Dr
Franklin NH 032351562

Call Sign: KB1JWC
Gregory P Couture
131 Victory Dr
Franklin NH 032351033

Call Sign: WB1EPJ
Mark R Williams
224 Victory Dr
Franklin NH 03235

Call Sign: W5CGU
John D Adamson Sr
420 Victory Dr
Franklin NH 03235

Call Sign: W5NJA
Norma J Adamson
420 Victory Dr
Franklin NH 03235

Call Sign: N2IBS
Steven A Mason
107 W Bow St
Franklin NH 03235

Call Sign: KB1IBK
David A Fleury
4 Wells St
Franklin NH 03235

Call Sign: KB1DQO
Matt G Gilman
6 Westview Dr. Unit 9
Franklin NH 03235

Call Sign: KA1TYU
Louise H Efthimiou
58 Winnipesaukee St
Franklin NH 03235

Call Sign: KA1TYV
John R Nyberg Sr
58 Winnipesaukee St
Franklin NH 03235

## FCC Amateur Radio Licenses in Freedom

Call Sign: K1MEZ
Roland D Goodwin
E Danforth Pond Rd
Freedom NH 03836

Call Sign: KB1VZB
Michael J Lee
6 Pleasant Dr
Freedom NH 03836

Call Sign: K1DDT

Michael J Lee
6 Pleasant Dr
Freedom NH 03836

Call Sign: KB1FUJ
William T Devine Iii
18 Powder Horn Lane
Freedom NH 03836

Call Sign: N1PZH
Joel J Clement
Rt 153
Freedom NH 03836

Call Sign: N1XUX
Lawrence J Claveau
95 West Danforth Rd
Freedom NH 038364123

Call Sign: WA1MAQ
James J Pittman
Freedom NH 038360521

Call Sign: KB1STD
Wesley W Maynard
Freedom NH 03836

Call Sign: KB1VRR
Brian R Taylor
Freedom NH 03836

## FCC Amateur Radio Licenses in Freehold

Call Sign: W2DC
Paul A Reveal
2206 Applewood Dr
Freehold NH 07728

## FCC Amateur Radio Licenses in Fremont

Call Sign: N1HIJ
Jeffrey A Hopkinson
96 Bean Rd

Fremont NH 03044

Fremont NH 030443319

Fremont NH 03044

Call Sign: K1RPK
Frederick M Grover
Box 206b
Fremont NH 03044

Call Sign: KB1CVD
Neal L Beede
59 Main St
Fremont NH 03044

Call Sign: N1WYB
Norman J Martineau Jr
424 Whittier Dr
Fremont NH 03044

Call Sign: WA1ZMB
Roland M Lambert Sr
Box 207a Rfd 1
Fremont NH 03044

Call Sign: K1CGH
John L Lennon
337 Main St
Fremont NH 03044

Call Sign: KA1LPY
Leland C Lepore
23 Wildwood Dr
Fremont NH 03044

Call Sign: W1GUE
Edward E Goyette
22 Cooper Dr
Fremont NH 03044

Call Sign: KA1ZQB
Robert P Kelly
488 Main St
Fremont NH 03044

Call Sign: AB1JS
Jack J Santos
192 Copp Dr
Fremont NH 03044

Call Sign: KB1SGL
Brett A Hunter
363 North Rd
Fremont NH 03044

Call Sign: KB1PSW
Joel L Dulude
George Mills NH 03751

Call Sign: KB1UDR
Megan C Guarnieri-Cleary
97 Godfrey Ln
Fremont NH 03044

Call Sign: K1PDS
Harold J Black
18 Pond Ln
Fremont NH 03044

Call Sign: N2BYT
Burr F Rockwell
276 Prospect Hill Rd
Georges Mills NH 03751

Call Sign: AB1MR
Michael W Fortuna
21 Hawthorne Dr
Fremont NH 03044

Call Sign: KB1UXM
Richard D Butler
23 Poplin Dr
Fremont NH 03044

Call Sign: K1DKC
L Darrell Kenison Jr
Georges Mills NH 03751

Call Sign: N1WZY
Moriah L Marshall
Georges Mills NH
037510289

Call Sign: N1EDU
David F Barker
7 Louise Ln
Fremont NH 03044

Call Sign: KA1SUE
Warren L Mc Leod
204 Scribner Rd
Fremont NH 03044

Call Sign: KB1SFM
Linda L Tanner
Georges Mills NH 03751

Call Sign: AB1DP
Michael R Noyes
6 Main St
Fremont NH 030443319

Call Sign: N1ISE
Stephen J Valliere
34 Whitman Dr
Fremont NH 03044

Call Sign: W1MRN
Michael R Noyes
6 Main St

Call Sign: N1MBO
Ruth B Valliere
34 Whitman Dr.

Call Sign: W1WNJ
William C Madden
15 Bacon Dr Apt 15
Gilford NH 03246

Call Sign: WE1Q
Hamilton B Fay
17 Bedford Ave
Gilford NH 03246

Call Sign: W1ONL
Allan C Richardson
31 Bedford Ave
Gilford NH 03246

Call Sign: K1OBP
Richard F Wholey
703 Belknap Mt. Rd
Gilford NH 03249

Call Sign: WB9LFB
Thomas L Kokx
165 Belknap Mtn Rd
Gilford NH 03246

Call Sign: KB1FLY
Michael T Harvey
714 Belknap Mtn Rd
Gilford NH 03249

Call Sign: K1RJZ
Richard J Zach
170 Belknap Point Rd  Unit-
44
Gilford NH 03249

Call Sign: K1DRZ
Dean R Zach
170 Belknap Point Rd Unit-
44
Gilford NH 03249

Call Sign: KA1OTX
Robert F Wilton
Box 86p
Gilford NH 03246

Call Sign: K1NUJ
Kenneth T Slater
12 Breton Rd Unit 5d

Gilford NH 03249

Call Sign: K1CNH
Gilford Middle High School
Amateur Radio Club
32 Carriage Rd
Gilford NH 03246

Call Sign: W1SVI
Raymond E Wilton
9 Chanticleer Shores
Gilford NH 03246

Call Sign: KB1GQR
Joanne M Buckner
105 Chestnut
Gilford NH 03249

Call Sign: KB1FUN
James M Buckner
105 Chestnut Dr
Gilford NH 03249

Call Sign: WA1AA
Christoph J Janker
115 Chestnut Dr
Gilford NH 03249

Call Sign: W1XKZ
Dale C Eddy
201 Chestnut Dr
Gilford NH 03249

Call Sign: KB1TKO
Michael J Hardy
1 Coach Rd
Gilford NH 03249

Call Sign: KB1COL
Jonathan C Wixson
3 Damson Ln
Gilford NH 03246

Call Sign: KB1TKN
Leslie Suranyi Jr

18 Doris Dr
Gilford NH 03249

Call Sign: KZ1I
David F Metz
94 Edgewater Dr
Gilford NH 03246

Call Sign: N1EZK
Lee A Duncan
29 Elderberry Dr
Gilford NH 032466408

Call Sign: W1LAD
Lee A Duncan
29 Elderberry Dr
Gilford NH 032496408

Call Sign: KA1UYF
Henry T W Kitchen
800 Gilford Ave
Gilford NH 03246

Call Sign: KA1QVQ
John M Kitchen
800 Gilford Ave Rt 11a
Gilford NH 03246

Call Sign: N1MBH
John S Kitchen
800 Gilford Ave Rt 11a
Gilford NH 03246

Call Sign: N1MHU
Gerow G Crowell Jr
26 Gilman Dr
Gilford NH 03246

Call Sign: KB1CSU
Arthur C Johnson
58 Gunstock Hill Rd
Gilford NH 032467558

Call Sign: KB1RKO
Carole H Johnson

58 Gunstock Hill Rd
Gilford NH 03249

Call Sign: KB1GQS
Martin Snow
187 Gunstock Hill Rd
Gilford NH 03249

Call Sign: KB1GQX
Steven R Snow
187 Gunstock Hill Rd
Gilford NH 03249

Call Sign: N1JMZ
Lionel R Corno
38 Heather Ln
Gilford NH 03246

Call Sign: KB1RZV
Judith A Perrier
33 High View Circle
Gilford NH 03249

Call Sign: KB1SAA
Dennis O Caldwell
33 High View Circle
Gilford NH 03249

Call Sign: N1JKU
John W Stephenson
22 Hook Rd
Gilford NH 03246

Call Sign: N1FAE
Karen T Lallier
161 Intervale Rd
Gilford NH 032467435

Call Sign: K1GSU
Allen O Weiss
19 Knollwood Dr
Gilford NH 03247

Call Sign: K1ELM
Charles E Hamlyn

Lake Breeze Pk
Gilford NH 03246

Call Sign: KB1RYI
Kathleen A Merriam
2393 Lake Shore Rd 11
Gilford NH 03249

Call Sign: KB1DZD
Michael J Benoit
2600 Lake Shore Rd Box
109
Gilford NH 03246

Call Sign: KB1RJX
Philip L Stephenson
55 Linda Lane
Gilford NH 03249

Call Sign: KB1RJY
Grant E Stephenson
55 Linda Lane
Gilford NH 03249

Call Sign: KB1IFK
Robert P Dean
22 Lockes Island
Gilford NH 032497713

Call Sign: N1ZRP
Arnold D Witbeck
48 Longridge Rd
Gilford NH 03246

Call Sign: WB1GNA
Samuel L Sargent
20 Mitchell Rd
Gilford NH 03246

Call Sign: WA1GAG
Thomas P Wuelfing
210 Morrill St
Gilford NH 032496422

Call Sign: K1RE

Ronald M Egalka
32 Northview Rd
Gilford NH 03247

Call Sign: N1HTR
Matthew C Egalka
32 Northview Rd
Gilford NH 03247

Call Sign: N1MAZ
Frank E Quimby
17 October Ln
Gilford NH 032496427

Call Sign: N1FAT
Alger A Conger
40 Old Lake Shore Rd
Gilford NH 03246

Call Sign: KB1AVO
Robert W De Camp
22 Olde English Ln
Gilford NH 03246

Call Sign: KB1COJ
Christopher J Wilson
75 Pinecrest Dr
Gilford NH 032462222

Call Sign: N1ZXE
Timothy D Fernholz
114 Pinecrest Dr
Gilford NH 03246

Call Sign: KB1RZZ
Austin R Schinlever
143 Sagamore Rd
Gilford NH 03249

Call Sign: WA1ZSR
Howard R Epstein
231 Sagamore Rd
Gilford NH 03249

Call Sign: N1XNT

Sean M Coffin Ii
63 San Born Rd
Gilford NH 03246

Call Sign: AB1AR
Alger A Conger
9 Sargent Pl Lot 41
Gilford NH 03246

Call Sign: KB1JCL
Robert P Carollo
17 Sleeper Hill Rd
Gilford NH 03249

Call Sign: KB1OYC
Cynthia M Carollo
17 Sleeper Hill Rd
Gilford NH 03249

Call Sign: NY1H
Robert P Carollo
17 Sleeper Hill Rd
Gilford NH 03249

Call Sign: K1CIN
Cynthia M Carollo
17 Sleeper Hill Rd
Gilford NH 03249

Call Sign: N1XBD
James A Craver
35 Sleeper Hill Rd
Gilford NH 03246

Call Sign: N1SWI
Timothy W Jalbert
51 Sleeper Hill Rd.
Gilford NH 03249

Call Sign: KE1MP
Timothy W Jalbert
51 Sleeper Hill Rd.
Gilford NH 03249

Call Sign: KB1CSS

Jack G Garneau
29 Swain Rd
Gilford NH 03249

Call Sign: KB1PNY
Bernadette A Garneau
29 Swain Rd
Gilford NH 03249

Call Sign: KB1VVK
Alar Kangur
35 Valley Dr
Gilford NH 03249

Call Sign: W1KWM
Marvin K White
71 Varney Pt
Gilford NH 03246

Call Sign: N1UBI
Eugene J Driscoll
25 Village Lane
Gilford NH 03249

Call Sign: K1MPK
Edgar A Kenney
26 Vincent Dr
Gilford NH 032466441

Call Sign: KB1QLX
William F Firth
62 White Birch Dr
Gilford NH 03249

Call Sign: N1WMH
Daniel R Carsen
83 White Birch Dr
Gilford NH 03249

Call Sign: N1SFL
Michael B Swift
Gilford NH 03246

Call Sign: N1YTB
Jeffrey A Cote

Gilford NH 03247

Call Sign: W1TYE
Donald L Onofrio
Gilford NH 03247

Call Sign: W1BTO
Michael B Swift
Gilford NH 03247

## FCC Amateur Radio Licenses in Gilmanton

Call Sign: KA1QHK
Suzanne T Christie
118 Allens Mill Rd
Gilmanton NH 032379202

Call Sign: WB1EBF
William F Christie
118 Allens Mill Rd
Gilmanton NH 032379202

Call Sign: N1WXS
Daniel J Adel
Allens Mills Rd
Gilmanton NH 03237

Call Sign: N1VB
Joel E Bjork
244 Allen's Mills Rd
Gilmanton NH 03237

Call Sign: AB2HJ
Joel E Bjork
Allen's Mills Rd
Gilmanton NH 03237

Call Sign: N1WMJ
Brendan M Mann
Box 70
Gilmanton NH 03237

Call Sign: W1TXU
Wilbur L Buchanan

87 Deer Dr
Gilmanton NH 03237

Call Sign: KB1UXU
Richard A Lucas
119 Deer Dr
Gilmanton NH 032375425

Call Sign: N1UJD
Jason M Plourde
60 Fox Dr
Gilmanton NH 03237

Call Sign: N1MVC
David J Brobst
35 Major Dr
Gilmanton NH 03237

Call Sign: KB1TKM
Allan R Mistler
604 Meadow Pond Rd
Gilmanton NH 03237

Call Sign: KB1WIK
PHILIP E Mcintyre
52 MEETINGHOUSE RD
Gilmanton NH 03237

Call Sign: KB1AVN
Jonathan J Hall
254 Meetinghouse Rd
Gilmanton NH 03237

Call Sign: KA1QLG
William D Tetreault Ii
Middle Route
Gilmanton NH 03237

Call Sign: N1TAC
James E Garfield
6 Mohegan Trail
Gilmanton NH 03237

Call Sign: KB1CYJ
Robert E Collins

23 Mohegan Trail
Gilmanton NH 03237

Call Sign: K2HZN
Robert Mac Guffie
70 Province Rd
Gilmanton NH 03237

Call Sign: K1FWS
Robert P Herlihy
17 Spruce Ave
Gilmanton NH 03237

Call Sign: KA1EPX
Timothy K Woods
Gilmanton NH 03237

Call Sign: N1RGF
Catherine S Gustafson
Gilmanton NH 03237

Call Sign: KB1GNK
Joy E Power
Gilmanton NH 032370035

Call Sign: KB1RKC
Kathleen A Brooks
Gilmanton NH 03237

**FCC Amateur Radio
Licenses in Gilman Iron
Works**

Call Sign: N1PKR
Marilyn R Deschenes
Box 810
Gilmanton Iron Works NH
03837

Call Sign: KB1SKW
Timothy W Robbins
226 Crystal Lake Rd
Gilmanton Iron Works NH
03837

Call Sign: N1AQP
Russell C Royce
Crystal Lake Rd
Gilmanton Iron Works NH
03837

Call Sign: KA1OEO
James T White Jr
33 Elm St
Gilmanton Iron Works NH
03837

Call Sign: KB1QWQ
Philip G Jones
79 Levitt Rd
Gilmanton Iron Works NH
03837

Call Sign: KB1LWP
Richard R Maltais
30 Middle Route
Gilmanton Iron Works NH
03837

Call Sign: N1MAW
Richard R Maltais
30 Middle Route
Gilmanton Iron Works NH
03837

Call Sign: N1DCD
Bryan D Miller
14 Pine Rd Crystal Lk
Gilmanton Iron Works NH
03837

Call Sign: WB1GDY
Kurt E Lautenschlager
Gilmanton Iron Works NH
03837

**FCC Amateur Radio
Licenses in Gilsum**

Call Sign: KB1SPT

Jonathan R Bialek
887a Route 10
Gilsum NH 03448

Call Sign: N1ZXR
Ariel E Piedmont
26 Emerson Brook Dr
Gilsum NH 03448

Call Sign: W1FYR
Alan C Merrill
116 Hammond Hollow Rd
Gilsum NH 034487602

Call Sign: KA1ZM
Martin Hanft
Nash Corner Rd
Gilsum NH 03448

### FCC Amateur Radio Licenses in Glen

Call Sign: K1RAR
W Francis Pingree
7 Birch Ledge Rd
Glen NH 03838

Call Sign: KB1BJI
La Vonne C Wright
44 Popple Hill Dr
Glen NH 03838

Call Sign: N1SPS
Edward S Wright
44 Popple Hill Dr Box 419
Glen NH 03838

Call Sign: KB1OKG
Philip I Marie Jr
783 Westside Rd
Glen NH 03838

Call Sign: AA1AU
Frank Grech
Glen NH 03838

Call Sign: KD1UO
Donald E Nelson
Glen NH 03838

Call Sign: KE1AT
Gary R Shirk
Glen NH 03838

### FCC Amateur Radio Licenses in Goffstown

Call Sign: N1MXE
Tate J Keegan
145 Addison Rd
Goffstown NH 03045

Call Sign: NG1T
William E Gillis Jr
37 Alene Ln
Goffstown NH 03045

Call Sign: K1PWD
Albert W Holland
Apple Tree Dr
Goffstown NH 03045

Call Sign: WA1DRI
Shirley B Holland
Apple Tree Dr
Goffstown NH 03045

Call Sign: N1THK
Hector R Palacios
761 Back Mountain Rd
Goffstown NH 03045

Call Sign: K1SNH
Bryan P King
774 Back Mountain Rd
Goffstown NH 030456105

Call Sign: KX1B
Bryan P King
774 Back Mountain Rd

Goffstown NH 030456105

Call Sign: KB1GTK
New Hampshire Microwave
Radio Assn
774 Back Mtn Rd
Goffstown NH 03045

Call Sign: K1GHZ
New Hampshire Microwave
Radio Assn
774 Back Mtn Rd
Goffstown NH 03045

Call Sign: KB1HHW
Anthony F Difranco
637 Black Brook Rd
Goffstown NH 03045

Call Sign: W1OCV
Edward S Albrechinski
223 Bog Rd
Goffstown NH 030450405

Call Sign: KA1YBS
Timothy D'apice
43 Checkerberry Ln
Goffstown NH 03045

Call Sign: KB1DJY
Richard S Barnes
26 Church St
Goffstown NH 030451703

Call Sign: N1YXI
Michael G Choquette
Church St
Goffstown NH 03045

Call Sign: KB1RGV
Christopher Hemmah
74 Cove St
Goffstown NH 03045

Call Sign: KB1RKQ

Ashley M Conley
6 Crestwood Lane
Goffstown NH 03045

Call Sign: KB1PPE
Michael J Sullivan
102 Donald Dr
Goffstown NH 03045

Call Sign: KB1ULH
Richard A Nadeau
217 Elm St
Goffstown NH 03045

Call Sign: K1RAN
Richard A Nadeau
217 Elm St
Goffstown NH 03045

Call Sign: KA1DYB
Warren Proctor
13 First Ave
Goffstown NH 03045

Call Sign: KB1RIN
Barbara A Doody
17 Foch St
Goffstown NH 03102

Call Sign: N1XEO
Ralph A Fellows
1 Foxtail Ln
Goffstown NH 03045

Call Sign: KB1ULO
Gary R Chapdelaine
61 Gold Finch Rd
Goffstown NH 03045

Call Sign: KB1UWG
Edward H Hieber
90 Gorham Pond Rd
Goffstown NH 03045

Call Sign: K1VO

Andrew G Boucher
102 Gorham Pond Rd
Goffstown NH 03045

Call Sign: KB1SGM
Anthony C Marts
112 Gorham Pond Rd
Goffstown NH 03045

Call Sign: KB1ULK
Howard A Wheeler
20 Hemlock Dr
Goffstown NH 03045

Call Sign: N1NSE
Richard R Dumais
92 Henry Bridge Rd
Goffstown NH 03045

Call Sign: KD1HD
Keith G Koerber
53 High St
Goffstown NH 03045

Call Sign: N1YEK
Joyce C Koerber
53 High St
Goffstown NH 03045

Call Sign: K1MLR
Robert L Merrill
85 High St
Goffstown NH 030450306

Call Sign: WI1O
Robert L Merrill
85 High St
Goffstown NH 030450306

Call Sign: N1SNA
Brenda M Crowling
236 Kennedy Hill Rd
Goffstown NH 03045

Call Sign: KB1RMC

Eric C Roy
83 Leach Hill Rd
Goffstown NH 03045

Call Sign: KB1CZW
Kenneth C Lucas
45 Main St
Goffstown NH 03045

Call Sign: KB1CZX
Cynthia L Lucas
45 Main St
Goffstown NH 03045

Call Sign: KB1THQ
Micah J Lucas
45 Main St
Goffstown NH 03045

Call Sign: KB1TYW
Timothy M Taber
208 Mast Rd
Goffstown NH 03045

Call Sign: K1TMT
Timothy M Taber
208 Mast Rd
Goffstown NH 03045

Call Sign: N1YRC
Edwin P Nothnagle
446 Mast Rd
Goffstown NH 03045

Call Sign: KB1RIR
Ronald H Michaud
5 Mercier Ct
Goffstown NH 03045

Call Sign: KB1SCO
Meridith L Suitor
26 Miles Ave
Goffstown NH 03045

Call Sign: KB1DBH

Donald R Lewis
101 Monarch Ave
Goffstown NH 03045

Call Sign: KB1MXI
Richard G Christie
149 Moose Club Park Rd
Goffstown NH 03045

Call Sign: KB1VON
Thomas B Linehan
489 Mountain Rd
Goffstown NH 03045

Call Sign: N1VRZ
Jon C Barton
492 Mountain Rd
Goffstown NH 03045

Call Sign: KB1DXD
Sandra L Cox
36 N Mast St
Goffstown NH 030451712

Call Sign: KB1WTG
Tamara L Mcshea
11 N Mast St 2nd Flr
Goffstown NH 03045

Call Sign: KB1ULN
Wilfred P Brodeur Jr
25 N Mast St Apt 3
Goffstown NH 03045

Call Sign: N1HAI
Willis C Mack
163 New Boston Rd
Goffstown NH 030452011

Call Sign: KB1SPR
Robert S Lindsey
8 New Rd
Goffstown NH 03045

Call Sign: KB1TKZ

Gloria J Lindsey
8 New Rd
Goffstown NH 03045

Call Sign: W1VF
Robert S Lindsey
8 New Rd
Goffstown NH 03045

Call Sign: N1SJG
Kristen M Mann
1 Oakwood Lane Unit 7
Goffstown NH 03045

Call Sign: KA1LK
David W Smith
5 Pineridge St
Goffstown NH 030451814

Call Sign: KB1SBO
Jennifer A Fox
42 Range Rd
Goffstown NH 03045

Call Sign: KB1SCR
Brian E Fox
42 Range Rd
Goffstown NH 03045

Call Sign: NU1F
Brian E Fox
42 Range Rd
Goffstown NH 03045

Call Sign: N1FOX
Jennifer A Fox
42 Range Rd
Goffstown NH 03045

Call Sign: W1WUR
Roger E Couturier
12 Reed St Apt 305
Goffstown NH 030451959

Call Sign: KB1WNC

Edward C Myers
45 Ridgewood Dr
Goffstown NH 03045

Call Sign: KN1I
Kenneth G Aldrich
16 Riverledge Dr
Goffstown NH 03045

Call Sign: KB1PKG
Paul G Morrissette
80 Riverledge Dr
Goffstown NH 03045

Call Sign: N1ZBQ
Mark F O Dowd
50 Rochambeau
Goffstown NH 03102

Call Sign: N1MQO
Kenneth R Pratte
505 Shirley Hill Rd
Goffstown NH 03045

Call Sign: KB1FID
Russell S Vanderhorst Mr.
12 Shirley Park Rd
Goffstown NH 03045

Call Sign: KB1SBP
Carolyn C Vanderhorst
12 Shirley Park Rd
Goffstown NH 03045

Call Sign: N1ARI
Ariana M Blanchette
29 Shore Dr
Goffstown NH 03045

Call Sign: NI1E
Marc A Bourque
30 Shore Dr
Goffstown NH 03045

Call Sign: KB4UTV

John H Pate Jr
3 South Mast St
Goffstown NH 03045

Call Sign: WB1FPA
Thomas W Howey
4 Stacey Ln
Goffstown NH 030452172

Call Sign: K4GHP
Michael D Miller
35 Stephen Dr
Goffstown NH 030452176

Call Sign: AB1JT
Michael D Miller
35 Stephen Dr
Goffstown NH 030452176

Call Sign: W1EAA
Michael D Miller
35 Stephen Dr
Goffstown NH 030452176

Call Sign: K1SI
Christopher M Garon
8 Third Ave.
Goffstown NH 03045

Call Sign: KB1GTP
Paul R Nault
18 Thomas Dr
Goffstown NH 03045

Call Sign: K1PRN
Paul R Nault
18 Thomas Dr
Goffstown NH 03045

Call Sign: KB1ULM
Karen J Pratt
90 Tibbetts Hill Rd
Goffstown NH 03045

Call Sign: KE1G

William A Freeman
420 Tibbetts Hill Rd
Goffstown NH 030453023

Call Sign: KB1WAR
Danielle R Finco
501 Tibbetts Hill Rd
Goffstown NH 03045

Call Sign: KB1GKO
Chris A Aylesworth
11 Timberwood Dr #206
Goffstown NH 03045

Call Sign: N1YZD
Robert K Hammond
2 Timberwood Dr 204
Goffstown NH 03045

Call Sign: KB1CSG
David A Karam
1 Timberwood Dr Unit 108
Goffstown NH 03045

Call Sign: KB1PST
Bradford A Wise
229 Tirrell Hill Rd
Goffstown NH 03045

Call Sign: KB1GYY
Jesse D Lucas
23 W Union St
Goffstown NH 03045

Call Sign: KB1WWS
Douglas R Chapman
572 Wallace Rd
Goffstown NH 03045

Call Sign: KB1HHD
William L Parker
41030 Washington St
Goffstown NH 03045

Call Sign: K1NDA

Roderick D Morrison Jr
360 Worthley Hill Rd
Goffstown NH 030452192

Call Sign: KA1VIW
Brenda L Lesmerises
Goffstown NH 03045

Call Sign: KC1HH
Robert L Merrill
Goffstown NH 03045

Call Sign: N1FJF
Sarah L Merrill
Goffstown NH 03045

Call Sign: N1HEM
Donald R Boston
Goffstown NH 03045

Call Sign: KB1FWY
William R Losefsky
Goffstown NH 03045

Call Sign: KB1HHY
Judi Hull
Goffstown NH 030450145

Call Sign: N1WL
William R Losefsky
Goffstown NH 03045

Call Sign: KB1JEH
Central Nhares Club
Goffstown NH 030450119

Call Sign: KB1JEI
Ncs Nhares Club
Goffstown NH 030450119

Call Sign: KB1JEJ
Command Nhares Club
Goffstown NH 030450119

Call Sign: KB1JEK

Grafton Nhares Club
Goffstown NH 030450119

Call Sign: KB1JEL
Coos Nhares Club
Goffstown NH 030450119

Call Sign: KB1JEM
Cheshire Nhares Club
Goffstown NH 030450119

Call Sign: KB1JEN
Hillsborough Nhares Club
Goffstown NH 030450119

Call Sign: KB1JEO
Greater Manchester Nhares
Club
Goffstown NH 030450119

Call Sign: KB1JEP
Strafford Nhares Club
Goffstown NH 030450119

Call Sign: KB1JEQ
Capital Area Nhares Club
Goffstown NH 030450119

Call Sign: KB1JER
Sullivan Nhares Club
Goffstown NH 030450119

Call Sign: KB1JES
Rockingham Nhares Club
Goffstown NH 030450119

Call Sign: KB1JET
Red Team Nhares Club
Goffstown NH 030450119

Call Sign: KB1JEU
Sec Nhares Club
Goffstown NH 030450119

Call Sign: KB1JHQ

Nhares Communication
Vehicle Club
Goffstown NH 03045

Call Sign: KB1KLF
West Rockingham Nhares
Club
Goffstown NH 030450119

Call Sign: KB1LZU
Granite State Amateur
Radio Association
Goffstown NH 03045

Call Sign: KB1MEV
Donna Losefsky
Goffstown NH 03045

Call Sign: KB1MEX
Christopher J Peploe
Goffstown NH 03045

Call Sign: KB1MEY
Mary E Peploe
Goffstown NH 03045

Call Sign: N1DDL
Donna Losefsky
Goffstown NH 03045

**FCC Amateur Radio
Licenses in Gonic**

Call Sign: WB0USO
Hal D Hoffner
4 Durham Ln
Gonic NH 03839

Call Sign: WA1YQO
Richard S Akerman Sr
Gonic NH 038397417

**FCC Amateur Radio
Licenses in Gorham**

Call Sign: KB1RIV
Barbara J Warren
11 Alpine St
Gorham NH 03581

Call Sign: KH6GR
Noel C Stahl
16 Alpine St
Gorham NH 03581

Call Sign: KB1MGU
Androscoggin Valley
Amateur Radio Club
16 Alpine St
Gorham NH 03581

Call Sign: AB1IO
Bruce G Pfendler
20 Androscoggin St Apt 3
Gorham NH 03581

Call Sign: N1TQO
Donald L Lader Jr
2 Bangor St
Gorham NH 03581

Call Sign: KA1BCR
Norman L Ely
30 Bangor St
Gorham NH 03581

Call Sign: KA1LJC
Charles M Reed
8 Broadway
Gorham NH 03581

Call Sign: N1ZGK
Stewart W Shaw
12 Cascade Flat
Gorham NH 035811013

Call Sign: KB1EMK
Louise A Shaw
12 Cascade Flats
Gorham NH 03581

Call Sign: KB1EUZ
David P Fontaine
7 Country Ln
Gorham NH 03581

Call Sign: KB1WPQ
Benjamin J Carlson
65 Crestwood Dr
Gorham NH 03581

Call Sign: W1ZME
Lee F Carroll
43 Evans St
Gorham NH 035810450

Call Sign: KB1PNA
Janice A Ely
88 Jimtown Rd
Gorham NH 03581

Call Sign: KB1FCZ
Michael M Pelchat
75 Lancaster Rd
Gorham NH 03581

Call Sign: KB1RSV
Justin R Mosher
292 Main St Apt 34
Gorham NH 03581

Call Sign: KB1TUO
Martin E Boyle
10 Mcfarland St
Gorham NH 03581

Call Sign: W9AYL
Natasha L Thompson
P.O. Box 294
Gorham NH 035810294

Call Sign: KA1DMN
Yves L Zornio
6 Spring Rd
Gorham NH 03581

Call Sign: KB1AFO
Jeffrey D Schall
Gorham NH 03581

Call Sign: N7EBG
Andrew E Schneider
Gorham NH 03581

Call Sign: KB1IBN
William N Westerlund
Gorham NH 035810051

## FCC Amateur Radio Licenses in Goshen

Call Sign: KA1ZSF
Betsy A Edes
Ball Park Rd
Goshen NH 03752

Call Sign: KB1AGW
John H Hooper
Box 105
Goshen NH 03752

Call Sign: KB1BIR
Nellie L Edes
Box 11k Ball Park Rd
Goshen NH 03752

Call Sign: KA1YHS
Corrie L Winterholer
Box 128
Goshen NH 03752

Call Sign: KB1AGX
Chuck A Rissala
Box 175
Goshen NH 03752

Call Sign: KB1SKJ
Robert O Johnson
360 Center Rd
Goshen NH 03752

Call Sign: KA1VCV
Daniel R Sherman
Center Rd
Goshen NH 03752

Call Sign: KA1EHB
Donald L Dazet
Cross Rd
Goshen NH 03752

Call Sign: KB1BJG
Desiree J Wright
Gen Del
Goshen NH 03752

Call Sign: KA1VCZ
Ian P Le Clair
General Delivery
Goshen NH 03752

Call Sign: KA1VCW
Kent W Stetson
Grand View Rd
Goshen NH 03752

Call Sign: N1IAF
Miles P Stetson
Grandview Rd
Goshen NH 03752

Call Sign: KB1BKL
Justin S Gonyea
308 Mill Village Rd N
Goshen NH 03752

Call Sign: KB1TLL
Nadine Lewis
464 Mill Village Rd N
Goshen NH 03752

Call Sign: KB1FKB
Daniel P Gonyea
308 Mill Village Rd North
Goshen NH 03752

Call Sign: KB1TBS
Charles A Lewis Sr
464 Mill Village Rd North
Goshen NH 03752

Call Sign: KA1WEK
Tammy D Magoon
Province Rd
Goshen NH 03752

Call Sign: KB1WLQ
Clark R Wamsley
49 Rand Pond Rd
Goshen NH 03752

Call Sign: KB1CYY
Jessie L Gagnon
171 Rand Pond Rd
Goshen NH 03752

Call Sign: KB1AZM
Ben L Carleton
Rt 10
Goshen NH 03752

Call Sign: KB1AZR
Joshua C Starcher
Rt 31
Goshen NH 03752

Call Sign: KB1CZA
Matthew P Blackwood
274 Washington Rd
Goshen NH 03752

Call Sign: KA1WEN
Alicia L Koscielniak
Goshen NH 03752

Call Sign: KA1YFZ
Ryan K Hall
Goshen NH 03752

Call Sign: KA1ZSE

Julie A Young
Goshen NH 03752

Call Sign: KB1AZL
Stacy J Koscielniak
Gosehn NH 03752

Call Sign: KB1AHT
Mike T Sherman
Goshen NH 03752

Call Sign: KB1AZS
Matthew D O Clair
Goshen NH 03752

Call Sign: KB1CBZ
Julie B Heath
Goshen NH 03752

Call Sign: KB1VOC
Thomas J Dicampo
Goshen NH 03752

**FCC Amateur Radio Licenses in Grafton**

Call Sign: N1PZR
William E Harp
Box 765
Grafton NH 03240

Call Sign: W1ZPN
Jeffrey L Hunziker
Kilton Pond
Grafton NH 03240

Call Sign: KA1CIV
Daniel A Lees
107 Livingston Hill Rd
Grafton NH 03240

Call Sign: WA1QEH
Louis C Zannini
21 Lower Meadow Rd
Grafton NH 032400262

Call Sign: KC2QMZ
Robert H Forshee
80 Main St
Grafton NH 03240

Call Sign: NN1G
Robert H Forshee
80 Main St
Grafton NH 03240

Call Sign: N1XXX
Paul D Hathaway
Slab City Rd
Grafton NH 03240

Call Sign: N1WBD
Robert M Hale
61 Slab City Rd.
Grafton NH 03240

Call Sign: N1SCJ
Edward J Colby
85 Turnpike Rd
Grafton NH 032400216

Call Sign: KB1PER
Daniel A Bergamini
364 Turnpike Rd
Grafton NH 03240

Call Sign: K1QXF
Grahame J Kulas
Grafton NH 03240

Call Sign: KB1RZF
Charles J Niemi
Grafton NH 03240

**FCC Amateur Radio Licenses in Grantham**

Call Sign: N1WJR
Matthew R Smith
82 Al Smith Rd

Grantham NH 03753

Call Sign: KA1HQC
Glenn A Campbell
42 Bright Slope Way
Grantham NH 03753

Call Sign: KB1LPP
Eric J Rauert
63 Brockridge Dr
Grantham NH 03753

Call Sign: KB1GNZ
Eric T Covill
631 Dunbar Hill Rd
Grantham NH 03753

Call Sign: K0JAL
Jerry A Lineback
1 General Court
Grantham NH 03753

Call Sign: W1ATC
Henry J Mc Carthy
Greensward Dr
Grantham NH 03753

Call Sign: KD3QV
Friedrich Dintelmann
436 Rd Around The Lake
Grantham NH 03753

Call Sign: W1SIB
Joseph F Gardner
Split Rock Rd Box 1044
Grantham NH 03753

Call Sign: WB2RDJ
Spotswood D Bowers Iii
21 Wedgewood Dr Box 929
Grantham NH 037530929

Call Sign: KB1GWQ
Andrew W Hobgood
16 Whitetail Ridge

Grantham NH 03753

Call Sign: K1GLE
Shirley E Mission
Grantham NH 037530948

Call Sign: K1TI
Paul D Terwilliger
Grantham NH 03753

Call Sign: KA1FXU
James H Lindholm
Grantham NH 03753

Call Sign: N1KZD
Howard C Llewellyn
Grantham NH 037531185

Call Sign: W2BMI
Donato C Ian
Grantham NH 03753

Call Sign: WB2VZD
David W Wright
Grantham NH 03753

Call Sign: K2RGY
George W Bond
Grantham NH 03753

Call Sign: KB1FVK
David W Wright
Grantham NH 03753

Call Sign: KB1KSS
Jo Ann M Rauert
Grantham NH 03753

Call Sign: KB1LLK
Marie A Bahrenburg
Grantham NH 03753

Call Sign: KB1RAH
Michael L Hughes
Grantham NH 03753

Call Sign: KB1VYB
Bryan D Weber
Grantham NH 03753

Call Sign: WW1I
Bryan D Weber
Grantham NH 03753

## FCC Amateur Radio Licenses in Greenfield

Call Sign: N1IWV
Edward J Anderson
104 Gould Hill Rd.
Greenfield NH 03047

Call Sign: KA1XK
Christopher C Horne
75 New Boston Rd
Greenfield NH 03047

Call Sign: WA3YHH
Randolph K Beltz
126 Old Bennington Rd
Greenfield NH 03047

Call Sign: KA1CXM
Richard M Pavlik
162 Old Bennington Rd
Greenfield NH 03047

Call Sign: N1PKC
Thomas F Shiel
51 Thomas Dr
Greenfield NH 030474722

Call Sign: KA1IYR
Crotched Mountain
Amateur Radio Club
1 Verney Dr
Greenfield NH 03047

Call Sign: N1PQB
Kristin C Driscoll

Verney Dr
Greenfield NH 03047

Call Sign: N1XOX
Michael J Szymanowski
125 Zephyr Rd
Greenfield NH 03047

Call Sign: N1QGP
Katherine R Cousins
Greenfield NH 03047

Call Sign: N1PPX
Gena M Kachadoorian
Greenfield NH 03047

Call Sign: WB1ENV
Joseph R Plourde
Greenfield NH 030470091

## FCC Amateur Radio Licenses in Greenland

Call Sign: N1LBG
Ronald Gallant
329 Bayside Rd
Greenland NH 03840

Call Sign: KA1QF
John P Hirtle
Box 129
Greenland NH 03840

Call Sign: KD1CR
Joseph H R Girard
11 Caswell Dr
Greenland NH 03840

Call Sign: KA1QCC
Richard C Hartmann
46 Caswell Dr
Greenland NH 03840

Call Sign: KB1VXP
John P Rand

20 Dearborn Ave
Greenland NH 03840

Call Sign: KB1RCY
Adam R Carr
240 Great Bay Rd
Greenland NH 03840

Call Sign: KB1RCX
Russell T Carr
240 Great Bay Rd
Greenland NH 03840

Call Sign: KB1SOC
Vaughan Morgan Iii
16 Holly Lane
Greenland NH 03840

Call Sign: WA1QWV
Peter S Ostromecky
55 Mcshane Ave
Greenland NH 03840

Call Sign: WA1UCI
Stanley F Ostromecky
29 Meadow Ln Bbt
Greenland NH 03840

Call Sign: KB1GHR
Richard C Eisfeller
10 Palm Dr
Greenland NH 03840

Call Sign: KB1SOE
Rosemary A Mackenzie
353 Portsmouth Ave
Greenland NH 03840

Call Sign: KC1JF
Daniel A Lapanne
1125 Portsmouth Ave
Greenland NH 03840

Call Sign: N1GJB
Birlem B Pomroy

450 Portsmouth Ave. Apt.
1
Greenland NH 038402222

Call Sign: KD1CS
Birlem B Pomroy
450 Portsmouth Ave. Apt.
1
Greenland NH 03840

Call Sign: KB1MHU
Richard W Hazzard
21 Post Rd
Greenland NH 03840

Call Sign: KA1RWH
Richard W Hazzard
21 Post Rd
Greenland NH 03840

Call Sign: K1RWH
Richard W Hazzard
21 Post Rd
Greenland NH 03840

Call Sign: W1JSM
Donald F Brown
416 Post Rd
Greenland NH 03840

Call Sign: WA1PSR
Scott M Hirtle
463 Post Rd
Greenland NH 03840

Call Sign: KB1LXX
Derek I Simpson
25 September Dr
Greenland NH 038402503

Call Sign: KB1OMQ
Jerilyn L Simpson
25 September Dr
Greenland NH 03840

Call Sign: KA1NUG
Nelson E Ramsdell
61 September Dr
Greenland NH 03840

Call Sign: N1GTM
Douglas A Wilson
10 Tidewater Farm Rd
Greenland NH 03840

Call Sign: N1QAT
Richard L Violette
164 Tuttle Lane Apt 1
Greenland NH 03840

Call Sign: N1HKK
Richard C Csernelabics
333 Winnicut Rd
Greenland NH 03840

Call Sign: W1WQM
Port City Amateur Radio
Club
Greenland NH 038400159

Call Sign: NM1JY
Port City Amateur Radio
Club
Greenland NH 038400159

Call Sign: N1SGZ
Donald T Williams
48 Adams Ave
Greenville NH 03048

Call Sign: KB1MZ
Edward W Brown
49 Adams Ave
Greenville NH 030483015

Call Sign: KB1JLD
Lee E Wilborg

99 Crestwood Ln
Greenville NH 03048

Call Sign: N1VPV
Charles P Fisher Jr
426 Fitchburg Rd
Greenville NH 03048

Call Sign: KB1WWQ
James W Reissfelder
774 Fitchburg Rd
Greenville NH 03048

Call Sign: WA1VVV
Lucien J Noel
766 Fitchburg Rd Rt 31
Greenville NH 03048

Call Sign: KB1RGW
George P Lacroix
33 High St
Greenville NH 03048

Call Sign: N1FPX
Philip G Alix
High St
Greenville NH 03048

Call Sign: KB1DWG
Penny M Lashua
220 Hillcrest Dr
Greenville NH 030483336

Call Sign: N1OIV
Edward L Smith Iii
61 Main St
Greenville NH 03048

Call Sign: N1CUG
Marcel H Caron
54 Main St Apt 112
Greenville NH 03048

Call Sign: WA1TYN
Douglas J Mc Kown

54 Main St. Apt. 110
Greenville NH 03048

Call Sign: NQ1Z
Michael J Donahue
56 Temple Rd
Greenville NH 03084

Call Sign: WB1ABI
Peter J Kenney
202 Tobey Hwy
Greenville NH 03048

Call Sign: N1ZZE
David E Martin
Greenville NH 03048

Call Sign: KB1PEX
Richard A Clark Jr
Greenville NH 03048

Call Sign: KB1RTO
Jonathan L Bouley
Greenville NH 03048

Call Sign: W2GIK
Richard E O Connor
21 Halls Brook Rd
Groton NH 03266

Call Sign: KB1GYA
Eleanor L Glidden
350 Brown Rd
Groveton NH 03582

Call Sign: KB1TTI
Sara J Cookson
5 First St
Groveton NH 03582

Call Sign: N1XGL
Harold D Hopps
82 Hillside Ave
Groveton NH 03582

Call Sign: N1SJX
Herbert J Pitts
280 Lost Nation
Groveton NH 03582

Call Sign: KB1VLM
Steven I Boudle
29 West St
Groveton NH 03582

Call Sign: KK4AWT
Alan R Morrissette
15 Winter St
Groveton NH 03582

## FCC Amateur Radio Licenses in Guild

Call Sign: KA1IIA
Robert L Provost
Guild NH 03754

## FCC Amateur Radio Licenses in Haksett

Call Sign: N1YAW
Gary C Lambert
23 Sherwood Dr
Haksett NH 03106

## FCC Amateur Radio Licenses in Hampstead

Call Sign: N8GUS
John W Schultheis
14 Andrew Cir
Hampstead NH 03841

Call Sign: N1WAW

Neill G Ross
5 Beach Rd
Hampstead NH 03841

Call Sign: WA1MGL
Dennis A Morrison
37 Beverly Dr
Hampstead NH 03841

Call Sign: W4AHD
David W Hargreaves
191 Buttrick Rd
Hampstead NH 03841

Call Sign: KB1HVR
Aine Blanchard
143 East Rd
Hampstead NH 03841

Call Sign: KB1LSS
Edward F Zaremba Iii
342 East Rd
Hampstead NH 03841

Call Sign: N1UFC
Matthew F White
Ells Shore Rd
Hampstead NH 03841

Call Sign: KB1KOW
Patricia M Smith
78 Granite Village
Hampstead NH 03841

Call Sign: KA1OSM
George M Lambrou
66 Hickory Rd
Hampstead NH 03841

Call Sign: N1IGH
Edward C Danielson
14 Holiday Ln
Hampstead NH 03841

Call Sign: KB1WMF

Christopher G Mccune
34 Holiday Ln
Hampstead NH 03841

Call Sign: N1ZQS
Ronald K Clayton Sr
98 Kent Farm Rd
Hampstead NH 03841

Call Sign: N1WLL
Edwin L Fournier
44 Lexington Dr
Hampstead NH 03841

Call Sign: KB1SGU
Eric Persson
112 Main St
Hampstead NH 03841

Call Sign: N1IVJ
Charles H Littlefield
223 Main St
Hampstead NH 03841

Call Sign: NM1W
James P Mc Hale
356 Main St
Hampstead NH 03841

Call Sign: KB1TFJ
John J Curley
13 Matthews Dr
Hampstead NH 03841

Call Sign: KA1OUE
Nancy K De Luca
40 Redcoat Dr
Hampstead NH 03841

Call Sign: WB1GOB
Dennis D De Luca
40 Redcoat Dr
Hampstead NH 03841

Call Sign: N2MGI

Matt Parker
28 Sawmill Ln
Hampstead NH 03841

Call Sign: K1SOJ
Brian G Eastman
31 Sawyer Rd
Hampstead NH 03841

Call Sign: K1FRS
William P Chandler
32 Shore Rd
Hampstead NH 03841

Call Sign: W1AXP
William P Chandler
32 Shore Rd
Hampstead NH 03841

Call Sign: WB1HFU
Richard H Breinlinger
51 Washpond Rd
Hampstead NH 03841

Call Sign: W1CCT
Kenneth H Clark
25 West Rd
Hampstead NH 03841

Call Sign: W1CDL
Thelma F Lycett
15 Westwood Dr
Hampstead NH 03841

Call Sign: W1DKS
Philip S Lycett Jr
15 Westwood Dr
Hampstead NH 03841

Call Sign: KB1WFM
Henry L Morin
Hampstead NH 03841

**FCC Amateur Radio
Licenses in Hampton**

Call Sign: N1EDA
Irving K Strout Jr
Anns Ln
Hampton NH 03842

Call Sign: N1QEA
Robert A Nalen
27 Ashworth Ave
Hampton NH 03842

Call Sign: N1LSX
Christopher E Perkins
86 Ashworth Ave
Hampton NH 03842

Call Sign: KB1UQS
Hampton Beach Amateur
Radio
100 Brown Ave
Hampton NH 03842

Call Sign: KB1UQT
Hampton Beach Amateur
Radio
100 Brown Ave
Hampton NH 03842

Call Sign: K1HBR
Hampton Beach Amateur
Radio
100 Brown Ave
Hampton NH 03842

Call Sign: N1JPU
Verlin W Balsiger Jr
14 Cliff Ave
Hampton NH 03842

Call Sign: KB1UBC
Casey Bradshaw
11 Colonial Circle
Hampton NH 03842

Call Sign: N4LCQ

William T Kelleher
7 Dearborn Ave
Hampton NH 03842

Call Sign: KA1VB
Roger W Smith
13 Edgewood Dr
Hampton NH 038423925

Call Sign: KB1LDO
Christine T Karmen
21 Elaine St
Hampton NH 03842

Call Sign: KB1KXQ
John L Karmen Iii
13 Evergreen Rd
Hampton NH 03842

Call Sign: KB1SEU
Robert L Lamothe
225 Exeter Rd
Hampton NH 03842

Call Sign: KB1BOB
Robert L Lamothe
225 Exeter Rd
Hampton NH 03842

Call Sign: N1SKY
David C Mackensen
31 Forest Dr
Hampton NH 03842

Call Sign: N1LKF
Douglas T Wood
29 Gale Rd
Hampton NH 038421013

Call Sign: KC7ASC
Roxanne M Dockey
60 Hampton Meadows
Hampton NH 03842

Call Sign: AB1IH

John J Nigrelli
68 Hampton Meadows
Hampton NH 03842

Call Sign: AB1JN
John J Nigrelli Mr.
68 Hampton Meadows
Hampton NH 03842

Call Sign: AJ1Z
Kurt B Kaiser
53 Hampton Towne Est
Hampton NH 03842

Call Sign: KB1SOA
Christin W Kaiser
53 Hampton Towne Est
Hampton NH 03842

Call Sign: W1CWK
Christin W Kaiser
53 Hampton Towne Est
Hampton NH 03842

Call Sign: K1QI
Kurt B Kaiser
53 Hampton Towne Est
Hampton NH 03842

Call Sign: N1RKJ
Calvin W Locke Jr
4 Hemlock Haven
Hampton NH 038421723

Call Sign: KB1MWB
James E Bray
34 Hemlock Haven
Hampton NH 03842

Call Sign: K8TOW
James E Bray Jr
34 Hemlock Haven
Hampton NH 03842

Call Sign: KA1BHC

Kenneth W Zahrndt
76 Hemlock Haven
Hampton NH 038421727

Call Sign: K1KL
Kevin M Lyons
7 Heritage Dr
Hampton NH 038421017

Call Sign: N1QZW
Judith P Mascioli
7 Heritage Dr
Hampton NH 03842

Call Sign: KA1IZO
Sarah J Hunter
167 High St
Hampton NH 03842

Call Sign: W1NNO
Douglass E Hunter
167 High St
Hampton NH 03842

Call Sign: W1NPJ
Lloyd H Farrell
241 High St
Hampton NH 03842

Call Sign: WI1L
Daniel J Herzog
467 High St 18
Hampton NH 03842

Call Sign: KA1ZTL
Todd A Biggins
2 Hilda Dr
Hampton NH 03842

Call Sign: WA1PKQ
Robert D Calkins
8 Josephine Dr
Hampton NH 03842

Call Sign: N1UGS

Robert E O Brien
536 Lafayette Rd 3
Hampton NH 03842

Call Sign: W1MRD
Robert L Simons
9 Lamprey Terrace
Hampton NH 03842

Call Sign: KB1TPX
Bisbano J Michael Sr
16 Landing Rd
Hampton NH 03842

Call Sign: WA1ZCQ
Carl F Achin
200 Landing Rd
Hampton NH 038424124

Call Sign: KB1NUB
Gregory M Mclaughlin
210 Landing Rd
Hampton NH 03842

Call Sign: KB1INK
Jesse M Clifford
54 Locke Rd
Hampton NH 03842

Call Sign: WB1HHS
John D Haughton
76 Locke Rd
Hampton NH 03842

Call Sign: KA1YCT
Michael R Prince
18 Longwood Dr
Hampton NH 03842

Call Sign: WB1FPD
John N Mac Innes Iii
12 M St Right Rear
Hampton NH 03842

Call Sign: KA1FNN

Jonathan M TRUE
31 Mill Rd
Hampton NH 03842

Call Sign: N1QZG
Kevin F Motley
960 Ocean Blvd
Hampton NH 03842

Call Sign: KB1WBP
Brian E Coffen
7 Penniman Ln
Hampton NH 03842

Call Sign: W1DJ
Harold W Wills
1 Pine Rd
Hampton NH 03842

Call Sign: KA1BBN
Evelyn A Benson
7 Ridgeview Ter
Hampton NH 03842

Call Sign: WA1IVT
Melvin Clamp
3 Robin Ln
Hampton NH 03843

Call Sign: KB1WEU
Kevin Sluder
19 Taylor St
Hampton NH 03842

Call Sign: KN1JLK
Kevin Sluder
19 Taylor St
Hampton NH 03842

Call Sign: W1BQ
Alan W Baker
30 Towle Farm Rd Unit 8
Hampton NH 03842

Call Sign: KB1RNI

Thomas P Gudaitis
3 Tucker Lane
Hampton NH 03842

Call Sign: NN1T
Thomas P Gudaitis
3 Tucker Lane
Hampton NH 03842

Call Sign: W1TG
Thomas P Gudaitis
3 Tucker Lane
Hampton NH 03842

Call Sign: W1VVV
Thomas P Andrews Jr
17 Twin Dr
Hampton NH 038431783

Call Sign: W1SGQ
Peter D Corson
5 Wentworth Ave
Hampton NH 03842

Call Sign: KA8TIH
Constantine Fantanas
451 Winnacunnet Rd #304
Hampton NH 03842

Call Sign: KB1KNX
Ellis G Beatty
457 Winnacunnet Rd Apt
108
Hampton NH 03842

Call Sign: WZ1H
John Raleigh
139 Woodland Rd
Hampton NH 03842

Call Sign: AA1CA
Thomas J Doubek
Hampton NH 038430392

Call Sign: K1MIB

Emily M Wallace
Hampton NH 03842

Call Sign: K1UQX
Richard W TRUE
Hampton NH 03842

Call Sign: KA1WHY
Donald Phillips
Hampton NH 038431795

Call Sign: N1ZGH
Ernest G Woodburn
Hampton NH 03843

Call Sign: KB1GNU
Thomas P Andrews Jr
Hampton NH 038431783

### FCC Amateur Radio Licenses in Hampton Beach

Call Sign: W1UXR
Henry E Dumaine
23 Dumas Ave Grt Boarshd
Hampton Beach NH 03842

Call Sign: WA1TYD
Bradley E Louth
Duston Ave
Hampton Beach NH 03842

Call Sign: AA7CM
PAMELA J Taylor
11 M St # C
Hampton Beach NH 03842

### FCC Amateur Radio Licenses in Hampton Falls

Call Sign: KB1NQB
Calvin M Lord
29 Brimmer Lane
Hampton Falls NH 03844

Call Sign: N6VW
Roy M Pueschel
68 Brown Rd
Hampton Falls NH 03844

Call Sign: KB1MVT
James E Macionski
2 Crestview Dr
Hampton Falls NH 03844

Call Sign: W8LM
Lawrence E Macionski
2 Crestview Dr
Hampton Falls NH 03844

Call Sign: N1ZOP
John R Clemons
39 Drink Water Rd
Hampton Falls NH
038442116

Call Sign: K1YKQ
C Francis Leary
177 Drinkwater Rd
Hampton Falls NH 03844

Call Sign: WA1MAD
Marie B Leary
177 Drinkwater Rd
Hampton Falls NH 03844

Call Sign: K3MWB
Martin W Barrett
2 Elton Ln
Hampton Falls NH 03844

Call Sign: K1AX
James R Casian
175 Exeter Rd
Hampton Falls NH 03844

Call Sign: KB1JXN
Kenneth J Browne
8 Frying Pan Ln

Hampton Falls NH 03844

Call Sign: AA1LN
Nicholas J Thomas
3 Merchant Rd
Hampton Falls NH 03844

Call Sign: N1LCL
Deborah L Thomas
3 Merchant Rd
Hampton Falls NH
038440273

Call Sign: NT1A
Nicholas J Thomas
3 Merchant Rd
Hampton Falls NH 03844

Call Sign: N1YGF
Erin M Kliegle
39 Mill Ln
Hampton Falls NH 03844

Call Sign: KB1KCD
John J Beaton
33 Nason Rd
Hampton Falls NH
038440016

Call Sign: KB1KCE
Marion J Hardy
33 Nason Rd
Hampton Falls NH
038440016

Call Sign: KB1MIP
Paul A Michael
8 Pevear Ln
Hampton Falls NH 03844

## FCC Amateur Radio Licenses in Hancock

Call Sign: KB1SWW
Jon P Grosjean

117 Depot Rd
Hancock NH 03449

Call Sign: K1BUR
Parker H Starratt
62 Duncan Rd
Hancock NH 034496101

Call Sign: KB1UQJ
William Welch
28 Evergreen Hill Rd
Hancock NH 03449

Call Sign: WB5JMJ
Michael B Matteson
5 Kimball Rd
Hancock NH 03449

Call Sign: N1PNW
David H Clarke
Ledge Rd
Hancock NH 03449

Call Sign: KA1TNN
Bruce D Smith
39 Longview Rd
Hancock NH 03449

Call Sign: KC1AX
Ralph C Neary
116 Peterborough Rd
Hancock NH 03449

Call Sign: KB1QGK
Mark T Parker
73 Prospect Hill
Hancock NH 03449

Call Sign: W1BYK
Mark T Parker
73 Prospect Hill
Hancock NH 03449

Call Sign: N1EHJ
Virginia F Williams

146 Prospect Hill Rd
Hancock NH 034495211

Call Sign: KB1ZP
Dwight H Williams
146 Prospect Hill Rd
Hancock NH 034495211

Call Sign: N1JZM
Thomas J Villeneuve
62 Vatcher Rd
Hancock NH 03441

Call Sign: N1THH
Kathleen K Villeneuve
62 Vatcher Rd
Hancock NH 03449

Call Sign: KA1DNP
Richard B Bell
Hancock NH 03449

Call Sign: KB1ABJ
Roberta I Bell
Hancock NH 03449

Call Sign: N1OGG
Rebecca J Randolph
Hancock NH 03449

Call Sign: N1OOQ
Thomas F Randolph
Hancock NH 03449

Call Sign: W2NSD
Wayne Green Ii
Hancock NH 03449

**FCC Amateur Radio
Licenses in Hanover**

Call Sign: KB1IML
Wolfgang Gick
7 Austin Ave Apt 1
Hanover NH 03755

Call Sign: KB1JXW
Max Wild
7 Austin Ave Apt 1
Hanover NH 03755

Call Sign: KB1RAE
Claire Mckenna
Bartmouth College Hb 1774
Hanover NH 03755

Call Sign: KA1ZAP
Nicholas A H Swogger
Burnside Reservoir Rd
Hanover NH 03755

Call Sign: N9ELC
Mark W Buck
9 Carriage Ln
Hanover NH 03755

Call Sign: KE6FF
Carey E Heckman
7 Choate Rd
Hanover NH 037551701

Call Sign: W1EAR
Carey E Heckman
7 Choate Rd
Hanover NH 037551701

Call Sign: KB1PUB
Nicholas A Harper
3 Crowley Ter
Hanover NH 03755

Call Sign: KB1HVJ
Glenn T Nofsinger
8000 Cummings Hall
Hanover NH 03755

Call Sign: KB1QOK
Rachel A Hochman
Dartmouth College
Hanover NH 03755

Call Sign: KB1TLK
Jeffrey I Spielberg
Dartmouth College
Hanover NH 03755

Call Sign: KB1HVI
Alexandra M Kern
Dartmouth College
Hanover NH 03755

Call Sign: KB1WEO
Patrick R Yukman
Dartmouth College
Hanover NH 03755

Call Sign: WB1ABP
Eric J Dennison
19 Dresden Rd
Hanover NH 03755

Call Sign: KB1AYT
Donald O Kollisch
93 E Wheelock St
Hanover NH 03755

Call Sign: KB9WUW
Dane P Owen
16 Etna Rd
Hanover NH 03755

Call Sign: N1SCS
Alex J Pollock
14 Goodfellow Rd
Hanover NH 037554800

Call Sign: N1SIZ
Wayne F Benoit
1 Grant Rd
Hanover NH 03755

Call Sign: KA3ZMT
Eric A Kratochvil
4 Greensboro Rd
Hanover NH 03755

Call Sign: KB1MWP
David E Danna
669 Hanover Ctr Rd
Hanover NH 03755

Call Sign: N1PNE
Daniel W Collison
4 Heneage Ln
Hanover NH 03755

Call Sign: KB1IWG
Samuel J Reisner
3074 Hinman
Hanover NH 03755

Call Sign: KB1UBB
Jonathan H Guinther
2187 Hinman Box
Dartmouth College
Hanover NH 03755

Call Sign: KB1RAG
Louis H Buck
4890 Hinmen Hall Dartmath
College
Hanover NH 03755

Call Sign: K1JJT
John M Stephens
6 Kingsford Rd
Hanover NH 03755

Call Sign: KQ6ZY
John M Wilson
5 Ladd Rd
Hanover NH 03755

Call Sign: KB1LRH
Paul Thompson Sr
14 Ledge Rd
Hanover NH 03755

Call Sign: KB1LSO
Paul Thompson Jr

14 Lege Rd
Hanover NH 03755

Call Sign: KA3EEX
Sean W Smith
13 Low Rd
Hanover NH 03755

Call Sign: WC1M
Richard L Green
190 Lyme Rd
Hanover NH 037556602

Call Sign: WA1DCM
Frank D Browning Jr
80 Lyme Rd 154
Hanover NH 03755

Call Sign: N8TM
Timothy C Prince
80 Lyme Rd 173
Hanover NH 03755

Call Sign: K2DGW
Margaret E B Stephenson
80 Lyme Rd Apt 363
Hanover NH 03755

Call Sign: W1DGC
J Gregg Stephenson
80 Lyme Rd Apt 363
Hanover NH 03755

Call Sign: AB1O
Richard W Olmsted Sr
80 Lyme Rd Apt 440
Hanover NH 03755

Call Sign: NB1F
John W Brown
80 Lyme Rd; Apt. 259
Hanover NH 037551231

Call Sign: KB1MWQ

Nicholas A Sinnott-
Armstrong
9 Montview Dr
Hanover NH 03755

Call Sign: KE1KI
Marc A Kenton
5 Mulherrin Farm Rd
Hanover NH 037554907

Call Sign: KB1IXE
Peter L Abdu
16 N Balch St
Hanover NH 03765

Call Sign: KB1IXF
William A Abdu
16 N Balch St
Hanover NH 03765

Call Sign: K1ZLL
L David Minsk
24 Rayton Rd
Hanover NH 03755

Call Sign: KB1IFU
Stephen R Rogers
22 Rennie Rd
Hanover NH 03755

Call Sign: W1STV
Stephen R Rogers
22 Rennie Rd
Hanover NH 03755

Call Sign: KB1AMC
Eugene A Fucci Sr
12 Rip Rd
Hanover NH 03755

Call Sign: KB1RAF
Nathan O Loewke
3 Smith Rd
Hanover NH 03755

Call Sign: KB1JYI
Niklas W Gick
South Park St
Hanover NH 03755

Call Sign: WA2DLS
Donald P Silver
26 Stonehurst Common
Hanover NH 037553232

Call Sign: KB1MOV
William B Brown
4 Storrs Rd
Hanover NH 03755

Call Sign: KB1MRK
Ari S Brown
4 Storrs Rd
Hanover NH 03755

Call Sign: W1ET
Dartmouth Amateur Radio
Assn
63 Sudikoff Hall
Hanover NH 037558000

Call Sign: N7SVD
Bruce R Huber
16 Valley Rd
Hanover NH 03755

Call Sign: N1USV
Billian M Marinov
27 West
Hanover NH 03755

Call Sign: AA1XO
Stanley D Dunten
19 Woodmore Dr
Hanover NH 03755

Call Sign: KB1EFC
Charles B Wilber
Hanover NH 037550985

Call Sign: N1NRB
Adam T Strohl
Hanover NH 037550049

Call Sign: W1FN
Twin State Radio Club Inc
Hanover NH 03755

Call Sign: KB1QOL
Phillip J Bracikowski
Hanover NH 03755

Call Sign: KB1WDG
Wrtc 2014
Hanover NH 03755

Call Sign: WR1TC
Wrtc 2014
Hanover NH 03755

## FCC Amateur Radio Licenses in Harrisville

Call Sign: KA1BFT
Orville R Bailey
Harisville NH 03450

Call Sign: KV1N
Lawrence C Mc Clure Jr
11 Keltic Way
Harrisville NH 03450

Call Sign: KB1JNQ
Mark A Eaton
121 Main St 2
Harrisville NH 03450

## FCC Amateur Radio Licenses in Harts Location

Call Sign: K1SLJ
Marion L Varney
Route 302
Harts Location NH 03812

## FCC Amateur Radio Licenses in Haverhill

Call Sign: K1THJ
William F Koch Jr
293 Dartmouth College
Hwy
Haverhill NH 03765

## FCC Amateur Radio Licenses in Hebron

Call Sign: W1ISK
Emily P Hanscom
Box 49
Hebron NH 032419700

Call Sign: KB1DJX
Arthur E Cummings
34 Cilley Brook Lane
Hebron
Hebron NH 03241

Call Sign: W1DOK
Sherwood M Kidder
133 Hobart Hill Rd
Hebron NH 03241

Call Sign: KA1YAC
Ramona L Dillon
247 Hobart Hill Rd
Hebron NH 03241

Call Sign: KA1YAD
Robert E Dillon
247 Hobart Hill Rd
Hebron NH 03241

Call Sign: KB1SRX
James R Spoerl
74 Sarah Lane
Hebron NH 03241

Call Sign: N1KDP
Gary R Filteau

Hebron NH 032410213

Call Sign: KB1UXV
Marek L Makoski
293 Bacon Rd
Henniker NH 03242

Call Sign: KB1RIJ
Larry P Beagle
30 Bennett Rd
Henniker NH 03242

Call Sign: KA1UXE
Suzanne Dobbins
11 Colby Crossing
Henniker NH 03242

Call Sign: AF1T
Dale P Clement
2 Corbin Rd
Henniker NH 032423367

Call Sign: W1MKY
Michele A Clement
49 Corbin Rd
Henniker NH 03242

Call Sign: N1GJF
Clifford L Eisner Sr
8 Cross Rd
Henniker NH 03242

Call Sign: KB9DGB
Timothy S Firkowski
9 Cross Rd
Henniker NH 03242

Call Sign: KA1QXR
Geoffrey A Lundy
514 Davison Rd
Henniker NH 03242

Call Sign: KA1PBQ
Melissa J Muzzy
13 Evergreen Circle
Henniker NH 03242

Call Sign: KO1X
Michael J Muzzy
13 Evergreen Circle
Henniker NH 03242

Call Sign: K1BGI
Kenneth E Dermon
18 Hemlock Corner
Henniker NH 03242

Call Sign: KB1IVO
Michele A Bergh
22 Hemlock Corner Loop
Henniker NH 03242

Call Sign: W1PS
William R Hall Jr
144 Longview Dr
Henniker NH 03242

Call Sign: N1ZID
Joseph W Kangas
99 Old Hillsboro Rd
Henniker NH 03242

Call Sign: KA1TFE
Mary B Santini
23 Old W Hopkinton Rd
Henniker NH 03242

Call Sign: N1HQT
Maria B Cann
23 Old W Hopkinton Rd
Henniker NH 03242

Call Sign: W2LX
Stuart D Cowan
22 Pine Hill Rd
Henniker NH 03242

Call Sign: N1GAQ
Glenn A Hammond
7 Ray Rd
Henniker NH 03242

Call Sign: NS1E
James D Mc Elroy
130 Rush Rd
Henniker NH 03242

Call Sign: K1LAS
Louise E French
1213 Rush Rd
Henniker NH 03242

Call Sign: KC1JD
Brian J Dobson
25 Shore Dr
Henniker NH 03242

Call Sign: KB1MFZ
Steven T Cote
58 Tanglewood Dr
Henniker NH 03242

Call Sign: KB1MGA
Craig A Cote
58 Tanglewood Dr
Henniker NH 03242

Call Sign: KB1PKX
Joshua N Locke
511 Tanglewood Dr
Henniker NH 03242

Call Sign: K1XLG
Joshua N Locke
511 Tanglewood Dr
Henniker NH 03242

Call Sign: W1JL
Joshua N Locke
511 Tanglewood Dr
Henniker NH 03242

Call Sign: N1XIP
Robert S Stanley
21 Warner Rd
Henneker NH 03242

Call Sign: K1DFQ
Wilfred L French
69 Warner Rd
Henniker NH 03242

Call Sign: KB1CAH
Henniker Community
School Radio Club
15 Western Ave
Henniker NH 03242

Call Sign: KB1MGB
Douglas W Tackett
34 Western Ave
Henniker NH 03242

Call Sign: KA1VCX
Erich A Adler
121 White Birch Rd.
Henniker NH 03242

Call Sign: K1BKE
Contoocook Valley Radio
Club
Henniker NH 032420088

Call Sign: K1JYI
George H Beardsley
Henniker NH 03242

Call Sign: N1KPT
Richard C Chapin
Henniker NH 03242

Call Sign: KB1MNF
Cv Radio Club
Henniker NH 03242

Call Sign: K1DFQ
Cv Radio Club

Henniker NH 03242

Call Sign: N1LTG
Luc H Boissonnault
Box 1195
Hill NH 03243

Call Sign: KA1FUA
William F Watson
51 Crescent St
Hill NH 03243

Call Sign: K1QLK
Daniel A Huntley
28 Crescent St.
Hill NH 03243

Call Sign: K1VZI
Lee R Herterich
138 Dearborn Rd
Hill NH 03243

Call Sign: KB1RZM
Gordon P Kempe
Hill NH 03243

Call Sign: K1CKL
Sidney E Blanchard
505 2nd Nh Tnpk
Hillsboro NH 03244

Call Sign: KB2UNE
Edward M Paquette
11 B Blair Ave
Hillsboro NH 03244

Call Sign: K1GCA
George C Arvanetaki
91 Barden Hill Rd

Hillsboro NH 03244

Call Sign: KB1BOD
Robert W Studivan
339 Beard Rd
Hillsboro NH 03244

Call Sign: AA1VW
Robert W Studivan
339 Beard Rd
Hillsboro NH 03244

Call Sign: W1MFF
Ralph W Johnson Jr
23 Boulder Rd
Hillsboro NH 03244

Call Sign: KA1GYK
Alfred C Avery
89 Center Rd
Hillsboro NH 03244

Call Sign: N1IVH
Ronald F Trice
371 Center Rd
Hillsboro NH 03244

Call Sign: W1JQX
Walter E French
Center Rd Apt 23
Hillsboro NH 03244

Call Sign: KA1SGR
James E Cartwright
Gay Ave
Hillsboro NH 03244

Call Sign: WA1JYV
Jodi SCALTRETO
17 Gould Pond Rd
Hillsboro NH 03244

Call Sign: KA1RZE
Roland J Bovio Sr
215 Henniker St

Hillsboro NH 03244

Call Sign: WA1OUB
Robert T Mobile
33 Kimball Hill Rd
Hillsboro NH 03244

Call Sign: K1SIX
Robert T Mobile
33 Kimball Hill Rd
Hillsboro NH 03244

Call Sign: N1TCD
Paula B Bliss
Longwoods Park
Hillsboro NH 03244

Call Sign: KB1OA
Jon F Lannon
207 North Rd
Hillsboro NH 03244

Call Sign: N1SKZ
Thomas M Matisko
66 Patten Hill Rd
Hillsboro NH 03244

Call Sign: KB1SZM
Louis A Mayfield
22 Raccoon Ally
Hillsboro NH 03244

Call Sign: N1UMO
Dennis E Caugnaro
Rfd 1
Hillsboro NH 03244

Call Sign: N1WEF
Andrew S Young
221 Stowe Mtn Rd
Hillsboro NH 03244

Call Sign: N1WEJ
W James Young
221 Stowe Mtn Rd

Hillsboro NH 03244

Call Sign: WB6THS
Jeffrey R Abare
27 Union St
Hillsboro NH 03244

Call Sign: W1FJE
Thomas W Laffin
93 W Main St
Hillsboro NH 03244

Call Sign: WA3LDI
Christopher A Sieg
96 W Main St
Hillsboro NH 03244

Call Sign: WB1HAA
Franklin D Ross
421 W Main St
Hillsboro NH 03244

Call Sign: KC1GF
Richard S Johnson
12 Walnut St.
Hillsboro NH 032441752

Call Sign: W2YQS
Russel H Brush
102 West Main St
Hillsboro NH 03244

Call Sign: N1MPO
Glenn A Stevens
Hillsboro NH 03244

Call Sign: N1SLQ
Jason M Brodsky
Hillsboro NH 032441310

Call Sign: NC1O
Michael A Brodsky
Hillsboro NH 03244

Call Sign: W1GIL

Guilford Mitchell
Hillsboro NH 032441313

Call Sign: WB2VHZ
John E Lind
Hillsboro NH 03244

Call Sign: KB1MKO
James A Minnich Jr
Hillsboro NH 032441219

Call Sign: KB1ODV
David R Wood
Hillsboro NH 03244

Call Sign: K1MAS
David R Wood
Hillsboro NH 03244

Call Sign: KA1UHL
Richard M Prunier
Hillsborough NH 03244

Call Sign: KB1VLK
Stormy E Gleason
Hillsborough NH 03244

**FCC Amateur Radio
Licenses in Hinsdale**

Call Sign: KB1FUT
Kevin L Stupak
779 Brattleboro Rd
Hinsdale NH 03451

Call Sign: N1ZOJ
Jamie P Denno
19 Cedar St.
Hinsdale NH 03451

Call Sign: KB1PNM
Rebecca J Eldred
19 Cedar St.
Hinsdale NH 03451

Call Sign: N1TZX
John A Boden
20 Dodge Ave
Hinsdale NH 03451

Call Sign: K1OUW
Shirley A De Angelis
31 Indian Acres Dr
Hinsdale NH 03451

Call Sign: N1NCJ
Patrick L O Connor
485 Plain Rd
Hinsdale NH 034512129

Call Sign: KB1SMP
Curtis S Levasseur
46 Emerson Dr
Hinsdale NH 03451

Call Sign: KB1SPF
Arthur G Rizzi
110 Indian Acres Dr
Hinsdale NH 03451

Call Sign: N1PBX
Conrad L Kruse
583 Plain Rd
Hinsdale NH 03451

Call Sign: W1TDG
Raymond A Wilson
9 Fox Run Rd
Hinsdale NH 03451

Call Sign: KB1XU
Dale W Shipp
6 Maple Ln
Hinsdale NH 03451

Call Sign: KB1MKY
Alexis J Capezza
846 Plain Rd.
Hinsdale NH 03451

Call Sign: N1TGB
Clifford E Hastings Ii
50 High St
Hinsdale NH 034510638

Call Sign: KB1USR
Martin L Boucher
72 Middle Oxbow Rd
Hinsdale NH 03451

Call Sign: KI4LDR
John A Capezza
846 Plain Rd.
Hinsdale NH 03451

Call Sign: N1WYW
Cynthia A Hastings
50 High St
Hinsdale NH 03451

Call Sign: K1HIN
Victor C Dwyer
178 Monument Rd
Hinsdale NH 03451

Call Sign: K1KEH
Catherine M Schill
Sargent Hill Rd
Hinsdale NH 03451

Call Sign: KB1MRE
Stephen A Hastings
50 High St
Hinsdale NH 034510638

Call Sign: KB1WUZ
William A Horsch
177 Northfield Rd
Hinsdale NH 03451

Call Sign: WA1RVK
Robert P Schill
Sargent Hill Rd
Hindale NH 03451

Call Sign: N1UOR
Mark W Curtiss
68 High St
Hinsdale NH 03451

Call Sign: KC4HTJ
Josh D Hodges
110 Old Brattleboro Rd.
Hinsdale NH 03451

Call Sign: W1HZL
Robert H Schill
Sargent Hill Rd
Hinsdale NH 03451

Call Sign: N1VWU
Cindy L Curtiss
68 High St
Hinsdale NH 03451

Call Sign: KB1KZS
Andrew D Bark
285 Oxbow Rd
Hinsdale NH 03451

Call Sign: N1NHF
Ralph L Desrosiers
7 Springbrook St
Hinsdale NH 03451

Call Sign: K1JWH
Joseph J De Angelis
21 Indian Acres Dr
Hinsdale NH 03451

Call Sign: KB1OVK
Michael E Hill
416 Plain Rd
Hinsdale NH 03451

Call Sign: N1NPD
Michael J Greenia
Thicket Hill
Hinsdale NH 03451

Call Sign: N1JWV
Mary Jane Keniston
Thicket Hill L12
Hinsdale NH 03451

Call Sign: KB1OVJ
Andrew J Hall
10 Woodlawn Lane
Hinsdale NH 03451

Call Sign: K1JRG
Roger E Jasienowski
Hinsdale NH 03451

Call Sign: N1XPS
Daniel F Stark
Hinsdale NH 03451

Call Sign: KB1SKT
Walter P Joyner Iv
Hinsdale NH 03451

## FCC Amateur Radio Licenses in Holderness

Call Sign: N1DYL
Peter J Nicola
64 Black Bare Trail
Holderness NH 03245

Call Sign: WA1ZDV
Jack J Barbera Jr
58 Hardhack Rd
Holderness NH 03245

Call Sign: KB1LEN
Shirley S Barbera
58 Hardhack Rd
Holderness NH 03245

Call Sign: KB1RZ
Richard G Hodges
34 Hodges Rd
Holderness NH 03245

Call Sign: WB1EBI
Malcolm T Taylor
1103 N.H. Route 113
Holderness NH 03245

Call Sign: N1OWC
David A Holt
90 Nh Rte 175
Holderness NH 03245

Call Sign: KB1OYG
Bethany S Veith
16 Perch Pond Rd
Holderness NH 03245

Call Sign: K1ATE
Bethany S Veith
16 Perch Pond Rd
Holderness NH 03245

Call Sign: KB1QLZ
William A Veith
16 Perch Pond Rd
Holderness NH 03245

Call Sign: N1JLR
David E Court E
88 Perch Pond Rd
Holderness NH 03245

Call Sign: KA1SIM
William J Jensen
Route 3
Holderness NH 03245

Call Sign: N1RGE
Peter J Furmanick
Holderness NH 03245

Call Sign: WB2JWU
Peter Hamersma
Holderness NH 03245

Call Sign: KB1QLV
Angela A Francesco

Holderness NH 03245

## FCC Amateur Radio Licenses in Hollis

Call Sign: KB1KCR
Todd M Bubar
14 Alsun Dr
Hollis NH 03049

Call Sign: AF1B
Leslie Getto
35 Alsun Dr
Hollis NH 03049

Call Sign: AB1OC
Fred Kemmerer
39 Baldwin Ln
Hollis NH 03049

Call Sign: KB1VMQ
Anita J Kemmerer
39 Baldwin Ln
Hollis NH 03049

Call Sign: AB1QB
Anita J Kemmerer
39 Baldwin Ln
Hollis NH 03049

Call Sign: N2XIO
John A Watson
89 Blood Rd
Hollis NH 030496530

Call Sign: K0UNJ
Thomas J Harris
1 Broad St
Hollis NH 03049

Call Sign: N1TRO
Thomas J Harris
1 Broad St
Hollis NH 03049

Call Sign: KB1VD
Robert G Krupp
32 Deer Run Rd
Hollis NH 03049

Call Sign: K9NX
David C Henderson
187 Depot Rd
Hollis NH 03049

Call Sign: AK1K
R Sterling Eanes
207 Depot Rd
Hollis NH 03049

Call Sign: N1NCN
Marshall S Thomas
214 Depot Rd
Hollis NH 03049

Call Sign: KB7ULE
Bright C K Foo
264 Depot Rd
Hollis NH 03049

Call Sign: KB1PHX
Bonita Currier
96 Dow Rd
Hollis NH 03049

Call Sign: KB1PHZ
William P Currier
96 Dow Rd
Hollis NH 03049

Call Sign: WC1I
William P Currier
96 Dow Rd
Hollis NH 03049

Call Sign: KV4GH
Eric G Forrest
33 Emerson Lane
Hollis NH 03049

Call Sign: K1KFW
Alfred L Poulin
32 Farley Rd
Hollis NH 03049

Call Sign: KA1HLD
John M Swaney
136 Farley Rd
Hollis NH 03049

Call Sign: WA1QDC
John S Baker
255 Farley Rd
Hollis NH 03049

Call Sign: KA1CM
Daniel L Murphy
10 Farm Pond Ln
Hollis NH 03049

Call Sign: N1DLM
Daniel L Murphy
10 Farm Pond Ln
Hollis NH 03049

Call Sign: KA1PDV
Richard D Watson Jr
22 Fletcher Ln
Hollis NH 03049

Call Sign: N1FBX
Stan J Penner
28 Fletcher Ln
Hollis NH 03049

Call Sign: N1TZC
Gerald J Walsh
53 Flint Pond Dr
Hollis NH 03049

Call Sign: K1LL
Paul Gifford
16 Hazel St
Hollis NH 03049

Call Sign: K1CHR
Cheshire Nhares Club
32 Hazel St
Hollis NH 03049

Call Sign: K1HIL
Hillsborough Nhares Club
32 Hazel St
Hollis NH 03049

Call Sign: WD4JZO
James T Blaine
32 Hazel St
Hollis NH 030496510

Call Sign: KB1KXL
Jeffrey M Kabel
28 Irene Dr
Hollis NH 03049

Call Sign: K1OG
Christopher R Ogren
77 Irene Dr
Hollis NH 03049

Call Sign: K1CVH
Christopher R Ogren
77 Irene Dr
Hollis NH 03049

Call Sign: KC2AON
Donald J Purcell
53 Iron Works Lane
Hollis NH 030496447

Call Sign: AB1DS
Donald J Purcell
53 Iron Works Lane
Hollis NH 030496447

Call Sign: N1CR
Robert M Barry
68 Jewett Ln
Hollis NH 03049

Call Sign: KA1BFR
Robert J Green
64 Laurel Hill Rd
Hollis NH 03049

Call Sign: K1NL
Paul Gifford
51 Lorna St
Hollis NH 03049

Call Sign: KB1VYP
Ruslan R Nabioullin
50 Louise Dr
Hollis NH 03049

Call Sign: K1DZ
Richard V Kemper
5 Marshalls Way
Hollis NH 03049

Call Sign: WA1GES
Dennis D Poulin
11 Mill Rd
Hollis NH 03049

Call Sign: AA1D
Edmund M De Lacy
5 Milton Pl
Hollis NH 03049

Call Sign: WA1LFD
Kevin J Kelly
43 Milton Pl
Hollis NH 030496127

Call Sign: KK6EQ
William H Almond
60 Milton Place
Hollis NH 03049

Call Sign: WB1ECB
William S Opalka
105 Mooar Hill Rd
Hollis NH 03049

Call Sign: N1TRO
Alexander W Harris Jr
93 N Pepperell Rd
Hollis NH 03049

Call Sign: W2BOE
Donald L Merwede
67 Nartoff Rd
Hollis NH 03049

Call Sign: N1ALT
Donald V Hurt
28 Old Runnels Bridge Rd
Hollis NH 03049

Call Sign: N1IBD
John R Marien
30 Orchard Dr
Hollis NH 030496101

Call Sign: KB1RTV
Aaron G Hill
20 Patch Rd
Hollis NH 03049

Call Sign: KA1RON
Aaron G Hill
20 Patch Rd
Hollis NH 03049

Call Sign: WB1ADR
R Lee Hill
20 Patch Rd
Hollis NH 03049

Call Sign: N1BA
R Lee Hill
20 Patch Rd
Hollis NH 03049

Call Sign: K1WKG
Robert E Fiero
11 Pierce Ln
Hollis NH 03049

Call Sign: AB1AV
William B Noyce
98 Pine Hill Rd
Hollis NH 03049

Call Sign: N1KDU
Craig A Neth
123 Pine Hill Rd
Hollis NH 03049

Call Sign: N1THJ
Dale A Neth
123 Pine Hill Rd
Hollis NH 03049

Call Sign: KB1PBG
William C Stephan
145 Pine Hill Rd
Hollis NH 03049

Call Sign: WB1FRY
Paul M Haskell Sr
300 Pine Hill Rd
Hollis NH 03049

Call Sign: KA1DP
Robert R Jehu
293 Pinehill Rd
Hollis NH 030495924

Call Sign: N1NH
James P Belanger
32 Plain Rd
Hollis NH 03049

Call Sign: N1DMA
Neil A Rosenberg
60 Plain Rd
Hollis NH 03049

Call Sign: KB1EIM
Nancy K Rosenberg
60 Plain Rd
Hollis NH 030496248

Call Sign: KB1CRJ
William D Norcott
18 Powers Rd
Hollis NH 030496100

Call Sign: KB1UMW
John F Heden
43 Proctor Hill
Hollis NH 03049

Call Sign: KA1JMG
Jennifer R Belanger
17 Proctor Hill Rd
Hollis NH 034900275

Call Sign: KA1WSA
New England Vhf Uhf
Society
19 Proctor Hill Rd
Hollis NH 03049

Call Sign: KB1UMV
Ryan F Heden
43 Proctor Hill Rd
Hollis NH 03049

Call Sign: KK1O
Steven Toli
41 Rail Way
Hollis NH 03049

Call Sign: N1GHJ
Stephen K Brede
105 Richardson Rd
Hollis NH 03049

Call Sign: KA1RWQ
Paul H Gill Jr
103 Rideout Rd
Hollis NH 03049

Call Sign: KB1RTP
Stephen M Davidson
155 Rideout Rd
Hollis NH 03049

Call Sign: NX1W
Alan J Kirby
54 Ridge Rd
Hollis NH 030496040

Call Sign: KA1OMJ
Harland A Muzzey Jr
81 Ridge Rd
Hollis NH 03049

Call Sign: KA1OMK
Laurie E Brown
16 Silver Lake Rd
Hollis NH 03049

Call Sign: N1VQQ
Timothy G Martineau
Silver Lake Rd
Hollis NH 03049

Call Sign: KB1FQI
Anthony G Capodilupo
16 Spaulding Ln
Hollis NH 03049

Call Sign: KB1ODJ
Stephen A Mccalmont
5 Truell Rd
Hollis NH 03049

Call Sign: N1TW
Stephen A Mccalmont
5 Truell Rd
Hollis NH 03049

Call Sign: KB1PJD
Andrew M Mccalmont
5 Truell Rd
Hollis NH 03049

Call Sign: KB1PTJ
Alexander K Mccalmont
5 Truell Rd
Hollis NH 03049

Call Sign: KB1VBU
Austin H Mccalmont
5 Truell Rd
Hollis NH 03049

Call Sign: N4CZW
Jeffery N Mac Donald
Truell Rd
Hollis NH 03049

Call Sign: K1YET
Stewart K Jackson
21 Van Dyke Rd
Hollis NH 03049

Call Sign: KW1DX
David A Pyle
26 Van Dyke Rd
Hollis NH 030496183

Call Sign: K1DUZ
Richard L King
8 Van Dyke Rd Box 505
Hollis NH 03049

Call Sign: N1XWB
Raymond R Benson
71 Wheeler Rd
Hollis NH 03049

Call Sign: N1YUC
Charles C Benson
71 Wheeler Rd
Hollis NH 03049

Call Sign: WA1LZZ
Peter Redes
77 Wheeler Rd
Hollis NH 03049

Call Sign: K1VLB
Michael J Hopkins
203 Wheeler Rd
Hollis NH 03049

Call Sign: W1FAO
Richard C Anthony Sr
65 White Pine Dr
Hollis NH 03049

Call Sign: WA1SYO
Lorna J Anthony
65 White Pine Dr
Hollis NH 03049

Call Sign: N1SUW
Thomas Luteran
129 Wright Rd
Hollis NH 03049

Call Sign: K1RTC
Richard G Mills
Hollis NH 03049

Call Sign: KB1EEU
John J Slater Iii
Hollis NH 03049

Call Sign: N1FT
Richard W Critz Jr
Hollis NH 03049

Call Sign: K1SMD
Stephen M Davidson
Hollis NH 03049

**FCC Amateur Radio
Licenses in Hooksett**

Call Sign: WA4WWR
Richard A Woolverton
24 Barberry St
Hookset NH 03106

Call Sign: KB1MSC
Michael H Holton
29 Bartlett St
Hooksett NH 03106

Call Sign: KA1ERN
Ronald F Poloske
9 Berry Hill Rd
Hooksett NH 03106

Call Sign: W1NBB
Sam K Lackoff
4 Birchwood Ln
Hooksett NH 03106

Call Sign: KB1NIO
Glen A Laramie
21 Bulland Dr
Hooksett NH 031061652

Call Sign: KB1OTG
Glen A Laramie
21 Bulland Dr
Hooksett NH 031061652

Call Sign: KA1UJQ
Daniel E Demers
3 Bullard Dr
Hooksett NH 03106

Call Sign: K1DED
Daniel E Demers
3 Bullard Dr
Hooksett NH 03106

Call Sign: N1YMZ
Sarah B Given
22 Bullard Dr
Hookseh NH 03106

Call Sign: WA0SKN
Alan H Kreifels
6 Cedar St
Hooksett NH 03106

Call Sign: N1ORB
Jennifer A Williams
97 Corriveau Dr
Hooksett NH 03106

Call Sign: N1UYI
Bryan H Williams
97 Corriveau Dr
Hooksett NH 03106

Call Sign: AA1YG
Donald P Cornellier
67 Crescent St
Hooksett NH 031061722

Call Sign: KB1ESY
Clive O Stephenson
28 Dale Rd Apt G-1
Hooksett NH 03106

Call Sign: KB1ESZ
Elizabeth J Fernyhough
28 Dale Rd Apt G-1
Hooksett NH 03106

Call Sign: W1VAU
Walter C Chase
1 Donald St
Hooksett NH 03106

Call Sign: N1CKX
Vernon S Henry
21 Donald St
Hooksett NH 031061537

Call Sign: KB1VOV
Jeanne M Wurtele
8 Dorris Dr
Hooksett NH 03106

Call Sign: KB1VHK
Christina M Simpson
12 Evelyn St
Hooksett NH 03106

Call Sign: KB1WAU
Thomas Simpson
12 Evelyn St
Hooksett NH 03106

Call Sign: N1KXT
Scott F Oneto
3 Forest Hills Rd
Hooksett NH 03106

Call Sign: KB1GZA
Joshua A Robertson
361 Hackett Hill Rd
Hooksett NH 03106

Call Sign: KB1GZE
Allan W Young
1160 Hooksett Rd 23
Hooksett NH 03106

Call Sign: KB1VOO
Cinthia M M Oneto
3 Forest Hills Rd
Hooksett NH 03106

Call Sign: KB1HPL
Timothy J Robertson
361 Hackett Hill Rd
Hooksett NH 031062516

Call Sign: N1LGO
James A Fitzgerald
1465 Hooksett Rd Box 159
Hooksett NH 03106

Call Sign: KB1QXH
Dale B Clement
122 Goffstown Rd
Hooksett NH 03106

Call Sign: KA1PWR
Nelson A Charest
23 Harvest Dr
Hooksett NH 03106

Call Sign: N1VSA
Rachel E Schor
1465 Hooksett Rd Unit 432
Hooksett NH 03106

Call Sign: KB1OOS
Lanette Mech
27 Granite St
Hooksett NH 03106

Call Sign: KB1IXG
Sean D Hallinan
31 Harvest Dr
Hooksett NH 03106

Call Sign: WA2IZM
Jonathan D Schor
1465 Hooksett Rd Unit 432
Hooksett NH 031061825

Call Sign: KA1NKD
Lanette Mech
27 Granite St
Hooksett NH 03106

Call Sign: KB1JYP
Enver J Silkman
1137 Hooksett Rd
Hooksett NH 03106

Call Sign: W2IZM
Jonathan D Schor
1465 Hooksett Rd Unit 432
Hooksett NH 031061825

Call Sign: WA1YIQ
William R Schor
17 Grant Dr
Hooksett NH 03106

Call Sign: AA1NH
Mark P Faulkner
1407 Hooksett Rd
Hooksett NH 03106

Call Sign: KC6NPK
Jonathan M Healey
17 Johns Dr
Hooksett NH 03106

Call Sign: N4KCA
Michael D Young
21 Grant Dr
Hooksett NH 03106

Call Sign: K1NIN
Darin L Ninness
1465 Hooksett Rd #240
Hooksett NH 03106

Call Sign: N1NGI
Marc A Pinsonneault
1 K Ave
Hookseh NH 031061148

Call Sign: N1TYJ
Rene J Chandonnet
12 Greystone Terrace
Hooksett NH 031062186

Call Sign: KB1OCE
Richard E Sterry
1465 Hooksett Rd 130
Hooksett NH 03106

Call Sign: KB1UBG
Sherri A Gaudette
4 Lancelot Dr
Hooksett NH 03106

Call Sign: KB1GYZ
Daniel S Robertson
361 Hackett Hill Rd
Hooksett NH 03106

Call Sign: KA1CYG
William J Bradley Sr
1465 Hooksett Rd 212
Hooksett NH 031061829

Call Sign: N1VQK
Jean J Labonville
38 Lantern Lane
Hooksett NH 03106

Call Sign: N1KHR
Everett R Hardy
298 Londonderry Tpke
Hooksett NH 03106

Call Sign: N1SIM
Carol J Hardy
298 Londonderry Tpke
Hooksett NH 03106

Call Sign: KB1QGH
Lynne O Brien
267 Londonderry Turnpike
Hooksett NH 03106

Call Sign: N1BUC
Paul N Bouchard
117 Mammoth Rd
Hooksett NH 031061152

Call Sign: N1OUO
Donald W Langlais
130 Mammoth Rd Apt 26
Hooksett NH 03106

Call Sign: N1QXL
Oscar J Lessard Sr
13 Martins Ferry Rd
Hooksett NH 03106

Call Sign: KB1CMF
Robert B Watts
8 Morrill Rd
Hooksett NH 03106

Call Sign: KB1QGF
Jeffrey J Hill
10 Mountain View Rd
Hooksett NH 03106

Call Sign: KB1QGE
Anne E Hill
10 Mountain View Rd
Hooksett NH 03106

Call Sign: WB2UID
Michael J Murphy
38 N Reading St
Hooksett NH 03104

Call Sign: WU2D
Michael J Murphy
38 N Reading St
Hooksett NH 03104

Call Sign: W1KSA
Clyde R Sorensen
19 Nancy Ln
Hooksett NH 03106

Call Sign: N1GTD
Gerard J Hallahan
28 Pinnacle St
Hooksett NH 03106

Call Sign: AA1YN
Lee D Scott
51 Pleasant St
Hooksett NH 031061453

Call Sign: KB1WID
Timothy P Alexander
33 Prescott Heights
Hooksett NH 03106

Call Sign: N1WEI
Ronald G Adams
10 Rockforest Dr
Hooksett NH 03106

Call Sign: W1SGD
James L Tift
14 S Main St
Hooksett NH 03106

Call Sign: WB3EER
Robert K Beltz
4 Sargent Dr
Hooksett NH 03106

Call Sign: KB1RVA
Randall Cima
3 Seasons Dr
Hooksett NH 03106

Call Sign: KB1NKB
Harry S Newman
36 Sherwood Dr
Hooksett NH 03106

Call Sign: KB1VVV
Serge Croteau
14 Springer Rd
Hooksett NH 03106

Call Sign: KB0TBN
John J Narkis
9 Spruce Ct
Hooksett NH 03106

Call Sign: KB0TBO
Maria E Narkis
9 Spruce Ct
Hooksett NH 03106

Call Sign: N3FXP
Scott W Cousens
502 W River Rd #43
Hooksett NH 03106

Call Sign: N1FST
Timothy M Huff
45 Whitehall Rd
Hooksett NH 03106

Call Sign: N1VRO
Edward J Kelly
45 Whitehall Rd
Hooksett NH 03106

**FCC Amateur Radio
Licenses in Hopkinton**

Call Sign: KB1TYT
Donald L O'brien

860 Briar Hill Rroad
Hopkinton NH 03229

Call Sign: KB1HGZ
David A Hubbard
117 Brockway Rd
Hopkinton NH 03229

Call Sign: KB1GOC
Scott W Flood
74 Buckingham Ln
Hopkinton NH 03229

Call Sign: N1FSN
Lee Hancock
Hatfield Rd
Hopkinton NH 03229

Call Sign: WA1UKV
Robert C Fair
797 Hopkinton Rd
Hopkinton NH 03229

Call Sign: N1RKL
David W Purington
86 Hutchins Hill
Hopkinton NH 03229

Call Sign: KB1DGC
John R Scholl
207 Irish Hill Rd
Hopkinton NH 032292204

Call Sign: W1EBS
Eugene A Slusser
232 Putney Hill Rd
Hopkinton NH 03229

Call Sign: WB1ASC
John S Brookfield Jr
688 Rollins Rd
Hopkinton NH 03229

Call Sign: KA1BET
William H Burroughs

18 Tamarack Rd
Hopkinton NH 03229

**FCC Amateur Radio
Licenses in Hudson**

Call Sign: KB1IDB
Louise V Dillon
5 A Mark St
Hudson NH 03051

Call Sign: KB1IDC
Kevin J Dillon
5 A Mark St
Hudson NH 03051

Call Sign: KB1UXP
Christopher R Farrell
20 Adam Dr
Hudson NH 03051

Call Sign: KB1UXQ
Michael P Farrell Sr
20 Adam Dr
Hudson NH 03051

Call Sign: KB8BAL
David L Hickmott
2 Anna Louise Dr
Hudson NH 03051

Call Sign: N1TMZ
Carol A Bushong
2 Anna Louise Dr
Hudson NH 03051

Call Sign: KB1PRD
Reginald E Pepin
87 B Pelham Rd
Hudson NH 03051

Call Sign: W1PRZ
Reginald E Pepin
87 B Pelham Rd
Hudson NH 03051

Call Sign: K1HEI
Richard J Guerra
32 B St
Hudson NH 03051

Call Sign: KA1ZRC
Mike P Painter
30 Barretts Hill Rd
Hudson NH 03051

Call Sign: N1ZHA
Keith A Ladd Sr
Barretts Hill Rd
Hudson NH 03051

Call Sign: KA1IOZ
Gary Buonomo
Beechwood Rd
Hudson NH 03051

Call Sign: KB1DAL
James E S Wilkins
112 Belknap Rd
Hudson NH 030514466

Call Sign: N1WAU
Kenneth M Butler
8 Belknap Terrace
Hudson NH 03051

Call Sign: K1QZA
Raymond J Sukey
8 Blackstone
Hudson NH 03051

Call Sign: KB1RGC
Alan W Dupont
20 Blackstone St
Hudson NH 03051

Call Sign: N1XWC
John R Delano
18 Bluberry Ln
Hudson NH 03051

Call Sign: KB1DFM
James C Conrad
32 Bonnie Heights
Hudson NH 03051

Call Sign: W1FX
Daniel J Norton
8 Burton St
Hudson NH 03051

Call Sign: K1FGF
Kenneth B Fredholm
17 Cheney Dr
Hudson NH 03051

Call Sign: WB1EKF
Chad D Hunter
54 Bonnie Heights Dr
Hudson NH 03051

Call Sign: WB1ELQ
Farrell T Woods Jr
162 Bush Hill Rd.
Hudson NH 03051

Call Sign: KA1RGB
Jenness N Keller
1 Chiswick Rd
Hudson NH 03051

Call Sign: KA1SHF
Gary A Christiansen
34 Boyd Rd
Hudson NH 03051

Call Sign: W1UBH
George H Abbott
318 Central St
Hudson NH 03051

Call Sign: KB1DYJ
David T Tyler
34 Clement Rd
Hudson NH 030513942

Call Sign: KG1N
Lynwood D Gilcreast
38 Boyd Rd
Hudson NH 03051

Call Sign: KB1TQL
Alan E Lutz
15 Chagnon Lane
Hudson NH 03051

Call Sign: W3WDX
Samuel A Millar
39 Cottonwood Dr
Hudson NH 03051

Call Sign: KB1QYM
Aaron J Brace
25 Breakneck Rd
Hudson NH 03051

Call Sign: AE1NH
Alan E Lutz
15 Chagnon Lane
Hudson NH 03051

Call Sign: KA1RTV
Mark R Boette
19 Cranberry Ln
Hudson NH 03051

Call Sign: WA1MHE
Aaron J Brace
25 Breakneck Rd
Hudson NH 03051

Call Sign: N1TEY
Jules J Gagne
Chagnon Lane
Hudson NH 03051

Call Sign: KA1KDI
Geoffrey K Ross
8 Daniel Webster Dr
Hudson NH 03051

Call Sign: KB1RAU
Kari Brace
25 Breakneck Rd
Hudson NH 03051

Call Sign: N1JEF
Stewart A Kroner
17 Chagnon Ln
Hudson NH 030513433

Call Sign: N1EUR
Linda S Reed
15 Daniel Webster Dr
Hudson NH 03051

Call Sign: K0TV
Jeremy L Muller
61 Burns Hill Rd
Hudson NH 03051

Call Sign: N1RXS
Diana L Kroner
17 Chagnon Ln
Hudson NH 030513433

Call Sign: WA1HJR
Leonard K Leach
108 Derry St
Hudson NH 03051

Call Sign: K1DJN
Philip E Andrews
1 Burns Hill Rd  Apt. 22
Hudson NH 03051

Call Sign: N1EGC
Paul M Davis
Chandler Ct
Hudson NH 03051

Call Sign: N1KDT
David R Franco
3 Dugout Rd
Hudson NH 030513506

Call Sign: N1EMC
David R Franco
3 Dugout Rd
Hudson NH 030513506

Call Sign: WB1ENY
Robert J Bielawa
18 Farmington Dr
Hudson NH 03051

Call Sign: AB1DF
Sadakazu Tanabe
22 Friars Dr
Hudson NH 03051

Call Sign: KB1CR
Edmund J Bielawski
7 Easthill Dr
Hudson NH 03051

Call Sign: KB1VHJ
Timothy P Bradley
Farnum Ct
Hudson NH 03051

Call Sign: KB1HOT
Mark A Dudas
32 Gabrielle Dr
Hudson NH 03051

Call Sign: WA1PDI
Brian E Bedard
6 Edgewood Dr
Hudson NH 03051

Call Sign: KB5STH
Jonathan J Meyer
59 Ferry St
Hudson NH 03051

Call Sign: KB1VHM
David L Dupont
1 Garrison Farm Rd
Hudson NH 03051

Call Sign: N1ORI
Robert S Bergemann Jr
909 Elm Ave
Hudson NH 03051

Call Sign: WA1ZJR
Joseph J Hogan
332 Fox Hollow Dr
Hudson NH 03051

Call Sign: KB1PEV
Andrew P Cloutier
25 George St
Hudson NH 03051

Call Sign: AB1MX
Paul G Dumont Jr
10 Fairway Dr
Hudson NH 03051

Call Sign: K1BSB
Ralph A Mack
11 Frenette Dr
Hudson NH 03051

Call Sign: KE1HS
Jack H Duffy Jr
46 Glasgow Cir
Hudson NH 030513759

Call Sign: K1NOB
Paul G Dumont Jr
10 Fairway Dr
Hudson NH 03051

Call Sign: KT1E
Lorraine A Mack
11 Frenette Dr
Hudson NH 03051

Call Sign: NF1L
Jack H Duffy Jr
46 Glasgow Cir
Hudson NH 030513759

Call Sign: N1ECD
Shiam Lal
16 Fairway Dr
Hudson NH 03051

Call Sign: KA1QMD
Johanna M Sousa
21 Frenette Dr
Hudson NH 03051

Call Sign: K1SLT
Michael J Golini
1 Glasgow Circle
Hudson NH 03051

Call Sign: NW1G
Huguette M Chandra
16 Fairway Dr
Hudson NH 03051

Call Sign: KB1KQQ
Front Porch Group
21 Frenette Dr
Hudson NH 03051

Call Sign: KA1LTQ
Alfred T Augeri
43 Glasgow Circle
Hudson NH 03051

Call Sign: N1APT
Robert J Costello
17 Fairway Dr
Hudson NH 03051

Call Sign: K1QU
Front Porch Group
21 Frenette Dr
Hudson NH 03051

Call Sign: KA1IWR
Robert F Hoaglund
44 Glen Dr
Hudson NH 03051

Call Sign: KB1VBN
Michael C O'keefe
57 Glen Dr
Hudson NH 03051

Call Sign: N1LAJ
John Skribiski
16 Gowing Rd
Hudson NH 03051

Call Sign: KA1MQ
James C Freed
4 Greenfield Dr
Hudson NH 03051

Call Sign: N1LOI
Patricia L Dunn
4 Griffin Rd
Hudson NH 03051

Call Sign: WB2FSK
Charles B Dunn
4 Griffin Rd
Hudson NH 03051

Call Sign: W1CBD
Charles B Dunn
4 Griffin Rd
Hudson NH 03051

Call Sign: KA1YYK
Robert L Graves Sr
4 Grigas St
Hudson NH 03051

Call Sign: K1TMC
Margery L Hardy
8 Hardy Ln
Hudson NH 03051

Call Sign: N1KOS
William A Zaharchuk
8 Hartson Cir
Hudson NH 03051

Call Sign: N1TVR
Kenneth S Wilde Jr
20 Hawkview Rd
Hudson NH 03051

Call Sign: KA1THZ
David J Smith
21 Hawkview Rd
Hudson NH 03051

Call Sign: WA1VVM
Michael J Krebs
26 Hazelwood Rd
Hudson NH 030513430

Call Sign: N1WWV
Robert Robbins
43 Hazelwood Rd
Hudson NH 03051

Call Sign: N1XEU
Lucille W Robbins
43 Hazelwood Rd
Hudson NH 03051

Call Sign: KB1LS
Raymond A Claise
34 Heritage Cir
Hudson NH 03051

Call Sign: KB1TBU
Scott B Larose
4 Hickory St
Hudson NH 03051

Call Sign: K1TCX
David C Mores
86 Highland St
Hudson NH 030514129

Call Sign: N1TAA
Carl R Murphy
14 Hilindale Dr
Hudson NH 03051

Call Sign: N1WDB
Donna M Murphy
14 Hilindale Dr
Hudson NH 03051

Call Sign: KB1ITO
David B Shaw
10 Holly Ln
Hudson NH 03051

Call Sign: KB1KOU
Thomas R Zirlott
11 Hopkins Dr
Hudson NH 03051

Call Sign: N1LJN
Bryan R Cote
22 Ledge Rd
Hudson NH 03051

Call Sign: N1DQQ
Dennis C Donah
34 Library St
Hudson NH 030514243

Call Sign: KA1WWL
Howard Blake
8 Linda St
Hudson NH 03051

Call Sign: KB1UMM
Stephen W Thompson
5 Linden St
Hudson NH 03051

Call Sign: KB1ST
Stephen W Thompson
5 Linden St
Hudson NH 03051

Call Sign: W1RCC
Donald H Gowdy
1 Lorraine St
Hudson NH 03051

Call Sign: N1XWD
Richard P Fortier
145 Lowell Rd
Hudson NH 03051

Call Sign: N1FEA
Ralph G Burgess
283 Lowell Rd
Hudson NH 03051

Call Sign: KB1QYK
Jeffrey B Wallace Jr
Lowell Rd
Hudson NH 03051

Call Sign: W1TED
Ted L Trost
142 Lowell Rd Unit 17-323
Hudson NH 03051

Call Sign: KB1HAC
Krista F Trost
142 Lowell Rd Unit 17-323
Hudson NH 03051

Call Sign: KB1RUE
Howard Chain
142 Lowell Rd Unit 17-333
Hudson NH 03051

Call Sign: K9NPD
Howard Chain
142 Lowell Rd Unit 17-333
Hudson NH 03051

Call Sign: AA1GR
Jeffrey L Dauphinais
4 Maureen Ln
Hudson NH 030513445

Call Sign: N1SUS
Ronald V Falcone
16 Mc Kinney Dr
Hudson NH 03051

Call Sign: WA1TGN
Robert A Kravitz
2 Meadow Dr
Hudson NH 03051

Call Sign: N1BNK
Bertram G Ryland
13 Meadowlark Dr
Hudson NH 03051

Call Sign: AB1NW
Jay W Tarbotton
7 Mountain View Dr
Hudson NH 03051

Call Sign: KB1DAJ
Dale C Earl
17 Mountain View Dr
Hudson NH 03051

Call Sign: AA1WF
Dale C Earl
17 Mountain View Dr
Hudson NH 03051

Call Sign: K1DCE
Dale C Earl
17 Mountain View Dr
Hudson NH 03051

Call Sign: AA1BD
David R Day
37 Musquash Rd
Hudson NH 03051

Call Sign: N1OCQ
Brian R Alley
25 Old Coach Rd
Hudson NH 03051

Call Sign: W1ZRE
Paul F Gauvreau
145 Old Derry Rd
Hudson NH 03051

Call Sign: KB1UCZ
Alexandre Pare
15 Oliver Dr
Hudson NH 03051

Call Sign: KB1WEI
Patrick A Mcghie
7 Patricia Dr
Hudson NH 03051

Call Sign: KB1SEG
Robert R Marceau
37 Pinewood Rd
Hudson NH 03051

Call Sign: KB1EZI
Gregory C Katsohis
16 Ponderosa Dr
Hudson NH 03051

Call Sign: KB1HHJ
Deborah C Katsohis
16 Ponderosa Dr
Hudson NH 03051

Call Sign: N1DDC
Roland P Labbe
Quail Run Dr
Hudson NH 03051

Call Sign: KB1LKE
Davis W Murphy Sr
40 Rangers Dr
Hudson NH 03051

Call Sign: W1SBX
Davis W Murphy Sr
40 Rangers Dr
Hudson NH 03051

Call Sign: KB1EDD
Michael A Yuoska
65 Rangers Dr
Hudson NH 03051

Call Sign: W1QFD
Michael A Yuoska
65 Rangers Dr
Hudson NH 03051

Call Sign: N1PVA
Bernard L Follansbee Jr
3 Rega St
Hudson NH 03051

Call Sign: K1LO
Lawrence H Olsen
20 Richman Rd
Hudson NH 03051

Call Sign: W1OJP
Robert Bellville
8 Rita Ave
Hudson NH 030515029

Call Sign: W1QJH
Gerard L Le Boeuf
28 River Rd
Hudson NH 030515227

Call Sign: W1YSC
Lorette E Le Boeuf
28 River Rd
Hudson NH 030515227

Call Sign: KD6LIG
Rhodri A R Elliott
21 Riviera Rd
Hudson NH 03051

Call Sign: WA1ZSJ
Andrew R Schindler
26 Robin Dr
Hudson NH 03051

Call Sign: KG7HF
Paul R Decker
59 Robinson Rd
Hudson NH 03051

Call Sign: KB1OGL
Brittany L Decker
59 Robinson Rd
Hudson NH 03051

Call Sign: KB1RGE
Claudia F Decker
59 Robinson Rd
Hudson NH 03051

Call Sign: KA1TH
Carl F Piepora
126 Robinson Rd
Hudson NH 03051

Call Sign: KA1KPM
Sherry L Kahn
147 Robinson Rd
Hudson NH 03051

Call Sign: NV1Z
Richard B Kahn
147 Robinson Rd
Hudson NH 03051

Call Sign: KB1WEQ
Brian Mattor
24 Roosevelt Ave Apt 25
Hudson NH 03051

Call Sign: WA1POU
Walter F Davidson
4 Saint Francis Pl
Hudson NH 03051

Call Sign: KB1KOY
William B Abbott
48 School St
Hudson NH 030514153

Call Sign: KG1K
Sadakazu Tanabe
37 Sheffield St
Hudson NH 03051

Call Sign: KA1TID
Ronnie K Fordham
15 Shelley Dr.
Hudson NH 03051

Call Sign: KB1ESK
Joseph J Field
22 Speare Rd
Hudson NH 03051

Call Sign: K1BWA
Joseph J Field
22 Speare Rd
Hudson NH 03051

Call Sign: W1JOF
Allan R Tastula
20 Spruce St
Hudson NH 03051

Call Sign: KB1IBZ
David J Ainley
10 St Mary Dr
Hudson NH 030915077

Call Sign: N1EWW
Robert D Nunes
12 St Mary Dr
Hudson NH 03051

Call Sign: WA2IYO
Patricia O Barber
8 Stevens Dr
Hudson NH 03051

Call Sign: WA2ROJ
William J Barber Jr
8 Stevens Dr
Hudson NH 03051

Call Sign: NE1B
William J Barber Jr
8 Stevens Dr
Hudson NH 030513126

Call Sign: KB1REV
Motorola Amateur Radio
Club - New England
8 Stevens Dr
Hudson NH 03051

Call Sign: K1MOT
Motorola Amateur Radio
Club - New England
8 Stevens Dr
Hudson NH 03051

Call Sign: N1SFT
Craig T Bailey
13 Travers St
Hudson NH 03051

Call Sign: N1NKF
Jeffery L Clegg
39 Trigate Rd
Hudson NH 03051

Call Sign: KB1OCF
Peter A Dolloff
9 Village Ln
Hudson NH 030513848

Call Sign: KB1WWP
William R Phillips
5 Washington St.
Hudson NH 03051

Call Sign: W1WCR
Victor A Misek
142 Wason Rd
Hudson NH 03051

Call Sign: KA1FYB
John R Brunelle
Hudson NH 03051

Call Sign: KA1ULJ
Johnathan P Mondoux
Hudson NH 03051

Call Sign: W1WH
Leonard W Haeseler
14 Sanders Rd
Hudston NH 03051

## FCC Amateur Radio Licenses in Intervale

Call Sign: KB1OOO
Marc A Vaillant
962 Hurricane Mtn Rd
Intervale NH 03845

Call Sign: KE8KW
Kenneth G Smith
Intervale NH 038450905

Call Sign: N1HWK
Bruce Hill
Intervale NH 03845

Call Sign: N1IME
Kevin S Bennett
Intervale NH 03845

Call Sign: KB1VMN
Peter A Villaume
Intervale NH 03845

## FCC Amateur Radio Licenses in Jackson

Call Sign: W1PNR
William D Beal Jr.
692 Dundee Rd
Jackson NH 038460001

Call Sign: KB1KSJ
Mount Washington
Observatory Arc
P O Box One
Jackson NH 038460001

Call Sign: W1BVU

Robert K Temple
Thorn Hill Rd
Jackson NH 03846

Call Sign: N1HRE
Anne D Peterson
19 Windy Hill Dr
Jackson NH 03846

Call Sign: AG1Z
William A Harris
Jackson NH 03846

Call Sign: N1DQA
Benjamin W English Jr
Jackson NH 03846

Call Sign: N1DQM
Robert E Cheney
Jackson NH 03846

Call Sign: N1FXY
Douglas C Bates
Jackson NH 03846

Call Sign: N1VLS
Judith T English
Jackson NH 03846

Call Sign: K1REC
Robert E Cheney
Jackson NH 03846

Call Sign: KB1VIG
Edward C Jariz
Jackson NH 03846

## FCC Amateur Radio Licenses in Jaffery

Call Sign: KA1ZKX
Stephen G Capizzano
Jaffery NH 034520661

Call Sign: KC5FCC

Janet M Brown
49 Amos Fortune Rd
Jaffrey NH 03452

Call Sign: KJ5JJ
Craig L Brown
49 Amos Fortune Rd
Jaffrey NH 03452

Call Sign: N0CUH
Christopher M Edscorn
15 Carriage Hill Dr
Jaffrey NH 03452

Call Sign: N1YVC
Luke V Edscorn
15 Carriage Hill Dr
Jaffrey NH 03452

Call Sign: KB1ELD
Jeffrey W Mungovan
51 Darcie Dr
Jaffrey NH 034521944

Call Sign: KA1IAY
Harold G Sands
369 Dublin Rd
Jaffrey NH 03452

Call Sign: KC5OTX
Peter G Lauzon
28 Erin Lane
Jaffrey NH 03452

Call Sign: KB1CYG
David E Barker
590 Fitzwilliam Rd
Jaffrey NH 03452

Call Sign: KB1TQX
Dennis P Campbell
45 Forest Park
Jaffrey NH 03452

Call Sign: KA1KPJ

A Josephine Hollis
75 Forest Pk
Jaffrey NH 03452

Call Sign: KA1GAV
Ross G Kenyon
30 Gilmore Pond Rd
Jaffrey NH 03452

Call Sign: K1ONG
Peter W Reed
416 Gilmore Pond Rd
Jaffrey NH 03452

Call Sign: N1XDW
Nicholas C Kemmis
643 Gilmore Pond Rd
Jaffrey NH 03452

Call Sign: K1BJF
Barry J Furnival
158 Great Rd
Jaffrey NH 03452

Call Sign: KB1EGX
Deborah E Bennett
87 Heath Rd
Jaffrey NH 034520404

Call Sign: WB1NH
Wayne D Bennett
87 Heath Rd
Jaffrey NH 034520404

Call Sign: WB1RLB
Roberta L Bennett
87 Heath Rd
Jaffrey NH 03452

Call Sign: N1NTV
Steven R Flood
142 Main St #304
Jaffrey NH 03452

Call Sign: W1SRF

Steven R Flood
142 Main St Apt 304
Jaffrey NH 03452

Call Sign: KB1FGG
Carl D Hedman
22 Moore Pike
Jaffrey NH 03452

Call Sign: N1GCF
Henry S Gallup
100 Mountain Rd
Jaffrey NH 03452

Call Sign: KB1BIM
Thomas E Cook
17 Mountain Rd Apt 6
Jaffrey NH 03452

Call Sign: KE1HG
Charles E Whitney
115 North St
Jaffrey NH 03452

Call Sign: KB1RZJ
Jonathan P Vitello
361 North St
Jaffrey NH 03452

Call Sign: K1ZAK
Susan Cornell
15 Parsons Lane
Jaffrey NH 03452

Call Sign: KB1BJB
Agnes V Hautanen
35 Pinecrest Rd
Jaffrey NH 03452

Call Sign: K1JWM
Jeffrey W Mungovan
Po Box 223
Jaffrey NH 03452

Call Sign: KB1RKM

Elvin R Ramey
88 Prospect St
Jaffrey NH 03452

Call Sign: KB1OY
Paul J Sturges Sr
3 Windy Fields Lane
Jaffrey NH 03452

Call Sign: N1POF
Curtis W Hunnewell
Jaffrey NH 03452

Call Sign: KB1SXH
Timothy P Algeo
Jaffrey NH 03452

## FCC Amateur Radio Licenses in Jefferson

Call Sign: KB2VIX
Patrick J Kawonczyk
49 Ingerson Rd
Jefferson NH 03583

Call Sign: N2MMU
Grace A Kawonczyk
49 Ingerson Rd
Jefferson NH 03583

Call Sign: WB2FAS
Peter J Kawonczyk
49 Ingerson Rd
Jefferson NH 03583

Call Sign: WB8WGA
Robert W Ball
23 Ingerson Rd.
Jefferson NH 03583

Call Sign: KB1IMJ
Carl J Rod
129 Meadow Rd
Jefferson NH 03583

Call Sign: AB1IG
Carl J Rod
129 Meadow Rd
Jefferson NH 03583

Call Sign: KB1PSX
Antonio J Dangelo
187 Presidential Highway
Jefferson NH 03583

Call Sign: K1AJD
Antonio J Dangelo
187 Presidential Highway
Jefferson NH 03583

Call Sign: WB1GQQ
Alan P Balog
1973 Presidential Hwy
Jefferson NH 03583

Call Sign: KA1YDN
Kevin L Staines
Jefferson NH 03583

Call Sign: N1OTK
Linda A Staines
Jefferson NH 03583

## FCC Amateur Radio Licenses in Keene

Call Sign: N1FFQ
Robert I Smith
22 Arch St
Keene NH 03431

Call Sign: WB1AMI
Joseph L Skiffington
109 Ashvelot St Apt 3
Keene NH 03431

Call Sign: KB1SEK
Bruce W Pollock
14 Barrett Ave
Keene NH 03431

Call Sign: N1NGE
Carol A Beaver
37 Beaver St
Keene NH 03431

Call Sign: W1ECA
Harry J Reed Jr
Box 286
Keene NH 03431

Call Sign: N1GAN
Eric R Carlson
Box 29
Keene NH 03431

Call Sign: KA2NIK
John I Mc Kenney
Box 68
Keene NH 03431

Call Sign: KB2FF
Richard E Seifert
5 Central Sq Ter
Keene NH 03431

Call Sign: KB1IVX
Lisa K Henkel
40 Central Square #5
Keene NH 03431

Call Sign: N1UCQ
Bruce Mac Donald
39 Central Square Pmb #225
Keene NH 03431

Call Sign: KG4JOT
Wade H Penny Iii
205 Chapman Rd
Keene NH 03431

Call Sign: KG4KXD
Ryan W Penny
205 Chapman Rd

Keene NH 03431                  Keene NH 03431                  Keene NH 03431

Call Sign: KA1USR               Call Sign: KA1UMK               Call Sign: W1ZIS
Roger E Hill                    Donald V Wilson                 Roger E Emery
12 Chickadee Ct                 14 Forest View Rd               19 Hastings Ave
Keene NH 034311625              Keene NH 03431                  Keene NH 03431

Call Sign: N1PEJ                Call Sign: N1NHL                Call Sign: KQ1I
Jason A Bueckner                Joseph F Majewski               Aaron A Lipsky
215 Church St / Apt# 1          11 Fox Cir                      64 Hastings Ave
Keene NH 03431                  Keene NH 03431                  Keene NH 03431

Call Sign: KA1TWX               Call Sign: KB1QAE               Call Sign: KB1SIZ
Bruce F Graves                  Joshua R Boulanger              Judith A Sloan
5 Colonial Dr                   24 Fox Circle                   38 High St
Keene NH 03431                  Keene NH 03431                  Keene NH 03431

Call Sign: W1HCX                Call Sign: K1EEN                Call Sign: KB1CYE
David F Putnam                  Joshua R Boulanger              Charles C Luebkeman
150 Court St                    24 Fox Circle                   30 Hilltop Dr
Keene NH 03431                  Keene NH 03431                  Keene NH 034314910

Call Sign: KA1QQE               Call Sign: KB1VVE               Call Sign: KB1FVO
Robert Hook                     Don A Koivula                   Bernard A Cote
248 Court St                    168 George St                   3 Imelda Ave
Keene NH 03431                  Keene NH 03431                  Keene NH 03431

Call Sign: KB1TYV               Call Sign: KB1II                Call Sign: KB1FVP
Charles Kirk                    Alexander J Bonica              Karyn M Cote
9 Cranberry Rd                  51 Green Acres Rd               3 Imelda Ave
Keene NH 03431                  Keene NH 03431                  Keene NH 03431

Call Sign: N1IPK                Call Sign: N1KWF                Call Sign: KB1POP
Patrick F Laughlin              Randall R Lake                  Timothy E Guyot
16 Crescent St                  73 Gunn Rd                      8 James Hill Dr
Keene NH 03431                  Keene NH 03431                  Keene NH 03431

Call Sign: N1BYD                Call Sign: N1PNX                Call Sign: KD1LQ
Geoffrey S Molina               Barbara J Lake                  Clark O Dexter
222 Darling Rd                  73 Gunn Rd                      137 Jordan Rd
Keene NH 03431                  Keene NH 03431                  Keene NH 03431

Call Sign: N1AGI                Call Sign: KB1GTQ               Call Sign: N1YMP
Wesley E Clark                  Bryan J Lake                    William K Chaffee Sr
61 Dickinson Rd.                73 Gunn Rd                      8 June St

Keene NH 03431       Keene NH 03431       Keene NH 03431

Call Sign: KA1BGI
Richard G Beatty
176 Liberty Ln
Keene NH 03431

Call Sign: N1XKN
David R Crossmon
17 Melody Ln
Keene NH 034315014

Call Sign: N9IZK
Roger A Goss
81 Oriole Ave.
Keene NH 03431

Call Sign: K6BGI
Richard G Beatty
176 Liberty Ln
Keene NH 03431

Call Sign: K1JKF
Richard P Miinch Jr
32 Mill Rd
Keene NH 03431

Call Sign: KB1MLW
Karen D Manuel
105 Oriole Dr
Keene NH 03431

Call Sign: N1PNZ
Colin R Lyle
383 Main St
Keene NH 03431

Call Sign: WB3DCA
Steven B Konick
19 Newbury Lane
Keene NH 03431

Call Sign: KB1ECA
Lee J Dexter
P.O. Box 201
Keene NH 03431

Call Sign: N1NGC
Deborah L Reynolds
52 Manchester St
Keene NH 03431

Call Sign: N1LUR
Richard C Hebert
65 Nims Rd
Keene NH 03431

Call Sign: N2KTM
James H Faux
22 Pako Ave
Keene NH 034315015

Call Sign: K1IOJ
Lemuel R Cummings
27 Marguerite St
Keene NH 03431

Call Sign: N1RCH
Richard C Hebert
65 Nims Rd
Keene NH 03431

Call Sign: KC2MZS
Josephine S Faux
22 Pako Ave
Keene NH 034315015

Call Sign: K1TQY
Dawn M Cummings
27 Marguerite St
Keene NH 03431

Call Sign: N1NCI
Dale R Paquin
111 North St
Keene NH 03431

Call Sign: N1POG
Conrad A Perreault
177 Pako Ave
Keene NH 03431

Call Sign: KE5BGA
Thomas A Baldwin
456 Marlborough St
Keene NH 03431

Call Sign: KB1FNR
Barbara C Paquin
111 North St
Keene NH 03431

Call Sign: KB1FLN
Cheshire County Dx Arc
661 Park Av #4
Keene NH 03431

Call Sign: KF6HWS
Christopher P Cake
19 Meeting House Rd
Keene NH 03431

Call Sign: KB1JIP
Joyce E Torrey
21 Oriole Ave
Keene NH 03431

Call Sign: KB1NKG
Bruce I Beliveau
372 Park Ave
Keene NH 034311557

Call Sign: KA1DWZ
Richard A Crossmon
17 Melody Ln

Call Sign: KB1JIQ
Clinton A Juniper
21 Oriole Ave

Call Sign: N1EHB
George Broesder
671 Park Ave Apt 43

Keene NH 03431

Call Sign: KB1RZC
Jeremiah F Rohr
38 Park Ave Apt E
Keene NH 03431

Call Sign: N1VFM
Robert G Crossmon
87 Pearl St
Keene NH 03431

Call Sign: N1CGE
Paul T Reagan
Rd 1
Keene NH 03431

Call Sign: KB1MZN
Garry J Emge
42 Reservoir St
Keene NH 03431

Call Sign: KB1VQH
Jeffrey V Clough
36 Sparrow St
Keene NH 03431

Call Sign: KB1CYH
Jason D Adams
48 Stanhope Ave
Keene NH 03431

Call Sign: KD1RT
Peter C Doyle
119 Stearns Rd
Keene NH 03431

Call Sign: W1UGP
Frederick A Norris
5 Surry Hill Dr
Keene NH 034314932

Call Sign: KA7E
James A Feld
274 W. Surry Rd.

Keene NH 03431

Call Sign: N1PPM
Donald W Smith Jr
566 Washington St
Keene NH 03431

Call Sign: N1RGH
Jules A Hebert
610 West St
Keene NH 03431

Call Sign: N1JRB
Chris Drakiotes
8 Wetmore St
Keene NH 03431

Call Sign: KV1S
Aubrey V Gould
Windsor Court
Keene NH 03431

Call Sign: KD6RGW
John E Mulhollen
Keene NH 03431

Call Sign: N1HRY
Russell F Calkins
Keene NH 03431

Call Sign: N1NGF
John F Mc Hugh
Keene NH 03431

Call Sign: WB1GFM
Alice A Braley
Keene NH 034310352

Call Sign: KB1QMV
David A Campbell
Keene NH 03431

Call Sign: W1DXX
David A Campbell
Keene NH 03431

Call Sign: KB1UCS
Kenneth W Steeves
59 Amesbury Rd
Kensington NH 03833

Call Sign: N1PMO
Myles C Empey
Campry Rd
Kensington NH 03827

Call Sign: N1SDC
Rebecca A Hayden
45 Cottage Rd
Kensington NH 03827

Call Sign: N1VTW
Adam D Silvestri
45 Cottage Rd
Kensington NH 03827

Call Sign: WA1STH
Stephen J Silvestri Jr
45 Cottage Rd
Kensington NH 03827

Call Sign: WA1YWL
Paul F Avery Jr
Drinkwater Rd
Kensington NH 03833

Call Sign: W1DID
Alvin J Zink Jr
7 Hobbs Rd
Kensington NH 03833

Call Sign: N1FOK
John W G Tuthill
18 Hobbs Rd
Kensington NH 03833

Call Sign: N1WMZ

Gregory R Sinclair
4 Kady Ln
Kensington NH 03833

Call Sign: N1QVV
Carol A Empey
Lamprey Rd
Kensington NH 03827

Call Sign: KA1GJU
Kriss A Kliegle
25 Muddy Pond Rd
Kensington NH 038336817

Call Sign: WA1FUU
Eric M Young
205 N Haverhill Rd
Kensington NH 03833

Call Sign: W1FUU
Eric M Young
205 N Haverhill Rd
Kensington NH 03833

Call Sign: W1EGB
Ellis G Beatty
23 Osgood Rd
Kensington NH 03833

Call Sign: K1RX
Mark S Pride
120 South Rd
Kensington NH 03833

Call Sign: KA1JBL
Albert Cerniauskas
133 South Rd
Kensington NH 03827

Call Sign: KB1MHR
Robert A Soper
169 South Rd
Kensington NH 03833

**FCC Amateur Radio
Licenses in Kingston**

Call Sign: WA1PST
Herbert F Holland Sr
12 Bartlett St
Kingston NH 03848

Call Sign: K1DGI
Gladys I Washburn
29 Circuit Dr
Kingston NH 03848

Call Sign: K1OHQ
George D Washburn
29 Circuit Dr
Kingston NH 03848

Call Sign: W1PAY
James T Rankin
28 Clark Rd
Kingston NH 03848

Call Sign: N1XEJ
Bonnie P Taylor
29 Clark Rd
Kingston NH 038483657

Call Sign: N1CHG
Murray E Hale
24 Con Cannon Rd
Kingston NH 03848

Call Sign: WB1EOF
Patricia E Warrington
27 Exeter Rd
Kingston NH 03848

Call Sign: W1JV
John L Vander Sande
5 Lantern Lane
Kingston NH 038483246

Call Sign: KE1BR
David E Sanford

15 Little River Rd
Kingston NH 03848

Call Sign: N1RUW
Peter G Buckley
38 Little River Rd
Kingston NH 03848

Call Sign: KB1JYO
Dana L Merrill
9 Madison Ave
Kingston NH 03848

Call Sign: KB1KJJ
Robert L Merrill
11 Madison Ave
Kingston NH 03848

Call Sign: W1DK
David E Sanford
2 Meadow Wood Rd
Kingston NH 03848

Call Sign: KB1KTS
Dennis A Parker
3 Meeks Rd
Kingston NH 03848

Call Sign: N1RMB
Paul J Bean
51 Mill Rd
Kingston NH 03848

Call Sign: KD1FM
Robert H Bowes
5 New Boston Rd
Kingston NH 03848

Call Sign: AB1KB
Edward A La Pointe
92 North Rd
Kingston NH 03848

Call Sign: NS1P
Edward A La Pointe

92 North Rd
Kingston NH 03848

Call Sign: K1PWR
Warren D Smith
17 Old Mill Rd
Kingston NH 03848

Call Sign: N1YBN
David A Mascioli
1 Towle Rd
Kingston NH 03848

Call Sign: N1YVQ
Lorainne J Mascioli
1 Towle Rd
Kingston NH 038483460

Call Sign: N1QVA
Paul A Genovese
9 W Shore Park Rd
Kingston NH 03848

Call Sign: N1RDB
Michael C Le Page
5 Wrights Rd
Kingston NH 03848

Call Sign: N1AUX
Michael C Lepage
5 Wrights Rd
Kingston NH 03848

Call Sign: N1WRN
Joy G Lepage
5 Wrights Rd
Kingston NH 03848

Call Sign: KB1PZT
Mia S Lepage
5 Wrights Rd
Kingston NH 03848

Call Sign: N1MSL
Mia S Lepage

5 Wrights Rd
Kingston NH 03848

Call Sign: N1QWG
Peter A Southwick
Kingston NH 03848

Call Sign: WB1ENQ
Edwin G Warrington
Kingston NH 03848

Call Sign: KB1INL
Gary M Avery
Kingston NH 03848

## FCC Amateur Radio Licenses in Lacaster

Call Sign: KB1CRZ
Carlos Silva
34 Prospect St
Lacaster NH 03584

## FCC Amateur Radio Licenses in Laconia

Call Sign: KB1RJW
Patience E Hathaway
72 Anthony Dr
Laconia NH 03246

Call Sign: KB1FBP
Edward L Ohearn Jr
73 Ashley Dr
Laconda NH 03246

Call Sign: WB1ELT
Barry E Salway
214 Belvidere St
Laconia NH 03246

Call Sign: AA1YI
Barry E Salway
214 Belvidere St
Laconia NH 03246

Call Sign: WA1TVP
Andrew C Nuttle
Bh 11
Laconia NH 03246

Call Sign: W1GFC
Robert J Gilson
13 Birchwood Way
Laconia NH 03246

Call Sign: N1BVI
Robert D Berry
154 Blueberry Ln Apt 7
Laconia NH 03246

Call Sign: W1EDW
Thomas S Edwards Iii
40 Cherry St
Laconia NH 03246

Call Sign: KA1OLT
Harold N Kelley
24 Chester Ct
Laconia NH 03246

Call Sign: WB2TFY
Ruth D Thistle
17 Colonial Rd
Laconia NH 03246

Call Sign: WB2TGB
Robert S Thistle
17 Colonial Rd
Laconia NH 03246

Call Sign: K1VSS
Roger J Landry
22 Cottonwood Ave
Laconia NH 03246

Call Sign: N1NLY
Robert M Whittemore
77 Court St
Laconia NH 03246

Call Sign: N1UXI
Linda R Boisoneault
77 Eastmun Rd
Laconia NH 03246

Call Sign: KA1YLD
Richard E Kallum
41 Elm St
Laconia NH 03246

Call Sign: N1SZK
Robert A Cunningham
398 Elm St
Laconia NH 03246

Call Sign: N1RVI
Armand T Tardif
9 Emerald Dr
Laconia NH 03246

Call Sign: K1IZM
Fred T Davidson
11 Fern Lane
Laconia NH 032464087

Call Sign: K1OMC
Robert A Woodman
35 Fore St
Laconia NH 03246

Call Sign: KB1RZN
Adam J Smith
117 Franklin St
Laconia NH 03246

Call Sign: KB1GQU
Gertrude Marshall
21 Gilbert St
Laconia NH 03246

Call Sign: KB1GQT
John A Marshall
21 Gilbert St.
Laconia NH 03246

Call Sign: KB1RZT
Andrew D Groleau
14 Gillette St
Laconia NH 03246

Call Sign: WA1DHL
Horace T Bradford
59 Harvard St
Laconia NH 032463056

Call Sign: KB1ESH
Thomas E Laflamme
378 Hillcrest Dr
Laconia NH 03246

Call Sign: KB1VVP
Michael L Wheeler
281 Holman St
Laconia NH 03246

Call Sign: N1QXH
Warren C Sommers
319 Holman St
Laconia NH 03246

Call Sign: N1JAA
Michael A Swancott
Howard St
Laconia NH 03246

Call Sign: KB1JWB
Michael T Smith
54 Jackson St
Laconia NH 03246

Call Sign: KB1RKS
Linda M Sarette
14 Kensington Dr
Laconia NH 03246

Call Sign: KB1RKT
Douglas A Sarette
14 Kensington Dr
Laconia NH 03246

Call Sign: N1LT
Richard P Christopher
38 Kensington Dr
Laconia NH 03246

Call Sign: N1PKG
Mary E Christopher
38 Kensington Dr
Laconia NH 03246

Call Sign: W1CNH
Central New Hampshire
Amateur Radio Club
38 Kensington Dr
Laconia NH 03246

Call Sign: W1JY
Central New Hampshire
Amateur Radio Club
38 Kensington Dr
Laconia NH 03246

Call Sign: N1MAY
Louis A Laverdure
17 Kinsman Dr
Laconia NH 032462591

Call Sign: N4GUM
Evelyn L Hughes
29 Kinsman Dr
Laconia NH 03246

Call Sign: KB1QLU
Michael R Fecteau
89 Lafayette St
Laconia NH 03246

Call Sign: KB1RZL
Katheryn C Fecteau
89 Lafayette St
Laconia NH 03246

Call Sign: N1KFS
Margaret A Dare

2 Ledgecroft Pl
Laconia NH 03246

74 North
Laconia NH 03246

20 Pine Brook Ln
Laconia NH 03246

Call Sign: W1FWQ
George A Davison
5 Ledgecroft Pl
Laconia NH 03246

Call Sign: KB1RKX
Nicholas Shastany
133 North St
Laconia NH 03246

Call Sign: W1DBS
David B Stamps
20 Pine Brook Ln
Laconia NH 03246

Call Sign: KB1IYD
Francis C Morrill
17 Marshall Ct
Laconia NH 03246

Call Sign: KB1RKY
Michael A Shastany
133 North St
Laconia NH 03246

Call Sign: AA1NZ
Thomas L Bates
459 Province Rd
Laconia NH 03246

Call Sign: KA1TUN
Mark A Carwell
35 Marshall Ct
Laconia NH 03246

Call Sign: KB1POX
Ernest R Boisvert
171 North St
Laconia NH 03246

Call Sign: N1XDE
Andy A Bates
459 Province Rd
Laconia NH 03246

Call Sign: N1LHU
Carolyn A Carwell
35 Marshall Ct
Laconia NH 03246

Call Sign: N1ZGL
Megan M Schmucker
194 North St
Laconia NH 03246

Call Sign: KB1RZP
Casey R Walker
52 Province St
Laconia NH 03246

Call Sign: N1SFQ
Eric D Fabian
846 Meredith Center Rd
Laconia NH 03246

Call Sign: K1KM
Ralph J Rosen
1496 Old North Main St
Laconia NH 03246

Call Sign: KA1UDL
Herbert F Stover
350 Shore Dr
Laconia NH 03246

Call Sign: WB1HLG
Fred H Fabian Jr
846 Meredith Center Rd
Laconia NH 03246

Call Sign: KB1VVL
Jennifer A Muzzey
1480 Old North Main St 20
Laconia NH 03246

Call Sign: KA1HHK
Max W K Rothemund
578 Shore Dr
Laconia NH 03246

Call Sign: KA1VIK
Erik M Balfe
380 Mile Hill Rd 23
Laconia NH 03246

Call Sign: KB1RZW
Steven R Bohrer
38 Parker St
Laconia NH 03246

Call Sign: KA1HHL
Judith A Rothemund
578 Shore Dr
Laconia NH 03246

Call Sign: W1ETX
Frank W Martines
155 Morningside Dr
Laconia NH 032462653

Call Sign: W1KRZ
Warren P Ray Jr
212 Paugus Park Rd
Laconia NH 03246

Call Sign: KB1RZR
David R Jorgensen
41 Spruce St
Laconia NH 03246

Call Sign: K1OIZ
William J Thrippleton

Call Sign: KB1QHE
David B Stamps

Call Sign: N1CRZ
James D Robinton

43 Sterling Dr
Laconia NH 03246

Call Sign: KB1AVM
Clark S Metivier
17 Summer St
Laconia NH 032463132

Call Sign: KB1GQQ
Sylvia Metivier
17 Summer St
Laconia NH 03246

Call Sign: N1XBE
Clark S Metivier
19 Summer St
Laconia NH 03246

Call Sign: KB1RKP
Amy N Beaudoin
25 Taylor St
Laconia NH 03246

Call Sign: KB1EX
Guy M Arnold
5 The Meadows
Laconia NH 03246

Call Sign: KB1VXD
Christopher B Reynolds
33 Tilton Ave
Laconia NH 03246

Call Sign: KA1DWV
John W Lodge
25 Union Ave
Laconia NH 032463510

Call Sign: KB1RSP
Boy Scout Amateur Radio
Club 68
291 Union Ave
Laconia NH 03246

Call Sign: W1YHE

Haven L Foote
25 Union Ave Apt 701
Laconia NH 03246

Call Sign: KB0ASK
Kevin L Winslow Mr
765 Union Ave.  Apt. 501
Laconia NH 03246

Call Sign: N1FSU
Brenda J Schmucker
30 Walker St
Laconia NH 03246

Call Sign: N1NYH
Charles H Mc Allister
79 Warren St
Laconia NH 03246

Call Sign: N1NYI
William D Mc Allister Jr
79 Warren St
Laconia NH 03246

Call Sign: N1PZQ
Jennifer K Mc Allister
79 Warren St
Laconia NH 03246

Call Sign: N1WYT
William D Mc Allister
79 Warren St
Laconia NH 03246

Call Sign: KB1RZY
Norma J Mcallister
79 Warren St
Laconia NH 03246

Call Sign: KB1RZO
Benjamin R Mitchell
20 Webster St
Laconia NH 03246

Call Sign: N1WXR

Philip J Kerr
547 Weirs Blvd
Laconia NH 03246

Call Sign: KB1UJC
Genaro S Pingol Jr
257 Weirs Blvd 13
Laconia NH 03246

Call Sign: KB1FBO
Kimberly A Green
11 West St Apt 2
Laconia NH 03246

Call Sign: KB1BPK
Bruce S Colbath
58 Whipple Ave
Laconia NH 032463348

Call Sign: W1PJU
Gordon W Boutilier
73 Wildwood Rd
Laconia NH 03246

Call Sign: N1RVH
Thomas A Tardif
121 Winter St
Laconia NH 03246

Call Sign: KB1RKR
Nicholas F Callaghan
169 Winter St
Laconia NH 03246

Call Sign: KQ1Z
Paul G Patterson
Laconia NH 032476067

Call Sign: N1JJW
Ronald A Baker Iii
Laconia NH 03247

Call Sign: N1ZHY
Wanda K Durst
Laconia NH 03247

Call Sign: N1ZXD
Andrew D Johnson
Laconia NH 03247

Call Sign: W1ALX
Walter F Alden
Laconia NH 03247

Call Sign: W1JNG
Thomas S Edwards Jr
Laconia NH 03247

Call Sign: W1CEN
Central Nhares Club
Laconia NH 03247

Call Sign: KB1RZU
Janet V Payne
Laconia NH 03247

Call Sign: KB1UIZ
Craig F Devlin
Laconia NH 03247

## FCC Amateur Radio Licenses in Lakeport

Call Sign: KB1GQP
Jack H Severance
126 Washington St
Lakeport NH 03246

## FCC Amateur Radio Licenses in Lancaster

Call Sign: KB1MDD
Edward I Sanders
36 Bunker Hill St
Lancaster NH 03584

Call Sign: K1UQD
George E Nugent
77 Bunker Hill St
Lancaster NH 03584

Call Sign: N1OSK
Louise Force
12 Cottage St
Lancaster NH 03584

Call Sign: WB1ASL
Richard C Force
12 Cottage St
Lancaster NH 03584

Call Sign: N1XSR
Cheryl A La Bonte
10 Elm St
Lancaster NH 03584

Call Sign: KB1KDC
Frister Van Bergen
33 Elm St
Lancaster NH 03584

Call Sign: KB1SKY
Andrew J Buteau
33 Elm St
Lancaster NH 03584

Call Sign: KA1TNP
David O Falkenham
59 Elm St
Lancaster NH 03584

Call Sign: N1ROD
Steven P Jones
122 Elm St
Lancaster NH 03584

Call Sign: KB1TTG
David B Richter
130 Elm St
Lancaster NH 03584

Call Sign: N1YZH
Jean A Janney
29 Fletcher St
Lancaster NH 03584

Call Sign: N1PT
David F Haas
8 Grove St
Lancaster NH 03584

Call Sign: W1BFJ
John F Bean
1219 Lancaster Rd
Lancaster NH 03584

Call Sign: N1YZF
John E Plunkett
134 Lost Nation Rd
Lancaster NH 03584

Call Sign: N1XIS
Robert F Wilson
558 Lost Nation Rd
Lancaster NH 03584

Call Sign: KB1CCK
Richard A Sargent
Lost Nation Rd
Lancaster NH 03584

Call Sign: KB1RTN
Jesse M White
65 Main St
Lancaster NH 03584

Call Sign: W1YFL
Richard G Emmons
37 Portland St
Lancaster NH 03584

Call Sign: N1ZUN
David M Phillips
S Lancaster Rd
Lancaster NH 03584

Call Sign: W1YCZ
Daniel J Truland
25 Summer St
Lancaster NH 03584

Call Sign: N1UZA
Eduard L Labonte
45 Summer St
Lancaster NH 03584

Call Sign: WA1ED
Eduard L Labonte
45 Summer St
Lancaster NH 03584

Call Sign: WB2LJW
Anthony J Goceliak
Lancaster NH 035840544

Call Sign: KB1VNC
Brent D Field
Lancaster NH 03584

**FCC Amateur Radio
Licenses in Lebanon**

Call Sign: KE1LF
Wallace M Kimura
241 Bank St Ext
Lebanon NH 03766

Call Sign: KI6OKQ
Jin Young Park
4 Cedarwood Ln Apt 205
Lebanon NH 03766

Call Sign: N1PWR
Dominic J Coloutti Jr
46 Church St
Lebanon NH 03766

Call Sign: N1CVJ
Mark M Nunlist
20 Dorset Ln
Lebanon NH 03766

Call Sign: KB1VUN
Eric W Hansen
44 Dunsinane Dr

Lebanon NH 03766

Call Sign: N1SLZ
Nancy T Morley
6 Garnet St
Lebanon NH 03766

Call Sign: W1YJD
David P Morley
6 Garnet St
Lebanon NH 03766

Call Sign: WA1TLN
Russell A Mc Allister
40 Hardy Hill Rd
Lebanon NH 03766

Call Sign: KB1RSW
Charles D Young
3 High St
Lebanon NH 03766

Call Sign: KA1CRP
David E Landry
4 Jefferson Pl
Lebanon NH 03766

Call Sign: WA1PGW
Timothy M Brewer
Liberty Ln
Lebanon NH 03766

Call Sign: W1YGA
Charles M Harrington
121 Mascoma St 4
Lebanon NH 03766

Call Sign: N2ESV
William B Martin Jr
121 Mascoma St Apt 113
Lebanon NH 03766

Call Sign: W1USK
Richard S Guyer
8 Melrose St

Lebanon NH 037660444

Call Sign: WA1JOP
Edward L Hirsch
Meriden Rd
Lebanon NH 03766

Call Sign: K1HH
Alexander A Mc Donald
Methodist Hill
Lebanon NH 03766

Call Sign: KB1KEQ
Charles A Freeman
29 Morse Rd
Lebanon NH 037662325

Call Sign: K1QE
Charles A Freeman
29 Morse Rd
Lebanon NH 037662325

Call Sign: K1DL
Richard H Lang
43 Nottingham Cir
Lebanon NH 03766

Call Sign: KA1WDX
Howard M Green
20 Pine St
Lebanon NH 03766

Call Sign: W1GN
David Littlewood
241 Poverty Ln Apt 4
Lebanon NH 03766

Call Sign: WD4HCD
Mary B Davis
54 Renihan Meadows
Lebanon NH 03766

Call Sign: N1ZDV
Peter J Nestler
31 Wellington Cir

Lebanon NH 03766

Call Sign: KB1MRB
Parker D Sorenson
97 Wellington Cir
Lebanon NH 03766

Call Sign: KB1NWI
Michael H Nestler
31 Wellington Circle
Lebanon NH 03766

Call Sign: KB1NWJ
Elizabeth A Nestler
31 Wellington Circle
Lebanon NH 03766

Call Sign: WB9MHI
Dean C Sorenson
97 Wellington Circle
Lebanon NH 03766

Call Sign: WC1W
Dean C Sorenson
97 Wellington Circle
Lebanon NH 03766

Call Sign: KB1QEJ
Michael A Kokko
5 Wheatley St
Lebanon NH 03766

Call Sign: N1RGG
Laurel S Letter
84 Young St
Lebanon NH 03766

Call Sign: WA1PFK
Sidney S Letter
84 Young St
Lebanon NH 03766

Call Sign: KB1SKQ
Lisa-Ann Larson
Lebanon NH 03766

## FCC Amateur Radio Licenses in Lee

Call Sign: N1DRX
Richard T Mikoloski
13 Allen Ave
Lee NH 03824

Call Sign: N1IOX
Seamus E Casey
62 Calef Highway #119
Lee NH 03861

Call Sign: N2ZUZ
Dana A Partis
592 Calef Hwy
Lee NH 03824

Call Sign: N1PMN
Robert J Horton
Duff Thompson Lane
Lee NH 03824

Call Sign: WA1MNZ
Dennis R Blidberg
8 Earle Dr
Lee NH 03824

Call Sign: K4KGZ
Robert S Munger Jr
45 High Rd
Lee NH 03824

Call Sign: KR1C
Steven P Longworth
1 Mast Rd
Lee NH 03861

Call Sign: W1KBP
Herbert M Craddock
206 N River Rd
Lee NH 03824

Call Sign: KB1IVR

Linda A Parkhurst
83 Pine Knoll Village
Lee NH 03824

Call Sign: N1YOF
Emily L Parkhurst
83 Pine Knoll Villiage
Lee NH 03824

Call Sign: N1WLD
Wayne D Parkhurst
83 Pine Knoll Vlg
Lee NH 03824

Call Sign: W1OKU
Henry B Hagman
9 Pinecrest Estates
Lee NH 038246735

Call Sign: WA7DET
Thomas K Smith
4 Plumer Ln
Lee NH 038246210

Call Sign: N9NC
Thomas F Poland
6 Radford Dr
Lee NH 03861

Call Sign: KE1FQ
Richard L Messeder
Riverside Farm Dr
Lee NH 038616215

Call Sign: KB1NVR
Andras K Fekete
47 Sheep Rd
Lee NH 03824

Call Sign: N1ZGE
Gilbert L Chase Jr
186 Stepping Stone Rd
Lee NH 038246611

Call Sign: N1GXQ

James M Minor
142 Stepping Stones Rd
Unit 1
Lee NH 03861

Call Sign: KA1DCB
William A George
36 Tamarack Rd
Lee NH 03861

Call Sign: N1IWP
Scott K Pittroff
80 Turtle Pond Rd
Lee NH 03861

Call Sign: NE1EE
Richard L Messeder
147 Wadleigh Falls Rd
Lee NH 038616223

Call Sign: KB1PFX
George W Bryant Sr
3 Whittier Ln
Lee NH 03861

Call Sign: KA1VFV
Edward N Bruno
Box 4
Lempster NH 03606

Call Sign: KB1BIS
Tamara L Brown
Box 96b
Lempster NH 03606

Call Sign: N1STZ
Alan D Rauscher
24 Cutler Rd
Lempster NH 03605

Call Sign: KA1WEQ
Zachary B Tirrell

699 Dodge Hollow Rd
Lempster NH 03605

Call Sign: KA1WEO
Erica L Lake
General Delivery 11
Lempster NH 03606

Call Sign: KB1EFX
Autumn N Murray
377 Hurd Rd
Lempster NH 03605

Call Sign: KA1WEP
Rikki L Shepard
Lempster St
Lempster NH 03606

Call Sign: KB1CYZ
Timothy A Whitman
Rt 10
Lempster NH 03605

Call Sign: KB1FKA
Seth J Roberts
28 Second Nh Tplk
Lempster NH 03605

Call Sign: N1JOZ
Mary B Woloschuk
53 Unity Springs Rd
Lempster NH 036053130

Call Sign: K1THC
Bruce L Cragin
1357 Us Rte 10
Lempster NH 03605

Call Sign: KA1VCY
Jerri S Bruno
Lempster NH 03605

Call Sign: KA1VYH
Brandon E Kirk
Lempster NH 03605

Call Sign: KB1FKC
Isaiah B Whitman
Lempster NH 03605

Call Sign: KB1RDC
Geoff N Clark
Lempster NH 03605

Call Sign: KB1UFL
Charles F Easterly
Lempster NH 03605

Call Sign: WA1GJG
Glen A Parker
Us Rt 3
Lincoln NH 03251

Call Sign: KB1ENP
Donald S Thompson
Lincoln NH 03251

Call Sign: W1DST
Donald S Thompson
Lincoln NH 03251

Call Sign: N1QZS
Cheyenne T Greatorex
25 Bergin Ter
Lisbon NH 03585

Call Sign: N1YBH
James E Clark Jr
147 Dickinson St
Lisbon NH 035856205

Call Sign: KB1SLJ
Mary E Ruppert
319 Hurd Hill Rd

Lisbon NH 03585

Call Sign: N1TJX
Michael S Magwire Sr
431 Presby Rd
Lisbon NH 03585

Call Sign: WA1DPP
Robert J Howarth Jr
1930 Route 302
Lisbon NH 035857100

Call Sign: W1LJN
Leonard J Nyberg Jr
125 Savageville Rd
Lisbon NH 03585

Call Sign: N1ZGJ
David N Stiles
106 School St
Lisbon NH 03585

**FCC Amateur Radio
Licenses in Litchfield**

Call Sign: KB1TEK
Haralambos Syrstatides
29 Aldrich St
Litchfield NH 03052

Call Sign: N1QXG
Elizabeth R Scofield
9 Amsterdam Cir
Litchfield NH 03051

Call Sign: N1NSD
Peter P Campbell
8 Bixby Rd
Litchfield NH 030522625

Call Sign: N1LHS
Kenneth F Acker
33 Blue Jay Way
Litchfield NH 03051

Call Sign: K1LYR
Richard Parr Jr
12 Carriage Rd
Litchfield NH 03052

Call Sign: KB1VAZ
Kenneth G Ux
28 Century Lane
Litchfield NH 03052

Call Sign: K1KUX
Kenneth G Ux
28 Century Lane
Litchfield NH 03052

Call Sign: N1GFT
John P Daigle
3 Century Ln
Litchfield NH 03103

Call Sign: N1MNH
Leo D Mc Killop
17 Century Ln
Litchfield NH 03103

Call Sign: KB1VXB
Eric L Sherwin
29 Century Ln
Litchfield NH 03052

Call Sign: KB1INZ
Dante J Abbene
25 Chatfield Dr
Litchfield NH 03052

Call Sign: WA0AFX
William L Parker
5 Concord Coach Lane
Litchfield NH 03052

Call Sign: N1WMW
Paul R Ellis
12 Corning Rd
Litchfield NH 03052

Call Sign: W1HAY
Francis J Repko
12 Forest Ln
Litchfield NH 03052

Call Sign: N1VQW
Mark Pilant
15 Foxwood Ln
Litchfield NH 03052

Call Sign: KB1EON
Theresa A Kelley
15 Foxwood Ln
Litchfield NH 03052

Call Sign: KB1EOO
Adam S Pilant
15 Foxwood Ln
Litchfield NH 03052

Call Sign: K9PPL
Theresa A Kelley
15 Foxwood Ln
Litchfield NH 03052

Call Sign: KC1YP
Roberto L Landrau Jr
5 Josiah Dr
Litchfield NH 03052

Call Sign: N1EN
Roberto L Landrau Jr
5 Josiah Dr
Litchfield NH 03052

Call Sign: KB1LDM
Dave S Pflaum
7 Masquah Dr
Litchfield NH 030522412

Call Sign: KA1KGH
Charles J Purwin
5 Mc Questen
Litchfield NH 03052

Call Sign: N1DDH
Horace W Seymour Iii
13 Mike Ln
Litchfield NH 03052

Call Sign: KB1OCC
Brian M Mccue
11 Newstead St
Litchfield NH 03052

Call Sign: N1DDF
Richard J L Quinn
6 Nightingale Ln
Litchfield NH 03051

Call Sign: N1BWO
John Manning Jr
7 Oak Dr
Litchfield NH 03052

Call Sign: N1AKS
Donald L Clark
14 Old Stage Rd
Litchfield NH 030522364

Call Sign: N1KRA
Ralph E Howe Jr
31 Page Rd
Litchfield NH 03051

Call Sign: N1RKF
James E Gilbertson
145 Page Rd
Litchfield NH 03052

Call Sign: N1ANL
Bernard F Biron
77 Pinecrest Rd
Litchfield NH 030522334

Call Sign: WV1G
Carl P Kimball
14 Reid Lane
Litchfield NH 030521084

Call Sign: KB1PKE
David W Franklin
16 Roberts Rd
Litchfield NH 03052

Call Sign: WA1MOY
Wayne A Auger
19 Roberts Rd
Litchfield NH 03052

Call Sign: WB3HYD
Harry P Mc Kasson Jr
7 Rocky Hill Dr
Litchfield NH 03051

Call Sign: KB1GKN
Russell T Blanchette
3 Sata Way
Litchfield NH 03052

Call Sign: N1XEW
Stephen J Bazzocchi
16 Steven Way
Litchfield NH 03052

Call Sign: KE1EV
Richard E Carter Jr
74 Talent Rd
Litchfield NH 03052

Call Sign: KB1FZK
Joann L Carter
74 Talent Rd
Litchfield NH 03052

Call Sign: KB1FZL
Linda M Carter
74 Talent Rd
Litchfield NH 03052

Call Sign: N1RVF
Cheryl D Pecor
96 Talent Rd
Litchfield NH 03052

Call Sign: N1BKL
Robert H Baker
96 Talent Rd.
Litchfield NH 03052

Call Sign: KB1GQH
Ariana M Blanchette
8 Woodburn Dr 1
Litchfield NH 03052

Call Sign: KA1QBN
Anne Galimi
13 Woodburn Rd
Litchfield NH 03051

Call Sign: KA1QBO
Joseph J Galimi
13 Woodburn Rd
Litchfield NH 03052

Call Sign: W1TA
Nashua Mike & Key Club
13 Woodburn Rd
Litchfield NH 03051

Call Sign: KA1LGO
Mary L Jean
Woodburn Rd
Litchfield NH 03052

## FCC Amateur Radio Licenses in Littleton

Call Sign: N1OUM
Judith A Donovan
Bethlehem Rd
Littleton NH 03561

Call Sign: N1XED
Richard M Wiggin
90 Bishop St
Littleton NH 03561

Call Sign: N1QWD
Timothy J Crowan

Box 208
Littleton NH 03561

131 Grove St
Littleton NH 03561

1 Manns Hill Rd
Littleton NH 03561

Call Sign: KU1D
Harry C Mc Dade
Box 314
Littleton NH 03561

Call Sign: KA2TYO
Mary H Menzies
40 Hatch Brook Ln
Littleton NH 035615511

Call Sign: KA1RVU
William H Gilmore
Manns Hill Rd
Littleton NH 03561

Call Sign: N1JJV
David J Laflamme
Box 331
Littleton NH 03561

Call Sign: WA2PXX
Douglas M Menzies
40 Hatch Brook Ln
Littleton NH 035615511

Call Sign: KA1DSD
Theodore P Mc Dade
Manns Hill Rd
Littleton NH 03561

Call Sign: N1KQK
Rick J Pineo
17 Bronson St
Littleton NH 03561

Call Sign: WB1HLE
Edwin F Estle
40 Herbert Ln
Littleton NH 035619518

Call Sign: KA1DSB
Phyllis E Rogers
40 Maple St
Littleton NH 03561

Call Sign: KB1CJL
Thomas B Merritt
19 Church St
Littleton NH 035610516

Call Sign: KB1TTH
Robert D Decker
274 Hilltop Rd
Littleton NH 03561

Call Sign: KC8MID
Donald R Wogaman
1178 Monroe Rd
Littleton NH 035613013

Call Sign: W8HIF
Thomas B Merritt
19 Church St
Littleton NH 035610516

Call Sign: KB1CE
Michael T Dinardo
793 Hilltop Rd
Littleton NH 03561

Call Sign: KB1NDV
Dierdre E Wogaman
1178 Monroe Rd
Littleton NH 03561

Call Sign: W1TAC
Leo Labonte
54 Fairview St
Littleton NH 03561

Call Sign: KA1YAH
Robert L Haley
72 Joe Lahout Ln Apt 43
Littleton NH 03561

Call Sign: N1LEN
Vincent A Satinsky
Mt Eustis Rd
Littleton NH 03561

Call Sign: K1WGO
Robert J Koczur
403 Grandview Rd
Littleton NH 03561

Call Sign: W1NMM
Armand R Pageau
70 Kilburn St
Littleton NH 03561

Call Sign: N1IMC
Thomas C Berry
29 N Fairview St
Littleton NH 03561

Call Sign: N1IMD
Michael S Thompson
131 Grove St
Littleton NH 03561

Call Sign: KA1FJD
Royce A Haskell
77 Kilburn St
Littleton NH 03561

Call Sign: N1RCC
Timothy J Cronan
Old Franconia Rd
Littleton NH 03561

Call Sign: KU1D
Michael S Thompson

Call Sign: KA1SIF
Emelyn S Gilmore

Call Sign: N1YCA
Andrew D Belmore

153 Old Partridge Lake Rd
Littleton NH 03561

Call Sign: N1SWC
Barbara L Kirkland
Partridge Lake
Littleton NH 03561

Call Sign: KA1RUA
Robert E Kirkland
406 Partridge Lake Rd
Littleton NH 03561

Call Sign: N2EHZ
Patricia L Jansen
10 Pest House Rd
Littleton NH 03561

Call Sign: N1JHZ
Robert C Black
268 Pleasant St
Littleton NH 03561

Call Sign: N1WNP
Thomas J Black
Pleasant St
Littleton NH 03561

Call Sign: KB1RXL
Gail J Perkins
349 Railroad St
Littleton NH 03561

Call Sign: KB1GNY
William N Clewes
141 Riverview
Littleton NH 03561

Call Sign: K1EME
Gloria J Sencabaugh
343 South St
Littleton NH 03561

Call Sign: K1UAQ
William A Sencabaugh

343 South St
Littleton NH 03561

Call Sign: KB1NXU
Littleton Amateur Radio
Club
343 South St
Littleton NH 03561

Call Sign: K1EME
Littleton Amateur Radio
Club
343 South St
Littleton NH 03561

Call Sign: N1MTK
Annette L Hicks
453 South St
Littleton NH 03561

Call Sign: N1IDV
James S La Rose
77 St. Johnsbury Rd.
Littleton NH 03561

Call Sign: KI2J
Michael E Dow
59 Tuck Ln
Littleton NH 035614517

Call Sign: N1JHX
Fred S Hibbard
91 Tuck Ln
Littleton NH 03561

Call Sign: N1SHP
Lillian M Rayno
215 Washington St
Littleton NH 03561

Call Sign: WG1X
Robert L Rayno
215 Washington St
Littleton NH 03561

Call Sign: K1HR
Lyle E Bulis
Littleton NH 03561

Call Sign: KA1FGL
Clarence W Sleeper Jr
Littleton NH 03561

Call Sign: N1KQL
Brian T Bulis
Littleton NH 03561

Call Sign: WB1DVD
Gilbert E Donovan Sr
Littleton NH 03561

Call Sign: N1IMD
Michael S Thompson
Littleton NH 03561

Call Sign: W1US
Michael S Thompson
Littleton NH 03561

## FCC Amateur Radio Licenses in Lochmere

Call Sign: KB1UIX
Paul Boudreau
39 River Rd
Lochmere NH 03252

## FCC Amateur Radio Licenses in Londonbery

Call Sign: KA1HVH
Richard M Desmarais
17 Longwood Ave
Londonberry NH 03053

Call Sign: KB1WIH
Donald C Levesque Iii
526 A Mamoth Rd
Londonderry NH 03053

Call Sign: KB1QHW
Brian P Crowley
15 Acropolis Ave
Londonderry NH 03053

Call Sign: W1RRR
Brian P Crowley
15 Acropolis Ave
Londonderry NH 03053

Call Sign: KB1ULJ
Jose A Sosa Sr
90 Adams Rd
Londonderry NH 03053

Call Sign: N1OUY
Joseph E Arcidiacono
17 Alexander Rd Rfd 8
Londonderry NH 03053

Call Sign: KB1KIG
Eugene S Jastrem
19 Anderson Circle
Londonderry NH 03053

Call Sign: KB1WAV
Eric T Smith
9 Anthony Dr
Londonderry NH 03053

Call Sign: N1ASZ
David L Critchley
13 Apple Blossom Dr
Londonderry NH 03053

Call Sign: N1KEO
Sandra D Critchley
13 Apple Blossom Dr
Londonderry NH 03053

Call Sign: N1UZT
Harold J Morrissette Jr
20 Ash St
Londonderry NH 03053

Call Sign: N1HJM
Harold J Morrissette Jr
20 Ash St
Londonderry NH 03053

Call Sign: KB1PYC
Jason R Caldon
10 Auburn Rd
Londonderry NH 03053

Call Sign: KB1SGT
Joanne M Paradis
55 Auburn Rd
Londonderry NH 03053

Call Sign: KB1SBQ
Ken W Fongeallaz
89 Auburn Rd
Londonderry NH 03053

Call Sign: N1MVH
Douglas V Thompson Sr
Auburn Rd
Londonderry NH 03053

Call Sign: WD8DZH
Michael A Schroeder
71 Auburn Rd Rfd 1
Londonderry NH 03053

Call Sign: N1KTO
Bill M Steinhart
4 Baldwin Rd
Londonderry NH 03053

Call Sign: KB1FJU
Chad L Council
37 Bancroft Rd
Londonderry NH 03053

Call Sign: KA1UQH
Reginald H Silver
27 Bartley Hill Rd
Londonderry NH 03053

Call Sign: N1TRX
Charles A Barbeau
44 Bartley Hill Rd
Londonderry NH 03053

Call Sign: WI1E
John Paul J Hagerty
54 Bartley Hill Rd
Londonderry NH
030532424

Call Sign: KB1HSC
Henry J Fackovec
23 Beacon St
Londonderry NH 03053

Call Sign: K1YMH
Andre A Morneau
21 Bockes Rd
Londonderry NH 03053

Call Sign: N1FDA
Roger B Higgins
Box 151
Londonderry NH 03053

Call Sign: N1VRW
Ryan C Boda
Buttrick Rd
Londonderry NH 03053

Call Sign: N1WWR
John R Mac Donald
8 Carousel Court
Londonderry NH 03053

Call Sign: KJ1RE
Sydney L Stenger
2 Carousel Ct
Londonderry NH 03053

Call Sign: KB1FZT
Luis E Aguilar
6 Carousel Ct
Londonderry NH 03053

Call Sign: AA1XW
Luis E Aguilar
6 Carousel Ct
Londonderry NH 03053

Call Sign: KN1W
Luis E Aguilar
6 Carousel Ct
Londonderry NH 03053

Call Sign: KG5CE
Sydney L Stenger
2 Carousel Ct.
Londonderry NH 03053

Call Sign: KE1LZ
Sydney L Stenger
2 Carousel Ct.
Londonderry NH 03053

Call Sign: KA1KRK
Steven M Inza Sr
20 Chestnut Hill Dr
Londonderry NH 03053

Call Sign: KB1MSB
Steven M Inza
20 Chestnuthill Dr
Londonderry NH 03053

Call Sign: K5ECR
Brandon C Wilson
Cohas Terrace
Londonderry NH 03053

Call Sign: KB1VFX
Alexander Apostol
34 Colonial Dr
Londonderry NH 03053

Call Sign: KD7FQK
Thomas C Arnold
5 Columbia Dr
Londonderry NH 03053

Call Sign: K1FWE
John S Webster
4 Connors St
Londonderry NH 03053

Call Sign: KB1MXB
John P Matuszewski
5 Cortland St
Londonderry NH 03053

Call Sign: KB1APU
Gregory G Vogel
15 Cortland St
Londonderry NH 03053

Call Sign: WA3TBG
Bradford W Thomas
5 Danbury Court
Londonderry NH 03053

Call Sign: K1JC
Joseph A Ciarcia
3 Darrow Way
Londonderry NH 03053

Call Sign: KA1VNF
Timothy E Hennessy
6 Davis Dr
Londonderry NH 03053

Call Sign: N1BPO
Gary N Stapleford
28 Devonshire Ln
Londonderry NH 03053

Call Sign: KD1EX
William L Clark Jr
1 Dresden Way
Londonderry NH 03053

Call Sign: KB1EOK
Wayne A Hall
5 East Eglin Blvd
Londonderry NH 03053

Call Sign: KE4QEO
Karen L S Robinson
13 Elwood Rd
Londonderry NH
030533129

Call Sign: W1NEB
John E Robinson
13 Elwood Rd
Londonderry NH
030533129

Call Sign: WA1PFI
John S Welch
27 Elwood Rd
Londonderry NH 03053

Call Sign: W1TOA
Wayne M Lambert
2 Evergreen Circle
Londonderry NH 03053

Call Sign: K1DCI
Irwin E Swain
5 Fairway Rd
Londonderry NH 03053

Call Sign: KB1SJO
Kristie J Sweeney
148 Fieldstone Dr
Londonderry NH 03053

Call Sign: N1RKT
Tracy S Walters
17 Grenier Blvd.
Londonderry NH 03053

Call Sign: N1NUM
Robert E Pepper
32 Hall Rd
Londonderry NH 03053

Call Sign: N1CHI
Ruby Smith

92 Hall Rd
Londonderry NH 03053

Call Sign: N1CJW
Wesley Smith
92 Hall Rd
Londonderry NH 03053

Call Sign: KB1MTB
Roger W Fillio
3 Hampshire Ln
Londonderry NH 03053

Call Sign: KB1LHC
Adam F Hollows
4 Hardy Rd
Londonderry NH 03053

Call Sign: N1XHP
Robert J Pizani Jr
3 Harmony Dr
Londonderry NH 03053

Call Sign: N1IFL
James J Bowes
16 Harvey Rd
Londonderry NH 03053

Call Sign: KA1TSK
James A Sucke
237 High Range
Londonderry NH 03053

Call Sign: WA1HUM
Dana G Tremblay
216 High Range Rd
Londonderry NH 03053

Call Sign: KB1RWV
J Alden Benson Ii
6 Hillcrest Lane
Londonderry NH 03053

Call Sign: KB1VOB
Sylvia F Benson

6 Hillcrest Ln
Londonderry NH 03053

Call Sign: KB1MAU
Paul Dimarco
30 Holstein Ave
Londonderry NH 03053

Call Sign: WA1SVU
Scott W Saunders
4 Homestead Ln
Londonderry NH 03053

Call Sign: N1LFR
Eugene S Jastrem 3rd
19 Horseshoe Lane
Londonderry NH 03053

Call Sign: KB1RGG
Paul A Bocchiaro
78 Hovey Rd
Londonderry NH 03053

Call Sign: KB1FWT
George M Bahan
124 Hovey Rd
Londonderry NH 03053

Call Sign: N6RTY
Richard L Ouellette
4 Hunter Blvd Box 83
Londonderry NH 03053

Call Sign: N1SJH
Denise M O Kula
9 Jay Dr
Londonderry NH 03053

Call Sign: N3CLZ
Gary A Okula
9 Jay Dr
Londonderry NH 03053

Call Sign: WB1BQE
Albert M Lawler Jr

2 Jersey St
Londonderry NH 03053

Call Sign: KB1AUE
Jean M Gabaree
2 Jersey St
Londonderry NH 03053

Call Sign: KA1LAT
Peter V Reilley
20 King Arthur Dr
Londonderry NH 03053

Call Sign: KA1ZCU
David J Aubin
2 King Charles Dr
Londonderry NH 03053

Call Sign: WA2PMY
Thomas P Grodt
5 King Henry Dr
Londonderry NH 03053

Call Sign: KA1KGI
Janusz K Purwin
18 King John Dr
Londonderry NH 03053

Call Sign: N1SJL
Laurel B Bookman
8 King Phillip Dr
Londonderry NH 03053

Call Sign: KA1FRD
William L Robertson
6 King Richard Dr
Londonderry NH 03053

Call Sign: KB1NMF
Robert P Agusto
13 King Richard Dr
Londonderry NH 03053

Call Sign: NE1H
Robert P Agusto

13 King Richard Dr
Londonderry NH 03053

13 Lexington Ave
Londonderry NH 03053

6 Meetinghouse Dr
Londonderry NH 03053

Call Sign: KB1RCE
Kimberly A Agusto
13 King Richard Dr
Londonderry NH 03053

Call Sign: KA1WIO
Richard A Cardner
24 Litchfield Rd
Londonderry NH 03053

Call Sign: K1DDE
Shelby L Gregg
6 Meetinghouse Dr
Londonderry NH 03053

Call Sign: KB1RCL
Alexander R Agusto
13 King Richard Dr
Londonderry NH 03053

Call Sign: K1ENG
Richard M Desmarais
17 Longwood Ave
Londonderry NH 03053

Call Sign: K1COF
Stephen D Ham
12 Mill Rd
Londonderry NH 03053

Call Sign: WA1HBI
David G Mahoney
5 Lafayette Rd
Londonderry NH 03053

Call Sign: KB1VDN
Kathleen M Brissenden
16 Mallard Ln
Londonderry NH 03053

Call Sign: N1ZSM
David L Colglazier
6 Moulton Dr
Londonderry NH 03053

Call Sign: KB1WLD
Nicholas Robinson
3 Larch Ln
Londonderry NH 03053

Call Sign: KA1YRU
James W Haggerty
45 Mammoth Rd
Londonderry NH 03053

Call Sign: N1YRL
Brian M Hassick
7 Moulton St
Londonderry NH 03053

Call Sign: KB1TPC
Michael A Pettergill Jr
3 Laurel Hill Rd
Londonderry NH 03053

Call Sign: W1GQ
Bruce E Jewett
125 Mammoth Rd
Londonderry NH 03053

Call Sign: KB1MAV
John W Pappas
7 Noonan Dr
Londonderry NH 03053

Call Sign: N1YYD
Andrew R Keller
39 Lawson Farm Rd
Londonderry NH 03053

Call Sign: N1TRJ
David A Noblet
8 Manasquan Cr
Londonderry NH 03053

Call Sign: WB1AIW
Linwood B Davis
38 Noyes Rd
Londonderry NH 03053

Call Sign: N1FZZ
Roger D Ritter
3 Leelynn Cir
Londonderry NH 03053

Call Sign: N1EMW
Charles D French
6 Maplewood Dr
Londonderry NH 03053

Call Sign: KB1LBO
Timothy J Moore
44 Old Derry Rd
Londonderry NH 03053

Call Sign: N1XEM
Russell C Lawson Jr
6 Leelynn Cir
Londonderry NH 03053

Call Sign: KB1RWU
Richard P Semaski
5 Mckinley Ave
Londonderry NH 03053

Call Sign: K1TJM
Timothy J Moore
44 Old Derry Rd
Londonderry NH 03053

Call Sign: KB1MMI
Brendan Turcotte

Call Sign: KB1SZK
Shelby L Gregg

Call Sign: K1AVQ
Joseph R Gorton Jr

50 Old Derry Rd
Londonderry NH 03053

Call Sign: KD9AW
Miguel A Garcia
67 Old Derry Rd
Londonderry NH 03053

Call Sign: KB1TBX
Alert Amateur Radio Club
67 Old Derry Rd
Londonderry NH 03053

Call Sign: W1ESC
Robert W Simoneau
77 Old Derry Rd
Londonderry NH
030532219

Call Sign: W1HMP
Wayne E Weston
97 Old Derry Rd
Londonderry NH 03053

Call Sign: K4MH
Henry B Poole Jr
89 Old Nashua Rd
Londonderry NH 03053

Call Sign: WA1RKT
Eric Poole
89 Old Nashua Rd
Londonderry NH 03053

Call Sign: KA1TRP
Persis C Martin
36 Olde Country Village
Londonderry NH 03053

Call Sign: W2AHO
Walter C Martin
36 Olde Country Village
Londonderry NH 03053

Call Sign: KA1TFF

Paul M Mc Carthy
6 Page Rd
Londonderry NH 03053

Call Sign: N1GAL
Gary E Watson
81 Pendleton Lane
Londonderry NH 03053

Call Sign: W1GCJ
Albert J Lombardi
95 Pillsbury Rd
Londonderry NH 03053

Call Sign: N1RNX
Timothy J Bolduc
181 Pillsbury Rd
Londonderry NH 05053

Call Sign: N1QGS
John R Bolduc
181 Pillsbury Rd
Londonderry NH 03053

Call Sign: KB1LCV
Scott E Feinberg
186 Pillsbury Rd
Londonderry NH 03053

Call Sign: KB1LVQ
Steven A Feinberg
186 Pillsbury Rd
Londonderry NH 03053

Call Sign: AA1RS
James W Paquette
190 Pillsbury Rd
Londonderry NH 03053

Call Sign: KA1TOQ
Diana M Faucher
10 Pine St
Londonderry NH
030533804

Call Sign: KB1SO
Raymond E Faucher Jr
10 Pine St
Londonderry NH 03053

Call Sign: WA1COP
William S Koury
4 Plummer Dr
Londonderry NH 03053

Call Sign: N1YHX
Kathleen L Donovan
25 Raintree Dr
Londonderry NH 03053

Call Sign: KB1DYF
Pamela A Hall
91 Rockingham Rd
Londonderry NH
030532211

Call Sign: KB1UBE
Robert B Spencer
17 Rolling Ridge Rd
Londonderry NH 03053

Call Sign: N1RCA
Louis L Broad
22 Ross Dr
Londonderry NH 03053

Call Sign: KB1APQ
Wesley J Lundquist
11 Rossini Dr
Londonderry NH 03053

Call Sign: KB1SGK
Remi W Fortin
7 Shasta Dr
Londonderry NH
030533010

Call Sign: KB1VOF
Pauline C Fortin
7 Shasta Dr

Londonderry NH 03053

Call Sign: KC1YC
Laurence A Mc Caig
79 South Rd 4
Londonderry NH
030533847

Call Sign: KG4SHO
Joyce I Ozelius
79 South Rd 4
Londonderry NH 03053

Call Sign: KB1KDR
William Luzunari
3 Southwood Dr
Londonderry NH 03053

Call Sign: KB1UFP
Matthew M Derkrikorian
8 Sparhawk Dr
Londonderry NH 03053

Call Sign: K1NOM
Ray A Crowell
29 St Andrews Way
Londonderry NH 03053

Call Sign: KB1VNV
Russell J Stockdale
1 State Tree Circle
Londonderry NH 03053

Call Sign: AA1UI
Douglas A Hansel
37 Stonehenge Rd
Londonderry NH 03053

Call Sign: KC6LIX
Janet D Huttula
5 Stoney Point Dr
Londonderry NH 03053

Call Sign: KC6LOE
Greg A Huttula

5 Stoney Point Dr
Londonderry NH 03053

Call Sign: N1JKN
Guy F Williams
4 Thornton Rd
Londonderry NH 03053

Call Sign: KB1HOJ
Joseph R Levesque
3 Tokanel Dr
Londonderry NH 03053

Call Sign: W1GLJ
Joseph C Ghiloni Jr
5 Tranquil Dr
Londonderry NH 03053

Call Sign: KA1RTH
John G Caldwell
134 Treadway Ln
Londonderry NH 03053

Call Sign: KB1TFO
Chris M Oliverio
1 Troley Car Lane
Londonderry NH 03053

Call Sign: WB1HGE
Dennis Doucette
28 Trolley Car Ln
Londonderry NH 03053

Call Sign: KA1MGO
Stephen A D Urso
42 Trolley Car Ln
Londonderry NH
030532931

Call Sign: N1FCJ
Joseph J Musto
3 Tyler Dr
Londonderry NH
030532503

Call Sign: AA1MV
Keith W Allen
12 Vista Ridge Dr 33
Londonderry NH 03053

Call Sign: KB1WGF
David L Lacaillade
14 Vista Ridge Dr Unit 66
Londonderry NH 03053

Call Sign: N1DQS
Jay S Dunham
12 Wallace Cir
Londonderry NH 03053

Call Sign: KB1WEL
Jeffery K Locke
10 Welch Rd
Londonderry NH 03053

Call Sign: AB1O
Jeffery K Locke
10 Welch Rd
Londonderry NH 03053

Call Sign: KB1FEM
Lynne E Durland
114 West Rd
Londonderry NH
030533141

Call Sign: N1NAZ
George A Moranian
114 West Rd
Londonderry NH 03053

Call Sign: KB1RGF
Mary E Carr
7 Westwood Dr
Londonderry NH 03053

Call Sign: KE1CS
Stephen W D Esopo
19 Wiley Hill Rd
Londonderry NH 03053

Call Sign: K1SWD
Stephen W D Esopo
19 Wiley Hill Rd
Londonderry NH 03053

Call Sign: W1END
Eldon H Burkinshaw
1 Willow Ln
Londonderry NH
030533309

Call Sign: KB1VAY
Jonathan S Kane
27 Wilshire Dr
Londonderry NH 03053

Call Sign: KB1WHS
Richard C Maynard
10 Wilson Rd
Londonderry NH 03053

Call Sign: N1PPT
Solomon P Kamerman
5 Wimbledon Dr
Londonderry NH 03053

Call Sign: KB1OTI
Sean M Fichera
202 Winding Pond Rd
Londonderry NH 03053

Call Sign: N1ZWZ
Jose L Figueroa
29 Winterwood Dr
Londonderry NH 03053

Call Sign: KA1KDU
Richard F White
14 Woodland Dr
Londonderry NH
030534010

Call Sign: KB1DJV
Denise K Unkles

Londonderry NH 03053

Call Sign: N1EZ
Steven R Berry
Londonderry NH 03053

Call Sign: N1GBD
Joanna K Souza
Londonderry NH 03053

Call Sign: N3PLZ
John F Kruczak
Londonderry NH 03053

Call Sign: W1GS
William J Good Jr
Londonderry NH
030531289

Call Sign: N1RNX
John R Bolduc
Londonderry NH 03053

Call Sign: KB1TZF
Mark D'amico
Londonderry NH 03053

## FCC Amateur Radio Licenses in Loudon

Call Sign: N1JRZ
Donald E Taylor
301 Bear Hill Rd
Loudon NH 03307

Call Sign: KA1YMX
Nathan J Small
73 Bee Hole Rd
Loudon NH 03307

Call Sign: KA1ZUD
Harris H Gamble
62 Berry Rd
Loudon NH 033071100

Call Sign: N1FTC
Mark L Mc Cormack
Box 158
Loudon NH 03301

Call Sign: N1YSJ
Donald J Bonin
7002 Clinton
Loudon NH 03301

Call Sign: N1YSK
Donald W Bonin
7002 Clinton
Loudon NH 03301

Call Sign: KB1TDB
Douglas M Kerr
200 Love Joy Rd
Loudon NH 03307

Call Sign: W1YED
Donald L Knight
501 Love Joy Rd
Loudon NH 03301

Call Sign: KB1MRO
Gary E Martell
7097 Oak Hill Rd
Loudon NH 03307

Call Sign: N1DIM
Richard I Nelson
7225 Oak Hill Rd
Loudon NH 03301

Call Sign: N1HOF
James C Buck
7312 Oak Hill Rd
Loudon NH 03301

Call Sign: N1VMB
Brenda J Floyd
26 Redwood Rd 219
Loudon NH 03301

Call Sign: W1EGO
David H Deans
281 Rt 129
Loudon NH 033011325

Call Sign: N1WEB
Brian S Grimaldi
7001 Sanborn Rd
Loudon NH 033011618

Call Sign: AA6LC
Roger M Nichols
31 Violet Way
Loudon NH 033070844

## FCC Amateur Radio Licenses in Lyman

Call Sign: N1JJN
Kenelm J Parker
319 Hurd Hill Rd
Lyman NH 03585

## FCC Amateur Radio Licenses in Lyme

Call Sign: KB1QQU
Samuel C Colbeck
311 Goose Pond Rd
Lyme NH 03768

Call Sign: K1SCC
Samuel C Colbeck
311 Goose Pond Rd
Lyme NH 03768

Call Sign: KB1GDC
Christopher N Tausanovitch
58 Hardscrabble Lane
Lyme NH 03768

Call Sign: KB1GDD
Alexander W Tausanovitch
58 Hardscrabble Rd
Lyme NH 03768

Call Sign: KB1HWN
Nicholas A Ligett
40 Isaac Perkins Rd
Lyme NH 03768

Call Sign: KB1HWO
Steven D Ligett
40 Isaac Perkins Rd
Lyme NH 03768

Call Sign: KB1GDB
Jason O Reeves
314 Orford Rd
Lyme NH 03768

Call Sign: KB1IWT
Keith C Borgstrom
61 River Rd
Lyme NH 03768

Call Sign: W1ZRD
Keith C Borgstrom
61 River Rd
Lyme NH 03768

Call Sign: KB1CML
Chris J Hilbert
Lyme NH 037680157

## FCC Amateur Radio Licenses in Lyme Center

Call Sign: KA1TYQ
Barbara A Barreiro
412 Dorchester Rd
Lyme Center NH 03768

## FCC Amateur Radio Licenses in Lyndeborough

Call Sign: KA1QDG
Margaret H Tenney
Beasom Rd
Lyndeborough NH 03082

Call Sign: K1LZF
Robert T Johnson
Box 197
Lyndeborough NH 03082

Call Sign: N1VPQ
Andrew J Button
Box 429
Lyndeborough NH 03082

Call Sign: K1LKS
Lois E Kenick
30 Bracketts Crossroad
Lyndeborough NH 03082

Call Sign: N1VLE
David F Rokes
270 Center Rd
Lyndeborough NH 03082

Call Sign: KA1BFH
Leonard F Zecchini
714 Center Rd
Lyndeborough NH
030826316

Call Sign: AB1OL
Robert W Johnson
20 Cram Hill Rd
Lyndeborough NH 03082

Call Sign: K1YCC
Robert W Johnson
20 Cram Hill Rd
Lyndeborough NH 03082

Call Sign: N1RKA
Steven M Brown
Cram Rd
Lyndeborough NH 03082

Call Sign: W1FON
Steven M Brown
Cram Rd

Lyndeborough NH 03082

Call Sign: KB1ICG
Christopher T Ouellette
291 Forest Rd
Lyndeborough NH 03082

Call Sign: N1XOW
Richard V Richelo Jr
544 Forest Rd #2
Lyndeborough NH 03082

Call Sign: KB1OUB
Lisa Mendham
82 Herrick Rd
Lyndeborough NH 03082

Call Sign: KB1PPC
Edward B Mendham
82 Herrick Rd
Lyndeborough NH 03082

Call Sign: W1RE
Robert A Edry
462 Mountain Rd
Lyndeborough NH 03082

Call Sign: N1FLX
Michael T Decubellis
588 Mountain Rd
Lyndeborough NH 03082

Call Sign: N1KCV
Jeffrey L Jordan
649 Mountain Rd
Lyndeborough NH 03082

Call Sign: KB1QBD
Jeremy M Slater
232 New Rd
Lyndeborough NH 03082

Call Sign: KB1TQJ
Jeremy M Slater
232 New Rd

Lyndeborough NH 03082

Call Sign: KB1PJY
Andrew M Steere
363 Old Temple Rd
Lyndeborough NH 03082

Call Sign: K2VS
Carol L Wright
122 Putnam Hill Rd
Lyndeborough NH 03082

Call Sign: KE1NH
Carol L Wright
122 Putnam Hill Rd
Lyndeborough NH 03082

Call Sign: K2KID
Jamie Z Wright
122 Putnam Hill Rd
Lyndeborough NH 03082

Call Sign: K2VT
Randall W Wright
122 Putnam Hill Rd
Lyndeborough NH 03082

Call Sign: KX1NH
Randall W Wright
122 Putnam Hill Rd
Lyndeborough NH 03082

Call Sign: NX1D
William A Kinton
Lyndeborough NH 03082

Call Sign: KB1CFG
Laura Gene Edry
262 Old Mountain Rd
Lyndoborough NH 03082

## FCC Amateur Radio Licenses in Madbury

Call Sign: K1DKD

Robert S Jones
1 Freshet Rd
Madbury NH 03820

Call Sign: KB1MIR
Richard S Jones
9 Freshet Rd
Madbury NH 03820

Call Sign: K1DKD
Richard S Jones
9 Freshet Rd
Madbury NH 03820

Call Sign: K1PQO
Richard T Spurling
45 Freshet Rd
Madbury NH 03823

Call Sign: W1RTS
Richard T Spurling
45 Freshet Rd
Madbury NH 03823

Call Sign: KA1UVD
John J Nachilly
83 Hayes Rd
Madbury NH 03820

Call Sign: N1HNG
Thomas K Perley
192 Littleworth Rd
Madbury NH 03823

Call Sign: KB1VRY
Jennifer T Perley
192 Littleworth Rd
Madbury NH 03823

Call Sign: WA1OPL
Mark A Ward
Mill Hill Rd
Madbury NH 03823

Call Sign: KC4UCQ

Walter C Elly
15 Moss Lane
Madbury NH 03823

Call Sign: WA1SZE
David B Raynes
54 Old Stage Rd
Madbury NH 03820

Call Sign: KB1NNU
Brian P Raynes
60 Old Stage Rd
Madbury NH 03823

Call Sign: KB1RVE
Arul Mahadevan
3 Raynes Farm Rd
Madbury NH 03823

## FCC Amateur Radio Licenses in Madison

Call Sign: KB1JYZ
David W Aibel
249 Conway Rd.
Madison NH 03849

Call Sign: KB1IIR
William J Quigley
1753 East Madison Rd
Madison NH 03849

Call Sign: KB1RAW
Mt Washington Valley Ares
1753 East Madison Rd
Madison NH 03849

Call Sign: K1MWV
Mt Washington Valley Ares
1753 East Madison Rd
Madison NH 03849

Call Sign: W1JLH
Edward P Craugh
51 Little Shore Dr

Madison NH 03849

Call Sign: KB1IFI
Michael S Dunker-Bendigo
50 Rt 113
Madison NH 03849

Call Sign: N1NLX
David J Williams
Madison NH 03849

Call Sign: KB1KDA
Randy P Sherman
Madison NH 03849

Call Sign: KB1RJC
Herman W Weber
Madison NH 03849

Call Sign: KB1RJD
Merle E Weber
Madison NH 03849

## FCC Amateur Radio Licenses in Manchester

Call Sign: KC2MBU
Thomas G Grice
112a Auburn St.
Manchester NH 03103

Call Sign: W4LUG
Lee R Herrington
200 Alliance Way 206
Manchester NH 03102

Call Sign: W3LX
Everett M Adams
200 Alliance Way Apt 408
Manchester NH 031028405

Call Sign: W6FO
John T Croteau
423 Amherst St
Manchester NH 03104

Call Sign: N1ESE
John T Croteau
423 Amherst St
Manchester NH 03104

Call Sign: KB1TCZ
Christopher S Erickson
170 Amherst St 18
Manchester NH 03104

Call Sign: N1ZWX
James E Romano
135 Apple Brook Way
Manchester NH 03109

Call Sign: KB1CZQ
Brad C Cox
259 Ash St
Manchester NH 031043774

Call Sign: W1JBM
Maurice H Deschenes Sr
282 Ashland St
Manchester NH 03104

Call Sign: N1WAE
Kimberly L Shaw
702 Auburn St Apt 8
Manchester NH 03103

Call Sign: KB1WTU
New Hampshire Digital D
Star
354 B Kennard Rd
Manchester NH 03104

Call Sign: W1KBU
Conrad R Proulx
446 Bartlett St
Manchester NH 03102

Call Sign: KB1GIS
Andrew R Starin
432 Bartlett St Apt 2

Manchester NH 03102

Manchester NH 03109

Manchester NH 03103

Call Sign: NR1I
Charles L Franck
607 Beacon St
Manchester NH 03104

Call Sign: K1JJN
Robert F Molloy
66 Bellevue St
Manchester NH 03103

Call Sign: N1SJO
David L Towne
145 Blaine St
Manchester NH 03104

Call Sign: N1JHI
Joseph A Lore Jr
653 Beacon St
Manchester NH 03104

Call Sign: KB1EOR
Stephen C Shea
564 Belmont St
Manchester NH 03104

Call Sign: KB1UIU
Robert A Macdonald
149 Blaine St
Manchester NH 03102

Call Sign: N1SMB
Allen F Stewart
611 Beacon St # 1
Manchester NH 03104

Call Sign: KB1JPK
William P Brown
835 Belmont St
Manchester NH 03104

Call Sign: N1LPU
Robert A Macdonald
149 Blaine St
Manchester NH 03102

Call Sign: K1GLO
Donald A Dennis
499 Beech St
Manchester NH 03104

Call Sign: WB1GJA
Robert G Rebolledo
888 Belmont St
Manchester NH 03104

Call Sign: KB1THU
Peter M Dusaitis
99 Blevens Dr
Manchester NH 03104

Call Sign: KB1JPW
Andrew F Fairaizl
714 Beech St
Manchester NH 03104

Call Sign: W1WMK
Clarence W Farr
548 Belmont St 1
Manchester NH 03104

Call Sign: WA1N
Peter M Dusaitis
99 Blevens Dr
Manchester NH 03104

Call Sign: W1FVQ
Aime A Beaudry
862 Beech St
Manchester NH 03104

Call Sign: N1FCZ
Richard C Bell Jr
55 Benjamin St
Manchester NH 03109

Call Sign: KB1AZH
David D Flagg
423 Blevens Dr
Manchester NH 03104

Call Sign: W1WYZ
Clarence W Arnold
813 Beech St A303
Manchester NH 03104

Call Sign: AB1DH
Richard C Bell Jr
55 Benjamin St
Manchester NH 03109

Call Sign: N1USI
Stephen D Jones Jr
247 Blodget St.
Manchester NH 03104

Call Sign: N1ULS
Joshua D Penney
186 Beech St. #3
Manchester NH 03103

Call Sign: W1ZIZ
Harvey B Schow
88 Birchwood Rd
Manchester NH 031043910

Call Sign: KA1VBS
Robin L Sargent
335 Blucher St
Manchester NH 03102

Call Sign: K1PWF
Michael J Bober Jr
51 Belgrade St

Call Sign: KA1WWN
Maurice A Paquin
40 Blackstone St

Call Sign: N1WDS
John Mullen
461 Bodwell Rd

Manchester NH 03109          Manchester NH 031025126          Manchester NH 03103

Call Sign: N1ZUB            Call Sign: KA1IHE              Call Sign: N1ZDY
William R Tharp            William J Beidler             Stephen J Lee
1070 Bodwell Rd           185 Brennan St               134 Brunelle Ave
Manchester NH 03109        Manchester NH 03109           Manchester NH 03103

Call Sign: N1HKQ           Call Sign: KB1RGR             Call Sign: WA1AB
Linda M Hoffman           John A Canry                 Costas J Routos
1495 Bodwell Rd 27        185 Bridge St                178 Brunelle Ave
Manchester NH 03109        Manchester NH 03104           Manchester NH 031034605

Call Sign: N1AYH           Call Sign: KB1TCW             Call Sign: WB1GUH
Kenneth A Lucia           Daniel S Ward                Colin J Werner
1555 Bodwell Rd 44        185 Bridge St Apt 2          239 Brunelle Ave
Manchester NH 03109        Manchester NH 03104           Manchester NH 03103

Call Sign: KF4VTS          Call Sign: KB1FUG             Call Sign: KB1PDF
Brian D Fowler            John E Marcel                Clancy J Mcmahon
1555 Bodwell Rd Unit 16   491 Bridge St Apt 2          826 Bryant Rd
Manchester NH 03109        Manchester NH 03104           Manchester NH 03109

Call Sign: KB1PSI          Call Sign: KG1B              Call Sign: KB1QVN
Brian D Fowler            William J Knowles            Walter P Held
1555 Bodwell Rd Unit 16   683 Brown Ave                715 Calef Rd
Manchester NH 03109        Manchester NH 03103           Manchester NH 03103

Call Sign: KA1SHK          Call Sign: N1FTX             Call Sign: N1UEV
Brian S Beaudry           Richard R Roy                Travis J Roy
30 Bow St                1657 Brown Ave               555 Canal St # 1305
Manchester NH 03103        Manchester NH 03103           Manchester NH 03101

Call Sign: N1PIL           Call Sign: N1JS              Call Sign: KA1HTS
Timothy A Rowe            Joseph Santangelo            Janice L Brown
70 Bow St                3020 Brown Ave Unit 13       2132 Candia Rd
Manchester NH 03103        Manchester NH 031036948       Manchester NH 031095702

Call Sign: KB1DPZ          Call Sign: N1WOL             Call Sign: W1VTP
William H Thorpe Jr       Eva D Grimaldi               Alan H Brown Sr
106 Boynton St           134 Brunell Ave              2132 Candia Rd
Manchester NH 03101        Manchester NH 03103           Manchester NH 03109

Call Sign: KA1NXT          Call Sign: N1ISI             Call Sign: N1VEA
Howard F Darms           Denis L Labore               John R Dussault
159 Boynton St           51 Brunelle Ave              165 Candia Rd 2

Manchester NH 03109

Call Sign: NS1S
James H Steinmetz
549 Central St
Manchester NH 031033435

Call Sign: N1ASM
Steven A Moulton
45 Chase Way
Manchester NH 03104

Call Sign: KB2NV
Renald L La Rochelle
175 Chestnut St #312
Manchester NH 03101

Call Sign: N1GCH
Pamela A Stiles
880 Cilley Rd
Manchester NH 03103

Call Sign: N1KLX
Bryan H Mancuso
983 Cilley Rd
Manchester NH 03103

Call Sign: K1ANH
Rudolph A Cartier
1035 Cilley Rd
Manchester NH 03103

Call Sign: N1KOM
John C Caswell
435 Cilley Rd Apt 2
Manchester NH 03103

Call Sign: N1QZA
Richard A Zamoida
327 Circle Rd
Manchester NH 03103

Call Sign: KB1FSJ
Cheryl A Marcellino
332 Circle Rd

Manchester NH 03103

Call Sign: KB1POB
Steven R Hunt
350 Circle Rd
Manchester NH 03103

Call Sign: W1CDX
Steven R Hunt
350 Circle Rd
Manchester NH 03103

Call Sign: KB1QQW
European Psk Club (Us
Section)
350 Circle Rd
Manchester NH 03103

Call Sign: W1EPC
European Psk Club (Us
Section)
350 Circle Rd
Manchester NH 03103

Call Sign: K1MPQ
Andre L Bilodeau
507 Clay St
Manchester NH 03103

Call Sign: N1YBL
Paul R Scarlett
458 Cohas Ave
Manchester NH 03109

Call Sign: K1HWP
Joseph J Gaudet
572 Coral Ave
Manchester NH 03104

Call Sign: W1IUU
Walter J Sakowicz
749 Corning Rd
Manchester NH 03109

Call Sign: N1KOU

Robert P Norway
7 Country Club Dr 39
Manchester NH 03102

Call Sign: KB1PJZ
Brett Rudolf
22 Country Club Dr Apt 12
Manchester NH 03102

Call Sign: N1TRL
James H Joyce
19 Country Club Dr S27
Manchester NH 031028804

Call Sign: WB7TLE
Joseph F Gabler
189 Cranwell Dr
Manchester NH 031094516

Call Sign: KA1UDH
Ernest L Castle Iv
95 Crawford St
Manchester NH 03103

Call Sign: WA1YZW
Ernest L Castle Iii
95 Crawford St
Manchester NH 031094219

Call Sign: WA1PCV
Gary P Wallin
11 Crestview Rd
Manchester NH 031041804

Call Sign: W1GPW
Gary P Wallin
11 Crestview Rd
Manchester NH 031041804

Call Sign: WB1ADF
William A Wagner Jr
175 Crosbie St
Manchester NH 03104

Call Sign: KB1BTM

Daniel A Desfosses
33 Croteau Ct
Manchester NH 03104

Call Sign: KB2CPZ
Elizabeth A Mc Donnell
Croteau Ct
Manchester NH 03104

Call Sign: N1VEI
Edward L Szumiesz
14 Davignon St
Manchester NH 03102

Call Sign: K1ELS
Edward L Szumiesz
14 Davignon St
Manchester NH 03102

Call Sign: N1GCU
Robert M Ritter
99 Dawson Ave
Manchester NH 03104

Call Sign: N1GZW
Diane M Ritter
99 Dawson Ave
Manchester NH 03104

Call Sign: KA1FRT
John Lis
104 Day St
Manchester NH 031042877

Call Sign: KB1HAK
Rich T Ivey
182 Delaware Ave
Manchester NH 03104

Call Sign: N1IOG
Susan P Sparks
95 Derryfield Ct
Manchester NH 03104

Call Sign: N1IOH

Roland J Sparks
95 Derryfield Ct
Manchester NH 03104

Call Sign: NL7S
William G Feetham
770 Dix St
Manchester NH 03103

Call Sign: K1BIP
Donald A Conley Sr
90 Donahue Dr
Manchester NH 03103

Call Sign: WA1ZNZ
Judith A Conley
90 Donahue Dr
Manchester NH 03103

Call Sign: KA1KGB
Sean C Duclos
95 Donahue Dr
Manchester NH 03103

Call Sign: KX1L
John G Duclos
95 Donahue Dr
Manchester NH 03103

Call Sign: N1UJA
Michael R Chick
320 Douglas St 12
Manchester NH 03102

Call Sign: KA1XD
Paul M La Rochelle
486 Dubuque St
Manchester NH 03102

Call Sign: KB1VXU
Norman R Dery
40 Dudley St
Manchester NH 03103

Call Sign: KB1LVH

James A Medlock
139 Dunbar St
Manchester NH 031037318

Call Sign: AF1MR
James A Medlock
139 Dunbar St
Manchester NH 031037318

Call Sign: N1UJC
Jerry R Methvin
186 Dunbarton Rd 8
Manchester NH 03102

Call Sign: KB1MLV
Robert A Phillips
186 Dunbarton Rd Unit 2
Manchester NH 03102

Call Sign: AE1OU
Robert A Phillips
186 Dunbarton Rd Unit 2
Manchester NH 03102

Call Sign: WB1CMC
Todd R Byron
80 Dunbarton Rd.
Manchester NH 03102

Call Sign: KB1MXC
Kimberly A Labrie
431 E High St
Manchester NH 03104

Call Sign: KB1VLN
Derek M Sanders
47 Eagle Nest Way
Manchester NH 03104

Call Sign: N1ZGN
Matthew J Sapienza
285 East High St Apt 1
Manchester NH 03104

Call Sign: N1QXQ

Ernest E Cullen
175 Eastern Ave
Manchester NH 03104

Call Sign: KB1VHI
Justin A Rodriguez
167 Eastern Ave 201
Manchester NH 03104

Call Sign: N1WAC
Francis Lombardo Iii
144 Eastern Ave Apt 303
Manchester NH 031046620

Call Sign: N1HSV
Susan M Lavoie
147 Eastern Ave Apt 303
Manchester NH 03104

Call Sign: KC1GK
John J Brown
30 Edgemere Ave
Manchester NH 03103

Call Sign: KB1LCU
Joseph G Areyzaga
126 Edmond St
Manchester NH 03102

Call Sign: K1JGA
Joseph G Areyzaga
126 Edmond St
Manchester NH 03102

Call Sign: KD7FII
Thomas J Haynes
345 Edward J Roy Dr 112
Manchester NH 03104

Call Sign: N1ZNY
Victor Santamaria
245 Edward J. Roy Dr Unit
108
Manchester NH 03104

Call Sign: WA1PJG
Michael J Kane
1404 Elm St  Apt 18
Manchester NH 03101

Call Sign: KB1UVR
Michael J Kane
1404 Elm St  Apt 18
Manchester NH 03101

Call Sign: WA1PJG
Michael J Kane
1404 Elm St  Apt 18
Manchester NH 03101

Call Sign: WA1PJG
Michael J Kane
1267 Elm St Apt 4
Manchester NH 03104

Call Sign: WB2HED
Joseph J Dengel
816 Elm St No. 354
Manchester NH 031012101

Call Sign: KB2CVR
Michael J Arnold
816 Elm St.#284
Manchester NH 03101

Call Sign: KA1QZX
Anthony P D Agostino Mr
223 Elmwood Ave
Manchester NH 031036531

Call Sign: N1RPN
Arthur E Joly Jr
English Village Rd 104
Manchester NH 03102

Call Sign: N1KDB
Chad D Sandford
English Village Rd Apt 102
Manchester NH 03102

Call Sign: AA1JE
Ronald M Rioux
112 English Village Rd.
#204
Manchester NH 03102

Call Sign: N1PRG
Joseph L Labbe
25 Falls Ave
Manchester NH 03103

Call Sign: K1BHX
Louis D Michaud
144 Fieldcrest Rd
Manchester NH 03102

Call Sign: AB1BG
Michael R Prince
137 Fleming St
Manchester NH 03104

Call Sign: KC8LEL
Robert H Meader
323 Franklin St Apt 208
Manchester NH 03101

Call Sign: K1EAB
Eric A Boucher
251 Fremont St
Manchester NH 03103

Call Sign: KB1RMD
Derek J Lemay
1840 Front St
Manchester NH 03102

Call Sign: KA1UFC
Jeffrey S Steinmetz
461 Front St 1st Flr
Manchester NH 03102

Call Sign: KB1IIV
Jeffrey S Steinmetz
461 Front St 1st Flr
Manchester NH 03102

Call Sign: N1ICH
Peter C Hoefler
181 Gabrielle St
Manchester NH 03103

Call Sign: KB2RWT
Bradford C Goodwin Jr
59 Garden Dr #14
Manchester NH 03102

Call Sign: K1NJW
Norman J Wood Jr
100 George St
Manchester NH 03102

Call Sign: N1FIL
Richard A St Jean
100 Gilhaven Rd
Manchester NH 03104

Call Sign: K1DFL
Donald A Girard
21 Glen Ridge Ave
Manchester NH 03102

Call Sign: KB1MXE
David J Mezakowski
84 Golfview Dr
Manchester NH 03102

Call Sign: KE4BQO
Daniel P Mcdevitt
472 Granite St 12
Manchester NH 03102

Call Sign: N1YVD
George A Gould
125 Greeley
Manchester NH 03102

Call Sign: K1SBF
Donald H Pomeroy
255 Greeley St
Manchester NH 03102

Call Sign: WA1YIY
Phillip C Bowen
65 Green Acres Dr
Manchester NH 03109

Call Sign: N1OOL
Jeffrey F Des Rosiers
109 Green Acres Dr
Manchester NH 03109

Call Sign: KB1MER
Kimberly A Des Rosiers
109 Green Acres Dr
Manchester NH 03109

Call Sign: N1VJH
Michael E Gallant
190 Green Acres Dr
Manchester NH 03109

Call Sign: KB1HMY
Christie D Gallant
190 Green Acres Dr
Manchester NH 03109

Call Sign: N2URL
Ingrid K Leydens
30 Greenview Dr Apt 18
Manchester NH 03102

Call Sign: KA1COT
Joanne E Belliveau
111 Greenwood Ct
Manchester NH 03109

Call Sign: WA1ZSX
Gerard A Belliveau
111 Greenwood Ct
Manchester NH 03109

Call Sign: N1RVD
Stanley Papachristou
26 Greystone Way
Manchester NH 03104

Call Sign: KB1RWG
Bradford J Hazen
185 Grove St -2
Manchester NH 03103

Call Sign: KB1GZB
Kenneth A Robertson
361 Hackett Hill Rd
Manchester NH 03106

Call Sign: KA1VNE
Thomas Gibbons
1240 Hall St
Manchester NH 03104

Call Sign: KE1IX
Alan R Paige
1335 Hall St
Manchester NH 031042729

Call Sign: KB1LEA
Wayne R Watjus
60 Hamburg St
Manchester NH 03102

Call Sign: KC1EQ
John R Butler Jr
855 Hanover St
Manchester NH 03104

Call Sign: KA9HNR
Daniel J Bisinger
350 Hanover St  Apt. 2
Manchester NH 03104

Call Sign: N1UZS
Randy A Miller
855 Hanover St 115
Manchester NH 03104

Call Sign: N1KDW
Andrew C Bennett
855 Hanover St 153
Manchester NH 03104

Call Sign: KB1TQO
Ernest L Castle Iv
855 Hanover St 425
Manchester NH 03104

Call Sign: N1ETG
Ernest L Castle Iv
855 Hanover St 425
Manchester NH 03104

Call Sign: N1VPS
Norman D Deschenes
200 Hanover St Apt 313
Manchester NH 031046129

Call Sign: KB1NWN
Norman R Hutchinson
855 Hanover St Pmb 429
Manchester NH 03104

Call Sign: N1LTF
Robert A Witham Sr
627 Harvard St
Manchester NH 03103

Call Sign: N1IDS
William E Waitt
270 Hayward St
Manchester NH 03103

Call Sign: N1INK
Claudia R Waitt
270 Hayward St
Manchester NH 03103

Call Sign: KA1IHC
Keith A Morrissette
17 Hevey St
Manchester NH 03102

Call Sign: WA1AQS
Calvin C Thompson
33 Hevey St
Manchester NH 03102

Call Sign: N1PRI
Jay S Thompson
38 Hevey St
Manchester NH 03102

Call Sign: N1RKS
Brenda M Thompson Mrs
38 Hevey St
Manchester NH 03102

Call Sign: W1XC
Norval D Stapelfeld
680 Hevey St
Manchester NH 031023116

Call Sign: KA1PAT
Paul W Gunther
784 Hevey St
Manchester NH 031023118

Call Sign: N1FVF
John Mazur
24 Hillcroft Rd
Manchester NH 03104

Call Sign: W1COL
Frank M Mroz
209 Hillhaven Rd
Manchester NH 031042806

Call Sign: AA1ZD
Michael J Egan
68 Hollis St
Manchester NH 03101

Call Sign: KB1CFM
South New Hampshire
Contest Club
287 Holt Ave
Manchester NH 03109

Call Sign: WB1BSA
C/O L L Lee Museum-571
New Hampshire Scouting

Amateur Radio Service
Club
Holt Ave
Manchester NH 03103

Call Sign: KB1HHU
Steve Bartlett
497 Hooksett Rd Suite 372
Manchester NH 03104

Call Sign: N1SM
Steven P Morin
314 Hoyt St
Manchester NH 03103

Call Sign: KB1GPT
Smoke Signals Arc
314 Hoyt St
Manchester NH 03103

Call Sign: W1MFD
Smoke Signals Arc
314 Hoyt St
Manchester NH 03103

Call Sign: KB1OU
Donald R Morin
336 Hoyt St
Manchester NH 031033031

Call Sign: KB1DLQ
Andrew J Thomits
151 Hunters Village Way
Manchester NH 03103

Call Sign: KB1DYG
John C Williams
356 Huse Rd
Manchester NH 03103

Call Sign: N1SJJ
William F Donovan
377 Huse Rd 2
Manchester NH 03103

Call Sign: N1ORD
Paul R Richard
379 Huse Rd 33
Manchester NH 03103

Call Sign: KA1LAO
James P Pinfield
383 Huse Rd 9
Manchester NH 03103

Call Sign: W1CPH
Roger A San Soucie
246 Island Pond Rd
Manchester NH 03109

Call Sign: N1KCC
Linda S Blumberg
72 Jackson St
Manchester NH 03102

Call Sign: KA1WBI
Gary R Eastman
9 Jeff Ln Rfd 3
Manchester NH 03103

Call Sign: NA1Z
Shirley M Perry
24 Joliette St
Manchester NH 03102

Call Sign: KB1GTX
Stanley D Broad
199 Kelley St Apt 3
Manchester NH 03102

Call Sign: W1QDA
Raymond H Jackson
44 Kenberma St
Manchester NH 031036020

Call Sign: N1KIM
Reese C Fowler
Kennard Rd
Manchester NH 03104

Call Sign: W1RCF
Reese C Fowler
Kennard Rd
Manchester NH 03104

Call Sign: KB1FAC
Robert S Jacobs
20 Killdeer Dr
Manchester NH 03104

Call Sign: KB1GOG
Sandra D Jacobs
20 Killdeer Dr
Manchester NH 03104

Call Sign: KD1RD
Paul D Dussault
31 Kimball St
Manchester NH 03102

Call Sign: KB1QAL
Jason A Turcotte
39 Kimball St
Manchester NH 03102

Call Sign: N1TZN
Christine M Geithner
47 Kingston St
Manchester NH 03102

Call Sign: N1SBN
CHRISTINE M Dobbins
72 KINGSTON ST
Manchester NH 03102

Call Sign: KB1FDZ
Kevin E Gagnon
72 Kingston St
Manchester NH 031024132

Call Sign: KB1GKM
Garrett M Gagnon
72 Kingston St
Manchester NH 03102

Call Sign: AA1OH
Lynn A Shackelford
50 L English Vlg Rd 104
Manchester NH 03102

Call Sign: N1YVG
Richard B Mercer
235 Lake Ave
Manchester NH 03103

Call Sign: KA1DQL
Joseph A Bouchard
392 Lake Ave
Manchester NH 031034821

Call Sign: KB1BHU
Tiffani L Frisella
645 Lake Ave
Manchester NH 03103

Call Sign: N1XRN
Colin T Egan
967 Lake Shore Rd
Manchester NH 03109

Call Sign: KB1TPP
Francis P O'rourke
1294 Lakeshore Rd
Manchester NH 03109

Call Sign: KB1TSZ
Jeffrey E O'rourke
1294 Lakeshore Rd
Manchester NH 03109

Call Sign: KB1VDT
Stephen E Stanley
31 Lamonte St
Manchester NH 03104

Call Sign: KC1LW
Thomas R Friedman
53 Lancelot Ave
Manchester NH 03104

Call Sign: KC2DPY
Reynaldo A Betances
91 Laurel St
Manchester NH 03103

Call Sign: N1RHX
Gary P Nalen
200 Laurel St
Manchester NH 03103

Call Sign: KA1SMM
Gloria M Plummer
233 Laurel St
Manchester NH 03103

Call Sign: KB1UXY
Henry L Pelchat
442 Laurel St
Manchester NH 03103

Call Sign: N1YOI
David S Smith
476 Laurel St
Manchester NH 03103

Call Sign: N1XEK
Robert L Olson
55 Lavista St
Manchester NH 031033935

Call Sign: WA1DJT
Bertrand L Carbonneau
310 Laxson Ave
Manchester NH 03103

Call Sign: K1WJH
Henry D Brinn
12 Liane St
Manchester NH 031022574

Call Sign: K1RDM
Richard D Miller Jr
219 London St
Manchester NH 031045581

Call Sign: KB1JIA
Walter D Finnegan
357 Lowell St
Manchester NH 03104

Call Sign: K1FQS
Walter D Finnegan
357 Lowell St
Manchester NH 03104

Call Sign: N1UJB
Todd J Hannemann
440 Lowell St
Manchester NH 03104

Call Sign: W1NKI
Michael J Kane
80 Lowell St ,3n
Manchester NH 03101

Call Sign: KA1KFX
William A Brock
80 Lowell St A4a
Manchester NH 03101

Call Sign: W1NKI
William A Brock
80 Lowell St A4a
Manchester NH 03101

Call Sign: KB1VSF
Allan D Warner Jr
797 Mammath Rd Apt 44
Manchester NH 03104

Call Sign: N1IQT
Nathaniel B Burnham
251 Manchester St
Manchester NH 03103

Call Sign: KA1LGK
Lydia J Callahan
375 Manchester St  Apt 2f
Manchester NH 03101

Call Sign: N1BGG
John J Callahan Iii
375 Manchester St  Apt 2f
Manchester NH 03101

Call Sign: KB1USJ
John J Callahan Iv
375 Manchester St 2f
Manchester NH 03103

Call Sign: KA1ZGK
Maxine A Carder
296 Massabesic St
Manchester NH 03103

Call Sign: N1YVB
Richard R Paquette
690 Massabesic St
Manchester NH 03103

Call Sign: N1VPW
Mathew A Gauvin
715 Massabesic St
Manchester NH 03103

Call Sign: KB1UPI
Christopher S Howe
197 Mast Rd
Manchester NH 03102

Call Sign: W1CSH
Christopher S Howe
197 Mast Rd
Manchester NH 03102

Call Sign: KB1BIP
Nicole J Pepin
485 Mast Rd
Manchester NH 03102

Call Sign: WR1A
Gary W Hunter
84 Mc Carthy St
Manchester NH 03104

Call Sign: N1MWW
Deborah A Forrest
114 Medford St
Manchester NH 031094326

Call Sign: N1UVX
Roger E D Amours
71 Middle St
Manchester NH 03101

Call Sign: KA1VOM
Paul Bradt
52 Monroe St
Manchester NH 03104

Call Sign: KB1HBH
Jeffrey H Hirsch
59 Memorial Dr
Manchester NH 03103

Call Sign: KB1IVP
Brian T Weymouth
139 Middle St Suite 1
Manchester NH 031011927

Call Sign: N1TRW
John P Bourque
828 Montgomery St
Manchester NH 03102

Call Sign: N1USO
Mark S Mc Cormack
156 Merrimack St
Manchester NH 03103

Call Sign: W1ID
Gerald C Lemay
238 Milford St
Manchester NH 03102

Call Sign: N1WIS
Aaron J Bourque
828 Montgomery St
Manchester NH 03102

Call Sign: KE4OTM
Stephen M Ingle
569 Merrimack St
Manchester NH 03103

Call Sign: KA1NBW
Normand L Brien
367 Millstone Ave Apt 8
Manchester NH 031027184

Call Sign: N1SSS
Michael A Joseph
390 Mystic St
Manchester NH 031035804

Call Sign: KE4RBW
Karen L Ingle
569 Merrimack St
Manchester NH 03103

Call Sign: N1SJN
Harry B Smith
150 Minot St
Manchester NH 03109

Call Sign: N1VRP
Daniel R Snodgrass
11 N Adams St
Manchester NH 031042532

Call Sign: KB1VUG
Steve Black
524 Merrimack St Unit 3
Manchester NH 03103

Call Sign: N1EOV
Reinhard R Meyer
80 Mirror St
Manchester NH 03104

Call Sign: N1PQC
Skot P Jervis
245 N Main St
Manchester NH 03102

Call Sign: KB1VHG
Scott G Johnston
6 Miami Ct
Manchester NH 03103

Call Sign: KA1CKX
Charles H Oliver Jr
202 Mitchell
Manchester NH 03102

Call Sign: K1ATL
Robert F Francoeur
1805 N River Rd
Manchester NH 031041645

Call Sign: N1NEV
Norman R Pilotte
4 Michael St
Manchester NH 03104

Call Sign: N1VRX
Jean L Vallee
357 Mitchell St
Manchester NH 03103

Call Sign: W1YES
John D Richards
2021 N River Rd
Manchester NH 03104

Call Sign: N1UBJ
Denise A Pilotte
4 Michael St
Manchester NH 03104

Call Sign: KB1AZK
Christopher R Gonyea
44 Mitchell St.
Manchester NH 031036519

Call Sign: KB1HHF
Silvio M Pupino
2500 N River Rd
Manchester NH 03106

Call Sign: N1VQT
Ken P Merrill
42 Newbury Rd
Manchester NH 03103

Call Sign: W1HJI
Herbert V Cushing
1405 No River Rd
Manchester NH 03104

Call Sign: N1KTQ
Charles T Robinton
346 Normand St
Manchester NH 03109

Call Sign: N1PXH
Roger M Tetu
44 Norris St
Manchester NH 03103

Call Sign: K1RDR
Anthony F Gallo
171 North Acres Rd.
Manchester NH 03104

Call Sign: N1BTB
Christie Goudas
111 North Adams St
Manchester NH 03104

Call Sign: KW1S
Wayne M Lambert
215 North St
Manchester NH 03104

Call Sign: KB1ARM
Ronald V Pelleteri Jr
5 Northbrook Dr #511
Manchester NH 03102

Call Sign: KB1QMJ
Manchester High School
West Arc
9 Notre Dame Ave
Manchester NH 03102

Call Sign: WE1ST
Manchester High School
West Arc
9 Notre Dame Ave
Manchester NH 03102

Call Sign: KB1BPQ
Manchester High School
West Arc
9 Notre Dame Ave
Manchester Hs West
Manchester NH 03102

Call Sign: K9IDA
Alan D Kaplan
220 Oak St
Manchester NH 03104

Call Sign: KB4CJV
J Stewart Laird
632 Oak St
Manchester NH 031042623

Call Sign: W1ZPA
Henri J Chapdelaine
180 Oakland Ave
Manchester NH 031094408

Call Sign: KB1NX
Helen K Fowler
Old Hackett Hill Rd
Manchester NH 03102

Call Sign: KA1PJL
Lionel F Gallant
59 Old Hackett Hill Rd Apt
40
Manchester NH 031028989

Call Sign: KB1RZG
Michael B Shallow
151 Oneida St
Manchester NH 03102

Call Sign: K1MBS
Michael B Shallow
151 Oneida St
Manchester NH 03102

Call Sign: KA1PXG
Henry Gelzer
48 Orange St
Manchester NH 03104

Call Sign: KE1AM
David L Crook
248 Orange St
Manchester NH 03104

Call Sign: KB1DJZ
Christopher Blue
370 Orange St
Manchester NH 03104

Call Sign: KB1RII
Catherine Bailey
50 Orange St Apt 2r
Manchester NH 03104

Call Sign: N1QZM
Benjamin L Sisneroz
40 Orchard St
Manchester NH 03102

Call Sign: WA7IRI
Henry W De Jong
280 Paquette Ave
Manchester NH 031041755

Call Sign: N1WAA
Jim A Emond
399 Paquette Ave
Manchester NH 03104

Call Sign: N1KUU
Frank N Pizzutillo
17 Parenteau St
Manchester NH 03103

Call Sign: N1LIA
Donna D Pizzutillo
17 Parenteau St
Manchester NH 03103

Call Sign: K1EEH
Tracy A Chase
33 Parenteau St
Manchester NH 031032352

Call Sign: KB1HPJ
Debra L Beland
109 Patterson St
Manchester NH 031025045

Call Sign: KB1HYM
Andrew J Beland
109 Patterson St
Manchester NH 03102

Call Sign: KA1ZQG
Beverly A Parker
1654 Paule Ave
Manchester NH 03104

Call Sign: N1ZDX
Shawn J Caswell
366 Pearl St
Manchester NH 03104

Call Sign: KB1DTG
Warren P Kelley
90 Pearl St 3
Manchester NH 031011409

Call Sign: WD1V
John D Seney
144 Pepperidge Dr
Manchester NH 031036150

Call Sign: KB1CYD
Cushcraft Amateur Radio
Club
48 Perimeter Rd
Manchester NH 03103

Call Sign: AA1ZF
Joseph R Levesque
13 Pheasant Lane
Manchester NH 03109

Call Sign: KB1TQM
Kevin K Woods
122 Pheasant Lane
Manchester NH 03109

Call Sign: KB1OUA
Kenneth L Mandigo
30 Phinney Ave
Manchester NH 03109

Call Sign: WA1DOJ
Kenneth J Grinnell Jr
218 Pickering St
Manchester NH 03104

Call Sign: N1JLH
Christopher S Erickson
539 Pine St
Manchester NH 03104

Call Sign: KB1DIF
Jude I Mcquaid
604 Pine St
Manchester NH 03104

Call Sign: W1BT
Julian Lovejoy
718 Pine St
Manchester NH 03104

Call Sign: KA1UUN
Lawrence E Mc Derby
729 Pine St
Manchester NH 03104

Call Sign: KB1PPD
Stephen R Sheaffer
135 Pine St 3
Manchester NH 031036220

Call Sign: KD1LB
David P Erickson
8 Pond Dr
Manchester NH 03103

Call Sign: N1FLB
Lisa J Erickson
8 Pond Dr
Manchester NH 03103

Call Sign: N1MSW
De Witt Mercer Jr
37 Pond Dr
Manchester NH 03103

Call Sign: N1ZGB
Paul M Erickson
79 Pond Dr
Manchester NH 03103

Call Sign: N1ZGC
Christine I Erickson
79 Pond Dr
Manchester NH 03103

Call Sign: KB1OTX
Leonard J Baradziej
466 Proctor Rd
Manchester NH 03109

Call Sign: KB1UXI
Benjamin Adler
350 Propect St
Manchester NH 03104

Call Sign: WD1J
James D Devereux
99 Prout Ave
Manchester NH 03103

Call Sign: K1MNT
Lee D Parmenter
36 Provencher St
Manchester NH 03102

Call Sign: N1TRG
Gene M Tatham
152 Purdue St
Manchester NH 031033076

Call Sign: N1BOF
Richard D Markwith
251 Putnam Rd
Manchester NH 03102

Call Sign: N1GKO
Steven J Patrick
57 Quarry Way
Manchester NH 03106

Call Sign: N1ZGM
Daniel K Schanda
62 Rand St
Manchester NH 03109

Call Sign: N1RVC
David P Laroche
151 Ray St Apt 2b
Manchester NH 03104

Call Sign: AB1BM
Richard D Tenney
147 Reed St
Manchester NH 03102

Call Sign: KB1ULL
Elizabeth M Larrabee
456 Reservoir Ave
Manchester NH 03104

Call Sign: KD0PXE
Nicholas C Sandberg
94 Revere Ave
Manchester NH 03169

Call Sign: KB1WHX
Nicholas C Sandberg
94 Revere Ave
Manchester NH 03169

Call Sign: KA1ABN
Claire F Manning
Rfd 3
Manchester NH 03103

Call Sign: N1QLW
Jeremy P Hitchcock
633 River Rd
Manchester NH 03104

Call Sign: KB1UXS
Irene V Kaye
96 River Rd 207
Manchester NH 03104

Call Sign: N1HSU
Charles G Bridgewater
218 Riverbank Rd
Manchester NH 03103

Call Sign: N1XWI
Erich M Odowd
50 Rochambeau St.
Manchester NH 03102

Call Sign: KB1UOD
Harrison C Williams
151 Rosegate Farm Dr
Manchester NH 03109

Call Sign: KB1USC
Allen R Williams
151 Rosegate Farm Dr
Manchester NH 03109

Call Sign: WA1BLR
Daniel J Gingras
203 Rosegate Farm Dr
Manchester NH 03109

Call Sign: N1ICM
Sean H Gingras
203 Rosegate Fm Rd
Manchester NH 03109

Call Sign: KB1CZY
Robin E Maloney
12 Roy St
Manchester NH 031021433

Call Sign: K1YXP
Nassery T Noufel
6 Roycraft Rd
Manchester NH 03103

Call Sign: KB1PSS
George J Brome
256 Russell St
Manchester NH 03104

Call Sign: K1MCP
Francis X Gagne
50 S Belmont St
Manchester NH 031034630

Call Sign: KA1IJN
Edward O Leduc Sr
319 S Hall St
Manchester NH 03103

Call Sign: K1AEJ
Robert F Cooper
390 S Main St
Manchester NH 03102

Call Sign: K5WPR
Glen H Wall
262 S Mammoth Rd
Manchester NH 03109

Call Sign: KB1RMB
Michael Talalia
1029 S Mammoth Rd 13
Manchester NH 03109

Call Sign: N1OOK
John G Wynne
297 S Willow St
Manchester NH 03103

Call Sign: N1JLK
Donald R Henry
89 Seames Dr
Manchester NH 03103

Call Sign: KA1ICS
Roger E Lemay
191 Seames Dr
Manchester NH 031033945

Call Sign: N1KPQ
Donald P Seguin
141 Second St
Manchester NH 03102

Call Sign: KB1RIP
August J Gomes
335 Sewall St
Manchester NH 03103

Call Sign: N7FMH
Freddie M Hillhouse Jr
116 Sharon St
Manchester NH 03102

Call Sign: N1XEH
Damian L Vaillancourt
431 Shasta St
Manchester NH 03103

Call Sign: KA0GKK
F James Gray
53 Shepherd Rd
Manchester NH 03104

Call Sign: N1KDZ
Richard E Bennett
33 Sherman St
Manchester NH 03102

Call Sign: WA1MYQ
Scott J Mitchell
185 Sibley Ter
Manchester NH 03103

Call Sign: KB1QFZ
Tiffany M Picard
213 Silver St
Manchester NH 03103

Call Sign: KB1SCQ
Melissa A Morris
470 Silver St Apt 122
Manchester NH 03103

Call Sign: N1NLT
James R Mc Hugh
11 Smyth Ln
Manchester NH 03104

Call Sign: KA1QP
Leo Paul A Chauvin
110 So Lincoln
Manchester NH 03103

Call Sign: AA1VY
Leo Paul A Chauvin
110 So Lincoln
Manchester NH 03103

Call Sign: KB1WIL
Brian M Richards
797 Somerville St
Manchester NH 03103

Call Sign: KA1TTM
Ruth C Demeritt
632 Somerville St Apt 3
Manchester NH 03103

Call Sign: KB1CTV
Stephen T Austin
678 South Porter St
Manchester NH 03103

Call Sign: N1JKT
Carl P Kimball
134 South Taylor St
Manchester NH 03103

Call Sign: KB1NMC
Eric Novak
93 Springdale  Rd
Manchester NH 03103

Call Sign: N1FUH
Lynn M Coons
64 Springdale Rd
Manchester NH 03103

Call Sign: K1NOV
Eric Novak
93 Springdale Rd
Manchester NH 03103

Call Sign: KB1RQZ
Robert J Defosses
287 Spruce St -1
Manchester NH 03103

Call Sign: N1FIJ
Robert H Raiche
305 Stark Ln Rt 12
Manchester NH 03102

Call Sign: KA1BOB
Robert H Raiche
305 Stark Ln Rt 12
Manchester NH 03102

Call Sign: KB1LSQ
William C Glidden
14 Sterling Ave
Manchester NH 03103

Call Sign: KB1DGD
Joey A Murray
97 Sullivan St
Manchester NH 03102

Call Sign: N1UBC
Barry J Glennon
73 Sunnyside St
Manchester NH 03103

Call Sign: W1YES
Barry J Glennon
73 Sunnyside St
Manchester NH 03103

Call Sign: N1OMD
Donald A Phinney
15 Tamarack Ct
Manchester NH 03103

Call Sign: KA1KGA
Hervey J Desmarais
211 Tarrytown Rd Apt 19
Manchester NH 031032768

Call Sign: N1LOE
James E Webb
121 Taylor St
Manchester NH 03103

Call Sign: KB1OHE
Bruce J Taylor
57 Tennyson Dr
Manchester NH 03104

Call Sign: N1NMK
David M Bolduc
125 Theophile St
Manchester NH 03102

Call Sign: KB1HIE
Armand A Pinard
181 Thornton St
Manchester NH 03102

Call Sign: N1TXI
Gerald R Soucy
340 Titus Ave
Manchester NH 03103

Call Sign: KA1ZND
Jeremy J Caswell
16 Town House Rd
Manchester NH 03275

Call Sign: N1YGG
Michael J Sullivan
243 Trolley St
Manchester NH 03103

Call Sign: WS1P
Michael J Sullivan
243 Trolley St
Manchester NH 03103

Call Sign: N1OVB
Chris A Love
429 Trolley St
Manchester NH 03103

Call Sign: W1CAL
Chris A Love
429 Trolley St
Manchester NH 03103

Call Sign: KA1OVH
Dennis H Murphy
144 Union St
Manchester NH 03103

Call Sign: N1TLG
Samuel T Jones
959 Union St
Manchester NH 03104

Call Sign: W1HPM
Nh Fm Association Inc
1052 Union St
Manchester NH 03104

Call Sign: WA1HYC
Stoddard B E Chase
1064 Union St
Manchester NH 03104

Call Sign: KB1VHH
Philip A St Hilaire
1069 Union St
Manchester NH 03104

Call Sign: N1YVF
Daniel A Sinclair
235 Union St 3rd Floor
Manchester NH 03103

Call Sign: N1YVE
Michael A Tardiff
168 Valley St
Manchester NH 03103

Call Sign: KB1MAZ
Robert G Muise
170 Valley West Way
Manchester NH 03102

Call Sign: N1FVN
Donald A Devereux
269 Varney St
Manchester NH 03102

Call Sign: K1RMC
Mark S Starin
457 Varney St
Manchester NH 03102

Call Sign: KB1IOR
Uss Cassin Young Amateur
Radio Club
457 Varney St
Manchester NH 03102

Call Sign: N1TFS
Sean William J Toker
Village Circle Way
Manchester NH 03102

Call Sign: K1YXE
Homer G Dodge
51 Vinton St
Manchester NH 031033927

Call Sign: N1OZF
Mary E Whittemore
311 Vinton St

Manchester NH 03103

Call Sign: WB1EDI
Barry L Whittemore
311 Vinton St
Manchester NH 03103

Call Sign: NE1F
Mary E Whittemore
311 Vinton St
Manchester NH 03103

Call Sign: NF1O
Barry L Whittemore
311 Vinton St
Manchester NH 03103

Call Sign: W6JCF
Wallace E Mitchell
341 Vinton St
Manchester NH 031033949

Call Sign: KB1NKY
Arc Bsa Troop 135
311 Vinton St C/O Barry
Whittemore
Manchester NH 03103

Call Sign: KB1NH
Arc Bsa Troop 135
311 Vinton St C/O Barry
Whittemore
Manchester NH 03103

Call Sign: KA1WNL
Cynthia M Ruhsam
11 W Appleton Ave
Manchester NH 03104

Call Sign: KB1GOL
Claude P Pelletier
34 W North Ct
Manchester NH 03104

Call Sign: KC1PD

Brooks J Tanner
21 W.Auburn St
Manchester NH 03101

Call Sign: N1XFA
Benjamin M Mc Keon
118 Walker St
Manchester NH 03102

Call Sign: KB1CFF
Manchester Boys & Girls
Airwaves Amat Rad Clb
114 Walnut St
Manchester NH 03104

Call Sign: KB1AFD
David C Kleinchmidt
118 Walnut St
Manchester NH 03104

Call Sign: N1VQX
Donald A Rene
357 Walnut St
Manchester NH 03104

Call Sign: KA1SXM
Maureen F Dionne
426 Walnut St
Manchester NH 03104

Call Sign: WB1EEY
Edward E Bourque Sr
300 Ward St
Manchester NH 03104

Call Sign: KB1UMJ
Mark E Masse
9 Warner St
Manchester NH 03102

Call Sign: N1UZL
Floyd A Dicey
76 Warren Ave
Manchester NH 03102

Call Sign: N1DRV
Eric W Bennett
163 Wedgewood Ln
Manchester NH 03109

Call Sign: KB1IRU
Jason T Nelson
55 Wellington Terrace Dr
Manchester NH 03104

Call Sign: KD1SV
Kevin M Staley
68 West Elmhurst Ave
Manchester NH 03103

Call Sign: AB1QC
Kevin M Staley
68 West Elmhurst Ave
Manchester NH 03103

Call Sign: KB1TFQ
Anne M Tremblay
62 West Rosedale Ave
Manchester NH 03103

Call Sign: K1JYH
Frank Basoukas
86 West Rosemont Ave
Manchester NH 03103

Call Sign: K1GQH
Roger A Guillemette
32 Westminster St
Manchester NH 031036634

Call Sign: KB1DKA
Jody M Rivard
156 Westwood Dr
Manchester NH 031036138

Call Sign: KB1PMU
Michael P Arnold
72 Wheelock St
Manchester NH 03102

Call Sign: KB1TZE
Walter N Alford Jr
193 Whipple St
Manchester NH 03102

Call Sign: N1OML
Arthur C Des Meules
205 Wilmot St
Manchester NH 03103

Call Sign: KB0ZGG
Dana P Lemieux
349 Wilson St
Manchester NH 03103

Call Sign: KA1IHD
Adrian A Bisson Jr
155 Woodbine Ave
Manchester NH 03103

Call Sign: N1EAF
Gertrude A Durette
180 Woodbury St. Apt. 211
Manchester NH 03102

Call Sign: W1UDB
Richard E Durette
180 Woodbury St. Apt. 211
Manchester NH 03102

Call Sign: KB1WLG
Carmine R Sarno Jr
35 Woodview Way
Manchester NH 03102

Call Sign: N1ZWT
Mary Jane Komisarek
29 Wyoming Ave
Manchester NH 031036446

Call Sign: KB1BQK
Amoskeag Radio Club
Manchester NH 03108

Call Sign: KE1FF

David J Ceplinskas
Manchester NH 031050212

Call Sign: N1HIS
Denise M Des Rosiers
Manchester NH 03108

Call Sign: N1HJC
Thomas D Crowley
Manchester NH 031085331

Call Sign: N1KHP
Kevin A Aldrich
Manchester NH 03105

Call Sign: N1RXY
Sara M Whiting
Manchester NH 03105

Call Sign: N1TRK
Donna M Leger
Manchester NH 03108

Call Sign: N1TRS
Kenneth R Clarke
Manchester NH 03105

Call Sign: N2MLQ
Alexander B Latzko
Manchester NH 031050507

Call Sign: NU1G
Nelson R Lesmerises
Manchester NH 03105

Call Sign: W1HMT
Irving P Gray
Manchester NH 031084038

Call Sign: W8KKU
Charles W Marty
Manchester NH 03105

Call Sign: KB1FBL
Kokopelli ARC

Manchester NH 031085973

Call Sign: AF1G
Kokopelli ARC
Manchester NH 031085973

Call Sign: KB1FSK
Robert C Hoitt
Manchester NH 03108

Call Sign: KB1IMH
Lawrence S Ricard
Manchester NH 031084005

Call Sign: KB1JRB
Manchester Area Radio
Club
Manchester NH 031084367

Call Sign: N1AFD
Manchester Area Radio
Club
Manchester NH 031084367

Call Sign: KB1JZY
New Hampshire Scouting
Club
Manchester NH 03108

Call Sign: KB1LNN
Dale M Crowley
Manchester NH 03108

Call Sign: KB1NEC
Zane Sundquist
Manchester NH 03105

Call Sign: KB1SFI
Oscar Duran
Manchester NH 03108

Call Sign: KB1THT
Alan M Thorpe
Manchester NH 031084535

Call Sign: KB1VEM
Charles R Stevens
Manchester NH 03105

### FCC Amateur Radio Licenses in Manson

Call Sign: N1UOX
Steven B Warshauer
955 Brookline Rd
Manson NH 030484401

### FCC Amateur Radio Licenses in Marlborough

Call Sign: KA1OFA
Daniel R Mc Wethy
25 Chesham Rd
Marlborough NH 03455

Call Sign: N1JUL
Dino Drakiotes
16 Church St
Marlborough NH 03455

Call Sign: K1AHX
Frank H Gibson
17 Collins Dr.
Marlborough NH 01742

Call Sign: WB9RRT
Larry R Antonuk
29 Forrest Dr
Marlborough NH 03455

Call Sign: KB1NXE
James T Philopena
265 Frost Hill Rd
Marlborough NH 03455

Call Sign: KB1HUO
Jim A Poulette
General Delivery
Marlborough NH 03455

Call Sign: KB1CYM
Wayne F Crowell
468 Jaffrey Rd
Marlborough NH
034552803

Call Sign: KB1BHP
Joseph Puleo
51 Mc Kinley Cir
Marlborough NH 03455

Call Sign: KA1NUA
Charles I Despres
44 Monadnock Dr
Marlborough NH 03455

Call Sign: KB1EKA
Daniel E Clark
31 Mountain Dr
Marlborough NH 03445

Call Sign: W1WWW
Charles D Tousley
361 Old Chesham Rd
Marlborough NH 03455

Call Sign: KB1HGN
Larry Lindsley
180 Old Harrisville Rd
Marlborough NH 03455

Call Sign: N1RCR
Roger T Packard
102 Old Nelson Rd
Marlborough NH 03455

Call Sign: KB6NYC
Robert A Cameron
50 Oliver Rd
Marlborough NH 03455

Call Sign: KB1FWX
Anne B Mullett
46 Terrace St
Marlborough NH 03455

Call Sign: W0RCQ
Charles R Buffler
126 Water St
Marlborough NH 03455

Call Sign: KA1SIG
Robert G Brown
Marlborough NH 03455

### FCC Amateur Radio Licenses in Marlow

Call Sign: K1ZS
David W Wilbur
8 Flagg Rd
Marlow NH 03456

Call Sign: N1NHP
Brandon J Little
Forest Rd
Marlow NH 03456

Call Sign: N1HZX
Paul E Brown
40 Mill St
Marlow NH 03456

Call Sign: KC8DIO
Christopher L Leech
Marlow NH 03456

Call Sign: N1WRS
Joseph F Scharf
Marlow NH 03456

Call Sign: W1KWF
James P Fay
Marlow NH 03456

Call Sign: WA1FHB
David Mc Lanahan
Marlow NH 03456

Call Sign: WA1NTU

Laurence D Leech
Marlow NH 03456

Call Sign: WA1WJE
Timothy J Symonds
Marlow NH 034560164

Call Sign: KB1NLL
James C Pokorny
Marlow NH 03456

Call Sign: W1HNX
James C Pokorny
Marlow NH 03456

Call Sign: KB1RZH
Cheryl A Pokorny
Marlow NH 03456

## FCC Amateur Radio Licenses in Mason

Call Sign: K1CWF
Charles W Fifield Iii
388 Black Brook Rd
Mason NH 03048

Call Sign: W1NJG
Ralph F Tibbetts
382 Briggs Rd
Mason NH 03048

Call Sign: KA1LPB
James W Losee
397 Brookline Rd
Mason NH 03048

Call Sign: KA1LPC
Joan M Losee
397 Brookline Rd
Mason NH 03048

Call Sign: KB1AER
Andrew J Losee
397 Brookline Rd

Mason NH 03048

Call Sign: KB1AVR
Christine M Losee
397 Brookline Rd
Mason NH 03048

Call Sign: KA1FUI
Vivian E Wilborg
791 Brookline Rd
Mason NH 03048

Call Sign: W1ZC
Richard B Wilborg
791 Brookline Rd
Mason NH 03048

Call Sign: KA1EKN
Edward P Hamel
955 Brookline Rd
Mason NH 030484401

Call Sign: KB1ECO
Matthew W Crehan
955 Brookline Rd
Mason NH 030484401

Call Sign: N1UOW
Anita H Crehan
955 Brookline Rd
Mason NH 030484401

Call Sign: K1ID
James R French
204 Darling Hill Rd
Mason NH 03048

Call Sign: N1PKO
Kenneth J French
204 Darling Hill Rd
Mason NH 03048

Call Sign: KM1I
Kenneth J French
204 Darling Hill Rd

Mason NH 03048

Call Sign: N1STY
Stuart R Sherman
47 Gilman Hill Rd
Mason NH 03048

Call Sign: N1USL
Linda M Sherman
47 Gilman Hill Rd
Mason NH 03048

Call Sign: N1RZX
Alfred D Nickerson
214 Greenville Rd
Mason NH 03048

Call Sign: N1EUX
Alden T Greenwood
773 Greenville Rd
Mason NH 03048

Call Sign: KB2IJN
Brenda L Ferro
1001 Greenville Rd
Mason NH 03048

Call Sign: KU2A
Nicholas A Ferro Jr
1001 Greenville Rd
Mason NH 03048

Call Sign: KC1XX
Matthias Strelow
814 Hurricane Hill Rd
Mason NH 03048

Call Sign: WA1TVG
John A Diefenbach
231 Meeting House Hill Rd
Mason NH 030484118

Call Sign: K1TLV
John A Diefenbach
231 Meeting House Hill Rd

Mason NH 030484118

Call Sign: N1THN
Stephen R Hoffman
345 Meeting House Hill Rd
Mason NH 030484118

Call Sign: W1UP
James E Gaudet
315 Meetinghouse Hill Rd
Mason NH 03048

Call Sign: KA1CQO
Nancy A Gaudet
Meetinghouse Hill Rd
Mason NH 03048

Call Sign: KB1RTX
John J Molak
71 Old County Rd
Mason NH 03048

Call Sign: KM0LAK
John J Molak
71 Old County Rd
Mason NH 03048

Call Sign: K1IEQ
Kenneth D Harmon
471 Old Turnpike Rd
Mason NH 03048

Call Sign: WN1R
Anatoly V Stepanov
471 Old Turnpike Rd.
Mason NH 03048

Call Sign: KA1YHI
Thomas L Jones
439 Sand Pit Rd
Mason NH 03048

Call Sign: N3LEE
Lee M Lemoine
466 Townsend Rd

Mason NH 030484804

Call Sign: KA1PLM
Ivan E Johnson
2 Valley Rd
Mason NH 030484608

Call Sign: KD1AW
Robert S Fyfe
2 Valley Rd
Mason NH 03048

Call Sign: KB1CZP
Bay Haven Radio Klub
984 Valley Rd
Mason NH 03048

Call Sign: W2OPB
Bay Haven Radio Klub
984 Valley Rd
Mason NH 03048

Call Sign: AA1LL
Paul E Gili
984 Valley Rd
Mason NH 03048

Call Sign: KA1NPS
Linda L Cotter Cranston
731 Wilton Rd
Mason NH 030484202

Call Sign: KB1NW
Scott W Cranston
731 Wilton Rd
Mason NH 030484202

Call Sign: KA1UGW
Jennifer R Schongar
923 Wilton Rd
Mason NH 03048

**FCC Amateur Radio
Licenses in Melvin Village**

Call Sign: K1KZL
Paul E Magrath
68 County Rd
Melvin Village NH 03850

Call Sign: WA2LLR
William T Smith Iii
342 Gwh
Melvin Village NH 03850

Call Sign: N1TTC
Daniel W Caron
360 Middle Rd
Melvin Village NH
038500205

Call Sign: W1RSR
Robert S Reed
2 Union Wharf Rd
Melvin Village NH 03850

Call Sign: KT1A
John Gribbel Iii
Melvin Village NH 03850

Call Sign: N1ZIQ
Robert S Reed
Melvin Village NH 03850

**FCC Amateur Radio
Licenses in Meredith**

Call Sign: N1UWC
Christine K Peer
210 Black Brook Rd.
Meredith NH 03253

Call Sign: N1WEA
Stephen D Peer
210 Black Brook Rd.
Meredith NH 03253

Call Sign: NC1T
Frank B Bowser
19 Bonney Shores Rd

Meredith NH 03253

Call Sign: W1KZ
Chester T Francis
31 Boynton Rd  Unit 6
Meredith NH 03253

Call Sign: KB1VVT
David E Parker
9 Cataldo Rd
Meredith NH 03253

Call Sign: AC4SD
Anthony J Mika
12 Cattle Landing Rd
Meredith NH 03253

Call Sign: K1NCZ
Daniel A Perednia
114 Cattle Landing Rd Box
324
Meredith NH 03253

Call Sign: KB1EOJ
John J Fishman
13 Christy Ln
Meredith NH 03253

Call Sign: KF4ZRX
Alexander A Noordergraaf
87 Collins Brook Rd
Meredith NH 03253

Call Sign: KB1RKE
Thomas B Murphy
97 Collins Brook Rd
Meredith NH 03253

Call Sign: K1OHO
Roy W Frank
100 Cummings Cove Rd
Meredith NH 032536703

Call Sign: K1DKO
Bruce H Hack

22 Dale Rd
Meredith NH 032536802

Call Sign: KA1WBB
John F Jones
25 Dale Rd
Meredith NH 03253

Call Sign: K1FDX
Patricia A Rosha
56 Dale Rd
Meredith NH 03253

Call Sign: K1MNE
Adrian C Rosha Jr
56 Dale Rd
Meredith NH 03253

Call Sign: N1JHH
Elmer A Sperry Iii
20 Dollofff Brook Rd
Meredith NH 03253

Call Sign: KB1RZQ
Mark A Donohoe
64 Eaton Ave
Meredith NH 03253

Call Sign: KB1UJA
Sally A Porter
125 Edgerly School Rd
Meredith NH 03253

Call Sign: KB1GQN
Jason D Cornelissen
2 Flanders Rd
Meredith NH 03253

Call Sign: N1RCQ
Clifford D Dickinson
7 Lower Terrace Ave
Meredith NH 03253

Call Sign: KB1MMP
William J Carakatsane

25 Lower Waldron Rd
Meredith NH 03253

Call Sign: WB1ESE
Robert A Peelstrom Jr
82 Main St
Meredith NH 03253

Call Sign: N1DOB
James E Mc Glinchey
27 Meredith Bay Dr
Meredith NH 03253

Call Sign: AB1AH
Timothy P Golden
61 Meredith Center Rd
Meredith NH 03253

Call Sign: N1PKK
Michael I Sidney
129 Meredith Center Rd
Meredith NH 03253

Call Sign: KD4KME
Raymond D Montana
59 Meredith Neck Rd
Meredith NH 03253

Call Sign: N1SFN
Patricia A Montana
59 Meredith Neck Rd
Meredith NH 03253

Call Sign: K2ITX
Douglas C Mertz
144 Meredith Neck Rd
Meredith NH 03253

Call Sign: KF2W
Marc H Levey
80 Pease Rd
Meredith NH 03253

Call Sign: W1CGC
William J Hartford

128 Pinnacle Park Rd
Meredith NH 03253

Call Sign: KB1COM
Kenneth W Hamel
28 Pollard Shores Rd
Meredith NH 03253

Call Sign: KB1DCW
Uscg Northeast Region
28 Pollard Shores Rd
Meredith NH 03253

Call Sign: WA1LQX
Edward J Wilson Jr
94 Powers Rd
Meredith NH 03253

Call Sign: W3ATB
Tim J Carter
100 Swain Rd.
Meredith NH 032534614

Call Sign: K1BWP
David S Sticht
58 Tracy Way
Meredith NH 03253

Call Sign: WA1KUN
Joseph H Jeffrey
7 Trinity Rd
Meredith NH 03253

Call Sign: N1HQE
Linda J Mac Kay
92 Tucker Mountain Rd
Meredith NH 03253

Call Sign: N1HQF
Thomas E Mac Kay
Tucker Mt Rd
Meredith NH 03253

Call Sign: W1SKE
Thomas E Mac Kay

92 Tucker Mtn Rd
Meredith NH 03253

Call Sign: K1TEM
Thomas E Mac Kay
92 Tucker Mtn Rd
Meredith NH 03253

Call Sign: K1DIR
Robert M Knowles
52 Veasey Shore Rd.
Meredith NH 03253

Call Sign: W1GOU
Robert D Gage
89 Windsong Place
Meredith NH 03253

Call Sign: KB1BLT
Mariette J Lauer
Meredith NH 032530990

Call Sign: N1JNB
Michael Huntgeburth
Meredith NH 03253

Call Sign: N1MBA
Beverley H Lapham Iii
Meredith NH 03253

Call Sign: WB7BWP
David S Sticht
Meredith NH 03253

Call Sign: WB7PSG
Karen J Sticht
Meredith NH 03253

Call Sign: W1QN
James D Platt
1254 Route 120
Meriden NH 03770

Call Sign: N8RPD
William Daugherty
120 Underhill Rd
Meriden NH 03770

Call Sign: AA1IP
Bradley J Thompson
202 Whitaker Rd
Meriden NH 037700307

Call Sign: N1SMC
Dolores A Currier
Meriden NH 03770

Call Sign: W1KUA
Douglas R Plummer
Meriden NH 03770

Call Sign: KB1SKP
Robin M Marsh
Meriden NH 03770

Call Sign: W1MUO
Richard L Gysan
Meridith NH 03253

Call Sign: KB1DOQ
Donald J Collins
30 B Currier Rd
Merrimack NH 03054

Call Sign: AA1OC
William O Studley Iii
133 Baboosic Lake Rd
Merrimack NH 03054

Call Sign: WA1NNB
William C Richardson
149 Baboosic Lake Rd
Merrimack NH 03054

Call Sign: W1NNB
William C Richardson
149 Baboosic Lake Rd
Merrimack NH 03054

Call Sign: AA1LM
Robert J Koontz
249 Baboosic Lake Rd
Merrimack NH 03054

Call Sign: KB1MXF
Stephen D Jencks
263 Baboosic Lake Rd
Merrimack NH 030540533

Call Sign: K1SDJ
Stephen D Jencks
263 Baboosic Lake Rd
Merrimack NH 030540533

Call Sign: N1XUM
John T Koontz
249 Baboosie Lake Rd
Merrimack NH 03054

Call Sign: N1JKC
Daniel P Doyon
20 Back River Rd
Merrimack NH 03054

Call Sign: N1GSN
Paul E Mondoux
71 Back River Rd
Merrimack NH 03054

Call Sign: KB1VJS
Mark Villiard
3 Balsam Lane
Merrimack NH 03054

Call Sign: KA1FRC
Elizabeth A Hummel
139 Bedford Rd
Merrimack NH 03054

Call Sign: WA1NGA
William C Hummel
139 Bedford Rd
Merrimack NH 03054

Call Sign: KE1EB
Michael W Zaharee
10 Beebe Ln
Merrimack NH 03054

Call Sign: N1ZBS
Linda D Zaharee
10 Beebe Ln
Merrimack NH 03054

Call Sign: K3UTP
Richard L Leidich
11 Beebe Ln
Merrimack NH 03054

Call Sign: KB1HDI
David M Zaharee
10 Beebe Ln Dept L-1
Merrimack NH 03054

Call Sign: N1LTB
Bruce C Morrison
41 Belmont Dr
Merrimack NH 03054

Call Sign: KB1OFE
Paul A Giroux
16 Berkley St
Merrimack NH 03054

Call Sign: K2TLV
Gerald R Bogle
30 Berkley St
Merrimack NH 03054

Call Sign: KB1CMM
Robert E Grant
7 Birch St
Merrimack NH 03054

Call Sign: N1ZBM
Donald E Grant Iii
7 Birch St
Merrimack NH 03054

Call Sign: N1ZBN
Joy K Grant
7 Birch St
Merrimack NH 03054

Call Sign: KB1HMP
Julie Grant
7 Birch St
Merrimack NH 03054

Call Sign: N1UBD
Donald E Grant Ii
7 Birch St
Merrimack NH 03054

Call Sign: N1LHX
Kenneth F Hall
7 Birchwood Dr
Merrimack NH 03054

Call Sign: KB1QCS
James W Wendell
4 Blueberry Court
Merrimack NH 03054

Call Sign: W1VAW
James W Wendell
4 Blueberry Court
Merrimack NH 03054

Call Sign: N1JUR
Eric J Pfeifer
22 Boulder Way
Merrimack NH 03054

Call Sign: KA1PXB
Michael V Lospennato
5 Bowers Landing Dr 304
Merrimack NH 03054

Call Sign: N1QAZ
Richard A Moul
17 Bradford Dr
Merrimack NH 03054

Call Sign: N2QDV
David A Markson
16 Brant Dr
Merrimack NH 030543300

Call Sign: K1HI
Rexford C Lint
26 Brek Dr
Merrimack NH 03054

Call Sign: KB1NSW
Richard B Mcaroy
35 Brek Dr
Merrimack NH 03054

Call Sign: K1FIH
Patricia M Carson
15 Briarwood Dr
Merrimack NH 03054

Call Sign: KB1TJW
Timothy J Westley
4 Brookside Dr
Merrimack NH 03054

Call Sign: KB1TDK
Daniel S Ketchie
6 Brookside Dr
Merrimack NH 03054

Call Sign: AB1LS
Daniel S Ketchie
6 Brookside Dr
Merrimack NH 03054

Call Sign: KA1UC
Charles J Knox
11 Buttonwood Ln
Merrimack NH 03054

Call Sign: K1CJK
Charles J Knox
11 Buttonwood Ln
Merrimack NH 03054

Call Sign: KB1FZP
Gary R Mccoy
28 Cambridge Dr
Merrimack NH 03054

Call Sign: KB1MEZ
Gregory N Roberts
9 Cardinal Ct
Merrimack NH 03054

Call Sign: KF2TW
John B May
8 Castleton Ct
Merrimack NH 03054

Call Sign: N2YLQ
Robert J May
8 Castleton Ct
Merrimack NH 03054

Call Sign: KB1KXJ
Daral R Makahusz
7 Cedar Ln
Merrimack NH 03054

Call Sign: KB2ZVL
Kevin J Burns
33 Chestnut Circle
Merrimack NH 03054

Call Sign: KB1IDS
Miguel A Martorell
3 Chocorua Ln
Merrimack NH 03054

Call Sign: N1OC
Miguel A Martorell
3 Chocorua Ln
Merrimack NH 03054

Call Sign: N7VBP
Paul A Anzalone
1 Chororua Lane
Merrimack NH 03054

Call Sign: N1OB
Paul A Anzalone
1 Chororua Lane
Merrimack NH 03054

Call Sign: N1RYU
James A Szymczak
4 Cobblestone Place
Merrimack NH 03874

Call Sign: KA1BWI
Eric G Dolley
6 Collins Ave
Merrimack NH 03054

Call Sign: KB1PXD
William J Kimura
17 Conifer St
Merrimack NH 03054

Call Sign: N1AMC
William J Kimura
17 Conifer St
Merrimack NH 03054

Call Sign: N1TAQ
Peter B Grunewald
15 Cota Rd
Merrimack NH 03054

Call Sign: W1OF
Brian C Mitchell
20 Cota Rd
Merrimack NH 03054

Call Sign: N1WIR
Tracy A Lundstedt
48 Cota Rd
Merrimack NH 03054

Call Sign: KB1HHZ
Leatrice T Lebaron
9 Craig Dr
Merrimack NH 03054

Call Sign: KG1V
George L Gardner
23 Craig Dr
Merrimack NH 030543955

Call Sign: KE1KD
Scott L Babb
25 Cramer Hill Rd
Merrimack NH 03054

Call Sign: N1NVW
Holli M Babb
25 Cramer Hill Rd
Merrimack NH 03054

Call Sign: WB1N
Edwin B Smith
1 Cummings Rd
Merrimack NH 03054

Call Sign: WA2FCO
Ruth A Marcel
9 Cummings Rd
Merrimack NH 03054

Call Sign: WB2BON
Emmanuel J Marcel
9 Cummings Rd
Merrimack NH 03054

Call Sign: N1GHZ
Chris A Nissen
9 Dahl Rd
Merrimack NH 03054

Call Sign: KB1RHB
Dana A Knight
17 Dahl Rd
Merrimack NH 03054

Call Sign: KB1KC
Robert W Smart
21 Dalton Ct
Merrimack NH 03054

Call Sign: KB1DTF
James W Lajoie
573 Daniel Webster Hwy
Merrimack NH 030543426

Call Sign: N1ZZA
Judith J Volner
5 Deer Run
Merrimack NH 03054

Call Sign: WA1VIB
James W Volner
5 Deer Run
Merrimack NH 03054

Call Sign: KB1GYU
Raymond E Bonett
5 Donald Rd
Merrimack NH 03054

Call Sign: KB1PSE
Jillian T M Daniels
4 Donovan Court
Merrimack NH 03054

Call Sign: W1TIG
Jillian T M Daniels
4 Donovan Court
Merrimack NH 03054

Call Sign: N1THR
Robert D Bragdon
11 Douglas St
Merrimack NH 03054

Call Sign: WB3JOP
Cheryl V Liss
3 Dover St
Merrimack NH 030543129

Call Sign: N1LIC
Philip L Wetzel
4 Drouin Way
Merrimack NH 030544616

Call Sign: WB1GMD
George A Futterleib
3 Essex Green Ct
Merrimack NH 03054

Call Sign: W1CSI
Codem Radio Amateur Club
7 Executive Park Dr
Merrimack NH 03054

Call Sign: N1FBW
Ralph Canillas Jr
7 Fairway Dr
Merrimack NH 030541616

Call Sign: KC1YJ
Stephen W Holman
50 Fairway Dr
Merrimack NH 03054

Call Sign: KB1ISE
Russell S Holman
50 Fairway Dr
Merrimack NH 03054

Call Sign: KA1UDT
Errol H Upton
4 Falcon Dr
Merrimack NH 03054

Call Sign: N1QZK
Dennis C Cook
15 Farmer Rd
Merrimack NH 03151

Call Sign: KA1WY
Robert L Mc Naught
10 Fernwood Dr
Merrimack NH 03054

Call Sign: KE1CY
Bruce C Chadbourne
8 Forest Dr
Merrimack NH 030543230

Call Sign: KI1X
John W Hagerty Iii
8 Greenwood Dr
Merrimack NH 030542949

Call Sign: KB1IVN
William F Barnes
Hummingbird Dr Bldg 10
Merrimack NH 03054

Call Sign: KB1FAD
Laurance M Miller
10 Four Seasons Ln
Merrimack NH 03054

Call Sign: KA1RUW
Russell J Vassar Jr
4 Griffin St
Merrimack NH 03054

Call Sign: N1NEG
Kenneth J Winograd
15 Hutchinson Rd
Merrimack NH 03054

Call Sign: N1IHU
Alan C Legerlotz
11 Four Winds Rd
Merrimack NH 03054

Call Sign: KB1KXI
David M Berry
5 Gull Ln
Merrimack NH 03054

Call Sign: KB1KXG
Mark J Esselman
145 Indian Rock Rd
Merrimack NH 03054

Call Sign: KB1GYO
Alan C Legerlotz
11 Four Winds Rd
Merrimack NH 03054

Call Sign: KA1QXM
Rose A Napolitan
6 Gunstock Ridge
Merrimack NH 03054

Call Sign: K1PHJ
Reuben S Streeper
160 Indian Rock Rd
Merrimack NH 03054

Call Sign: AA1UR
Daniel D Principe
14 Four Winds Rd
Merrimack NH 03054

Call Sign: W2FGK
Alan Saeger
26 Hansom Dr
Merrimack NH 03054

Call Sign: N1NCP
Lawrence P Fletcher
7 Ivy Dr
Merrimack NH 03054

Call Sign: W1ZV
Daniel D Principe
14 Four Winds Rd
Merrimack NH 03054

Call Sign: N1VPH
Henry D Wade
11 Harrington Dr.
Merrimack NH 03054

Call Sign: KB1EJC
Steven C Mikolajczuk
104 Jay Rd
Merrimack NH 03054

Call Sign: K1DMU
Lyle M Kaufman
3 Glen Forest Dr
Merrimack NH 03054

Call Sign: K1RUN
David H Doherty
6 Highland Green
Merrimack NH 03054

Call Sign: N1RKV
Duane L La Flotte
30 Jessica Dr
Merrimack NH 03054

Call Sign: KB1WOY
Jeffrey S Kelley
5 Greatstone Dr
Merrimack NH 03054

Call Sign: N4XTC
David H Doherty
6 Highland Green
Merrimack NH 03054

Call Sign: K1BBE
Wayne M Kibbe
118 Joppa Rd
Merrimack NH 03054

Call Sign: KG6CIH
Christopher E Lumens
25 Greatstone Dr
Merrimack NH 03054

Call Sign: KX1C
David H Doherty
6 Highland Green
Merrimack NH 03054

Call Sign: W1PO
Daniel W Szymanowski
124 Joppa Rd
Merrimack NH 03054

Call Sign: KA1PQK
James T Francis Jr
4 Klara Dr
Merrimack NH 03054

Call Sign: K1LQ
Diane J Troyer
61 London St
Merrimack NH 03054

Call Sign: N1FMN
John J Mc Cormack Jr
18 Lorraine Rd
Merrimack NH 030544613

Call Sign: KA1AHO
Raymond L Johnson Jr
7 Madison Ln
Merrimack NH 030543018

Call Sign: KB1OWI
Sean M Hogan
36 Maidstone Dr
Merrimack NH 03054

Call Sign: K1EQN
Sean M Hogan
36 Maidstone Dr
Merrimack NH 03054

Call Sign: W1CUL
John T Apostolos
3 Majestic Ln
Merrimack NH 03054

Call Sign: KA1KLZ
Gregory R Staradub
33 Mallard Point Rd
Merrimack NH 03054

Call Sign: KB1DBG
Kenneth E Williams
36 Marty Dr
Merrimack NH 03054

Call Sign: AB1BE
Kenneth E Williams
36 Marty Dr
Merrimack NH 03054

Call Sign: KB1DN
Richard D Groves
47 Marty Dr
Merrimack NH 03054

Call Sign: N1QFO
Matthew M Sartin
23 Mc Elwain St
Merrimack NH 03054

Call Sign: N1RKM
Larry E Sartin
23 Mc Elwain St
Merrimack NH 03054

Call Sign: N1QFP
Eugene T Sartin
23 Mc Elwain St Suite 2
Merrimack NH 03054

Call Sign: KB1INY
Paul A Bell
7 Merrimack Dr
Merrimack NH 03054

Call Sign: W1HPB
Paul A Bell
7 Merrimack Dr
Merrimack NH 030544849

Call Sign: KB1JQQ
Dolores A Bell
7 Merrimack Dr
Merrimack NH 030544849

Call Sign: W1DOL
Dolores A Bell
7 Merrimack Dr
Merrimack NH 030544849

Call Sign: N1ZUU
Alan Chan
46 Merrimack Dr
Merrimack NH 03054

Call Sign: WA1TGX
Robert J Lynch
42 Middlesex Rd
Merrimack NH 03054

Call Sign: KB1UIV
Daniel Moran
Mill St
Merrimack NH 03054

Call Sign: K1VLU
James M Grady Sr
1 Mitchell St
Merrimack NH 03054

Call Sign: N1RBF
Patrice M Ellis
2 Mockingbird Ct
Merrimack NH 03054

Call Sign: N1QXD
Mark D Ellis
2 Mockingbird Ct
Merrimach NH 03054

Call Sign: KB1MEU
Carl G Hindy
14 Monadnock Ln
Merrimack NH 03054

Call Sign: W1PSY
Carl G Hindy
14 Monadnock Ln
Merrimack NH 03054

Call Sign: K1WVO
Michael Ryan Jr
6 Morningside Ave
Merrimack NH 030544202

Call Sign: KB1QYX
David W Michaels
8 Nathan Hale Ln
Merrimack NH 03054

Call Sign: K1GK
Gary T Kozinski
17 Nathan Hale Ln
Merrimack NH 03054

Call Sign: N1ONC
Bethany A Simons
18 Naticook Rd
Merrimack NH 03054

Call Sign: WA1TYB
Allen K Simons
18 Naticook Rd
Merrimack NH 03054

Call Sign: KB1LVO
Thomas J Mahon
31 Naticook Rd
Merrimack NH 03054

Call Sign: AB1NS
Thomas J Mahon
31 Naticook Rd
Merrimack NH 03054

Call Sign: KB1FXL
Brian M Boerner
57 Naticook Rd
Merrimack NH 03054

Call Sign: KB1GZZ
Knoll Crest Farm Radio
Club
57 Naticook Rd
Merrimack NH 03054

Call Sign: W2SUQ
Brian M Boerner
57 Naticook Rd
Merrimack NH 03054

Call Sign: KB1HYN
Amanda B Boerner
57 Naticook Rd
Merrimack NH 03054

Call Sign: KB1ESL
Melissa L Chevalier
91 Naticook Rd
Merrimack NH 03054

Call Sign: W1GRY
Gary J Chevalier
91 Naticook Rd
Merrimack NH 03054

Call Sign: N1KOT
Vincent G Piekunka
206 Naticook Rd
Merrimack NH 03054

Call Sign: KB1THS
Duncan E Morrill
19 Old Kings Rd
Merrimack NH 03059

Call Sign: WV1J
Duncan E Morrill
19 Old Kings Rd
Merrimack NH 03054

Call Sign: K1FKS
Edward R Walker Sr
4 Owls Ct
Merrimack NH 03054

Call Sign: KB1JNL
Eric W Choate
5 Packard Dr
Merrimack NH 03054

Call Sign: N1GLC
Eric W Choate
5 Packard Dr
Merrimack NH 03054

Call Sign: N1ZBO
Roger P L Heureux
14 Paige Dr
Merrimack NH 03054

Call Sign: KB1EFL
Martha A Wagner
1 Parker Dr
Merrimack NH 03054

Call Sign: N1ZYZ
Mark A Wagner
1 Parker Dr
Merrimack NH 03054

Call Sign: N1ZYY
Matthew A Wagner
1 Parker Dr
Merrimack NH 03054

Call Sign: KB1SRD
Richard A Todd
45 Parkhurst Rd
Merrimack NH 03054

Call Sign: K1HXA
Richard A Todd
45 Parkhurst Rd
Merrimack NH 03054

Call Sign: K1EEE
Michael R Rancourt
60 Pearson Rd
Merrimack NH 03054

Call Sign: KB1MPS
Thomas M Rancourt
60 Pearson Rd
Merrimack NH 03054

Call Sign: KJ4DS
Wayne F Cashwell
30 Peaslee Rd
Merrimack NH 030544517

Call Sign: AB1EM
Wayne F Cashwell
30 Peaslee Rd
Merrimack NH 030544517

Call Sign: NW1C
Wayne F Cashwell
30 Peaslee Rd
Merrimack NH 030544517

Call Sign: W1RDB
Daniel A Benard
81 Peaslee Rd
Merrimack NH 030546815

Call Sign: KB1VMA
Brian W Jennings
5 Pebble Ct
Merrimack NH 03054

Call Sign: N1PDM
Harry E Smith
12 Peter Rd
Merrimack NH 03054

Call Sign: N1RZB
David J Moge
34 Peter Rd
Merrimack NH 03054

Call Sign: N1YXV
Matthew P Day Mr
6 Quincy Dr
Merrimack NH 03054

Call Sign: W1CWC
Craig W Child
Railroad Ave
Merrimack NH 03054

Call Sign: KB1DZT
R Keith Beal
16 Reeds Ferry Way
Merrimack NH 030542839

Call Sign: K1DVM
Cedric F Onsruth
20 Reeds Ferry Way
Merrimack NH 030540880

Call Sign: KB1UBD
Lawrence D Bradshaw
6 Roberta Dr
Merrimack NH 03054

Call Sign: KE4ZLQ
Elizabeth R Bodman
18 Roundtree Dr
Merrimack NH 03054

Call Sign: NU1U
Ronnie Martin
5 Royal Court
Merrimack NH 030544252

Call Sign: KA1USU
Kathie W Martin
5 Royal Ct
Merrimack NH 03054

Call Sign: N1JOQ
Nathaniel L Fairbanks
5 Sandhill Dr
Merrimack NH 03054

Call Sign: KD6KWB
Gregory P Hassett
30 Sandpiper Lane
Merrimack NH 03054

Call Sign: W1RFB
Frank C Hassett
30 Sandpiper Lane
Merrimack NH 030544878

Call Sign: KB1HHH
John A Barrett
3 Savage Ln
Merrimack NH 03054

Call Sign: KE4RXW
David H Doherty
1 Scituate Place #3
Merrimack NH 03054

Call Sign: K1RUN
David H Doherty
1 Scituate Place 3
Merrimack NH 03054

Call Sign: K1VVV
David H Doherty
1 Scituate Place 3
Merrimack NH 03054

Call Sign: WA1CIR
John H Heaney Iii
5 Seaverns Bridge Rd
Merrimack NH 03054

Call Sign: N1ZKO
James M Eden
19 Seaverns Bridge Rd
Merrimack NH 03054

Call Sign: AB1NE
Gregory W Maglathlin
21 Seaverns Bridge Rd
Merrimack NH 03054

Call Sign: KB1PQD
Justin G Ruddock
60 Shelburne Rd
Merrimack NH 03054

Call Sign: K1XLT
Justin G Ruddock
60 Shelburne Rd
Merrimack NH 03054

Call Sign: WA1YXH
Michael G Bobblis
2 Short St
Merrimack NH 03054

Call Sign: W1SU
John J Cuneo Jr
28 Souhegan Dr
Merrimack NH 03054

Call Sign: AB1KW
Henri (Rik) Van Riel
50 Springfield Circle
Merrimack NH 03054

Call Sign: KB1LKH
Michael P Fesko
52 Springfield Circle
Merrimack NH 03054

Call Sign: KB2OOP
Ryan M Workman
2 Spruce St
Merrimack NH 03054

Call Sign: K1RTL
Richard T Leshner Jr
6 Spruce St
Merrimack NH 03054

Call Sign: N1CWJ
Norman E Rowe
2 Suncook Terrace Apt. 32
Merrimack NH 03054

Call Sign: N1IYI
William F Cashman
9 Surrey Ln
Merrimack NH 03054

Call Sign: K1QLV
Bradford L Cross
4 Tiffany Ln
Merrimack NH 03054

Call Sign: N1SMY
William J Ham
5 Timber Ln
Merrimack NH 030543221

Call Sign: KB1EDF
Desmond A Johnson
12 Timber Ln
Merrimack NH 03054

Call Sign: WK1V
Desmond A Johnson
12 Timber Ln
Merrimack NH 03054

Call Sign: WA4WIJ
Mary Jane F Warren
4 Tomahawk Dr
Merrimack NH 03054

Call Sign: WB4MDC
William J Warren
4 Tomahawk Dr
Merrimack NH 030542335

Call Sign: WA1IJO
Arnold L Robinson
99 Turkey Hill Rd
Merrimack NH 03054

Call Sign: K1HXA
Frederick A Todd
11 Valleyview Dr
Merrimack NH 03054

Call Sign: N1SIX
Raymond A Lajoie
6 W Chamberlain Rd
Merrimack NH 03054

Call Sign: N1UCS
Susan S Lajoie
6 W Chamberlain Rd
Merrimack NH 03054

Call Sign: KA1MXB
Peter R Cross
10 W Chamberlain Rd
Merrimack NH 030544014

Call Sign: KB1JKM
Michael M Cox
6 Walace Dr
Merrimack NH 03054

Call Sign: NB1HF
Neal E Blaiklock
26 Waterville Dr
Merrimack NH 03054

Call Sign: KA1PNT
William L Crenshaw
7 Westminster Ln
Merrimack NH 03054

Call Sign: KB1HBB
Edmundo E Martinez
14 Westminster Ln
Merrimack NH 030542366

Call Sign: WA1EYP
Michael Cobuccio
16 Westminster Ln
Merrimack NH 03054

Call Sign: KA1QZU
Richard H Rhoades
17 Westminster Ln
Merrimack NH 03054

Call Sign: KA1RAG
Christopher Rhoades
17 Westminster Ln
Merrimack NH 03054

Call Sign: W2HQD
Ralph S Reed Jr
50 Wilson Hill Rd
Merrimack NH 03054

Call Sign: KB1MRG
Gregory H Gardner
5 Windsor Dr
Merrimack NH 03054

Call Sign: K2TE
Edward C Deichler
86 Wire Rd
Merrimack NH 030540323

Call Sign: N1EJF
James S Godron
75 Woodward Rd
Merrimack NH 03054

Call Sign: KB1KCV
Ronald R Kimball
5 Wren Court
Merrimack NH 03054

Call Sign: N0RK
Ronald R Kimball
5 Wren Court
Merrimack NH 03054

Call Sign: K1WTK
John R Peschier
Merrimack NH 03054

Call Sign: N1BFL
Robert D Siebert Iii
Merrimack NH 030540458

Call Sign: N1MEP
Karen L Peterson
Merrimack NH 03054

Call Sign: N1THU
Brian W Simons
Merrimack NH 030540068

Call Sign: N1VLC
Stuart L Hollander
Merrimack NH 03054

Call Sign: N1VRV
Robert J Briggs
Merrimack NH 03054

Call Sign: N8INO
R Craig Peterson
Merrimack NH 030541120

Call Sign: W1FBW
Ralph Canillas Jr
Merrimack NH 030541616

Call Sign: KD5SMI
Michal Tomec
Merrimack NH 03054

Call Sign: N1PA
Paul A Anzalone
Merrimack NH 03054

Call Sign: KB1NYZ
Emergency Warning
Amateur Radio Network
Merrimack NH 03054

Call Sign: NN1PA
Emergency Warning
Amateur Radio Network
Merrimack NH 03054

Call Sign: W1LA
Tadmuck Swamp Vhf
Society
Merrimack NH 03054

Call Sign: KB1PAZ
Tracy A Claus
Merrimack NH 03054

Call Sign: KB1VLU
New England Digital Voice
Merrimack NH 03054

Call Sign: NE1DV
New England Digital Voice
Merrimack NH 03054

Call Sign: KB1WJI
Ewarn

Merrimack NH 03054

Call Sign: NE1DS
Ewarn
Merrimack NH 03054

Call Sign: KB1WNH
Ewarn
Merrimack NH 03054

Call Sign: KB1WRF
Ewarn
Merrimack NH 03054

## FCC Amateur Radio Licenses in Middleton

Call Sign: WD6GDK
Earle V Dudley Iii
Box 2820
Middleton NH 03887

Call Sign: NA1D
Mary A Saliga
173 Drew Dr
Middleton NH 03887

Call Sign: NA1E
Daniel R Saliga
173 Drew Dr
Middleton NH 03887

Call Sign: N1LZS
Charles H Wyatt Jr
Middleton Hill Rd
Middleton NH 03887

Call Sign: KB1AUI
Leonard E Arkerson
155 New Durham Rd
Middleton NH 03887

Call Sign: KA1KHX
Milton E Rich
237 Ridge Rd

Middleton NH 03887

Call Sign: KB1M
Walter G Peckham
322 Ridge Rd
Middleton NH 03887

## FCC Amateur Radio Licenses in Milan

Call Sign: KB1EUY
Kevin J Shyne
39 Chandler Lodges Rd
Milan NH 03588

Call Sign: N1WBA
Gregory S Meserve
788 Milan Rd
Milan NH 03588

Call Sign: N1FZK
Craig D Dube
255 W Milan Rd
Milan NH 03588

Call Sign: KX1S
Craig D Dube
255 W Milan Rd
Milan NH 03588

Call Sign: KY1S
Gail A Dube
255 W Milan Rd
Milan NH 03588

Call Sign: KB1GCW
Gail A Dube
255 West Milan Rd
Milan NH 03588

## FCC Amateur Radio Licenses in Milford

Call Sign: N1WIV
Michael J Gase

4 Acacia Ln
Milford NH 03055

Call Sign: WB1ERF
Ronald J Mariano Sr
178 Annand Dr
Milford NH 03055

Call Sign: N1DHK
Jack E Tripp
78 Armory Rd
Milford NH 030553405

Call Sign: KB3JID
David T Mattox
197 Badger Hill Dr
Milford NH 03055

Call Sign: KB1LKJ
David T Mattox
197 Badger Hill Dr
Milford NH 03055

Call Sign: KC1SG
Joel B Chappell
21 Billings St
Milford NH 03055

Call Sign: KB1UXN
Jennifer K Chandler
57 Birchwood Dr
Milford NH 03055

Call Sign: WS1R
Glendon A Moncrief
12 Border St
Milford NH 03055

Call Sign: N6LVT
Kevin L Johnson
60 Brookview Dr
Milford NH 030554601

Call Sign: N6MCA
Jean M Johnson

60 Brookview Dr
Milford NH 030554601

Call Sign: W1KLJ
Kevin L Johnson
60 Brookview Dr
Milford NH 030554601

Call Sign: KJ1I
Kevin L Johnson
60 Brookview Dr
Milford NH 030554601

Call Sign: KB1GWF
Michael J Silva
3 Carriage Ln
Milford NH 03055

Call Sign: WA1RYP
Roland A Gilbert
81 Chappell Dr
Milford NH 030553207

Call Sign: WE1O
Franklin M Davy
35 Christine Dr
Milford NH 03055

Call Sign: N1BFQ
David O Warren
20 Clark Rd
Milford NH 03055

Call Sign: N1TRP
John H Gordon Jr
66 Clark Rd
Milford NH 030553812

Call Sign: KB1GWD
Mathew P Lagro
170 Colburn Rd
Milford NH 03055

Call Sign: KB1HCF
James A Pfeiffer

207 Colburn Rd
Milford NH 03055

Call Sign: KA1OTN
Russell J Santos
245 Colburn Rd
Milford NH 03055

Call Sign: N1UJF
Joseph J Santos
245 Colburn Rd
Milford NH 03055

Call Sign: KB1DNX
Peter W Dowson
245 Colburn Rd
Milford NH 03055

Call Sign: K1TSV
Russell J Santos
245 Colburn Rd
Milford NH 030553544

Call Sign: N1XRL
Christopher J Cramer
68 Colburn Rd.
Milford NH 03055

Call Sign: N1UEG
Carlos A Barberis
123 Comstock Dr
Milford NH 03055

Call Sign: KB1SKZ
Jeff P Marshall
51 Cortland Rd
Milford NH 03055

Call Sign: KC1IY
Richard C Everhart
45 Crestwood Ln
Milford NH 030553514

Call Sign: W1RCE
Richard C Everhart

45 Crestwood Ln
Milford NH 030553514

Call Sign: W5RCE
Richard C Everhart
45 Crestwood Ln
Milford NH 030553514

Call Sign: KA1RUS
Sara C Everhart
Crestwood Ln
Milford NH 03055

Call Sign: KA1SOC
Kimberly L Koch
27 Crosby St
Milford NH 03055

Call Sign: KA1GAX
James E Coughlin
20 Dearborn St
Milford NH 03055

Call Sign: NE1K
Raymond P Regan
344 Elm St #11
Milford NH 03055

Call Sign: K1IE
William C Wrocklage
344 Elm St Unit 23
Milford NH 03055

Call Sign: KA1VQF
Norman R Norcross Jr
545 Elm St Unit13
Milford NH 03055

Call Sign: WA1SKI
Robert D Maciorowski
5 Farley St
Milford NH 03055

Call Sign: WA1RBM
Richard B Stetson

188 Federal Hill Rd
Milford NH 030553518

Call Sign: KA1BDL
Thomas E Gay Iii
18 Fern Ct
Milford NH 03055

Call Sign: WA1THG
John E Preble Sr
21 Foster Rd
Milford NH 03055

Call Sign: N1MAX
Dana R Schult
39 Highland Ave
Milford NH 03055

Call Sign: KC3NG
Renee M Culver
27 Iris Rd
Milford NH 03055

Call Sign: WA1YFB
Philip O Gendron
179 Jennison Rd
Milford NH 03055

Call Sign: W1POG
Philip O Gendron
179 Jennison Rd
Milford NH 03055

Call Sign: KC1F
Stuart R Santelmann
20 Larch Rd
Milford NH 03055

Call Sign: KB0LQM
Thomas C Perkins
7 Lincoln St
Milford NH 03055

Call Sign: W1FMF
Thomas C Perkins

7 Lincoln St
Milford NH 03055

51 Mont Vernon St
Milford NH 03055

321 Osgood Rd
Milford NH 03055

Call Sign: K1JPK
John P Krass
51 Lovejoy Rd
Milford NH 03055

Call Sign: N1MEO
Fletcher W Seagroves Jr
163 Mont Vernon St
Milford NH 03055

Call Sign: KE1KT
Bernard J Cass
399 Osgood Rd
Milford NH 030553435

Call Sign: KA1RUK
William E Barry
Mason Rd
Milford NH 03055

Call Sign: N1AFD
Richard G Fontaine
17 Mooreland St
Milford NH 03055

Call Sign: N1PUY
Edward M Hardy
615 Osgood Rd
Milford NH 03055

Call Sign: N2AZF
Jeff H Blake
110 Melendy Rd
Milford NH 03055

Call Sign: K1SSA
Paul T Frawley
439 N River Rd Unit 10
Milford NH 03055

Call Sign: N1QCI
Barbara A Hardy
615 Osgood Rd
Milford NH 03055

Call Sign: WA1ZRP
Theodore W Meedzan
26 Melendy Rd 56
Milford NH 030553470

Call Sign: KB1GWC
Ian P Johnson
354 Nashua St
Milford NH 03055

Call Sign: KB1GFM
Seth D Ambrose
14 Oxbridge Way
Milford NH 03269

Call Sign: KE1THR
E Keith Roberts
26 Melendy Rd Lot 78
Milford NH 03055

Call Sign: KB1QVL
Charles R Patterson
362 Nashua St
Milford NH 03055

Call Sign: KB1KXN
Roy A Golisano
44 Park St
Milford NH 03055

Call Sign: W1RDP
Harold C Densmore
35 Merrimack Rd
Milford NH 03055

Call Sign: KB1GNH
Stuart H Urie
614 Nashua St  161
Milford NH 03055

Call Sign: N1FQU
Charita A Ughu
90 Patch Hill Lane
Milford NH 030554137

Call Sign: WB1FPL
Lois B Densmore
35 Merrimack Rd
Milford NH 03055

Call Sign: KB1IDV
Michael E Thornton
561 North River Rd
Milford NH 030555012

Call Sign: KB1NBE
Donald P Stetson
333 Ponemah Hill Rd
Milford NH 030553529

Call Sign: KB1GIT
Steven M Santinelli
214 Mile Slip Rd
Milford NH 03055

Call Sign: WB1R
Bruce R Auge
68 Osgood Rd
Milford NH 03055

Call Sign: KB1SPQ
Francis Watson
29 Prospect St
Milford NH 03055

Call Sign: KE1KW
Terry R Parker

Call Sign: KB1PYB
David E Anderson

Call Sign: K1PLJ
Thea G Conant

59 Quarry Cir
Milford NH 03055

Call Sign: KB1GWG
Scott P Powers
23 Radcliffe Dr
Milford NH 03055

Call Sign: KB1LDK
Robert Stanton Jr
76 Stable Rd
Milford NH 03855

Call Sign: KI4ZYK
SEAN E Mccandless
25 SUMMER St
Milford NH 03055

Call Sign: K3RQ
George A Murphy
156 Summer St
Milford NH 03055

Call Sign: N1EQJ
Norman S Bragner Sr
31 Wellesley Dr
Milford NH 03055

Call Sign: W1LLD
Everett A Whitney
70 West St
Milford NH 03055

Call Sign: K1MHS
Milford High School
Amateur Radio Club
100 West St
Milford NH 03055

Call Sign: KG4IOG
Charles T Roberts
93 West St Apt 1
Milford NH 03055

Call Sign: KA1JDH

Janet R Levy
Milford NH 030550085

Call Sign: N1BFK
William J Sconce
Milford NH 030550085

Call Sign: N1YEP
Linda E Russell
Milford NH 03055

Call Sign: N1NHR
Charles R Patterson
Milford NH 030557521

## FCC Amateur Radio Licenses in Milton

Call Sign: KB1IDF
William T Gordon
4 Bolan Rd
Milton NH 03851

Call Sign: KT1N
William T Gordon
4 Bolan Rd
Milton NH 03851

Call Sign: W1KKT
Frank R Nutter
49 Charles St
Milton NH 038511252

Call Sign: N1OYP
Peter R Wilfert
Charles St
Milton NH 03851

Call Sign: K2MZE
Joseph Arnone Jr
74 Evergreen Valley Rd
Milton NH 038514509

Call Sign: KB1FFC
Clinton S Lurvey

74 Hare Rd
Milton NH 03851

Call Sign: WA1TFS
Clinton S Lurvey
74 Hare Rd
Milton NH 03851

Call Sign: AA1ZO
Clinton S Lurvey
74 Hare Rd
Milton NH 03851

Call Sign: W1JIC
David E Dickinson
356 Mason Rd
Milton NH 03851

Call Sign: WA1EUS
David L Merrill
177 Middleton Rd
Milton NH 03851

Call Sign: K1DEB
Deborah E Miller
8 Rookery Rd
Milton NH 03851

Call Sign: KB1VIH
Justin P Bellen
Tappon Ct
Milton NH 03851

Call Sign: WB1FPG
Robert D Sylvester Jr
41 Thurston Rd
Milton NH 03851

Call Sign: N3JDJ
Thomas L Mc Dougall Jr
White Mountain Highway
Milton NH 03851

Call Sign: KC7VKL
Paula M Dunn

62 White Mtn Hwy
Milton NH 03851

Call Sign: KB1IBO
Paula M Dunn
62 White Mtn Hwy
Milton NH 03851

Call Sign: AB1EU
Paula M Dunn
62 White Mtn Hwy
Milton NH 03851

Call Sign: AK1X
Paula M Dunn
62 White Mtn Hwy
Milton NH 03851

Call Sign: N1HDK
Bernard H Liberi Jr
Milton NH 03851

Call Sign: N1JLN
Bruce D Welch
Milton NH 03851

Call Sign: KB1KXP
Leslie O Chase
Milton NH 03851

Call Sign: N1JPB
Justin P Bellen
Milton NH 03851

## FCC Amateur Radio Licenses in Milton Mills

Call Sign: KB1TFH
Justin M Mayrand
246 Applebee Rd
Milton Mills NH 03852

Call Sign: N1DOA
Robert A Durso
334 Jug Hill Rd

Milton Mills NH 03852

## FCC Amateur Radio Licenses in Mirror Lake

Call Sign: W2HKF
Robert V Gould
Bennett Farm Rd
Mirror Lake NH 03853

Call Sign: K1FKF
Fred C Hunt
Mirror Lake NH 038530453

## FCC Amateur Radio Licenses in Monroe

Call Sign: KB1HDE
Gary A Merwin
1743 Coppermine Rd
Monroe NH 03771

Call Sign: KB1CRQ
Matt P Gibson
44 Plains Rd
Monroe NH 03771

Call Sign: KB1DZR
Deborah J Sanders-Dame
301 Smutty Hollow
Monroe NH 037719715

Call Sign: KA1JOZ
Brian R Dame
301 Smutty Hollow Rd
Monroe NH 03771

## FCC Amateur Radio Licenses in Mont Vernon

Call Sign: KA1IWL
Donald J Labonte
5 Carleton Rd
Mont Vernon NH 03057

Call Sign: N1IWN
Edward M Wetmore
11 Cross Rd
Mont Vernon NH 03057

Call Sign: KA1WJD
Manizheh Mehrabani
19 Harwood Rd
Mont Vernon NH 03057

Call Sign: KB1OIS
Bahnou Upton
19 Harwood Rd
Mont Vernon NH 03057

Call Sign: KB1OTB
Dahnesh F Upton
19 Harwood Rd
Mont Vernon NH 03057

Call Sign: WB1CMG
David M Upton
19 Harwood Rd Rr 1
Mont Vernon NH 03057

Call Sign: KB1GOO
George B Tocher
1 Hazen Rd
Mont Vernon NH 03057

Call Sign: N1FSM
John M Churin
13 Joe English Rd
Mont Vernon NH 03057

Call Sign: N1LKM
Susan J Bazarnick
12 Levesque Ln
Mont Vernon NH 03057

Call Sign: KB1GWI
James A Dewitt
15 Mason Rd
Mont Vernon NH 03057

Call Sign: KB1KGA
Ross N Keatinge
111 North Main St
Mont Vernon NH 03057

Call Sign: W1JOB
Harry F Chisholm
Old Milford Rd
Mont Vernon NH 03057

Call Sign: AD1W
Shawn T Diehl
Old Milford Rd
Mont Vernon NH
030570224

Call Sign: KB1NVN
Sam D Peret
11 Pine Knoll
Mont Vernon NH 03057

Call Sign: KC2TV
Anthony A Immorlica Jr
6 Purgatory Rd
Mont Vernon NH 03057

Call Sign: KA1COM
Arthur J Gregor
15 Purgatory Rd
Mont Vernon NH
030571500

Call Sign: W1VUW
Wayne A Kearsley
15 Rangeway Rd
Mont Vernon NH
030571520

Call Sign: W1YFU
Richard Quintal
78 Salisbury Rd
Mont Vernon NH
030570360

Call Sign: N1ORF

Anthony R Koch
Second St
Mont Vernon NH 03050

Call Sign: WA1HCO
Jeffrey R Millar
37 Spring Hill Rd
Mont Vernon NH
030571605

Call Sign: N1TRD
Herbert S Archer Iii
41 Spring Hill Rd
Mont Vernon NH 03057

Call Sign: KB1MVZ
Peter Viscarola
216 Tarn Rd
Mont Vernon NH 03057

Call Sign: K1PGV
Peter Viscarola
216 Tarn Rd
Mont Vernon NH 03057

Call Sign: AB7Q
David L Herrick
18 Tater St
Mont Vernon NH 03057

Call Sign: WA1BXM
David L Herrick
18 Tater St
Mont Vernon NH 03057

Call Sign: KB1WLF
Paul F Silva
70 Tater St
Mont Vernon NH 03057

Call Sign: N1HPF
Leslie A Zaraza
74 Tater St
Mont Vernon NH 03057

Call Sign: KD1ME
John G Griffith Iv
7 Trappist Cir
Mont Vernon NH 03057

Call Sign: W1IBI
Steven E Holzman
7 Westgate Rd
Mont Vernon NH 03057

Call Sign: KB1KGJ
Jeff Perkins
Mont Vernon NH
030570309

**FCC Amateur Radio
Licenses in Moultonboro**

Call Sign: W1JAQ
Melvin H Coffin
Ganzy Ln
Moultonboro NH 03254

Call Sign: W1NBL
Richard C Patten
46 Patten Hill Rd.
Moultonboro NH 03254

Call Sign: KA1SDM
Jeffery A Szymujko
Rfd Box 419
Moultonboro NH 03254

Call Sign: KB1CDJ
Fred W Fraser Jr
163 Shaker Jerry Rd
Moultonboro NH 03254

Call Sign: KF4ZGO
Steve A Lamesch
Skyland Park
Moultonboro NH 03254

Call Sign: KB1ECJ
Richard L Moren

Moultonboro NH
032540388

Call Sign: N1RRS
Michael J Ayers
Moultonboro NH 03254

Call Sign: W1KBO
George P Jowdy
Moultonboro NH 03254

Call Sign: W1RLM
Richard L Moren
Moultonboro NH
032540388

Call Sign: K1WPM
Douglas M Aiken
9 Bentley Rd
Moultonborough NH 03254

Call Sign: KB1CZV
Laura T Burke
44 Birch Lane
Moultonborough NH 03254

Call Sign: WB0AT
William J Burke
44 Birch Lane
Moultonborough NH 03254

Call Sign: K1VBD
Irving P Meredith
3 Blake,Rd
Moultonborough NH 03254

Call Sign: K1GVU
Edward Dobson
Box 677
Moultonborough NH 03254

Call Sign: N1YEF
Frederic A Mollins
395 Long Island Rd
Moultonborough NH 03254

Call Sign: N5PKY
Thomas E Potwin
52 Mountain View Dr
Moultonborough NH
032540516

Call Sign: KB1PRK
Bruce G Essler
61 Sheltie Crossing
Moultonborough NH 03254

Call Sign: AB1HY
Bruce G Essler
61 Sheltie Crossing
Moultonborough NH 03254

Call Sign: WA1NVV
Bruce G Essler
61 Sheltie Crossing
Moultonborough NH 03254

Call Sign: N1GN
Thomas G N Bethel
171 Skyline Dr
Moultonborough NH 03254

Call Sign: WA2PHS
John H Weinmann
7 Summit View Dr
Moultonborough NH 03254

Call Sign: K2RCV
John J Meehan
Moultonborough NH
032540615

Call Sign: KB1MSL
Alan E Walts
Moultonborough NH 03254

Call Sign: N1LYG
Michael J Colasurdo
Aten Rd
Munsonville NH 03457

Call Sign: KA1TWK
Steven C Bosworth
Box 598
Munsonville NH 03457

Call Sign: W1TLU
Edmund A Gianferrari
Box North Shore Rd
Munsonville NH 03457

Call Sign: KB1GSP
Hope A Lothrop
225 Murdough Hill Rd
Munsonville NH 03457

Call Sign: W1DLE
Ronald E Lyon
12 Olde Towne Rd
Munsonville NH 034575134

Call Sign: N1YLF
William J Ennis
110 A Concord St
Nashua NH 03060

Call Sign: AA1WR
James D Mc Elroy Sr
20 A Northwest Blvd  PMB
294
Nashua NH 030634066

Call Sign: N1WRE
James D Mc Elroy Sr
20 A Northwest Blvd 294

Nashua NH 030634066

Call Sign: N1ERJ
Rodney C Adams
20 A Northwest Blvd 347
Nashua NH 03063

Call Sign: NO1Q
William E Faulkner Iii
3 Addison Rd
Nashua NH 03062

Call Sign: KF1E
Norman O Dionne
101 Allds St
Nashua NH 030606301

Call Sign: N1KOP
Pamela Green
78 Allds St 2
Nashua NH 03060

Call Sign: K5PSZ
James M Mc Nulty
10 Allds St 319
Nashua NH 03060

Call Sign: K1RZO
Ruth M Mc Namara
10 Allds St Apt 112
Nashua NH 030604734

Call Sign: W1PEX
Daniel A Mac Donald
10 Allds St Apt 215
Nashua NH 03060

Call Sign: N1FRM
Roger D Gray
10 Allds St Apt 321
Nashua NH 03060

Call Sign: WA1VLV
Robert P Mulliken
43 Almont St

Nashua NH 03060

Call Sign: N1DNG
Neverett S Smith Sr
55 Amherst St
Nashua NH 03060

Call Sign: WB1EXS
Philip T Kennedy
132 Amherst St
Nashua NH 03064

Call Sign: KA1SSR
William S Hammond
19 Amherst St Apt B
Nashua NH 030642604

Call Sign: KB1WMQ
Dave Ridley
379 Amherst St Pmb 323
Nashua NH 03063

Call Sign: N1VLD
David G Le Vine
3 Amherst St Ste 283
Nashua NH 03063

Call Sign: K1QGF
Robert W Guerrette
135 Amherst St.
Nashua NH 03064

Call Sign: KB1VOA
Solomon P Belanger
36 And One Half Russell St
Nashua NH 03060

Call Sign: KA1SMI
Emile Broome Jr
31 Anvil Dr
Nashua NH 03060

Call Sign: KF4QQJ
Matthew D Chan
15 Arthurs Lane

Nashua NH 03062

Call Sign: WB1FMJ
Arthur A Dunham
190 Ash
Nashua NH 03060

Call Sign: KB1ESQ
Vernon Q Mitchell
5 Austin Circle
Nashua NH 03063

Call Sign: KA1DTZ
Walter M Kolosha
5 Autumn Leaf Dr  #20
Nashua NH 03060

Call Sign: KD1MD
Thomas E Southworth Sr
12 B Webster St
Nashua NH 03060

Call Sign: KB1DOL
Lee J Richardson
13 Bangor St
Nashua NH 03063

Call Sign: N1QET
Charles G Tarr Jr
9 Barisano Way
Nashua NH 03063

Call Sign: KA2CTQ
Brian R Findlay
4 Barnesdale Rd
Nashua NH 03062

Call Sign: KA1WOS
James R Hennessey
238 Bartemus Tr
Nashua NH 03063

Call Sign: KB8TZB
Andrew E Applegate Mr.
23 Bartemus Trail

Nashua NH 03063          Nashua NH 03062          Nashua NH 03062

Call Sign: WA1KSW        Call Sign: KE4SEY        Call Sign: KB1ICD
Thomas Sobell           George A Davison Iii      Adam J Pfeifer
66 Bartemus Trail       6 Beaver St              Black Oak Dr
Nashua NH 03063         Nashua NH 03063          Nashua NH 03062

Call Sign: KB1RDI        Call Sign: W1FWQ         Call Sign: KL0KP
Jeffrey A Dell          George A Davison Iii      Dylan D Van Lone
158 Bartemus Trail      6 Beaver St              19 Blackstone Dr 1914
Nashua NH 03063         Nashua NH 03063          Nashua NH 03063

Call Sign: KA1MEN        Call Sign: K1TCD         Call Sign: KA1DOR
Barry C Robinson        Kenneth E Churbuck       David L Taylor
252 Bartemus Trail      17 Bedford St            7 Blackstone Dr 32
Nashua NH 030627642     Nashua NH 03063          Nashua NH 03063

Call Sign: KQ1M          Call Sign: KB1UVF        Call Sign: KA1YNA
C Norman Smith          Michael S Degraw-Bertsch George J Cassista
278 Bartemus Trail      24 Berkeley St           1538 Blackstone Dr.
Nashua NH 03063         Nashua NH 03064          Nashua NH 03063

Call Sign: KA1WWJ        Call Sign: WA1HHU        Call Sign: N1UOD
Richard A Gagne         Juan M Valdes            Donald E Shepard
3 Bartemus Trl Apt 207  37 Berkeley St           18 Bloomingdale Dr
Nashua NH 03063         Nashua NH 03061          Nashua NH 03060

Call Sign: KA1RAN        Call Sign: W0TTR         Call Sign: KA1PKI
Robyn L Stowell         Bradley W Bonn           Theodore B Takacs
27 Bates Dr             24 Berkeley St.          64 Blossom St
Nashua NH 03060         Nashua NH 03064          Nashua NH 03060

Call Sign: KB1UBF        Call Sign: K1FMS         Call Sign: N1DGQ
Patrick M Dunn          Douglas W Green          Francis A Swiech
28 Bay Ridge Dr Apt  B  2 Birchwood Dr           20 Bluestone Dr
Nashua NH 03062         Nashua NH 03060          Nashua NH 030606820

Call Sign: N1FEP         Call Sign: N1AI          Call Sign: KA1VIO
Jonathan C Kaplan       David Cherkus            Thomas J Krupinski
24 Bayridge Dr Apt D    Black Oak Circle         54 Bluestone Dr
Nashua NH 03062         Nashua NH 03062          Nashua NH 03060

Call Sign: N1QHH         Call Sign: KB1EOQ        Call Sign: KD1YS
Joseph W Gaudreau       Diane L Robinton         Philip J Parcell Sr
26 Bayridge Dr Apt E    Black Oak Dr             2 Bond St

Nashua NH 03064        Nashua NH 03062        Nashua NH 03060

Call Sign: KB1HSD
Donald L Charlantini
7 Boxwood Ct
Nashua NH 03063

Call Sign: K2JGL
William C Severn
2 Browning Ave
Nashua NH 030622401

Call Sign: KI5EN
Judith P Mason
12 Cabot Dr
Nashua NH 03064

Call Sign: K1JQ
Donald L Charlantini
7 Boxwood Ct
Nashua NH 03063

Call Sign: KB1TCV
Arthur C Jeck
4 Bruce St
Nashua NH 03064

Call Sign: K1KFP
William L Twining
23 Cabot Dr
Nashua NH 030601633

Call Sign: KA1GFH
Donald K Mathieson
17 Briarwood Dr
Nashua NH 03063

Call Sign: KB1VHN
Terry D Newport
17 Bryant Rd
Nashua NH 03062

Call Sign: KB1QBE
David E Sonia
36 Cambridge Rd
Nashua NH 03062

Call Sign: KB1MZX
Raymond J Lanza
4 Briley Place
Nashua NH 03063

Call Sign: W1YQ
Terry D Newport
17 Bryant Rd
Nashua NH 03062

Call Sign: WA1UMI
Mildred E Fletcher
330 Candlewood Park
Nashua NH 03062

Call Sign: KB1HXK
Kenneth P Minasian
15 Broad St
Nashua NH 030642002

Call Sign: N1GI
Samir K Amin
31 Burgundy Dr
Nashua NH 03062

Call Sign: WA1QXH
Bernard A Fletcher
330 Candlewood Pk
Nashua NH 03062

Call Sign: KB1HYS
Edward J Mullin
275 Broad St
Nashua NH 03063

Call Sign: N1FHW
Matthew L Goldworm
5 Burke St
Nashua NH 03060

Call Sign: KB1WVT
Raymond E Freeman
6 Cannon Dr
Nashua NH 03062

Call Sign: N1VFF
Alden K Tibbetts
344 Broad St
Nashua NH 03060

Call Sign: KA1WFI
Maurice J Collard
4 Burns St
Nashua NH 030642515

Call Sign: N1IYB
Steven M Johnson
220 Cannongate Iii Rd
Nashua NH 03063

Call Sign: W3IVP
Robert D Blynn
310 Brook Village Rd 5
Nashua NH 03062

Call Sign: KA1VRJ
Donald E Hurd
9 Burns St
Nashua NH 03060

Call Sign: KB1IOG
Noel A Gervais
25 Carlene Dr
Nashua NH 03062

Call Sign: KA1KKC
Frank G Fontaine Jr
310 Brookvillage Rd 25

Call Sign: KA1VRK
Patricia A Hurd
9 Burns St

Call Sign: N1OZM
Oliver B Mc Mahon
6 Carlisle Rd

Nashua NH 03062               Nashua NH 03060               Nashua NH 03062

Call Sign: WA1UCM              Call Sign: KA1PIT             Call Sign: W1CTJ
Jeffrey G Adams               Scott R Harris               Charles T Jaglinski Jr
7 Carmine Rd                  23 Charlotte St              36 Cherry Hollow
Nashua NH 03063               Nashua NH 03060              Nashua NH 03062

Call Sign: WA1UCN             Call Sign: KA1RRV            Call Sign: W1SMN
Phyllis S Adams              Deborah P Harris             John R Halbert
7 Carmine Rd                 23 Charlotte St              8 Cherryfield Dr
Nashua NH 03063              Nashua NH 03060              Nashua NH 030621101

Call Sign: KA1CK             Call Sign: K7GN              Call Sign: KB1RFY
Edward F Durant             Layne La Baume               Lawrence E Moore Iii
19 Carroll St               7 Chatham St                 26 Cherrywood Dr
Nashua NH 030633104         Nashua NH 03063              Nashua NH 03062

Call Sign: KB1LCF            Call Sign: AE1N              Call Sign: W1AIO
Robert R Crawford Ii        Layne La Baume               Thomas W Penney
4 Casco Dr Apt D            7 Chatham St                 21 Cheryl St
Nashua NH 030624768         Nashua NH 030631157          Nashua NH 03062

Call Sign: WB1CSV            Call Sign: KA1O              Call Sign: NM1N
Daniel L Viens              Gregory W Papadeas           Edward J Los
27 Chadwick Cir Apt C       4 Chaucer Rd                 7 Cheyenne Dr
Nashua NH 03062             Nashua NH 030622403          Nashua NH 03063

Call Sign: KB1KTP           Call Sign: K7TB              Call Sign: W1DET
Carsten Turner             John R Larsen                Donald R Peters
8 Chadwick Cr Apt G        7 Cherokee Ave               51 Cheyenne Dr
Nashua NH 03062            Nashua NH 03062               Nashua NH 03063

Call Sign: N1WIU            Call Sign: KA7PIO            Call Sign: W1YSH
Christopher R Carlstrom    Joyce A Larsen               Ronald A Cadieux
115 Chandler St            7 Cherokee Ave               48 Chickie St
Nashua NH 03060            Nashua NH 03062               Nashua NH 03062

Call Sign: KC0QZC           Call Sign: KB1TUD            Call Sign: WA1RLP
Matthew J Tingler          Charles T Jaglinski Jr       Brian J Smith
3 Chapel Hill Dr           36 Cherry Hollow             16 Cliff Rd
Nashua NH 03063            Nashua NH 03062               Nashua NH 03060

Call Sign: W1ZZC            Call Sign: KC1JAG            Call Sign: N1JOF
Wilfrid L Fortin           Charles T Jaglinski Jr       LISA M Smith
17 Chapman St              36 Cherry Hollow             2 Clocktower Pl # 135

Nashua NH 03060

Nashua NH 03063

Nashua NH 03062

Call Sign: N1WMX
Arthur P Pepin
2 Clocktower Pl 101
Nashua NH 03060

Call Sign: K1PGM
Harold C Longendorfer
76 Coburn Woods
Nashua NH 03063

Call Sign: N1JKT
John K Trainer
70 Conant Rd.
Nashua NH 03062

Call Sign: N1NPY
James F Fennell Iii
1 Clocktower Pl 515
Nashua NH 03060

Call Sign: KB1FZQ
Sharon E Murray-Block
109 Coburn Woods
Nashua NH 03063

Call Sign: KB1QZL
Greater Nashua Chapter
American Red Cross
28 Concord St
Nashua NH 03064

Call Sign: KB1RUA
Carol A Rolf
2 Clocktower Pl 522
Nashua NH 03060

Call Sign: N1VLB
Willard A Flagg
146 Coburn Woods
Nashua NH 03063

Call Sign: K1NRC
Greater Nashua Chapter
American Red Cross
28 Concord St
Nashua NH 03064

Call Sign: KG6CII
David L Cantrell Jr
2 Clocktower Pl Apt 129
Nashua NH 03060

Call Sign: N1YEH
Madeline R Flagg
146 Coburn Woods
Nashua NH 03063

Call Sign: WA1VXD
Thomas W Cantwell
160 Concord St 5a
Nashua NH 03060

Call Sign: WB2EJB
Jeffrey H Bienstock
1 Clocktower Pl Apt 224
Nashua NH 030603376

Call Sign: NK1M
William I Hallahan
9 Coleridge Rd
Nashua NH 03062

Call Sign: N1YHY
Clayton R Seace
21 Congress St 14
Nashua NH 03062

Call Sign: KD1GR
Scott A Garman
2 Clocktower Pl Apt 332
Nashua NH 030603381

Call Sign: KB1QNK
Walter Fabian
8 Collier Court
Nashua NH 03062

Call Sign: N1GHQ
Jenifer C Fredericksen
45 Congress St 24
Nashua NH 03062

Call Sign: KB8REF
Christopher M Yanni
1 Clocktower Place Apt 528
Nashua NH 03060

Call Sign: N1OBB
Robert W Jeffrey Jr
1 Commercial St
Nashua NH 03060

Call Sign: KB1GEE
Samir K Amin
45 Congress St 26
Nashua NH 03062

Call Sign: NY8O
Evan S Wieder
5 Cobble Hill Rd
Nashua NH 03062

Call Sign: WA1DEI
George E Fisher
95 Conant Rd
Nashua NH 03062

Call Sign: AA1XT
Samir K Amin
45 Congress St 26
Nashua NH 03062

Call Sign: KB1AI
Robert L Maynard
60 Coburn Woods

Call Sign: N1MPL
John K Trainer
70 Conant Rd.

Call Sign: KB1HYL

Albert W Grant
27 Congress St 30
Nashua NH 03062

Call Sign: N1WDV
Jerry L Kramer
49 Congress St 9
Nashua NH 030627761

Call Sign: KD4SKE
Donald E Kulling
4 Copperfield Dr
Nashua NH 03062

Call Sign: KA1ZSN
Terralissa A Lee
16 Cortez Dr
Nashua NH 03062

Call Sign: KB1RGD
Linda L Doyle
33 Cox St
Nashua NH 03064

Call Sign: N1VQF
Joseph P Jepsen
87 Cox St
Nashua NH 03060

Call Sign: WA1RZW
Charles L Warrington
34 Cushing Ave
Nashua NH 03064

Call Sign: N1FGP
John H Gaffey
54 Cypress Lane Apt 11
Nashua NH 03063

Call Sign: KA1FG
John W Hardy Iii
163 Cypress Ln
Nashua NH 03063

Call Sign: KB1WCH

Jared D Erb
28 Danbury Rd
Nashua NH 03064

Call Sign: AB1LY
Eric B Phelps
4 Danforth Rd 10
Nashua NH 03060

Call Sign: K1KHQ
Lawrence E Pihl
131 Daniel Webster
Highway #712
Nashua NH 03060

Call Sign: KC9FKU
Richard A Whitnable
131 Daniel Webster Hwy
Apt 225
Nashua NH 030605224

Call Sign: KC5OJW
Joel D Martin
78 Deerwood Dr
Nashua NH 03063

Call Sign: N1QMZ
Eric L Plumley
15 Delude St
Nashua NH 03060

Call Sign: N6JPF
Jeffrey N Stah
5 Derry St
Nashua NH 03063

Call Sign: N1HMC
John F Heden
54 Dexter St
Nashua NH 03060

Call Sign: N1VQE
Richard W Jacobus
5 Dixville St
Nashua NH 030632514

Call Sign: N1PPZ
Craig M Adams
36 Dogwood Dr
Nashua NH 03062

Call Sign: N1MOW
Lawrence R Daddario
48 Dorchester Way
Nashua NH 03064

Call Sign: KA1VPP
Daniel P Swanson
47 Drury Ln
Nashua NH 03060

Call Sign: W1DAO
Kenneth A Wallace
5 Dryden Ave
Nashua NH 03060

Call Sign: W1DAT
Natalie E Wallace
5 Dryden Ave
Nashua NH 03060

Call Sign: N1HRI
Douglas A Willis
60 Dunbarton Dr
Nashua NH 030632052

Call Sign: WB2EYB
Nicholas Zoda Jr
6 Dustin Dr
Nashua NH 03062

Call Sign: N1VSG
William D Foster
131 Dw Hwy Apt 459
Nashua NH 03060

Call Sign: N1VSH
Barbara A Foster
131 Dw Hwy Apt 459
Nashua NH 03060

Call Sign: N1TOC
Nanu Swamy
42 E Bayridge Dr
Nashua NH 03062

Call Sign: KA1NDR
William D Bouchard
27 E Dunstable Rd
Nashua NH 03060

Call Sign: N1JUW
Michael T Byrne
42 E Dunstable Rd
Nashua NH 03060

Call Sign: KB1QBC
Gene A Fricke
102 E Hollis St 3a
Nashua NH 03060

Call Sign: N1TSN
Melissa G Floyd
15 E Pearl St 1
Nashua NH 03060

Call Sign: NO1P
Thomas Stewart
10 Eastbrook Dr
Nashua NH 03060

Call Sign: N1LBC
James E Mahoney Ii
13 Eastbrook Dr
Nashua NH 03060

Call Sign: K1CKD
Milton H Ahrendt
6 Edith Ave
Nashua NH 03060

Call Sign: N1EFL
Philip L Hall
8 Edson St
Nashua NH 03060

Call Sign: KB1RFU
Patricia R Westaway
20 Elaine Dr
Nashua NH 03062

Call Sign: N1FFW
James J Seagraves
33 Elgin St
Nashua NH 03060

Call Sign: N1GCD
Dawn L Burgoyne
46 Elgin St
Nashua NH 03060

Call Sign: KB3JUV
Justin T Kates
84 Elm St #2
Nashua NH 03060

Call Sign: WA1VEZ
William L Quick
3 Fairhaven Rd
Nashua NH 030605305

Call Sign: N1FHL
Connie O Stowell
36 Fairview Ave
Nashua NH 03060

Call Sign: NK1C
Robert D Stowell
36 Fairview Ave
Nashua NH 03060

Call Sign: WA2JLR
Patricia M Smith
9 Fenwick St
Nashua NH 03063

Call Sign: KB1TMX
Robert E Lozeau
21 Ferson
Nashua NH 03060

Call Sign: KA1SGS
Harold J Lalmond
19 Forest Park Dr
Nashua NH 03060

Call Sign: W1NAZ
Harold W Lalmond
19 Forest Park Dr
Nashua NH 030604325

Call Sign: KA1CRN
Lawrence A Artz
7 Fountain Ln
Nashua NH 03062

Call Sign: KA1NFM
Michael F Jones
7 Foxglove Ct
Nashua NH 03062

Call Sign: K1WER
David R Brindle
14 Friar Tuck Ln
Nashua NH 030622164

Call Sign: KA1QLM
Doris F Brindle
14 Friar Tuck Ln
Nashua NH 030622164

Call Sign: KB1PYH
Charles A Morse Jr
6 Fulton St
Nashua NH 03060

Call Sign: KB1KAY
Treff E Leblanc
12 FULTON ST
Nashua NH 03060

Call Sign: WB5SIL
John D Ralph
10 Galway Rd
Nashua NH 03062

Call Sign: K1FQL
Martin R Blustine
3 Gilboa Lane
Nashua NH 030607364

Call Sign: N1TRQ
John J De Paulis Jr
41 Gillis St
Nashua NH 03060

Call Sign: N1FER
Mary Elizabeth Restivo
51 Gillis St
Nashua NH 03060

Call Sign: W1TQ
David W Foner
51 Gillis St
Nashua NH 03060

Call Sign: K1QEF
Robert K Mc Killip Sr
77 Gillis St
Nashua NH 03060

Call Sign: KB1BGV
Craig P Chabot
83 Gilson Rd
Nashua NH 03062

Call Sign: N1LTI
Stephen A Fenton
9 Gingras Dr
Nashua NH 03060

Call Sign: KB1QFM
Charles M Ward
13 Grand Ave
Nashua NH 03060

Call Sign: N1JUK
Christopher P Arguin
10 Greenock Ln
Nashua NH 030623008

Call Sign: N1MFP
Peter A Arguin
10 Greenock Ln
Nashua NH 03062

Call Sign: N1HAJ
Colleen G Gaffey
6 Greenwood Dr
Nashua NH 03062

Call Sign: KB2TMJ
Peter W Gousios
24 Hall Ave
Nashua NH 030642139

Call Sign: W9JAT
Clyde R Sorensen
15 Hamlett Dr  #15
Nashua NH 03062

Call Sign: KA1CAW
Judith A Kozyra
6 Hamlett Dr Apt 24
Nashua NH 03062

Call Sign: KB1ITM
Eccles V Pridgen Jr
Hampshire Dr
Nashua NH 03063

Call Sign: N1MVF
Forrest A Kenney
Hampshire Dr
Nashua NH 03063

Call Sign: N1KPB
Bruce T Haldane
Hampshire Dr
Nashua NH 03063

Call Sign: KB1QHM
Sean R Payne
24 Hampshire Dr Apt D
Nashua NH 03063

Call Sign: NJ1H
William E Bordy
21 Hampton Dr
Nashua NH 030632720

Call Sign: W1SKI
Francis J Skorupski
88 Harbor Ave
Nashua NH 03060

Call Sign: N1WJU
Paul E Anderson
11 Harris St
Nashua NH 03060

Call Sign: KB1HWR
Michael J Lindeman
Hartford Ln
Nashua NH 03063

Call Sign: KC2JCB
Scott D Reynolds
22 Hassel Brook Rd
Nashua NH 03060

Call Sign: KA1LW
Joseph R Famularo Jr
65 Hawthorne Village Rd
Nashua NH 030622272

Call Sign: WB1DXP
Ernest J Charest
1 High Pine Ave
Nashua NH 03063

Call Sign: KD1JI
Roger J Jacobson
15 High Pine Ave
Nashua NH 03063

Call Sign: N1XY
Roger J Jacobson
15 High Pine Ave
Nashua NH 03063

Call Sign: KD7ZQQ
David W Moser
139 Hills Ferry Rd
Nashua NH 03061

Call Sign: KA1JJA
Steven M Lapinskas
11 Hillside Dr
Nashua NH 03060

Call Sign: KA1ZCD
Jackie M Dubois
31 Holbrook Dr
Nashua NH 03060

Call Sign: KA1VYI
Joseph L Desjardins
13 Holly Dr
Nashua NH 03063

Call Sign: N6ZDX
Gregory R Ellis
6 Hollyhock Ave
Nashua NH 03062

Call Sign: KA1NJD
Louis S Antonucci
22 Howard St
Nashua NH 03060

Call Sign: N1IWO
William R Thomas Jr
15 Hunt St
Nashua NH 03060

Call Sign: KB2FBE
Daniel J Abbis
4 Indian Fern Dr
Nashua NH 03062

Call Sign: KB1FWW
Peter D Lacey
10 Indian Rock Rd
Nashua NH 03063

Call Sign: KB1HHM
Peter D Lacey
10 Indian Rock Rd
Nashua NH 03063

Call Sign: AA1ZU
Peter D Lacey
10 Indian Rock Rd
Nashua NH 03063

Call Sign: W1OMZ
Philip D Labombarde
60 Indian Rock Rd
Nashua NH 03060

Call Sign: N1RVA
Jarrod D Laflotte
33 Intervale St
Nashua NH 03060

Call Sign: KH2DI
Tsunenori Shibata
8 Ipswich Circle
Nashua NH 03063

Call Sign: WH2ALN
Koichi Tanaka
8 Ipswich Circle
Nashua NH 03063

Call Sign: KB1GDA
Spaceflight Systems
Corporation Arc
19 Iroquois Rd
Nashua NH 03063

Call Sign: W1SSC
Spaceflight Systems
Corporation Arc
19 Iroquois Rd
Nashua NH 03063

Call Sign: KA1DT
David P Knight

3 Ivy Lane
Nashua NH 03063

Call Sign: WA1TON
David G Mack
5 Jennifer Dr
Nashua NH 03062

Call Sign: KB1HPI
James P Carbone
35 Jennifer Dr
Nashua NH 03062

Call Sign: KB1JPQ
James P Carbone
35 Jennifer Dr
Nashua NH 03062

Call Sign: AB1DG
James P Carbone
35 Jennifer Dr
Nashua NH 03062

Call Sign: N1KDR
David A Long
10 Jill Dr
Nashua NH 03062

Call Sign: KB1DOT
John M Yurcak
12 Jill Dr
Nashua NH 03062

Call Sign: K9AEN
John M Yurcak
12 Jill Dr
Nashua NH 03062

Call Sign: K1FUB
William F Fleury
17 Jill Dr
Nashua NH 03062

Call Sign: KB1RTR
Kevin A Duhamel

39 June St
Nashua NH 03060

Call Sign: N1UQJ
Janet A Rice
11 Kanata Dr
Nashua NH 03063

Call Sign: W1AOC
Robert C Rice
11 Kanata Dr
Nashua NH 03063

Call Sign: N1KZQ
Christopher M Grant
9 Kessler Farm Dr 214
Nashua NH 03063

Call Sign: KB1OUD
Heidi R Roy
11 Kessler Farm Dr 235
Nashua NH 03063

Call Sign: N1DAS
David K Sterrett
22 Kessler Farm Dr 685
Nashua NH 03063

Call Sign: KA1VUA
Penelope M Syriac
11 Kessler Farm Dr Apt 263
Nashua NH 03063

Call Sign: N1GDD
Francis J Murphy Jr
26 Kessler Farm Dr Apt 425
Nashua NH 030637134

Call Sign: N1KGR
Michael J Wilcox
34 Kessler Farm Dr Apt 564
Nashua NH 03063

Call Sign: KE7EUI
Nathan J Rackliffe

4 Kittery Dr
Nashua NH 03062

Call Sign: K7NJR
Nathan J Rackliffe
4 Kittery Dr
Nashua NH 03062

Call Sign: KA1NDT
James J Callahan
20 Knowlton Rd
Nashua NH 03063

Call Sign: W1UAB
Maurice R Bruneau
315 Lake St
Nashua NH 030604135

Call Sign: NE1I
Robert A Raymond
26 Langholm Dr
Nashua NH 03062

Call Sign: KA1VQX
Nancy L Campbell
96 Langholm Dr
Nashua NH 03062

Call Sign: NF1M
Robert C Campbell Sr
96 Langholm Dr
Nashua NH 030623072

Call Sign: WA1IEA
John A Sirvydas
20 Laurel Ct
Nashua NH 03062

Call Sign: N1HTM
William P Joiner
40 Laurel Ct
Nashua NH 03062

Call Sign: W1QKA
Roland G Lachance

48 Learned St
Nashua NH 03060

Call Sign: KB1VVW
Robert J Masek
165 Ledge St
Nashua NH 03060

Call Sign: KU2W
Roger A Morby
31 Ledgewood Hills Dr
Nashua NH 03062

Call Sign: KA1TIA
T Andrew Cott
77 Ledgewood Hills Dr
Nashua NH 030624437

Call Sign: KG1J
Arnold D Seifer
16 Ledgewood Hills Dr Apt
303
Nashua NH 030624452

Call Sign: KB1URE
Don Elkins
21 Leeann St
Nashua NH 03062

Call Sign: KB1TFP
Jose P Pinilla
9 Leewood Trl
Nashua NH 03062

Call Sign: KA1UEY
Michael P Berry
12 Lessard St
Nashua NH 03060

Call Sign: N1PGQ
William L Dobens
15 Lewis St
Nashua NH 03060

Call Sign: N1CKY

Nicholas A Albano
71 Linton St
Nashua NH 03060

Call Sign: WG1C
Norman L Stone
34 Lochmere Ln
Nashua NH 03063

Call Sign: N1BVO
Ralph N Keyslay
12 Lojko Dr
Nashua NH 03062

Call Sign: N1UH
Ralph N Keyslay
12 Lojko Dr
Nashua NH 03062

Call Sign: N1NBO
Donald R Fairchild
40976 Louisburg Sq
Nashua NH 03060

Call Sign: K1PPE
George P Stylianos
17 Lovell St
Nashua NH 03060

Call Sign: N1ILT
William K Riley
12 Lutheran Dr
Nashua NH 03063

Call Sign: KA1OML
Paul A Pearson
43 Lynn St
Nashua NH 03060

Call Sign: KB1KXH
Joseph Tringali
12 Mac Donald Dr
Nashua NH 03062

Call Sign: W1GIO

Joseph Tringali
12 Mac Donald Dr
Nashua NH 03062

Call Sign: W1RHS
Joseph A Guilbeault
407 Main Dunstable Rd
Nashua NH 030621881

Call Sign: KB1TFK
Beau Dionne
417 Main Dunstable Rd
Nashua NH 03062

Call Sign: N1IMZ
Emery W Hart
364 Main St
Nashua NH 03060

Call Sign: N1QZO
Joseph A Dumont
580 Main St
Nashua NH 03060

Call Sign: KA1YCO
John P Griffin Jr
369 Maindunstable Rd
Nashua NH 03062

Call Sign: N1WWT
Brian M Mc Kenna
3 Major Dr
Nashua NH 03060

Call Sign: KB1ANI
Robert W Donlon
16 Mapleleaf Dr
Nashua NH 03062

Call Sign: AA1AM
Kevin S Reynolds
6 March St
Nashua NH 030605352

Call Sign: KA1WCX

Rand Kmiec
4 Marcia Dr
Nashua NH 03062

Call Sign: N1IBV
Andrew A Balamotis
5 Marcia Dr
Nashua NH 03062

Call Sign: WB1G
Judith S Gauthier
8 Marcia Dr
Nashua NH 030621832

Call Sign: WA1VVK
Arthur P Landry Ii
6 Margaret Cir
Nashua NH 03062

Call Sign: KJ4XF
Robert R Mc Guirk
15 Marian Ln
Nashua NH 03062

Call Sign: KA1QQM
Lee C Hauenstein
4 Masefield Rd
Nashua NH 03062

Call Sign: N1GVM
Robert A Wilkie
18 Melissa Dr
Nashua NH 03062

Call Sign: N1HMW
Iris P Del More
17 Meredith Dr
Nashua NH 03063

Call Sign: WQ1W
Noel B Del More
17 Meredith Dr
Nashua NH 03063

Call Sign: KA1SQK

Peter W Naranjo
18 Meredith Dr
Nashua NH 03063

Ryan E Robinson
6 Mizoras Dr
Nashua NH 03062

Jonathan M Currier
6 New Searles Rd
Nashua NH 03062

Call Sign: N1RKQ
John R Tacconi
3 Merrill St
Nashua NH 03060

Call Sign: KB1LVD
Lara A Thompson
1 Monza Rd
Nashua NH 03064

Call Sign: KA1WHO
Jeremy T Stashluk
11 New Searles Rd
Nashua NH 03062

Call Sign: KB1RFV
Richard D Watts Jr
13 Merrimack St
Nashua NH 03060

Call Sign: KA1UY
Joseph R Cannarella
29 Monza Rd
Nashua NH 03060

Call Sign: WQ1M
William A Stashluk
11 New Searles Rd
Nashua NH 03062

Call Sign: KA1TPN
Dennis Puleo
9 Millbrook Dr
Nashua NH 03062

Call Sign: WB2ZHC
Matthew A Goglia
33 Musket Dr
Nashua NH 03062

Call Sign: K1HGK
Hilary F Johnson
48 New Searles Rd
Nashua NH 030623441

Call Sign: KB1HLT
Dennis Puleo
9 Millbrook Dr
Nashua NH 030621621

Call Sign: N1ZZD
Brian S Mc Carthy
65 Musket Dr
Nashua NH 03062

Call Sign: N1ROJ
Shih Hao Chong
49 New Searles Rd
Nashua NH 03062

Call Sign: KA1YSI
Richard A Derosier
4 Millpond Dr
Nashua NH 03062

Call Sign: AB1Z
John A Carroll
77 Musket Dr
Nashua NH 030621442

Call Sign: N1RVB
Wai Ling Hew
49 New Searles Rd
Nashua NH 03062

Call Sign: AB1JM
Stephen J Adams
220 Millwright Dr
Nashua NH 03063

Call Sign: W1PK
John A Carroll
77 Musket Dr
Nashua NH 030621442

Call Sign: KB1GIG
Susan A Erler
8 Newcastle Dr # 10
Nashua NH 03060

Call Sign: KB1SPK
Jemima G Adams
220 Millwright Dr
Nashua NH 03063

Call Sign: N1IYJ
Kevin J Gray
24 Natick St
Nashua NH 03063

Call Sign: K1WD
William H Davis
21 Newcastle Dr 10
Nashua NH 03060

Call Sign: KB1VOY
Lillian E Adams
220 Millwright Dr
Nashua NH 03063

Call Sign: N1SZX
Victoria A Bergeron
1 New Castle Dr 6
Nashua NH 03060

Call Sign: KA1RLC
James W Doolittle
25 Newcastle Dr 8
Nashua NH 03060

Call Sign: N1TSO

Call Sign: KB1EFF

Call Sign: KA1DJZ

Gregory V Carlson
10 Newcastle Dr Apt 2
Nashua NH 03060

Call Sign: KB1LMU
Maulin P Patel
5 Newfields St
Nashua NH 03063

Call Sign: W2NFX
Sarah J Gow
114 Newton Dr
Nashua NH 03063

Call Sign: KB1RGB
Richard J Fulton
22 Nightingale Rd
Nashua NH 03062

Call Sign: KD4GYO
Robert J Lyons Jr
35 Nightingale Rd
Nashua NH 03062

Call Sign: N1IMN
Dorothy L Peabody
35 Nightingale Rd
Nashua NH 03062

Call Sign: N1IMO
Bernard J Peabody
35 Nightingale Rd
Nashua NH 03062

Call Sign: N1GBA
Kenneth L Cable
5 Niquette Dr
Nashua NH 030622318

Call Sign: KB1KLM
Richard Parr Jr
56 Norma Dr
Nashua NH 03062

Call Sign: KA1ITQ

Thomas D Royer
15 Normandy Way
Nashua NH 03063

Call Sign: N1IKS
Robert M Muir
18 Northwood Dr
Nashua NH 03063

Call Sign: N1TZD
Justin D Marrese
25 Norwich Rd
Nashua NH 03062

Call Sign: N1UZR
Anthony M Marrese
25 Norwich Rd
Nashua NH 03062

Call Sign: N1VQP
Anthony M Marrese Jr
25 Norwich Rd
Nashua NH 03062

Call Sign: KA1MXW
William P Warrington
67 Nottingham Dr
Nashua NH 030622161

Call Sign: WB3BHT
Wai L Hom
79 Nottingham Dr
Nashua NH 03062

Call Sign: W1WFP
Robert E Newcomb
6 Nova Rd
Nashua NH 030601145

Call Sign: WB1EMY
Roberta M Newcomb
6 Nova Rd
Nashua NH 030601145

Call Sign: W1BXM

Guy W Bowden
12 Nutting St
Nashua NH 030601562

Call Sign: N1VEC
Thomas P Gorman
26 Oak Grove Trail
Nashua NH 03062

Call Sign: KD1GL
Donald P Cornellier
8 Oakdale Ave
Nashua NH 03062

Call Sign: WA1UJL
George H Dailey
1 Ohio Ave
Nashua NH 030605144

Call Sign: N1SUD
George F Cook
6 Oldham Lane
Nashua NH 03063

Call Sign: KA1GOZ
Donald K Dillaby
27 Palisade Dr
Nashua NH 030622119

Call Sign: N1FX
Michael A Di Fonzo
68 Palm St
Nashua NH 03060

Call Sign: N1TZE
James L Gilbertson
88 Palm St
Nashua NH 03060

Call Sign: WA1MUN
George C Ware
135 Palm St
Nashua NH 03060

Call Sign: WP4JIO

Jocelyn I Rivera Montalvo
67 Palm St Apt 23
Nashua NH 030603867

Call Sign: K1FMP
John R Burns Jr
126 Peele Rd
Nashua NH 03062

Call Sign: N4COY
William W Lana
29 Pemberton Rd
Nashua NH 03063

Call Sign: N1XOV
Joseph P Fallis
215 Pine St
Nashua NH 03060

Call Sign: N1FAL
Joseph P Fallis
215 Pine St
Nashua NH 03060

Call Sign: KB1VHB
Joseph P Fallis
215 Pine St
Nashua NH 03060

Call Sign: N1RQX
Claude M Kallanian
258 Pine St
Nashua NH 03060

Call Sign: KA9GHT
Randy L Ward
24 Pinehurst Ave
Nashua NH 03062

Call Sign: KA9GHV
Bernice E Ward
24 Pinehurst Ave
Nashua NH 03062

Call Sign: N1TZF

Dawn R Frazier
7 Plum Dr
Nashua NH 03062

Call Sign: KA1SRE
David R Fielding
3 Pluto Ln
Nashua NH 030621197

Call Sign: WA1USU
Theresa E Fielding
3 Pluto Ln
Nashua NH 03062

Call Sign: K1BXZ
David A Shaw
10 Pluto Ln
Nashua NH 03062

Call Sign: NE1F
Ann M Shaw
10 Pluto Ln
Nashua NH 03062

Call Sign: N1GHP
Brian G Nadeau
6 Pond View Cir
Nashua NH 03063

Call Sign: KB1TSA
David D Wong
2 Pond View Circle
Nashua NH 03063

Call Sign: N1FPU
John W Andrick Jr
5 Pope Circle
Nashua NH 03063

Call Sign: WB1FPK
Paul M Haskell Jr
21 Portchester Dr
Nashua NH 03062

Call Sign: N1WWX

John A Tastula
37 Prescott St
Nashua NH 03064

Call Sign: KB1WBZ
Lowell A Williams
9 Profile Cir
Nashua NH 03063

Call Sign: KC0DOT
Seth J Dewey
66 Profile Cir
Nashua NH 03063

Call Sign: NF1D
Thomas W Powers
32 Ramsgate Ridge
Nashua NH 03063

Call Sign: N1TLT
Dana A Groff
5 Rancourt St
Nashua NH 03060

Call Sign: N1KTK
Joellyn V Crowley
44 Raven St
Nashua NH 03060

Call Sign: K1YBM
Henry Stanley
20 Rene Dr
Nashua NH 03061

Call Sign: KA1MHU
Paul J Trudel
15 Ridgefield Dr
Nashua NH 03062

Call Sign: KA1NRT
Donald L Doucette
16 Robert Dr
Nashua NH 03063

Call Sign: KA1YBV

James A Pappas Jr
54 Robinhood Rd
Nashua NH 03062

Call Sign: N1DXG
Johnathan O Vail
2 Rockland St
Nashua NH 03064

Call Sign: KB1CRA
Allen C Cappone
4 Roedean Dr # 203
Nashua NH 03063

Call Sign: KB1MTU
Bryan P Halter
40 Royal Crest Dr - 11
Nashua NH 03060

Call Sign: N1TSM
Jamie M Clark
42 Royal Crest Dr 8
Nashua NH 03060

Call Sign: N1RKC
Thomas F Corbett Iii
41 Royal Crest Dr 9
Nashua NH 03060

Call Sign: KB1FZR
Vasudev S Ponnuchetty
31 Royal Crest Dr Apt #1
Nashua NH 03060

Call Sign: KB1UCH
Kenta T Hood
42 Royal Crest Dr Apt 1
Nashua NH 03060

Call Sign: KB1KCS
Murali K Balusu
4 Royal Crest Dr Apt 11
Nashua NH 03060

Call Sign: N1IKT

Michael J Canavan Sr
60 Saint Camille St
Nashua NH 03060

Call Sign: N1SUA
Krishna Mangipudi
20 Salmon Brook Dr
Nashua NH 03062

Call Sign: N1PQM
Keith C Davis
9 Sapling Cir Apt 9
Nashua NH 03062

Call Sign: AA1LZ
William J Claytor Jr
8 Sapling Cr #15
Nashua NH 03062

Call Sign: N1SXD
Philip A Greenwood Sr
62 Saywer St
Nashua NH 03060

Call Sign: KB1MWZ
Carol B Rodrigues
15 Scarborough Dr
Nashua NH 03063

Call Sign: N1RVE
Dana P Nickerson
9 Scotia Way
Nashua NH 03062

Call Sign: WA1SPP
Joshua L Segal
31 Scott Ave
Nashua NH 030622443

Call Sign: KC1WS
Joseph B Krasucki Jr
174 Searles Rd
Nashua NH 03062

Call Sign: N1KES

Joseph F Krasucki
174 Searles Rd
Nashua NH 03062

Call Sign: KA1HOV
John R Halbert
190 Searles Rd
Nashua NH 030623048

Call Sign: N1YWO
Richard P Wiik
40 Seminole Dr
Nashua NH 030633523

Call Sign: KB1GQM
Ralph F Schwarz
14 Shadowbrook Dr
Nashua NH 030624517

Call Sign: N1CU
Ralph F Schwarz
14 Shadowbrook Dr
Nashua NH 030624517

Call Sign: N1TVB
Laurie S Sealund
1 Shady Lane
Nashua NH 03062

Call Sign: NO1V
Ernest L Cote
17 Shady Ln
Nashua NH 030622327

Call Sign: N1ABA
Robert J Wolf
17 Shawnee Dr
Nashua NH 030621875

Call Sign: KB1WHV
David A Schimel
22 Shelburne Rd
Nashua NH 03063

Call Sign: KB1WKL

David A Schimel
22 Shelburne Rd
Nashua NH 03063

Call Sign: K1LGS
David A Schimel
22 Shelburne Rd
Nashua NH 03063

Call Sign: KB1WOF
Mark P Devins
19 Shingle Mill Dr
Nashua NH 03062

Call Sign: WB2QZM
Nelson S Allan
107 Shore Dr
Nashua NH 03062

Call Sign: K1ALH
Alan L Hess
111 Shore Dr
Nashua NH 030621339

Call Sign: WA1ZJJ
Rimantas A Bajercius
7 Silver Dr. #5
Nashua NH 03060

Call Sign: W1GEL
Anthony W Schott
Snow Cir
Nashua NH 03062

Call Sign: N9HAD
Bob J Goemans
Snow Circle
Nashua NH 03062

Call Sign: KB1UGV
Robert D Lansing
33 Spindlewick Dr
Nashua NH 03062

Call Sign: N1BAO

Michael D Lemieux
87 Spindlewick Dr
Nashua NH 03062

Call Sign: W1UHF
Michael D Lemieux
87 Spindlewick Dr
Nashua NH 03062

Call Sign: KB1WOC
Michael L Comella
3 Spit Brook Rd Apt E5
Nashua NH 03062

Call Sign: N1VCF
Michael L Comella
103 Spit Brook Rd Apt E5
Nashua NH 03062

Call Sign: KE4UYZ
David S Decker
103 Spit Brook Rd B-12
Nashua NH 03062

Call Sign: N1CLT
Earl L Komar
103 Spitbrook Rd Bldg D
Apt 8
Nashua NH 03062

Call Sign: W1LMS
Donald M Sheehan
14 Spring St
Nashua NH 03060

Call Sign: WA1GVH
John M Strakhovsky
715 St James Pl
Nashua NH 03062

Call Sign: WA1ESC
Charles E Merchant
11 Stanley Ln
Nashua NH 03062

Call Sign: KB1TFN
Chandrasekar Kathirvelu
74 Stillwater Dr
Nashua NH 03062

Call Sign: KB1PYD
Mark T Dorobiala
297 Stonebridge Dr
Nashua NH 03063

Call Sign: KB1SEE
Linda J Dorobiala
297 Stonebridge Dr
Nashua NH 03063

Call Sign: KB1PHB
Paul O Mosier
290 Stonebridge Dr.
Nashua NH 03063

Call Sign: KB1JCU
David R Sullivan
12 Stonybrook Rd
Nashua NH 03063

Call Sign: W1DUB
James G Kantargis Sr
45 Summer
Nashua NH 030602444

Call Sign: K1HAP
Edward S Gerow
24 Tampa St
Nashua NH 03060

Call Sign: KE1LO
Lawrence F Leonard
78 Tampa St
Nashua NH 030542549

Call Sign: W1PE
Lawrence F Leonard
78 Tampa St
Nashua NH 030642549

Call Sign: K1QP
Lawrence F Leonard
78 Tampa St
Nashua NH 030642459

Call Sign: KA1YSM
Thomas G Keller
1 Taschereau Blvd
Nashua NH 03062

Call Sign: N1QXE
Paul S Keddy
40 Taschereau Blvd
Nashua NH 03062

Call Sign: KA1RDO
Walter K Adasczik
5 Teak Dr
Nashua NH 03062

Call Sign: W1TWO
Paul W Warrington
41 Temple St Apt 207
Nashua NH 03060

Call Sign: K1KTN
Paul A Giroux
45 Tenby Dr.
Nashua NH 03062

Call Sign: W2MRJ
George W Engert
60 Tennyson Ave
Nashua NH 03062

Call Sign: WA4QCP
Barry C Weinstein
48 Tennyson Ave.
Nashua NH 03062

Call Sign: KD1TD
Patrick M Mc Connell
196 Tinker Rd
Nashua NH 03063

Call Sign: KA1WHR
Paul C Gardner
151 Tolles St
Nashua NH 03064

Call Sign: N1JII
David L Vogel
10 Torrey Rd
Nashua NH 03063

Call Sign: WA1MXT
Alfred J Lajoie Jr
19 Twelfth St
Nashua NH 03060

Call Sign: N1XWJ
Thomas A Rodier
34 Underhill St
Nashua NH 03060

Call Sign: N1YHW
Michael J Catalanotti
68 Underhill St
Nashua NH 03060

Call Sign: AD1D
David A Zlotek
42 Vespa Lane
Nashua NH 03064

Call Sign: N1TZG
Mark A Flanagan
29 Vespa Ln
Nashua NH 03060

Call Sign: KB1AII
Phillip J Pelland
2 Vieckis Dr
Nashua NH 03062

Call Sign: N1HIB
Ronald D Fussell
15 Vieckis Dr
Nashua NH 03062

Call Sign: W1ZUB
Stuart E Jeans
29 Vieckis Dr
Nashua NH 03062

Call Sign: KB1MXL
Steven C Foster
3 Vilna Ave
Nashua NH 03064

Call Sign: W1SCF
Steven C Foster
3 Vilna Ave
Nashua NH 03064

Call Sign: K1HDO
Maurice R Cote
10 W Hobart St
Nashua NH 03060

Call Sign: N1RKG
Edward W Grygorcewicz
617 W Hollis St
Nashua NH 03062

Call Sign: KB1HD
Samuel J Tobias
33 Walden Pond Dr
Nashua NH 03060

Call Sign: W1DZZ
Clarence D Hackney Jr
85 Walden Pond Dr
Nashua NH 030602877

Call Sign: KE1AD
Walter J Hynes Iii
25 Walkeridge Dr
Nashua NH 03062

Call Sign: KB1RFX
Stephen A Mroz
6 Watersedge Dr
Nashua NH 03063

Call Sign: WA1BEC
William C Mallard Jr
8 Watersedge Dr
Nashua NH 03063

Call Sign: N1DCZ
Andrew H Sallet
10 Wellesley Rd
Nashua NH 03062

Call Sign: W1TG
Andrew P Sallet
10 Wellesley Rd
Nashua NH 030621318

Call Sign: WA1WON
Mark A Sallet
10 Wellesley Rd
Nashua NH 03062

Call Sign: N1MET
Leonard A Dube Sr
583 West Hollis St
Nashua NH 030621342

Call Sign: W1ADS
Donald F Ayers
859 West Hollis St
Nashua NH 03060

Call Sign: KA1SAQ
David A Verville
70 West Hollis St  Apt 11
Nashua NH 03060

Call Sign: N1ZZG
Jeffrey M Arnold
2 Westminster Dr
Nashua NH 03064

Call Sign: N2DX
Phillip J Poynor
4 Westminster Dr
Nashua NH 03064

Call Sign: KE1E
Gregory A Hackney
109 Westwood Dr
Nashua NH 030623422

Call Sign: N1GP
Richard R Koch
43 Wethersfield Rd
Nashua NH 03062

Call Sign: N1WWQ
Gloria L Koch
43 Wethersfield Rd
Nashua NH 03062

Call Sign: KB1LXF
Marc W Morin
15 Winchester St
Nashua NH 03063

Call Sign: N1VPY
George S Guild
5 Woodfield St
Nashua NH 03062

Call Sign: KA1KLX
Elizabeth Y Olapurath
6 Woodfield St
Nashua NH 03062

Call Sign: KE1Z
John C Olapurath
6 Woodfield St
Nashua NH 03062

Call Sign: W2MFI
Raymond Schmitt
22 Woodland Dr
Nashua NH 03063

Call Sign: K1ABC
Paul F Macdonald
Nashua NH 030607068

Call Sign: KA1BDB

Stephen E Halpin
Nashua NH 03060

Call Sign: KC1VR
Henry A Rowe
Nashua NH 03060

Call Sign: KE1ABC
Patricia M Mac Donald
Nashua NH 030607068

Call Sign: KZ1O
David B Bushong
Nashua NH 030608055

Call Sign: N1FD
Nashua Area Radio Club
Nashua NH 03061

Call Sign: N1TSP
Danny E Rondon
Nashua NH 030613148

Call Sign: N2ULL
Steven C Obenhofer
Nashua NH 03061

Call Sign: WA2MYU
John P Georges
Nashua NH 03060

Call Sign: KB1FLX
Daniel J Cushing
Nashua NH 03061

Call Sign: KB1HIF
Michael J Rush
Nashua NH 030611034

Call Sign: WB1AS
Adam I Schoolsky
Nashua NH 030610095

Call Sign: KB1LDJ
Ionel Vasilescu

Nashua NH 030607248

Call Sign: KB1MNU
Adam Freiband
Nashua NH 030607272

Call Sign: WA1AJF
Adam Freiband
Nashua NH 030607272

Call Sign: KF5KHI
Luke Bussanmas
Nashua NH 03060

Call Sign: K1HIF
Michael J Rush
Nashua NH 030611034

## FCC Amateur Radio Licenses in Nelson

Call Sign: W1VE
Gerald B Hull
455 Lead Mine Rd
Nelson NH 03457

Call Sign: KB1GSQ
Richard J Lothrop
225 Murdough Hill Rd
Nelson NH 03457

## FCC Amateur Radio Licenses in New Boston

Call Sign: N1FLY
James E Fowler
114 Beard Rd
New Boston NH 03070

Call Sign: N1MQL
Joseph W Constance Jr
300 Bedford Rd
New Boston NH 03070

Call Sign: KY1P

John A Slusarz Sr
549 Bedford Rd
New Boston NH 03070

Call Sign: NR1M
Steven J O Neill
655 Bedford Rd
New Boston NH 030705121

Call Sign: AD1H
James M Hansen
31 Briar Hill Rd
New Boston NH 03070

Call Sign: WB1GLG
Patricia A Hansen
31 Briar Hill Rd
New Boston NH 03070

Call Sign: KB1ESM
John Aylesworth
179 Bunker Hill Rd
New Boston NH 03070

Call Sign: N1JUP
Alden W Miller
236 Chestnut Hill Rd
New Boston NH 03070

Call Sign: KB1HZX
Alden W Miller
236 Chestnut Hill Rd
New Boston NH 03070

Call Sign: WA1MAT
John H Reeves
13 Depot St
New Boston NH 03070

Call Sign: N1WJA
Frank R Wilson Jr
9 Greenfield Rd
New Boston NH 03070

Call Sign: N1WEE

Louis B Lanzillotti
16 High St
New Boston NH 030704011

Call Sign: N1YEI
Louis B Lanzillotti Ii
16 High St
New Boston NH 03070

Call Sign: N1BDD
Timothy J Lannan
31 Houghton Ln
New Boston NH 03070

Call Sign: WA4MXI
Robert M Fletcher
27 Howard Ln
New Boston NH 03070

Call Sign: NI1D
Paul Koning
408 Joe English Rd
New Boston NH 03070

Call Sign: WB2AQP
David C Salerno
51 Kennedy Lane
New Boston NH 03070

Call Sign: KB1UXX
Leander B Nichols
342 Lyndeboro Rd
New Boston NH 03070

Call Sign: WB2DWD
Robert R Seastream
255 Mont Vernon Rd
New Boston NH 03070

Call Sign: WA6HVL
John A Shea
5 Mont Vernon Rd.
New Boston NH 03070

Call Sign: KB1EHD

Paul A Dickson
284 Old Coach Rd
New Boston NH 03070

Call Sign: WK1J
Richard J Powell
50 Popple Rd
New Boston NH 03070

Call Sign: KB1QVO
Michael D Sousa
30 Rustic Ln
New Boston NH 03070

Call Sign: N1MXA
Nola S Page
155 S Hill Rd
New Boston NH 03070

Call Sign: W1UGV
Gardner S Page
155 S Hill Rd
New Boston NH 03070

Call Sign: KB1LVP
Charles R French
111 Saunders Hill Rd
New Boston NH 030704100

Call Sign: K1CRF
Charles R French
111 Saunders Hill Rd
New Boston NH 030704100

Call Sign: WA1HCE
David A Reeder
7 South Hill Rd
New Boston NH 03070

Call Sign: KA1UFC
Jeffrey S Steinmetz
170 South Hill Rd
New Boston NH 0307

Call Sign: KB1QLW

George E Nicolaou
301 South Hill Rd
New Boston NH 03070

Call Sign: N1FIK
Alan K Shuman
323 Weare Rd
New Boston NH 030700681

Call Sign: N1YPP
Denis R Desharnais
58 Whipplewill Rd
New Boston NH 03070

Call Sign: N2CVS
Lawrence D Lopez
New Boston NH 030700370

Call Sign: W1AE
Paul R Donaldson
New Boston NH 03070

Call Sign: W1AKS
New Hampshire Radio
Active In Disaster Incident
Operations
New Boston NH 03070

Call Sign: W1SEC
Nh Ares
New Boston NH 03070

Call Sign: K1HUL
Judi Hull
New Boston NH 03070

Call Sign: K1CMD
Command Nhares Club
New Boston NH 03070

Call Sign: K1MHT
Greater Manchester Ares
Club
New Boston NH 03070

Call Sign: K1NCS
Ncs Nhares Club
New Boston NH 03070

Call Sign: K1COM
Nhradio Communications
Vehicle
New Boston NH 03070

Call Sign: K1AKS
Alan K Shuman
New Boston NH 030700681

## FCC Amateur Radio Licenses in New Castle

Call Sign: KB1CNC
Craig Mahler
69 Cranfield St
New Castle NH 038540232

Call Sign: WA2DTN
Paul R Doe
80 Cranfield St
New Castle NH 03854

Call Sign: KB1HPM
Reginald E Whitehouse
24 Elm Court
New Castle NH 038540142

Call Sign: K1LLR
Geoffrey Potter
59 Little Harbor Rd
New Castle NH 03854

Call Sign: K1UY
Geoffrey Potter
59 Little Harbor Rd
New Castle NH 03854

Call Sign: W1CSW
Andrew B White
40 Vennard's Court
New Castle NH 038540091

Call Sign: N1YEB
Charles E Legare
New Castle NH 03854

Call Sign: KB1WYK
Sandra S Bisset
New Castle NH 03854

Call Sign: KB1WYN
Wallace E Mallett
New Castle NH 03854

## FCC Amateur Radio Licenses in New Durham

Call Sign: K1NRG
Greg Kelley
407 Berry Rd
New Durham NH 03855

Call Sign: N5WLU
Tom X Goss
396 Birch Hill Rd
New Durham NH 03855

Call Sign: KG4OGO
Debra L Pasternack
198 Brackett Rd
New Durham NH 03855

Call Sign: N3CAN
Marc D Behr
204 Brackett Rd
New Durham NH
038552330

Call Sign: KB1NSU
Jonathan B Roy
24 Main St Apt 2
New Durham NH 03855

Call Sign: N1EUN
Robert J Nelson Jr
64 Merrymeeting Lake Rd

New Durham NH 03855

Call Sign: AA1QD
Dale G Drake
78 Middleton Rd
New Durham NH
038552323

Call Sign: WA1YQQ
Richard E Leonard Jr
51 Miller Rd
New Durham NH 03855

Call Sign: KB1ERA
David E Mohr
27 Mml Ro
New Durham NH 03855

Call Sign: K1JFM
Henry G Munsey
189 N Shore Rd
New Durham NH 03855

Call Sign: KB1QOX
Greg Kelley
407 Ridge Rd
New Durham NH 03855

Call Sign: WK1W
Ronald W Coburn
163 Ridge Rd Top
New Durham NH
038552454

Call Sign: KB1IIQ
Rupert W Grahn
8 Sunset Ln
New Durham NH 03855

## FCC Amateur Radio Licenses in New Hampton

Call Sign: KA1DCU
Roxana C Krueger
445 Blake Hill Rd

New Hampton NH 03256

Call Sign: WA1YNV
Thomas A Krueger
445 Blake Hill Rd
New Hampton NH 03256

Call Sign: KB1IAK
Louis S Abdu
713 Blake Hill Rd
New Hampton NH
032564428

Call Sign: KB1IFL
Bette Abdu
713 Blake Hill Rd
New Hampton NH
032564428

Call Sign: N1RBZ
Jonathan K Bristow
N
New Hampton NH 03256

Call Sign: KC7TSA
Jeannie J Busby
949 Nh 132 N
New Hampton NH 03256

Call Sign: N1POL
Mark F Kozak
62 Riverwood Dr
New Hampton NH 03256

Call Sign: KB1LEM
Robert P Carter
1040 Rt 132 N
New Hampton NH 03256

Call Sign: N2ITL
Elena M Worrall
178 Straits Rd
New Hampton NH 03256

Call Sign: N2IRO

David P Worrall
178 Straits Rd
New Hampton NH 03256

Call Sign: NT1Q
William H Combs
Straits Rd
New Hampton NH
032560100

**FCC Amateur Radio
Licenses in New Ipswich**

Call Sign: N1UBR
Albert M Chalk
257 Ashburnham Rd
New Ipswich NH 03071

Call Sign: KB1TFL
Mark D Dupuis
151 Ashburnhan Rd
New Ipswich NH 03071

Call Sign: KA1HVJ
Richard L Szmauz
Box 642
New Ipswich NH 03071

Call Sign: KB1SZJ
Howard B Christle
186 Fox Farm Rd
New Ipswich NH 03071

Call Sign: K1QHH
Joseph G Thomas
Goen Rd Rfd Box 244
New Ipswich NH 03071

Call Sign: KB1HEB
Dorothy A Gable
41 Green Farm Rd
New Ipswich NH 03071

Call Sign: KB1HED
Timothy J Gable

41 Green Farm Rd
New Ipswich NH 03071

Call Sign: N3LLO
Matthew A Zinicola
55 Green Farm Rd
New Ipswich NH 03071

Call Sign: N1MZY
Everett W Parmenter Jr
23 Greenbriar Rd
New Ipswich NH 03071

Call Sign: KB1JPT
Dawn E Ronayne
84 Greenbriar Rd
New Ipswich NH 03071

Call Sign: KB1EII
Debra M Barnett
160 Greenville Rd
New Ipswich NH 03071

Call Sign: WB1AGI
Leo T Meedzan
67 Hubbard Pond Rd
New Ipswich NH 03071

Call Sign: N1ZIC
Frederick J Meshna
43 Ken St
New Ipswich NH 03071

Call Sign: N1VEJ
Jonathan R Grovesteen
122 Lower Pratt Pond Rd
New Ipswich NH 03071

Call Sign: KB1RTT
Mary A Fish
37 Main St
New Ipswich NH 03071

Call Sign: N1VET
Charles R Kay

151 Main St
New Ipswich NH 03071

Call Sign: N1JDM
Sean P Mc Inerney
83 Mason Rd
New Ipswich NH 03071

Call Sign: KB1ABI
Jean R St Pierre
15 Matson Rd
New Ipswich NH 03071

Call Sign: K1SDL
Gregory M Cain
24 Middle  Pratt Pond Rd
New Ipswich NH 03071

Call Sign: KB1JIF
Gayle-Ann Rust
116 Mountain View Dr
New Ipswich NH 03071

Call Sign: KB1HBI
David L Rust
116 Mountain View Dr
New Ipswich NH 03071

Call Sign: WR1I
David L Rust
116 Mountain View Dr
New Ipswich NH 03071

Call Sign: KB1KYJ
Wapack Trail Amateur
Radio Association
116 Mountain View Dr
New Ipswich NH 03071

Call Sign: W1ARA
Wapack Trail Amateur
Radio Association
116 Mountain View Dr
New Ipswich NH 03071

Call Sign: KC7TRZ
Jerry L Busby
949 Nh Route 132 N
New Hampton NH 03256

Call Sign: KB1MDQ
Douglas E Ford
335 Old Country Rd
New Ipswich NH 03071

Call Sign: WN1FIT
Anthony J Mcdonald
39 Old Tenny Rd. Apt # 101
New Ipswich NH 03071

Call Sign: N1QDZ
Joseph M Swick
14 Old Wilton Rd
New Ipswich NH 03071

Call Sign: WA1GMN
Paul M Chizinski
112 Old Wilton Rd
New Ipswich NH
030713422

Call Sign: N1ZIB
Timothy A Traffie
65 Perry Rd
New Ipswich NH 03071

Call Sign: W1UPL
Abbott L Rodenhiser
216 Perry Rd
New Ipswich NH
030714027

Call Sign: KB1MBU
Gregg S Wayman
8 Philmart Dr
New Ipswich NH 03071

Call Sign: KB1JSI
Brady D Anderson
203 Poor Farm Rd

New Ipswich NH 03071

Call Sign: KA1MBE
William A Birch
30 Porter Hill Rd
New Ipswich NH
030713732

Call Sign: KB1IDO
Tamara S Andrew Birch
30 Porter Hill Rd
New Ipswich NH
030713732

Call Sign: AB1CO
Tamara S Andrew Birch
30 Porter Hill Rd
New Ipswich NH
030713732

Call Sign: KB1AVT
Gregory M Cain
44 Pratt Pond
New Ipswich NH 03071

Call Sign: KB1PSV
Lance E Deplante
300 River Rd
New Ipswich NH 03071

Call Sign: K2HZB
Lance E Deplante
300 River Rd
New Ipswich NH 03071

Call Sign: KB1ABM
Frances S Riggs
189 Temple Rd
New Ipswich NH 03071

Call Sign: N1QXN
William C Rhodes
20 Timber Top Rd Apt 5
New Ipswich NH 03071

Call Sign: WB1HBW
John M Clark
91 Timbertop Rd
New Ipswich NH 03071

Call Sign: N1FQQ
Robert L Close
93 Timbertop Rd
New Ipswich NH 03071

Call Sign: K1SRR
Robert L Close
93 Timbertop Rd
New Ipswich NH 03071

Call Sign: N1VKC
David C Mathewson
140 Turnpike Rd
New Ipswich NH 03071

Call Sign: KB1HYR
Brett L Markham
283 Turnpike Rd
New Ipswich NH 03071

Call Sign: NI1NH
New Ipswich Ares Club
661 Turnpike Rd
New Ipswich NH 03071

Call Sign: KB1OTW
New Ipswich Emergency
Communications Group
661 Turnpike Rd
New Ipswich NH 03071

Call Sign: KB1ABL
Joseph D Howard
Turnpike Rd
New Ipswich NH 03071

Call Sign: N1IFU
Carl M Traffie
17 Wheeler Rd

New Ipswich NH
030713847

Call Sign: N1YJU
David W Somero
53 Wheeler Rd
New Ipswich NH 03071

Call Sign: KB1RFC
Stephen B Hughes
44 Whittemore Hill Rd
New Ipswich NH 03071

Call Sign: KA1YIB
Daniel C Olson
Willard Rd
New Ipswich NH 03071

Call Sign: KB1ABK
George M Standley
9 Wyman Rd
New Ipswich NH 03071

Call Sign: NN1M
Norman E Saucier
32 Wyman Rd
New Ipswich NH 03071

Call Sign: K1QJS
James L Hicks
New Ipswich NH 03071

Call Sign: KA1JBB
Thomas G Bryan
New Ipswich NH 03071

Call Sign: N1IQC
Frank J Danisienka
New Ipswich NH 03071

Call Sign: KB1EOI
William J Edmonds
New Ipswich NH
030710159

Call Sign: KB1HIA
Richard A Lehtonen
New Ipswich NH 03071

Call Sign: KB1LSI
Sw Nh Fists Club
New Ipswich NH 03071

Call Sign: W1FFF
Sw Nh Fists Club
New Ipswich NH 03071

Call Sign: KB1RTZ
Christine M Pillsbury
New Ipswich NH 03071

Call Sign: KB1IDW
New Ipswich Town Hall
661 New Ipswich Ares Club
Turnpike
New Ipswick NH 03071

Call Sign: KB1NZW
Derek L Rust
116 Mountain View Dr
New Ipwich NH 03071

## FCC Amateur Radio Licenses in New London

Call Sign: KB1ICL
John M Bock
103 Andover Rd
New London NH 03257

Call Sign: N1WEK
Richard Guerringue
125 Bog Rd
New London NH
032570368

Call Sign: N1GEP
Reade Williams
16 Fenwood Dr

New London NH
032571099

Call Sign: W1GUX
Robert R Buckley
11 Gay Farm Rd
New London NH
032574316

Call Sign: KB1JGZ
David F Harris
438 Hall Farm Rd
New London NH 03257

Call Sign: W0LYI
John P Walsh
82 Hilltop Pl
New London NH
032571128

Call Sign: KA1QKJ
Dan H Allen
120 King Hill Rd
New London NH
032574411

Call Sign: KB1JCP
Dan H Allen
120 King Hill Rd
New London NH
032574411

Call Sign: N1UM
Dan H Allen
1300 King Hill Rd
New London NH 03257

Call Sign: KA1QXB
Richard N Sweetland
115 Knights Hill Rd
New London NH
032574574

Call Sign: W1ARD
John B Wilson

296 Lamson Lane
New London NH 03257

Call Sign: N1UJZ
Christopher J Andrews
1 Meadow Ln
New London NH 03257

Call Sign: K1NTT
Robert F Cole
Murray Pond Rd
New London NH 03257

Call Sign: N1SG
Steven M Greenbaum
500 Otterville Rd
New London NH 03257

Call Sign: N1QYT
Karen D Ryan
70 Pine Hill Rd.
New London NH 03257

Call Sign: WA1FAF
Mark S Ryan
70 Pine Hill Rd.
New London NH 03257

Call Sign: K2AQ
Howard F Malone
98 Rowell Hill Rd
New London NH 03257

Call Sign: KB2TLH
Ryan M Malone
98 Rowell Hill Rd
New London NH 03257

Call Sign: K1KLM
Kathleen L Malone
98 Rowell Hill Rd
New London NH 03257

Call Sign: KA1QLC
Clark W Collins Jr

Rowell Hill Rd Box 334
New London NH 03257

Call Sign: KB1ICJ
Paul J Diekmann
24 Sawyer Ln
New London NH 03257

Call Sign: N1AMC
Vincent R Sproul
140 Seamans Rd
New London NH 03257

Call Sign: N1LIL
Walter Angoff
64 Surrey Lane
New London NH
032570245

Call Sign: K1WM
William G Mc Fadden
New London NH
032571395

Call Sign: KB1DXA
Adam L Le Clair
New London NH 03257

Call Sign: KV1G
Edgar R Condict
New London NH
032571110

Call Sign: N1CLB
George H Bailey
New London NH 03257

Call Sign: N1VOV
John H Wiltshire
New London NH
032570129

Call Sign: WA1ZCN
David B Colter

New London NH
032571109

Call Sign: KB1ICK
Gregory M Barthol
New London NH
032570093

Call Sign: W1EU
Edgar R Condict
New London NH
032571110

Call Sign: KB1SYE
Charles P Adams Jr
New London NH 03257

**FCC Amateur Radio
Licenses in New Market**

Call Sign: N1ZGI
Larry A Wickens
326 Ash Swamp Rd
New Market NH 03857

Call Sign: KT1V
Theodore J Demopoulos
Bass St
New Market NH 03857

Call Sign: N8AYZ
John W Good Jr
283 Great Bay Woods
New Market NH 038572425

Call Sign: KB1MSN
John W Good Jr
283 Great Bay Woods
New Market NH 038572425

Call Sign: N1FIW
Donald H Gebo
40 Riverbend Rd
New Market NH 03857

## FCC Amateur Radio Licenses in Newbury

Call Sign: AC1H
Kenneth D Tentarelli
27 Bowles Rd
Newbury NH 032556110

Call Sign: N1ZDU
Mark J Hilton
130 Bowles Rd
Newbury NH 03255

Call Sign: N1ZDT
Richard K Laporte
106 Chalk Pond Rd
Newbury NH 03255

Call Sign: KA1ZSM
Robert R Bergeron
190 Chalk Pond Rd
Newbury NH 03255

Call Sign: KE6RDD
Ken Schuster
626 Chalk Pond Rd.
Newbury NH 032555710

Call Sign: W1EVE
Charles F Rayner
9 North Face Dr
Newbury NH 03255

Call Sign: N1QA
Douglas T Martin
38 Ramblewood Dr
Newbury NH 03255

Call Sign: N1VZQ
Diane L Foster
56 Southgate Rd
Newbury NH 032555307

Call Sign: N1KQA
Lois C Ritchie
Newbury NH 03255

Call Sign: N1NEA
Donald F Falkowski
Newbury NH 03255

Call Sign: N1YBM
Fred L O Connor
Newbury NH 03255

Call Sign: WA1EVT
Warren P Ritchie
Newbury NH 03255

Call Sign: KB1FZD
Melanie M Bell
Newbury NH 03255

Call Sign: KB1FJK
Robert J Bell
Newbury NH 03255

Call Sign: AA1XC
Robert J Bell
Newbury NH 03255

Call Sign: KB1TTK
Clyde J Bacon
Newbury NH 03255

## FCC Amateur Radio Licenses in Newcastle

Call Sign: WB1EOX
Samuel B Fuller
168 Portsmouth Ave Box 271
Newcastle NH 03854

## FCC Amateur Radio Licenses in Newfields

Call Sign: N1NMU
Robert J Devantery
159 Exeter Rd
Newfields NH 03856

Call Sign: KB1IHR
Lewis M Bond Iii
81 Halls Mill Rd
Newfields NH 03856

Call Sign: KA1RRR
William R Davis Iii
10 Main St  P.O. Box 1003
Newfields NH 03856

Call Sign: N1YLV
John M Hayden
Newfields NH 038560003

Call Sign: N1ZWY
Gary Rosa
Newfields NH 03856

Call Sign: KB1UWW
William C Bragg
Newfields NH 03856

## FCC Amateur Radio Licenses in Newington

Call Sign: KA9TME
Frederick W Harvey
23 Beane Ln
Newington NH 03801

Call Sign: KB1UAJ
Frederick W Harvey
23 Beane Ln
Newington NH 03801

Call Sign: N1YCF
Paul J Downey
16 Capt Lndg
Newington NH 03801

Call Sign: K1SCQ
Steven C Quinn
56 Captains Landing

Newington NH 03801

Call Sign: KD6DVV
William A Black
51 Captains Landing Rd
Newington NH 03801

Call Sign: W1KTV
George J Newick
34 Fabyan Point Rd
Newington NH 038012729

Call Sign: KA1CVU
Robert W Hill
168 Little Bay Rd
Newington NH 038012709

Call Sign: KB1FQF
Glenn A Myrick
55 Old Dover Rd
Newington NH 03801

Call Sign: KB1FK
Albert T Libby
148 Old Dover Rd
Newington NH 03801

Call Sign: KA1PQD
Gail M Klanchesser
Old Post Rd
Newington NH 03801

## FCC Amateur Radio Licenses in Newmarket

Call Sign: N1WMV
Mark J Darrigo Jr
Bass St
Newmarket NH 03857

Call Sign: KB1AGP
Karen S Blue
Bass St
Newmarket NH 03857

Call Sign: KD1JR
Gary M Blue
Bass St
Newmarket NH 03857

Call Sign: KB1SNW
Daniel A Stonesifer
9 Bennet Way 12
Newmarket NH 03857

Call Sign: WA1NXZ
Frederick J Thibeau
7 Channing Way
Newmarket NH 03857

Call Sign: KB1RVG
Jeffrey R Cantara
31 Doe Farm Ln
Newmarket NH 03857

Call Sign: KA2NBW
Diana Virgona
29 Gordon Ave
Newmarket NH 038571802

Call Sign: N1ZXZ
Rick Miller
110 Grant Rd
Newmarket NH 03857

Call Sign: KB1SNZ
Charles A Smart
181 Grant Rd
Newmarket NH 03857

Call Sign: KA1PQE
Robert K Bresideski
24 Great Hill Dr,
Newmarket NH 038572057

Call Sign: KB1SPL
James D Antonino Sr
33 Johnson Dr
Newmarket NH 03857

Call Sign: KB1VCH
Wichyein Tritarntipvikul
12 Joy Farm Ln
Newmarket NH 03857

Call Sign: KB1VCI
Khumron Thongsuk
12 Joy Farm Ln
Newmarket NH 03857

Call Sign: AB1OE
Thanawat Rungaroonwan
12 Joy Farm Ln
Newmarket NH 03857

Call Sign: KB1VLV
Sonthaya Phanthanyakij
12 Joy Farm Ln
Newmarket NH 03857

Call Sign: KF1I
Wichyein Tritarntipvikul
12 Joy Farm Ln
Newmarket NH 03857

Call Sign: KB1VTO
Khumron Thongsuk
12 Joy Farm Ln
Newmarket NH 03857

Call Sign: KB1VWH
Kriangkrai Suriyakrai
12 Joy Farm Ln
Newmarket NH 03857

Call Sign: AB1PE
Khumron Thongsuk
12 Joy Farm Ln
Newmarket NH 03857

Call Sign: KB1WMM
Anothai Burinkul
12 Joy Farm Ln
Newmarket NH 03857

Call Sign: KB1RUB
Mark A Thompson
109 Langs Lane
Newmarket NH 03857

Call Sign: KB1PYE
Samuel J Fitzpatrick
9 Osprey Ln
Newmarket NH 03857

Call Sign: KC1XC
George P Demosthenes Jr
Rfd 2
Newmarket NH 03857

Call Sign: KC5HBI
Joseph A Faletra
2 Lee Hook Rd 1
Newmarket NH 038572127

Call Sign: W1SJF
Samuel J Fitzpatrick
9 Osprey Ln
Newmarket NH 03857

Call Sign: N1UXD
Robert D Allard
19 Riverbend Rd
Newmarket NH 038571412

Call Sign: W1HIE
Leodor A Boisvert
175 Main St
Newmarket NH 03857

Call Sign: W1FMR
James M Fitton
71 Pear Tree Ln
Newmarket NH 03857

Call Sign: N1YVU
Mary N Allard
19 Riverbend Rd
Newmarket NH 03857

Call Sign: KA1SNG
Elaine L Camire
20 Maplecrest
Newmarket NH 03857

Call Sign: KB1KBD
Joel L Huntress
904 Piscassic St
Newmarket NH 038571189

Call Sign: WA1YKL
Steven D Donnell
210 S Main St
Newmarket NH 03857

Call Sign: W1JUI
Edward Camire Sr
20 Maplecrest
Newmarket NH 038571402

Call Sign: N1JLH
Joel L Huntress
904 Piscassic St
Newmarket NH 038571189

Call Sign: N1LCK
Earl E Miller Iii
8 Sleepy Hollow
Newmarket NH 03857

Call Sign: KB1AIY
Chandler Robbins
7 Moody Pt Dr
Newmarket NH 03857

Call Sign: KB1VTP
Darin Bennett
Piscassic St Apt 107
Newmarket NH 03857

Call Sign: KI4TKS
Nicole R Hoover
225 South Main St
Newmarket NH 03857

Call Sign: K1DKE
Normand E Boisvert
2 Mt Pleasant St
Newmarket NH 03857

Call Sign: KB1UIW
Nathan Smith
Piscassic St Apt 305
Newmarket NH 03857

Call Sign: KB1QPJ
Gail P Wasiewski
236 South Main St
Newmarket NH 03857

Call Sign: N1BHB
Barbara E Cote
171 New Rd
Newmarket NH 03857

Call Sign: KG4SIZ
William J Bell
Piscassicst - 310
Newmarket NH 03857

Call Sign: KB1BEE
Brian N O Donnell
16 Stonewall Way
Newmarket NH 03857

Call Sign: WB1HJP
Armand G Cote
171 New Rd
Newmarket NH 03857

Call Sign: N1PEZ
Michael G Gardner
13 Railroad St Apt 6
Newmarket NH 03857

Call Sign: WW1V
Robert M O Donnell
16 Stonewall Way
Newmarket NH 03857

Call Sign: KB1EUB
Andrew N O Donnell
16 Stonewall Way
Newmarket NH 03857

Call Sign: N1GCJ
Luis O Alvarez
Newmarket NH 03857

**FCC Amateur Radio
Licenses in Newport**

Call Sign: W1WNH
Richard P Cota
54 Alexander Ave.
Newport NH 03773

Call Sign: WB1DSX
Todd R Stetson
Allan
Newport NH 03773

Call Sign: NN1R
John Tom Hill Amateur
Radio Club
77 Anderson Rd
Newport NH 03773

Call Sign: WB1DKX
Michael H Geschwindner
39 Belknap Ave
Newport NH 03773

Call Sign: N1PHR
Matthew M Blanchard Sr
6 Blood Rd
Newport NH 03773

Call Sign: KB1AJC
Cynthia W Herschlein
Box 191g
Newport NH 03773

Call Sign: K1YDH
Edward Zarebski

Box 192
Newport NH 037738301

Call Sign: KB1BBQ
Joshua B Fox
Box 198a
Newport NH 03773

Call Sign: KB1BIQ
Nicole M Smith
Box 199
Newport NH 03773

Call Sign: KA1YER
Kristie L Pockett
Box 202
Newport NH 03773

Call Sign: KB1AJH
Karrie L Pockett
Box 202
Newport NH 03773

Call Sign: KA1WEM
Kimberly L Carnevale
Box 221
Newport NH 03773

Call Sign: KA1YEP
Julie A Carnevale
Box 221
Newport NH 03773

Call Sign: KA1WEL
Bridget A Hamilton
Box 228a
Newport NH 03773

Call Sign: N1UUL
Dorothy B Mitchell
Box 254
Newport NH 037730254

Call Sign: N1TYY
Helen J Blood

534 Bradford Rd
Newport NH 03773

Call Sign: N1YMR
Dolores S Lader
738 Bradford Rd
Newport NH 03773

Call Sign: K1RO
Mark J Wilson
12 Breezy Point Rd
Newport NH 03773

Call Sign: N1OJS
Jean F Wilson
12 Breezy Point Rd
Newport NH 03773

Call Sign: KB1SFP
Annette L Boutin
14 Campus St
Newport NH 03773

Call Sign: WB1BZU
John J Kowalczyk
Cash St
Newport NH 03773

Call Sign: KA1VFW
Edmund C Davis Iii
E Rd 2
Newport NH 03773

Call Sign: W1EEF
Richard W Doremus Jr
5 Golf Club Rd
Newport NH 03773

Call Sign: N1BNY
Robert L Huneven
896 Hurd Pond Rd
Newport NH 037737717

Call Sign: K1NH
William L Halleck

13 Moore Rd
Newport NH 03773

Call Sign: N1CB
Carl H Breuning
54 Myrtle St
Newport NH 03773

Call Sign: WA1WEY
Cheryl A Breuning
54 Myrtle St
Newport NH 03773

Call Sign: KA1IIM
Cheryl L Wilder
54 Myrtle St
Newport NH 03773

Call Sign: N1PHN
Joseph L Moulton Sr
181 Oak St
Newport NH 03773

Call Sign: N1VOW
Russell J Mitchell
83 S Main St
Newport NH 037731810

Call Sign: KA1YEO
Kurt D Haselton
177 S Main St
Newport NH 03773

Call Sign: AJ1S
Andrew J Stenberg
529 South Main St
Newport NH 037732906

Call Sign: W4PAS
Richard G Whynall
5 Spruce St
Newport NH 03773

Call Sign: N1RX
Bruce C Beford

178 Summer St
Newport NH 037731219

Call Sign: KB1KSK
Sullivan County Amateur
Radio Group
178 Summer St
Newport NH 037731219

Call Sign: WU1W
Sullivan County Amateur
Radio Group
178 Summer St
Newport NH 037731219

Call Sign: KU1R
Sullivan County Amateur
Radio Group
178 Summer St
Newport NH 037731219

Call Sign: KB1UVQ
Linda A Beford
178 Summer St
Newport NH 03773

Call Sign: KA1ORB
Linda A Beford
178 Summer St
Newport NH 03773

Call Sign: KA1NHM
Robert E Magnuson Jr
198 Summer St
Newport NH 03773

Call Sign: K2AJV
Joseph L Hartmann Jr
Summer St
Newport NH 03773

Call Sign: W2FYB
Albert T Rooney S J
Memorial Radio Club
Summer St

Newport NH 03773

Call Sign: N1YSY
Paul F Reilly
41 Syndicate St
Newport NH 03773

Call Sign: KB1UFH
Robin F Geschwindner
133 Turkey Hill Rd
Newport NH 03773

Call Sign: KB1UFI
Richard M Geschwindner Jr
133 Turkey Hill Rd
Newport NH 03773

Call Sign: N1SSH
Robert L Haight Jr
Newport NH 03773

Call Sign: K1SWL
David J Benson
Newport NH 03773

**FCC Amateur Radio
Licenses in Newton**

Call Sign: KA1WDY
Frederick J Wheeler Iii
50 Amesbury Rd
Newton NH 03858

Call Sign: KB1PAY
Ronald L Jones
103 Amesbury Rd
Newton NH 03858

Call Sign: KB1KVU
Ann Byers
8 Bartlett St
Newton NH 03858

Call Sign: AB1DR
Ann Byers

8 Bartlett St
Newton NH 03858

Call Sign: K1QO
Ann Byers
8 Bartlett St
Newton NH 03858

Call Sign: KD1ZT
Robert J Daigle
5 Durgin Dr
Newton NH 03858

Call Sign: N1ALM
Dana B Allison
4 Hadley Rd
Newton NH 03858

Call Sign: K1SAP
David A Crawford
60 Heath St
Newton NH 038583400

Call Sign: KA1JHI
Robert A Littlefield
72 Heath St
Newton NH 03858

Call Sign: WB1ELP
John C Mattson
58 Highland St
Newton NH 03858

Call Sign: KA1LCR
Anthony J Lamoly
18 Maple Ave
Newton NH 03858

Call Sign: N1VQG
Eileen M Lamoly
18 Maple Ave
Newton NH 03858

Call Sign: KB1MHT
Andrew N Stover

13 N Main St
Newton NH 03858

Call Sign: N1IAN
Tom D A Gynan
26 New Boston Rd
Newton NH 03858

Call Sign: N1IPJ
John A Gynan
26 New Boston Rd
Newton NH 03858

Call Sign: K1JZD
William R Cronk Sr
171 S Main St
Newton NH 03858

Call Sign: N2EWW
Mary Anne R Lapierre
2 Sarah's Way
Newton NH 038583426

Call Sign: N2EWX
Russell R Lapierre
2 Sarah's Way
Newton NH 038583426

Call Sign: K1EPJ
David R Le Duc
24 Tanglewood Dr
Newton NH 03858

Call Sign: N1IX
David R Le Duc
26 Tanglewood Dr
Newton NH 03858

Call Sign: K1KOL
William A Baker
16 Thornell Rd
Newton NH 03858

Call Sign: KB1JZT
Douglas W Mcgeoch

2 Valley Dr
Newton NH 03858

Call Sign: KA1KAN
Marion D Cipolle
20 Whippoorwill Dr
Newton NH 038583314

Call Sign: W1SZ
David J Cipolle
20 Whippoorwill Dr
Newton NH 03858

Call Sign: KB1LHF
Luke D Cipolle
20 Whippoorwill Dr
Newton NH 03858

## FCC Amateur Radio Licenses in Newton Junction

Call Sign: N1ZOU
Jacqueline N Leo
6w Main St
Newton Junction NH 03859

Call Sign: KA1IQK
Gordon A Cheney
23 W Main St
Newton Junction NH 03859

Call Sign: AA1PY
Scott L Smulski
Newton Junction NH 03859

Call Sign: KA1YLG
Andrew W Gaunt
Newton Junction NH
038590013

Call Sign: N1PWD
Carlos R Gonzalez Iii
Newton Junction NH 03859

Call Sign: K1UZ
Scott L Smulski
Newton Junction NH 03859

Call Sign: KB1RJB
Lorraine S Macdonald
84 Allard Farm Circuit
North Conway NH 03860

Call Sign: N1MUD
Jonathan Hively
301 Birch Hill Rd
North Conway NH 03860

Call Sign: N1NEY
Brian C Jaworski
Box 1526
North Conway NH 03860

Call Sign: KB1RST
Holly A Gaudette-Fitch
119 Dandi View Rd
North Conway NH 03860

Call Sign: KB1RSU
Dane K Fitch
119 Dandi View Rd
North Conway NH 03860

Call Sign: KB1EZJ
Gregory S Fitch
119 Dandiview Rd
North Conway NH 03860

Call Sign: W1DRG
John T Putnam
221 Dandiview Rd
North Conway NH
038605604

Call Sign: W1LQQ
Charles E Gagnon Jr

307 Echo Acres
North Conway NH 03860

Call Sign: KB1OPF
John M Ferris
252 Grove St
North Conway NH 03860

Call Sign: KB1OPK
Cheryl A Ferris
252 Grove St
North Conway NH 03860

Call Sign: KM4DB
David A Klemp
77 Grove St Unit 16
North Conway NH 03860

Call Sign: KB1JBZ
Kory J Kimble
60 Lamplighter Park
North Conway NH 03860

Call Sign: KA1LIA
David A Badger
Maple St
North Conway NH 03860

Call Sign: KB1CND
John R Philbrick
2 Red Ridge Ln
North Conway NH 03860

Call Sign: KB1SAZ
Tom M Baptiste
1230 West Side Rd
North Conway NH 03860

Call Sign: N1KZR
Mark A Ewing
605 White Mt Highway
N Conway NH 03860

Call Sign: KE4WVR
JANIS M Mccarvill

3852 White Mtn. Hwy. Apt.
#308
North Conway NH 03860

Call Sign: KA1SVV
Robert M Ormond
North Conway NH 03860

Call Sign: KB1CRO
Jeffrey S Fongemie
North Conway NH
038602351

Call Sign: N1WCU
Marc R Chauvin
North Conway NH 03860

Call Sign: N1XEN
John R Fulp
North Conway NH 03860

Call Sign: KB1OGT
David G Mandel
North Conway NH 03860

Call Sign: KB1QKC
James E Crawford
North Conway NH 03860

Call Sign: KB1RIW
Joseph W Larue
North Conway NH 03860

Call Sign: KB1RJE
Nickolas A James
North Conway NH 03860

Call Sign: KB1RJG
Dawn James
North Conway NH 03860

Call Sign: KB1TPY
Robert W Dutton
North Conway NH 03860

## FCC Amateur Radio Licenses in North Danville

Call Sign: WA1DFM
Frederick F Rogers
97 Sandown Rd
North Danville NH
038190309

## FCC Amateur Radio Licenses in North Hampton

Call Sign: KB1SNY
Julie E Johnson
1 Apricot Way
North Hampton NH 03862

Call Sign: KB1VMP
Bryan Yeaton
130 Atlantic Ave
North Hampton NH 03862

Call Sign: N1YLI
Daniel R Shepard
186 Atlantic Ave
North Hampton NH 03862

Call Sign: KA1LNN
Ralph A Martin
13 Cherry Rd
North Hampton NH 03862

Call Sign: KB1VGQ
Ralph S Martin
15 Cherry Rd
North Hampton NH 03862

Call Sign: W1GLY
Scott C Seely
114 Exeter Rd
North Hampton NH 03862

Call Sign: W1UNC
Raymond L Belanger

21 Hobbs Rd
North Hampton NH 03862

Call Sign: KB1IDT
Christopher A Sloane
40 Hobbs Rd
North Hampton NH 03862

Call Sign: K1FOO
Christopher A Sloane
40 Hobbs Rd
North Hampton NH 03862

Call Sign: KB1MHQ
Kae A Sloane
40 Hobbs Rd
North Hampton NH 03862

Call Sign: K1KAE
Kae A Sloane
40 Hobbs Rd
North Hampton NH 03862

Call Sign: K1YU
Christopher A Sloane
40 Hobbs Rd
North Hampton NH 03862

Call Sign: KA1FLI
Richard E Cumming
Hobbs Rd
North Hampton NH 03862

Call Sign: N1HAB
David J Farrell
21 Kimberly Dr
North Hampton NH
038622239

Call Sign: K1GAR
John N Mac Innes Iii
52 Lafayette Rd - Apt 4
North Hampton NH 03862

Call Sign: WA1MQW

Ralph L Sherouse Jr
182 Mill Rd
North Hampton NH 03862

Call Sign: KB1FXA
Cartier Amateur Radio
Team
4 Park Circle
North Hampton NH 03862

Call Sign: N1TON
Arthur W Pelletier Iii
154 Post Rd
North Hampton NH
038622035

Call Sign: KB1EOG
William E Coffey
221 Post Rd
North Hampton NH
038622038

Call Sign: AC1BD
William E Coffey Mr
221 Post Rd
North Hampton NH
038622038

Call Sign: KB1MJA
Vincent P Corbett Iii
51 South Rd
North Hampton NH 03862

Call Sign: W1CBT
Vincent P Corbett Iii
51 South Rd
North Hampton NH 03862

Call Sign: N1QEY
David W Parkhurst
63 South Rd
North Hampton NH 03862

Call Sign: K1WZR
Richard H Morris

85 South Rd
North Hampton NH 03862

Call Sign: W3CMU
Edwin C Mac Neil
60 Walnut Ave
North Hampton NH 03862

Call Sign: KB1SOF
Vincent P Corbett
134 Walnut Ave
North Hampton NH 03862

Call Sign: N1DUN
Eileen A Turchan
North Hampton NH 03862

Call Sign: W1TH
Theodore M Turchan
North Hampton NH 03862

Call Sign: WA1ZNA
David J Marinelli
North Hampton NH 03862

Call Sign: N1HIT
New Hampshire
Interconnect Team
North Hampton NH
038620051

### FCC Amateur Radio Licenses in North Haverhill

Call Sign: WK1Z
John T Flynn
5 Allagash Rd
North Haverhill NH 03774

Call Sign: KZ1Q
Donald B Stapelfeld Sr
2040 Lime Kiln Rd.
North Haverhill NH 03774

Call Sign: KB1SKK
Carleton W Torrey
48 Oak Ridge Park
North Haverhill NH 03774

Call Sign: KB1VZW
Forrest J Boucher
18 Terrace Dr
North Haverhill NH 03774

Call Sign: WA8MWZ
William D Lindsey
125 West Side Dr
North Haverhill NH 03774

Call Sign: N1QGC
Wayne S Mc Danolds
North Haverhill NH 03774

Call Sign: WA1SMC
Henry F Bartkowski
North Haverhill NH 03774

### FCC Amateur Radio Licenses in North Salem

Call Sign: N1ETJ
Richard G Rossi
30 Gillis Ter
N Salem NH 030730576

Call Sign: K1RCT
Warren R Martel
143 Haverhill Rd
North Salem NH 03073

Call Sign: KA1ALZ
Donald G Bozeman
67 Shore Dr
North Salem NH 03073

Call Sign: N1CSH
Marilyn A Richardson
North Salem NH 03073

Call Sign: N1THT
Thomas D Sharpe
North Salem NH 03073

Call Sign: WA1SOT
James M Richardson Jr
North Salem NH 03073

Call Sign: KB1NVQ
Theodore W Hatem
North Salem NH
030730406

Call Sign: K1KKY
Theodore W Hatem
North Salem NH
030730406

Call Sign: K1QI
Thomas D Sharpe
North Salem NH 03073

Call Sign: N1CE
Thomas D Sharpe
North Salem NH 03073

Call Sign: KB1UAP
Pcom
North Salem NH 03073

Call Sign: KB1URC
Nh-Star
North Salem NH 03073

### FCC Amateur Radio Licenses in North Sandwich

Call Sign: KB1GNJ
Ian J Fair
49 Maple Ridge Rd
North Sandwich NH 03259

Call Sign: K3CK
David A Eaton

228 Whiteface Rd
North Sandwich NH 03259

Call Sign: KA1GS
George D Kopperl
235 Whiteface Rd
North Sandwich NH
032593603

Call Sign: N1XIK
Lisa H Morgan
381 Whiteface Rd
North Sandwich NH 03259

Call Sign: N1DCT
Richard R Morgan
381 Whiteface Rd
North Sandwich NH 03259

Call Sign: KB1PJE
Herbert W Sallet
North Sandwich NH
032590078

Call Sign: N1YZE
Russell N Boyce Jr
Box 283
North Stratford NH 03590

Call Sign: N1LSW
Jack J Komisarek
Box 372
North Stratford NH 03590

Call Sign: KE1LN
Allan M Briqueler
555 Fuller Rd
North Stratford NH 03590

Call Sign: KC2GUL
Abbie J Woods

545 Fuller Rd.
North Stratford NH 03590

Call Sign: KB1WLA
Jon L Smith
337 Us Route 3
North Stratford NH 03590

Call Sign: N1SWZ
Jon L Smith
337 Us Route 3
North Stratford NH 03590

Call Sign: N1XZQ
Michael A Parrow
North Stratford NH 03590

Call Sign: N1ZKP
Annette M E Parrow
North Stratford NH 03590

Call Sign: K2AMB
Adam Bronstein
5 Davis Court
North Sutton NH 03260

Call Sign: N1YPZ
Eric T Schultz
375 North Rd.
North Sutton NH 03260

Call Sign: N1ZCN
Louise P Schultz
375 North Rd.
North Sutton NH 03260

Call Sign: KA1HUW
Heather L Rowe
North Sutton NH 03260

Call Sign: W1OHA
Paul I Cleveland

North Sutton NH
032600089

Call Sign: KB1OTA
Daniel A Sundquist
North Sutton NH 03260

Call Sign: KB1KOX
Neil L Goodell
53 Joslin Rd
N Swanzey NH 03431

Call Sign: W1PTX
Neil L Goodell
53 Joslin Rd
N Swanzey NH 03431

Call Sign: AE1P
Neil L Goodell
53 Joslin Rd
N Swanzey NH 03431

Call Sign: KB1UPS
Joshua R Goodell
53 Joslin Rd
N Swanzey NH 03431

Call Sign: N1BAC
Arnold E Johnson
43 Old Homestead Hwy
North Swanzey NH 03431

Call Sign: K4KCM
Donald R Bjorklund
17 Sylvan Way
North Swanzey NH 03431

Call Sign: KB1PMW
Charles L Underhill

8 East St
North Walpole NH 03609

## FCC Amateur Radio Licenses in North Woodstock

Call Sign: KA1QDL
Martha S Talbot
8 Courtney Rd
North Woodstock NH
03262

Call Sign: KB1OXL
Artemas L Latham Iii
15 Scenic View Dr
North Woodstock NH
03262

Call Sign: N1ALL
Artemas L Latham Iii
15 Scenic View Dr
North Woodstock NH
03262

Call Sign: N1PMY
Joseph F Cardullo Jr
Young St
North Woodstock NH
03262

## FCC Amateur Radio Licenses in Northfield

Call Sign: KB1RKN
Ross A Starkweather
67 Bean Hill Rd
Northfield NH 03276

Call Sign: KB1HYJ
Donald E Girard
283 Concord Rd
Northfield NH 03276

Call Sign: WA1NUU

Irving T Atwood Jr
1 Fiske Rd.
Northfield NH 03276

Call Sign: N1PKN
Fred G French Jr
75 Forrest Rd
Northfield NH 032764050

Call Sign: K1TFH
Clifton H Mills Jr
107 Greenwood Dr
Northfield NH 032764712

Call Sign: N1PKM
Fred G French Sr
Northfield Village Apt 35
Northfield NH 03276

Call Sign: KB1CSW
Jason A Webster
575 Oak Hill Rd
Northfield NH 03276

Call Sign: KB1CSX
John A Webster Jr
575 Oak Hill Rd
Northfield NH 03276

Call Sign: W1DDI
Mark E Persson
426 Shaker Rd
Northfield NH 032762809

Call Sign: KB1MGK
Katelyn N Vander Clute
89 Silver Ln
Northfield NH 03276

Call Sign: KB1MGL
Douglas C Vander Clute
89 Silver Ln
Northfield NH 03276

Call Sign: W1YVY

William E Merrill Jr
25 Spring St Apt 30
Northfield NH 03276

Call Sign: NC1F
Carl P Nordmark
25 Spring St Apt 31
Northfield NH 032761626

Call Sign: K1NHB
Brian A Sargent
35 Summer St Apt 24
Northfield NH 032761615

Call Sign: KB1CVP
Michael E Dangelo
80 Turnpike Rd
North Field NH 03276

Call Sign: K1LGU
Roger A Gagnon
34 Woodlawn Ave
Northfield NH 032764724

## FCC Amateur Radio Licenses in Northwood

Call Sign: K1EEM
Erin E Madison
813 1st New Hampshire
Tpk #2
Northwood NH 03261

Call Sign: KA1LJG
Roy E Wentworth
555 1st Nh Tpke
Northwood NH 03261

Call Sign: KA1BXA
George V Donatello
45 Bennett Bridge Rd
Northwood NH 03261

Call Sign: KA1SZV
Kathleen M G Lord

4 Bow St
Northwood NH 03261

Call Sign: KD6FPZ
Paul S Castellani Jr
181 Bow St
Northwood NH 03261

Call Sign: KA1LKP
Ethel L Wentworth
Box 242
Northwood NH 03261

Call Sign: N1NIU
Dorothy J Berg
Box 3192
Northwood NH 03261

Call Sign: KA1EPK
Marion F Masten
Box 422a
Northwood NH 03261

Call Sign: WA1PQF
Henry R Masten Jr
Box 422a
Northwood NH 03261

Call Sign: KA1LJF
Ann L Nary
Box 541
Northwood NH 03261

Call Sign: N1LZR
Ren W Horne
35 Denmark Dr
Northwood NH 03261

Call Sign: W1REN
Ren W Horne
35 Denmark Dr
Northwood NH 03261

Call Sign: W1ELW
Robert V Lindquist Sr

549 First Nh Tpk
Northwood NH 032613301

Call Sign: N1QVS
Frank B Gagne Jr
3 Gary Rd
Northwood NH 03261

Call Sign: N1QZN
Kathleen Gagne
3 Gary Rd
Northwood NH 03261

Call Sign: N7PQO
Michael L Savage
153 Lower Deerfield Rd
Northwood NH 03261

Call Sign: KB1LTD
Bernard E Gynan Sr
177 Lower Deerfield Rd
Northwood NH 03261

Call Sign: N1NZA
William D Fowler
480 Mountain Ave
Northwood NH 03261

Call Sign: WB1APP
Robert A Distasio
88 Old Barnstead Rd
Northwood NH 032613117

Call Sign: KB1PUY
James R Lindquist
138 Rochester Rd
Northwood NH 03261

Call Sign: W1TQQ
James R Lindquist
138 Rochester Rd
Northwood NH 03261

Call Sign: KA1LLP
Norman E Nary

41 Sky Farm Rd
Northwood NH 03261

Call Sign: K1NEN
Norman E Nary
41 Sky Farm Rd
Northwood NH 03216

Call Sign: KB2DYH
Jon G Gabay
108 Sunset Dr
Northwood NH 03261

Call Sign: KB1HMJ
John A Blackwell
32 Temperance Hill Dr
Northwood NH 03261

Call Sign: KB1IWA
Susan D Bielski
32 Temperance Hill Dr
Northwood NH 03261

Call Sign: W1AMO
Susan D Bielski
32 Temperance Hill Dr
Northwood NH 03261

Call Sign: W1JAB
John A Blackwell
32 Temperance Hill Dr
Northwood NH 03261

Call Sign: N1NNI
Stanley E Somers
182 Winding Hill Rd
Northwood NH 03261

Call Sign: KB0ZCX
Russell J Kelsea
Northwood NH 03261

Call Sign: N1NMR
Norman D Dodge Jr
Northwood NH 03261

Call Sign: KB1GNL
Joseph E Kramas
Northwood NH 03261

Call Sign: K1JEK
Joseph E Kramas
Northwood NH 03261

Call Sign: KB1HQU
Saddleback Repeater
Associates Inc.
Northwood NH 03261

---

**FCC Amateur Radio
Licenses in Nottingham**

---

Call Sign: KB1CRG
Gary J Fruchter
54 Barderry Ln
Nottingham NH 03290

Call Sign: KB1OPG
Frederick J Manley Jr
3 Camelot Court
Nottingham NH 03290

Call Sign: KB1OPH
Patricia C Manley
3 Camelot Court
Nottingham NH 03290

Call Sign: KB1DNR
William R Hodgson Jr
1 Devonshire Dr
Nottingham NH 032906304

Call Sign: W1WRH
William R Hodgson Jr
1 Devonshire Dr
Nottingham NH 032906304

Call Sign: KC1TQ
George H Rouff
35 Garland Rd. Apt.1

Nottingham NH 032906106

Call Sign: KA6FFJ
Richard A Lane
22 Gile Rd
Nottingham NH 03290

Call Sign: KB1LTR
Jarrod R Lane
22 Gile Rd
Nottingham NH 03290

Call Sign: KR1L
Richard A Lane
22 Gile Rd
Nottingham NH 03290

Call Sign: K1TB
Theodore Brassard
10 S Summer St
Nottingham NH 03290

Call Sign: WD1K
Garry P Anderson Sr
24 Smoke St
Nottingham NH 03290

Call Sign: KB1KDT
Robert J Horton
49 Sofia Way
Nottingham NH 03290

Call Sign: NG1V
Robert A T Scott
19 South Summer St
Nottingham NH 03290

Call Sign: KA1TCA
David N Groshans
Star Route Box 44
Nottingham NH 03290

Call Sign: N1ATV
Amateur Television Of
Manchester

2 Tuckaway Shore Rd
Nottingham NH 03290

Call Sign: WA1WOK
Herbert M Calvitto
2 Tuckaway Shores Rd
Nottingham NH 03290

Call Sign: KB1QEY
Granite State Network
2 Tuckaway Shores Rd
Nottingham NH 03290

Call Sign: KA1INX
Gregory J Raymond
Nottingham NH 03290

Call Sign: N1QLP
Daniel J Raymond
Nottingham NH 03290

Call Sign: KB1IVW
William Stevens
Nottingham NH 03290

---

**FCC Amateur Radio
Licenses in Orford**

---

Call Sign: N1ASE
Katharine C Baker
Baker Rd
Orford NH 03777

Call Sign: N1SME
Steven L Bilski
Box 75
Orford NH 03777

Call Sign: N1GMC
Edmond S Cooley
236 Dame Hill Rd
Orford NH 037774608

Call Sign: KA1OAX
Lawrence R Wilsey

1153 Rt 25a
Orford NH 037774360

Call Sign: KA1IM
Stuart C Corpieri
Orford NH 037770214

Call Sign: KB1MZY
Lorine E Giangola
Orford NH 03777

## FCC Amateur Radio Licenses in Orfordville

Call Sign: N1USW
Gregory R Kirscher
Box 137b
Orfordville NH 03777

## FCC Amateur Radio Licenses in Ossipee

Call Sign: K1MMF
Peter W Rollock
Box 399
Ossipee NH 03864

Call Sign: N1NDP
Michael J Coakley
14 Elm St Ext.
Ossipee NH 03864

Call Sign: W1VDF
John A Howell
108 Foggs Ridge Rd
Ossipee NH 03864

Call Sign: KB1WNW
David R Marshall
220 Foggs Ridge Rd
Ossipee NH 03864

Call Sign: NJ1B
Joseph L Bradley
345 Granite Rd

Ossipee NH 03864

Call Sign: KB1LDU
Kenneth D Adams
45 Watervillage Rd
Ossipee NH 03864

Call Sign: K1SAX
James A Brennan Jr
Ossipee NH 03864

Call Sign: KC1ER
James D Spencer
Ossipee NH 03864

Call Sign: N1CCR
Barry Dudelson
Ossipee NH 03864

Call Sign: KB1JJD
Robert C D Amico
Ossipee NH 03864

Call Sign: KB1RBQ
Richard G Hart
Ossipee NH 038640117

Call Sign: K1UFB
Robert C D Amico
Ossipee NH 03864

Call Sign: KB1BLI
Helen M Howell
108 Foggs Ridge Rd
Ossispee NH 03864

## FCC Amateur Radio Licenses in Pelham

Call Sign: WA1CEH
Richard C Burton Sr
1 Albert St
Pelham NH 03076

Call Sign: KB1RIO

Joseph E Durkin
Appaloosa Ave
Pelham NH 03076

Call Sign: KB1IYI
Randy S Rutherford
13 Applewood Rd
Pelham NH 03076

Call Sign: KQ1U
Ronald J Sousa
6 Armand Dr
Pelham NH 03076

Call Sign: W1MBG
Francis J Keslo
5 Belvina Cir
Pelham NH 03076

Call Sign: N1DXC
Garret D White
19 Brett Circle
Pelham NH 03076

Call Sign: KB1RIK
Jennifer L Betts Cantara
7 Bush Hill Rd
Pelham NH 03076

Call Sign: KI1M
Peter A Cantara
7 Bush Hill Rd
Pelham NH 03076

Call Sign: NE1RD
B. Scott Andersen
9 Cara Lane
Pelham NH 03076

Call Sign: KB1SRA
Brian B Razzetti
1 Christopher Ln
Pelham NH 03076

Call Sign: KB1SQY

Gary L Muller
19 Clark Circle
Pelham NH 03076

Kevin J O'sullivan
27 Greenmeadow Dr
Pelham NH 03076

Peter W Daniels
52 Ledge Rd
Pelham NH 03076

Call Sign: KB1SQZ
Liam W Muller
19 Clark Circle
Pelham NH 03076

Call Sign: KA1VMR
Kenneth K Albertson
190 Hobbs Rd
Pelham NH 03076

Call Sign: KB1FZN
David W Law
4 Longview Circle
Pelham NH 03076

Call Sign: N1LWH
Paul K Ciampa
3 Colonial Dr
Pelham NH 03076

Call Sign: KA1SBA
Richard J Schroeder
14 Independence Dr
Pelham NH 03076

Call Sign: KB1KCU
Michael D Scott
19 Longview Circle
Pelham NH 03076

Call Sign: KB1NEF
Richard R Feola
13 Countryside Dr
Pelham NH 03076

Call Sign: WA1OFB
William R Cussick
15 Jeremy Hill Rd
Pelham NH 03076

Call Sign: W1ASR
Donn A Clark
Main St
Pelham NH 03076

Call Sign: KA1WAE
Gilbert H Monty
4 Crescent Circle
Pelham NH 030762309

Call Sign: KA1LLO
William T Lord
19 Jeremy Hill Rd
Pelham NH 03076

Call Sign: K1JDR
Peter Milonopoulos
296 Mammoth Rd
Pelham NH 03076

Call Sign: KB1UX
John F Mara
18 Debbie Dr
Pelham NH 03076

Call Sign: WA1F
Frank A Reed
131 Jeremy Hill Rd
Pelham NH 03076

Call Sign: WB1DDE
Charles B Ward
360 Mammoth Rd
Pelham NH 03076

Call Sign: KB1UXT
Ronald C Knight
6 Doreen Dr
Pelham NH 03076

Call Sign: KM1H
Carl W Huether
169 Jeremy Hill Rd
Pelham NH 03076

Call Sign: KA1PEF
Alice R Kirby
Meadow Knoll
Pelham NH 03076

Call Sign: KA1UJB
Leo J Zegouros
293 Gage Hill Rd
Pelham NH 03076

Call Sign: WA1GZN
Ross K Whynot Jr
66 Keyes Hill Rd
Pelham NH 030762115

Call Sign: KB1DDN
Peter R Gamache
50 Mammoth Rd
Pelham NH 030763276

Call Sign: KA1UQY
Raymond J Guilbault
6 Glenside Dr
Pelham NH 03076

Call Sign: KA1HVA
Samuel E Messery
Keyes Hill Rd
Pelham NH 03076

Call Sign: WA1ILV
Armand R Berard
134 Old Gage Hill
Pelham NH 03076

Call Sign: KB1SMG

Call Sign: WA2QYD

Call Sign: K1QPB

Virginia R Traversy
25 Old Gage Hillard S
Pelham NH 03076

Call Sign: KB1RGA
Tibor F Ivanyi
23 Primrose Ln
Pelham NH 03076

Call Sign: K1ZUW
John J Walterbach
21 Simpson Mill Rd
Pelham NH 03076

Call Sign: N1LJ
Bryan R Cote
85 Sky View Dr
Pelham NH 03076

Call Sign: K1EER
Donald W Hornbeck
1 Timber Lane
Pelham NH 030760877

Call Sign: KA1NDL
Samuel R Gabour
4 Webster Ave
Pelham NH 03076

Call Sign: N1MPZ
Istvan P Peteranecz
16 Wellesley Dr
Pelham NH 030762921

Call Sign: K1OR
John C Swiniarski
3 Wheaton Dr
Pelham NH 03076

Call Sign: K1OJL
Dennis P Perrotta
8 Wheaton Dr
Pelham NH 03076

Call Sign: WA1KOE

Carol A Perrotta
8 Wheaton Dr
Pelham NH 03076

Call Sign: KN1E
John H Wolfenden
9 Willow St
Pelham NH 03076

Call Sign: N1PMG
Brian R Key
20 Windham Rd
Pelham NH 030762370

Call Sign: KE5ASE
Bernard J Jones
60 Wyndridge Circle
Pelham NH 03076

Call Sign: N1HBI
Richard A Dean
Pelham NH 03076

Call Sign: N1RKH
John C Lavery
Pelham NH 03076

Call Sign: WA1LHA
Harry K Wetherbee
Pelham NH 030761022

Call Sign: W1DTV
Bruce R Kerrigan
Pelham NH 03076

Call Sign: W1SO
Bruce R Kerrigan
Pelham NH 03076

Call Sign: KB1MSV
Ellen J Kerrigan
Pelham NH 03076

Call Sign: W1CVB
Ellen J Kerrigan

Pelham NH 03076

Call Sign: W1DTV
Ellen J Kerrigan
Pelham NH 03076

## FCC Amateur Radio Licenses in Pembroke

Call Sign: KB1KLO
Nhrc A.R.S.
415 4th Range Rd
Pembroke NH 03275

Call Sign: W1CUM
Nhrc A.R.S.
415 4th Range Rd
Pembroke NH 03275

Call Sign: AA1DY
Robert M Montmarquet
347 Academy Rd
Pembroke NH 03275

Call Sign: KB1AZF
Angela M Montmarquet
347 Academy Rd
Pembroke NH 03275

Call Sign: N1NKH
Brian R Montmarquet
347 Academy Rd
Pembroke NH 03275

Call Sign: N1YNA
James R Fallon
348 Academy Rd
Pembroke NH 03275

Call Sign: KB1UFJ
Tyler A Dupuis
349 Academy Rd
Pembroke NH 03275

Call Sign: WA2ZAE

Ernest L Lopez
643 Borough Rd
Pembroke NH 03275

Call Sign: K1MOW
Joseph O Beckett
203 Brickett Hill Rd
Pembroke NH 03275

Call Sign: KB1BBM
Jason C Menard
65 Broadway
Pembroke NH 03275

Call Sign: KK1RR
Richard L Rumphrey
98 Broadway
Pembroke NH 032751217

Call Sign: KB1BBK
David J Brent
167 Buck St
Pembroke NH 03275

Call Sign: KB1BGQ
Michael J Young
193 Buck St
Pembroke NH 03275

Call Sign: W1VBX
Norman W Littlefield
407 Buck St
Pembroke NH 03275

Call Sign: KB1VOH
Lawrence M Hall
456 Buck St
Pembroke NH 03275

Call Sign: KB1SCP
Corey Girard
Cardigan Dr.
Pembroke NH 03275

Call Sign: KA1EHA

R Gregg Chadwick
736 Cross Country Rd
Pembroke NH 03275

Call Sign: KB1BBN
Jody P Bonenfant
8 Donald Ave
Pembroke NH 03275

Call Sign: N1SIN
Luke M Bonenfant
8 Donald Ave
Pembroke NH 03275

Call Sign: KD1HX
Michael J Gallant
9 Donna Dr
Pembroke NH 03275

Call Sign: KB1IBL
Steven A Moulton
38 Donna Dr
Pembroke NH 032753109

Call Sign: KA1OKQ
Peter J Gailunas
415 Fourth Range Rd
Pembroke NH 03275

Call Sign: KB1DIV
Ronald H Brotman
211 Friendship Ave
Pembroke NH 03275

Call Sign: N1VJC
Robert A Heath
403 Girard Ave
Pembroke NH 03275

Call Sign: KB1BBO
Ryan D Ground
79 Glass St
Pembroke NH 03275

Call Sign: KB1BBL

Seth O Perdue
89 Glass St
Pembroke NH 03275

Call Sign: AA1BC
Paul A Taylor
645 Haleigh's Court
Pembroke NH 03275

Call Sign: KB1VOE
Robert A Fanny Jr
40 Mason Ave
Pembroke NH 03275

Call Sign: N1IZZ
Paul R Paradis
30 Melissa Dr
Pembroke NH 03275

Call Sign: N1RLK
Sherry M Paradis
30 Melissa Dr
Pembroke NH 03275

Call Sign: KB1POA
Stephen G Keith
474 N Pembroke Rd
Pembroke NH 03275

Call Sign: KB1MIY
John J Gilligan
817 N Pembroke Rd
Pembroke NH 03275

Call Sign: N1OVK
Allison L Hardy
433 Nadine Rd
Pembroke NH 03275

Call Sign: WV1S
Thomas C Hardy
433 Nadine Rd
Pembroke NH 03275

Call Sign: KB1FUH

Robert B Farley
310 North Pembroke Rd
Pembroke NH 032753604

Call Sign: K1CFI
Robert B Farley
310 North Pembroke Rd
Pembroke NH 032753604

Call Sign: W1CPL
Capital Area Nhares Club
310 North Pembroke Rd
Pembroke NH 032753604

Call Sign: KB1DYB
John P Woolf
246 Pembroke Hill Rd
Pembroke NH 03275

Call Sign: N1XIR
Cynthia A Ward
233 Pembroke St
Pembroke NH 032751339

Call Sign: N1IQF
David A Poitras
518 Pembroke St
Pembroke NH 03275

Call Sign: KB1GIA
David A Poitras
518 Pembroke St
Pembroke NH 03275

Call Sign: N1IQF
David A Poitras
518 Pembroke St
Pembroke NH 03275

Call Sign: KB1BGR
Amanda J Boudreau
383 Perley Ave
Pembroke NH 03275

Call Sign: W1ALE

Edward F Everett
885 Plausawa Hill Rd
Pembroke NH 03275

Call Sign: KB1NME
Jonathan C Hardy
21 Prospect St
Pembroke NH 03275

Call Sign: N1QHG
Susan Perry
26 Robin Wood Farm
Pembroke NH 03275

Call Sign: N1KIX
Steven R Eisenberg
21 Robinwood Farm
Pembroke NH 03275

Call Sign: KB1ATE
Jonathan C Hardy
26 Robinwood Farm
Pembroke NH 03275

**FCC Amateur Radio
Licenses in Penacook**

Call Sign: KC1BE
Norton J Stokes
25 Abbott Rd
Penacook NH 03303

Call Sign: KB1OEE
Danielle M Morse
29 Abbott Rd
Penacook NH 03303

Call Sign: KB1JAY
Francis P Guimont
38 Abbott Rd
Penacook NH 03303

Call Sign: W1FPG
Francis P Guimont
38 Abbott Rd

Penacook NH 03303

Call Sign: KA1DQT
Willis L Wheeler Jr
14 Bentwood St.
Penacook NH 033031804

Call Sign: KB1TMY
Alicia A Gargus
58 Community Dr
Penacook NH 03303

Call Sign: KB1ITN
Andrew C Schlegel
14 Electric Ave
Penacook NH 03303

Call Sign: N0ZDD
Guy P Oliveri
5 Heartwood Lane 98
Penacook NH 03303

Call Sign: KB1RIM
Joseph A Deshaies
33 Heartwood Ln 25
Penacook NH 03303

Call Sign: N1PIA
Paul A La Clair
82 High St
Penacook NH 03303

Call Sign: KB1RIT
Deborah A Yeager
99 High St
Penacook NH 03303

Call Sign: K1FDD
John E Marcel
60 Lilac St
Penacook NH 03303

Call Sign: K1NHF
New Hampshire Fire Radio
Net

60 Lilac St
Penacook NH 033031892

Call Sign: KB1LDL
Robert F Soucy
34 Maplewood Lane
Penacook NH 03303

Call Sign: WA1YNJ
Steven G Crane
116 Merrimack St
Penacook NH 03303

Call Sign: KB1RKU
James R Cole
32 Millennium Way
Penacook NH 03303

Call Sign: KB1HHG
Richard E Smith
19 Modena Dr
Penacook NH 03303

Call Sign: K1WYH
Richard E Smith
19 Modena Dr
Penacook NH 03303

Call Sign: N5FGO
Donald D Buchanan
78 Primrose Ln
Penacook NH 033032024

Call Sign: KB1FAB
Edgar F Brodeur
34 Shaw St
Penacook NH 03303

Call Sign: N1XRZ
Roger W Ziegler
3 Snow St.
Penacook NH 03303

Call Sign: K1VLF
James M Moran Sr

17 Tower Circle
Penacook NH 03303

Call Sign: N1NLU
Jason M Valley
219 Village St
Penacook NH 03303

Call Sign: W1OE
David J Fournier Sr
50 W Main St
Penacook NH 03303

Call Sign: KA1TEK
Mark A La Clair
99 Washington
Penacook NH 03303

Call Sign: KB1OOJ
New Hampshire Fire Radio
Net
75 Washington St
Penacook NH 033031566

Call Sign: N1JQC
Dennis J Flora
112 Washington St
Penacook NH 03303

Call Sign: N1QBP
Claudette B Flora
112 Washington St
Penacook NH 03303

Call Sign: N1NS
Warren E Marble
84 Washington St Bld 4 U
23
Penacook NH 03303

Call Sign: N1IHZ
Joseph E Burke
5 Wildflower Dr
Penacook NH 03303

Call Sign: W1INC
Joseph E Burke
5 Wildflower Dr
Penacook NH 03303

Call Sign: N1OOZ
James P Mc Kerley
Penacook NH 03303

Call Sign: WA1YQA
Bruce A Ricker
133 Lilac St
Pennacook NH 03303

Call Sign: AB1AQ
Bruce A Ricker
133 Lilac St
Pennacook NH 03303

## FCC Amateur Radio Licenses in Perry

Call Sign: N7IFN
Orion E Evans
9 Ash St
Perry NH 03038

## FCC Amateur Radio Licenses in Peterborough

Call Sign: WA2ESZ
Leo T Deeny
Box 143b
Peterborough NH 03458

Call Sign: KB1AVQ
Leslie R George
Box 332
Peterborough NH 03458

Call Sign: KA1LCB
Barbara W Wilson
Box 368
Peterborough NH 03458

Call Sign: WA5PMZ
William A Conkerton Jr
380 Brush Brook Rd
Peterborough NH 03458

Call Sign: KB1AVS
Edgar D Morrow
116 Burke Rd
Peterborough NH 03458

Call Sign: KA1UKM
Linda R Reneau
Concord St
Peterborough NH 03458

Call Sign: KA1VKU
Robert E Lyons
22 E Hill Rd
Peterborough NH 03458

Call Sign: W1RLY
Everett Clement
Elm Hill
Peterborough NH 03458

Call Sign: KB1LSU
Ann A Eaton
254 General Miller Rd
Peterborough NH 03458

Call Sign: N1HJG
James W Bail
19 Granite St 6
Peterborough NH 03458

Call Sign: N1OME
Tucker B Harding
34 Hall Ct
Peterborough NH 03458

Call Sign: KC0WDZ
Jeremiah T Vanderneut
35 High St
Peterborough NH 03458

Call Sign: KA1ADE
Michael C Wakefield
94 Kaufmann Dr
Peterborough NH
034581520

Call Sign: N1XDC
Gordon A Stone
26 Lounsbury Ln
Peterborough NH 03458

Call Sign: KB1IQF
David R Mitchell
4 Mercer Ave
Peterborough NH 03458

Call Sign: W1DB
C David Buren
357 Middle Hancock Rd
Peterborough NH 03458

Call Sign: KA1JOU
Kenneth D Fields
18 Old St Rd
Peterborough NH
034581636

Call Sign: WA1UMV
Stanley M Miastkowski
159 Old St Rd
Peterborough NH 03458

Call Sign: KB1JK
William H Clark Jr
141 Rivermead Rd
Peterborough NH 03458

Call Sign: KB1OBV
Denise L Lahey
750 Sand Hill Rd
Peterborough NH 03458

Call Sign: KB1OBW
David G Enos
750 Sand Hill Rd

Peterborough NH 03458

Call Sign: KB1OCQ
Pierre Colin
750 Sand Hill Rd
Peterborough NH 03458

Call Sign: KB1QAC
Dana S Whitaker
74 Spring Rd
Peterborough NH 03458

Call Sign: N1DSW
Dana S Whitaker
74 Spring Rd
Peterborough NH 03458

Call Sign: KA1JWF
Rally Dennis
110 Spring Rd
Peterborough NH 03458

Call Sign: K1NQZ
Ralph I Maxwell
76 Summer St
Peterborough NH 03458

Call Sign: KB1RTQ
Curtis M Dude
55 Union St
Peterborough NH 03458

Call Sign: K1PKW
George A Oickle Jr
475 Union St  Apt 13
Peterborough NH 03458

Call Sign: N1RWL
David R Torrey
20 Vine St
Peterborough NH 03458

Call Sign: N1STS
Daniel R Torrey
20 Vine St

Peterborough NH 03458

Call Sign: N1BEW
David S Buck
25 West Ridge Dr
Peterborough NH 03458

Call Sign: N0BH
Luke M Hopkins
81 Wilder Farm Rd.
Peterborough NH 03458

Call Sign: N1SGY
Donald J Stoops
208 Wilton Rd
Peterborough NH 03458

Call Sign: KC1DN
Henry J Butler
4 Winter St
Peterborough NH 03458

Call Sign: N1MZX
Jonathan M Hampson
Peterborough NH 03458

Call Sign: W1QQB
Edward R Hampson
Peterborough NH 03458

Call Sign: WA1VMZ
Elizabeth S Alpaugh Cote
Peterborough NH
034580458

Call Sign: KB1UCR
Ronald C Subka
Peterborough NH 03458

Call Sign: N1PPY
Anne C Thompson
27 Webb Rd
Petersburough NH 03458

## FCC Amateur Radio Licenses in Piermont

Call Sign: WB6MXL
Peter Erpelding
255 River Rd
Piermont NH 03779

Call Sign: K1CLD
William R Deal
Piermont NH 03779

Call Sign: KA1JSB
Donald A Smith
Piermont NH 03779

## FCC Amateur Radio Licenses in Pike

Call Sign: KA1VIG
Clifford G English Jr
555 Lily Pond Rd
Pike NH 03780

Call Sign: KB1MCC
Pamela B English
555 Lily Pond Rd
Piko NH 03780

Call Sign: KA1VII
Andrew S Cummings
Lime Kiln Rd
Pike NH 03780

Call Sign: N1IFQ
Julia M Cummings
Lime Kiln Rd
Pike NH 03780

Call Sign: K1DQJ
Augustin S L Etoile
Pike NH 03780

## FCC Amateur Radio Licenses in Pittsburg

Call Sign: W1AEB
Albert E Barnes
20 Back Lake Rd Apt 119
Pittsburg NH 03592

Call Sign: N1JMH
Louis A Peterson
Box 482
Pittsburg NH 03592

Call Sign: N1NOX
Allen H Kendall
Box 91c
Pittsburg NH 03592

Call Sign: WA2UTY
Robert B Emmons
Harry Lane
Pittsburg NH 03592

Call Sign: KA1YVU
Arthur E Jarrett
8 River Rd
Pittsburg NH 03592

Call Sign: W1RMH
Robert H Wright
216 River Rd
Pittsburg NH 03592

Call Sign: W1SJS
Anatole G Courchene
Rt 1
Pittsburg NH 03592

Call Sign: WA2ILB
Roger M Ziegler
44 Stewart Young Rd
Pittsburg NH 03592

Call Sign: KG4GKP
Gregory B Woody
Pittsburg NH 03592

Call Sign: WA1PXI
Edward C Towle
6 Berry Ave
Pittsfield NH 03263

Call Sign: KB1RKG
Fallon C Reed
103 Berry Pond Rd
Pittsfield NH 03263

Call Sign: KA1YMW
Mary E Reed
103 Berry Pond Rd
Pittsfield NH 03263

Call Sign: KK1KW
Frederick S Reed
103 Berry Pond Rd
Pittsfield NH 03263

Call Sign: KB1URR
Jacob M Henry
103 Berry Pond Rd
Pittsfield NH 03263

Call Sign: N1IMB
Nancy A Robinson
17 Bridge St Apt 1
Pittsfield NH 03263

Call Sign: KD1Q
Chester C Smith Sr
152 Clough Rd
Pittsfield NH 03263

Call Sign: N1QBN
Susan J Bleckmann
5 Fayette St
Pittsfield NH 03263

Call Sign: KA1WMY
Martin R Boisvert

3250 Loudon Rd
Pittsfield NH 03263

Call Sign: KB1DQJ
Samuel A Mc Keen
2 MANCHESTER ST APT 1
Pittsfield NH 03263

Call Sign: WB1DPF
Matthew E David
1030 S Pittsfield Rd
Pittsfield NH 03263

Call Sign: KB1JST
Joanne E Shurbert
64 Siel Rd
Pittsfield NH 03263

Call Sign: AA1F
Robert W Thrall
64 Siel Rd
Pittsfield NH 03263

Call Sign: KB1RZX
William D Allen Jr
11 Tarchee Dr
Pittsfield NH 03263

Call Sign: KB1GTV
Sherrie L Demmons
Tilton Hill Rd
Pittsfield NH 03263

Call Sign: N1QHB
David B Hiscock
1 Tiltonhill Rd
Pittsfield NH 03263

Call Sign: W1UEL
Neil W Hobey
Upper City Rd
Pittsfield NH 03263

Call Sign: KB1UNW

Louise A Merchant Hannan
23 Watson St
Pittsfield NH 03263

Call Sign: W1KD
Frank Lyman Jr
Pittsfield NH 03263

Call Sign: N1SMA
Frank H Currier
67 High St
Plainfield NH 03781

Call Sign: KB1IRM
Edward P Foltyn
125 High St
Plainfield NH 03781

Call Sign: W1EPF
Edward P Foltyn
125 High St
Plainfield NH 03781

Call Sign: N1HPX
Waltraud B Coli
73 Ledge Dr Box 354
Plainfield NH 03781

Call Sign: N1KDV
Douglas R Plummer
313 Old County Rd.
Plainfield NH 03781

Call Sign: N1AHF
David A Bridgham
55 Red Hill Rd
Plainfield NH 03781

Call Sign: N5EI
Edward A Feustel
385 River Rd
Plainfield NH 037815036

Call Sign: KC1DL
Satoshi Akagawa
294 Route 120
Plainfield NH 037815430

Call Sign: W1GRF
Grafton Nhares Club
812 Rt 12 A
Plainfield NH 03781

Call Sign: K1SGA
Southern Grafton Amateur
Radio Emergency Service
812 Rt 12 A
Plainfield NH 03781

Call Sign: KX1Y
William Daugherty
812 Rte. 12a
Plainfield NH 03781

Call Sign: N1DAU
Shawn L Wilder
158 Tallow Hill Rd
Plainfield NH 03781

**FCC Amateur Radio
Licenses in Plaistow**

Call Sign: N1QCR
Christopher S Coughlin
6 Birch St
Plaistow NH 03865

Call Sign: KE4VUV
Brett A Karaus
18 Canterbury Forest
Plaistow NH 03865

Call Sign: N1KUA
Steven S Kiarsis
39 Crane Crossing Rd
Plaistow NH 03865

Call Sign: N1ROL
Jennifer L Kiarsis
39 Crene Crossing Rd
Plaistow NH 03865

Call Sign: KB1KNL
Jay A Guzofski
15 Culver St 78
Plaistow NH 03865

Call Sign: N1SVN
Elizabeth M Reis
15 Culver St 81
Plaistow NH 03865

Call Sign: KA1RRZ
John M Doggett
8 Davis Park
Plaistow NH 03865

Call Sign: N1VPR
Francis R Cookson Jr
9 Davis Park
Plaistow NH 03865

Call Sign: KB1JLF
Peter P Nitchman
10 Dundee Dr
Plaistow NH 038652518

Call Sign: N2KIP
Peter P Nitchman
10 Dundee Dr
Plaistow NH 038652518

Call Sign: N1TCH
Peter P Nitchman
10 Dundee Dr
Plaistow NH 038652518

Call Sign: KD1SL
Anthony R Costanzo
3 Elm St
Plaistow NH 03865

Call Sign: KB1DBE
Neil K Rabideau
54 Forrest St
Plaistow NH 03865

Call Sign: AA1WG
Neil K Rabideau
54 Forrest St
Plaistow NH 03865

Call Sign: NR1N
Neil K Rabideau
54 Forrest St
Plaistow NH 03865

Call Sign: W1YVX
Raymond M Patnaude
5 Johnson Dr
Plaistow NH 03865

Call Sign: W1LS
Peter B Cunningham
13 Johnson Dr
Plaistow NH 03865

Call Sign: KB1APF
Carol D Paraskos
1 Lynwood St
Plaistow NH 03865

Call Sign: KD1HU
Evan J Paraskos Sr
1 Lynwood St
Plaistow NH 03865

Call Sign: WB1EZZ
Marco Fiore
20 Main St
Plaistow NH 038653003

Call Sign: K1SJZ
Donald Wendell
124 Main St
Plaistow NH 03865

Call Sign: N1TRZ
Marlene J Benson
296 Main St
Plaistow NH 038653034

Call Sign: N1TSA
Louis A Benson Jr
296 Main St
Plaistow NH 03865

Call Sign: KB1JUF
George A Croteau
309 Main St
Plaistow NH 03865

Call Sign: KB1OFC
Richard C Fowler
311 Main St
Plaistow NH 03865

Call Sign: KB1QKJ
Mark E Fowler
311 Main St
Plaistow NH 03865

Call Sign: W1JAG
Jay A Guzofski
2 May Ray Ave
Plaistow NH 03865

Call Sign: W1FNX
Jay A Guzofski
2 May Ray Ave
Plaistow NH 03865

Call Sign: W1ERP
John B Rubner Jr
120 Newton Rd Unit 2c
Plaistow NH 03865

Call Sign: KF4RJL
Henry F Cotter
233 Oak Ridge Rd Unit 19
Plaistow NH 03865

Call Sign: K1IFV
George S Maclauchlan
190 PLAISTOW RD
Plaistow NH 03865

Call Sign: K1LD
W David Gerns Sr
3 Rolling Hill Ave
Plaistow NH 03865

Call Sign: KA1OCK
Frederick O Nelson
5 Rose Ave
Plaistow NH 03865

Call Sign: N1TF
Thorvaldur Sveinbjornsson
5 Rustic Ln
Plaistow NH 03865

Call Sign: WA1VUN
Robert L Blouin
5 Seaver Brook Ln
Plaistow NH 03865

Call Sign: KA1RAE
Michelle R Cote
14 Smith Corner Rd
Plaistow NH 03865

Call Sign: W1QYR
Harry M Smith
6 Springview Ter
Plaistow NH 03865

Call Sign: KB1GTO
Steven J Rugoletti
12 Stanwood Ave
Plaistow NH 038652229

Call Sign: WB2MJG
Peter M Bealo
82 Sweet Hill Rd
Plaistow NH 03865

Call Sign: KA1TQE
Ethel M Backard
6 Sweet Hill Rd Box 343
Plaistow NH 03865

Call Sign: KA1SNK
Edwin F Ludke
16 Walton Rd
Plaistow NH 03865

Call Sign: KO1C
Robert O Hofland
Plaistow NH 03865

Call Sign: WA1IIO
Charles D Brown Jr
Plaistow NH 03865

**FCC Amateur Radio
Licenses in Plymouth**

Call Sign: WA1NMB
John F Archibald
20 Avery St
Plymouth NH 03264

Call Sign: K1OGU
Maxine A Andrews
Box 12
Plymouth NH 03264

Call Sign: KB1VVM
Christopher R Leland
105 Chaisson Rd
Plymouth NH 03264

Call Sign: KA1TBN
Joyce E Liptak
Chiasson Rd
Plymouth NH 03264

Call Sign: N1GFR
Gordon C Liptak
Chiasson Rd
Plymouth NH 03264

Call Sign: WB1FJW
Thomas N Morrison
66 Cross Country Ln
Plymouth NH 03264

Call Sign: N1ITD
Carol A Brook
1829 Dick Brown Rd
Plymouth NH 03264

Call Sign: WA1QHN
Frederick H Gould
557 Fairgrounds Rd
Plymouth NH 03264

Call Sign: KB3UZJ
Michael J Griffith
5 Fox Park Dr Apt 96
Plymouth NH 03264

Call Sign: WX1PSU
Michael J Griffith
5 Fox Park Dr Apt 96
Plymouth NH 03264

Call Sign: WX3TTX
Michael J Griffith
5 Fox Park Dr Apt 96
Plymouth NH 03264

Call Sign: N1PKL
John P Pinker
13 Hawthorne St
Plymouth NH 032641108

Call Sign: KB1VVN
Kathleen M Beriau
8 Ledgeview Way
Plymouth NH 03264

Call Sign: KB1JVY
Jeff S Ferguson
75 Main St Ste 4
Plymouth NH 03264

Call Sign: KB1SZN
Paul W Mutina
75 Main St Suite 4
Plymouth NH 03264

Call Sign: N1XNU
Steven N Kidder
391 Mayhew Tpk
Plymouth NH 03264

Call Sign: KB1NRT
Marika L Hughes
391 Mayhew Turnpike
Plymouth NH 03264

Call Sign: KB1TNA
James P Harrington
594 Mayhew Turnpike
Plymouth NH 03264

Call Sign: WB1HJL
Thurston M Plantinga
Reservoir Rd
Plymouth NH 03264

Call Sign: KB1UVN
Steven L Corum
93 River Rd
Plymouth NH 03264

Call Sign: KB1EUD
Kenneth L Corum
104 River Rd
Plymouth NH 03264

Call Sign: KB1MFA
Sean K Sargent
1095 River Rd
Plymouth NH 03264

Call Sign: AE1T
Peter G Drexel
9 Rogers St
Plymouth NH 03264

Call Sign: N1SFM
Patsy R Sargent
22 Sunrise Cir
Plymouth NH 03264

Call Sign: N1OVA
Samuel F Sargent
55 Sunrise Circle
Plymouth NH 03264

Call Sign: KB1LYW
Christine S Sargent
55 Sunrise Circle
Plymouth NH 03264

Call Sign: KB1SUZ
Edward J Hauser
53 Tenney Mt Rd
Plymouth NH 03264

Call Sign: K1TAM
Raymond E Welch Jr
31 Thurlow St
Plymouth NH 03264

Call Sign: K1PSC
Computer Science Dept Psc
Psc Radio Club
Plymouth NH 03264

Call Sign: N1ARA
Culver J Floyd
Plymouth NH 03264

Call Sign: N1SFP
Charles D Maddox
Plymouth NH 03264

Call Sign: W1LO
Warren P Stiles
Plymouth NH 03264

Call Sign: WA1NGN
James E Leahy Sr

Plymouth NH 03264

Call Sign: KB1IWD
David N Linn
1500a Lafayette Rd 308
Portsmouth NH 03801

Call Sign: K5CUI
Kristopher D Cui
536a Union St.
Portsmouth NH 03801

Call Sign: KB1KBC
George F Rinalducci
244 Austin St
Portsmouth NH 03801

Call Sign: KB1FRX
Seth Miles
245 Austin St
Portsmouth NH 03801

Call Sign: WA1DEW
David B Bateman
37 Baycliff Rd
Portsmouth NH 03801

Call Sign: KB1QPH
Dorothy A Chapman
40 Bedford Way Suite 102
Portsmouth NH 03801

Call Sign: KB1MVW
Venkata R Korada
13 Beechstone -4
Portsmouth NH 03801

Call Sign: K1LNU
Weston B Loundon Sr
7 Beechstone Apt 3
Portsmouth NH 03801

Call Sign: N6VFG
Cory N Miller
14 Beechstone Apt 3
Portsmouth NH 03801

Call Sign: N2HZN
Karen K Muldoon
25 Beechstone Apt 6
Portsmouth NH 03801

Call Sign: KA1VGH
Stephanie J W Hurd
31 Blue Heron Dr
Portsmouth NH 03801

Call Sign: WR1U
Gary E Hurd
31 Blue Heron Dr
Portsmouth NH 03801

Call Sign: KB1CVC
Mary L Bragg
44 Blue Heron Dr
Portsmouth NH 038013339

Call Sign: WA1VMJ
Wayne C Bragg
44 Blue Heron Dr
Portsmouth NH 038013339

Call Sign: N1DSJ
Wayne C Bragg
44 Blue Heron Dr
Portsmouth NH 038013339

Call Sign: W1MXA
John R Pope
60 Blue Heron Dr
Portsmouth NH 03801

Call Sign: KA1WSN
Judith E Tierno
135 Bow St
Portsmouth NH 03801

Call Sign: N1LCO
Blynn E Davidson
Box 1082
Portsmouth NH 03801

Call Sign: KB1KJL
Jan-Michael Ehrhardt
C/O Pcarc
Portsmouth NH 038021587

Call Sign: KB1KJM
Max E Holicki
C/O Pcarc
Portsmouth NH 038021587

Call Sign: KB1PEG
Philipp Fretz
C/O Pcarc
Portsmouth NH 03802

Call Sign: KB1PEH
Ramona Witzig
C/O Pcarc
Portsmouth NH 03802

Call Sign: KB1PEI
Andreas Ott
C/O Pcarc
Portsmouth NH 03802

Call Sign: KB1PEJ
Franziska Waltisberg
C/O Pcarc
Portsmouth NH 03802

Call Sign: KB1PEK
Rosemarie Bottcher
C/O Pcarc
Portsmouth NH 03802

Call Sign: KB1PEL
Markus Fretz
C/O Pcarc
Portsmouth NH 03802

Call Sign: KB1PTC  
Bruno Frutig  
C/O Pcarc  
Portsmouth NH 03802  

Call Sign: N1EDC  
Paul F Teague  
152 Essex Ave  
Portsmouth NH 03801  

Call Sign: N1LCN  
Richard W Hodgdon  
10 Kent St  
Portsmouth NH 03801  

Call Sign: KB1LUR  
Cristian F Valentini  
C/O Port City Arc  
Portsmouth NH 038021587  

Call Sign: WA1WJC  
Sullivan G Scott Jr  
165 F W Hartford Dr  
Portsmouth NH 03801  

Call Sign: WA1IMJ  
Cloyed T Straub Jr  
1971 La Fayette Rd  
Portsmouth NH 03801  

Call Sign: W1HCD  
Paul M L Desilets  
33 Clinton St  
Portsmouth NH 03801  

Call Sign: W1PIE  
David E Sawyer  
2 Fairview Dr  
Portsmouth NH 038013529  

Call Sign: WA1PLA  
Madelyn C Straub  
1971 Lafayette Rd  
Portsmouth NH 03801  

Call Sign: KB1QPG  
Robert E Tuley Jr  
26 Columbia Ct Apt 1  
Portsmouth NH 03801  

Call Sign: N1KCC  
Casey Hoch  
115 Flightline Rd  
Portsmouth NH 03801  

Call Sign: WA1MKH  
Wayne J Canino  
242 Leslie Dr  
Portsmouth NH 03801  

Call Sign: N1OJA  
Scott R Leonard  
103 Court St  
Portsmouth NH 03801  

Call Sign: KB8MAN  
Steven P Walker  
331 Grant Ave.  
Portsmouth NH 03801  

Call Sign: N1IXM  
Kathleen H Gordon  
454 Lincoln Ave  
Portsmouth NH 03801  

Call Sign: W1KCR  
Joel S Look  
140 Court St 617  
Portsmouth NH 038014447  

Call Sign: KA1WSE  
James H Riley  
Harbour Pl 7  
Portsmouth NH 03801  

Call Sign: WG1J  
Glen R Gordon  
454 Lincoln Ave  
Portsmouth NH 03801  

Call Sign: N1OIZ  
Sheila A Kearsey  
29 Doris Ave  
Portsmouth NH 03801  

Call Sign: N1ZNL  
Dora C Anthony  
1493 Islington St  
Portsmouth NH 03801  

Call Sign: KC1JG  
Ralph H Marler Jr  
75 Longmeadow Ln Apt 17  
Portsmouth NH 03801  

Call Sign: N1SDU  
Richard F Weaver  
107 Eastwood Dr  
Portsmouth NH 03801  

Call Sign: KB1HIG  
Jennifer K Rydeen  
610 Islington St 4  
Portsmouth NH 03801  

Call Sign: AG6DT  
Apiwat Jirawattanaphol  
399 Maplewood Ave  
Portsmouth NH 03801  

Call Sign: W1IMB  
Robert A Calkins  
206 Elwyn Ave  
Portsmouth NH 03801  

Call Sign: KB1HIH  
Michael K Rydeen  
610 Islington St 4  
Portsmouth NH 03801  

Call Sign: KI1F  
Apiwat Jirawattanaphol  
399 Maplewood Ave  
Portsmouth NH 03801

Call Sign: KB1VYM
Kittithat Saenwong
399 Maplewood Ave
Portsmouth NH 03801

Call Sign: KB1VYN
Sarawut Niruttinanont
399 Maplewood Ave
Portsmouth NH 03801

Call Sign: KB1VYO
Chanyut Unwiset
399 Maplewood Ave
Portsmouth NH 03801

Call Sign: K1NOS
Janet L Hanchett
35 Mariette Dr
Portsmouth NH 03801

Call Sign: K1UYA
Gordon H Hanchett
35 Mariette Dr
Portsmouth NH 03801

Call Sign: KB1BJS
Barclay Jackson
36 Marston Ave
Portsmouth NH 03801

Call Sign: W1LMD
Antonio Vaccaro Sr
815 Mc Gee Dr
Portsmouth NH 03801

Call Sign: W1CBM
Jordan Sandler
5 Meadow Rd
Portsmouth NH 038013123

Call Sign: KA1OWQ
Joseph M Verna
347 Meadow Rd
Portsmouth NH 03801

Call Sign: KA1TGQ
Ronald T Turner
94 Mendum Ave
Portsmouth NH 03801

Call Sign: N1AA
Richard A Kirkpatrick
777 Middle Rd Unit 32
Portsmouth NH 038014833

Call Sign: W1JUW
Frank L Pike
700 Middle St
Portsmouth NH 03801

Call Sign: KX0X
Joseph J Barrett
411 Middle St 6
Portsmouth NH 038015065

Call Sign: KB9YEO
Douglas Beesley
336 Miller Ave
Portsmouth NH 03801

Call Sign: KA1HDB
Stephen J Rammer
70 New Castle Ave
Portsmouth NH 03801

Call Sign: KB1HUA
Richard W Piller
Ocean Rd
Portsmouth NH 03801

Call Sign: N1TGH
Joseph W Harding
140 Osprey Dr
Portsmouth NH 03801

Call Sign: KB1LJU
James C Muddiman
Pcarc
Portsmouth NH 038431587

Call Sign: N1OIY
Raszelle D Fine
82 Pine St
Portsmouth NH 03801

Call Sign: WA1CXB
Wade M Burnette Sr
114 Pine St
Portsmouth NH 03801

Call Sign: KA1D
Christopher J Brown
45 Pleasant Point Dr
Portsmouth NH 03801

Call Sign: KB1DBA
Kent D Kasper
283 S St Apt 1
Portsmouth NH 03801

Call Sign: WA1UTO
R James Andrews
161 Sagamore Ave
Portsmouth NH 03801

Call Sign: KA1VAF
Carl D Jewell
565 Sagamore Ave 21
Portsmouth NH 03801

Call Sign: KB1PJ
David E Speltz
579 Sagamore Ave Unit 108
Portsmouth NH 03801

Call Sign: KB1SGN
JAMES J Mc GOVERN
19 SANDERLING WAY
Portsmouth NH 03801

Call Sign: W1MCG
James J Mc Govern
19 Sanderling Way
Portsmouth NH 03801

Call Sign: N1IOA
James J Mc Govern
19 Sanderling Way
Portsmouth NH 03801

Call Sign: KB1MRD
Joshua R Quinn
30 Sewall Rd
Portsmouth NH 03801

Call Sign: N1FWN
Steven C Quinn
30 Sewall Rd
Portsmouth NH 03801

Call Sign: W1NJN
Dino E Argentini
2 Shearwater Dr
Portsmouth NH 038013351

Call Sign: W1BOW
Wayne C Bragg
31 Shearwater Dr
Portsmouth NH 03801

Call Sign: KA1RNP
Sunyoung Kwon
436 Sherburne Rd
Portsmouth NH 03801

Call Sign: KC1MW
Alphonse T Lapanne
460 Sherburne Rd
Portsmouth NH 03801

Call Sign: KC1MX
Stella M Lapanne
460 Sherburne Rd
Portsmouth NH 03801

Call Sign: AB1PU
Thomas B Liebert
506 Sherburne Rd
Portsmouth NH 03801

Call Sign: NV1T
Thomas B Liebert
506 Sherburne Rd
Portsmouth NH 03801

Call Sign: NR1P
Barry Shore
91 South St
Portsmouth NH 03801

Call Sign: N1RIL
A Wilson Wood
928 South St
Portsmouth NH 03801

Call Sign: N1VNA
Richard J Tibbetts
928 South St
Portsmouth NH 03801

Call Sign: W1OQG
H Wayne La Chapelle
928 South St
Portsmouth NH 03801

Call Sign: W1FSY
Roger F Wood
1066 South St
Portsmouth NH 03801

Call Sign: N2KUB
Brett C Claydon
82 Spinnaker Way
Portsmouth NH 03801

Call Sign: KA1JCX
David R Heller
95 T J Gamester Ave
Portsmouth NH 03801

Call Sign: W1YFZ
David W Meehan
13 Taft Rd
Portsmouth NH 03801

Call Sign: KB1PFW
Katherine M Meehan
13 Taft Rd
Portsmouth NH 03801

Call Sign: W1YFZ
Katherine M Meehan
13 Taft Rd
Portsmouth NH 03801

Call Sign: KA1RTK
Harold V Clemens Jr
41 Taft Rd
Portsmouth NH 03801

Call Sign: WB2VWJ
John C Farrell
60 Union St
Portsmouth NH 03802

Call Sign: W1GGA
Richard C Wilder
58 Walker Bungalow Rd
Portsmouth NH 038015546

Call Sign: N1POJ
Raymond E Brulotte
75 Walker Bungalow Rd
Portsmouth NH 03801

Call Sign: N1UXE
Doyglas W Belanger
1610 White Cedar Blvd
Portsmouth NH 03801

Call Sign: N1TFR
Gail A Snow
Willard Ave
Portsmouth NH 03801

Call Sign: KA1BCK
Edward J Fournier
60 Wilson Rd
Portsmouth NH 03801

Call Sign: N1VEX
Leonard G Leighton
1338 Woodbury Ave
Portsmouth NH 038013229

Call Sign: KB1KKJ
Deney D Morganthal
1931 Woodbury Ave #168
Portsmouth NH 03801

Call Sign: KA9TND
Michael S Paris
1931 Woodbury Ave. #179
Portsmouth NH 03801

Call Sign: KB1GGL
Linda Paris
1931 Woodbury Ave. #179
Portsmouth NH 03801

Call Sign: KA1TGS
Richard B Collier
Portsmouth NH 03801

Call Sign: KA1TJG
Michael I Collier
Portsmouth NH 03801

Call Sign: KA1WTM
Edwin Shortz
Portsmouth NH 038026668

Call Sign: N1EAE
Mark G Goodreau
Portsmouth NH 03802

Call Sign: WA2WFZ
Mark L Anthony
Portsmouth NH 03802

Call Sign: NE1G
Mark G Goodreau
Portsmouth NH 03802

Call Sign: KB1QPN

Carol Berg
Portsmouth NH 03802

## FCC Amateur Radio Licenses in Randolph

Call Sign: KA1LZ
Douglas E Mayer
79 Boothman Lane
Randolph NH 03593

Call Sign: KD1JV
Steven Weber
580 Durand Rd
Randolph NH 03593

Call Sign: KB1EUX
Raymond F Cotnoir
31 Raycrest Dr
Randolph NH 03593

Call Sign: KB1RSX
Richard G Theberge Jr
1386 Us Rt 2
Randolph NH 03593

## FCC Amateur Radio Licenses in Raymond

Call Sign: KB1SEH
Tad Richardson
12 Bald Hill Rd
Raymond NH 03077

Call Sign: W1ANF
Kenneth L Freeland
45 Barberry Ln
Raymond NH 03077

Call Sign: W1SD
Stephen M Dallas
5 Blake Rd
Raymond NH 03077

Call Sign: W1NH

Robert C Mitchell Sr
55 Blueberry Hill Rd
Raymond NH 03077

Call Sign: WA1YEH
Elijah F Marden
94 Boxwood Ln Rte 27
Raymond NH 03077

Call Sign: KB1SWY
Elizabeth M Harmon
15 Cilley Rd
Raymond NH 03077

Call Sign: KB1PGE
Douglas Murphy
17 Clover Ct
Raymond NH 03077

Call Sign: KB1PGG
Scott W Murphy
17 Clover Ct
Raymond NH 03077

Call Sign: KB1POD
Ann M Murphy
17 Clover St
Raymond NH 03077

Call Sign: KB1IKO
Robert Mcconn
16 Country View Dr
Raymond NH 03077

Call Sign: KB1TWM
Scott D Cole
33 Epping St
Raymond NH 03077

Call Sign: K1LPX
Neal A Wiggin
4 Feng Dr
Raymond NH 03077

Call Sign: K1GAU

Robert W Mc Mullen
7 Forest Rd
Raymond NH 03077

Henry J Secorsky
111 Harriman Hill Rd
Raymond NH 03077

Edward Whitman
18 Manor View Dr
Raymond NH 03077

Call Sign: W1RWM
Robert W Mc Mullen
7 Forest Rd
Raymond NH 03077

Call Sign: N1UZM
Patricia A Maxwell
14 Harriman Rd
Raymond NH 03077

Call Sign: KD4CLJ
David K Bodman
48 Mildred Ave
Raymond NH 03077

Call Sign: N1XEL
Robert Morales
62 Freetown Rd
Raymond NH 03077

Call Sign: WB6YGQ
William T Buck
Heritage Way
Raymond NH 03077

Call Sign: KB1RQM
James C Rhodes
11 Morgan Farm Rd
Raymond NH 03077

Call Sign: KB1VAX
Chad R Pasho
62 Freetown Rd Unit 14
Raymond NH 03077

Call Sign: KA1JSJ
Lawrence H Wright Ii
10 Huckleberry Rd
Raymond NH 03077

Call Sign: KB1TXE
Hannah M Rhodes
11 Morgan Farm Rd
Raymond NH 03077

Call Sign: N1VWR
Lionell A Cascio
127 Greedn Rd
Raymond NH 03077

Call Sign: W1EGJ
Lawrence H Wright Ii
10 Huckleberry Rd
Raymond NH 030772034

Call Sign: K1JCR
James C Rhodes
11 Morgan Farm Rd
Raymond NH 03077

Call Sign: N1WDR
M Alan Seacole
33 Ham Rd
Raymond NH 03077

Call Sign: N1XUT
Keith A Norris
30 John St
Raymond NH 03077

Call Sign: KB1QFL
Louis H Steed
12 Morrison Rd
Raymond NH 03077

Call Sign: KB1SWV
Jill G Galus
56 Harriman Hill Rd
Raymond NH 03077

Call Sign: KA1DRB
Hermann Schodder
7 Katie Ln
Raymond NH 03077

Call Sign: KB1UFT
James N Forrestall
40 Mountain Rd
Raymond NH 03077

Call Sign: KR1D
William J Carney
61 Harriman Hill Rd
Raymond NH 03077

Call Sign: N1HKD
Thomas D J Castle
180 Lane Rd
Raymond NH 03077

Call Sign: KB1UXJ
Richard E Alexander
16 Nottingham Rd
Raymond NH 03077

Call Sign: KA1HNV
Michael J Secorsky
111 Harriman Hill Rd
Raymond NH 03077

Call Sign: N1YRB
Bertha A Dodier
19 Main St Apt 2
Raymond NH 030772330

Call Sign: N1WDX
William R Cameron
84 Old Mill Rd
Raymond NH 030771905

Call Sign: KR1L

Call Sign: N1HCT

Call Sign: N1KIG

Daren S Nielsen
Orchard St
Raymond NH 03077

Call Sign: WA1ZBY
Joseph Lamothe Jr
27 Parker Ave Hilltop Co
Op
Raymond NH 03077

Call Sign: WF1W
Francis J O Brien
12 Plains Rd
Raymond NH 03077

Call Sign: N1JLI
Sharon I Lonergan
18 Power St
Raymond NH 03077

Call Sign: KA1WXB
Bruce A Goldsmith
91 Prescott Rd
Raymond NH 03077

Call Sign: KB2WHQ
Michael L Hall
5 Prevere Rd
Raymond NH 030771562

Call Sign: KB1EOS
Edward B Thacher
17 Quinlan Farm Rd
Raymond NH 03077

Call Sign: WK1T
Warren A Simard
1 Richard Ct
Raymond NH 03077

Call Sign: KA1ORU
Matthew B Borsa
4 Richard Ct
Raymond NH 03077

Call Sign: K1RHK
William J Spiller
9 Riverside Dr
Raymond NH 03077

Call Sign: WB1EZL
Andrew M Fagen
3 Royal Lane
Raymond NH 03077

Call Sign: N1QWC
Robert G Heichlinger
16 Royal Lane
Raymond NH 03077

Call Sign: WA1RDG
Gerard M Antaya
1 Rt 27
Raymond NH 03077

Call Sign: N1ZGQ
Steve L Hayes
237 Rte 27 #4
Raymond NH 03077

Call Sign: W1LQY
Raymond F Muise
10 Sesame St
Raymond NH 03077

Call Sign: N1LTS
Donald J Abely
42 Sherman Dr
Raymond NH 03077

Call Sign: K1PF
Kenneth P Donnelly
237 St Rt 27
Raymond NH 03077

Call Sign: N1GIC
Chester J Goguen
237 State Rt 27
Raymond NH 03077

Call Sign: KB1OTY
Barbara J Haglind
192 State Rte 27
Raymond NH 03077

Call Sign: KB1KVG
Daryl W Averill
237 State Rte 27
Raymond NH 03077

Call Sign: WC1E
Daryl W Averill
237 State Rte 27
Raymond NH 03077

Call Sign: KA1HNU
Richard A Lewis Sr
Raymond NH 03077

Call Sign: KA1JJD
Arline J Clark
Raymond NH 03077

Call Sign: KA1JYP
Brian F Cyr
Raymond NH 03077

Call Sign: KD1SY
Robert G Bastien
Raymond NH 030770130

Call Sign: N1DNC
Peter H Merrow
Raymond NH 03077

Call Sign: N1UOA
John J Rusnak
Raymond NH 03077

Call Sign: WA1LNP
Gordon L Muise
Raymond NH 03077

Call Sign: WE1USA
Nh Me Vt Cw Contest Club

Raymond NH 03077

Call Sign: KB1KXM
Joseph V Gregorio
Raymond NH 03077

Call Sign: KB1WET
Joshua S Mann
Raymond NH 03077

Call Sign: W1DPT
Joshua Mann
Raymond NH 03077

## FCC Amateur Radio Licenses in Redstone

Call Sign: N1UOH
Roderick J Henry Jr
52 Mountain St
Redstone NH 03813

## FCC Amateur Radio Licenses in Richmond

Call Sign: KB1LMA
Michael C Pearsall
425 Athol Rd
Richmond NH 03470

Call Sign: WR1W
Norman E Woodward
170 Fish Hatchery Rd
Richmond NH 03470

Call Sign: KB1KWO
William P Pearsall
20 Old Homestead Hwy
Richmond NH 03470

Call Sign: KZ6V
Lolita L Shaw
29 Old Homestead Hwy
Richmond NH 03470

Call Sign: N1PNY
Mary E Shaw
29 Old Homestead Hwy
Richmond NH 03470

Call Sign: WA1NHP
Herbert B Shaw Iii
29 Old Homestead Hwy
Richmond NH 03470

Call Sign: K1RKC
Patricia A Newton
40 Pond Woods Rd
Richmond NH 03470

## FCC Amateur Radio Licenses in Rindge

Call Sign: KB1ECF
Peter J Whicker
130 Abel Rd
Rindge NH 03461

Call Sign: KB1EUS
Sarah A Whicker
130 Abel Rd
Rindge NH 03461

Call Sign: KB1DRC
Richard U Whicker
251 Abel Rd
Rindge NH 03461

Call Sign: KA1ZRK
Sean M Carroll
Box 1998
Rindge NH 03461

Call Sign: W1KOT
William A Farnsworth
Box 451
Rindge NH 03461

Call Sign: KA1ZKZ
Philip A Towle

Brigham Rd
Rindge NH 03461

Call Sign: N1AJY
Lawrence A Del Signore
88 Candlelight Rd
Rindge NH 03461

Call Sign: W1FOH
Donald F Tatro
17 Country Rd
Rindge NH 03461

Call Sign: KE6CZN
Fred K Chelminski
30 Danforth Rd
Rindge NH 03461

Call Sign: WA1HOG
Dennis M Hennigan
38 Foliage Way
Rindge NH 03461

Call Sign: KA1UBH
Kenneth A Raymond
74 Highland Dr
Rindge NH 03461

Call Sign: KB1LCT
Kenneth F Little
7 Jay Dr
Rindge NH 03461

Call Sign: W1KZE
James K Sullivan
8 Jericho Rd
Rindge NH 034615624

Call Sign: K1UIL
George I Chatfield
43 La Chance Circle
Rindge NH 03461

Call Sign: WA1EAC
Benjamin J Leon

18 Lakeview Dr
Rindge NH 03461

Call Sign: N1UB
Benjamin J Leon
18 Lakeview Dr
Rindge NH 03461

Call Sign: N1QZ
Charles E Ronayne
205 North St.
Rindge NH 03461

Call Sign: N1NCS
Donald J Lawrence
18 Old New Ipswich Rd
Rindge NH 03461

Call Sign: KB1EIH
Robin A Lawrence
36 Old New Ipswich Rd
Rindge NH 03461

Call Sign: KB1JSH
Steven J Hruska
358 Old New Ipswich Rd
Rindge NH 03461

Call Sign: KB1AHH
Joseph F Gosling
Old New Ipswich Rd
Rindge NH 03461

Call Sign: AA1LH
Bruce J Bennet
12 Red Gate Ln
Rindge NH 03461

Call Sign: N1NHM
Orion J Lawrence
Schinnacock Trl
Rindge NH 03461

Call Sign: N4QKD
Sherry D Durham

22 Skyview Dr
Rindge NH 03461

Call Sign: K1CRR
Ronald E Osimo
185 Thomas Rd
Rindge NH 03461

Call Sign: KB1BNT
James D Hoard
66 Tico Rd
Rindge NH 03461

Call Sign: WA1WRH
Joseph C Majewski
49 Todd Hill Rd
Rindge NH 034610167

Call Sign: KB1HWQ
Thomas F Mackesy
85 University Dr.
Rindge NH 034615039

Call Sign: KB1BNU
Jesse D Hoard
13 Wallace Rd
Rindge NH 03461

Call Sign: KB1FAR
Mark J Stone
180 Woodbound
Rindge NH 03461

Call Sign: NR1Q
Charles E Brault
65 Woodbound Rd
Rindge NH 03461

Call Sign: KB1BMQ
Amy B Bennet
Rindge NH 03461

Call Sign: N1SWL
Anne E Bennet
Rindge NH 03461

Call Sign: W1HR
Ham Radio Brasspounders
Rindge NH 034610209

Call Sign: W1JCC
John C Clark Jr
Rindge NH 03461

Call Sign: K1QX
John C Clark Jr
Rindge NH 03461

Call Sign: KB1SEP
Steven R Bailey
Rindge NH 03461

Call Sign: N1QVW
Ward C Bryant
468 Cathedral Rd.
Rindge, NH 03461

## FCC Amateur Radio Licenses in Rochester

Call Sign: N1YFL
Patrick E Snapp
14 A Highland St
Rochester NH 03868

Call Sign: KB1UFQ
John T Kenney
13 Alice Lane
Rochester NH 03867

Call Sign: K1LTM
John T Kenney
13 Alice Lane
Rochester NH 03867

Call Sign: KA1MMD
John T Wingate
22 Betts Rd
Rochester NH 03867

Call Sign: W4UZE
Daniel J Manteuffel Jr
116 Betts Rd
Rochester NH 03867

Call Sign: N1WUR
Matthew G Balentine
12 Birch Dr
Rochester NH 03867

Call Sign: KB1QIH
Robert R Beauchamp
55 Blue Hills Dr
Rochester NH 03839

Call Sign: N1YDX
Lee R Chasse
27 Broad St
Rochester NH 03867

Call Sign: KB1WWR
Robert B Betts
22 Brook Farm Vlg
Rochester NH 03839

Call Sign: KB1CQV
Justin D Manteuffel
Cedarbrook Village
Rochester NH 03867

Call Sign: KB1JYK
Gregory J Jandris
117 Chamberlain St
Rochester NH 03867

Call Sign: K1GOT
Lawrence A Ring Mr
93 Charles St
Rochester NH 03867

Call Sign: NU1J
Stanley C Aldrich
155 Charles St
Rochester NH 03867

Call Sign: KB1PUX
John A Baker Iii
108 Chestnut Hill Rd
Rochester NH 03867

Call Sign: N1SDX
William T Martell
213 Chestnut Hill Rd
Rochester NH 03867

Call Sign: N1ARR
Donald S Hawkins Jr
5 Colman
Rochester NH 03867

Call Sign: KB1KKL
John F Rodenhuis
68 Country Brook Ln
Rochester NH 03839

Call Sign: WA1AEC
Collin M Prescott Jr
20 Cove Ct
Rochester NH 038671201

Call Sign: WA1QGA
Denis J Hamel Jr
13 Crockett St.
Rochester NH 03867

Call Sign: K1ZPH
John L Myers
21 Cross Rd
Rochester NH 03867

Call Sign: KB1TDD
Charles J Hudson
102 Cross Rd
Rochester NH 03867

Call Sign: KA1STU
Gordon D Bennett
24 Crosswind Ln
Rochester NH 038675108

Call Sign: KB1MIN
Tami A Larock
3 Damours Ave
Rochester NH 03839

Call Sign: KB1MIO
Paul F Camelia
3 Damours Ave
Rochester NH 03839

Call Sign: KB1LL
Amedee S Landry
1 Dockside Ln
Rochester NH 03867

Call Sign: W1RTL
Donald B Wotton
8 Dodge St
Rochester NH 03867

Call Sign: KB1TDE
Robert V Alexander
111 Dry Hill Rd
Rochester NH 03867

Call Sign: K1RVA
Robert V Alexander
111 Dry Hill Rd
Rochester NH 03867

Call Sign: K1GRU
Norman N Charron
17 Fairway Ave
Rochester NH 038672226

Call Sign: KB1FWA
Matthew P Henderson
88 First Crown Point Rd
Rochester NH 03867

Call Sign: KB1ASY
Brian E Holdsworth
50 Flat Rock Bridge Rd
Rochester NH 03867

Call Sign: WA1GKQ
Francis M Burns
6 Forrest Ave
Rochester NH 03867

Call Sign: W1SRA
Saddleback Repeater
Associates Inc.
2 Fortier Dr
Rochester NH 03867

Call Sign: KB1RNQ
Marybeth E Serozynsky
2 Fortier Dr
Rochester NH 03867

Call Sign: N1PUK
Marybeth E Serozynsky
2 Fortier Dr
Rochester NH 03867

Call Sign: N1JEH
Shawn M Yeaton
2 Fortier Dr
Rochester NH 03867

Call Sign: KB1WBO
Matthew A Bonneau
109 Franklin St
Rochester NH 03867

Call Sign: KA1NVX
William R Delaney
25 Gooseberry Cir
Rochester NH 03867

Call Sign: KB1WJL
Donald R Hennessey
22 Gooseberry Circle
Rochester NH 03867

Call Sign: KB1VUL
Gary L Defoer
33 Highland St Apt 6
Rochester NH 03868

Call Sign: KB1BQT
Craig P Hossfeld
5 Isabella Ln
Rochester NH 03867

Call Sign: KB1NQZ
Michael J Listner
Lincoln St
Rochester NH 03867

Call Sign: KA1INH
James M Doherty
3 Lynn Ln
Rochester NH 03867

Call Sign: K1FDP
Arefg/Sim 157
7 Maplewood Ave
Rochester NH 03867

Call Sign: WA1FUG
Richard L Caverly
1 Meaderboro Rd
Rochester NH 03867

Call Sign: K0MHL
Marilyn K G Jones
30 Meaderboro Rd
Rochester NH 038674234

Call Sign: KB1COV
Jackson H Jones
30 Meaderboro Rd
Rochester NH 038674234

Call Sign: W0WRQ
Jackson H Jones
30 Meaderboro Rd
Rochester NH 038674234

Call Sign: KB1RNP
James G Webber Ii
132 Meaderboro Rd
Rochester NH 03867

Call Sign: KB1BQU
Maria H Rosendahl
209 Milton Rd 150
Rochester NH 03868

Call Sign: KB1KBF
Matthew E Leonard
6 Morton Ave
Rochester NH 03867

Call Sign: KE1JM
Eugene W Richard
36 Murray Dr
Rochester NH 03868

Call Sign: W1WBM
Maurice E Hale Jr
2 N Elderberry Ln Box 111
Rochester NH 03867

Call Sign: N1VBO
Kenneth F Doyle
6 Nola Ave
Rochester NH 038673314

Call Sign: AA1QW
Brian E Chaloux
217 North Main St Apt 3
Rochester NH 03867

Call Sign: N1ZPT
Norman F Whitehill Jr
167 Old Dover Rd
Rochester NH 03867

Call Sign: N1OEU
Steven M Herchenroder
292 Old Dover Rd
Rochester NH 03867

Call Sign: WG1B
William D Gipson
8 Orchard St.
Rochester NH 03867

Call Sign: N1XUQ
Jeffrey A Zajicek
5 Outlook Ln
Rochester NH 03867

Call Sign: KB1FAN
Dean H Libersky
514 Portland St
Rochester NH 03867

Call Sign: N1UBB
Matthew J Herrick
4 Royal Crest
Rochester NH 03867

Call Sign: N1YGH
Erin E Zajicek
5 Outlook Ln
Rochester NH 03867

Call Sign: KB1SNX
Julie Day
27 Regency Ct
Rochester NH 03867

Call Sign: N1KIO
Thomas J Saluti
38 Royal Crest
Rochester NH 03867

Call Sign: KA1FGM
James A Roese
4 Paradise Dr
Rochester NH 03867

Call Sign: WB1FGU
Philip D Sawyer
28 Richardson
Rochester NH 03867

Call Sign: N1FF
William D Gipson
13 Royal Crest Mhp
Rochester NH 03867

Call Sign: N1MPM
Karen L Staines
54 Partridge Green
Rochester NH 03867

Call Sign: WF1Q
Robert A Layton
18 Riverlawn Ave
Rochester NH 03867

Call Sign: KB1WMV
Richard C Rice
13 Royalcrest
Rochester NH 03867

Call Sign: KB1CKD
Christopher J Prenaveau
22 Patriots Way
Rochester NH 03839

Call Sign: KA1YZK
Janis A Marshall
37 Riverlawn Ave
Rochester NH 03868

Call Sign: K1STF
Strafford Nhares Club
387 Salmon Falls Rd
Rochester NH 03868

Call Sign: N1IRI
Shawn P Flaherty
13 Pine St
Rochester NH 03867

Call Sign: WA1RGP
Paul D Marshall
37 Riverlawn Ave
Rochester NH 038688617

Call Sign: KB1NHZ
Lawrence F Innman
387 Salmon Falls Rd
Rochester NH 03868

Call Sign: N1GXX
Stanley M Pridham
362 Portland St
Rochester NH 03867

Call Sign: K1WO
Paul D Marshall
37 Riverlawn Ave
Rochester NH 038688617

Call Sign: K1SRJ
Lawrence F Inman
387 Salmon Falls Rd
Rochester NH 03868

Call Sign: KB1VMD
Donna R Ellis
488 Portland St
Rochester NH 03867

Call Sign: KA1ZTR
Richard A Clough
21 Rochester Hill Rd
Rochester NH 03867

Call Sign: N1ZAD
Shawn M Staines
463 Salmon Falls Rd
Rochester NH 03868

Call Sign: K1DRE
Donna R Ellis
488 Portland St
Rochester NH 03867

Call Sign: KA1UUV
Stuart S Mann
149 Rochester Hill Rd
Rochester NH 03867

Call Sign: KA1PHC
Kevin K Mikoski
607 Salmon Falls Rd
Rochester NH 03868

Call Sign: KE1LS
Kevin K Mikoski
607 Salmon Falls Rd
Rochester NH 03868

Call Sign: WA1PTC
Mike K Staines
997 Salmon Falls Rd
Rochester NH 038685706

Call Sign: K1YPM
Neill A Williams
25 Seneca St Cocheco River
Estates
Rochester NH 038674332

Call Sign: KA1PJI
Shirley A Zinck
5 Sewell Rd
Rochester NH 03867

Call Sign: K1YQR
Edward H Nelson
7 Sewell Rd
Rochester NH 03868

Call Sign: K1IG
Edward H Nelson
7 Sewell Rd
Rochester NH 03868

Call Sign: W1EHN
Edward H Nelson
7 Sewell Rd
Rochester NH 03868

Call Sign: N1FOX
Nancy M Zakupowsky
14 Sewell Rd
Rochester NH 03867

Call Sign: N1YOE
Irving S Bergstrom
6 Snow St

Rochester NH 03867

Call Sign: WA1BTF
Lucille T Letourneau
17 St James Terrace
Rochester NH 03867

Call Sign: N1VEB
David S Winson
7 Stewart Ct
Rochester NH 03867

Call Sign: N1VRE
Barbara R Winson
7 Stewart Ct
Rochester NH 038671829

Call Sign: KA1ZJY
Steven D Tuttle
33 Summer St
Rochester NH 03867

Call Sign: KB1LOA
Kenneth F Thomas
14 Temple Dr
Rochester NH 03868

Call Sign: N1QXI
Terry T Long
214 Ten Red Rd
Rochester NH 03867

Call Sign: KB1AFA
Micheal J Demeritt
336 Ten Rod Rd
Rochester NH 03867

Call Sign: WA1UJC
Charles L Thompson Jr
728 Ten Rod Rd
Rochester NH 038678242

Call Sign: K1ACL
Alfred W La Vallee
13 Villanova Ln

Rochester NH 03867

Call Sign: W1SVL
Lawrence L Prado Jr
19 W Wind Estates
Rochester NH 03867

Call Sign: KB1SPH
Jeffrey A Lavoie
62 Washington St
Rochester NH 03867

Call Sign: KB1COU
Keith P Brooks
5 West Lane
Rochester NH 03867

Call Sign: N0QKN
Dale A Mills
60 Whitehall Rd
Rochester NH 03867

Call Sign: KB1QPD
Terry J Long
89 Whitehall Rd
Rochester NH 03868

Call Sign: KB1NJX
Elayne J Baillargeon-Ketel
107 Whitehall Rd
Rochester NH 038685712

Call Sign: KB1NKD
Stephen M Ketel
107 Whitehall Rd
Rochester NH 03868

Call Sign: W1EJB
Elayne J Baillargeon-Ketel
107 Whitehall Rd
Rochester NH 038685712

Call Sign: K1EAR
John W Sowden
105 Whitehouse Rd 7

Rochester NH 03867

Call Sign: KB1WER
Ann-Marie D Lavoie
105 Whitehouse Rd Lot 26
Rochester NH 03867

Call Sign: KB1NZG
David C Allen
105 Whitehouse Rd Lot -88
Rochester NH 03867

Call Sign: KB1STV
Michael F Lavoie
105 Whitehouse Rd Lot#26
Rochester NH 03867

Call Sign: N1AMD
Michael F Lavoie
105 Whitehouse Rd Lot#26
Rochester NH 03867

Call Sign: KA1UNL
Scott D Maltese
19 Willow Brook Apt
Lowell St
Rochester NH 03867

Call Sign: N1HOU
Bruce W Senter Sr
35 Winter St
Rochester NH 03867

Call Sign: N1NTK
James M Di Stefano
88 Woodland Green
Rochester NH 03868

Call Sign: WA1DDC
Steven P Urban
77 Woodland Grn
Rochester NH 038685719

Call Sign: KB1SZL
Donald E Laroche
595 Main St
Rollinsford NH 03869

Call Sign: KB7OHH
Steven W Thayer
690 Main St
Rollinsford NH 03869

Call Sign: KB1TDC
Timothy A Pinkham
880 Portland Ave
Rollinsford NH 03869

Call Sign: KB1WST
Ronald G Hargreaves
334 Rollins Rd
Rollinsford NH 03869

Call Sign: N1YOK
Oscar O Michaud
25 Silver Ln
Rollinsford NH 038695409

Call Sign: KB1COS
Richard C Kansky
41 South St
Rollinsford NH 038690642

Call Sign: W0IDE
Jeffry V Herring
43 Woods Run
Rollinsford NH 03869

Call Sign: KB1DEP
Brian G Stubbs
Rollinsford NH 038690712

Call Sign: N1QQG
Marilynn M Bueckner

397 Middletown Rd
Roxbury NH 034318706

Call Sign: N1NZR
W A Bueckner
397 Middletown Rd
Roxbury NH 034318706

Call Sign: KB1LVR
Bruce Angus
372 E Rumney Rd
Rumney NH 03266

Call Sign: N1MER
Alan J Hunter
Main St
Rumney NH 03266

Call Sign: N1IEH
Laurianne M Olcott
925 Quincy Rd
Rumney NH 03266

Call Sign: N1RBB
Richard B Barnes
1029 Quincy Rd
Rumney NH 032663541

Call Sign: KB1WJK
William J Taffe
1201 Quincy Rd
Rumney NH 03266

Call Sign: KA1VJU
David E Megin
535 School St
Rumney NH 03266

Call Sign: KB1GQV
Margaret M Brown
535 School St
Rumney NH 03266

Call Sign: W1RTM
Red Team Nhares Club
535 School St
Rumney NH 03266

Call Sign: KB1A
Tomio Morita
376 Stinson Lake Rd
Rumney NH 03266

Call Sign: W1TTX
James G Keyworth
Stinson Lake Rd
Rumney NH 03266

Call Sign: AA1UP
Tomio Morita
376 Stinson Lake Rd Box
95
Rumney NH 03266

Call Sign: KD1G
Galen R Courtney
61 Victory Ave
Rumney NH 03266

Call Sign: KC1RO
Galen R Courtney
61 Victory Ave Rt 25
Rumney NH 03266

Call Sign: W1BTN
Mary J Courtney
Rumney NH 03266

Call Sign: KB1JGS
John R Allen
1 Forest Green Rd
Rye NH 03870

Call Sign: KB1HUB

Ann L Stanford
6 Harborview Dr
Rye NH 03870

Call Sign: KB1HUC
Glen C Stanford
6 Harborview Dr
Rye NH 03870

Call Sign: K1RSC
John E Johnston
10 Lang Rd
Rye NH 038702328

Call Sign: WB8NTR
Laurence E Clark Jr
13 Mc Laughlin Dr
Rye NH 038702629

Call Sign: N1QJM
James W Beattie
1126 Ocean Blvd
Rye NH 03870

Call Sign: K1RNB
Franklin Merriman
79 Old Beach Rd
Rye NH 03870

Call Sign: WA1YDS
Franklin W Davis
76 Wallis Rd
Rye NH 03870

Call Sign: WA1KJE
Marjorie M Scully
113 Wallis Rd
Rye NH 03870

Call Sign: N1CKP
Stephen H Dyke
587 Wallis Rd
Rye NH 03870

Call Sign: AA1MI

Paul G Schreier
25 Washington Rd
Rye NH 03870

Call Sign: KB1MCD
John F Davis
195 Washington Rd
Rye NH 03870

Call Sign: K1RSC
John F Davis
195 Washington Rd
Rye NH 03870

Call Sign: KD1PN
Tyson J Mc Mahon
970 Washington Rd
Rye NH 03870

Call Sign: KA1TFY
John D Myles
Rye NH 03870

Call Sign: N8UDD
Deborah E Bowmar
Rye NH 03870

Call Sign: KB1PGI
Michael D Toews
Rye NH 03870

Call Sign: KB1MGM
Ralph A O Connor
112 Perkins Rd
Rye Beach NH 038710319

Call Sign: KB1LCJ
John J Leonard
Rye Beach NH 03871

Call Sign: KM1N
William A Longworth
21 Alfred Dr
Salem NH 03079

Call Sign: N1OCP
Theodore P Fazioli
21 Alta Ave
Salem NH 03079

Call Sign: N1ZBP
Richard G Lavoie
5 Anderson Ave
Salem NH 03079

Call Sign: K1ILB
Anthony S Coco
20 Atkinson Rd
Salem NH 03079

Call Sign: W1OFH
Eugene J Gaumont
18 Bannister Rd
Salem NH 03079

Call Sign: KB1DIT
Louis T Maguire Jr
16 Barron Ave
Salem NH 03079

Call Sign: W1LTM
Louis T Maguire Jr
16 Barron Ave
Salem NH 03079

Call Sign: WB1DDD
William J Thompson Sr
25 Bell Dr
Salem NH 03079

Call Sign: N1PMK
David C Quinney Sr
22 Beverly Ave
Salem NH 03079

Call Sign: W1MHD
Raymond F Jones Sr
19 Blake Rd
Salem NH 03079

Call Sign: WA1FHR
Donald M Buja
96 Bridge St
Salem NH 03079

Call Sign: N1LWF
Raymond F Bonney
2 Brookwood Dr
Salem NH 03079

Call Sign: N1CMD
David W Goodwin
36 Brookwood Dr
Salem NH 030793024

Call Sign: KA1IX
Ernest P Caramanis
45 Budron Ave
Salem NH 03079

Call Sign: K1SXJ
George F Pelich
10 Canobie Ave
Salem NH 03079

Call Sign: KB1JLG
David A Annicelli
10 Carmar Ln
Salem NH 03079

Call Sign: N1EXT
David A Annicelli
10 Carmar Ln
Salem NH 03079

Call Sign: WB1GGU
John Murphy
18 Centerville Dr
Salem NH 03079

Call Sign: KB1THN
David E Chandler
88 Chappy Ln
Salem NH 03079

Call Sign: KC1T
Warren P Floyd
14 Cindy Ave
Salem NH 03079

Call Sign: W1EUI
John J Keaney
10 Clifton Ave
Salem NH 03079

Call Sign: N1CAU
Peter P Ivas
16 Clifton Ave
Salem NH 03079

Call Sign: KB1DIS
Ryan C Johnson
15 Clinton St
Salem NH 03079

Call Sign: N1ERA
Michael P Arnold
99 Cluff Crossing Rd - Apt
# F3
Salem NH 03079

Call Sign: KB1OSF
Ken L Flesher
3 Corliss St
Salem NH 03079

Call Sign: KE1BA
Kenneth M Cody
21 Crescent St
Salem NH 03079

Call Sign: N1LFT
Kathleen R Cody
21 Crescent St

Salem NH 03079

Salem NH 03079

Salem NH 03079

Call Sign: N1TBN
Alan J Marchioni
47 Crestwood Cir
Salem NH 030794101

Call Sign: KB1FGH
James D Nicholson
Galway Lane
Salem NH 03079

Call Sign: W8AUE
Janet D Bruce
5 Hawk Dr
Salem NH 03079

Call Sign: KB1IEA
Christine E La Chance
10 Dana Rd
Salem NH 03079

Call Sign: KA1ENH
Eleanor S Martel
Geremonty Dr Rm 218b
Salem NH 03079

Call Sign: K1QOK
David M Carpenter
31 Henderson Cir
Salem NH 03079

Call Sign: N1USJ
Shihchin Lee
57 Duston Rd
Salem NH 03079

Call Sign: KB1DIR
Stephen D Terry
11 Gibney Cir
Salem NH 03079

Call Sign: N1GUL
Marie G Croteau
14 High St
Salem NH 03079

Call Sign: N1XPR
Jeffrey Lee
57 Duston Rd
Salem NH 03079

Call Sign: W1SDT
Stephen D Terry
11 Gibney Cir
Salem NH 03079

Call Sign: W1YGE
Royal A Roulston
20 Highland Ave
Salem NH 03079

Call Sign: W9UFW
Fred Stolte
5 Ermer Rd
Salem NH 03079

Call Sign: N1LTH
Christine R Mc Grath
8 Grove Ave
Salem NH 03079

Call Sign: KB1CIE
William E Fernandez
77 Hooker Farm Rd
Salem NH 03079

Call Sign: KB1FNJ
Thomas G La Plume
3 Frary St
Salem NH 03079

Call Sign: N1PVQ
Thomas Mc Grath
8 Grove Ave
Salem NH 03079

Call Sign: NN1F
Gordon W Mc Cann
17 Howard St
Salem NH 03079

Call Sign: KB1QIF
James E Lombardozzi
2 Freedom Dr
Salem NH 03079

Call Sign: N1SLP
Peter C Stillwaggon
78 Hagop Rd
Salem NH 03079

Call Sign: N1KPC
William R Shea
7 Jill Rd
Salem NH 03079

Call Sign: N1WRB
Norman P Lord Jr
2 Freedom Dr Apt-B
Salem NH 03079

Call Sign: N1NJA
Kathie A Glidden
25 Hampshire St Apt 18
Salem NH 09079

Call Sign: N1GVG
Robin L Williams
32 Joseph Rd
Salem NH 03079

Call Sign: N1GTX
Norman P Lord Jr
2 Freedom Dr Apt-D

Call Sign: KB1UXK
Janet D Bruce
5 Hawk Dr

Call Sign: N1GVH
Brian A Williams
32 Joseph Rd

Salem NH 03079                    Salem NH 03079                    Salem NH 03079

Call Sign: WB1FTV                 Call Sign: N1VN                   Call Sign: KA1KWT
Thomas R Raskow                   Craig F Lebeau                    Jeffrey D Gilman
36 Joseph Rd                      3 Lamplighter Ln                  9 Martin Ave
Salem NH 03079                    Salem NH 03079                    Salem NH 03079

Call Sign: KB1ERI                 Call Sign: W1GIN                  Call Sign: N1GZK
Michael J O Connell Sr            Edmund F Cook                     James E Lally
7 Kim Rd                          20 Lawrence Rd                    21 Meisner Rd
Salem NH 03079                    Salem NH 030793237                Salem NH 03079

Call Sign: N1SYG                  Call Sign: N1JDQ                  Call Sign: N1CUU
Timothy P Bradley                 Kevin E Wilson                    Carl S Heidenblad
3 Kyle Dr                         33 Lawrence Rd                    106 Millville Circle
Salem NH 03079                    Salem NH 03079                    Salem NH 03079

Call Sign: N1NV                   Call Sign: WA1KMU                 Call Sign: KB1FUV
Clifford J Mead                   Alex H Elm                        Michael J Banks
9 Kyle Dr                         87 Lawrence Rd                    25 Millville St
Salem NH 030792321                Salem NH 03079                    Salem NH 03079

Call Sign: KS1Q                   Call Sign: W1SIP                  Call Sign: KA1SNY
Robert F Leonard Iii              John L Brain Sr                   Roxanne E Marconi
87 Lake Shore Dr                  242 Lawrence Rd                   49 Millville St
Salem NH 03079                    Salem NH 03079                    Salem NH 03079

Call Sign: W1OA                   Call Sign: KA1OZG                 Call Sign: KB1HSF
Allan M Zecchini                  Robert F Blain Sr                 Michael W Wasiejko
60 Lake St                        2 Lois Ln                         134 Millville St
Salem NH 030792247                Salem NH 03079                    Salem NH 030792220

Call Sign: KB1GXS                 Call Sign: K1PTM                  Call Sign: N1CGR
Roberta A Lebeau                  Kendall W Colby                   Michael W Wasiejko
3 Lamplighter Lane                30 Mac Larnon Rd                  134 Millville St
Salem NH 03079                    Salem NH 03079                    Salem NH 030792220

Call Sign: KB1ESI                 Call Sign: WA1SDB                 Call Sign: KA1SNH
Craig F Lebeau                    Heidi A Greenlaw                  Dennis J Croteau
3 Lamplighter Ln                  368 Main St                       14 Mountain Ave
Salem NH 03079                    Salem NH 03079                    Salem NH 030791408

Call Sign: KB1ETD                 Call Sign: KB1UFK                 Call Sign: W1JBE
Ross F Lebeau                     Daniel F Yetter                   Daniel A Boudreau
3 Lamplighter Ln                  10 Marsh Ave                      5 Mulberry Rd

Salem NH 03079

Call Sign: N1XIH
Simon N Lloyd Hughes
224 N Broadway
Salem NH 03079

Call Sign: K1HRO
Ham Radio Outlet Amateur
Radio Club
224 N Broadway D-12
Salem NH 03079

Call Sign: KB1RUZ
Robert O Corey
399 N Main St
Salem NH 03079

Call Sign: N1YGX
William E Robbins
401 N Main St
Salem NH 03079

Call Sign: N1OVC
Janet A Minch
110 N Policy St
Salem NH 03079

Call Sign: KB1JHC
George E Hartz Iv
16 North Main St
Salem NH 03079

Call Sign: KB1PLE
Richard A Faust Iii
153 North Main St
Salem NH 03079

Call Sign: NR1F
Richard A Faust Iii
153 North Main St
Salem NH 03079

Call Sign: KC1IH
Lawrence M Weil

11 Palmer St
Salem NH 030791331

Call Sign: KA1SXE
Gus E Agudelo
14 Pleasant St
Salem NH 03079

Call Sign: KA1MLI
Kenneth A Takaki
64 Porcupine Cir
Salem NH 03079

Call Sign: N1FTZ
Stewart L Richardson
4 Rena Ave
Salem NH 030792030

Call Sign: AA1ZP
Stewart L Richardson
4 Rena Ave
Salem NH 030792030

Call Sign: W1ZQI
Joseph N Ouellette
15 Robert Ave
Salem NH 03079

Call Sign: KB1FPQ
Christopher R Page
215 S Broadway Suite 169
Salem NH 03079

Call Sign: KB1PLC
Mark W Rogers
28 School St
Salem NH 03079

Call Sign: K1LKP
Carmen C Drogo
52 School St
Salem NH 03079

Call Sign: KA1NKV
John M Klingler

149 School St
Salem NH 03079

Call Sign: KA1GK
Philip O Martel
23 Scotland Ave
Salem NH 03079

Call Sign: K1VVM
Brian J Vigars Sr
15 Shadow Lake Rd
Salem NH 03079

Call Sign: WA1CFT
Richard M Norley
97 Shannon Rd
Salem NH 030790350

Call Sign: WA1MDP
Stephen P Kutny
1 Shepard Ave
Salem NH 03079

Call Sign: N1DRK
Steven R Barker
8 Shepard Ave
Salem NH 03079

Call Sign: KA1JRH
Joseph A Rosa Sr
133 Shore Dr
Salem NH 03079

Call Sign: WB1CWK
Lynda S Paul Ms
347 Shore Dr
Salem NH 03079

Call Sign: KB1RFG
Jeffrey D Romano
8 South Shore Rd
Salem NH 03079

Call Sign: AB1CI
Charles E Perkett

16 Sunset Rd
Salem NH 030791704

Call Sign: KA1QQO
Frank C Calabria
10 Teague Dr
Salem NH 03079

Call Sign: KA1TDO
Peter J Calabria
10 Teague Dr
Salem NH 03079

Call Sign: KB1TCX
Jeremy S Lerner
12 Teague Dr
Salem NH 03079

Call Sign: N1FGT
Diane R Valcourt
19 Teague Dr
Salem NH 03079

Call Sign: NY1Z
Gerald L Valcourt Jr
19 Teague Dr
Salem NH 03079

Call Sign: KB1PRV
Kenneth S Rust
37 Teague Dr
Salem NH 03079

Call Sign: K1NWQ
Salvatore P Marino
24 Town Village Dr
Salem NH 03079

Call Sign: N1QYN
Keith W Cerretani
25 Townsend Ave
Salem NH 03079

Call Sign: KB1LVN
Thomas Newton

10 Trailer Home Dr
Salem NH 03079

Call Sign: N1JV
Thomas Newton
10 Trailer Home Dr
Salem NH 03079

Call Sign: KD1JE
Gilbert A Bergeron
23 Trailer Home Dr
Salem NH 03079

Call Sign: K1HVW
Richard G Favreau
17 Travelers Dr
Salem NH 03079

Call Sign: K1WV
William R Valentine
4 W Duston Rd
Salem NH 03079

Call Sign: KB1SWU
David J Dunham
73 W Passage Rd
Salem NH 03079

Call Sign: K1VYY
Robert E Dupre
28 Williams St
Salem NH 03079

Call Sign: N1HJF
Reno R Jandreau
19 Woodbury St
Salem NH 03079

Call Sign: N1JVZ
Fred A Kruse
Salem NH 03079

Call Sign: N1VQS
Frank X Mc Canna
Salem NH 03079

Call Sign: WA1AJH
Norman J Bistany
Salem NH 030791148

Call Sign: KB1IBT
Shawn D Stricker
Salem NH 03079

## FCC Amateur Radio Licenses in Salisbury

Call Sign: KB1WKW
John F Supry
63 Brookside Dr
Salisbury NH 03268

Call Sign: WW1WW
Woodrow S Beckford
250 Couchtown Rd
Salisbury NH 03268

Call Sign: W1ADI
Analog Devices Amateur
Radio Club
250 Couchtown Rd
Salisbury NH 03268

Call Sign: N1GCO
Edwin F Bowne
58 Old Turnpike Rd
Salisbury NH 03268

Call Sign: WA1SSJ
Wayne W Andrews
603 Old Turnpike Rd.
Salisbury NH 032680294

Call Sign: K1VZE
Russell A Mc Laughlin
1455 Raccoon Hill Rd
Salisbury NH 03268

Call Sign: KB1QGI
Kathryn P Michener

24 Searles Hill Rd
Salisbury NH 03268

Call Sign: K1KTE
Kathryn P Michener
24 Searles Hill Rd
Salisbury NH 03268

Call Sign: KB1QGJ
Sandt D Michener
24 Searles Hill Rd
Salisbury NH 03268

Call Sign: N1SPQ
John K Beaudoin
South Rd
Salisbury NH 03268

## FCC Amateur Radio Licenses in Sanbornton

Call Sign: K1VRL
John L Beck
Box 239
Sanbornton NH 03269

Call Sign: KB1GIZ
Johann S Busch
333 Brook Rd
Sanbornton NH 03269

Call Sign: W1JSB
Johann S Busch
333 Brook Rd
Sanbornton NH 03269

Call Sign: N1HQD
Louise A Jeffrey
51 Cogswell Rd Unit 1
Sanbornton NH 03269

Call Sign: N1VUI
Paul J Moore
11 Collieson Rd
Sanbornton NH 03269

Call Sign: N1UBH
Merrel A Collard
15 Hale Rd
Sanbornton NH 03269

Call Sign: WA1BAA
John T Wilson
109 Hale Rd
Sanbornton NH 03269

Call Sign: KB1SEJ
Cameron C Thompson
67 Hermit Woods Rd
Sanbornton NH 03269

Call Sign: KB1RKH
Scott T Taylor
117 Kaulack Rd
Sanbornton NH 03269

Call Sign: WA1HQR
Raymond A Beaupre
701 New Hampton Rd
Sanborton NH 032692014

Call Sign: N1UUX
Cedar L Sanderson
1168 New Hampton Rd
Sanbornton NH 03269

Call Sign: W1PID
James F Cluett
1241 New Hampton Rd
Sanbornton NH 03269

Call Sign: KB1JWF
Karney R Nazarian
46 Normandin Dr
Sanbornton NH 03269

Call Sign: W2AFC
Karney R Nazarian
46 Normandin Dr
Sanbornton NH 03269

Call Sign: N1EEB
Joseph S Malinowski Jr
146 Osgood Rd
Sanbornton NH 03269

Call Sign: WA1EAK
Russell F Tilton
26 Point Rd
Sanbornton NH 03269

Call Sign: N1GFD
Ron Desharnais
Sanbornton NH 03269

## FCC Amateur Radio Licenses in Sanbornville

Call Sign: W1WA
William A Dennis
Box 463
Sanbornville NH 03872

Call Sign: KA2KON
Stephen A Colello
119 Flynn Rd
Sanbornville NH 03872

Call Sign: K1BFE
Gordon E Wiggin
45 School St
Sanbornville NH 03872

Call Sign: N1STG
Patrick Renard
463 Stone Ham Rd
Sanbornville NH 03872

Call Sign: W1IP
Box 463 International
Police Assn Us Section Arc
Stoneham Rd
Sanbornville NH 03872

Call Sign: K1IP

Box 463 American Police
Network Arc
Sanbornville NH 03872

Call Sign: K1WR
Box 463 Wakefield
Wireless Association
Sanbornville NH 03872

Call Sign: KA1OFF
Linwood C Potter
Sanbornville NH 03872

Call Sign: KA8PVB
Robert J Gallagher
Sanbornville NH 03872

Call Sign: KB1BTL
Donald E Bergeron
Sanbornville NH 03872

Call Sign: W1OFR
Robert W Hooper
Sanbornville NH 03872

Call Sign: W1UDM
Bruce R Wiggin
Sanbornville NH
038720519

Call Sign: WA1TVR
Real P Frechette
Sanbornville NH 03872

FCC Amateur Radio
Licenses in Sandown

Call Sign: N1VNI
Edwin W Robbins Jr
3 Bunce Cir
Sandown NH 03873

Call Sign: KE1GQ
Elaine R Smith
1 Celeste Ter

Sandown NH 03873

Call Sign: KB1EOH
Edward C Couture
49 Elizabeth Rd
Sandown NH 038732033

Call Sign: KA1URV
William Zinck
271 Fremont Rd
Sandown NH 03873

Call Sign: K1MIZ
Charles R Cunningham
7 Glastombury Dr
Sandown NH 03873

Call Sign: N1WDU
Albert C Lake Jr
174 Hampstead Rd
Sandown NH 03873

Call Sign: W1KCE
Charles S Morrill
25 Hamstead Rd Box 14
Sandown NH 038732414

Call Sign: N1RKP
Keith C Spaulding
13 Higgins Ave
Sandown NH 03873

Call Sign: N1JLJ
Keith D Cronyn
2 Holmeswood Dr
Sandown NH 03873

Call Sign: KX1T
Alfred F Pariseau
44 Main St
Sandown NH 03873

Call Sign: N1KQW
Larry E Thigpen
618 Main St

Sandown NH 03873

Call Sign: KB1TUS
James T Passanisi
85 North Rd
Sandown NH 03873

Call Sign: N1OQF
Edward P Murphy Jr
25 Oakridge Rd
Sandown NH 03873

Call Sign: KB1CMN
Erin H Cruess
30 Odell Rd
Sandown NH 03873

Call Sign: KB1GKK
Jon A Mckenzie
30 Odell Rd
Sandown NH 03873

Call Sign: K1OZ
James R Spear
45 Penacook Rd
Sandown NH 03873

Call Sign: KB1OVA
Walter S Clifton
12 Royal Range Rd
Sandown NH 038732127

Call Sign: K3PYI
J Joseph Hurray
3 Schoolhouse Ln
Sandown NH 03873

Call Sign: N1FKG
Wendy D Hurray
3 Schoolhouse Ln
Sandown NH 03873

Call Sign: K1ZR
Shane E Mattson
27 Snow Lane

Sandown NH 03873

Call Sign: KA1MRL
Louis A Porcelli
18 Swmill Ridge
Sandown NH 03873

Call Sign: KA1JLF
Thomas E Rafuse
3 Timber Trail
Sandown NH 03873

Call Sign: KB1QYW
Charles L S Marshall
45 Waterford Dr
Sandown NH 03873

## FCC Amateur Radio Licenses in Sandwich

Call Sign: KA1EIJ
Donald R Casey
147 Mountain Rd
Sandwich NH 03227

Call Sign: K1ZKJ
William T Gill Iii
250 Mountain Rd
Sandwich NH 03227

Call Sign: KB1OKK
Louis G Brunelle
32 Palmer Hill Rd
Sandwich NH 03227

## FCC Amateur Radio Licenses in Seabrook

Call Sign: NI1O
Joseph H Dugan
15 Autumn Way
Seabrook NH 03874

Call Sign: W1FYW
Joseph Mc Clintock

24 Batchelder Rd 114 D 2
Seabrook NH 038744401

Call Sign: N1WLG
Rebecca L Daniel-
Maldonado
24 Batchelder Rd Bldg 114
Seabrook NH 03874

Call Sign: KB1PJC
James C Cameron
19 Blueberry Ln
Seabrook NH 03874

Call Sign: K1JYA
Nicholas D Ricci
209 Bristol St.
Seabrook NH 03874

Call Sign: N1KTF
Addison E D Entremont
25 Brooks Rd Extn
Seabrook NH 03874

Call Sign: N1CSG
Addison E D Entremont
25 Brooks Rd. Ext.
Seabrook NH 03874

Call Sign: AB1OR
Addison E D Entremont
25 Brooks Rd. Ext.
Seabrook NH 03874

Call Sign: KA1VAE
Larry A Kraus
112 Cimarron Apt B1
Seabrook NH 03874

Call Sign: KB1FUF
Robert E Mcdonald
118 Cimarron Dr
Seabrook NH 03874

Call Sign: K1JCJ

Robert E Mcdonald
118 Cimarron Dr
Seabrook NH 03874

Call Sign: K1TJK
Thomas J Kelly
89 Collins St
Seabrook NH 03874

Call Sign: KB1TZH
Bobbi-Sue Lauder
Cross Beach Rd
Seabrook NH 03874

Call Sign: KB1TZI
Joseph B Leonard Iii
Cross Beach Rd
Sea Brook NH 03874

Call Sign: KD4SQA
Robert A Beal
34 Dwight Ave
Seabrook NH 03874

Call Sign: N1DQT
Lewis J Thurlow
241 Folly Mill Rd
Seabrook NH 03874

Call Sign: KR1A
David B Savory
154 Garden St
Seabrook NH 03874

Call Sign: KB1PXE
Richard W Cooper
51 Gove Rd
Seabrook NH 038744108

Call Sign: W1MSN
Richard W Cooper
51 Gove Rd
Seabrook NH 038744108

Call Sign: W1ROC

Rockingham Nhares Club
919 Lafayette Rd Unit 15
Seabrook NH 03874

Call Sign: N1YI
George F Rinalducci
919 Lafayette Rd Unit 15
Seabrook NH 03874

Call Sign: WA1RRR
Robert C Le Blanc
11 Maple Ridge Rd
Seabrook NH 03874

Call Sign: KB1GCK
Jack D Gosselin
25 Maple Ridge Rd
Seabrook NH 03874

Call Sign: KB1TUN
John R Cameron
44 New Zealand Rd Apt 2
Seabrook NH 03874

Call Sign: KA1UTV
Roy M Kirkpatrick
47 Railroad Ave
Seabrook NH 03874

Call Sign: N1LFU
John A Andrewskiewicz
20 Raymond Dr
Seabrook NH 03874

Call Sign: KA1IV
Oscar M Chagnon
River
Seabrook NH 03874

Call Sign: KD1VR
Jason A Janvrin
49 Rocks Rd
Seabrook NH 038740343

Call Sign: WA1NH

Jason A Janvrin
49 Rocks Rd
Seabrook NH 038740343

Call Sign: KB1AKX
Roderick W Anspaugh
57 Rocks Rd
Seabrook NH 03874

Call Sign: N1PIQ
Charles A Anspaugh
57 Rocks Rd
Seabrook NH 03874

Call Sign: N1TJB
Virginia H Anspaugh
57 Rocks Rd
Seabrook NH 03874

Call Sign: KB1KSQ
David A Dearth
208 S Main St
Seabrook NH 03874

Call Sign: N1NKZ
James A Mazzola
200 South Maine St
Seabrook NH 03874

Call Sign: WA1YRM
Philip S Lycett Iii
8 Whittier Dr
Seabrook NH 03874

Call Sign: KA1DPI
Marie A Polito
Seabrook NH 03874

Call Sign: KA1FTZ
Mary P Vivenzio
Seabrook NH 03874

Call Sign: N1UXY
Edward C Szczesuil
Seabrook NH 03874

Call Sign: N1YXL
Thomas J Kelly
Seabrook NH 03874

Call Sign: WB1GLB
Kenneth C Vivenzio
Seabrook NH 03874

## FCC Amateur Radio Licenses in Sharon

Call Sign: KD1NY
John M Wilson Jr
32 Mc Coy Rd
Sharon NH 034587019

Call Sign: N1MZZ
David L Bowles
698 Route 123
Sharon NH 03458

Call Sign: W1CSB
Chester S Bowles
698 Rt 123
Sharon NH 03458

Call Sign: KB1LDR
Robert A Greenwood
69 Spring Hill Rd
Sharon NH 03458

## FCC Amateur Radio Licenses in Shelburne

Call Sign: N1JQA
Richard R Lussier Jr
679 North Rd
Shelburne NH 03581

Call Sign: N1BLU
John K Russell
4 Seyah Rd
Shelburne NH 03581

Call Sign: N1RNY
Robert E Smith
164 Caroline Rd
Silver Lake NH 03875

Call Sign: KB1IHP
Nathan R Warner
1627 Village Rd
Silver Lake NH 03875

## FCC Amateur Radio Licenses in Somersworth

Call Sign: N1HFE
John A Gaidos
165 Blackwater Rd
Somersworth NH 03878

Call Sign: KB1KNW
Christopher R Bergeron
39 Cinnamon Ridge Rd
Somersworth NH 03878

Call Sign: KB1COQ
Michael R Mc Grane
9 Colonial Dr
Somersworth NH 03878

Call Sign: N1XW
Michael R Mc Grane
9 Colonial Dr
Somersworth NH 03878

Call Sign: WA1ZFH
Jean R Danforth
162 Colonial Village
Somersworth NH 03878

Call Sign: K1DWZ
Kenneth H King
24 Coombs Rd
Somersworth NH 03878

Call Sign: KA1CNJ
John F Craig
36 Cornfield Dr
Somersworth NH 03878

Call Sign: WA1IPD
Paul J Desharnais
22 Cote St
Somersworth NH 03878

Call Sign: N1ZBF
Andrew R Lavertu
42 Crystal Springs
Somersworth NH 03878

Call Sign: KE4EAV
Monique T Dillon
6 Davis St.
Somersworth NH 03878

Call Sign: N0UUC
Robert E Dillon Jr
6 Davis St.
Somersworth NH 03878

Call Sign: N1SHH
Edward N De Jesus
5 East St
Somersworth NH 03878

Call Sign: KE1EQ
Wayne N Maxwell
27 Francoeur Dr
Somersworth NH 03878

Call Sign: W1WNS
Wayne N Maxwell
27 Francoeur Dr
Somersworth NH 03878

Call Sign: KB1DTN
Robert S Buck
33 Green St
Somersworth NH 03878

Call Sign: W1MPY
William P Marvin
257 Green St
Somersworth NH 03878

Call Sign: KB1QMZ
Garry D Gerossie Jr
27 Hanson St
Somersworth NH 03878

Call Sign: K1SLM
Garry D Gerossie Jr
27 Hanson St
Somersworth NH 03878

Call Sign: N1VZT
Audrey J Metcalf
440 High St
Somersworth NH
038781011

Call Sign: KB1QPI
William R Bokesz
82 Indigo Hill Rd
Somersworth NH 03878

Call Sign: KA5VAW
Michael P Parma
8 Laurel Lane
Somersworth NH 03878

Call Sign: WN1Y
Leo F Cavanaugh
103 Main St
Somersworth NH 03878

Call Sign: KB1GMK
David A Bosley Jr
198 Main St
Somersworth NH 03878

Call Sign: KB1JQC
Leonard F Ames
362 Main St

Somersworth NH 03878

Call Sign: KE1FG
Marc R Deschenes
388 Main St Unit A
Somersworth NH 03878

Call Sign: KB1TDI
Pascal J Bertrand
26 Myrtle St
Somersworth NH 03878

Call Sign: KB1QHF
Karen P Lauze Md
27 Otis Rd
Somersworth NH 03878

Call Sign: AB1JB
Karen P Lauze Md
27 Otis Rd
Somersworth NH
038782313

Call Sign: KB1YN
William P Kram
34 Otis Rd
Somersworth NH
038782314

Call Sign: N1AUX
Denis J Hamel
36 Pleasant
Somersworth NH 03878

Call Sign: KB1GNT
Lois F Ambrose
1 Pond Rd
Somersworth NH 03878

Call Sign: N1VQC
Paul E Hebert
17 Prospect St
Somersworth NH 03878

Call Sign: KA1TIO

Ralph R Sawyer Iii
130 Rocky Hill Rd
Somersworth NH
038782817

Call Sign: KB1NIN
Douglas T Martin
107 Rt 16 B
Somersworth NH 03878

Call Sign: W1DMX
Douglas T Martin
107 Rt 16 B
Somersworth NH 03878

Call Sign: N1BNC
Nathaniel A Lee
74 Salmon Falls Rd
Somersworth NH 03878

Call Sign: KC1FF
Donald F Gelinas
49 South St
Somersworth NH 03878

Call Sign: KB1BSM
Carl M Fortier
6 Summer St
Somersworth NH 03878

Call Sign: N1MMI
Rodney M Berry
29 Third St
Somersworth NH 03878

Call Sign: KB1WGE
Stephen M Rielly
709 Tri City Rd
Somersworth NH 03878

Call Sign: KA1YZI
Bruce A Chamberlin
8 Tri City Rd Apt 12
Somersworth NH 03820

Call Sign: KA1BTV
Donald K Black
55 Union St
Somersworth NH 03878

Call Sign: KA1YSO
Paul R Dusseault
Somersworth NH 03878

## FCC Amateur Radio Licenses in South Acworth

Call Sign: KB1DIB
Joel Bishop
42 Bishop Rd
South Acworth NH 03607

Call Sign: N1YTA
Justin B Thyme
Tucker Rd
South Acworth NH 03607

## FCC Amateur Radio Licenses in South Effingham

Call Sign: N1YEE
Thomas E Green
South Effingham NH 03882

## FCC Amateur Radio Licenses in South Hampton

Call Sign: WA1OWH
Peter A Perkins Mr.
129 Hilldale Ave.
South Hampton NH 03827

Call Sign: W1KGH
Randall H Spooner
Locust St
South Hampton NH 03827

Call Sign: N1ZQG

Jonathan D Baker
304 Main Ave
South Hampton NH 03827

## FCC Amateur Radio Licenses in South Sutton

Call Sign: KC1SU
Robert L Nelson
33 Foxchase Rd
South Sutton NH 03273

Call Sign: KB1EDM
Douglas W Prince
98 Pound Rd
South Sutton NH 03273

Call Sign: KB1LRI
Chris M Roy
South Sutton NH 03273

## FCC Amateur Radio Licenses in South Tamworth

Call Sign: KA1BQN
Christopher B Moneypenny
86 Mountain Rd
South Tamworth NH 03883

Call Sign: KA1TIW
James W Caswell
Rfd Bearcamp Pond Rd
South Tamworth NH 03883

## FCC Amateur Radio Licenses in Spofford

Call Sign: KA1MDB
Steven A Fisher
Box 548
Spofford NH 03462

Call Sign: KK1CW
Walter H Lau

53 Cady Ln
Spofford NH 03462

Call Sign: KB4FAM
Jay Motley
360 Rt 9a
Spofford NH 03462

Call Sign: WA2VSN
Walter J Lewandowski
4 Zinn Rd
Spofford NH 03462

Call Sign: N1POC
Louise L Hebert
Spofford NH 03462

Call Sign: N1POD
Douglas M Hebert
Spofford NH 03462

Call Sign: WA1UNN
Leonard Goodnow
Spofford NH 034620213

Call Sign: KB1NWT
John F Angil Ii
Spofford NH 03462

## FCC Amateur Radio Licenses in Springfield

Call Sign: KB1ICR
William E Watkins
256 Phil Brick Hill
Springfield NH 03284

Call Sign: KB1EGH
Clayton R Wood
Springfield NH 03284

Call Sign: KD1P
Kenneth R Downs
Springfield NH 032840352

Call Sign: W1KRT
Kenneth R Downs
Springfield NH 032840352

Call Sign: KB1UMT
Wanda L Lapoint
Springfield NH 03284

## FCC Amateur Radio Licenses in Stark

Call Sign: N1PND
Richard F Daley Jr
3 Percy Peaks Estates
Stark NH 03582

Call Sign: KB1DZQ
James R Eich
800 Stark Hwy
Stark NH 035826309

Call Sign: KB1IZA
Dennis A Croteau
1279 Stark Hwy
Stark NH 03582

## FCC Amateur Radio Licenses in Stewartstown

Call Sign: KB1FFY
Robert J Weir
531 Piper Hill Rd
Stewartstown NH 03576

## FCC Amateur Radio Licenses in Stoddard

Call Sign: W1BYG
Frank W Hogg
Box 478e
Stoddard NH 03464

Call Sign: K1HYL
Oliver P Quist
64 Deer Run

Stoddard NH 03464

Call Sign: KB1JCO
James L Kelly
270 N Hidden Lake Rd
Stoddard NH 034644505

Call Sign: N1WRP
Walter A Champney
71 Rt 123
Stoddard NH 03464

Call Sign: KA1IEP
Charlotte H Pratt
615 Rt 9
Stoddard NH 03464

Call Sign: WA1DKL
Bradley C Pratt Sr
615 Rt 9
Stoddard NH 03464

Call Sign: K1QLW
Bradley C Pratt Sr
615 Rt 9
Stoddard NH 03464

Call Sign: KB1EJZ
Anthony W Woislaw
1063 Shed Hill Rd
Stoddard NH 03464

Call Sign: KB1GHB
David B Holmes
135 Shedd Hill Rd
Stoddard NH 03464

Call Sign: KD2SJ
Donald J Haenichen Jr
Stoddard NH 03464

Call Sign: N2YNZ
Maryellen Haenichen
Stoddard NH 03464

## FCC Amateur Radio Licenses in Strafford

Call Sign: KB1WBM
Todd B Scruton
673 First Crown Point Rd
Strafford NH 03884

Call Sign: WX1S
Alfred J Coelho
927 First Crown Point Rd
Strafford NH 03884

Call Sign: KA1CVB
Leon A Duval Iii
39 Jodi Ln
Strafford NH 03884

Call Sign: KB1VCU
Lynn Darnell
70 Lake Shore Dr
Strafford NH 03884

Call Sign: W1JFP
Calvin W Stiles
1283 Parker Mountain Rd.
#1
Strafford NH 038846333

Call Sign: N1UVZ
Alan R Hackert
48 Parshley Lane
Strafford NH 03884

Call Sign: KB1JSA
Jeanne M Hackert
48 Parshley Lane
Strafford NH 03884

Call Sign: KB1RGU
Alexander Hackert
48 Parshley Lane
Strafford NH 03884

Call Sign: W2JMH

Jeanne M Hackert
48 Parshley Lane
Strafford NH 03884

Call Sign: WA1PTU
David J Carroll
211 Province Rd
Strafford NH 03884

Call Sign: W1JRO
Merrill F Steward
Province Rd
Strafford NH 03884

Call Sign: KB1DTQ
David F Palmer
216 Roller Coaster Rd
Strafford NH 03884

Call Sign: N1WUU
John M Cronk
20 Shiere Way
Strafford NH 03884

Call Sign: KB1OQL
LINDA J Mcphee SMITH
67 WHIG HILL Rd
Strafford NH 03884

Call Sign: K1OFB
Joseph F Carriere
Strafford NH 03884

Call Sign: KB1TY
Rimantas P Pauliukonis
Strafford NH 038840321

Call Sign: WA1BDL
Ronald W Foote
Strafford NH 03884

Call Sign: N1KTI
Arthur E Cook
66 Potato Hill Rd
Stratford NH 03590

## FCC Amateur Radio Licenses in Stratham

Call Sign: KA1FWT
Eric K Long
3 Alderwood Dr
Stratham NH 03885

Call Sign: W1WIW
Paul F Allen
66 Brookside Dr
Stratham NH 03885

Call Sign: KB1OMS
Charles M Landry
3 Brown Ave
Stratham NH 03885

Call Sign: KB1QOB
Joanne C Gretter
21 Butterfield Lane
Stratham NH 03885

Call Sign: KB1LSY
Bruce R Gretter
21 Butterfield Ln
Stratham NH 03885

Call Sign: KA1A
Donald L Meeves
18 Crestview Ter
Stratham NH 03885

Call Sign: K1AC
Donald L Meeves
18 Crestview Ter
Stratham NH 03885

Call Sign: KB1YJ
William F Clapp
31 Crestview Ter
Stratham NH 03885

Call Sign: KE1FA

Paul Wolf
19 Doe Run
Stratham NH 038852308

Call Sign: KB1EHB
Jeremy D Riecks
18 Doe Run Ln
Stratham NH 03885

Call Sign: KA1JV
David T Wimberly
1 Drury Plains Rd
Stratham NH 03885

Call Sign: K1EWK
Edward J Knapp Jr
22 Dumbarton Oaks
Stratham NH 03885

Call Sign: KB1LBU
Michael J Curtis
62 Dumbarton Oaks
Stratham NH 03885

Call Sign: N1ZWW
David M Sallet
88 High St
Stratham NH 03885

Call Sign: WA1UVX
Robert C Mc Carthy
133 High St
Stratham NH 03885

Call Sign: N1HNE
Justin T Horan Jr
2 Holmgren Crt
Stratham NH 03885

Call Sign: KB1NMD
Norman E Krebs
9 Jana Ln
Stratham NH 038852109

Call Sign: K1SFD

Norman E Krebs
9 Jana Ln
Stratham NH 038852109

Call Sign: KB1MNT
Roger B Thompson
4 Joyce Ln
Stratham NH 03885

Call Sign: K1PV
Roger B Thompson
4 Joyce Ln
Stratham NH 03885

Call Sign: NR1SS
David D Ball
10 Kirriemuir Rd
Stratham NH 03885

Call Sign: N1TOP
Malcolm G Cole Iii
12 Lamington Hill Rd
Stratham NH 03885

Call Sign: KA1DON
Mildred A Polito
6 Linwood Ln
Stratham NH 03885

Call Sign: WB1HJO
Charles A Polito Jr
6 Linwood Ln.
Stratham NH 03885

Call Sign: W3MAP
Mildred A Polito
6 Linwood Ln.
Stratham NH 03885

Call Sign: W3CAP
Charles A Polito Jr
6 Linwood Ln.
Stratham NH 03885

Call Sign: K1RTO

Scott M Standen
2 Long Hill Rd.
Stratham NH 03885

Call Sign: N1LTJ
David E Schricker
26 Pinewood Dr
Stratham NH 03885

Call Sign: WB1DHO
Raymond D Parsons Jr
355 Portsmouth Ave
Stratham NH 03885

Call Sign: KB1DTP
Timothy P Loomis
61 River Rd 2
Stratham NH 03885

Call Sign: WA1HOV
Barry L Watkins
4 Shirley Ln
Stratham NH 03885

Call Sign: N1CIO
R Lyndon Burnham Jr
1 Smith Farm Rd
Stratham NH 03885

Call Sign: KB1SGP
Blake A Nadilo
83 Stratham Heights Rd
Stratham NH 03885

Call Sign: KB1SGQ
Cory P Nadilo
83 Stratham Heights Rd
Stratham NH 03885

Call Sign: KB1SGR
Rudy Nadilo
83 Stratham Heights Rd
Stratham NH 03885

Call Sign: KB1SGV

Heather C Pierce
83 Stratham Heights Rd
Stratham NH 03885

Call Sign: N1FFA
Daniel A Parcell
37 Thornhill Rd
Stratham NH 03885

Call Sign: KB1UPT
Christopher M Pierce
111 Tidewater Farm Rd
Stratham NH 03885

Call Sign: KB1PMT
Raymond Dalrymple
39 Vineyard Dr
Stratham NH 03885

Call Sign: KB1JCB
Benjamin D Long
2 William Circle
Stratham NH 03885

### FCC Amateur Radio Licenses in Sugar Hill

Call Sign: KA2UDQ
Charles E Chase
115 Beaver Pond Trail
Sugar Hill NH 03586

Call Sign: K4FNJ
Robert T Brigman
23 Butternut Lane
Sugar Hill NH 03586

Call Sign: WA1YKM
Robert A Baumer
111 Nason Rd
Sugar Hill NH 03585

Call Sign: WA1CLK
Robert A Baumer
111 Nason Rd

Sugar Hill NH 03585

Call Sign: W1GJG
Glen A Parker
88 Streeter Pond Dr
Sugar Hill NH 03586

### FCC Amateur Radio Licenses in Sullivan

Call Sign: WB1CKZ
James J Wilder
Apple Hill Rd
Sullivan NH 03445

Call Sign: WS1A
Robert L Hummel
103 Gilsum Rd
Sullivan NH 03445

Call Sign: AB1EY
David W Swett
159 South Rd
Sullivan NH 03445

Call Sign: K1XYL
Gail E Hummel
Sullivan NH 03445

Call Sign: N1XOQ
George A Hall
Sullivan NH 034450084

Call Sign: KB1LBW
Gwendolyn E Hummel
Sullivan NH 03445

Call Sign: KB1SWX
George A Hall
Sullivan NH 03445

### FCC Amateur Radio Licenses in Sunapee

Call Sign: N1BDX

Eric P Franzen
Box 235
Sunapee NH 03782

Call Sign: WB1CNQ
Vernon E Hause
Box 452
Sunapee NH 03782

Call Sign: N1XRY
Dori A Lyman
11 Garnet St Apt 21
Sunapee NH 03782

Call Sign: KB1SKL
Thomas K Perron
94 Hamel Rd
Sunapee NH 03782

Call Sign: KA8WEO
Ryan D Crawford
4 Harding Hill Rd
Sunapee NH 037823816

Call Sign: K1HKR
Roger O Topliffe
458 Jobs Creek Rd
Sunapee NH 037823110

Call Sign: KB1GZM
Sunapee Amateur Radio
Club
104 Lake Ave
Sunapee NH 03782

Call Sign: KC7UQU
Lloyd R Hensrude
110 Lake Ave
Sunapee NH 03782

Call Sign: KA1NYP
Steven I Marshall
1029 Main St
Sunapee NH 037823026

Call Sign: N1WRI
Karen L Marshall
1029 Main St
Sunapee NH 037823026

Call Sign: WA1SDJ
John G Rooney
114 Marys Rd
Sunapee NH 03782

Call Sign: KA1FFX
John L Gosselin
118 New Province Rd
Sunapee NH 03782

Call Sign: WA1FBC
Maurice E Collins
33 North Rd
Sunapee NH 03782

Call Sign: N1STC
Alan J Soucy
516 North Rd
Sunapee NH 03782

Call Sign: W1VLL
Barry S Smith
330 Nutting Rd
Sunapee NH 03782

Call Sign: K1YOT
Alan L Peterson
82 Pine Ridge Rd
Sunapee NH 03782

Call Sign: N1CIR
Robert R Boyd
648 Rt 103
Sunapee NH 037823719

Call Sign: N1DRE
Claire G Boyd
648 Rt 103
Sunapee NH 037823719

Call Sign: K1DNZ
Warren J Sanborn Jr
74 Sleeper Rd
Sunapee NH 03782

Call Sign: KB1ICP
Benjamin G Hawkins
32 Sunny Ln
Sunapee NH 03782

Call Sign: KB1ICQ
Ralph B Hawkins
32 Sunny Ln
Sunapee NH 03782

Call Sign: K1KXX
Theodore J Sandberg
9 Wendell St Box 842
Sunapee NH 03782

Call Sign: K1JY
Lindsay M Collins
Sunapee NH 03782

Call Sign: N1OAI
Ruth M Collins
Sunapee NH 037820374

Call Sign: KB1ERF
Jeffrey E Brode Jr
Sunapee NH 03782

Call Sign: W1VMW
Veterans Memorial Wireless
Association
Sunapee NH 03782

Call Sign: W1VN
Veterans Memorial Wireless
Association
Sunapee NH 03782

| FCC Amateur Radio Licenses in Suncook |
| --- |

Call Sign: KA1ISK
Donald G Hamlin
310 Buck St
Suncook NH 03275

Call Sign: KB1VSD
Robert F Drew
205 Friendship Ave
Suncook NH 03275

Call Sign: KB1TZD
Jordan R Fanny
40 Mason Ave
Suncook NH 03275

Call Sign: N1CUB
Richard L Harkness Jr
Swamp Rd
Suncook NH 03275

Call Sign: WB1CTP
Paul E Chouinard
Swiftwater Dr
Suncook NH 032751828

Call Sign: KA2BPD
Lawrence G Heslin
Suncook NH 03275

Call Sign: N1GZY
Richard F Lansing
Suncook NH 03275

Call Sign: KB1HOE
David J Berube
Suncook NH 03275

Call Sign: KA1VGM
Lawrence A Levesque
134 Farm Rd
Surry NH 03431

Call Sign: AD1T
Cheshire County Dx Arc
151 Joslin Rd
Surry NH 03431

Call Sign: KA1QFA
Becky J W Huntley
151 Joslin Rd
Surry NH 03431

Call Sign: WA1ZYX
Joel T Huntley
151 Joslin Rd
Surry NH 03431

Call Sign: K1TQY
Cheshire County Dx Arc
151 Joslin Rd
Surry NH 03431

Call Sign: KB1QPC
Tyler J Huntley
151 Joslin Rd
Surry NH 03431

Call Sign: KA1HZF
George E Davis
95 Pond Rd
Surry NH 03431

Call Sign: KA1FZL
David L Lawrence
311 Pond Rd
Surry NH 034318119

Call Sign: W1EFK
David L Lawrence
311 Pond Rd
Surry NH 034318119

Call Sign: KC1QP
Knud E M Keller
Rt 12a
Surry NH 03431

Call Sign: KB1HJ
Wayne E Donnelly
Rfd 1
Sutton NH 03221

Call Sign: NU1A
Frank A Finger
102 Main St
Sutton Mills NH 03221

Call Sign: WA1YSM
Michael H Thompson
4 Blake Rd
Swanzey NH 03446

Call Sign: K1ZO
Douglas H Scribner
80 California Brook Rd
Swanzey NH 03446

Call Sign: KB1VYY
Robert G Dettelback
35 Centerview Dr
Swanzey NH 03446

Call Sign: N1ELO
Eric A May
6 Colonial Village Dr 6
Swanzey NH 03431

Call Sign: WB1AOU
Dennis J Carlson
160 Highland Circle Rd
Swanzey NH 03446

Call Sign: KA1MTM

Charles W Matthews
114 Lat Ln
Swanzey NH 034463245

Call Sign: N1YSW
Peter J Kelley
14 Maple St
Swanzey NH 03446

Call Sign: N1NGH
Linda L Thompson
23 Maple St
Swanzey NH 03446

Call Sign: KB1UID
Kenneth A Ayers
783 Old Homestead Hwy
Swanzey NH 03446

Call Sign: KB1EAO
Eric R Smith
388 Old Homestead Hwy
Apt 2
Swanzey NH 03446

Call Sign: KA1IEO
Janice A Sevene
77 Old Leonard Farm Rd
Swanzey NH 03446

Call Sign: KB1JAB
James O Tremblay
41 Perry Lane
Swanzey NH 03446

Call Sign: KB1OWH
Brian B Bohannon
4 Stonefield Ln
Swanzey NH 03446

Call Sign: KB1HPK
Sheldon S Bailey
851 W Swanzey Rd #23
Swanzey NH 03446

Call Sign: KB1URV
John A Glezen
742 W Swanzey Rd 204
Swanzey NH 03446

**FCC Amateur Radio
Licenses in Tamworth**

Call Sign: KB1RJA
Robert Horton
302 Chinook Trail
Tamworth NH 03886

Call Sign: AA1KA
John F Barnes
237 Depot Rd
Tamworth NH 03886

Call Sign: KB9NJX
Norman L Purdy
394 Great Hill Rd
Tamworth NH 03886

Call Sign: K1OBI
Louis R Ouellette
Mason Hill Rd
Tamworth NH 03886

Call Sign: KB1LXZ
Stephen C Lapete
Tamworth NH 03886

Call Sign: K1AME
Stephen C Lapete
Tamworth NH 03886

**FCC Amateur Radio
Licenses in Temple**

Call Sign: N1CWV
Stanley P Maynard
Box 47
Temple NH 03084

Call Sign: N3NPR

Glenn W Nielsen
54 Brown Rd
Temple NH 03084

Call Sign: N1MZV
Thomas R Charron
43 Flanders Lane
Temple NH 03084

Call Sign: KB1FKU
Peter E Thorngren
374 General Miller Hwy
Temple NH 03084

Call Sign: KB1RSG
Peter E Thorngren
374 General Miller Hwy
Temple NH 03084

Call Sign: KB1RUC
Barbara A Thorngren
374 General Miller Hwy
Temple NH 03084

Call Sign: KA1SX
Edward C Holz
Hudson Rd
Temple NH 030840041

Call Sign: W1JAZ
Vicente P Orlandella
212 Webster Hwy
Temple NH 03084

Call Sign: N1PHT
David A Yetman
Temple NH 030840192

Call Sign: KB1NKA
Martin T Connolly
Temple NH 03084

**FCC Amateur Radio
Licenses in Thornton**

Call Sign: N1YRO
Hope Dubois
13 Mill Brook Rd
Thornton NH 03223

Call Sign: N1PMI
William D Rowell Sr
Box 307a
Tilton NH 03276

Call Sign: N1FVK
J E Goodin
14 Circle Dr
Tilton NH 03276

Call Sign: KB1RKI
Roland D Dubord
4 Deer St 7
Tilton NH 03276

Call Sign: WA1DCN
Gordon H Kendall
19 Foot Hill Way
Tilton NH 03276

Call Sign: KA1OAR
Carolyn L Ekstrom
78 High St
Tilton NH 03276

Call Sign: WB1GXM
Conrad V Ekstrom Jr
78 High St
Tilton NH 03276

Call Sign: WB1DRU
Lionel A La Branche
9 Linden Ave
Tilton NH 03276

Call Sign: KB1MXD
Michael E Radcliffe

4 Marsh Hill Circle
Tilton NH 03276

Call Sign: N1ZHE
David M Carney
5 Northbrook Dr
Tilton NH 03276

Call Sign: N1FQP
Vincent M Kondrotas Jr
19 Northbrook Rd
Tilton NH 03276

Call Sign: K1MRU
Arthur E Dubia
70 Park St
Tilton NH 03276

Call Sign: KA1FKM
Richard L Batchelder
School St
Tilton NH 03276

Call Sign: KB1RFW
Marion E Vertigans
7 Vista Heights
Tilton NH 03276

Call Sign: N1XCJ
Wayne G Holway
77 Vista Heights
Tilton NH 03276

Call Sign: N1KPO
Ronald J Majewski
432 West Main St
Tilton NH 03276

Call Sign: W1SQY
Walter E Kimball
67 White Rock Cir
Tilton NH 032765315

Call Sign: N1EMS
Jason M Valley

9 Windsor Dr
Tilton NH 03276

Call Sign: W1BDC
Robert G Sanborn
139 Winter St
Tilton NH 03276

Call Sign: N1UAS
Victor A Farrington
Tilton NH 03276

Call Sign: KB1IFO
Joseph P Mahoney
Tilton NH 03276

Call Sign: KB1OYD
Susan L Williams
Tilton NH 03276

Call Sign: KB1PKL
Corey M Richardson
20 Central Sq
Troy NH 03465

Call Sign: KA1BBG
Brian J Foley
1 Central Square Po Box 1
Troy NH 03465

Call Sign: N1XAX
Martha K Silander
29 Fitzwilliam Rd
Troy NH 03465

Call Sign: KB1DXX
Rebecca M Campbell
11 Garden Way
Troy NH 03465

Call Sign: KB1CZL
Kierstin S Clark

40 Mackey Rd
Troy NH 03465

Call Sign: N1KWM
Mark A Clark
40 Mackey Rd
Troy NH 03465

Call Sign: N1NHB
Taimi S Clark
40 Mackey Rd
Troy NH 03465

Call Sign: N1WYV
Ian D Clark
40 Mackey Rd
Troy NH 03465

Call Sign: KB1EAX
Ne Topband Cw Club
209 Marlboro Rd
Troy NH 034650741

Call Sign: KB1EGB
Nh Me Vt Cw Contest Club
209 Marlboro Rd
Troy NH 034650741

Call Sign: N1POB
Patrick W Keating
267 Marlboro Rd
Troy NH 03465

Call Sign: W1GSY
Ralph L Eaton
15 Thayer Ave Box 755
Troy NH 03465

Call Sign: KB1AJS
Jeremy A Smith
11 Tolman Rd
Troy NH 03465

Call Sign: N1ZM
Robert A Smith

11 Tolman Rd
Troy NH 03465

Call Sign: KB1PNH
Neal S Richardson
Troy NH 03465

## FCC Amateur Radio Licenses in Tuftonboro

Call Sign: N1TPJ
Raymond E Hurt
Willand Rd
Tuftonboro NH 03816

Call Sign: N1TPI
Evan L Lawrence Hurt
Willand Rd
Tuftonboro NH 03816

## FCC Amateur Radio Licenses in Twin Mountain

Call Sign: WA1YFF
George F Stickney
13 Ridgeview Dr
Twin Mountain NH 03595

Call Sign: WA1EIO
James L Simpson
Rt 3
Twin Mountain NH 03595

Call Sign: KB1KXK
Glenn C Werner
Twin Mountain NH 03595

Call Sign: K1PCB
Glenn C Werner
Twin Mountain NH 03595

Call Sign: KB1LKD
Antonia Werner
Twin Mountain NH 03595

## FCC Amateur Radio Licenses in Union

Call Sign: KA1RSU
Janet E Shea
Union NH 03887

Call Sign: KA1ULI
Shawn N Perry
Union NH 03887

Call Sign: N1HNH
Virginia C Mc Neil
Union NH 03887

## FCC Amateur Radio Licenses in Unity

Call Sign: N1UUG
Kim G White
148 Skyline Rd.
Unity NH 03773

## FCC Amateur Radio Licenses in Wakefield

Call Sign: KB1FKT
Donald L Dodge
259 Crew Rd
Wakefield NH 03872

Call Sign: W1MIV
Charles E Tamm
Hilltop Dr
Wakefield NH 03872

Call Sign: K1LHL
Paul H Mc Nally
Lovell Lake Rd
Wakefield NH 03872

Call Sign: AA7ZI
Alan R King
99 Pray Hill Rd

Wakefield NH 03872

Call Sign: KB1DCR
Tamika T Hebert
140 Blackjack Crossing
Walpole NH 03608

Call Sign: N1MSO
Bethany A Hebert
140 Blackjack Crossing
Walpole NH 03608

Call Sign: WK1P
Paul J Hebert
140 Blackjack Crossing
Walpole NH 03608

Call Sign: K1PH
Paul J Hebert
140 Blackjack Crossing
Walpole NH 03608

Call Sign: N1SCT
Richard J Larson Jr
142 Blackjack Crossing
Walpole NH 03608

Call Sign: WB1FOR
Alfred Bertin
Box 145
Walpole NH 03608

Call Sign: W1UJN
Almon E Welch
20 High St
Walpole NH 03608

Call Sign: KA3KIX
Dennis E Mc Clary
Pleasant St
Walpole NH 036080148

Call Sign: KB1CYK
Cecil B Taylor Iii
22 Prospect Hill Rd
Walpole NH 03608

Call Sign: KB1JHH
Anthony J R Goodhue
63 River Rd
Walpole NH 03608

Call Sign: N1ZCO
Peter R Provencher Sr
86 Scorill Rd
Walpole NH 03608

Call Sign: W1VSO
William L Brackett
25 South St
Walpole NH 036080604

Call Sign: AA1NC
Raymond W Kimberly
511 Valley Rd
Walpole NH 03608

Call Sign: KA1TLP
Sandra J Kimberly
511 Valley Rd
Walpole NH 03608

Call Sign: KA1KST
James B Whittaker
Walpole NH 03608

Call Sign: KC0DBB
Colin R Skelding
Walpole NH 036080398

Call Sign: KB1JDS
Thomas A Bensenhaver
Walpole NH 03608

Call Sign: W1IRQ
Kenneth B Klinedinst
94 Bean Rd
Warner NH 03278

Call Sign: KC1NCR
Jeffrey A Cummings
268 Bean Rd
Warner NH 03278

Call Sign: K0YLW
Jeffrey A Cummings
268 Bean Rd
Warner NH 03278

Call Sign: KA1CJI
Michael P Saltmarsh
297 Bean Rd
Warner NH 03278

Call Sign: KC0NCR
Jeffrey A Cummings
268 Bean Rd.
Warner NH 03278

Call Sign: KB1MWS
Daniel S Coolidge
108 Bible Hill Lane
Warner NH 03278

Call Sign: KB1VJQ
David L Gallipeau
246 Birch Hill Rd
Warner NH 03278

Call Sign: N1PHZ
Philip H Doughty
Box 71
Warner NH 03278

Call Sign: KB1EOM
John W Johnson
Collins Rd
Warner NH 03278

Call Sign: KB1JPC
Michael D Sulas
6 Farrel Loop Apt 3
Warner NH 03278

Call Sign: WA2TDC
Bruce H Cudney
757 Kearsarge Mountain Rd
Warner NH 03278

Call Sign: W1BHC
Bruce H Cudney
757 Kearsarge Mountain Rd
Warner NH 03278

Call Sign: KA2DYC
Clara L Burroughs
845 Kearsarge Mountain Rd
Warner NH 03278

Call Sign: AK2X
Paul Migliore
Kearsarge Mtn Rd
Warner NH 03278

Call Sign: KA7RKR
Robert E Koski
278 Pumpkin Hill Rd
Warner NH 03278

Call Sign: AB1AA
Robert E Koski
278 Pumpkin Hill Rd
Warner NH 03278

Call Sign: N1KTP
David L Connors
90 Quimby Rd
Warner NH 032785000

Call Sign: KA1FPJ
Dzintra M Alksnitis
805 Rt 103 East Unit 6
Warner NH 03278

Call Sign: KB1ICS
Lawrence J Richard
444 Rt 103w
Warner NH 03278

Call Sign: N1UY
Chris M Roy
61 W Roby District Rd.
Warner NH 03278

Call Sign: KB1QFE
Frederick Moe
36 West Man St
Warner NH 03278

Call Sign: K1MOE
Frederick E Moe
36 West Man St
Warner NH 03278

Call Sign: KA1KNU
Debi Reger
Warner NH 03278

Call Sign: KA1KNV
Paul V Gunter
Warner NH 03278

## FCC Amateur Radio Licenses in Warrne

Call Sign: N1AYR
Richard N Cadieux
200 D South Main St
Warren NH 03279

Call Sign: WA1LJJ
Andrew G Bourassa
64 Lund Lane
Warren NH 03279

Call Sign: W1LJJ
Andrew G Bourassa
64 Lund Lane
Warren NH 03279

Call Sign: KB1GNG
Suzanne M Flagg
66 Mountain Meadow Rd
Warren NH 03279

Call Sign: N1HWU
Fred Heywood Iii
Warren NH 03279

## FCC Amateur Radio Licenses in Washington

Call Sign: K2DYG
Edward I Rumrill
Ashuelot Dr
Washington NH 03280

Call Sign: KA1PWL
Kenneth E Mc Neill
105 Bradford Springs Rd
Washington NH 03280

Call Sign: AA1HM
Robert J Zahn
494 Highland Haven Rd.
Washington NH 03280

Call Sign: W1ORE
John R Mc Kinnon
16 Mc Kinnon Rd
Washington NH 032800282

Call Sign: N4HTC
Franclyn B Garvin
85 Point Rd
Washington NH 03280

Call Sign: KB1NMV
Lindley C Rankine
1388 South Main St
Washington NH 03280

Call Sign: KA1HCN
Robert J Wright

Washington NH 03280

Call Sign: N1TNY
John Bates Iii
Washington NH 03280

Call Sign: WB2NAS
Thomas E Talpey
Washington NH 03280

Call Sign: KB1KYQ
Veterans Memorial Wireless
Association
Washington NH 03280

Call Sign: NT1I
John Bates Iii
Washington NH 03280

Call Sign: KB1WVI
Stepehen A Clarke
Washington NH 03280

## FCC Amateur Radio Licenses in Waterville Valley

Call Sign: KD2VX
Kathryn A Finch
21 Tripyramid Way #25
Waterville Valley NH
032150300

Call Sign: KF1WV
Kathryn A Finch
21 Tripyramid Way #25
Waterville Valley NH
032150300

## FCC Amateur Radio Licenses in Weare

Call Sign: K1QQ
Kenneth W Cronyn Iii
81 Anns Dr

Weare NH 03281

Call Sign: N1VQB
Robert A Heath Jr
28 Beech Hill Rd
Weare NH 03281

Call Sign: KB1NS
Raymond P Ainsworth
94 Beech Hill Rd
Weare NH 032814315

Call Sign: KB1OEH
Lana L Doughty
33 Blake Rd
Weare NH 03281

Call Sign: N1RNB
Freddy A J Cassier
60 Bogue Rd
Weare NH 03281

Call Sign: N1FXU
Roland J Dufour
164 Bogue Rd
Weare NH 032815600

Call Sign: N1SCP
Geert R Hoylaerts Conrad
60 Boque Rd
Weare NH 03281

Call Sign: N1TBG
Marleen R Y Van Huffel
60 Boque Rd
Weare NH 03281

Call Sign: N1PKJ
Brad R Barry
11 Boulder Hill Rd
Weare NH 03281

Call Sign: W1UNV
Donald E Thomson
139 Center Rd

Weare NH 03281

Call Sign: KC0DXJ
Alice R Morris
146 Colby Rd A
Weare NH 032815505

Call Sign: KI0CU
Paul W Marsh
146 Colby Rd A
Weare NH 032815505

Call Sign: KB1THO
Wayne R Davis
62 Collins Landing Rd 66
Weare NH 03281

Call Sign: KB1ISM
Stephen A Bourget
401 Concord Stage Rd
Weare NH 03281

Call Sign: KB1MXH
Rudolph D Bourget
401 Concord Stage Rd
Weare NH 03281

Call Sign: KB1KRI
Brian P Glidden
492 Concord Stage Rd
Weare NH 03281

Call Sign: KB1JXO
William E Dunbar
650 Concord Stage Rd
Weare NH 03281

Call Sign: N1HDF
William E Dunbar
650 Concord Stage Rd
Weare NH 03281

Call Sign: N1GQT
Henry E Sippel

732 Concord Stage Rd Lot
30
Weare NH 03281

Call Sign: N1KOV
Wilfred A Michaud
35 Cottage Rd.
Weare NH 03281

Call Sign: KB1OGB
Corey A Heath
80 Craney Hill Rd
Weare NH 03281

Call Sign: N1FBY
Alan E Fronk
93 Craney Hill Rd
Weare NH 03281

Call Sign: N1WWW
Alan R Sanborn
57 Etta Ln
Weare NH 03281

Call Sign: N1VRS
John E Siemanowicz Sr
17 Fieldstone Cir
Weare NH 03281

Call Sign: KB1SGS
Aaron T Nelson
57 Fieldstone Cir 3
Weare NH 03281

Call Sign: K1BX
Arthur K Hambleton
95 Guy S Lane
Weare NH 03281

Call Sign: KR5X
Hambleton Family Arc
95 Guys Lane
Weare NH 03281

Call Sign: KB1STB

Eric S Hambleton
95 Guys Lane
Weare NH 03281

Call Sign: KB1STC
Scott W Hambleton
95 Guys Lane
Weare NH 03281

Call Sign: KB1HID
David A Melton
138 Jewett Rd
Weare NH 03281

Call Sign: KB1MXA
Lawrence F Ouellette
200 Maplewold Rd
Weare NH 03281

Call Sign: N2JIP
Howard A Livingston
242 Maplewood Rd
Weare NH 03281

Call Sign: KB1SCN
Marc N Gervais
207 Mountain Rd
Weare NH 03281

Call Sign: KA1KDC
William W Fowler
124 Mountain School Rd
Weare NH 03281

Call Sign: N1JHG
Susan P Fowler
124 Mountain School Rd
Weare NH 03281

Call Sign: N1JKB
Leo R Brooks
80 Oak Ridge Rd
Weare NH 03281

Call Sign: N1QGT

Kenneth R Averill
417 Old Francestown Rd
Weare NH 03281

Call Sign: AB1GW
Douglas O Alwine
297 Quaker St
Weare NH 03281

Call Sign: KB1DIU
Lawrence A Damour Jr
159 Reservoir Dr
Weare NH 03281

Call Sign: N1PHV
Lawrence A Damour Sr
159 Reservoir Dr
Weare NH 03281

Call Sign: KB1GIK
Concord Fire Dept Arc
159 Reservoir Dr
Weare NH 03281

Call Sign: K1CFD
Concord Fire Dept Arc
159 Reservoir Dr
Weare NH 03281

Call Sign: N2AEV
Henry E Weeden
638 Reservoir Dr Box 30
Weare NH 03281

Call Sign: KB1IVZ
Robert D Kyer
401 Riverdale Rd
Weare NH 03281

Call Sign: N1QXF
Frank B Tillotson Jr
34 Sugar Hill Estates
Weare NH 03281

Call Sign: K1LYV

John N Van Loendersloot
201 Walker Hill Rd
Weare NH 03281

Call Sign: KB1OEF
Remi L Lisee
54 Wallingford Terrace
Weare NH 03281

Call Sign: W1RLL
Remi L Lisee
54 Wallingford Terrace
Weare NH 03281

Call Sign: W1ECC
Edward C Couture
47 Woodbury Rd
Weare NH 03281

Call Sign: W1JS
John E Sheehy Jr
Weare NH 032810400

Call Sign: W1MRQ
Ernest L Gray
Weare NH 03281

Call Sign: KB1KRJ
Diane M Lusardi
Weare NH 03281

Call Sign: KB1TYZ
Keith A Fellbaum
Weare NH 03281

**FCC Amateur Radio
Licenses in Webster**

Call Sign: KB1FSL
Jermey E Blaiklock
82 Detour Rd
Webster NH 03303

Call Sign: N1WJQ
Don M Hook

443 Gerrish Rd
Webster NH 03303

Call Sign: KB1TMZ
Sandra L Weld
8 Penacook Circle
Webster NH 03303

Call Sign: N1TFB
Lee W Demarest
266 Pond Hill Rd
Webster NH 03303

**FCC Amateur Radio
Licenses in Weirs Beach**

Call Sign: KA1JVS
Robert E Gorman
178 Channel Ln
Weirs Beach NH 03247

Call Sign: WB1FYE
Edward L O Hearn
1 Pendleton Beach Rd
Weirs Beach NH 03246

Call Sign: AA1EO
Edward L O Hearn
1 Pendleton Beach Rd
Weirs Beach NH 03246

Call Sign: N1HSS
Bruce H Smith
Weirs Beach NH 03247

**FCC Amateur Radio
Licenses in Wentworth**

Call Sign: N1UJI
Brian A Du Bois
469 Atwell Hill Rd
Wentworth NH 03282

Call Sign: W1QR
Richard N Cadieux

33 Dancing Bones Rd
Wentworth NH 03282

Call Sign: KB1EOU
Beverly F Walker
578 N Dorchester Rd
Wentworth NH 03282

**FCC Amateur Radio
Licenses in West
Chesterfield**

Call Sign: W1JEV
Alfred A Dascomb
461 Gulf Rd
West Chesterfield NH
03466

Call Sign: K1BWC
Gordon M Scallion
79 Spaulding Hill Rd
West Chesterfield NH
03466

Call Sign: KB1DXF
Gary E Penfield
24 Stoneleigh Hts
West Chesterfield NH
03466

Call Sign: N1BGV
Lowell Laporte
West Chesterfield NH
03466

Call Sign: N1SJK
Norman C Cobb Jr
West Chesterfield NH
034660036

**FCC Amateur Radio
Licenses in West Franklin**

Call Sign: N1PKD
Arlin K Taylor

9 Pemigewasset St
West Franklin NH 03235

Call Sign: N1PKE
Kevin P Feeley
61 Range Rd
West Franklin NH 03235

Call Sign: N1WIZ
Robert P Towne Sr
123 South Main St.  Apt.4
West Franklin NH 03235

Call Sign: N1TBE
Karen L Plummer
Box 82c
West Lebanon NH 03784

Call Sign: WB1EIB
Thomas H Andersen Iii
44 Crafts Ave
West Lebanon NH
037841112

Call Sign: KA8YRU
Theodore L Beach
15 Estabrook Cir
West Lebanon NH
037841201

Call Sign: KB1CMB
Russell L Pool
Longley Heys Poverty Ln
West Lebanon NH 03874

Call Sign: KD4PIE
Sally S Dean
5 Mack Ave
West Lebanon NH 03784

Call Sign: N0JSR
James C Dean

5 Mack Ave
West Lebanon NH 03784

Call Sign: N1CIV
Robert P Jacobson
94 Main St
West Lebanon NH 03784

Call Sign: KB1JYR
Regina Y Watkins
94 Main St
West Lebanon NH 03784

Call Sign: N1SMF
Stanley Liang
100 Maple St
West Lebanon NH 03784

Call Sign: N1SMG
Linda S Liang
100 Maple St
West Lebanon NH 03784

Call Sign: KB0QVT
George P Thomas Jr
4 Meadowbrook Village #2
West Lebanon NH 03784

Call Sign: KB1VAS
Gary Chiasson
3 Timothy St
West Lebanon NH 03784

Call Sign: N1TPQ
Jeffrey O Clayman
39 Village Green
West Lebanon NH 03784

Call Sign: N1MSP
David M Henderson
West Lebanon NH 03784

Call Sign: W1USJ
William V Jarvis
West Lebanon NH 03784

Call Sign: KB1ELY
Michael G Balog
West Lebanon NH 03784

Call Sign: KA1WTL
John E Rines
Box 19
West Nottingham NH
03291

Call Sign: N1NFX
Elwood A Bearce Jr
14 Old Mill Rd
West Ossipee NH
038900169

Call Sign: WA1IRC
Donald Halpin
Rte 16
West Ossipee NH 03890

Call Sign: KA1IYM
William E Clegg Jr
West Ossipee NH 03890

Call Sign: KA1RJZ
Zachary R Smith
West Ossipee NH 03890

Call Sign: N1LCS
Herbert J Ross
West Ossipee NH 03890

Call Sign: N1JCB
Leonard E Shurtleff
West Ossipee NH 03890

Call Sign: AB1PW
Walter A Brown
West Ossipee NH 03890

### FCC Amateur Radio Licenses in West Peterboro

Call Sign: KB1NKF
Carl R Moberg
18 Altemont St
West Peterboro NH 03468

### FCC Amateur Radio Licenses in West Springfield

Call Sign: N1LVE
Francis E La Point
West Springfield NH 03284

### FCC Amateur Radio Licenses in West Swanzey

Call Sign: N1PSX
Theodore P Bothwell
37 Centerview Dr
West Swanzey NH 03469

Call Sign: N1BAE
Ruth S Pratt
99 Lat Ln
West Swanzey NH 03469

Call Sign: WA1YZN
Bruce R Bohannon
315 Matthews Rd
West Swanzey NH 03446

Call Sign: KA1DHA
Kenneth R Sevene
77 Old Leonard Farm Rd
West Swanzey NH 03446

Call Sign: W1ARH

Kenneth R Sevene
77 Old Leonard Farm Rd
West Swanzey NH 03446

Call Sign: WA1OEV
Italo L Giovanella
155 Partridgeberry Ln
West Swanzey NH 03469

Call Sign: WD4GAM
Arthur N Graves Sr
11 Pine St Extension
West Swanzey NH 03469

Call Sign: KB2HPO
Michael R Carey
47 Swanzey Lake Rd
West Swanzey NH
034462552

Call Sign: KB1CYI
Dylan H Bush
Watson Rd
West Swanzey NH 03469

Call Sign: KB5STC
George A Dragoon
West Swanzey NH 03469

### FCC Amateur Radio Licenses in Westmoreland

Call Sign: W1BHL
Wayne G Thompson
37 Capron Rd
Westmoreland NH 03467

Call Sign: KA2RWT
Edward J Kaliski
474 Glebe Rd
Westmoreland NH 03467

Call Sign: WB3KJV
James M Clark
18 Old Morre Rd

Westmoreland NH 03467

Call Sign: KB1SFO
Allen J Parker
1284 River Rd North
Westmoreland NH 03467

Call Sign: KB1AJP
Allen J Parker
1284 River Rd North
Westmoreland NH 03467

Call Sign: WS1V
Clinton Spaar Iii
428 Route 63
Westmoreland NH
034674419

Call Sign: KA1VCC
Rufus J Stacey
Rte 63
Westmoreland NH 03467

Call Sign: KC1TS
David B Perrin Jr
Westmoreland NH 03467

### FCC Amateur Radio Licenses in Whitefield

Call Sign: KA1LWL
Elaine B Koczur
Box 20
Whitefield NH 03598

Call Sign: N1SHT
Zbigniew Mroczko
Box 621
Whitefield NH 03598

Call Sign: KA1QJP
Virginia L Poole
Box 631
Whitefield NH 03598

Call Sign: N1HSG
John F Poole
Box 631
Whitefield NH 03598

Call Sign: KB1RIX
Kelley A Sweeney
50 Brown St
Whitefield NH 03598

Call Sign: WX2L
Timothy R Havens
43 Crane Rd
Whitefield NH 03598

Call Sign: N1RZ
Timothy R Havens
43 Crane Rd
Whitefield NH 03598

Call Sign: NA1CW
Timothy R Havens
43 Crane Rd
Whitefield NH 03598

Call Sign: KB1AFP
Joseph P Elgosin
19 Elm St
Whitefield NH 03598

Call Sign: KB1KDB
Robert A Mitten
20 Greenwood St
Whitefield NH 035983615

Call Sign: N1PCE
John E Ryan
29 Greenwood St
Whitefield NH 035980232

Call Sign: KB1RXK
Sam L Desjardins
39 Jefferson Rd
Whitefield NH 03598

Call Sign: KS1S
Stanley A Holz
117 Jefferson Rd
Whitefield NH 035989709

Call Sign: KB1FF
Clifford W Vendt
30 Maple St
Whitefield NH 03598

Call Sign: KB1VDR
John D Stock
45 Maple St
Whitefield NH 03598

Call Sign: N1BAP
John R Goodwin
9 Park St
Whitefield NH 03598

Call Sign: N1POA
Linda B Goodwin
17 Park St
Whitefield NH 03598

Call Sign: K1HNY
Arthur E Little
Whitefield NH 03598

Call Sign: KB1GXZ
Joseph E Jackson
Whitefield NH 03598

Call Sign: KB1KJG
Kristen G Van Bergen-
Buteau
Whitefield NH 03598

Call Sign: W1FVB
Frister Van Bergen
Whitefield NH 03598

Call Sign: N1KBO
Michael M Landry
22 View St.

Whitefield, NH 03598

FCC Amateur Radio
Licenses in Wilmont

Call Sign: KB1ICN
Randolph Prydekker
77 Atwood Rd
Wilmot NH 032874408

Call Sign: KB1EPM
Kristi S Upton
115 French Rd
Wilmot NH 03287

Call Sign: KF1Y
Stephen H Pink
59 Grace Rd
Wilmot NH 03287

Call Sign: KB1PDJ
Matthew M Franklin
326 Nh Rte 4a
Wilmot NH 03287

Call Sign: KB1ICO
Richard L Dumais
970 Rt 4a
Wilmot NH 03287

Call Sign: N1OGR
Peter L Burghardt
195 Village Rd
Wilmot NH 03287

Call Sign: KB1QFF
James D Fogg
18 Watershed Lane
Wilmot NH 03287

Call Sign: KB1EFB
Ian H Locke
7 White Pond Rd
Wilmot NH 03287

Call Sign: WA1NPZ
Robert N Principato
Wilmot NH 03287

Call Sign: AB1OH
Michael P Pelletier
Wilmot NH 03287

Call Sign: NM2G
Michael P Pelletier
Wilmot NH 03287

## FCC Amateur Radio Licenses in Wilmot Flat

Call Sign: N1TZP
Gerald W Trombley
7 Pancake St
Wilmot Flat NH 03287

## FCC Amateur Radio Licenses in Wilton

Call Sign: KA1DJS
Theodore F Brigham
476 Abbot Hill Rd
Wilton NH 03086

Call Sign: N1EVQ
Robert Kaladish
668 Abbot Hill Rd
Wilton NH 03086

Call Sign: KB1WIG
Alison Kaladish
668 Abbot Hill Rd
Wilton NH 03086

Call Sign: W1NLA
William J Mc Keown
Abbot Hill Rd
Wilton NH 03086

Call Sign: KA1IXM
Walter F Gardner

Box 103
Wilton NH 03086

Call Sign: KB1NGF
Donald R Lebrun
189 Burton Highway
Wilton NH 03086

Call Sign: KB1VXG
James A Kofalt
46 Celts Way
Wilton NH 03086

Call Sign: N1ZHB
Keith S Knight
309 Curtis Farm Rd
Wilton NH 03086

Call Sign: KA1GOV
Alexander A Lo Verme
85 Holt Rd
Wilton NH 030865139

Call Sign: K1VWJ
Richard L Searle
555 Lyndeborough Center Rd
Wilton NH 03086

Call Sign: WB1AKE
Dee Ann M Dubois
55 Maple St
Wilton NH 03086

Call Sign: N1MZW
Lawrence M Duval
117 Maple St
Wilton NH 03086

Call Sign: KA1KXL
Bruce C Bourdon
76 Marden Rd
Wilton NH 030865322

Call Sign: KB1MAY

Denis E Cote
963 Mason Rd
Wilton NH 03086

Call Sign: KB1PYF
Mark A Hastings
17 Peirce Ln
Wilton NH 03086

Call Sign: WB9TSZ
Richard F Thompson
59 Putnam Hill Rd
Wilton NH 03086

Call Sign: K1HE
Richard F Thompson
59 Putnam Hill Rd
Wilton NH 03086

Call Sign: KA1HLI
John C Baymore
22 Riverbend Way
Wilton NH 03086

Call Sign: KA1DQN
Erwin G Kann
266 Russell Hill Rd
Wilton NH 030860456

Call Sign: WA1RAJ
Carl D Walker
11 Samanthas Way
Wilton NH 03086

Call Sign: KT1F
Ross N Keatinge
29 Sleepy Hollow
Wilton NH 03086

Call Sign: KC1RM
James A Labrecque
87 Stiles Farm Rd
Wilton NH 03086

Call Sign: W1GMG

Robert K Jeffers
10 Stoney Brook Dr
Wilton NH 03086

Call Sign: KB1IHB
Joshua J Pieterse
227 Temple Rd
Wilton NH 03086

Call Sign: K1HDP
Winston L Center
Wilton NH 030860193

Call Sign: K1RIS
Richard L Sharkey
Wilton NH 03086

Call Sign: KA1TBY
Daniel St Laurent
Wilton NH 03086

Call Sign: KA1TJF
John F Shea
Wilton NH 03086

Call Sign: KB1CLQ
Chris C Caiazzi
Wilton NH 030860355

Call Sign: KB1GXM
Kate P Graumann
Wilton NH 03086

## FCC Amateur Radio Licenses in Winchester

Call Sign: WB1HJX
Gordon R Anderson
21a Richmond St
Winchester NH 03470

Call Sign: KB1KSF
Stanislaus J Wojnowski
124 B Keene Rd
Winchester NH 03470

Call Sign: KA1REL
Steve M Bonski
112 Back Ashvelot Rd
Winchester NH 03470

Call Sign: W1QWJ
Richard B Stevens
110 Bolton Rd
Winchester NH 034702602

Call Sign: KB1OPE
Alexander F Kulas
371 Burt Hill Rd
Winchester NH 03470

Call Sign: N1YXJ
Randy H Carlstrom
32 Goamko Dr
Winchester NH 03470

Call Sign: N1ICD
Gregory R Chappell
29 Kapper Dr
Winchester NH 03470

Call Sign: WB1HGT
Louis A Birtz
203 Manninghill Rd
Winchester NH 03470

Call Sign: N1XSQ
Kathleen L Hebert
260 S Scofield Mtn Rd
Winchester NH 03470

Call Sign: N1XWZ
Jennifer M Hebert
260 Scofield Mountain Rd
Winchester NH 03470

Call Sign: KB1EBN
Bruce J Golinski
260 Scofield Mtn Rd
Winchester NH 03470

Call Sign: W1NAC
Daniel E Clark
52 Warwick Rd  Apt 111
Winchester NH 03470

Call Sign: KB1SMS
Arlene W Crowell
8 Winchester Rd
Winchester NH 03470

Call Sign: N1VPB
Donald H Barrett
Winchester NH 03470

Call Sign: W9YRH
Dean W Dixon
Winchester NH 03470

Call Sign: W1VK
Dean W Dixon
Winchester NH 03470

## FCC Amateur Radio Licenses in Windham

Call Sign: WR1F
Srdjan Krstanovic
19 Aladdin Rd
Windham NH 03087

Call Sign: WA1YPK
Thomas M Nolan
12 Alpine Rd
Windham NH 03087

Call Sign: KB1LJY
Karen A Lambert
7 Appleton Rd
Windham NH 03087

Call Sign: KA1REN
Karen A Lambert
7 Appleton Rd
Windham NH 03087

Call Sign: N1IK
Brian M Lambert
7 Appleton Rd
Windham NH 03087

Call Sign: WA1YHO
Gary S Dallas
4 Aspen St
Windham NH 03087

Call Sign: KA1API
Jonathan L Kaplan
13 Atlantic Rd
Windham NH 03087

Call Sign: N1RD
Jeffrey D Struven
41 Blossom Rd
Windham NH 03087

Call Sign: AE1D
William K Mc Nally
7 Blueberry Rd
Windham NH 03087

Call Sign: KA1WHN
John P Jones Iii
6 Bristol Hill Rd
Windham NH 03087

Call Sign: WB9IIT
Stephen M Sirota
24 Brookview Rd
Windham NH 03087

Call Sign: K1DLM
David L Merchant
18 Burnham Rd
Windham NH 03087

Call Sign: K1QOB
Peter J Anderson
1 Cardinal Rd
Windham NH 03087

Call Sign: WA1Z
Robert G Raymond
4 Cardinal Rd
Windham NH 03087

Call Sign: N1FNX
Douglas M Chin
3 Carr Hill Rd.
Windham NH 03087

Call Sign: KB1TQN
Wayne A Moore Jr
131 Castle Hill
Windham NH 03087

Call Sign: WA1VPY
Paul S Hempstead
109 Castle Hill Rd
Windham NH 03087

Call Sign: N1XTQ
John J Dowd Jr
129 Castle Hill Rd
Windham NH 03087

Call Sign: K1WGD
Morton C Pearlman
20 Cobbetts Pond Rd
Windham NH 03087

Call Sign: K1YQM
Janice B Pearlman
20 Cobbetts Pond Rd
Windham NH 03087

Call Sign: WA1ZTE
Robert E Tadgell Jr
5 E Nashua Rd
Windham NH 030870521

Call Sign: N1FAD
Robert E Comtois
12 Edgewood Rd
Windham NH 03087

Call Sign: N1XWE
J E Gross Iii
25 Farrwood Rd
Windham NH 03087

Call Sign: N1XWF
Jesse E Gross Iv
25 Farrwood Rd
Windham NH 03087

Call Sign: N2HXU
Vance E Poteat
9 Fine View Rd
Windham NH 03087

Call Sign: N4VEP
Vance E Poteat
9 Fine View Rd
Windham NH 03087

Call Sign: WW1P
Vance E Poteat
9 Fine View Rd
Windham NH 03087

Call Sign: KB1IOC
Tracy L Poteat
9 Fine View Rd
Windham NH 03087

Call Sign: W1TLP
Tracy L Poteat
9 Fine View Rd
Windham NH 03087

Call Sign: N4VP
Vance E Poteat
9 Fine View Rd
Windham NH 03087

Call Sign: KB1EXO
Harold J Lalmond
25 Gaumont Rd
Windham NH 03087

Call Sign: KA1MBF
Pamela M Skinner
68 Gov Dinsmore Rd
Windham NH 03087

Call Sign: N1PMJ
Kevin D Reid
42 Governor Dinsmore Rd
Windham NH 03087

Call Sign: WA1YEG
Robert A Skinner
68 Governor Dinsmore Rd
Windham NH 03087

Call Sign: K1TR
Edward S Parsons
9 Grandview Rd
Windham NH 03087

Call Sign: KA1CHQ
Wayne R Casagrande
1 Hardwood Rd
Windham NH 03087

Call Sign: WE1F
Robert J Souza
17 Hardwood Rd
Windham NH 03087

Call Sign: KD1YA
Michael J Cardarelli
10 Haskell Rd
Windham NH 03087

Call Sign: K2KYR
Ronald J Casagrande
34 Hickory Lane
Windham NH 030871623

Call Sign: KA1VYX
Andrew K Freeston
13 Hidden Valley Rd
Windham NH 03087

Call Sign: W1VL
Andrew C Manti Jr
2 Highland Rd
Windham NH 030871804

Call Sign: N1BZP
John T Ramsay
9 Highland Rd
Windham NH 03087

Call Sign: KA1IPV
Roberta A Johnson
1 Jones Rd
Windham NH 03087

Call Sign: WB1CUQ
Ralph N Johnson
1 Jones Rd
Windham NH 03087

Call Sign: KB1QFJ
Edward L Clark
12 Karen Rd
Windham NH 03087

Call Sign: KB1LHD
Joshua B Heinzl
110 Kendal Pond Rd
Windham NH 03087

Call Sign: WA3UEN
Carl G Heinzl
110 Kendall Pond Rd
Windham NH 030871418

Call Sign: KB1LQA
Jonathan P Heinzl
110 Kendall Pond Rd
Windham NH 03087

Call Sign: KA1IOY
Joan R Normington
137 Kendall Pond Rd
Windham NH 03087

Call Sign: K1DG
Norman D Grant
144 Kendall Pond Rd
Windham NH 03087

Call Sign: AL1O
Tobias M Wellnitz
144 Kendall Pond Rd
Windham NH 03087

Call Sign: KB1KAA
Nigel S Cawthorne
144 Kendall Pond Rd
Windham NH 03087

Call Sign: KB1KBX
Analog Devices Amateur
Radio Club
144 Kendall Pond Rd
Windham NH 03087

Call Sign: KB1KGL
Long Island Dx Society
144 Kendall Pond Rd
Windham NH 03087

Call Sign: KA1LNW
Stephen W Cox
176 Kendall Pond Rd
Windham NH 03087

Call Sign: N1DBT
Carroll L Walsh
13 Kent St
Windham NH 03087

Call Sign: KB1JNM
Mark L Branoff
11 Leni Rd
Windham NH 030871526

Call Sign: N1WIY
Mark E Raposo
88 Londonderry Rd

Windham NH 03087                    Windham NH 030871299              Windham NH 03087

Call Sign: W1JEL                    Call Sign: W1ELX                  Call Sign: KB1WAT
Edmund C Harrington                 J S Dunn                         Jeffrey M Opper
136 Londonderry Rd                  12 Mockingbird Hill Rd           56 Overton Rd
Windham NH 03087                    Windham NH 030871219             Windham NH 03087

Call Sign: N1PQA                    Call Sign: WA1LCW                 Call Sign: KB1DYD
Joseph F Tauras                     Lane E Bickford                  Sheri A Robinton
7 Long Meadow Rd                    25 Nashua Rd                     8 Patricia St
Windham NH 030871398                Windham NH 03087                 Windham NH 03087

Call Sign: KD1DK                    Call Sign: KA1CTR                 Call Sign: N1TUF
Harvey R Champigny                  Lane E Bickford                  Mark E Robinton
92 Lowell Rd                        25 Nashua Rd                     8 Patricia St
Windham NH 03087                    Windham NH 03087                 Windham NH 03087

Call Sign: W1NIR                    Call Sign: N1ZBL                  Call Sign: AA1WE
Harvey H Champigny                  Gregory W George                 David L Allain
92 Lowell Rd                        82 Nashua Rd                     Po Box 392
Windham NH 03087                    Windham NH 03087                 Windham NH 03087

Call Sign: WA1YAV                   Call Sign: KB1OPN                 Call Sign: W1FEW
Gaetano Frittitta                   Ryan E Horgan                    Richard G Brown
Lowell Rd                           7 Netherwood Rd                  3 Princeton St
Windham NH 03087                    Windham NH 03087                 Windham NH 03087

Call Sign: N1QH                     Call Sign: W1QWR                  Call Sign: N1LHV
Gaetano Frittitta                   Howard I Matchett                Fernando A Frometa
Lowell Rd                           35 North Lowell Rd               138 Range Rd
Windham NH 03087                    Windham NH 03087                 Windham NH 03087

Call Sign: N1PMH                    Call Sign: WX1Z                   Call Sign: WB2JBO
Jeffrey W Walker                    Daniel K Rovell-Rixx             Reginald D Cumming
63 Marblehead Rd                    8 Oriole Rd                      178 Range Rd
Windham NH 03087                    Windham NH 03087                 Windham NH 03087

Call Sign: KB1OSI                   Call Sign: KA1FTX                 Call Sign: KA1AMP
Devin J Walker                      Benjamin S Doe                   Wayne D Burton
63 Marblehead Rd                    17 Oriole Rd                     179 Range Rd
Windham NH 03087                    Windham NH 03087                 Windham NH 03087

Call Sign: K1AR                     Call Sign: N1BGU                  Call Sign: KB1ESN
John H Dorr                         Steven L Thornton                George S Ingram
2 Mitchell Pond Rd                  25 Oriole Rd                     3 Rock Pond Rd

Windham NH 03087

Call Sign: WA1KKZ
George W Kimball
27 Rock Pond Rd
Windham NH 030872220

Call Sign: KB1PES
Michael J Sapienza
43 Rockingham Rd
Windham NH 03038

Call Sign: K1TRQ
Robert E Ironfield
11 Sawtelle Rd Box 608
Windham NH 03087

Call Sign: N1QGH
Peter J Kantsos
19 Sharon Rd
Windham NH 03087

Call Sign: W1MJS
Michael J Spitalere
4 Simpson Rd
Windham NH 03087

Call Sign: WB9YVJ
Susan L Noblet
52 Stacey Circle
Windham NH 030871648

Call Sign: N1BPN
Janet E Mattleman
27 Telo Rd
Windham NH 030871126

Call Sign: N1FEL
Brian T Sullivan
7 Tokanel Rd
Windham NH 03087

Call Sign: KB1PET
David E Norton
16 Tully St

Windham NH 030871521

Call Sign: W1BYI
David E Norton
16 Tully St
Windham NH 030871521

Call Sign: K1MOM
Jeanne V Schipelliti
13 Woodvue Rd
Windham NH 030872112

Call Sign: W1DAD
Peter Schipelliti
13 Woodvue Rd
Windham NH 030872112

Call Sign: KW2S
Spencer L Webb
Windham NH 03087

Call Sign: N1HZC
William R Gill
Windham NH 03087

Call Sign: N1QVY
William N Morgan Sr
Windham NH 03087

Call Sign: N1RNV
John C Charette
Windham NH 03087

Call Sign: N1YRA
Christopher J Brown
Windham NH 03087

Call Sign: WB1DDC
Robin A Cavusoglu
Windham NH 03082

Call Sign: KB1GOI
Albert P Lelis Jr
Windham NH 030870610

Call Sign: KB1HLU
Chandra A Webb
Windham NH 03087

Call Sign: W1STT
Richard R Feola
Windham NH 03087

Call Sign: KB1TJX
Jason Diesel
Windham NH 03087

## FCC Amateur Radio Licenses in Windsor

Call Sign: N1ZON
John Drake
31 Heartwood Lane
Windsor NH 03244

## FCC Amateur Radio Licenses in Winnisquam

Call Sign: AA1IT
Ronald V Pelleteri Jr
14 Route 3
Winnisquam NH
032890161

Call Sign: K1QLA
C Craig Mac Farland
Winnisquam NH 03289

Call Sign: W1PXM
Aime A Theberge
Winnisquam NH 03289

Call Sign: KB1JTK
Naturist New Hampshire
Winnisquam NH 03289

Call Sign: NU1DE
Naturist New Hampshire
Winnisquam NH 03289

Call Sign: KB1LGV
Richard A Grant
Winnisquam NH 03289

## FCC Amateur Radio Licenses in Wolfeboro

Call Sign: K1NEB
Douglas H Cady
5 Bassett Rd
Wolfeboro NH 03894

Call Sign: KB1DLX
Robert L Ness Jr
917 Beach Pond Rd
Wolfeboro NH 03894

Call Sign: WA1APL
George H Hall
29 Birch Hill Estates Rd
Wolfeboro NH 03894

Call Sign: W1TPC
Richard D Ackerman
Box 422
Wolfeboro NH 03894

Call Sign: KB1MSQ
Edward Graham V
164 Bryant Rd
Wolfeboro NH 03894

Call Sign: N1TPH
Joseph G Sayers
90 Canopache Rd
Wolfeboro NH 03894

Call Sign: W1DPT
George E Mann Jr
67 Center St
Wolfeboro NH 03894

Call Sign: KB1IZD
David C Devries
160 Center St

Wolfeboro NH 03894

Call Sign: KB1IZE
Devon M P Devries
160 Center St
Wolfeboro NH 03894

Call Sign: KB1QPK
Stacey Savage
258 Center St
Wolfeboro NH 03894

Call Sign: N1PHX
Thomas F Fortuna
9 College Rd
Wolfeboro NH 03894

Call Sign: KA5WHO
Dale G Smith
272 College Rd
Wolfeboro NH 03894

Call Sign: KC6TLA
Lawrence S Hebb Jr
23 Crystal Shore Rd
Wolfeboro NH 03894

Call Sign: W1EMN
Samuel S Sayward Sr
Forest Rd
Wolfeboro NH 03894

Call Sign: W1ZOA
Richard A Watson
475 Gov Wentworth Hwy
Wolfeboro NH 03894

Call Sign: N1EXU
Herbert G Baldwin
465 Governor Wentworth
Hwy
Wolfeboro NH 03894

Call Sign: W1ZVV
Herbert G Baldwin

465 Governor Wentworth
Hwy
Wolfeboro NH 03894

Call Sign: KB1EQZ
Toni E Russell
9 Haines Hill Rd
Wolfeboro NH 03894

Call Sign: K1TNG
Frederick E Joyce
387 N Main St
Wolfeboro NH 03894

Call Sign: WB1EZN
Arthur W Buckner Sr
407 N Main St
Wolfeboro NH 03894

Call Sign: AA1VQ
Arthur W Buckner Sr
407 N Main St
Wolfeboro NH 03894

Call Sign: N1YOH
Keith A Mandigo
541 N Main St
Wolfeboro NH 03894

Call Sign: W1STS
Scott D Karvonetz
6 Natures Way
Wolfeboro NH 03894

Call Sign: W1SVN
Scott M Doremus
123 Penn Air Rd
Wolfeboro NH 03894

Call Sign: W1VVE
Stephen Waterman Iii
20 Pleasant Valley Rd
Wolfeboro NH 03894

Call Sign: W1UR

Daniel G Morgan
451 Pleasant Valley Rd
Wolfeboro NH 03894

Call Sign: N1YEC
Stephen D Marsh
742 Pleasant Valley Rd
Wolfeboro NH 03894

Call Sign: N1YED
William M Marsh
742 Pleasant Valley Rd
Wolfeboro NH 03894

Call Sign: K1SC
Sanford H Cole Jr
80 Rollingwood Dr Apt 145
Wolfbrough NH 03894

Call Sign: K1CX
Elitist Contest Club
100 Spruce Rd
Wolfeboro NH 03894

Call Sign: K1GQ
Willard L Myers
100 Spruce Rd
Wolfeboro NH 03894

Call Sign: KA1VFL
Craig W Garland
9 Triggs Island
Wolfeboro NH 03894

Call Sign: N1TPK
Robert R Arndt
40 Union St
Wolfeboro NH 03894

Call Sign: N1TXR
KAREN E Arndt
40 UNION ST
Wolfeboro NH 03894

Call Sign: K1OLV

Henry J Colbath Jr
Wolfeboro NH 03894

Call Sign: KA1EEK
Eunice L Sayward
Wolfeboro NH 03894

Call Sign: KA1PJV
Erik H Arctander
Wolfeboro NH 03894

Call Sign: KA5ZLK
Lynn A Miffitt
Wolfeboro NH 03894

Call Sign: N1TPG
Robert E Levin Jr
Wolfeboro NH 03894

Call Sign: N1UVB
Theresa Taylor
Wolfeboro NH 03894

Call Sign: W1BST
Lakes Region Repeater
Association
Wolfeboro NH 03894

Call Sign: W3OXO
Charles E Sturtevant
Wolfeboro NH 038941415

Call Sign: KB1KZF
James F Miffitt
Wolfeboro NH 03894

FCC Amateur Radio
Licenses in Wolfeboro
Falls

Call Sign: KA1PJT
Arthur W Buckner Jr
Box 55
Wolfeboro Falls NH 03896

Call Sign: W1PWG
George A Servente
90 Cotton Valley Rd
Wolfeboro Falls NH 03896

Call Sign: N1MBD
Mildred L Buckner
L Grove St
Wolfeboro Falls NH 03896

Call Sign: KB1DLY
Helen J Stock
Wolfeboro Falls NH 03896

Call Sign: KB1DLZ
Peter C Mullen
Wolfeboro Falls NH
038960105

Call Sign: N1VAU
Clayton L Ferry
Wolfeboro Falls NH
038960777

Call Sign: N3FAH
Richard F Schafer
Wolfeboro Falls NH 03896

Call Sign: KB1EQX
Barbara A Lantz
Wolfeboro Falls NH
038960183

FCC Amateur Radio
Licenses in Woodsville

Call Sign: W1ZYZ
Mark E Doucet
4 Cromwell Dr
Woodsville NH 03785

Call Sign: KD1W
Timothy B Parker
122 Dartmouth Rd
Woodsville NH 03785

Call Sign: N1IMA
Gunnar Kryger
2 N Ct St
Woodsville NH 03785

Call Sign: KB1GUO
James C Westover
5 Smith St Apt 3
Woodsville NH 03785

Call Sign: WB1ALJ
Thomas F Dennehy
670 Swiftwater Rd
Woodsville NH 03785

Call Sign: KB1AMF
Douglas M Riggie
14 Terrace St
Woodsville NH 03785

Call Sign: AK1Z
Richard W Demick
4 Wilson Ave
Woodsville NH 03785

Call Sign: W6TH
Vito S Chiarappa
Woodsville NH 03785

www.ingramcontent.com/pod-product-compliance
Lightning Source LLC
Chambersburg PA
CBHW081144270326
41930CB00014B/3028

* 9 7 8 1 6 2 5 1 2 0 5 1 9 *